D0072720

WOMEN WRITERS OF THE WORLD
VOL. 1

WOMEN WRITING
IN DUTCH

GARLAND REFERENCE LIBRARY
OF THE HUMANITIES
VOL. 1439

Women Writers of the World

KATHARINA WILSON
Series Editor

WOMEN WRITING IN DUTCH
edited by Kristiaan Aercke

WOMEN WRITING IN DUTCH

edited by

Kristiaan Aercke

GARLAND PUBLISHING, Inc.
New York & London / 1994

Library of Congress Cataloging-in-Publication Data

Women writing in Dutch / edited by Kristiaan Aercke.
      p.   cm. — (Women writers of the world ; vol. 1)
(Garland reference library of the humanities ; vol.
1439)
    ISBN 0–8153–0231–2 (acid-free paper)
    I. Aercke, Kristiaan, 1959–   . II. Series. III. Series:
Garland reference library of the humanities ; vol. 1439.
PT5411.W66   1994
839.3'10809287'0904—dc20   93–37518
                                    CIP

Printed on acid-free, 250-year-life paper
Manufactured in the United States of America

Women Writing in Dutch

*is dedicated to
the "little people" who
were involved in its making*

Anaïs Aercke (August 5, 1992)
Sophia Parente (July 27, 1992)
William A.D. de Vroom-Hellwarth (Nov. 6, 1991)
Kyle Simons Baker (Sept. 24, 1991)
Marcus Nelson van der Sanden (Jan. 4, 1991)
Francesca Parente (Nov. 17, 1990)

Series Editor's Preface

The Garland series Women Writers of the World presents writers from diverse languages in modern English translations. Each volume in the series focuses on a particular language, country or distinct culture and offers a chronologically and generically representative selection of texts from its women writers. Each anthology commences with a general introduction, and the text selections are preceded by precise bio-critical introductions followed by bibliographies.

Given the broad range of the anthologies, the individual methodologies differ from volume to volume; still, throughout the series our efforts were aimed at making texts accessible to the English-speaking reader that in the past have been the domain of a few specialists in their respective linguistic fields.

Katharina M. Wilson
University of Georgia

Contents

On the Contributors

Kristiaan AERCKE is Assistant Professor of Comparative Literature at the University of Wisconsin-Madison. His main area of research and teaching is early modern and Baroque European literature. His publications include essays on medieval, Renaissance, Baroque, Belgian, fin-de-siècle and modernist literature. He has published translations of Anna Bijns, and a verse-translation with introduction and notes of Vondel's *Gijsbrecht van Amstel*, until recently Holland's "national play" (1991). Professor Aercke's book *Gods of Play: Baroque Festive Performances as Rhetorical Discourse* is forthcoming, and he is currently working on a translation of Vondel's *Maria Stuarda*.

Veerle FRAETERS holds degrees in Ancient History and Germanic Philology and is currently an Assistant-Lecturer of Middle Dutch literature in the Department of Germanic Philology at the Universitaire Faculteiten St-Ignatius, University of Antwerp. Dr. Fraeters wrote a licenciate thesis on Hadewijch's Stanzaic poems and is currently writing a doctoral dissertation on Middle Dutch alchemical texts. She publishes mainly on medieval mysticism and alchemy.

Theresia DE VROOM is Assistant Professor of English at Loyola Marymount University in Los Angeles, California, where she teaches medieval and Renaissance literature. She has published on Dutch medieval literature, including the works of Hadewych and the beast-epic *Van Den Vos Reynaerde*. At present, Professor de Vroom is writing a book on the development of tragicomedy in England at the end of the Renaissance.

Hermina JOLDERSMA is Associate Professor of German at the University of Calgary, Alberta, Canada. Her main area of published research is the (popular) literature of the early-modern period, with emphasis on 16th-century Netherlandic song. Her focus on women's experience in culture and literature in both the Netherlands and Germany extends beyond this point. Professor Joldersma has edited a special issue of the *Canadian Journal of Netherlandic Studies* on "Women Writers in the Netherlands and Flanders" (11 [2] Fall 1990).

James A. PARENTE, Jr. is Associate Professor of German at the University of Minnesota-Twin Cities. He has also taught at Princeton University and the University of Illinois-Chicago. He is a specialist in early modern German, Netherlandic, Scandinavian and Neo-Latin literature. Professor Parente is the author of *Religious Drama and the Humanist Tradition: Christian Theater in Germany and the Netherlands, 1500-1680* (1987), coeditor of *Literary Culture in the Holy Roman Empire, 1555-1720* (1991) and *Studies in German and Scandinavian Literature after 1500* (1993), and editor of *Socio-Historical Approaches to Early Modern German Literature* (1993). He has written articles on early modern German, Dutch, and Danish literature and is, at present, preparing a book on Neo-Latin drama in Germany and the Netherlands, 1480-1780.

Cornelia Niekus MOORE is Professor of German and Dutch, and Associate Dean of the Colleges of Languages, Linguistics and Literature, at the University of Hawaii. Her research interests include 16th- and 17th-century German and Dutch literature, especially as it affects the reading habits of women at that time.

André LEFEVERE is Professor in the Department of Germanic Languages and in the Comparative Literature Program at the University of Texas-Austin. He has held numerous visiting professorships and fellowships in Europe, the United States, and Australia. Professor Lefevere has done work on genre study, mysticism, and medieval literature in general. Most of his work has to do with translation and other forms of cultural transfer. He has translated Wolfram von Eschenbach's *Parzival* (1991) and a volume of the Dutch medieval mystic Jan van Ruusbroec's *Opera omnia* (1991) in the "Corpus Christianorum, Continuatio Medievalis" series. His views on translation and cultural transfer have most recently been expressed in *Translation, Rewriting, and the Manipulation of Literary Fame* (1992); *Translation, History, and Culture: A Source Book* (1992), and *Translating Literature: Practice and Theory in a Comparative Literature Context* (1992).

Jeanne K. HAGEMAN is Assistant Professor of French at the University of Alaska at Fairbanks. Her current interests involve research on eighteenth-century women authors and their role as educators. She is coediting an Anthology for a Women's Studies class in French.

Augustinus P. DIERICK, is Associate Professor of German and Dutch at Victoria College, University of Toronto, where he teaches German and Dutch language, literature and culture courses. In addition to articles on a great variety of Dutch and German literary subjects (including modern Heimatliteratur, Ingeborg Bachman, Hugo von Hofmannsthal, Thomas Bernhard, Ernst Weiss, the Dutch novel 1880-1910, novels on the Dutch East Indies, on the Second World War, Symbolism, Bordewijk,...), he has published a book on German Expressionist prose. Professor Dierick is presently finishing a book on Gottfried Benn, a project on the papers of Frans Coenen, and a study of German exiles in Holland 1933-1940.

Gary Lee BAKER is Assistant Professor in the Department of Modern Languages at Denison University, Ohio. He teaches German language and literature and has an active research interest in Dutch literature. He has published on Multatuli and on the German author Uwe Johnson. For the Roland Holst project, Professor Baker has enjoyed the collaboration of his colleague Judy COCHRAN, Associate Professor of French and Comparative Literature at Denison University. Professor Cochran is a specialist in classical and contemporary French literature who has published on Giono, Violette Leduc and Andrée Chedid. She is the translator-editor of a recently published volume of selected poems by Andrée Chedid.

Jolanda VANDERWAL TAYLOR is Assistant Professor in the Department of German at the University of Wisconsin-Madison, where she teaches Dutch and German. Her research interests include Dutch and German 20th-century literature. She has published essays on Alfred Döblin, W.F. Hermans, Marga Minco, Rinnes Rijke, and the Memory of the Second World War in Dutch Literature.

Johan P. SNAPPER presently holds the Queen Beatrix Chair of Dutch Language, Literature & Culture at the University of California-Berkeley. Besides numerous articles on German and Dutch writers, Professor Snapper has edited and written several books on Dutch literature, including *Post-War Dutch Literature: A Harp Full of Nails* (1971) and *De spiegel der verlossing in het werk van Gerard Reve* (1990). He is presently writing a monograph on Marga Minco.

Laureen NUSSBAUM is Professor emerita of Foreign Languages & Literatures, Portland State University, Oregon. Born in Germany, she emigrated first to the Netherlands and then to the United States. She has published on women in the work of Bertold Brecht, on *littérature engagée* of the 1930s, and on post-World War II documentary theater. Recently, Professor Nussbaum has focused on German writers in Dutch exile after 1933, which has led, for example, to various articles on Georg Hermann and to the publication of a book of his letters.

Basil D. KINGSTONE is Professor of French at the University of Windsor, Canada, where he teaches translation. He was associate editor of the *Canadian Journal of Netherlandic Studies* from 1985 to 1990, when he became the editor. His translation into French of Jef Last's *Mijn vriend André Gide*, with introduction and notes, is to be published by the Presses de l'Université de Lyon. He has also published articles on Dutch writers, translation of Quebec short stories, articles on language teaching, and a manual on translation (English-French, French-English).

Myra SCHOLZ-HEERSPINK is a free-lance translator residing in the Netherlands since 1974. She holds a Ph.D. in Germanic Literature from Indiana University-Bloomington, for which she wrote a dissertation on a medieval topic. Besides translations of poetry, she has also published articles on 16th- and 17th-century Dutch literature, and she is also a specialist on the work of Eva Gerlach.

Nikolaas VAN DER SANDEN teaches at the Dutch Studies Center, University of Minnesota-Twin Cities. He has a great interest in literary translation and has published translations of modern Dutch literature, in cooperation with the writers (such as Bert Jansen and Stefan Sanders). He has also published scholarly essays on Grimmelshausen's *Simplicius Simplizissimus*, on Heijermans' *Op hoop van zegen*, and on 17th-century travel accounts, both Dutch and German.

Acknowledgements

The editor would like to thank the following individuals, organizations and institutions whose contributions have made the production of *Women Writing in Dutch* possible.

* Katharina M. Wilson, Department of Comparative Literature, University of Georgia, for the original idea and for including the volume in her series "Women Writers of the World." * Department of Comparative Literature, University of Wisconsin-Madison, for unfailing material support. * Bruno Browning, Ph.D., Learning Support Services, University of Wisconsin-Madison, for expert computer assistance. * Mary E. Pollock, Athens, Georgia, for efficient preparation of the camera-ready copy. * Phyllis Korper, Senior Editor, Garland Publishing, Inc., New York, for seeing the volume through production. * Mr. A. te Boekhorst, Royal Netherlands Embassy, Washington D.C., for generous publication support. * Administratie Kunst (Muziek, Letteren, Podiumkunsten), Ministerie van de Vlaamse Gemeenschap, Brussels, for generous translation support. * The University of Wisconsin-Madison Graduate School for giving the editor conference travel grants.

We are grateful for permission to use excerpts * from *Anne Frank: The Diary Of A Young Girl*, by Anne Frank. Copyright 1952 by Otto H. Frank. Used by permission of Doubleday, a division of Bantam Doubleday Dell Publishing Group, Inc. * From *In A Dark Wood Wandering*, by Hella Haasse. Translation copyright 1989 by Edith Kaplan, Kalman Kaplan and Anita Miller. Used by permission of Academy Chicago Publishers, Ltd. * From *The Scarlet City*, by Hella Haasse. Translation copyright 1990 by Anita Miller. Used by permission of Academy Chicago Publishers, Ltd. * From the work of Monika van Paemel. Used and translated by permission of Meulenhoff Nederland bv, Amsterdam. * From the work of Eva Gerlach. Used and translated by permission of the author and

Introduction

Kristiaan P. Aercke

Several general theoretical concerns accompanied the making of the anthology *Women Writing in Dutch*. First, the question must be asked whether the anthology format is in itself a valid strategy for introducing writers to a new market (a related question being, does the American academic market need yet another anthology of "women writers?"). And secondly, is it justifiable, possible, or desirable to introduce writers via translations? In the light of current debates on canon revision, all three questions must be answered with a resounding yes.[1]

In 1979, the Dutch poet and critic Gerrit Komrij defined anthologizers in the introduction of his own anthology, *De Nederlandse Poëzie van de 19de en 20ste eeuw in 1000 en enige gedichten* ("Dutch Poetry from the 19th and 20th Centuries in 1000 Poems And Then Some More." Amsterdam: Bert Bakker). Komrij considered anthologizers (himself included), "people with prehensile hands, with a restless stare; they want to scrutinize *everything*, and tap all over this and that, only to drop things the very next moment. Occasional vampires" (my translation). His own anthology was in a sense also a restless but therapeutic undertaking, aimed at expressing sincere discontent with the existing anthologies of Dutch poetry. The average anthology, so Komrij implied, was overly rigid and canonical, and designed to perpetuate the notion that "poetry is the territory par excellence of emotional outpourings, lofty moods, waving banners, and pomp and circumstance" (my translation). In 1979, such a critical rejection of a long-standing tradition still sounded fairly revolutionary, and so was Komrij's selection for his own anthology, with which many readers did not agree, including his famous colleagues J. Bernlef, Remco Campert, Gerrit Kouwenaar, and Bert Schierbeek.

Anthologies offer a convenient format for presenting texts that are in some way related. Until very recently, the criteria used most often to combine selected texts in one volume were either the language in which they were written, or their general subject matter. But in all cases, the candidates for inclusion in mainstream anthologies had stood the test of time and the tests administered by the canonizing literary milieu. The anthology format thus generates both awe and a certain disdain — awe, because it is supposed to contain "the very best of *the* literature" (in the *florilegia* tradition), and disdain, because texts are generally reproduced only fragmentarily and incompletely and geared toward pedagogical use. A major shift in anthology policy has occurred in the United States since the early 1980s, in response to the now apparently unstoppable academic concern with canon revision. It is undeniable that political and economic ideologies have always determined the strategies of anthologizers, and they continue to do so. But the 1980s have seen the overthrow of the *discreetly* hidden ideologies which protected the conservative canon, as well as the near-triumph of the *aggressively innovative* strategies which are aimed at promoting women writers and members of specific cultural, racial, ethnic groups and/or sexual orientations. One can view this development from two angles. A positive, and perhaps naive, observer might say that the tremendous energy which publishers and academics have put into producing such books for classroom use is a sign of health: it shows academics in touch with the real world and perhaps even in the vanguard of social change. A more skeptical (and perhaps more realistic) observer could argue that this anthologizing energy is not so much the determining cause of canon revision as an effort to catch up with the pressures of a changing social reality.

Indeed, the truth is that social, political, and ideological concerns of the "real world" occasionally force the academe to adapt its programs. The increasing interest in "minority studies" (which is itself a belittling phrase) requires abundant supplies of texts to prove the validity and relevance of the subject. One may surmise that publishers as individuals and as businesses are willing to disregard their own ideologies, and jump on the wagon for the sake of image and profit by providing affordable, selected texts for classroom consumption. Given the rule that academics must publish lest they perish, they are understandably eager to initiate or collaborate with the anthologizing industry. The current boom in "women writers" anthologies thus should surprise no one, although it is a startlingly new phenomenon: this extensive campaign to disseminate and promote an apparently inexhaustible supply of texts which have as their *sole, predetermined* selection criterion the *gender* of their authors may well be the first undertaking of its kind since the invention of print itself.

Clearly, the "women writers" anthologies (and those of works by people who are conveniently lumped together in specific groups by the publishing business or by academics) have a function in the ongoing process of canon revision. The anthology format has always been an ideal tool for ideologically inspired revisionists of the canon for two related reasons: it offers on the one hand, a fairly attractive correlation of price and volume, and on the other, unequalled manipulative possibilities. With the latter I mean that the anthologizer has the power to screen twice for ideological "correctness": first, within the potential pool of writers to be included, and secondly, within the writings of each selected author. Thus, the "occasional vampire" collects scraps and fragments of an oeuvre to highlight the ideologically most desirable tidbits while diverting attention away from those aspects of the oeuvre that are less suitable to the goals and purposes of the anthology. For this reason, the anthology is a two-edged sword, capable both of preserving an existing canon and defending it, *and* of carving out a new canon.

In recent years, the latter function has clearly been in the ascendant. Fact is that canon revision, in the mind of many, has come to mean mainly one thing: to allow texts written by women and by members of specific groups to (re-)emerge systematically *at the virtual exclusion* of everything else. In spite of all good intentions and protestations to the contrary, the ideologies of such a new canon – as we find it represented in the new anthologies – are probably as artificial, as exclusive, and as politically determined as the old ones. Thus it is interesting to consider what happens when publishers and their anthologizers try to please both the "old" and the "new" canons at the same time. In 1989, Roger Lonsdale updated *The New Oxford Book of 18th-Century Verse*; also in 1989, Lonsdale published Oxford's volume *18th-Century Women Poets*. It was a conscious decision, in other words, to give the women "a book of their own" and to segregrate 18th-century British writers on the basis of gender, and gender alone. This case illustrates several important points. First, the isolation of women writers in the Lonsdale anthologies strongly suggests that Oxford's interests were political rather than intellectual and aesthetic. Secondly, it illustrates the tendency to isolate texts by women writers and then read or study them like "samples." The purpose of this isolation is to discover in women's writing the traces of a shared experience – for the greater part a negative experience since it stems from denial in historically patriarchal cultures – but an experience which is automatically assumed to be utterly distinct from the experiences that have shaped and determined male writing. The implication is not simply that women writers are presented as a separate genus, but rather that this genus is made out to be absolutely irreconcilable with an hypothetically diametrically opposite genus of "male writers."

Not only must we seriously ask ourselves whether canon revision *can* be successful if the *only* criterion for broadening the canon is that of gender (or race, or class, or ethnic origin, or...). but we must also wonder whether single-gender anthologies really solve the problem of historical underrepresentation and provide a good theoretical basis for the empowerment of women writers. Indeed, whereas the new type of anthologies certainly succeeds in increasing the visibility of selected women writers, it also seems to suggest that women writers *must* be introduced in bevies, the members of which are related first and foremost by their gender, and secondly, by

another feature, such as race, national origin, language, or historical
time period. In a way, such anthologies then simply perpetuate the
conventional rhetorical confession of artistic impotence with which
much women's writing from any period often begins or ends – in the
words of the 16th-century Antwerp poet and schoolteacher Anna
Bijns: "Artistic tempers, with art on your minds/Nothing here but
what in good faith was done./Now knowing this, relish its affection
even more./And in case of a fault, well, 't is a woman's work" (my
translation). There is safety in numbers, and anthologies may create
the impression that the selected women need the strength of numbers
to stand on their feet and that, if each of the writers represented were
really any good, she would have been given an edition or a volume
of her own instead of being lumped with a selection of members of
the same sorority. (Oxford, again, presents an interesting compromise
with the "Schomburg Library of 19th-Century Black Women Writers"
[approximately 40 titles, gen. ed. Henry Louis Gates, Jr.], as do also
Penguin and Daedalus Books with, respectively, the "Virago
(Modern) Classics" and the "Mothers of the Novel" series.) In spite
of these considerations, the contributors to *Women Writing in Dutch*
feel that the anthology format is a boon rather than a handicap. The
literature boasts so many great writers, male and female – but the
women are even less known abroad than the men. To introduce the
names of some of these and a sampling of their work is the *only*
ideology that has governed the making of *Women Writing in Dutch*.

   The irony is that some academics will consider *Women
Writing in Dutch* a risky enterprise *not* because it is an anthology of
women writers, but rather because these women were/are Western
Europeans, who wrote/are writing in Dutch, a Germanic language.
There are two aspects to this issue. First, in spite of an impressive
number of recent translations of literature written in Dutch and some
vigorous Dutch and Belgian governmental support to that purpose, the
American academe continues to label the Dutch language, and thus by
implication the literature written in Dutch, as "minor." Even
Comparatists, who should theoretically have a wider perspective than
other professional students of literature, are generally surprised to
learn, for example, that there are and always have been more

speakers of Dutch than of all the Scandinavian languages combined; that "Flemish" and "Dutch" are the same language, in spite of the false distinction which seems to be perpetuated by the Modern Language Association; and that the Low Countries have been a crucial European geographical and cultural axis from the early Middle Ages until today. But the second aspect is far more sensitive. Indeed, in spite of its professed response to the need for multi-cultural diversity, the "revised" literary canon in the U.S. is still quite provincial. Judging from the regularly appearing academic publishers' catalogs, canon revision is primarily a matter of internal politics, i.e., it is still concerned *only* with texts written in some variant of English. And in the case of Comparative Literature, an explicit political and ideological agenda of issues has redefined the strata of the "new" "multi-cultural" canon to favor (women) writers of color and/or from historically-geographically unempowered cultures and regions rather than from the many "minor" *Western European* literatures and cultures. Indeed, for reasons of ignorance or convenience, even seasoned Comparatists all too often undiscriminatingly lump all of the latter together in some vague *Gestalt*, the outlines of which have become rather unfashionable in the past decade.

Related to these concerns is the discussion of the function and value of literary translation. Clearly, since virtually nobody reads Dutch, our authors must be translated before we can even begin hoping that they, too, will be embraced in a future, freer, less prejudiced and genuinely multi-cultural canon. But the problem is that professional critics, literary scholars, and teachers often still consider translated literature no literature at all or, at best, barely acceptable for reasons of necessity, in introductory survey courses "World Masterpieces for Freshmen – prerequisites: none." In recent decades, literary scholarship and historiography have "rediscovered" ("given a voice to," "empowered," "problematized") untold numbers of texts, authors, and entire literatures that were previously considered "marginal" or, to use a better term, "peripheral." This includes writing by women, gay writing, detective fiction, western novels, children's literature, pornography. But the same courtesy has not been extended to other "peripheral" texts, such as literary translations. Indeed, whereas women writers have gained massive support and respect in serious literary studies, the translated text remains the pariah of the library, having squatter's rights at the most. And yet, this should not be the case. I would like to argue that a less provincial and therefore more sincere revision of the literary canon cannot take place without taking literary translation seriously. Indeed, as the poly-system theorists of Amsterdam, Antwerp, and Tel Aviv have argued since the 1970s, translations play an important (but underestimated and often even unperceived) role in the formation and reformation of the host canon. A similar point was raised in the 1920s by the Russian Formalists and the Prague School of Linguistics, who indicated that, if literature study is ever to be taken seriously as a science, it cannot continue to select only the most desirable specimens and the most appetizing samples for the purposes of research and criticism. Rather, literature study will have to become less evaluative and all-inclusive. Such a truly scientific – that is, non-evaluative, non-elitist – approach to literary history, theory and criticism cannot afford to ignore translations.

The reason for this is that translations are functional within the literary host system. Such a system is actually a "poly-system," or system of smaller systems, of which the configurations change continuously.[2] How does this polysystem work? The canonizing literary milieu (teachers, scholars, publishers, editors, critics, reviewers, and anthologizers) creates and maintains a form of system-stratification in the literary system of a given language: it distinguishes between canonized ("high") and non-canonized ("low") systems, which are allowed to be engaged in a continuous struggle. The "canonized" products are those that the literary milieu has declared (1) officially acceptable, (2) aesthetically valuable, and (3) capable of injecting new features in the literary repertory. "Non-canonized" products form the marginal or peripheral reservoir of a literary system: trivial or entertainment-, folk- or childrens' literature, pornography, adaptations of other works, and translations. Almost without exception, translations of texts that were or are canonized and central in their original system remain peripheral in the host system, even if they are instrumental in the creation of new, so-called "original" "masterpieces" in that host system. For example, Thomas North's translation of Plutarch's *Parallel Lives* from the French of

Amyot (1579), and John Florio's translation from Montaigne, *Essayes, or Morall, Politike and Millitarie Discourses* (1603, 1613), both have great independent artistic merit but, being translations, were never canonized. Yet, they were highly "functional," for example in being crucial sources to Shakespeare.

Now, dynamic relations exist between the various types and strata in literary systems. Systems are anything but static, and exchanges or transfers, feedback and creative impulses do occur continuously between "high" and "low" forms, between the "center" and the "periphery." The center is the standard, the curriculum; it contains the features that are canonized precisely because they are, or were at one time, innovating, challenging, difficult, capable of producing "high art," responsive to the changing needs of the polysystem. But when canonized features cease to be "functional" in this sense, they are often pushed out of the center and made to join the periphery. Once landed in the periphery, such features can of course continue to generate products (which are then called "epigonal" literature). In fact, what is called "new" in peripheral, non-canonized literature is merely the result of this general dynamic principle. For example, such features as indirect speech, or the flashback technique, were introduced in non-canonized literature (children's books, westerns, pornography, ...) only *after* they had been subjected to *such* thorough experimentation in canonized literature that they had ceased to be shocking or surprizing there (very much like Burke's theory that the culture of a "lower class" is an outdated, outmoded version of the culture of the class immediately above it on the social scale). Of course, the same dynamic principle also operates in reverse. Peripheral features often enter the center, fuel the system with new forms and ideas, and become canonized. Such interaction is not limited to the same system: features from a different system, which may already have been waiting in the periphery, often enter the center of a target system. This "conversion" activity occurs especially in historical periods when cultural systems are very much open to other systems. Thus the dynamics of system-change. As relations among elements of a system change, and as relations between the literary system itself and its surrounding cultural systems change, a continuous transfer occurs of features (i.e., genres, themes, technical procedures, etc.) from the canonized to the non-canonized strata of a system, and vice versa.

This dynamic, which is the object of study of polysystem theory, describes very well some of the current developments in canon revision. Dynamic interaction is very important for a literary system, for without it, the system ceases to develop synchronically and diachronically. It becomes predictable, stereotypical, dependent entirely on a fixed canon, and petrified. Such was precisely the fate of "high" Latin literature, or, apparently, Hebrew literature until the Israeli period, or Chinese literature until fairly recently. If a system becomes unresponsive to changes in the larger social-cultural system, it becomes exclusively "bookish" and, in a sense, disfunctional as literature. Hence the importance of literary translation as a theoretical and practical activity: since translated texts do influence the creation of new texts in the host language, they do contribute to the dynamics of the host canon. Translations, in other words, are functional products in the literary economy – just like anthologies. Together, they can be used as tools to "empower" or "give a voice to" texts, authors and entire literatures that are traditionally considered, say, "marginal" or "minor" out of ignorance or prejudice.

Women Writing in Dutch is the first volume of a series that is explicitly devoted to literatures other than English, under the general editorship of Katharina M. Wilson (University of Georgia), who has already seriously and successfully challenged academic provincialism in the United States by editing anthologies of translated works of women writers also in "minor" European languages. A medievalist, Professor Wilson edited *Medieval Women Writers* (Georgia, 1984), *Women Writers of the Renaissance and Reformation* (Georgia, 1987), and with the late Frank J. Warnke, *Seventeenth-Century Woman Writers* (Georgia, 1989): She has also edited the two-volume *Encyclopedia of Continental Women Writers* (Garland, 1991), which provides a cosmopolitan alternative to Blain's *The Feminist Companion to Literature in English (from the Middle Ages to the Present)* (Yale, 1990). Wilson's chronologically organized anthologies represent a wide selection of European literatures, in the French, Provençal, German, Austrian, English, Spanish, Italian, Hungarian, Dutch, Scandinavian, and Slavic languages.

The original title for the present volume, *Dutch Women Writers*, was dismissed as misleading for it emphasized nationality rather than language: the Southern Netherlands (Belgium) produced the first women writers in the language, and Flemish writers are producing work that is as outstanding as anything done by their sisters from the Northern provinces. Moreover, *"Women Writing in Dutch"* might help to dismiss the incorrect notion that Flemish and Dutch are different languages. In Fall 1990, the *Canadian Journal of Netherlandic Studies* (XI [ii] 1990) devoted a special issue to Dutch and Flemish women writers (special ed. Hermina Joldersma); several contributors to this issue considered the proposed anthology a useful follow-up project, in which they could develop their subject at greater length and present new translations.

In the following chapters, each contributor first presents a critical introduction to the writer and her work, emphasizing any combination of such issues as biography related to the work, education, relevance of the writer's work for her own and for our age, comparison with her (fe)male contemporaries, stylistics, major themes, critical reception at home and abroad (translations?), influence (by and on), modern theoretical approaches, place in the canon, relevance for gender studies, etc. This section is followed by (almost always) new translations of what the contributor judged to be characteristic and important sections of the writer's work: a representative set of poems, letters, chapters of a novel, or several short stories. Finally, each chapter contains an updated primary and secondary bibliography for further reading.

The chapters are arranged in chronological order, to begin with the medieval mystics: Veerle Fraeters (University of Antwerp-UFSIA) writes on Hadewijch, and Theresia de Vroom (Loyola Marymount University) on Beatrijs. Medieval mysticism is currently a prominent subject in literary and women's studies, and much has been published in recent years on the great sixteenth- and seventeenth-century mystics of the Spanish-speaking world. We hope to show that the medieval mystics of the Low Countries are equally interesting. Hadewijch already has name recognition in English, and some of her work is available in translation. The thirteenth-century beguine Beatrijs van Nazareth, however, is still less well known in the English-speaking world. The Renaissance is well represented by four authors. Hermina Joldersma (University of Calgary) writes on Anna Bijns, whose oeuvre contains not only the vitriolic Counter-reformational refrains for which she is mostly known, but also many tender or "foolish" love poems. The latter side of her oeuvre was artificially obscured: Bijns is thus also interesting from a feminist viewpoint for the fact that her work during her lifetime as well as her posthumous reputation were thoroughly manipulated by male clergymen. A very different personality is the intellectual and attractive *salon*-lady Maria Tesselschade Roemer Visscher, who is introduced by James A. Parente (University of Minnesota-Twin Cities). Maria Tesselschade Roemers Visscher was a lover of clever word-games à la Marino, the author of letters and poems in which she reacted to private and public events of importance, and an esteemed guest of P.C. Hooft's famous Muiderkring. Maria's sister Anna Roemers Visscher, also a writer, makes a prominent appearance in this chapter; in fact, in the critical literature she seems to play a more significant role than her sister. Furthermore, the learned and widely renowned Anna Maria van Schurman of Utrecht, in a chapter by Cornelia N. Moore (University of Hawaii-Manoa). Together with Marie de Gournay in France, Bathsua Makin in England, and Maria de Zayas y Sotomayor in Spain, Schurman was truly one of Europe's leading women scholars and, though deeply religious, one of the boldest participants in the famous *querelle des femmes* regarding the philosophically and theologically instituted views on women's inferiority to men. Our last Renaissance author, the mystic prose writer Maria Petijt, is introduced and discussed by André Lefevere (University of Texas-Austin). Known also as Maria a Sancta Teresia, Petijt recorded her spiritual genesis and progress in an interesting autobiography and in many letters to her spiritual director; the latter translated her text into Latin, thoroughly reworking it in the process. The eighteenth century is not the most exciting period in Dutch literature, but Jeanne Hageman (University of Alaska-Fairbanks) provides an interesting chapter on the novelist Elizabeth Wolff, the more talented partner of the duo Wolff-Aagje Deken. These two women are best known for their epistolary novel *Sara Burgerhart*, a very fine example of the genre, a novel of European quality. Two major poets represent the nineteenth century. Anna Louisa Geertruida Bosboom-Toussaint, poet and historical novelist, is discussed by Augustinus P. Dierick (University of Toronto). And Gary Lee Baker (Denison University) takes on the formidable Henriëtte Roland Holst-van der Schalk, who is known mainly for her essays and poetry, in which she explores contemporaneous socialism, and for her own social-democratic ideals. A reasonable variety of authors represent some tendencies of Dutch literature by women in the twentieth century. Hella Haasse is treated by Jolanda Vanderwal Taylor (University of Wisconsin-Madison). Haasse is a prolific novelist, one who is already known in North America; at least one of her novels in translation has been featured in the catalog of the "Book of the Month Club." There is a chapter on Marga Minco, by Johan P. Snapper (University of California-Berkeley). Of course we did not want to omit Anne Frank, who may at this time well be the best known Dutch woman writer in North America. It is fitting that Anne Frank is re-introduced in our book by Laureen Nussbaum (emerita; Portland State University), who was, as a young girl, an intimate friend of the Frank girls in Amsterdam. The contemporary generation is represented by three important writers: the Flemish novelist Monika van Paemel, by Basil Kingstone (University of Windsor-Ontario); the poet Eva Gerlach, by Myra Scholz-Heerspink; and Maria Stahlie, formerly Dutch writer-in-residence at the University of Minnesota, who will be discussed by Klaas van der Zanden, a former colleague of hers in Minneapolis.

Obviously, the present selection is not intended to be a final one. *Women Writing in Dutch* could, and probably should have included such writers as Anne M.G. Schmidt, Suster Bertken, Elisabeth Marain, the two sisters Loveling, Andreas Burnier, Hélène Swarth, Christine d'Haen, Kristien Hemmerechts, Doeschka Meijsing, Lieve Joris, Maria Rosseels, Patricia de Martelaere, Margaretha Droogleever Fortuyn-Leenmans, Renate Rubinstein, Mischa de Vreede, Astrid Roemer, and many, many others.[3] Regardless of the

limitations of the anthology format, however, it is to be hoped that
the articles on the women writers whom we *did* include will provide
new insights into the contribution that all of these authors have made
to literature written in Dutch. Strictly speaking, this anthology does
not introduce any "newly recovered" women writers, for they are
practically all fairly well canonized, but we hope nevertheless that the
careful re-examination of the texts by the contributors, the availability
of first-rate translations (many now for the first time), and the
intentional context of the volume will spark off debates about some
fundamental aspects of the role of women writers, and women in
general, in the artistic and social life of the Low Countries.

Notes

1. The main ideas of this introduction were presented first in a
paper read at the Dutch section of the 1991 Kentucky Foreign Language
Conference (University of Kentucky, Lexington), and then, revised, in a
paper read at the 6th Annual Wisconsin Symposium for Netherlandic Studies
(University of Wisconsin, Madison) in 1992.

2. The following résumé of polysystem theory is based entirely on
some of the writings of Itamar Even-Zohar. See especially his *Papers in
Historical Poetics*, Papers on Poetics and Semiotics No. 8 (Tel Aviv: The
Porter Institute for Poetics and Semiotics, 1978); "The Position of Translated
Literature Within the Literary Polysystem," in James S. Holmes et al., eds.
Literature and Translation: New Perspectives in Literary Studies (Leuven:
Acco, 1978), 117-27); and "Polysystem Theory," in *Poetics Today* 1: 1-2
(1979) 287-310 (with lengthy bibliography).

3. A considerable number of contemporary Dutch and Flemish
women writers, including some of those mentioned here, are introduced, via
capsule biographies and translated text-fragments, by Lucie Th. Vermij, ed.,
Women Writers from the Netherlands and Flanders, trans. Greta Kilburn
(Amsterdam: International Feminist Book Fair Press, 1992). This book also
contains much valuable information on available translations, cultural-

historical factors, the women's literary movement, and women writers of children's literature.

Hadewijch

Veerle Fraeters

In the thirteenth century, Hadewijch, a mystic woman from the Duchy of Brabant, wrote "visions," letters, and poems of high literary quality for a small circle of female friends.[1] Until the early sixteenth century, her work was often copied and quoted in *rapiaria*, collections of ideas from several writers and thinkers.[2] By the mid-sixteenth century, however, Hadewijch fell into oblivion. No *vita* prolonged her memory, as was the case with many a mystic woman of her days, probably because, being a beguine, she did not live in a monastic milieu. In 1838, two manuscripts of her work were discovered in the Royal Library of Brussels.[3] Another manuscript was found soon after,[4] and at the beginning of our century, the Flemish Jesuit Jozef van Mierlo started publishing critical editions. From that moment onward, a flood of studies on the literary and spiritual aspects of her works has been produced. She is now recognized as a principal and influential representative of *minnemystiek*, "love mysticism", and as a writer who, at the dawn of vernacular literary production, made an important and creative contribution to the Middle-Dutch language and its literature.[5] Since biographical information on Hadewijch is lacking, we must rely on her writing and on an understanding of her era in order to sketch the life and personality of this remarkable woman.

Throughout the early Middle Ages, unmarried women and widows retired, or were disposed of, in numerous nunneries that had been founded in the Merovingian and Anglo-Saxon kingdoms. These nunneries were run by the nuns and directed by abbesses, often masterful women of royal and aristocratic descent. Monks from monasteries attached to these nunneries provided the necessary services of sacraments.[6] Circumstances changed from the tenth century onwards: as the Church became more organised and ecclesiastically more right-minded, male dominance asserted itself. In the eyes of the churchmen, women could figure only in two paradoxical roles: the virgin who, like Mary, excels in purity, and the wicked Eve, unfit for spiritual vocation and a constant threat to man's chastity.[7] As a consequence, many nunneries were closed, or, alternatively, the nuns were strictly enclosed for "in appearing in the world they either made others desire them, or saw things which they themselves desired," according to the *vita* of Hugh, the early twelfth-century abbot of Cluny (Southern 311). Around the same time, the abbot of the Norbertine order of Prémontré decreed that, "recognizing that the wickedness of women is greater than all the other wickedness of the world,...for the safety of our souls, we will on no account receive any more sisters to the increase of our perdition, but will avoid them like poisonous animals" (Southern 314).[8]

Concurrently the troubadours started to sing in praise of their *domna*, the unattainable pure and perfect lady to whom they devoted their songs and submitted themselves. Some churchmen followed their tune. Robert d'Abrissel, a French preacher, gathered a following of women and founded a double monastery at Fontevrault in which the monks, for the sake of the safety of their souls, submitted themselves in penitent obedience to the nuns (Southern 312; Mommaers 1989:28-31). In general, however, the number of monastic foundations for women decreased, while more and more women — pushed, among other things, by the psychological need to identify with the Mary-aspect of the ambivalent female image of the time — felt compelled to devote their lives to a spiritual relationship with the divine.[9]

Still in the eventful twelfth century, a large number of people started to contest the display of opulence and power that characterized the Church and the monasteries. Many reform movements emerged, both orthodox and heterodox, which opted for the *vita apostolica*: the poor and humble life in imitation of the "primitive" Church. The claims of evangelical poverty could be met by mendicancy (e.g. by the mendicant orders of Saint Francis and Saint Dominic) or by manual work, which from the apostolic age onward had been incorporated into the religious life in order to discipline the body and instill a sense of humility (McDonnell 141-53). Neglected by the official institutions of the Church, many of the women in search of a religious life were inspired by these reform movements and were attracted by a life of evangelical poverty in imitation of Christ.

As a result, by the close of the twelfth century, cities all over Europe witnessed the new phenomenon of women — some at home, others alone — , leading a chaste and simple life devoted to spiritual growth and charity. Contemporaneous documents simply refer to them as *mulieres sanctae* (holy women) or *mulieres reliogiosae* (religious women). Gradually, they formed groups, submitting themselves to the government of a mistress. In Brabant and the Rhineland, where their presence and activities were most intense, they were called beguines.[10] They lived in chastity yet without taking public vows, in poverty yet ensuring self-sufficiency by manual work, and combining public works of charity with private contemplation within their small community.[11] This new way of life, a revolutionary combination of devotion and freedom uncontrolled by the Church, made the ecclesiastical authorities quite uneasy. The lifestyle of the beguines was an obvious critique of current Church practices; moreover, as spiritual leaders, they offered an alternative to the corrupt clergy. Jacques de Vitry, prominent churchman and theologian at the university of Paris, became a disciple of the beguine Marie d'Oignies in the diocese of Liège and he energetically defended her orthodoxy and that of the beguine movement. In 1216, he was able to obtain the pope's oral permission for *mulieres religiosae* of France and the German empire to live the common life.[12] This was the very beginning of the channelling of the beguine movement by the Church. By the mid-thirteenth century, more and more beguines were forced to live in an enclosure supervised by a pastor. These enclosures were called "beguinage." They comprised a church, a

cemetery, a hospital, convents for the younger beguines and
individual houses for the older ones.[13]

Hadewijch was a beguine of the early days, when the
movement was still unchannelled and contested. She was a gifted
visionary and mystic who tried to bestow her teaching of love on a
small community of fellow *mulieres religiosae*. But she seems to have
encountered great difficulties in fulfilling this task. In her works, she
often mentions the "false fellows" who caused her community to split
up (see in the Translations, paragraph 5 of Letter 29). Thus she
wrote:

> And this I entreat you urgently, and exhort you, and
> counsel you, and command you as a mother
> commands her dear child, whom she loves for the
> supreme honor and sweetest dignity of love, to cast
> away from you all alien grief, and to grieve for my
> sake as little as you can. What happens to me,
> whether I am wandering in the country or put in
> prison — however it turns out, it is the work of
> love.[14]

Scholars have debated whether this exile was a historical
event or a mere figure of speech, for "spiritual exile" was one of the
main themes of her works. Today, there is a consensus that
Hadewijch was actually expelled from her beguine community and
exiled because of the daring doctrine of love that she promoted.[15]
But what exactly did her mystical teachings contain?

Mysticism is of all time, for it is a dimension of human
consciousness, known to the mystic but unknown to most of us.
Comparative research has defined the basic patterns of mysticism.[16]
In a mystical experience one has direct contact with the divine and
one knows from this contact that everything is related, or originally
One.[17] A mystic, then, is a person who devotes his/her life to the
mystical way, which is twofold and consists of, first, exploring one's
own consciousness in order to experience the spiritual unity with the
divine, and second, constantly fertilizing one's practical life with the

strength and insight received from the mystical experience. The core of mysticism is one. Its actual manifestations differ according to the personality of the mystic and her/his historical context.

In the twelfth century, the monastic and cathedral schools which had been established during the Carolingian Renaissance became notable centers of learning where biblically revealed knowledge was infused with the study of Platonism and Aristotelianism. In these schools (some of which developed into universities), the (exclusively male) professors conducted heady scholastic disputes and tried to construct rational proofs of the existence of God.[18] But some monks followed the opposite path and focused not on scholastic reasoning and a rational understanding of God, but rather on spiritual growth and a direct experience of God. Two writers on mysticisim are worth mentioning here, because Hadewijch underwent their influence. Saint Bernard describes the relationship between God and the human soul as a love-relationship comparable to bridegroom and bride. Through this experience of love, one obtains knowledge of God.[19] His friend and disciple, William of Saint Thierry, who supported neo-Platonic ideas, conceives of the soul as *imago Dei*, the image of God: the soul is not spotted by sin but free, noble, pure and everlasting. Introspection into one's own soul must therefore be the way to an apprehension of God.[20] In their writings, many female mystics of the following centuries resemble the twelfth-century male mystics.[21] But the resemblance is never a simple echo, for in telling about their spiritual insights, the female mystics primarily start from their own experience.

Hadewijch never attempted to systematize her mystical doctrine. But on browsing through her works, the reader soon finds that *minne*, "love," is the central concept of her thinking. Its multiple and multiform presence — it can occupy nearly any function in a sentence and is often repeated in one and the same sentence, though in different grammatical functions — characterizes all her writings.[22] Hadewijch scholarship has had a hard time discovering which meanings this word *minne* might cover. The traditional reading of *minne* as God or Christ has proved too simplistic. De Paepe reversed the focus and defined *minne* as the never-ending dynamic love-relationship between the human soul and God (331). Recently, scholars have come to agree that the one word *minne* encompasses God, the lover, as well as the love-relationship between God and the human soul. As Hadewijch herself states apodictically in Letter 25 (paragraph 34): "Love is all."

In Hadewijch's view, *minne* is "a game that no one can truly explain" (Poem 40, stanza 7). In order for a game to be a game, it must be played in utter sincerity and total abandon. This absolute devotion secures a deep joy at the moment of victory, but at the same time, the player must always be ready to accept a loss. Time and again, Hadewijch expresses that the only correct attitude to life for the mystic lover is this passionate involvement combined with the readiness to accept blows and the courage to always go on. In *minne*, victory (the union with Christ) can only be tasted for a short while. The ultimate transcendence of God accounts for the fact that the game of love is actually a never-ending quest during which fruition and lack take turns, or as Hadewijch puts it (Poem 22, stanza 7):

> Inseparable satiety and hunger
> Are the appendage of lavish love,
> As is ever well known by those
> Whom love has touched by herself.

This paradox is intrinsically linked with another paradoxical aspect of *minne*. A true mystical life is comprised of contemplation *and* charity. These two complementary poles of the mystical life must constantly fertilize one another. The search for quietistic ecstatic unity with God on the one hand, and emotional activist charity on the other, are thus considered misinterpretations of the mystical life. The true mystic tries to make the two poles hold hands. In paragraph 117 of Letter 6 Hadewijch reminds the addressee that

> With the Humanity of God you must live here on
> earth, in the labors and sorrows of exile, while within
> your soul you love and rejoice with the omnipotent

and eternal Divinity in sweet abandonment. For the
truth of both is one single fruition. And just as
Christ's Humanity surrendered itself on earth to the
will of the Majesty, you must here with love
surrender yourself to both in unity. Serve humbly
under their sole power, stand always before them
prepared to follow their will in its entirety, and let
them bring about in you whatever they wish.

Minne is a game, says Hadewijch, that no one can truly
explain. Its paradoxical nature outwits reason and language. And as
for the short moments of fruition during which the human soul meets
God, and in which God speaks to the human soul, human language
is utterly deficient. This mystic law creates a tension that underlies all
Hadewijch's writings: they speak about the unspeakable. As a
consequence, the deficiency of language is an important theme of
Hadewijch's works:

> For earth cannot understand heavenly wisdom. Words
> enough and Dutch enough can be found for all the
> things on earth, but I do not know of any Dutch or
> any words that answer my purpose. Although I can
> express everything insofar as this is possible for a
> human being, no Dutch can be found for all I have
> said to you, since none exists to express these things,
> as far as I know. (Letter 17, paragraph 112).

Yet, in Letter 28, Hadewijch tried to reproduce the silent
communication between the human soul and God. The style of this
text, which is included among the translations, is very peculiar. Each
paragraph gives some qualities of God, which are then adorned with
repetitive specifications, so that each paragraph becomes as it were a
whirlpool of words that try to picture the soul's fruition of God. But
finally this joyful verbal glorification of God ends in "a blissful
silence." Words never succeed in trapping God. However, the play
with words betrays the joy the writer had in writing on this ineffable
event and evokes a similar feeling of joy in the reader who thus can

sense the delight of the blissful soul "led into a spiritual drunkenness, in which it is playing." Thus, Letter 28 is an exquisite example of the literary mastery all Hadewijch's writings bear witness to.

Literacy among medieval women was anything but widespread.[23] Women in convents often knew enough Latin to have access to religious sources. Laywomen were supposed to marry and bear children and only from the thirteenth century onwards did some of them receive elementary education in reading and writing in order to run their households more efficiently. Only women of patrician and bourgeois descent had the opportunity to receive a broader education. From her works we know that Hadewijch must have known Latin, for she quotes and translates Richard of Saint Victor and William of Saint Thierry. She was acquainted with the latest literary forms, especially the courtly love song, and she had command over the visionary genre and the epistolary style. She mastered her mother tongue, Dutch, to an astonishing degree. Her level of education was unusual and scholars agree that it points to an aristocratic descent (Mommaers 19-20).

But education alone does not a writer make. In a society that does not expect women to write, a woman will only put her thoughts to paper when she has a strong conviction and a belief that her voice is important and in need of being heard (Petroff 4). It is obvious then that the beguine communities provided the right breeding ground for women writers. The most gifted amongst the *mulieres sanctae* experienced visions and lived through the mystical union with God. This gave them a feeling of self-respect and the courage to communicate. The other members of the group were ready to believe in their authority and made a hungry audience and reading public for the literary renderings of their experiences, their insights and their advice. Medieval women's writing was thus canalized into certain genres, namely those allowing for personal expression and for communication with others, such as "visions," poetry, and letters. The fact that Hadewijch masterfully made use of each of these three different genres may be an indication of her literary gifts. Generally speaking, her visions and poems are more introverted and express her sufferings, her longings and her achievements. The letters are more extraverted and encourage her disciples to suffer willingly for the sake of Love.[24]

Hadewijch's 14 *Visions* form a carefully compiled book that mirrors the author's mystical journey and as such formed a spiritual guide for her circle of friends.[25] The visions which she received instructed her about her own position on the mystical way and thus contributed to a deeper understanding of herself and of her destiny. At the beginning of the first vision, Hadewijch is still "too childish and too little grown-up" (paragraph 1). She is led by an angel past seven trees that symbolize the virtues necessary for the true spiritual life. Later in the vision, Christ Himself reproaches her for complaining about her misery, and he announces that,

> as you desire to possess me wholly in my Divinity
> and Humanity, you shall desire to be poor, miserable
> and despised by all men (paragraph 268).

In the following visions, she is taught to discern the true nature of all things, of all human beings, and of God. She also receives insight into the difference between passionate charity and serene charity and into the right balance between charity and contemplation (see in Translations: Visions 2, 3 and 5). At the end of the volume, Hadewijch has reached perfection. In Vision 12, she sees herself as the bride of the divine and she becomes one with Him. And in Vision 13, the Virgin Mary speaks to her:

> Behold, everything is fulfilled. Penetrate all these
> attributes and fully taste love. For you cherished love
> with humanity; you adorned and led love with loyal
> reason; and, with this lofty fidelity and this entire
> power, you vanquished love and made love one. If
> you wish to have ampler fruition, you must leave
> your body here (paragraph 109).

The *Visions* are often considered one of the greatest achievements in Dutch artistic prose of the Middle Ages (Vanderauwera 190). Alliteration and assonance, and powerful imagery mark the textual surface. But it is exactly this artistry which makes them less accessible. Besides, they seem to lack logical structure. The composition of each vision, however, reflects the way Hadewijch perceived receiving visions. Each vision invariably starts with a laconic indication of time and place of the vision, usually a liturgical event on a church holiday. Then Hadewijch describes herself as being drawn "into the mind," a state characterized by the absence of normal coordinates of time and space. In this state she receives the vision: she sees what is shown to her and hears what is said to her. Afterwards she falls "out of the mind," into a momentary ecstatic experience of unity in which all discriminating consciousness and all senses fail her. Sometimes, as in Vision 5, she is pulled back "into the mind" and receives another vision. Finally, she comes "into herself" again, into daily reality marked by suffering.[26]

Hadewijch's 45 *Stanzaic Poems* are cast in the conventional forms of the courtly love lyric. She had complete control over all the formal techniques of the genre: nature opening, meter, rhyme scheme, tornada,[27] assonance, alliteration and repetition, and concatenation. Especially the skillful use of concatenation, repetition and paradox, gives the texture of her poems a rich density. The courtly figures of speech such as the unattainability of the lady, the complete obedience of the lover, and the complaints of the lack of fruition express wonderfully well the *minne*-relationship between the mystic lover and God. Hadewijch also made use of the theme of the knight-errant who courageously goes in search of enriching adventures full of adversity. This chivalric image symbolizes the total surrender and the courage which are characteristic of the mystic who wants to live the "game of love." But Hadewijch's poems are not courtly love songs; they are mystical love songs, a new genre which she created. Her poems in stanzas do not honor a courtly lady, they court *minne*. This accounts for a major change: whereas the troubadour's love songs were generally mere convention, Hadewijch really lived and longed for *minne*. The imagery of spiritual exile and desperate craving for union with the beloved thus obtains a depth alien to profane love songs. Also the function of the stanzaic poems differs from that of the courtly love songs.[28] The troubadour performs his songs to entertain a courtly public; the stanzaic poems were read out loud or sung out in Hadewijch's beguine circle. The "I" in the poems is not an empty pronoun. It refers to the mystic mistress Hadewijch, and it functions as a mirror for the beguines who also try to live for love. The "I" in the poem and the public are connected by one and the same quest for love. The poems thus become an instrument for meditation. This effect is heightened by the dense and sometimes hermetic textual surface of the poems: they can only be understood when the listener or reader makes a concentrated effort at understanding.[29]

This "autobiographical" turn might explain why Hadewijch's poems are still so appealing, while courtly love lyrics are often considered too formalistic by modern readers. The twentieth-century reader who is interested in the quest for God, or the quest for the self — for in order to meet God, Hadewijch dives into her own soul, the *imago dei* — can easily identify with the "I" and the "you" in the pronominal architecture of her texts. In the original context, they used to refer to like-minded souls.

The collection of "Letters" contains both letters proper and treatises. The former start with a *salutatio* which betrays the warm friendship Hadewijch must have felt for her addressee (or addressees), a woman (or women) of the small community of which Hadewijch once was the mistress.[30] Hadewijch tries to give these novices — pilgrims on the spiritual path — insight into themselves and into the laws of love. To the addressee of Letter 2, she says:

> You are still young, and you must grow a good deal, and it is much better for you, if you wish to walk the way of love, that you seek difficulty and that you suffer for the honor of love, rather than wish to feel love...Let no doubt or disappointment ever turn you away from performing acts of virtue; let no ill success cause you to fear that you yourself will not come to conformity with God. You must not doubt this, and you must not believe in men on earth, saints, or angels, even if they work wonders; for you were called early, and your heart feels, at least sometimes, that you are chosen and that God has

begun to sustain your soul in abandonment
(paragraph 66).

This quotation reveals that Hadewijch writes with great
authority.[31] She sternly urges her friend(s) to completely surrender
to love, and she advises to stop focusing on the mystical union and
instead to face the sufferings of daily life; on the other hand, she
warns her friend(s) against charity initiated by passion (see Letters 2,
3 and 5 in Translations). It is interesting to see how Hadewijch
transmits to her friends the insights she acquired from her own
visions, when she was immature herself. At the same time, the letters
painfully disclose how difficult it is for Hadewijch to cope with her
own actual and spiritual suffering. Her own desire for fulfillment and
her own sense of exile often overshadow the advice and
encouragement to the addressee.[32] In addition to the letters, this
volume also contains five "treatises," comments, really, on a certain
aspect of the spiritual life. Letter 28 (see Translations), is such a
treatise which attempts to render into language the "glorious feast"
that occurs when the soul meets God. Both the letters proper and the
treatises are put in prose of the utmost clarity though it shares the
formal artistry — repetition, assonance, alliteration — of her visionary
prose. Hadewijch has also written sixteen rhymed letters, commonly
called "poems in couplets." They start with a warm address to the
addressee and develop the same themes as the prose letters.

Female mystics are often studied in the light of how they
were influenced by male writers. However, their own influence on
other mystics is all too rarely the focus of scholarly research. The
following passage by Jan Van Leeuwen informs us that Hadewijch
was revered and her works studied in the circle of the famous
fourteenth-century mystic Jan van Ruusbroec (who gained
international recognition during his lifetime and still enjoys a
worldwide readership) to which Van Leeuwen belonged:

Thus says a holy and glorious woman called
Hadewijch, a true mistress. For the books of
Hadewijch are good and just for certain, born out of

God and revealed by Him...But Hadewijch's teaching
is not automatically beneficial, for too many are those
who cannot understand it: those whose inner eyes are
too much obscured, not opened yet by the love that
clings to God in the nudity and silence of fruition.[33]

The question then arises to what extent Hadewijch has
influenced the thinking and literary production of Ruusbroec. During
his editorial work at the dawn of the century, Jozef van Mierlo
discovered striking parallels of ideas and language between Hadewijch
and Ruusbroec.[34] But it was not until the 1980s that serious attempts
were made to study Ruusbroec's debt to Hadewijch.[35] In a recent
article, J. Reynaert has tried to work out Van Mierlo's remark.[36] As
for ideas, he concludes, Ruusbroec adopted, first, Hadewijch's
emphasis on true contemplation and charity inspired by pure love as
opposed to their false counterparts inspired by human passion, and
secondly, her precarious balance between true contemplation and true
charity as a necessary element of the mystical life. As for language,
Reynaert points to various images and expressions typical of
Hadewijch's description of the "mystical way" which are also to be
found in Ruusbroec's works. Without doubt, the writing of the
fourteenth-century mystic Ruusbroec is the "continuation and
development of Hadewijch" (van Mierlo 1922).

NOTES to the Introduction

I would like to express my gratitude to two colleagues at the
University of Antwerp: to Hilde Staels, for reading through this
chapter and through the translations with an eye to the English
language, and to Frank Willaert, whose critical suggestions for the
Introduction proved very useful.

1. Hadewych may have lived in Antwerp, for inside the cover of
one manuscript of her works (MS. C, cf. note 4), the inscription "Beata

Hadewigis de Antverpia" is written. However, the inscription dates from the sixteenth century.

2. Vanderauwera 191-2 gives a detailed survey of the fortunes of Hadewijch's works from the fourteenth to the early sixteenth century.

3. MS. A and MS. B, both from the fourteenth century, are catalogued in the Royal Library in Brussels under the numbers 2879-80 and 2877-78. The late-nineteenth-century, non-critical editions of Hadewijch's works were made on the basis of these two manuscripts.

4. MS. C, somewhat older than MS. B, is in the University of Ghent (number 941). An incomplete fourth manuscript, MS. R, from about 1500, was discovered in 1963 and is in the library of the Ruusbroecgenootschap, Antwerp (number 385 II).

5. For a complete bibliography of editions and related works up to 1987, see Gertrud J. Lewis, *Bibliographie zur deutschen Frauenmystik. Mit einem Anhang zu Beatrijs van Nazareth und Hadewijch von Frank Willaert und Marie-José Govers* (Bibliographien zur deutschen Literatur des Mittelalters 10) (Berlin: Erich Schmidt Verlag, 1989), 351-410.

6. R.W. Southern, *Western Society and the Church in the Middle Ages* (Harmondsworth: Penguin, 1978), 309-310.

7. On misogyny in the later Middle Ages, see e.g. Carolyn Walker Bynum, *Fragmentation and Redemption: Essays on Gender and the Human Body* (New York: Zone Books, 1991), 151-157.

8. On feminine monasticism, see Jean Leclercq, "Feminine Monasticism in the Twelfth and Thirteenth Centuries." *The Continuing Quest for God*, ed. W. Skudlarek (Collegeville, Minn.: The Liturgical Press, 1982), 114-126.

9. The social origin of the eruption of female spirituality in the later Middle Ages has been much debated and is known to scholars as the *Frauenfrage*. See especially McDonnell 81-100.

10. In Lombardy a *mulier sancta* was called "umiliata," in Northern Italy "bizocche," in the North of France "papelarde," in Western Germany "Coquenunne," and in the Low Countries "beguine." See Mommaers 32-33.

11. Charitable work meant mainly to care for the sick; manual work to obtain economic independence consisted of spinning, weaving and embroidering (McDonnell 145-149).

12. Mommaers 40-46. Petroff 173-175 describes the lives of the Beguines in Liège on the basis of the writings of Jacques de Vitry.

13. For a detailed history of the Church's increasing control over the beguine movement, see McDonnell 154-164. Beguinages can still be visited in Antwerp, Ghent, Louvain, and other places in Belgium.

14. All fragments quoted in this Introduction are cited from the Hart translation (1980).

15. Mommaers 39-58. See also Hart 5. Letter 5 also refers to Hadewijch's exile (see in Translations: Letter 5, paragraph 14).

16. The following remarks on mysticism are based on F. Staal, *Exploring Mysticism* (Harmondsworth: Penguin, 1975), 119-224; William James, *The Varieties of Religious Experience: A Study in Human Nature* (Glasgow: Fount Paperbacks, 1981); Evelyn Underhill, *Mysticism: A Study in the Nature and Development of Man's Spiritual Consciousness* (London: Methuen, 1957); and Paul Mommaers, *Wat is mystiek?* (Bruges: Emmaüs, 1977).

17. See in the Translations: "Before all unites with all, One has to taste sour sorrows" (Poem 17, stanza 13).

18. See Frederick C. Copleston, *A History of Medieval Philosophy* (Notre Dame: Univ. of Notre Dame Press, 1990), 87-103 and 277-279.

19. In her "List of the Perfect," Hadewijch mentions Saint Bernard as one of the twenty-one mature lovers with whom she has contact. Vision 12 is a beautiful example of nuptial mysticism.

20. Hadewych's Letter 18 contains a literal translation from a passage of William's *Liber de natura et Dignitate Amoris*. See Mommaers 1989:92.

21. Such as Julian of Norwich. See Jean Leclercq, "Preface" to *Julian of Norwich: Showings*, trans. Edmund Colledge and James Walsh (New York: Paulist Press, 1978).

22. In stanza 11 of Poem 37, one reads: "Minne wilt dat minne al minne met minnen mane:" "Love wants that love, with love, demands total love".

23. Neither was male literacy. On the extent of literacy among women from the early Middle Ages to the beguines of the later Middle Ages, see McDonnell 365-387. Petroff 4-58 provides an interesting picture from a cultural-psychological point of view on medieval women writing.

24. The distinction between the inner-directed poems and visions and the outer-directed letters is made by Elona K. Lucas, "Psychological and Spiritual Growth in Hadewijch and Julian of Norwich," *Studia Mystica* 9 (3) 1986, 3-20.

25. About the careful construction of the volume as a didactic instrument, see Willaert, "Hadewijch und ihr Kreis in den Visionen," *Abendländische Mystik im Mittelalter*, ed. Kurt Ruh (Stuttgart, 1986), 368-387.

26. For a comment on Vision 6 and a detailed survey of the different states the visionary finds herself, see Mommaers, ed. *De visioenen van Hadewych*, vol. 2 (1979), 65-72.

27. The tornada is a short concluding stanza that repeats some of the rhymes of the stanza preceding it. Hadewijch indicates the tornada by R/N, the sign used to mark the beginning of the responsory in liturgical books.

28. It is as yet unclear whether the stanzaic poems were performed as songs or whether they were merely read out loud. On the function of the stanzaic poems, see Willaert 275-297.

29. Wilhelm Breuer, "Philologische Zugänge zur Mystik Hadewijchs." *Grundfragen christlicher Mystik* eds. Margot Schmidt and Dieter R. Bauer. (Stuttgart-Bad Cannstatt: Frommann Verlag, 1987), 103-122.

30. Since Hadewijch never addresses the addressee by name, it is impossible to know whether her letters were written to one woman or to several.

31. On Hadewijch's authority, see Mommaers 1989:74-77.

32. Compare: "Alas, dear child! although I speak of excessive sweetness, it is in truth a thing I know nothing of, except in the wish of my heart--that suffering has become sweet to me for the sake of love. But she has been more cruel to me than any devil ever was. For devils could not stop me from loving God or loving anyone he charged me to help forward; but this he himself has snatched from me. What he is, he lives by, in his sweet self-enjoyment, and lets me thus wander far from this fruition, beneath the constant weight of nonfruition of Love, and in the darkness where I am destitute of all the joys of fruition that should have been my part." (Letter 1, paragraph 48).

33. Jan Van Leeuwen, *VII tekene der sonne* ("Seven Signs of the Zodiac"), as quoted by Jozef van Mierlo, *De visioenen van Hadewych*, vol. 2 (Louvain, 1925), 137.

34. Jozef van Mierlo, "Uit de geschiedenis onzer middeleeuwsche letterkunde: Hadewijch," *Dietsche Warande en Belfort* 22 (1922) 84-94.

35. In "Hadewijch als voorloopster van de Zalige Jan van Ruusbroec." *Dr. L. Reypens-Album*, (ed. A. Ampe (Antwerp, 1964), 55-74, S. Axters did study the links between Hadewijch and Ruusbroec, but in his conclusion he highlighted the different mentalities and temperaments of the two mystics. Of course, Hadewijch ends up being presented as the more dubious of the two.

36. J. Reynaert, "Ruusbroec en Hadewijch," *Ons Geestelijk Erf* 55 (1981), 192-233.

Translations by Veerle Fraeters[1]

From *VISIONS*

Vision 2

1. It was on a Pentecostal day that I received the Holy Spirit in such a way that I understood all love's will in all things, and all the ways of the will of heaven and the heavenly beings, and all the perfection of perfect justice, and all the defects of the damned. And of all those wills that I saw, I understood to what extent they belonged to truth and to untruth. And since then, I could feel everything about the lovers whom I saw,[2] in whichever of those wills they then were. And then I understood all languages spoken, seventy-two different ones. As for me, the manifold of all these ways has disappeared and fallen silent. But the onefold staring into him, and the burning of love, and the truth of his will, all this has since neither been quenched, nor silenced, nor been appeased in me.

18. Before that day, I always wished to know with regard to all my doings; I was pondering and repeating unceasingly: what is love, who is love?

20. In doing so, I had spent two years.

Vision 3[3]

1. After that, on Easter day, I went to God, and he embraced me inwardly, in my senses, and took me into the mind and transported me into the face of the Holy Spirit, which holds the Father and the Son in one being. From this integrated being of your face, I received all insights and read all verdicts passed on me.

8. And out of the face a voice resounded so terrible that it was heard all over and it said to me: behold, old one,[4] who called me and who sought me, look how I am love a thousand years before

the birth of men. Look and receive my spirit and see how I am love in all things. And if you, through all the paths of full love, fully bring yourself to me, as a pure human being as I was, then you will find fruition of me, being love. Until that day comes, you will love what I, love, am, and then you will be love, as I am love. And you will not live less than what I, love, am, all the days up to your death, in which you will become alive. United with me, you have received me and I have received you. Go and live what I am, and then come back and bring me full divinity and take fruition of me as I am.

25. And then I came into myself again and I understood all I have just said and I stayed to stare into my dear sweet love.

Vision 5

1. On the matins of the Ascension of Our Lady, I was transported into the mind for a short while, and the three highest heavens were shown to me, after which the three highest angels are named, the thrones, the cherubims and the seraphs.[5] And of the four animals, the eagle came to me, Saint John, the sweet evangelist,[6] and he said: Come and see the things that I saw while I was a human being. You have seen them wholly and unfolded, while I saw them wrapped up in images; you have contemplated them and you understand their essence.

12. And thinking about the words Saint John said to me hereafter, I fell with my face into a huge suffering, and the suffering cried out loud: Ah, ah, holy friend and true majesty! Why do you leave ours behind in foreign pieces,[7] why do you not flow through them thus bringing them into our unity. My whole will is with you and with you I hate and love the way you do,[8] for since you have given me insight once more, I am no longer a Lucifer, like those who are Lucifer now and demand that goodness and grace is given to them, while through their works and toils they are not worthy of it.[9] And they want to escape from work and yet take fruition of grace, and they pride themselves because you grant them a little of your goodness, so they think they are entitled to it and thus they fall from your heavenly majesty. This you made me understand.

30. In this I used to do wrong against the living and the dead, whom I passionately, following my passion and not following the right course, without heeding the rightful course, wanted to free from purgatory and from hell.[10] But blessed be you, since without blaming me, you made it come true for four from the living and the dead, who then belonged to hell. Your goodness was tolerant of my ignorance in this, and of my unpolished passion and of the unbridled charity for men that you, in you, gave to me. At that time I did not yet fully know your perfect justice. In not fully knowing it, in this I fell and became Lucifer, even if you did not blame me for it. This was the one case in which I fell down among men, so that I remained unknown to them and they were cruel to me. Through love I wanted to keep all the living and the dead from the depths of despair and of misbehaviour and I caused their pain to be lessened and the dead ones in hell to be sent to purgatory and those living in hell to be guided into heaven. Of this your goodness was tolerant and it showed me that because of this I was fallen among men.

52. When you took me into yourself and let me know how you are and hate and love in one being, then I forever realised how I, wholly with you, should hate and love and be in all beings. Since I know that now, I demand of you that you make ours all united with us.[11]

59. And the one seated on the throne in heaven said to me: These three thrones represent me in three persons: the thrones, man; the cherubims, the Holy Spirit; the seraphims, me in my full fruition. And he took me up out of the mind into the highest fruition in wonder out of the realm of reason. There I took delight in him as I will eternally.

65. That moment was short, and when I came back into my self again, He brought me in the mind, and said the following to me: As you take delight just now, you will take delight eternally.

68. And John said to me: Go to your burden and God will renew his old wonders in you.

71. And I came back into my suffering again with many a great woe.

Vision 12

1. During mass on Twelfth Day I was taken up out of myself into the mind. There I saw a city, big and wide and high and adorned with perfections, and in the middle of it, somebody was sitting on a round disc that was continuously disclosing itself and enclosing itself with mysteries. And the one seated on the disc was sitting there still, and inside the disc he was twirling around in an untold rotation. And the wheel in which the disc in which he was twirling was running, was so unheard-of deep and dark that nothing however horrible can bear comparison to it. And inside at the upper side, the disc was set with precious stones of purified golden colour and down in the darkness of its terrible turn, it was like formidable flames swallowing heaven and earth by which all things transient are consumed.[12]

21. And the one seated there, his face could be contemplated by no one but by him who belongs to the terrible flames of the disc and who has been thrown into the abyssal wheel below. And the face drew all the dead to it living and by it all things barren blossomed and contemplating it all the poor were given abundance and all the weak strength and in that face all those who were many and manifold became one.

29. And the one who sat enthroned there in the city, he was clothed in a gown whiter than white and on the breast of it was written his name: all beloveds' beloved. Then I fell down before the face to venerate the verity of the terrifying being that I saw there revealed.

35. Then a screaming eagle came flying by and said in a loud voice: "this love [i.e., Hadewych] does not yet know all that she will become." And another said: "this love does not yet know the nature of her highest path." And the third one said: "this love does not yet know the domain her bridegroom will endow her with." And the fourth one said to me: "endure and wait and do not fall into this face. Those who fall and venerate this face will receive grace, those who stand and contemplate this face will receive justice and will have power to perceive the abyssal depths, the awareness of which is so aweful for those who are not aware."

49. And then I was taken up by the voice of the eagle that had spoken to me. And into the city then came a big crowd, and everyone was beautifully adorned by his own deeds. These were all virtues escorting a bride towards her beloved. They had served her well and had preserved her spirit so that now they could present her fully to the almighty God who would take her as his bride. And she was clothed in a gown, made of the integrated will, always, without flaw, in the service of all virtues, and exhibiting all things that belong thereto: the gown was embellished with all those virtues and each of them had its symbol on it, and its name written and thus proclaimed.

65. The first one was faith that had lifted her out of her lowness.

67. The second one was hope that had made her rise above herself into the total trust in everlasting joys.

70. The third one, true loyalty, declared her noble, since never, however distressed, did she forsake fidelity.

73. The fourth one, love of one's fellow-man, declared her rich, since her acts of charity never failed, outward nor inward, and gifts in honor of charity never lacked her, for her total trust gained her access to all riches.

78. The fifth one, desire, testified to the wideness of her spiritual landscape, beautiful and blessed with full riches, so that she might well receive all the magnificence of heaven.

82. The sixth one, humility, declared her so deep and so unfathomable that she might well fully receive that magnifence in her unfathomable depth.

85. The seventh one, discernment, declared her so bright that she set each being in the rightful place, heaven in its height, hell in its depth, purgatory in its place, the angels in their orders, each human being in the place that comes to him on his way of trial and error. That she thus let God become, accorded well with the gown of the unified will.

93. The eighth one, her trustworthy mighty deeds, declared her so strong that nothing was beyond her and that on her own she conquered all opposing forces and made all highness low and all lowness high.

98. The ninth, reason, showed that she was well-ordered and that reason was the measure by which she continuously generated justice and that gave her insight in her beloved's dearest will and just like him she blessed and doomed all that he loved and all that he hated and she gave all that he gave and took all that he took.

105. The tenth one, wisdom, showed that she was capable of mastering to perfection all virtues which must be encountered to fully satisfy the beloved. It also showed that in the unity, that deep wheel there under the awesome terrible disc in which he who would receive the bride was sitting, that in that unity, she recognized each person of the trinity.

112. The eleventh one, peacefulness, showed and declared her beautiful bearing and that she was skilled in fervent embracing and in infinite kissing and in all the honours and encounters with which the loved one courts the beloved; and that with him, she was announced and born, and that both were born out of one another, and that with him, she grew up and with him she lived a human's life abiding the same pain, poverty, disdain, the same compassion for all those slain by the wrath of justice; and that both were fed by one another, inward and outward, and never found foreign comfort; and with him she died and with him she freed all prisoners and what he fettered she fettered and with him she arose and one with him she sailed to his Father and there with him she recognized his Father as Father and with him him as Son and with him the Holy Spirit as Holy Spirit and with him, like him, she knew them all as one and she knew the being in which they were one. All this was testified by her peacefulness, that she had thus lived and that henceforth she would live with him with love in love.

135. The twelfth one, patience, had kept her from all evil and from agony in all agonies that she knew were the instruments for good deeds and a new embrace. It showed her divine in essence and in deeds.

140. Thus was that gown of the integrated will adorned with all that belongs to the divine nature. And thus adorned, the bride came with that beautiful companion represented in symbols. On her breast she wore an ornament with the divine seal since she was acquainted with the undivided divine unity. It signified that she had

understood his hidden word of himself, out of that abyssal depth. And thus she entered the city with that company, guided between fruition of love and command of virtue; the command she brought there, the fruition she found there.

152. And while she was thus guided towards the highest seat, the eagle that had spoken to me said: now see through the face and become the entitled bride of the magnificent bridegroom and see yourself thus. And at once I saw myself received by the one there seated in the wheel on the spinning disc and I was one with him in the full knowledge of unity. When I was received, the eagle said: now you see, you almighty that I previously called beloved, that you did not know what you would become and what your highest road would be and what that huge domain would be that your bridegroom would endow you with. When you first fell in the face, you recognized it as merciless to the simple soul; when you stood up and looked through it, you saw yourself complete, together with us, the entitled bride sealed with love. You, almighty, have deeply received that hidden word, understood by Job: porro dictum est.[13]

172. By that abyss I saw myself swallowed. And there I received certainty about my being received, in this form, in my beloved, and my beloved also in me.

From *STANZAIC POEMS*

Stanzaic Poem 17

1

When season shall renew itself,
Hills and dales are still
Gloomy and dark all over,
Yet the hazel starts to bloom.
Though the lover meets misfortune,
It all will make him grow.

2

What help is joy or time to him
Who seeks delight in the name of love

And does not find worldwide
One to truly trust
And freely say to: love, it is you
Who can satisfy the bottom of my soul?
3
     How can joy embrace him
Whom love has put in custody,
While he would travel through love's wideness
And without worries freely take delight?
More than stars in heaven
Are love's sorrows then.
4
     The number of those sorrows is untold
The heavy burdens beyond weigh
No one is a match for that
And one had better just forsake.
Be it small, I also had my part to bear.
To live is a horror to me.
5
     How can life abhor and rue him
Who always has given all for all
And is driven away and led astray
To where he envisages no return,
And is crushed by a storm of despair.
What rue resembles such sorrows?
6
     Ah, you proud souls,[14] who go through all with love
And live freely under her protection,[15]
Have mercy upon the victim love has slain
And stabbed by exile and despair.
Ah, he who finds a way, may live freely by that way;
My heart lives in despair.
7
     For I saw rise up a shining cloud,
Well-shaped, above the clouded sky.
I fancied I would soon in full profusion
Play freely in the sun.[16]

Then my elation turned into illusion;
Who would blame me, should I die.
8
      Then night sank down over my day.
Oh woe, that I was ever born!
But he who gives his all to love,
Love will grant him love.
Although again I am shaken now,
God consoles all noble souls.
9
      At the beginning love contents.
When love first mentioned love to me,
Ah, how I, with my all, took delight in her all!
Then she made me be like the hazelnut-tree
Which in dark times blossoms early,
While one long awaits her fruit.
10
      He fares well, who can abide
Until love, with all, sees to his all.
Ah God, this does not trouble me,
It makes me so much happier
For I gave my all to love.
But woe only wounded me more.
11
      This for the lover is too hard:
To seek out love, and not know where to search,
Be it in darkness or in light,
In wrath or in love. Would love
Truly give her consolation,
That would satisfy the exiled soul.
12
      Ah, if my Sweet would give me sweetness in love,
Love would not be exhausted,
And then elation would not be illusion.
It would be a pity, if it were so.

Ah, God make the proud souls understand
What such a loss would mean.
13
      Ah, what I mean and meant to say,
God has shown the noble souls
Whom He granted pain from love
For fruition of love's nature.
Before all unites with all
One has to taste sour sorrows.
R/N[17]
Love's coming comforts, her withdrawal wears out;
That makes the adventure heavy.
Ah, how one can grasp all with all
Is unknown to foreign peasants.

Stanzaic Poem 22

1
      My need is huge and to men unknown.
They are cruel to me, for they want to keep me
From there where all love's powers summon me.
They do not know of it, and I cannot show them,
So I have to live up to what I am.[18]
In what love inspires my spirit,
In that I exist; for that I will exert myself.
2
      Whatever blows men bring me for love's sake,
I want to endure, without taking harm.
For, from the nobility of my soul I understand
That in suffering for high love, I win.
Therefore I gladly give myself
In pain, in repose, in dying, in living,
For I know the law of lofty fidelity.
3
      The law I discern in love's nature,
Throws my soul into adventure.
It has neither form, nor cause or shape,
Yet when one tastes it, it is real.[19]

It is the substance of my joy
For which I crave at all time.
I spend my days in much bitterness.
4
      I do not complain of pain from love:
It becomes me to always be her servant,
Whether she orders loud or still.
One can witness her only in appearance.
It is a wonder beyond grasp,
Which has so clasped my heart
And makes me roam a wild wasteland.
5
      More cruel a wasteland than love can shape
Her landscape into, has never been made.
For she makes one crave for her with lust
And taste her essence without knowing.
She reveals herself fleetingly;
One follows her and she remains unseen.
This keeps exiled hearts forever on guard.
6
      If I saved up some strength in following love's counsel
All lovers would know that I do wrong.
I can be master now of what I had to beg for then
And such great harm, could never be overcome.
Now in following my nature, I find delight
Which gives me love and ever new fervor.
Therefore my yearning will never be fulfilled.
7
      It weighs me down that I can not get
To witnessing love, unless I lose myself.
Even if lust would crush my heart,
And the power of love's need, I am not to hold myself back.
One day I must know what draws me
And often rudely wakes me up
When I am settling myself in repose.

8

      If somebody tried me, I would lay a complaint
Against myself: I cannot bear the way I should,
That love once guided me to lofty heights
And now encounters me with cruel blows.
I receive neither luck nor benefit from it.
I do not know whether it is love's own doing.
I fear the false and cruel pitfalls of disloyalty.[20]

9

      Small wonder I dread disloyalty:
It has hurt me more than I could ever fathom.
For my being withheld from what I intend,
Is due to disloyalty and to nothing else.
It has done me so much harm,
That, if ever I am to flee from it,
It can only be done by lofty fidelity.

10

      What does it help me to sing of love
And now for myself prolong my pain?
In whatever suffering love holds me,
Against her might I have no redress.
I avow all that he shall avow,
Whose heart love's power has stolen.
What does it help me to force my nature?

R/N

For my nature will always be
What it is, and win what belongs to it,
However narrow men may make its path.

Stanzaic Poem 32

1

      The flowers soon will open,
And many other kinds of bloom,
And one will doom the noble hearts
Who live under love's dominion.
My welfare I put at love's disposal
And my power in her hands.

From her I merely demand
To always remain in her chains.
2
        The one locked up now in true love's chains
— as is one's debt to love —
Will certainly, before long,
Be exposed to spiteful strangers.
They bring much suffering upon those
Who live under lofty love's protection.
But however cruel they are to them,
It amounts to little, thank God.
3
        He who will serve high love
Must spare no pain.
He will give his all,
To satisfy lofty love.
And if he happens to tarry somewhat
Then he might well know this truth:
That he clearly will never become
Master of true love.
4
        Love is master of many things,
She generously gives sour and sweet.
Since I first experienced her taste,
I am always at her feet.
I beg her that she may be pleased
By the way I suffer deadly pains
For her, all without cure,
And do not complain of it to strangers.
5
        One who would tell strangers
What we endure in honour of love,
Would disturb their peace of mind
And deeply hurt their nature.
For they do not understand
What we must suffer for true love

— Adventures, painful turns of fortune —
If she is to rejoice in our love.

6

      To those who seek to satisfy love,
I urge that they spare nothing
And fully abandon themselves,
So as to stand the storms with fervor,
In spite of all those faultfinders,
Who so much want to do them harm.
However heavy they may burden them,
They must forever remain free.

7

      Freedom can be perceived indeed
In the jousts and lofty deeds
Of him who with high spirits travels through,
When the storm of love stands up to him.
For in jousts one wins that prize
Of which one seems worthy, for love.
Love is such a strong support;
To suffer for her is only fair.

8

      Those who spare some pain in love,
For certain can never understand
What can be won by those
Who always are love's servants,
And accept her heavy blows
Of which they stay unhealed,
And rise up high and fall down deep,
Before they satisfy love.

9

      Base spirits and slow hearts
Will always be concealed
The magnificence known by those
Who live in love's desire.
For they launch assaults
In storm and in adventure,

And they deserve an outcome
In the loftiness of love.
10
     God, grant success to those who seek
To satisfy love's will
And readily accept
Her great and heavy burdens,
And always endure so much for her,
For they consider love worthy of it.
I wish that one day they may fathom
The wonders of love's wisdom.

From *LETTERS*

Letter 5

1. God be with you, my dear love, and may he give you comfort and peace in himself. What I would like to see now above all, is that God would support you with peace, and comfort you with His goodness and enlighten you with the pride of his spirit, as he will do, with pleasure even, if you trust him and sufficiently abandon yourself in him.

8. Ah, dear child, sink in him with all your soul and move out of all those things that are not love, whatever happens to you: for our blows are many, and if we can stand firm, we will grow mature.

13. To suffer all from all people, that is great perfection. But, God knows, the greatest perfection is to suffer from the false fellows who seem our inmates in the household of faith. Ah, this should not surprise you, though it hurts me, that those we had chosen to share the delight in our beloved, start to disturb and destroy our company so as to separate us, and they especially do not want me to be together with anyone else. My dear, how unspeakably sweet to me is love's nature, and the gifts I get from her. Ah, I can not refuse her anything; and you would abide and withstand her, who is said to conquer all things?

28. Ah dearest, why did not love keep you more closely under her control and swallow you up in her depth? O dear, sweet as love is, why do you not fall deep into her, and why do you not touch God deeply enough in the bottomless depth of his nature? Sweet love, for love, give yourself fully to God in love: this is necessary. For this lingering is harmful to both of us, yes, harmful to you and hard on me.

37. Ah, dear love, let not pain divert you from virtue. You are busy with so many things that do not matter. You waste too much time by hastily throwing yourself into the things that cross your path. I have not been able to get you to be moderate in this. When you feel like doing something, you always do it with so much haste, you carry on as if you could think of nothing else. Your helping and comforting all your friends, pleases me much, yes, do as much as you can, if at least, in this, you and them remain serene: that I would authorize with pleasure.[21]

49. I beg and urge you, by the true fidelity of love, that you do and do not all the things I told you and that, for our unconsoled sorrow, you comfort all the sorrowful ones with all your might. Above all, I order you to keep the law of love, eternally laid on us, intact and unharmed by all foreign sorrows and all grief.

Letter 7

1. Ah, I greet you, dear, with the love that is God, and with what I am and which also is somewhat God. And I am grateful to you for what you are and not grateful to you for what you are not. Ah dear, all things should be sought for through themselves: might through might, art through art, power through power, love through love, all through all, and always the like through the like: that alone and nothing else can satisfy them. Love alone and nothing else can satisfy us, and evermore we have to defy her with new storms, with all might, with all art, with all power, with all love, with all this together; and this is to enjoy love.[22]

14. Ah, sweet love, do not forget to devote yourself to our love with new works and let her work, even if we cannot sufficiently

enjoy her. She is onto herself enough, even if from the outside she is wanting to us. Love always rewards, even if she is often late. He who gives his all to love, will get her all, some in joy, some in sorrow.

Letter 19

1. God be with you. May he give you
True insight in love's ways,
And may he make you understand:
I belong to my beloved as my beloved belongs to me,
As says the bride in the Song of Songs [2:16].
The one who sufficiently gives way to love,
Will once conquer her completely.
I hope that this will still come true;
Though for us it seems to take so long,
Let us yet thank love for all.
The one who wants to taste true love,
— Be it in wandering or in arriving —
Must keep to neither paths nor ways.
The one who, searching for love's victory,
Wanders hills and dales,
With nothing but foreign comfort, in suffering, in pain,
In ways alien to human nature,
Will be carried by love's strong steed.
For reason cannot understand,
How love, with love, sees through the beloved
And how in everything love is free.
Yes, when she has reached this freedom,
— The freedom love can give —
She spares neither death nor life;
She wants love's all, and nothing less.
At this point I leave rhyme, sense is out.
27. For, with no sense can the substance of love, that I have in mind for you and wish you, be expressed. I do not say more; here, only one's soul can speak. Our subject is too wide, for we understand love to be God himself in nature. True love has never had any

substance. Without substance, but with God's rich freedom, she is forever providing riches, and working in high spirits, and growing in nobleness.

37. Ah, if only you would grow mature according to the dignity God has summoned you to before all beginning! How can you bear it that God with his nature takes delight in you, and you do not take delight in him. How I feel about that, is something I had better be silent about. Read what you have here, if you want. I will keep silent. God works according to his will. I can only say what Jeremia said: Lord, you have deceived me, and I like to have been deceived by you.[23]

46. The most untouchable soul is most akin to God. Keep yourself untouched by all humans in heaven and on earth until the day that God is lifted up from the earth and draws you up, with all, along with him. Some say that he meant his being lifted on the cross. But when God and the blissful soul are one, then with the blissful soul he is exalted above the earth in a most splendid way. For when to the soul nothing but God exists, and when it has no will left but to live according to his only will, and if the soul has come to nought, and with its will wills all he wills, and is swallowed by him and has come to nought, then he is exalted above the earth and draws all things to him. And thus with him the soul becomes all that he is.

62. The swallowed souls thus lost in him receive, in love, their other half, as the moon receives her light from the sun. The unified insight they then obtain from this new light, namely where they come from, where they live, this unified light takes possession of the other and thus two half souls become one. Then time has come. If you had waited for this light to chose your beloved, then this would have made you free. For, those who wait are gathered and clad in the unified light, in which God clads himself.

73. As for how these two half souls become one, much enters into this. I dare say no more. For, my misfortune with regard to love is too immense and besides the strangers might well plant nettles where roses should grow. Here I stop, God be with you.

Letter 28[24]

1. In the riches of the Holy Spirit's clarity, in *that* the blissful soul finds glorious feasts. These feasts exist in divine words, meeting, in divinity, the divinity of our Lord. These words give to every soul that hears and naturally understands them, four things, fully divine: they give her tenderness and sweetness and joy and delight and all in a true spiritual way.[25]

10. Whenever God gives the blissful soul that clarity, which makes her see him in his godhead, then she sees him in his eternity and in his greatness and in his wisdom and in his nobility and in his presence and in his overflowing and in his wholeness. She sees how God is in his eternity: God with natural godhead. She sees how God is in his greatness: majestic with natural majesty. She sees how God is in his wisdom: delighted with natural delight. She sees how God is in his nobility: clear with natural clarity. She sees how God is in his presence: sweet with natural sweetness. She sees how God is in his overflowing: rich with natural riches. She sees how God is in his wholeness: abundant with natural abundance. In all these she sees God in one person and in each of these she sees God in manifold godlike riches.

30. When she is in this contemplation, she has to keep her heart serene, however different she might be outwardly. Thus says the sweet soul who, with love and in great agony has been waiting for her Lord with expectancy. And her Lord has clarified her heart. And in that clarity she has come into full disclosure. And she speaks of feasts and she says out of delight: what is all to me but God? God is to me present, God is to me overflowing, God is to me whole. In the Son, God is present to me with sweetness, in the Holy Spirit, God is overflowing to me with riches, in the Father, God is whole to me with delight. Thus God is to me in three persons one Lord and one Lord in three persons, and with three persons in manifold godlike riches is he to my soul.

48. And she herself goes on: the soul who walks with God in his presence, she likes to speak of his tenderness and his sweetness and his greatness. The soul who walks on with God in his overflowing, she likes to speak of his love and his delight and his

nobility. The soul who yet walks on with God in his wholeness, she likes to speak of his heavenly riches and his heavenly joy and his heavenly abundance. The blissful soul who walks with all of these in God and with God walks in all of these, she knows all kinds of graces, and she is master, and delighted with the same delight in godlike riches as God is, who is an eternal Lord and who is all good and who is God and who made all things.

65. God is greatness and power and wisdom. God is goodness and presence and sweetness. God is subtlety and nobility and abundance. God is high in his greatness and complete in his power and delighted in his wisdom. God is wonderful in his goodness and whole in his presence and joy in his sweetness. God is true in his subtlety and abundant in his nobility and overflowing in his abundance. Thus is God in three persons with himself in manifold godlike riches. God is a blissful beatitude and he subsists with supreme power in wonderful exalted riches.

80. These are words that with delight well up, out of God's perfection. And what is God's perfection? That is the being of the godhead in unity, and the unity in wholeness and the wholeness in disclosure, and the disclosure in glory, and the glory in delight, and the delight in eternity. God's graces are all perfect. But he who understands this, how this is in God and in the heaven of heavens, he possesses the perfection of all kinds of graces. He who wants to speak of this, has to speak with his soul.

93. God delightfully abides in the midst of his glories. And therein he is in himself, ineffable with goodness, and with riches and with wonder. God is with himself in himself, expressing himself with full bliss, to the bliss of his creatures; for thus is God. And this is why heaven and earth are full of God to anyone who is so spiritual that he may contemplate God.

101. And the blissful soul with God saw God, and she saw God wholly and overflowing, and she saw God overflowing in wholeness and whole in overflowing. And she spoke with her wholeness and said: God is a great Lord in eternity, and his godhead consists in his being three persons. He is Father in his power, he is Son in his revelation, he is Holy Spirit in his glory. God gives in the Father, and he reveals in the Son and he makes one taste in the Holy

Spirit. In the Father God works powerfully, in the Son knowably, in the Holy Spirit subtly. Thus God works with three persons in one Lord and with one Lord in three persons and with three persons in manifold godlike riches and with manifold godlike riches in the soul delighted in Him, whom he has led into the mystery of his Father and he brings her into full delight.

121. Between God and the blissful soul that has become God with God exists a spiritual love. So whenever God reveals this spiritual love to the soul, then a tender friendship rises within her. That is: she feels within herself how God is her friend, before all despair and in all despair and above all despair, yes, above all despair, into the fidelity of his Father. Within this tender friendship a lofty confidence rises. Within this lofty confidence a fair sweetness rises. Within this fair sweetness a true joy rises. Within this true joy a godlike clarity rises. And so she sees and she sees not. She sees a subsistent, an overflowing, a total truth, which is God himself in eternity. She stands still and God gives and she receives. And what she then receives in truth, and in spirituality, and in tenderness, and in wonder, that can be conveyed to no one. And she must remain in stillness, in the freedom of this delight. What God then says to her of high spiritual wonder, that no one knows but God, who gives it to her, and the soul, who, like God, is spiritual above all spirituality.

146. Thus spoke a person in God: my soul, she is all torn by the power of eternity, and she is all melted by the friendship of paternity, and she is all poured out by the magnitude of God. That magnitude is without measure and the heart of my heart is a rich riches, which is God and the Lord in his eternity.

153. Thus spoke a soul in the friendship of God: I have heard the voice of delight. I have seen the land of clarity, and I have tasted the fruit of joy. Since this has been, all the senses of my soul have been waiting for high spiritual wonders and all my present prayers are always held in a sweet confidence, which is God himself in true truth. Since this is thus, I am extremely delighted with such a delight as is God in his godhead.

165. God is flowing with holiness above all holy ones in his own paternity. And from there he is giving his dearest children new riches, all full of glory. And since this is God, he can, today and

tomorrow and ever, give new riches, heard by no one, except by the persons who heard of it by himself in his eternity. God is in his persons, and God is in his faculties. God in his faculties is above without end and he is beneath without end and he is all around without end. God is in the midst of his persons fulfilling all his faculties with godlike riches. Thus is God in the persons with himself in manifold godlike riches. A bit of God, that *is* God, and therefore in his slightest gifts, God puts all his faculties in motion. Yes, a bit of God, that is God himself: he is in himself. The riches of God are manifold, and God is manifold in unity, and he is onefold in manifold. Since this is God, all his children are filled with delight, and always one is more delighted than the other, and all his children are filled with delight.

188. The blissful soul speaks with love of spiritual wisdom and she speaks sublimely with truth and she speaks powerfully with riches. God gives love and truth and riches out of the fullness of his godhead. God gives love with understanding, God gives truth with contemplation, God gives riches with fruition.

196. Thus spoke a soul in the presence of God: one God is of all heavens, and the heavens are disclosed and the faculties of this great God shine in the hearts of his intimates with tenderness and with sweetness and with joy. Then the blissful soul is led into a spiritual drunkenness, in which she is playing and conforming herself to the sweetness she feels within herself. She is a child of God and she is filled with delight.

207. Another soul my soul calls even more delighted. That is the soul who with truth and with nobility and with clarity and with loftiness is led into a blissful stillness. And in that blissful stillness she hears a great commotion of that wonder, which is God himself in eternity.[26] Both of them are children of God and are filled with delight in this life. He who has come so far with God, that he has love and works with wisdom in divine truth, he is often filled with such a delight, as is God. For in so far as he can see with wisdom, he loves with love, and in so far as he can love with love, he sees with wisdom and often he is working with wisdom and with love in God's riches; and this is a sublime delight. He who has been standing still with God so long, that he understands such wonders, as God is

in his godhead, he often seems to devout men who do not know this,[27] ungodly with godliness and unstable with stability and ignorant with knowledge.

231. I saw God as God and man as man. And then that did not make me wonder, that God was God and man was man. Then I saw God as man and I saw man godlike. Then that did not make me wonder, that man was blissfully filled with God. I saw how God to the very noblest man gave insight in suffering and in suffering took insight away. And where he took insight away from him, he gave him the sharpest insight of all insights. When I saw that, I found comfort with God in all suffering.

242. Thus spoke a soul in the riches of God: divine wisdom and total humility, in that exists great delight in the clarity of the Father, and that is great perfection in the truth of the Son, and that is great play in the sweetness of the Holy Spirit. From the moment the holiness of God made me fall silent, I have heard many things, and from the moment I heard many things, where did I keep them? Not in folly did I keep for myself what I kept. I have kept all things before and after. Thus I keep silent and rest in God until God bids me speak. I have unified all my diversity, I have individualized all my unity, and I have enclosed all my individuality in God, until the day someone will come with such discernment, who then asks me what I mean. And then I feel with God in God, that, while speaking, I am only all the more discerned (from Him) and for this reason I softly keep silent.

262. Thus spoke a soul in the freedom of God: I understood all expressions in one unity and then I stayed to play in the residence of the Lord, and I let his servants look after his kingdom. Ah, in those days, all landscapes of all lands flew into this land. That is what I call the season of delight. I stayed there and stood above all things and amidst all things, and I looked out above all things into the glory without end.

NOTES to the Translations

1. In order to facilitate cross-reference to the Middle-Dutch editions, the paragraphs of the prose texts are numbered. The paragraph numbers in the visions refer to *De visioenen van Hadewijch*, ed. van Mierlo (2 vols. Leuven, 1924-1925), which, though out of print, is still the standard authoritative edition. The paragraph numbers in the letters refer to *De brieven van Hadewijch*, ed. Mommaers (1990), which is based on *Hadewijch: Brieven. Vol. 1: Tekst en commentaar*, ed. Van Mierlo (2 vols. Antwerpen, 1947). While translating the poems, I have kept the original lines.

2. "Lovers" refer to persons who, like Hadewijch, devote themselves to the mystical love-process.

3. Scholars have pointed out that Visions 2 and 3 belong together. Both of them relate how Hadewijch received insight in all things and in God. See De Paepe 1967:151-152 and Mommaers, *Visioenen* vol. 2 (1979) 39.

4. "Old one:" lovers who have reached a certain degree of maturity in the mystical love-process are "old." The addressee of the letters is often called "young" by Hadewijch. In the first vision, Hadewijch says that at the time she received the vision, she was young and childlike, for she had not yet experienced enough suffering.

5. According to medieval geocentric cosmology, seven spheres revolve around the earth. The seventh sphere is bounded by three heavens inhabited by three different kinds of angels. God dwells in the infinite fiery abyss circling the highest heaven.

6. Medieval iconography often represented the four evangelists by animals; Saint John is symbolized by an eagle.

7. "Ours" refers to the beguines of Hadewijch's circle.

8. The notion that love and hate both live in the divine is one of the key elements of Hadewijch's mysticism.

9. Scholars have been puzzled by the Lucifer-reference. An interesting interpretation is provided by H.W.J. Vekeman, "Die ontrouwe maectse so diep... Een nieuwe interpretatie van het vijfde visioen van Hadewijch," *De Nieuwe Taalgids* 71 (1978), 385-409.

10. The mystical night, the period during which the mystic is crushed by despair, is here called "hell." Prompted by emotional charity, Hadewijch has wanted to help those in "hell."

11. Again, "ours" refers to the women of Hadewijch's beguine community. This passage alludes to Hadewijch's exile from the group.

12. Mommaers, ed. *De visioenen van Hadewijch*, vol. 1 (1979), 113-115, points out that in one and the same text, God is described as a terrifying abyss *and* as a loving bridegroom. For Hadewijch, says Mommaers, the "Eastern" conception of God as an undifferentiated self and the "Western" conception of God as a trinitarian person are not mutually exclusive.

13. Job 4:12, "secretly someone spoke to me."

14. The qualification "proud" or "high-spirited" often occurs in Hadewijch's works. It is drawn from the chivalric code and refers to the courage of completely giving oneself to a quest — in Hadewijch's case the quest for love — and the ability to bear the suffering that inevitably goes with it, without becoming desperate.

15. Since *minne*, the Middle-Dutch word for "love," is feminine, I chose to refer to it by means of the pronoun "she" whenever it is personified.

16. Just like many writers before her, such as Bernard of Clairvaux and William of Saint Thierry, Hadewijch constantly associates the Godhead with light. In the stanzaic poems, the light-metaphor refers not so much to illuminative power, but rather to emotional fulfillment, as is the case here. See J. Reynaert 1981:65-81.

17. "R/N" is the sign used to mark the beginning of the responsory in liturgical books.

18. For Hadewijch the soul is *imago Dei*, a spotless image of God and thus naturally and essentially good. The nature of the human soul exists in being united with God; to achieve that union, the soul has to surrender completely to the love-process. See also stanza 10 and R/N.

19. The nature of Love can never be grasped by reason, it can only be tasted. Its palpability is proof of the reality of Love (compare Saint Bernard's expression: Jesus is honey in the mouth.) The theme of the ineffability of love occurs through stanzas 3, 4 and 5.

20. Disloyalty is personified; it stands for the inability of the "I" to surrender herself completely to love, and is opposed to the "high fidelity" of stanza 9.

21. On emotional charity as opposed to true charity which is serene and driven by pure love, and not by "unpolished passion," compare paragraph 1 of Vision 5.

22. This is an elaboration of the Platonic maxim that "only like knows like."

23. Jer. 20:7.

24. Although Hadewijch's authorship of this letter has been called into question on stylistic grounds (see Reynaert 1981:425-427), modern scholarship generally ackowledges Hadewijch as the author. See Willaert, "Is Hadewijch de auteur van de XXVIIIe Brief?" *Ons Geestelijk Erf* 54 (1980) 26-38. See also Mommaers and Willaert, "Mystisches Erlebnis und sprachliche Vermittlung in die Briefen Hadewijchs," *Religiöse Frauenbewegung und mystische Frömmigkeit im Mittelalter*, eds. Dinzelbacher and Bauer (Cologne: Bohlau Verlag, 1988), 117-151 and especially 146-151.

25. The Middle-Dutch word *siele* is feminine and is always referred to as *si*, "she." The Dutch language thus allows for a subtle natural personification, while in English a reference to "the soul" as "she" immediately allegorizes the text. Yet, I have chosen to refer to "the soul" as "she" rather than "it," for this fits much better the nuptial union of the soul and God that is described in this letter.

26. In God, noise and silence are one. Hadewijch often turns to paradox in her attempt to describe the divine.

27. This is the theme of the "strangers," the "false fellows" (see also Letter 5, paragraph 13) who consider themselves religious, but cannot understand the mystical path of love.

Bibliography

Primary Works

Hadewijch. *Visioenen*. Ed. Jozef van Mierlo, S.J. 2 vols. Leuven: Vlaamsche Boekenhalle, 1924-25.
_____. *Strophische gedichten*. Ed. van Mierlo. 2 vols. Antwerp: Standaard, 1942.
_____. *Brieven*. Ed. van Mierlo. 2 vols. Antwerp: Standaard, 1947.
_____. *Mengeldichten*. Ed. van Mierlo. 2 vols. Antwerp: Standaard, 1952.
_____. *De visioenen van Hadewijch*. Trans., ed. Paul Mommaers. 2 vols. Bruges: Emmaüs, 1979.
_____. *Strofische gedichten*. Trans., ed. Norbert de Paepe. Leiden: M. Nijhoff, 1983.
_____. *Mengeldichten of rijmbrieven*. Trans. M. Ortmans-Cornet, introd. W. Corsmit. Bruges: Tabor 1988.
_____. *De brieven van Hadewijch*. Trans., ed. Paul Mommaers. Averbode: Altoria, 1990.

Translations

_____. Trans., introd. Columba Hart; pref. Paul Mommaers. *The Complete Works*. New York; Ramsey; Toronto: Paulist Press, 1980.

_____. Trans., introd. Ria Vanderauwera. "The Brabant Mystic Hadewijch." *Medieval Women Writers*. Ed. Katharina M. Wilson. Athens: Univ. of Georgia Press, 1984. 186-203. (Introductory essay, and translation of Letters 9, 11, 20, 25, and 26 and of stanzaic Poems 7, 12, 27, and 35).

_____. Trans. Eric Colledge. "Hadewijch of Brabant. Letters to a Young Beguine." *Medieval Women's Visionary Literature*. Ed. Elizabeth A. Petroff. New York; Oxford: Oxford Univ. Press, 1986. 189-194. (Translation of Letters 6 and 11).

Related Works

Bolton, Brenda M. "Mulieres Sanctae." *Women in Medieval Society*. Ed. Brenda M. Bolton et al. Philadelphia: Univ. of Pennsylvania Press, 1979. 141-158.

Dronke, Peter. *Women Writers of the Middle Ages: A Critical Study of Texts from Perpetua (+203) to Marguerite Porete (+1310)*. Cambridge: Cambridge Univ. Press, 1984.

Guest, Tanis M. *Some Aspects of Hadewijch's Poetic Form in the "Strofische Gedichten"*. The Hague: Martinus Nijhoff, 1975.

Lucas, Elona K. "Psychological and Spiritual Growth in Hadewijch and Julian of Norwich." *Studia Mystica* 9 (3) 1986. 3-20.

McDonnell, Ernest W. *The Beguines and Beghards in Medieval Culture With Special Emphasis on the Belgian Scene*. New York: Octagon Books, 1969.

Mommaers, Paul. *Hadewijch*. Averbode: Altoria, 1989.

Paepe, Norbert de. *Hadewijch: Strofische gedichten. Een studie van de minne in het kader der 12de en 13de eeuwse mystiek en profane minnelyriek*. Ghent: Koninklijke Vlaamse Academie, 1967.

Petroff, Elizabeth Avilda. Ed. *Medieval Women's Visionary Literature*. New York; Oxford: Oxford Univ. Press, 1986.

Reynaert, Joris. *De beeldspraak van Hadewijch*. Tielt; Bussum: Lannoo, 1981.

Wakefield, Ray M. "The Beguine Sisters." *Canadian Journal of Netherlandic Studies* 3 (1981-82). 67-70.

Weevers, Theodoor. *Poetry of the Netherlands in its European Context, 1170-1930.* London: Athlone, 1960. 27-38.

Willaert, Frank. *De poëtica van Hadewijch in de Strofische Gedichten.* Utrecht: 1984.

Wilson, Katharina M. Ed. *Medieval Women Writers.* Athens: Univ. of Georgia Press, 1984.

Beatrijs of Nazareth

Theresia de Vroom

We know more about Beatrijs of Nazareth (1200-1268) than about many of her contemporaries because of a biography that was written by her "brother and servant," a confessor of the Nazareth convent where she had been prioress. This anonymous priest did not know Beatrijs personally but had available to him her *Levensboek* (or diary) as well as contemporary accounts of her by her religious sisters, among them her own sister, Christine.[1] The biographer tells us that he did very little to Beatrijs's original diary, only "polishing the style of a stuttering tongue" and expanding it with the figures of style of Latin rhetoric.[2]

Beatrijs was born at Tirlemont (Tienen) in the Liège diocese. Her mother, Gertrude, was renowned for her piety and her charity; her father, Barthelémy, with the assistance of his three daughters, Beatrijs, Christine and Sybille, founded several convents after the death of his wife and he oversaw the affairs of the convents of Florival (Bloemendael), Val des Vierges (Maagdendael), near Oliplinter in Brabant, as well as Nazareth, near Lier.[3] Barthelémy followed the rule of the Cistercians as did all his children.

According to her biographer, Beatrijs was a remarkable little girl. Beatrijs's mother educated her at home and then may have sent her to a school in her home town although the text of the biographer is not explicit.[4] It was said that by the age of five, she knew by heart the Book of Psalms, which in those days served as a first reading book.[5] When her mother died Beatrijs was seven years old and her father shortly thereafter took her to live with a small group of Beguines in Zoutleeuw (Leau) and she was sent to a Latin school to be educated in the *artes liberales* until the age of eight or nine. She then was moved by her father to the Cistercian monastery of Bloemendael where she continued her studies, completing the *trivium*, grammar, rhetoric and dialectic, and the *quadrivium*, music, geometry, arithmetic, and astronomy.

When Beatrijs had reached her fifteenth year, she asked the abbess of the community if she could become a novice and make her profession. Although she was fervent in her desire to enter the convent formally, her superiors decided that Beatrijs was yet too young, too lacking in strength, and lacking as well the finances for the necessary expenses. The latter objection presents an unclear portrait of both the order and the financial status of her father. At the time when Beatrijs asked to become a novice, dowries were not universally accepted, at least not in the Cistercian order.[6] Further, Beatrijs's lack of funds does not support the image of Barthelémy as founder of the Bloemendael convent and certainly not his image as its financial benefactor.[7]

Beatrijs was not easily dissuaded. In spite of the hesitations on the part of the abbess, who "turned pale with amazement" at the request, Beatrijs managed to convince the Chapter and was authorized to take the habit on Holy Thursday, 1215.[8] She took her vows a year later and was sent to the convent at La Ramée to learn the art of calligraphy and manuscript illumination at the scriptorium there. It was at La Ramée that Beatrijs met and formed a close friendship with Ida de Nivelles, who was also still a novice, but being older than Beatrijs, guided her young friend devotedly. Although Beatrijs's life is studded with similar close friendships (following the Cistercian fashion of Aelred de Rievaulx's *De spiritali amictia*[9]) Ida was extraordinary to her; she was Beatrijs's sister and her spiritual mother:

> The venerable Ida of Nivelles.... It was to this blessed woman that the devout girl attached herself inseparably with a bond of love. Every day she carefully sought a word of edification from her

mouth, and when she had it, she sowed it in the fertile soil of her heart. So it was that from their close companionship together a certain alliance of spiritual love was contracted between them which, even afterwards remained intact as long as they lived. Ida of Nivelles learned by revelation of the Holy Spirit that our Beatrijs would doubtless be taken by the Lord as His special spouse and that the fullness of His grace would be poured superabundantly into her soul. Therefore Ida gave herself wholly to Beatrijs's service and took Beatrijs wholly to herself, forming her with all possible solicitude by good advice. Nor was the devout girl ungrateful for such benefits, but returned the service as best she could, loving Ida as a mother, following her as a leader and embracing her as a teacher, since she was daily charmed by her sweet speech and carefully instructed by her word and example.[10]

In the Latin text the difference between the two women is more pronounced than the English translation brings out. Ida is called *beata femina*, blessed woman, and Beatrijs *devota juvencula*, devout girl. Ida is *magni meriti domina euidem loci monialis*, a woman (strictly a "lady" in the unspoiled sense of the word in the thirteenth-century) of great merit and a nun of La Ramée.

Beatrijs remained in contact with Ida throughout her life; the messenger between the two women may have been Barthelémy, since one of his daughters remained a nun at La Ramée.[11] When Beatrijs had left La Ramée, between the ages of seventeen and eighteen, she fell into the depression (*torpor*) described in her biography.[12] She sought Ida's advice, and according to Ida's biographer the following dialogue took place between the older woman and God:

Ida began in a tender low voice to ask God on behalf of a certain beloved sister of hers who, as she learned from her, was burdened in the mind with a grievous trouble. The Lord answered her: 'What are you

asking of me daughter? If you wish to enquire about
her sins, they are already forgiven.' To this Ida
replied, 'Lord, I wish to know even more. If I have
found favor in your eyes, show me some proof of her
salvation.' Then the Lord replied out of His gentle
kindness: 'Behold I am showing you the glorious,
ineffable, happy place which I shall give her in the
end without end. Tell her, therefore, from me not to
be deeply troubled in her heart but let her live in
peace. As a sign I have sent her such an abundant
blessing of my grace when she was near the door of
the church that failing in body and asleep in the arms
of love she could not move from that spot.' Christ's
virgin rejoiced at hearing this.[13]

Here both Beatrijs's and Ida's biographers corroborate the same event
suggesting both the credibility and the significance of Beatrijs's
depression. Further, because no diary or writings by Ida have
survived, scholars have suggested that the source of some of Ida's
biography may indeed have been Beatrijs herself and the several
"friends" whom Ida's biographer addresses in his prologue to her life.
He writes:

I am transmitting this written account of Christ's
beloved to all her friends so that in it as in a most
clear mirror they may be able to see living again the
one they have loved and tried to imitate. But I think
it should be transmitted particularly to those who
loved her specially, and for whom she had a special
love.[14]

Beatrijs remained at Florival until 1221. She then joined her
father, brother, and sisters, as well as several other religious women,
in the Val de Vierge convent at Oplinter where she professed her final
vows in 1225. According to the *Life*, Beatrijs spent six months
before going to the new convent with her sisters, copying the
liturgical books that the community would need. From 1226 onward,

Beatrijs lived at the convent at Nazareth where she was prioress from 1237 until August 29, 1268, the date of her death. We have little information of her years at the Nazareth convent in her biography, save the retelling of two of her visions (see Translations) and the assurance from the biographer that she accomplished her duties there "in a perfect manner."

In a recent essay on women's autobiographical writings, Patricia Meyer Spacks says:

> The struggle of men, their autobiographies suggest,
> is to surmount limitations; the struggle of women,
> often to circumvent them, to operate so smoothly
> within limits that they seem to have no hampering
> effect.[15]

The distinction between the writing of women and men is perhaps more difficult to assess in the early periods of literary history than in the later ones. Generic possibilities and subjects, especially in Medieval religious literature are essentially the same for both women and men. Beatrijs of Nazareth, like her contemporaries, Hadewijch, Angela of Foligno, St. Hildegard, and so forth, wrote in genres that were also employed by men: biographies of saints, treatises on the life of prayer, letters of spiritual encouragement, dramas illustrating the history of faith, mystical accounts of visions, and so forth. They chose subjects which too were the province of male writers before them and contemporaneous with them. Discussions of the special burden of women's lot, sometimes circumscribed by family management, childbirth and feminine romantic fantasy, find little place in the first writings by women in the Middle Ages. And yet the religious women of this period wrote a great deal and their writings produced some of the finest examples of spiritual and mystical literature of all time.[16] Their work, of which Beatrijs of Nazareth's spiritual autobiography, *The Seven Manners of Loving*, is an excellent example, is written within the confines of a patristic Christian tradition, a tradition that considered women inferior to men both physiologically and spiritually. A tradition whose position on women as religious spokespersons is summed up by John Gerson (1429):

> ...the female sex is forbidden on apostolic authority [1 Tim. 2:12] to teach in public, that is either by word or by writing.... All women's teaching, particularly formal teaching by word and writing, is to be held suspect unless it has been diligently examined, and much more fully than men's. The reason is clear: common law — and not any kind of common law, but that which comes from on high — forbids them. And why? because they are easily seduced, and determined seducers; and because it is not proved that they are witnesses to divine grace.[17]

Gerson's comments reflect the general position of the high Middle Ages. In this light a woman who writes spiritual literature is already in the position of challenging male authority. For a woman to write, then, even if in direct imitation of a male model, is to raise oneself up, to be a woman outside the confines of sexual inferiority and spiritual inequality, and to take upon oneself the male domain of spiritual teachings and leadership.

Women religious writers of the Middle Ages were largely celibate, which exempted them from the charge of feminine weakness and aligned them with the *vir*tue of men.[18] Women wrote religious literature because there was an audience for their writing, perhaps one composed primarily of women or laypeople more generally, who were excluded from officiating in the religious rituals of the Church.[19] Women wrote in the setting of a convent or a beguinage because it gave them an opportunity for education and with it a modicum of independence: financial, religious, political and social.[20] But what women wrote and why is essentially defined by their inferior position in relation to men and by their identity as women. As I have already suggested, women wrote because it essentially gave them equal status with men in the domain of spiritual matters. But further, women wrote religious literature because it gave them a subject that captured them and gave them focus: that subject is the nature of Divine Love as expressed in erotic and spiritual terms.

The subject of the writings of Beatrijs of Nazareth is the attainment of Divine Love. The author guides the reader through seven steps or manners which reach higher and further in each successive step toward the unity of the soul with God and its fulfillment in Divine Love. In the *Seven Manners*, Beatrijs characterizes her soul's plight by overwhelming longing. Almost every sentence is shaped by longing and with it the lack or loss associated with one not yet completely fulfilled by love. Throughout the work, the soul is "unfulfilled and unsatisfied"(10); she "searches ... what she lacks in her longing to be like love" (3). "What she longs to do is above impossible, unobtainable by all created" (10), and "far above her power, and above human reason, and above all sense" (11). Beatrijs's characterization of the perfect love places the soul (herself) in a constant state of longing and with it the realization that she is lacking. The absence which shapes Beatrijs's narrative is characteristic of her fellow female mystical writers. In it the position of woman in medieval society is figured: unempowered, overwhelmed, and essentially "longing." At the same time, this woman or soul ultimately attains Divine Love. She who is characterized by lack and longing and incapableness, proves herself to be entirely capable, fulfilled and satisfied at the end of the narrative. While the author's soul begins indeed as a lowly creature, it ends as the hero of its own spiritual life, united and one with God. In this overcoming of its own nature, the soul as a figure for the feminine reveals its heroism in its/her ability to endure, suffer and finally, to be rewarded.

In the *Seven Manners* Beatrijs discusses the ecstasy that is linked to suffering. Her biographer tells us that she inflicted various kinds of punishments on herself — sleeping on stones, flagellating herself, walking on ice, binding thorns between her breasts and loins, eating only dry bread when she was ill, and so forth. In the Fifth Manner of Loving, Beatrijs describes the pains of being overtaken by love:

> At the same time love becomes so boundless
> overflowing in the soul, it is so powerfully and so
> violently moved in the heart, that it seems to the soul
> that the heart is wounded many times and that these
> wounds are inflicted anew every day in bitter pain
> and with renewed intensity. And so it seems to the
> soul that her veins are bursting, that her blood drains
> away, her marrow withers, her bones crack, her
> chest is burned, and her throat is parched, so that the
> face and body feel the heat from within and this is
> the furor of love. She feels at the same time, that an
> arrow pierces the heart and runs to the throat and
> further to the brain....(20)

The two metaphors which shape the above description are those of
penetration and dissolution. While these are indeed descriptions of
female erotic and sensual experience, the imagery also identifies the
sufferer with Christ and his passion. The figure of the crucified Christ
is linked to the passive experience of the mystic because he is a man
violated by the violence of other men.[21] Angela Foligno would
describe Christ's passion in similar terms:

> There appeared to me the image of the blessed God
> and Man crucified, as if newly taken down from the
> cross; his blood appeared so fresh and bright red and
> flowing as if it were right now pouring forth from his
> recent wounds. Then there also appeared in all the
> joints of the blessed body such a dissolution of the
> tendons and union of the limbs from the horrible
> stretching of those virgin limbs at the homicidal
> hands of those traitors above the suffering cross, that
> the nerves and junctures of the bones of that most
> holy body seemed all loosened from their proper
> harmonious union ... but there was no break in the
> skin.[22]

In a similar way, Beatrijs, so her biographer tells us, would imitate the suffering Christ:

> The fervor of this desire inflamed her mind so much that as often as she remembered [Christ's death and her own exile, she cried]. And her heart, for a long period of time laid open by desire, and her arteries, also opened, frequently brought [to her] a horror of death, since they could not be brought back to their natural condition, because of the impediment of her desire.... Indeed such was the wounded devotion [*sauciata deuotio*] of this holy woman, such the desire for celestial joys, such the affection, at once wounded and languishing in love [*vulnerata simul et amors languens*], that, in the fervor of her desire, rivers of copious blood frequently poured from her mouth and nostrils.... So finally this violent desire continually dominated her mind, ever growing, until very often, destitute of the obedience of her corporeal senses, she was not able to discern by their services what was outside her....[23]

In her identification with Christ's passion, Beatrijs transcends the limitations of her sex and indeed becomes God-like. At the end of her travail in the *Seven Manners* she will comment that "she feels a radiant purity, and a spiritual satisfaction, and the freedom from longing, and a discriminating wisdom and a *gentle equality between our Lord* and the close knowledge of God" (my emphasis; 26). Her joy comes as naturally to her as a creature behaves on earth:

> And just like a fish that swims in the width of the current and rests in its depths, and like a bird that boldly flies in the open spaces and in the heights of the air, in the same way she feels her spirit walking freely in the widths and depths, in the open spaces and in the heights of love (28).

The plight of the soul culminates in her union with God, fearless and free: "And then love makes the soul so bold and so free that she fears neither man nor enemy, neither angel nor saint, or God Himself on all she does and leaves undone...." (30). And finally: "This is the freedom of conscience, and the sweetness of the heart and the goodness of the senses, and the nobility of the soul, and the spirit's exaltation and the beginning of everlasting life" (32).

In the Medieval writings by and about Beatrijs of Nazareth we find a remarkable example of mystical and feminine expression. In the *Seven Manners of Loving* (and her biographer corroborates it) feminine desire is transformed into spiritual longing which in turn reshapes the identity of the mystic. Beatrijs, through her passionate suffering, is able to identify herself with Christ. She is able to "proceed to divinity through a humanity that is intensely physical,"[24] and in doing so she transcends the inferiority of her sex, to the point of equality, not only with man, but with God.[25] Beatrijs of Nazareth's *Seven Manners of Loving* is ultimately a feminine fantasy of divinity that allows the author to collapse the distinctions between gender and more importantly between (wo)man and God. At the conclusion of her spiritual autobiography, Beatrijs is united and transformed by God, she is "one with Him in spirit in indistinguishable faithfulness and everlasting love" (50).

NOTES to the Introduction

I would like to thank Dr. Joseph G. Jabbra and the Office of the Academic Vice President at Loyola Marymount University for generously supporting this work in the form of a summer faculty research grant.

1. Reypens, ed. *Vita Beatricis, Prologus*, par. 1, 13.

2. Reypens, ed. *Vita Beatricis*, III, par. 274, 185.

3. Reypens, *Vita Beatricis*, I, pars. 8-15; 17-21, 193-6.

4. The *Vita* reads: "ab eius matre ... scolari studio mox censuit applicandam." Henriquez, ed. 19, 58-61.

5. Reypens, ed. *Vita Beatricis*, I, par. 19, 23-4.

6. De Granck 1983 note 18.

7. De Granck 1983 note 19.

8. Reypens, ed. *Vita Beatricis*, I, par. 45-8, 38-41. On the subject of adolescent novices see: Joseph H. Lynch, "The Cistercians and Underage Novices," *Citeaux* 24, 1973. 283-297.

9. Such friendships were found in the ecstatic feminine experience of the thirteenth century as well as in the discipline of Cistercian spirituality. See: Aelred de Rievaulx, "De spiritali amictia." *Opera omnia*, eds. A. Hoste and C.H. Talbot (Turnhout: Brepols 1971). Vol. I. 285-350.

10. Henriques, ed. *Vita Beatricis*. 50, 35-56.

11. "Sub eodem quoque tempore, misso nuncio venerabili, cuius supra mentionem fecimus, Yde Nyvellensi." Henriquez, ed., *Vita Beatricis*. 67, 5.

12. Henriquez, ed. *Vita Beatricis*. 60-64.

13. Henriquez, ed. *Vita Beatricis*. 212.

14. *Catalogus codicum hagiographicorum Bibliothecae regiae Bruxellensis*. Pars I. Codices Latini membranei. Tomus II. Brussels, 1889. 222-3.

15. Patricia Meyer Spacks, "Reflecting Women," *Yale Review* 63 (1973) 27.

16. Elizabeth Petroff begins her study with the observation that "Women were not the only writers of devotional and didactic literature but they did write some of the best," (1). In *The Medieval Lyric*, Peter Dronke comments, "It is to women that we owe some of the highest flights of

Mystical poetry in the Middle Ages." (New York: Harper and Row, 1969) 81.

17. Quoted in Bynum (1982) 135-136. Bynum goes on to say that, "Female as well as male authors accepted such generalizations, although religious women were usually little deterred by them." She gives several examples of female writers who were drawn to write, "in spite of their sex" (136).

18. St. Jerome suggests that to be a celibate woman was indeed to become like a man. For a translation of Jerome's letters on the education of virgins, see: Susan Groag Bell, ed., *Women from the Greeks to the French Revolution.* (Belmont, California: Wadsworth Press, 1973) 90-5. Joan of Arc would say that her dressing as a man was indeed to align herself with "*vir*tue," a word entirely rooted in the male domain as its Latin origins attest.

19. Petroff 4.

20. Wilson ix.

21. Petroff 12.

22. Quoted in Petroff 13.

23. Quoted in Bynum 162-3.

24. Bynum (1987) 165. In this study on the significance of eating and food to medieval women, Bynum discussed Beatrijs's transformation into Christ in relation to images of eating and drinking, especially as they relate to her reception of the sacrament of the Eucharist (161-5).

25. For a discussion of the absolute equality between men and women, male and female, mother and son in heaven and the implications of this equality in relation to the power of the Virgin in the cosmic order see Petroff 19.

Translated by Theresia de Vroom

The *SEVEN MANNERS OF LOVING*

There are seven manners of loving, which come down from the highest and return back again to the heavens above.

I. The First Manner of Loving

1

The first is a longing that is thrust forth from love; it must rule in our hearts for a long time before it can conquer all adversity; before it can work love's power and judgment and grow within us in holiness.

2

This manner is a longing that surely comes from love; it shows that the good soul will faithfully serve the Lord, follow him in holiness, and truly love him, as long as she does everything in her power to attain and to keep the purity and nobility and the freedom in which she was made by her Creator, in His image and likeness; this the soul must love and truly keep. Here and in this way, the soul longs to lead her entire life, and here to work and wax, to climb into the heights of love and closer to the knowledge of God, to the point of the completeness she was made for and is called to by her Creator. Hereafter the soul rises late and early and so she delivers herself always. And her questions, her teaching, her petitions, and her thoughts to God are: how can she reach and how may she attain the closest resemblance to love, adorned with all its virtues and with that purity that is the true nobility of love.

3

This soul searches all the while what she is and what she would like to be, what she possesses and what she lacks in her longing to be like love. And with great desire and with all the strength that she has, so she longs to keep and to protect herself from all that could burden or hinder her as she works to this end. And never does her heart rest from seeking or from asking, learning, gaining and keeping everything that may help her and bring her to love.

4

This is the most earnest desire of the soul that is put here, and to this end the soul must work and labor until it is sufficient. Granted by God, because she is sincere and faithful, the soul may from this time forward, without the hindrance of past misdeeds, serve love with a free conscience, and with a pure spirit, and with clear understanding.

5

This kind of longing is of such great purity and nobility that it surely comes from love and not from fear. Because fear makes us work and suffer, to do and leave undone, out of dread of the anger of our Lord and of the judgment of our righteous judge, or of the everlasting punishment, or the eternal plagues. But love, in all that it does, stands for purity and exaltation, and the highest nobleness, as it itself is in its own true nature, that it possesses and uses; and in this way, love teaches those that serve it.

II. The Second Manner of Loving

6

The soul has still another manner of loving, which is that she offers herself to serve the Lord for nothing, only with love and without any reason, without any payment in grace or glory. And the soul is like the maiden that serves her Lord out of great love for Him, and not for payment, satisfied that she may serve Him, and that He lets her serve Him. In this way the soul longs to serve love with love, without measure and above measure, beyond human desire and reason, with all service performed faithfully.

7

When the soul is in this state, she is so fervent in her longing, so ready to serve, so happy in her labor, so sweet in her sorrow, so glad in her suffering; and with everything that she is the soul longs only to love Him and so she asks only to do and to serve in the service of love and for its honor.

III. The Third Manner of Loving

8

The next manner of loving comes to the good soul "as" a time of much suffering and exists in great anguish; now the soul longs to do enough for love, to follow in complete honor, in all service, in complete obedience and in complete submission to love.

9

This desire becomes all the while more stormy in the soul, and in this way the soul understands with great longing all the things [she has] to do and all the pains that follow; all to suffer and to endure, and all these things [accomplished] without measure and withholding nothing, all following love in this way.

10

In this state the soul is ready to serve in all ways, willing and unafraid in labors and suffering, even so the soul remains unfulfilled and unsatisfied in all her deeds. But above all else that which causes her the most pain: that despite her great longing, the soul cannot do enough for love, that she falls short so much in loving.

Yet she knows certainly, that this is above human ability, above all her power to do because what she longs to do is above impossible, unobtainable by all created, that is, that she might do as much as all mankind on the earth, and as all the spirits in heaven, and all creation that are above and below, and do beyond all telling more than they, in service, in loving and in glorifying the wonder of love. And because she falls so far short in her labors, she wants with powerful longing to bring fulfillment. But that satisfaction cannot be granted her.

11

She knows certainly that what she longs to fulfill is far above her power, and above human reason, and above all sense, but still she cannot pace herself, nor restrain herself, nor calm herself. She does all she can, she thanks and praises love, she works and labors for love, she sighs and she longs for love, she gives herself entirely to love. and all her works are fulfilled in love. All this does not give her any rest and it is her heart's greatest suffering, that she must long but that she cannot prevail; and because of this the soul must remain in the sorrow of the heart, and live unsatisfied. And so it seems to her as if she lives dying and dying feels the pains of hell; and all her life is hellish, and without grace, unsatisfied because of the horror of her desires that she cannot enact, nor quiet, nor satiate. In suffering she must remain until she is ready, when the Lord will comfort her, and put her in another manner of loving and longing, and in better knowledge of Himself. And then she must work for that which was given to her by our Lord.

IV. The Fourth Manner of Loving

12

It is the custom of our Lord now in the fourth manner of loving to give sometimes great joy, sometimes great sorrow, of this we will now say something.

13

Sometimes it happens that love is sweetly awakened in the soul and joyfully arises and stirs itself in the heart without any help from human actions. And so then the heart is so tenderly touched by love, and so powerfully torn by love. and so completely gripped by love, and so powerfully overcome by love, and so dearly embraced in love, that it is entirely conquered by love.

14

Now the soul feels a great closeness to God and a clarity of understanding, and a wonderful richness, and a noble freeness, and an abundant sweetness, and a great pressing of stronger love, and an overflowing of greater fulfillment. And then the soul feels that all her senses are blessed in love and her will has become love, and that she has sunk down so deeply and is so engulfed in everlasting love, that she has entirely become love.

15

The beauty of love has adorned the soul, the power of love has consumed her, the sweetness of love has submerged her, the righteousness of love has engulfed her, the nobleness of love has embraced her, the purity of love has beautified her, and the eminence of love has drawn her up and enclosed her, so that the soul must be entirely love and do nothing else than love.

16

When the soul feels herself to be full of mystical joy and in great fullness of heart, the spirit will sink entirely in love, the body seems to pass away, the heart to melt, and all its power to dissipate. And so powerfully is the soul conquered by love, that she often cannot support herself, and often her limbs and her senses lose their powers.

17

And just as a vessel that is full, if it is stirred, it quickly overflows and spills, so at times the soul is touched and overpowered by this great fullness of heart that in spite of herself, she bursts and overflows.

V. The Fifth Manner of Loving

18

In the fifth manner of loving it sometimes happens that the soul is powerfully woken up, and storm-like rises up violently, with great furor, as if it would break the heart with its strength and pull the soul out of herself and above herself in the exercise of love, and in the uses of love. And then in addition the soul is drawn in the longing of love to fulfill the great works, the pure works, of love and also the desires of the many promptings of love. Or sometimes the soul longs to rest in the sweet embrace of love, and in the freeness of joy, and in the satisfaction of having God's love, so the heart and its desires long for this state, and earnestly look for it and truly strive for it.

19

When the soul is in this state, she is so strong in spirit and understands much in her heart; she is so holy in her body, and quick in her workings, so capable of doing things outside and inside [the body], so that it seems to the soul herself that all she does and is busy doing will be done, even if the outside [the body] is idle. At the same time the soul feels such strong stirrings from within, and such utter dependence on love, and great impatience in her longing, and many sorrows from great frustration; or she feels sorrow from the great feelings of love itself, without knowing why, or it may be that she is

so moved to long for love, or because she is filled with dissatisfaction that she cannot know the final fulfillment of love.
20

At the same time love becomes so boundless and so overflowing in the soul, it is so powerfully and so violently moved in the heart, that it seems to the soul that the heart is wounded many times and that these wounds are inflicted anew everyday in bitter pain and with renewed intensity. And so it seems to the soul that her veins are bursting, that her blood drains away, her marrow withers, her bones crack, her chest is burned, and her throat is parched, so that the face and body feel the heat from within and this is the furor of love. She feels at the same time, that an arrow pierces the heart and runs to the throat and further to the brain as if it would miss the soul's desires.
21

And in the same way the soul feels the devouring fire that already pulls her in and consumes her with overpowering strength; [she feels] love working violently in the soul, sparing nothing and without measure, and all in her pulling and tearing.
22

And at this time the soul is tormented and her heart grows sick and all her power dwindles, and yet this is how the soul is fed and love is nourished and the spirit transcends herself, because love is so high above all understanding, above all that the soul can do or suffer. Even though at this time the soul may long to break the ties of love, she cannot in any way be unbound. But the soul is so fettered with the ties of love, by the expanse of love she is so completely conquered, that she cannot rule herself with measure or reason, she cannot reason through understanding, nor balance desire with reason, nor keep up with or endure this wisdom.
23

Because the more that is given from above, the more that is demanded of the soul, and the more that is revealed to her, so much more the soul is filled with longing to come close to the light of truth, and the purity, and the nobleness, all in the domain of love. And all the time the soul will be torn and drawn and never will it be satisfied nor rest. For that which most tears and torments her, is that which is to her most healing and sweet; that which cuts the deepest alone gives her healing.

VI. The Sixth Manner of Loving
24

When she, the bride of our Lord, has come further and climbed higher to greater holiness, she will feel another manner of loving, that is both closer and higher in its understanding. She will feel that love has conquered all the shortcomings in her, and that she has bettered those shortcomings and mastered her senses, and adorned her nature, and increased and raised her being, and that she has become great, all without her own pleasure being revealed; and also, that she has occupied the heart securely, and she can use it to rest, and will practice [loving] there freely.
25

When the soul is in this state, it seems to her that many things are trivial, and easy to do or to leave undone, to suffer and to endure what is necessary, all to be worthy of love, and so it is easy for her to practice love.
26

Then in this way she [the soul] feels a great strength and a radiant purity, and a spiritual satisfaction, and the freedom from longing, and a discriminating wisdom and a gentle equality between our Lord and the close knowledge of God.
27

And then is she [the soul] just like a housewife who has put all her household in good order, and wisely protects it, and keeps it prudently, and well disposes it; and she lets in and she lets out, and she does and she leaves according to her will; so it is with the soul, she is love and love reigns in her, mighty and powerful, working and resting, doing and leaving, outside and inside according to love's will.
28

And just like a fish that swims in the width of the current and rests in its depths, and like a bird that boldly flies in the open spaces and in the heights of the air, in the same way she feels her spirit

walking freely in the widths and depths, in the open spaces and in the heights of love.
29

The power of love has drawn and guided the soul, sheltered and protected it, and it has given her the prudence and the wisdom, the sweetness and the strength of love. Yet at the same time love has hidden the soul's power [from herself], until that time when she climbs to greater heights and when she entirely herself has become free, and when love even more powerfully reigns within her.
30

And then love makes the soul so bold and so free that she fears neither man nor enemy, neither angel nor saint, or God himself in all she does or leaves undone, in all her work or rest, and she feels that the love that is inside her is awake, and works just as much in the body when it is awake or asleep: she knows well and she feels, that love is not found in the labor nor in the suffering of those in whom it rules.
31

But all those that want to come to love, they must search it in fear, and follow it with loyalty, exercising themselves with longing, and they may not spare themselves great labors, and much affliction, enduring the discomfort of suffering. And all the small things she must see as great, until worthy, until she has come to that point, that love reigns within her, [when] the power of love works [in her], the power that makes all things small, and all labor easy, and suffering sweet, and pays all debts.
32

This is the freedom of conscience, and the sweetness of the heart and the goodness of the senses, and the nobility of the soul, and the spirit's exaltation, and the beginning of everlasting life.
33

This is how the angels live, and after this follows everlasting life, that God because of his goodness may grant to us all.

VII. The Seventh Manner of Loving

34

Still the blessed soul has another [a seventh] manner of higher loving, one that gives her no little work inside. That is that she is drawn above humanity in love, and above human desire and reason, and above all the workings of our hearts, and only is drawn by everlasting love into the eternity of love, and into the incomprehensible width and the inaccessible height and the profound abyss of divinity, that is in all things, and that remains incomprehensible above all things, and that is unchanging, all-being, all-powerful, all-knowing, and all-powerful in its might.

35

Herein is the blessedness of the soul, so deeply sunk in love, and so strongly drawn in longing that her heart is so pressed and impatient within, her soul flows and liquifies out of love, her spirit is possessed with the violence of great longing. And to this end draw all her desires, so she will be in the uses of love. This she demands sincerely of God and this she desires ardently from God, and this she truly longs for. Because love knows no end, nor rest, nor peace in being.

36

Love pulls her up and holds her under, it releases her and oppresses her, it gives death and brings life, it gives health and wounds the soul again. It makes her mad and then wise again. In this way love pulls her into a higher being, in this way she climbs up in spirit above time and eternity and is raised up above the gifts of love in the eternity of love which is without time, and she is set above all human manners of love, and above her own nature in longing she is able to be above herself.

37

There is all her being and all her desire, all her longing, and her love: in this certain truth and in this pure clearness, and in this noble highness, and in this rich beauty, and in the sweet company of the highest spirits that already overflow with the superfluity of love, who have their being in bright knowledge, and in it they possess and they use their love.

38

     The will [of the soul] is there above, amongst these spirits, in her desire she goes there, and most [she desires to be amongst] the burning seraphim, [but it is] in the great divinity, and in the exalted Trinity, that her beloved rest and dearest dwelling-place is.

39

     She [the soul] searches [for the Lord] in His majesty, she follows Him there and beholds Him with heart and spirit. She knows Him, she loves Him, she longs for Him so desperately that she can hear neither saints nor men, neither angels nor creatured things, except in that common love of Him with which all love Him. And Him alone has the soul chosen to love above all, and below all, and inside all, so that with all longing of her heart and with all the strength of her spirit, she so longs to see Him, and to have Him, and to delight in Him.

40

     And because of this, the earth is for her a great suffering, a powerful prison, a heavy torment. She despises the world; the world hates her, and that which belongs to the earth cannot please her nor satisfy her. And that is her greatest pain, that she must be so far away, and seem so strange. She cannot forget her suffering, her longing cannot be satisfied, her yearning she quells in sadness, and her desires are martyred, she is tormented beyond measure and without respite.

41

     Because of this she is in a state of great yearning and powerful longing to be let out of the world's suffering, and to be unbound from her body, and so she says with a sorrowing heart as the apostle said: "*Cupido dissolui et esse sum cristo.*" That is, "I long to be unbound and to be with Christ."

42

     This longing in her is great and strong, and that which she must endure is hard and long, and the suffering that her longing causes her is indescribably great, and still she must live in hope and in hope she yearns and pines.

43

Ah, holy longing of love, how strong you are in a loving soul! It is a blessed passion and a sharp torment and a long torment and a murderous death and a dying life.

44

There above she cannot yet come and below she may not rest or stay, to think of Him [God] is a longing she cannot endure. And His absence fills her with tormented longing. And so she must live with great sorrow.

45

And therefore, she will not nor cannot be consoled, as the prophet says: "*Renuit consolari anima mea et cetera*," that is, "My soul refuses to be comforted." So the soul refuses every consolation even that from God Himself and from His creatures because all the comfort which she might receive strengthens further her love and draws her longing to a higher being, and it renews her desire to be love and to exist in the uses of love and without comfort to live in suffering. And so she remains unsatisfied and unconsoled by all gifts, because she still has not attained the promised love.

46

This is a hard and laborious life, because she will take no consolation here, but longs only to achieve what it seeks so restlessly.

47

Love has drawn her and pulled her and taught her to go love's way and the soul has followed them faithfully. In the meantime, in great suffering and with much labor, with great desire and cruel longing; in much impatience and greater dissatisfaction; in sorrow and in suffering and in powerful torment; in seeking and in searching, and in wanting and in having; in climbing and in drawing back, in following and in pursuing; in need and in pain, in fear and in anxiety, in woe and in desolation; in great faith and in great doubt; in love and in loss, so the soul is ready to bear all. In death and in life she will suffer love and in the feelings of her heart she bears many cruel pains and because of love she desires to come to her true home.

48

And when the soul has seen all this suffering, then her refuge will be celestial glory. Because it is the end of the work of love that the soul longs to be close to love, striving to be near love, where it can be nearest to love.

49

Because of this the soul always wishes to follow love, to know love and to use love, and that cannot happen while she is here [on earth] in this suffering. Therefore she desires to leave this life and find her home, where she has already made her dwelling, there where she with love and desire can find rest. Because she knows well that there all hindrances will be removed, and that she will there, in love, by love be received.

50

For there the soul will look upon that which she has so sorrowfully longed for: she will have Him for her eternal reward. He whom she has so faithfully served, and she shall use Him with complete satisfaction, He whom she has embraced in her soul with great love. And there she shall go in the joy of her Lord, just as St. Augustine says, "*Qui in te intrat, in gaudium domini sui et cetera,*' that is, "O Lord, Who goes in the joy of the Lord goes into Him, and he shall not fear, for in Him who is perfect shall all perfection be had."

51

Then the soul is united with her bridegroom and becomes one with Him in spirit in indistinguishable faithfulness and everlasting love.

52

And who has practiced with Him in a time of grace, shall use Him in everlasting glory, where there is nothing else but praise and love. To this may God bring all of us. Amen.

From the *Vita Beatricis*

A Trinitarian Vision — How in her Desire, Beatrice
Aspires to the Knowledge of the Holy Trinity

Par. 215:1-2
And for a particular time she had been filled with a desire for this understanding, it happened on the day of the Most Holy Nativity of the Lord, applying all her heart's powers to meditation, she began to ponder deeply on the mystery of our Lord's Incarnation, when all of a sudden, in ecstasy, she was carried up into the celestial spheres, born aloft by the Divine Spirit, her own spirit being in an instant raised to the contemplation of an excellent vision. What did she see? From the omnipotent and eternal Father there came forth a great river from which flowed in all directions numerous streams and rivulets which offered water to drink "springing up into life everlasting" (John 4:14). Some drank from the river itself, others from the streams, while others quenched their thirst at the rivulets. But she who was privileged to see things was able to drink at all waterways. While drinking, she immediately grasped, with the inner most point of her mind, the meaning of all these images.

Par. 216
The River was the Son of God Himself, Our Lord Jesus Christ, eternally created by the Father, born in the time of His Mother for the redemption and salvation of mankind. The streams were the signs of our reestablishment, the stigmata of the Lord's Passion which He deigned to suffer on the wood of the Cross for us sinners. The rivulets then are the graces which the Giver of all things good never ceases throughout the centuries to bestow upon His faithful ones, to help them do His will.

Those drinking at the river are those who, distinguished for their more perfect lives, followed the Redeemer's footsteps with unwavering zeal; those drinking at the streams are those who, thanks to compassion, progress by remembrance of the Lord's Passion. And those drinking at the rivulets are those who strive to transform the graces they have received into works of charity, thus fulfilling God's will. The number of persons drinking, with their different manners of doing so, is ordered according to the hierarchy of merits, for Christ gave drink to the first from His very person, He restored the second category with the sweet chalice of His passion and He satiated the others with the delightful gifts of His graces and with the heavenly sweetness of His comfort.

She also saw that some refused to drink, wishing to approach neither the river, nor the streams, nor the rivulets, thus remaining parched and empty on account of their stubbornness. These are the people who, by the stains of grave sins and the practice of evil deeds, have voluntarily separated from the community of the chosen, despising the Lord Who does not despise them. Parched and empty and knowing nothing of heavenly delight, they remain attached exclusively to their earthly pleasures and desires.

Par. 217

After seeing all this, the Lord's handmaid, having carefully followed with a sharp eye, the course of the river back to the source of eternity whence it began, had the privilege of understanding what she had wished to understand of the mystery of the Holy Trinity: how the Lord, the Son of God, was created eternally by the Father and, in the course of time, born in time of a mother; how the Holy Spirit proceeds equally from the Father and the Son, how the difference of the Persons coalesced in one single Essence of Divinity, eternity, and majesty, as well as all the other holy and sacred mysteries of the Divine Trinity, venerated in perfect faith on this earth by our Holy Mother the Church. All things thanks to the revelation of the Holy Spirit, Beatrijs's soul was able to fully grasp, at one and the same time.

Returning back to herself (after the ecstasy) with her own strength, Beatrijs would like to continue meditating on these mysteries. The Lord discourages her from this and orders her to devote her cares and attentions to others.

Par. 218

... Having accepted as a divine gift this task of charity, it seemed to her that in a most excellent manner, her heart dilated and expanded, as if it should cover the whole world, at the cost of bursting. From then onwards she clasped to her heart the whole human race, as if she had captured it in an enormous net. I think that this term of capturing signifies nothing other than the breadth of charity, so that she became debtor — as the Apostle says (Rom. 1:14) — "towards both the wise and the foolish." According to the grace she had received, in all purity of faith and heart, she dedicated herself to the service of each one, according to his needs. And she undertook these duties of charity with devotion, and with even greater devotion she carried them out.

Vision of the World as a Wheel — How She Saw the Whole World Placed Beneath Her Feet, Like a Wheel

Par. 234

After she had spent a long time in the accomplishment of her duties as prioress, it happened one day that she heard a nun reading those words of St. Bernard in which he says that "Many are those who suffer torments for Christ's sake but few are those who love themselves perfectly for Christ's sake." She kept in her memory the words of this holy man and for two days she often pondered over them. But by herself she was not at all able to discover their correct meaning, wondering how man's love applied to himself could in some way be more important than bearing the sufferings of the Passion for Christ. As man, whether he be good or evil, naturally loves himself for "no man hates his own flesh" (Eph. 5:29), this brief addition "for Christ's sake" seemed to her to give special significance to these words, because experience alone, and not the subtlety of the human intelligence can discover the meaning of this addition.

Par. 235

Realizing that, through the efforts of meditation, she did not succeed in finding the deepest sense of these words, God's servant then turned to prayer, ardently beseeching the Lord to illuminate her on this matter. In His goodness, what could He refuse His chosen handmaid, in her arduous search and fruitful zeal? The grace of divine love not only gave her what she asked for, but it also enlightened her, revealing to her the manifold secrets of the divine mysteries.

Par. 236

As soon as she was raised aloft into ecstasy, she saw placed beneath her feet the whole machine of the world as if it were a wheel. She saw herself placed above it, her eyes of contemplation magnetized towards the incomprehensible Essence of the Divinity, while the innermost point of her intelligence, in an admirable manner, considered the eternal and true God, the uncreated Most High, the Lord in the majesty of His substance. She was so adequately positioned between God and man that, below God, but higher than the whole world, she trampled upon terrestrial things, remaining inseparably united to the Divine Essence by the embraces of charity.

In this union in which she became "one in single spirit with God" (I. Cor. 6:17) she realized that she had reached that purity, freedom of spirit and glory for which she had been created from the very beginning. And as if her spirit had been transferred entirely within the Divine Spirit, she thus understood that, for a short while, she was united to the Most High Deity and rendered entirely celestial.

Par. 237

Coming back to herself, she retained in her memory the sweetness of this contemplation, delighting in it, without, however, experiencing it again. And remembering what she had seen and understood, comforted by the indescribable divine sweetness, she reposed peacefully in the arms of the Beloved, burning with the fire of love. Then she understood the sense of the words cited above, but less by intelligence than by experience, with the purified eye of the spirit, and she became aware that she loved herself perfectly for Christ's sake, but that there are few who reach this summit for perfect love.

NOTES to the Translation

We know that The *Seven Manners of Loving* was written by Beatrijs of Nazareth because in one of the last chapters of his *Vita*, Beatrijs's biographer gives a Latin adaptation of her work (III, pars. 246-261). It is thanks to this translation that it was possible for scholars to identify the author of the Middle Dutch text which was rediscovered in 1895 in a document called the *Limbourg Sermons*. Beatrijs's treatise is written in prose and in the Brabant dialect. Both Reypens and Wackers have discussed the problems of the text of the *Seven Manners*, in particular the problem presented by the "Seventh Manner" which seems to be a summary of the first six manners and therefore possibly a later addition.

There is one complete translation in English of the *Seven Manners* by E. College (1965) and a translation of only the "Seventh Manner" by Sheila Hughes (1989 via the French translations of Emilie Zum Brunn and Georgette Epiney-Burgard). Both translations work to make sense of a text that indeed seems strange to modern readers and in that sense both translations are useful. In places I find both hasty and inexact. In the present translation, I have tried as much as possible to maintain the exact language and sense of the Dutch text. At times this makes for awkward and even cryptic reading but in these instances the original is just as unclear and unwieldy. The text of the *Seven Manners* is alien, strange and remarkable; I have tried to preserve all these senses in my translation.

Beatrijs often uses repetition of phrase, syntax, and mood in her treatise. Again I have translated these repetitions as literally as possible in order to preserve the sense of the original. The effect in the Dutch is that repetition works as a kind of prayer or contemplative meditation, repeating the degrees or varieties of experience in a similar form that both shapes and defines experience more fully and at the same time coaxes the reader into a meditative spirit. In the Dutch (as in Latin) the soul, "siele" is feminine. I have taken the liberty of translating it as feminine, with the attendant pronoun, "she," which is also used in the Dutch. This is indeed a liberty since key terms such as "minne" (love), for example, are also feminine and I do not translate them as reflecting gender. But because it is a woman's soul that is discussed and because I examine the *Seven Manners* above as distinctive in its feminine quality, I have chosen to translate the subject of the treatise, the soul, as reflecting its female nature.

For the translation of selections from the *Vita Beatricis*, I have relied on the fine translation by Sheila Hughes (again taken from the French by Zum Brunn and Epiney-Burgard). With the exception of partial translations in Bynum's *Holy Feast and Holy Fast* (1987), there are no other translations of the *Vita* in English of her biography.

Bibliography

Primary Works

Anon. *Vita Beatricis: De autographie van de Z. Beatrijs van Tienen O. Cist, 1200-1268.* Ed. L. Reypens. Antwerp: Ruusbroec-Genootschap, 1964.

Anon. *Vita Beatricis*. Ed. Chr. Henriquez. *Quinque Prudente Virgines.* Antwerp, 1630 1-167.

Beatrijs. *Seven mannieren van minnen.* Ed. L. Reypens and J. Van Mierlo. Louvain: De Vlaamse Boekenhalle, 1926.

_____. *Van seven manieren vanheiliger minnen.* Ed. H.W. Vekeman and J.J. Th. M. Tersteeg. Zutphen: N.V.W.J. Thieme & Cie., 1971.

Related Works

Bynum, Caroline Walker. *Holy Feast and Holy Fast: The Religious Significance of Food to Medieval Women.* Berkeley; Los Angeles: Univ. of California Press, 1987. 115-128, 160-165.

_____. *Jesus as Mother: Studies in the Spirituality of the High Middle Ages.* Berkeley; Los Angeles: Univ. of California Press, 1982.

College, E. Ed., trans. *Mediaeval Netherlands Religious Literature.* Leyden: Sythoff, 1965.

Dronke, Peter. *Women Writers of the Middle Ages.* Cambridge: Cambridge Univ. Press, 1984.

Granck, R. de, "Chronological Data in the Lives of Ida of Nivelles and Beatrice of Nazareth." *Ons Geestelijk Erf*, 57 (1983). 15-29.

_____. "The Cistercian Nuns of Belgium in the Thirteenth Century." *Cistercian Studies* 5 (1970). 169-187.

Petroff, Elizabeth Alvilda. Ed. *Medieval Women's Visionary Literature*. New York; Oxford: Oxford Univ. Press, 1986.

McDonnell, E.W. *The Beguines and Beghards in Medieval Culture With Special Emphasis on the Belgian Scene*. New York: Octagon Books, 1969.

Reypens, L. "De 'Seven manieren van minnen' geinterpoleerd." *Vita Beatricis*, See Primary Works. Bijlage IX, 237-256.

Wackers, P. "Het interpolatie probleem in de 'Seven manieren van minnen' van Beatrijs van Nazareth." *Ons Geestelijk Erf* 45 (1971). 21-230.

Wilson, Katharina M., Ed. *Medieval Women Writers*. Manchester: Manchester Univer. Press; Athens: Univ. of Georgia Press, 1984.

Zum Brunn, Emilie and Georgette Epiney-Burgard. *Women Mystics in Medieval Europe*. trans. Sheila Hughes. New York: Paragon Books, 1989.

Anna Bijns

Hermina Joldersma

In 1985, the dramatic and controversial launching of a major prize for the female voice in Dutch literature, the Anna Bijns Prize, marked the advent of a radical reappropriation of the sixteenth-century author after whom the prize was named. If previous scholarly appreciation for her work had rested on her inimitable articulation of the counterreformational cause, and on the unparalleled animation and linguistic virtuosity with which she inspired the standard refrain form of contemporary rhetorical poetics, post-Prize reception of Anna Bijns has catapulted both author and work into the thick of late twentieth-century literary life. Several of her many pithy formulations serve as pertinent mottos for the award. "No better friend than cash in hand" is entirely appropriate for a prize of 10,000 Dutch guilders which seeks in part to rectify the gender imbalance in the awarding of other literary prizes. "O God, what rumors reach our ears," a reference to the Reformist foment in sixteenth-century Antwerp, speaks volumes about the vitriolic discussion concerning "the female voice in literature" ignited by the establishment of the Prize.[1]

For the poet herself, this grand celebration of Anna Bijns as sister, as feminist *avant la lettre*, cannot be ignored in the future academic interpretation of her life and work, for it constitutes a necessary first step in modern appreciation for "older," i.e. pre-Romantic literature, a step which Hans Robert Jauss has called "the

immediate or prereflective reader experience" (Jauss 182). For the
four founders of the Prize (E. de Waard, R. Dorrestein, A.
Meulenbelt, and C. van Tuyll), this "prereflective reader experience"
is based less on Jauss's concept of aesthetic pleasure in the texts than
on a personal identification with Bijns as female author. But by
adopting Anna Bijns as patroness of a modern literary award they
have initiated a renewed discussion of her work. And because the
Prize celebrates the female experience and the female imagination in
literature, they have insured that this renewed discussion will
necessarily include some consideration of her "female voice." Of
course, they are not the first to focus "prereflectively" on Bijns's
gender, for past (exclusively male) scholarship has always drawn
attention to the fact that Anna Bijns was a woman.[2] Both past (male)
and current (female) readers focus on Bijns's emotionality as one
distinctive feature of her "woman's voice," but it is clear that readers
vary widely in their evaluation of this emotionality. The late-
twentieth-century founders of the Prize root their reading in an
instinctive empathy with the first independent woman writer in Dutch
who "chose neither the protection of marriage nor that of a convent
life [but] lived her life as her own woman" and who seems to have
paid an emotional and financial price for that independence
(Dorrestein 59). Hence, for example, they value the vehemence of
Bijns's attacks on Luther, because these refrains reveal a woman who
"singlehandedly and with the keenest and most powerful verbal means
at her disposal fought for a cause in which she deeply believed" (De
Waard 5). They see her coarse language — which was criticized by
previous scholars as showing a "lack of discrimination in choice of
imagery" (Roose 357) — as illustrating "the female voice" in practice;
with it Bijns appropriated "male verbal territory" as her own, instead
of being "forced into silence, euphemism, or circumlocution" as
female writers often are (Showalter 255-256). As an example, De
Waard cites Bijns's much criticized image of the despondent lover as
a cow ("With a cow's sluggish gait I sway about"),[3] and she argues
that, had the twentieth-century (male) poet Gerrit Achterberg included
it among his many far-fetched metaphors, it would have been
considered stunningly original (35-6).[4] Particularly irritating for
feminist critics is the double standard evident in the recurring and

unduly lengthy debate about the experiential basis for Bijns's love poetry. "Love poems?" writes De Waard, "How could she, being the virtuous old maid that she was, ever have written such passionate stuff? Did she just make them up? Then they are bad poetry. Didn't she make them up? Then **she** was a bad woman! A discussion which never plays a role in the interpretations of male literature" (De Waard 35; cf. Dorrestein 60). De Waard sums up the feminist view of scholarship on Bijns with these words: "The work of Anna Bijns is an as yet unexplored gold mine. It might be that the establishment of a foundation and a prize with her name on it will finally encourage (female and male) scholars to turn their attention to that research" (35-6).[5]

Mining the gold from Bijns's work presents a formidable challenge, for its considerable stylistic, linguistic, and cultural distance from modern Dutch cannot be entirely overcome by personal sympathy. Rather, bridging this distance entails moving beyond the "prereflective reader experience" to a second stage of reading, to what Jauss calls coming to terms with "the astounding or surprising otherness of the world opened up by the text" (182). If we are not to misread Bijns as a twentieth-century feminist (also not intended by the founders of the Prize), we must move from a naive identification to an understanding of the otherness of Bijns's sixteenth-century world. Methodologically, this entails "the reconstruction of the horizon of expectation of the addressees for whom the text was originally composed" (Jauss 182). For Bijns this work of reconstructing the horizon of sixteenth-century expectations is still a relatively open field. In particular, most of the otherwise valuable scholarship on her work has made two assumptions which will require a fundamental reassessment: that Bijns's work can be judged by late nineteenth- or early twentieth-century notions of appropriate female behavior, and that a post-Romantic aesthetic privileging personal experience as the basis for "real" literature ought also to be valid for the sixteenth century.[6] Before exploring these problems in greater depth, however, another significant hindrance requires mention: the lack of a readily available, reliable, complete, and comprehensive modern edition presenting a clear picture of Bijns's texts as they have been shaped by the rather complex transmission of her work. Her first volume of 23 poems was also the first volume of rhetorical refrains ever to be published in the Low Countries (1528; translated into Latin in 1529). The second edition (1548) incorporated a second book with an additional 24 counterreformational poems. A third volume appeared in 1567. There were numerous editions and reprintings during her lifetime, with the first collected edition of the three books appearing in 1646. During the seventeenth century, her third book was adapted for school use. In addition, other texts are scattered through an astonishing number of contemporary manuscript codices.[7] Such modern reprints as do exist constitute a rather bewildering thicket of partial nineteenth-century editions, to which critical discussions on textual reliability or authorship must be sought in yet other studies.[8] A comprehensive edition would provide a sound basis for the philological work needed to convey the richness and charm of her poetry to an audience unfamiliar with its sixteenth-century context. In the meantime, scholars must also keep in mind that Bijns's "woman's voice" (whatever that may be) has always been filtered through male literary tastes, from the Minorites who first edited the counterreformational poems, through earlier compilers who included (or failed to include) her in the tradition,[9] to modern scholars who have established the parameters of discussion.[10] Clearly, future interpretation would benefit tremendously from a carefully crafted critical edition.

But the reconstruction of sixteenth-century expectations is only the second step in Jauss's approach to older literature and "cannot in itself be the absolute goal of understanding, if the knowledge of the otherness of a distant text-world so gained is to be more than simply a sharpened variation of historical reification" (Jauss 182). The necessary third step consists of seeking the "possible meaning [of the text] for us," the modern readers. It is at this juncture that the reinterpretation set in motion by the founders of the Anna Bijns Prize becomes particularly fascinating. For, says Jauss, the reconstruction of "otherness" can have two effects on this meaning: the text may prove to be "unreadable" for modern tastes and "drop out of the canon of contemporary aesthetic experience" (183), or it may prove to have "a significance which reaches further historically, which surpasses the original communicative situation"

(182). Jauss emphasizes that this significance (or lack thereof) is never absolute, but is rather "the never-completed result of a process of progressive and enriching interpretation" dependent on reader's expectations (183). In the case of Bijns's work, it is clear that though (male) scholars have insisted on its significance for modern readers, the way in which they did so was less than convincing, since both Bijns's femaleness and her sixteenth-century aesthetic were stumbling blocks. The result has been a most curious juxtaposition of praise and apologetic criticism, well represented by Roose's conclusion: "As a poet she does still have something to offer the modern reader, too; she can repeatedly move him and, despite her shortcomings, which, in our opinion, particularly curtail the effect of her amorous refrains, we hail her as one of the most important poets of the sixteenth century, as a writer who deserves a place of honour in the history of Netherlandic literature" (367). This statement was made almost three decades ago, and important developments in the study of both sixteenth-century and women's literature have reshaped the expectations of twentieth-century readers.[11] These developments will also inform appreciation for the modern significance of Bijns's work.

One change will lie in the area of biography, although there is general admiration for the picture lovingly constructed around the turn of the last century by Jos Van den Branden, city archivist of Antwerp.[12] The facts themselves are tantalizingly sparse. Anna Bijns was born in 1493. In the same year, her parents, hosemaker Jan Bijns Lambertszoon and his wife Lijsbeth Voochs, acquired the house "The She-Wolf" on the Great Market in Antwerp. In 1495 a second daughter, Margriete, was born, and in 1497 a son, Maarten. Jan Bijns died in 1516, and a year later Margriete married the silversmith Jan Pauwels, for which she requested her share of the inheritance left by their father. The house on the Great Market was sold, and the three remaining family members settled into a less central location on the Keizerstraat, in the house "Patience" where Maarten, then twenty, opened a school. Anna's mother died in 1530. Maarten married in 1536, and in the same year Anna moved across the street into a tiny house called "Het Roosterken," where she opened her own school, joining the St. Ambrosius guild for teachers.[13] Owned by Jan van Severdonck, pastor of the Cathedral of Our Lady, the house was given to Bijns under favorable conditions upon his death in 1541. Until 1573 Bijns taught school there; in the fall of that year she sold it, entrusting the money to the merchant couple Stollaert-Boots in exchange for their agreement to look after her until her death. She died in 1575 at the age of 82, and was given a pauper's burial. The last record relating to her is the "Obiit" placed after her name in the records of the St. Ambrosius guild.

The timeless portrait that emerges from these specifically sixteenth-century facts bears the startlingly familiar contours of an intelligent person shaped by the straitened material and intellectual circumstances of what might be called, with appropriate reservations, the lower middle-class: just enough material security to allow a foray into a world beyond mere subsistence, too little to permit a leisurely exploration of that world; just enough intellectual stimulation to inspire articulate defense of old ideas, too little to participate as equal partner in the contemporary exchange of new thought. In addition, Bijns's sex closed off to her those avenues which could serve to broaden the horizons of her male peers, such as the journeyman's travels or membership in the poetic guilds, the Chambers of Rhetoric.[14] Bijns's family background confirms this interpretation. Her father's occupation as hosemaker would place the family in one of the numerically smaller and less prestigious trades.[15] Yet, he seems to have been loyal to the station which permitted him a measure of success, as is suggested by the fact that he named his eldest daughter after Saint Anna, the guild's patron saint, and that he achieved some status as officer within the guild. His death meant the loss of the trade, since women were generally not allowed to participate in the trades on any kind of equal footing,[16] and resulted in a lower standard of living for his dependents. Jan Bijns's death was probably a more significant factor in the family's financial decline than Margriete's marriage and demand for her share of the inheritance, which have usually been blamed. Of course, son Maarten could theoretically have continued his father's business; he chose instead to set up a school. His school's financial success, not otherwise documented, may be inferred from the fact that Anna seems to have had much time for writing: such of her poems as are dated are most often from this time.[17] One poem does bear the revealing postscript "In the year fifteen hundred and twenty-nine / At two at night this poem was done" (B/vH 259), but while this may imply that household or teaching duties kept Bijns from writing during the day, it may also testify to a character which could not desist until a poetic inspiration had been formed to satisfaction.

Anna's own school may be pictured as very much in keeping with the circumstances of her station. It seems to have been moderately successful financially: although a significant portion of what money she did have in her old age must have come from the sale of a building she had inherited, the school itself earned her a measure of financial independence for 44 years.[18] Yet the school was curtailed by her own limitations. Antwerp teachers were allowed to charge students tuition depending on what they were able to teach them, with basic religious instruction beginning at 20 nickels per year, while writing brought in 32 nickels, and fees for extras such as arithmetic and geometry were arranged between teacher and parents (Roose 41). Because Anna's own education, presumably from the Minorites, seems to have consisted of religious instruction and letters in Dutch,[19] the education she could provide her students was limited as well, and it is probably correct to assume that Bijns could not have charged more than 32 nickels per child, an income further limited by the small size of the building (Marain 19). It is instructive to compare this to the enterprise of a younger colleague, Pieter Heyns, who in 1555, at the age of 18, opened a school for girls. He averaged about 50 students a year, of which about half were boarders, the other half day-girls. Heyns was able to teach them reading, writing, arithmetic, French and Dutch, with music lessons costing extra. He himself was completely bilingual, and "enjoyed a great reputation not only as a school master but also as a member of a chamber of rhetoric" (Voet 396-398). Clearly, Anna's school could not have offered much competition.

Particularly Bijns's dealings with Stollaert-Boots reveal her as a semi-poor woman maintaining a fierce independence only by being thrifty to the point of miserliness and by juggling meager finances with careful suspicion. In exchange for her money, this couple was to care for her in their house until her death, also supplying her with clothing and linen. In addition, after her death her nephews

(Maarten's children) and their offspring were to receive eight Carolus guilders each, a certain sum was to go to the Minorites, and Bijns herself was to receive a dignified burial. On September 10, 1573, the agreement was to be officially signed before the city magistrates, but Bijns suddenly refused; it seems that she wanted to retain control over her own personal possessions until her death, while the couple had already counted on being able to use them as their own. It took over two months for the parties to reach an agreement, during which time Bijns had an inventory made of all her furniture, so that nothing could be touched without her permission. But even at the next signing, on November 26, she raised another concern: if she were to become so ill that the Stollaerts could no longer care for her in their house, the place to which they might move her would have to meet with her approval.[20] Only when the Stollaerts agreed to this was the arrangement finalized. De Waard points out that given this record of prior mistrust and disagreement, Bijns probably did not spend two happy years with the Stollaerts, as has generally been assumed (31-2). Considering that the lady Stollaert, by then a widow, broke the agreement to bury Bijns with commensurate dignity but instead gave her the cheapest possible burial, it would hardly seem that her last days were serenely happy.

Given a background in which a conservatist stance ensured material survival, it should come as no surprise that Bijns adopted a similar attitude on the issues of the day. For the sixteenth century was a time of major change on virtually every front, from church affairs (Luther's Reformation) through learning (Humanism and the Renaissance) and information technology (the printing press) to economics (a shift from feudalism to capitalism), with their attendant changes in the social fabric of society. As one of the major international centres of Europe, Antwerp was an early participant in many of these changes. Its sizeable German community, for example, ensured that Luther's ideas were at work in the city only six months after his famous 95 theses were first made public in 1517 (Voet 164-166; Aercke 1987). Antwerp was home to half of the 135 printers active in the the Netherlands from 1500 to 1540 (Voet 395); already the biggest commodity market of the West, it "automatically became the greatest financial centre of Renaissance Europe" (Voet 337). Some of these changes, such as modern financial practices and Humanist innovations in knowledge, are hardly reflected in Bijns's work, though when they are, she is critical:

> Bankruptcy — as common a practice
> Among the Dutch as among the French;
> Five years of grace, that's the guarantee given,
> Of two loans obtained hardly one is repaid
> (B/vH 42);

> What is the use of studying many books?
> What is the use of acquiring many goods
> Or of following in the skies
> The course of the stars and planets?
> What is the use of measuring the earth
> Or of learning many hidden secrets
> Through astronomy?
> (Meijer 80, his translation).

Rather, it is the Reformation to which she turns her attention and energy, and if she is a fierce defender of the old in this battle, she does permit the Minorites to disseminate that defense using the most modern and ideologically risky technology of the time, the printing press.[21] This may be one reason why only her counterreformational and religious poetry was published during her lifetime, even though she devoted equal poetic energy to love, friendship and marriage, and her male peers did publish such poetry. Perhaps she felt, in the words of the 1546 Index, that such literature "would better not be read than read in these perilous times, and better out of the hands of the common folk and young people, than in them" (Reusch 30). It is also true, of course, that the sixteenth century was one period in which, in the name of "the equality of all believers," women were for a short time permitted to "embrace forbidden roles and activities in the name of the revitalized Christian faith."[22] Only Bijns's polemical poetry was eminently useful to the (male) Roman Catholic hierarchy during these turbulent times.

Bijns's counterreformational poetry is a genial transformation of theological dispute into polemical exhortation and emotional debate. For though she touches on virtually all of the most significant tenets of reformational teaching (Roose 244-247), she does so almost exclusively in the context of a sarcastic unmasking of the evils of "Lutherie," the term she coined for all manifestations of the Reformation. So, for example, she criticizes the Reformational rejection of fasting, confession, or celibacy:

> Luther teaches not fasting but feasting
> And the sweetness of overindulging one's palate
> (B/vH 8);
>
> One need not confess, or shed even one tear
> Since Christ has paid all
> (B/vH 161);
>
> So he (Luther) allowed monks to wed nuns
> For he, too, wanted to get his hands on a woman
> (B/vH 166).

Often it seems, however, that her concern for the primacy of the Roman Catholic church and its teachings was at least equalled, if not surpassed, by her very legitimate fear of the effect of reformational ideas on the social order. She saw very clearly that Luther's idea of the priesthood of all believers, which entailed the right and duty to read and interpret Scripture, would lead to an irrevocable fragmentation of what had up to that time been, at least nominally, one cohesive system of belief and order. Religious fragmentation did indeed begin almost immediately, as various Protestant sects (Lutheran, Anabaptist, Calvinist) placed emphases on different parts of Scripture. Bijns is right when she comments: "Prince, they're all sheets cut from the same cloth / And the Anabaptists have sprouted from the Lutherans" (B/vH 143). She also considered Luther's doctrine responsible for social upheaval, for protesters often justified their actions by quoting from Scripture. Most specifically, she cites the German peasant wars in 1525:

> He [Luther] wants to deny his responsibility[23]
> For the peasants rising up against their masters,
> For he first taught them that they needed no ruler,
> Which caused the peasants to long for freedom.
> (B/vH 142-143).

Anabaptism also roused her ire, and it is understandable that she, who worked so hard to garner and preserve what was hers, would be as horrified as the rest of her contemporaries at the Anabaptist belief in the communal ownership of property, put into brief and disastrous practice in Münster in 1535. Except for one poem on free will (1527; B/vH 75-78), Bijns does not seek to refute the various Protestant doctrines with rational argument. Recognizing quite rightly that for most of her contemporaries emotion, rather than reason, was the prime mover for the Reformation's popular appeal, she "admonished and chided the mass of the newly converted," playing on their emotions with "constant apostrophes — direct questions, repetitions and exclamatory remarks — and a careful choice of hyperbolic imagery" (Aercke 1987:372). Piling image upon image, question upon question, "she tried to create disgust for the Reformation through the presentation of the heretical life as disgusting and disease-ridden on the material and spiritual level" (Aercke 1987:371).

Though many of her poems were written long before their publication, her three collections reflect the fortunes of reformational and counterreformational thought in Antwerp through the course of four decades. Book I (1528) opens with two poems in praise of the Virgin Mary, then continues with a number of general laments about the deterioration of faith and morals. "How topsy-turvy the world has become," she complains,

> What's it all coming to, how can it make me glad
> In thinking on it the heart crimps up in fear
> When contemplating the days which are now before
> > our eyes
> (B/vH 12).

The remaining poems in the collection attack Luther and his
teachings; while the tone is already sharp, her efforts are directed
mainly at believers who have ventured from the narrow way: "O
Christian folk, have you gone so wrong?" (B/vH 36). She also
addresses the very corruption in the Church which inspired reform,
contrasting current practices with her perception of the pure poverty
of the Early Church "when abbots lived like mice / In caves and
holes" (B/vH 39). Bijns treats the lower clergy more benignly than
their superiors, but she does blame them for not speaking out as
eloquently as they should:

> Alas! They're mostly just dumb dogs.
> They cannot bark — that is why God's law
> Is now neglected and brushed aside!
> (B/vH 60; trans. Aercke 1987:369).

It may be that Bijns, or at least her editors, believed that her
poems might be useful to inspire the kind of preaching necessary to
stem the Reformational cause. As Aercke has argued, the volume's
"organization and especially the abundance of biblical and scriptural
source references and allusions to the patristic authors in the margins
make the volume a useful tool for the writing of sermons" (1987:369-
370).

Book II (1548) was published at a time when Calvinism and
Anabaptism were beginning to make their presence felt in Antwerp,
yet it constitutes a more focussed and sharper attack specifically on
Luther and his teachings. Some of the poems are direct responses to
similar verses from the reformational camp (e.g. B/vH 146, 157),
though, once, Bijns hints that she did not waste good money on such
drivel:

> It's for the love of truth that this poem's been made,
> Though my memory may have forgotten this or that;
> If I had had that Lutheran refrain at hand,
> I'd no doubt have repaid its author all the better
> (B/vH 109).

The insistence with which she attacked the Lutheran camp is represented stylistically by a formally somewhat unusual refrain, which explains "This is why the world is in the state it's in" by means of 100 lines beginning with "Because" (B/vH 147-153). Not included in the collection of 1548 is a poem become famous in the modern reception of her work: "Yet, When Compared, Martin Rossom Comes Out Best" (trans. Aercke 1987:384-386). In this poem Bijns compares two Martins, Luther, and van Rossum, the Gelderland commander who had in 1542 ransacked his way across Brabant before laying unsuccessful siege to Antwerp for three days.[24] That this otherwise exceptionally effective poem was excluded from the 1548 edition is not as surprising as one might first suppose. In 1548 emotions were still running high, and though Bijns may have drawn inspiration from a proverb "Two Martins have created strife the whole world through / The one plagues the church, the other the farmers" (Roose 216), it was a far cry from criticising both in one breath to actually letting van Rossum come out the better, however theologically correct the argument that to murder souls is more heinous than to murder bodies. Furthermore, it has been remarked that Bijns, for all her participation in the vehement polemics common to reformational debate in general, in contrast to others never attacked identifiable individuals from her own environment. While this may be attributed to nobleness of character, as W.J.C. Buitendijk does (in Roose 251), it might also mean that she was well aware of her vulnerability as a single older woman without male protection in a society where such was not the norm, and was careful not to make personal enemies. Her editors may have concurred or have had their own reservations; their vulnerability to attack became all too clear when the Franciscan monastery in Antwerp was burned by Reformed militants in 1567.

While Book III (1567) continues some of the earlier anti-Lutheran polemics, many of its poems address a theme always present but not developed in the other books, the faith in God which inspired the defense to which Bijns had devoted so much energy.[25] Her non-polemic religious poetry, of which some is to be found only in manuscripts, reveals her unshakeable faith that the creature finds meaning only in the creator, that human beings are nothing without

God, and that turning away from God ensures disaster. The emphasis on "prayer and piety, pity and regret" in the 1567 collection "matched the contemporaneous mea culpa attitude of some in the Catholic camp, who interpreted the apparent success of the Reformation despite harsh opposition as a divine affliction" (Aercke 1987: 373). This emphasis, of course, reveals as much about editorial as about authorial intention, for many of these poems, too, were written in the 1520s. Bijns's keen awareness of the inadequacies of human nature before God seems to have been at the centre of her religious experience. She often depicts these inadequacies in very drastic terms:

> I live unreasonably, as a beast,
> Rooting in mud just like a swine
> (B/vH 357);

> I have little concern for my own salvation
> Though the body's at church, the soul's outside...
> I'd much rather hear harps and lutes
> Drums and flutes and other instruments
> Than the word of God, so full of virtue
> (B/vH 362).

Roose is entirely correct in pointing out that while Bijns does seem to be speaking of herself in such lines, it is not likely that she was such a drastic sinner (282). Indeed, it seems that her real concern was not so much any specific sin as it was the all-pervasiveness of human inadequacy and the impossibility of living up to one's Godly nature in this life. In this she shows herself to be a thoroughly sixteenth-century writer rather than a medieval one, for in her poetry there is no time for the restful contemplation or ecstatic celebration of anticipated heavenly joys so common to the cloistered mystical tradition.[26] Instead, all of her poems are characterized by struggle, and only her faith that God will finally prevail keeps her from total despair. It is the existential urgency of a human being who can imagine but cannot attain perfection which makes her religious poetry still readable today, both for those who share the Christian belief structure which shaped her world view, and for those who do not.[27]

Strong emotion and struggle also characterize her poems on friendship, love, and marriage. In these, more than in the religious ones, Bijns draws on medieval literary tradition in its specifically early-modern shape. Her love poems employ all the conventions of medieval courtly love poetry, which is inspired by the constitutive unattainability of the (female) love object: glorification of the beloved, self-abasement of the lover, confessions of steadfast troth, fear of ruinous "gossips," lament about lack of solace, and finally, the element of "hope" as the most positive emotion allowed the lover. Bijns's unique contribution lies in the way she reshapes (male) late-medieval convention with a "woman's voice," a substantial topic for which only a few introductory remarks must suffice here. For example, it has been argued that her view of love (in the love poems) is more cynical than that common to the tradition generally (e.g. Roose 192); if this is indeed so, one might consider whether this greater cynicism expresses the sixteenth-century female experience of love. It is also significant that far more women are the main speakers in her work than in that of other writers, and that she is the only *woman* to have a woman speak. A similar consideration of Bijns's "woman's voice" would benefit her satires on marriage. These texts are to be situated in a literary tradition of the battle for domination between the sexes, a tradition reaching back to Socrates and Xanthippe but gaining in momentum in the changing social fabric of the sixteenth century.[28] Bijns's texts are only some of many castigating a variety of real or imagined transgressions against social norms governing male/female relationships. A preliminary reading suggests that Bijns's woman's voice comes through in at least some of the poems, even when a male persona speaks. In one, for example, Bijns has the husband lament that his wife treats him badly. Most of his complaints, however, concern work with which wives must contend as a matter of course: making beds, cooking, scrubbing floors, even rinsing out poopy diapers. His complaint "I've been wived: would I had died from the plague!" is a pun with implications far exceeding a simple complaint about being married, and reader sympathy for the husband must extend to "wifehood" as well.

Relatively unique in sixteenth-century literature are Bijns's poems celebrating friendship. Some of the themes were adopted from the love complaints, such as the sorrow which separation brings or the pain caused by the faithless fickleness of friends. Yet these poems are far more than the sum total of their component parts, and the intensity of the friendship they posit as their theme is so uncommon that, as Roose has remarked, critics have often misread them as love poems (176). Some poems, such as "It lightens the heart, when the tongue can voice its need a bit" (J/vH 76) seem to focus more on the problems associated with communicating such sorrow to one's friends than on the sorrow itself, as these lines indicate: "I might unburden myself to my friends, but if they love me / I'll just sadden them" (J/vH 78). Though Roose interprets this poem to be about love, for "what else could the sorrow be, about which she says that, if she were to express it, people would laugh?" (179), one can imagine a melancholic heart or an inner sorrow to have many other causes, not the least of which could be the actual social loneliness a single woman such as Bijns might have experienced. The friendship poems are especially intriguing because some of them maintain a strict gender neutrality in person. In "When gone, a loved one's the source of great pain" (J/vH 22-24), for example, the persona could be either male or female, and could address either a woman or a man. Perhaps Bijns's singleness, combined with her so beneficial friendships to the Minorites (who were, after all, male, and yet at least theoretically non-sexual in their celibacy) inspired a unique vision of a friendship not defined by gender boundaries. Formal expression of this friendship is also to be found in the many acrostics of male names in her work, most of them of the Minorites and often linked with ANNA (Roose 43-52).

One literary problem meriting further investigation is the nature of the I-persona in Bijns's work. Certainly the first person is all-pervasive, for with perhaps two exceptions ("Make Merry and Leap the Scythe," trans. Aercke 1987:380-381, and "'Tis better to fart than to be harmed," J/vH #46, 105-106), all poems are thus composed. Scholars have assumed this poetic "I" to be identical with Bijns in the counterreformational poems, and, with some qualifications, also in the religious and friendship poems; in the misogamist poems they have taken it as voicing her opinions, if not representing her person; in the love poems, however, they have held the I-persona to be a strictly fictional voice. Only Jonckbloet posited, in his 1873 history of Dutch literature, that Bijns's love poetry must have been based on experience, and that this experience must have been an illicit and unhappy affair in her youth (Roose 185). In subsequent discussion, Jonckbloet's thesis alternatively found mild support or vehement opposition. The opposition seems to have taken two approaches, autobiographical or literary. Autobiographical objections argued that a moral single woman would not have engaged in such an affair or at most may have had a non-physical attachment (Roose 185-188); the literary objections, articulated most convincingly by Van Mierlo, argued that the poems were literary fiction and ought to be read entirely within the context of the literary tradition (see also Roose's conclusion, 187). This argument is not, however, an entirely satisfactory solution to the intricacies of Bijns's relationship to her I-persona, for it does not address the fact that all of Bijns's work must be read in a similar context, and does not justify reading her love poems differently than the others. Rather, such justification must lie in the nature of different literary traditions, and in Bijns's unique manipulation of those traditions. Sixteenth-century literature is especially challenging in this regard, since medieval literary conventions undergo significant alteration in the changing social and ideological conditions of that century. Indeed, some literary forms, particularly polemic verse, were so changed by the subject matter of the Reformation and the medium of print that they constitute the beginnings of new traditions; here, perhaps, lies one justification for equating only the I-persona in Bijns's counterreformational poetry with Bijns herself. Like few of her contemporaries, she seems to have understood the potential power of a personal subject in literature, and employed that personal subject to full advantage in the most important controversy of the day. Bijns's skillful use of the I-persona would suggest that her work, far from being primarily "the swan-song of medieval literature" (Meijer 82), is a much more complex embodiment of the watershed between the medieval and the modern world.

In the larger context of sixteenth-century literature, Bijns's significance transcends both achievements for which she has usually been noted, namely her articulation of the counterreformational cause and her mastery of the unwieldy refrain form. To be sure, these achievements should not be minimized: she was the first, most articulate, and most convincing Catholic voice in Dutch of the century, and her linguistic virtuosity lent her formally correct poetry a liveliness unmatched by her contemporaries. Her poems are formally conservative, adhering either to the multi-stanza refrain with the thematic tag-line or aphorism concluding each stanza, or to the ABC poem of (usually) 26 stanzas. In other aspects, however, they traverse new territory. Despite the constrictions of an intricate, carefully executed rhyme scheme, Bijns was the first to attempt, and achieve, some approximation of natural speech. She did this by introducing "a variant of the French alexandrine into Dutch poetry, emphasizing rhythm without rigid syllable count," by using enjambment, and by employing the caesura to serve "as a natural breathing pause rather than a syntactic gap" (Aercke 1987:375). Linguistically, too, she traverses new ground; if the lack of a Humanist education meant that she did not participate in Renaissance literature, by the same token it ensured that she used the vernacular at her disposal to full advantage, often creating striking images by unusual juxtapositions, or even inventing new but eminently expressive words. In her use of the vernacular she was more like her arch-enemy Luther than she would have appreciated, for he, too, was one of the first to consciously manipulate the language of the common folk for his purposes. All in all, Bijns's work is characterized by "a naturally dramatic union of passion in theme and expression" (Aercke 1987:375). Yet Bijns is able to express this passion in different ways, and it is striking how her poetic voice varies considerably from theme to theme: exhorting or despairing in the counterreformational poems, gentle or forlorn in the friendship poems, derisive and mocking in the marriage poems. It is indeed a testimony to her remarkable poetic gift that her poems seem to be less exercises in rhetorical virtuosity, as is so often true for her contemporaries, but more the expression of individual thought and especially feeling.

If it is in the unique manipulation of contemporary literary convention that we begin to discern the individual expression of Anna Bijns and discuss her significance for modern readers, it is also here that we must seek the existence and significance of her female voice. In certain respects, viewing Bijns against the background of contemporary literary convention is a two-edged sword, for one must bear in mind that "women shared a great deal with the men of their own class, and identified with the aims and aspirations of their fathers and husbands" (Wiesner 318). This, as I have argued, is partially true for Bijns; in many ways she remained true to the material and intellectual situation of the lower middle class. At the same time, Bijns had the relatively unique experience of being fatherless for almost 60 years, and of never having married. In other words, if all women experienced a difference from those "fathers and husbands" in that they "could not themselves achieve the same aims" (Wiesner 318), Bijns, without traditional male attachment, must more than once in her life have consciously experienced the difference her gender made to the world around her. This awareness comes to subtle, possibly unconsious expression in her work. It is there quite obviously in the misogamist poems: the drudgery of household tasks is depicted with an eye to detail rooted in personal experience, and a woman's loss of freedom through marriage is described so convincingly that one must agree, "Unyoked is best! Happy the woman without a man!" (trans. Aercke 1987:382-383). There are also simply more women present in Bijns's poetry than in that of her contemporaries. For example, Bijns employs the form of the moralizing *Standenrevue*, a late-medieval genre in which all contemporary social groups are castigated for a particular fault, to criticize what she considers the worst sins of the Reform-minded. Her use of the *Standenrevue* is typically sixteenth century in that a certain disorder in the organization of social groups reflects the changing social order of that century. In one poem, for example, Bijns concentrates on abbots, princes and lords, and merchants (B/vH 39-41), while in another she castigates tradespeople such as smiths, shoemakers, carpenters, masons, tinworkers, etc., throwing in "drunken chums" and other choice slanderings for good measure (B/vH 29-32). It has been remarked that she was particularly hard on the women who followed and promoted reformational teaching (Roose 247). This is not true; rather, if Bijns seems to be hard on women, it is because she included them much more regularly and systematically in the *Standenrevue* than her (male) contemporaries did. In contrast to the latter, she does not forget women as a special group, and if she castigates "doctoren" — common men who presume to interpret Scripture like their educated superiors — , she will not leave out "doctorinnen," who neglect their spinning for their studies, and who have the audacity to hold classes in their homes (B/vH 31; cf. 63-67). Again and again one is struck by Bijns's insistence on "inclusive language" and imagery: she holds Adam and Eve equally responsible for sin in the world (eg. B/vH 7, 21, 64, 71, 96, 324), and virtually always uses male and female terms in pairs (eg. "lutherianen oft lutherinnen" [B/vH 65], "clercken ende clergessen" [B/vH 115], "men and women" [B/vH 70; "nuns become whores, monks become ruffians" [B/vH 168]). To some extent the double figure of speech is sixteenth-century rhetorical practice, and also for Bijns may have aided rhyme and rhythm. Nevertheless, Bijns was singularly consistent and inventive in this regard. Already mentioned was the greater voice accorded women in her love poems; whether this voice differs from that of her male speakers must yet be investigated. Bijns's female voice might also be evident in imagery; De Waard cites one striking example in which Bijns extends to the household realm the Biblical image of one rotten limb (of the body) infecting the others, "Just as moths in one garment infest all the other clothes" (22; from J/vH 63).

Bijns's female voice is, of course, not part of a single tone giving voice to a single reality, but rather one voice in "a complete choir" unified in its description of what may be wide varieties of female experience by a common perspective of describing this experience from "inside out" rather than "outside in" (Meulenbelt 144-145). Hearing Bijns's female voice will mean extending Jauss's concept of otherness to include the otherness of gender as well as the otherness of time. But working through this double refraction is well worth the effort, for it enables the modern reader to see Bijns as a quintessentially sixteenth-century author, whose ambivalent reaction to the major changes of her time finds echo in modern ambivalence about equally dramatic change, and a sixteenth-century woman whose life and work embody a female version of sixteenth-century reality more than recognizable as female reality even today. As one of the major voices of her time, her voice adds significantly to our understanding of this intriguing century, and in no small measure to a better understanding of our own.

NOTES to the Introduction

1. See Dorrestein, Meulenbelt, and particularly my article "The Anna Bijns Prijs (1985-)" in the *Canadian Journal of Netherlandic Studies* XIII, ii (Fall 1992). 29-34. My information about the Prize was gleaned from the Publications of the "Anna Bijns Stichting". Selected portions of Bijns's work have been reworked as an "Anna Bijns Triptych" for soprano and flute/alto flute, which was performed at the first ceremonial awarding of the annual Prize to Josepha Mendels in 1986, as well as at the official formation of the Flemish branch of the Anna Bijns Foundation in 1991. Accompanying the Flemish celebration (which included a walk-about to unveil plaques at the three Antwerp houses in which Anna Bijns resided during her life) was the world première of *Het Roosterken*, a radio play about the author written by the Flemish poet Elisabeth Marain. The only known visual representation of Anna Bijns, a tiny sixteenth-century pen-and-ink caricature of a sharp-nosed visage with tongue impertinently protruding, has achieved new status as a silver sculpture by the artist Maja van Hall; this sculpture is the "Anna Bijns Trophy" which accompanies the monetary award. And even popular culture has gotten into the act: in 1986, the first "Anna Bijns Festival" (a mammoth gala occasion at the Amsterdam Schouwburg celebrating women in the arts) inspired the "Anna Bijns Cocktail" (Campari with Caveno Bianco, or alternatively Campari with soda or orange juice) which contributed its share to the tenor of the festivities.

2. Gender bias in previous scholarship is in certain respects tediously predictable, but it seems necessary to deal with this bias at least once for every author. The all-pervasive attention to Bijns's femaleness is represented — though by no means exhausted — by the following remarks (my emphasis). Basse criticizes the tendency of her anti-reformational polemics to degenerate into "a coarseness unexpected *in a woman*" (57). Schneiderwirth intends his brief study to elucidate "the personality of this unique *woman*, teacher, and poet" (8). Van Mierlo's otherwise decidedly

laudatory discussion of her work mentions that Bijns is "surprisingly well-versed *for a woman*" (328). Knuvelder acquires a sympathy for "*this woman*" when he reads her love poetry, in which she reveals herself as "*a woman* who craves the joy of love,*" "who abases herself, who is prepared to travel every road of suffering which her beloved requires of her" (460). Meijer believes that "her attacks on Luther are so bitter, so personal, and so invariably below the belt that one has to restrain oneself from concluding that *she was taking a frustrated love out on him*" (81). Roose seeks to explain Bijns's intertwining of tender and coarse sentiments by pointing to the fact that "Anna Bijns was *a woman*, and there is no other single psychological characteristic which can so decidedly be attributed to *women* than greater emotionality" (200-1). Roose concludes that "she was a *woman*. Those who have written about Anna Bijns have often been caught off guard by the masculine militance voiced in her work, and have often overlooked this *feminine* characteristic. Nevertheless, this characteristic manifested itself repeatedly" (365). (Roose [d. 1991: see Porteman] wrote most extensively and most representatively on Bijns.)

3. Translated by Aercke as "I walk as ponderously as if I were a cow" (Aercke 1987:374).

4. Consider the magnaminity of Meijer's opinion "that Achterberg has proved once and for all that there is no such thing as a non-poetic image" (Meijer 369).

5. Such research has already begun outside the Netherlandic countries, and particularly in the United States. See the various articles by Aercke, which in turn were used by the German Reimöller for her talk.

6. Bijns's "womanness" has already been discussed; representative for the latter view may be Roose, who laments that sixteenth-century rhetorical poetry repressed the expression of personal feeling and considered didacticism and moralism as essential (327).

7. Roose (71) lists 16 manuscripts; Aercke (1987:375) states that there are 17.

8. Roose mentions that Bogaers and van Helten went beyond merely rectifying printers's errors in their edition (65), and he says that Soens's edition of manuscript A contains a host of unfortunate errors (73). In addition, one must consult both Roose and Van Mierlo (*Sprokkelingen* [1950]) for discussion on whether all of the poems in Soens's edition are to be ascribed to Bijns.

9. Bijns's friend Matthys de Castelein did not mention her among the Flemish rhetoricians who wanted to see their works in print (Aercke 1987: 375). Johan van Beverwijck did include her in *Van de Wtnementheyt des Vrouwelicken Geslachts* ("On the Excellence of the Female Sex;" Dordrecht, 1693; Roose 165).

10. Such a parameter is the discussion concerning the biographical basis for her love poetry; another might be the criteria used to determine questions of authorship.

11. A classic for understanding sixteenth-century literature on its own terms is still Barbara Könneker's *Die deutsche Literatur der Reformationszeit. Kommentar zu einer Epoche* (München: Winkler, 1975). In her lengthy introduction, Könneker argues that the medium of print combined with the message of the Reformation to effect a radical transformation of literature, in that the potential of "word as weapon" was first fully realized. This function in turn affected literary form. For the study of women in this period, the essays in *Rewriting the Renaissance. The Discourses of Sexual Difference in Early Modern Europe* (Eds. M.W. Ferguson, M. Quilligan, and N.J. Vickers. Chicago: Univ. of Chicago Press, 1986) offer a variety of approaches and many further references.

12. Jos Van den Branden. *Anna Bijns: Haar Leven, Hare Werken, Haar Tijd 1493-1575* (Antwerp, 1911). My sketch is based on the use made by Aercke (1987), De Waard, and Roose of Van den Branden's work.

13. The St. Ambrosius guild was established in 1530, probably as a means for city authorities to control and safeguard education with respect to Reformational teaching (Voet 395-396); its medal is pictured in Voet 284.

14. Bijns' relationship to these Chambers is still subject to debate, although Roose is probably correct in assuming that Bijns was not a member (171).

15. In Antwerp there was a sharp distinction, indeed, a running feud between the hosemakers and their rivals, the tailors, and it seems that the latter had greater status and numbers than the former. City records of 1584 show 479 tailors and 124 hosemakers (Voet 297), and while tailors were represented on the city's "Monday Council" on their own, the hosemakers were grouped together with others in the guild of the woolworkers (Voet 281, 285). A 1511 medal for the guild of the hosemakers shows three pairs of breeches on the reverse, with the initials of the patron saint, S.AN [Anna], on the obverse (Voet 284).

16. "Where women practiced a trade they generally formed a group apart" (Voet 281) and were quite restricted in what they were allowed to do. To my knowledge, no history of women's work in the sixteenth-century Lowlands, similar to Merry Wiesner's *Working Women in Renaissance Germany* (New Brunswick, NJ: Rutgers Univ. Press, 1986), is as yet available.

17. Dating bears further study. Though Book III has a number of poems from the mid-1540s, most dated poems are from the 1520s, suggesting that Bijns had little time and energy for writing once she had started her own school (Roose 171, 76).

18. While it may have been unusual for a woman to run her own school, Antwerp did have quite a number of female teachers. In 1584, the city authorities fixed the number of teachers at 80 men and 60 women (Voet 396).

19. While her knowledge of Scripture was relatively detailed, her work does not show acquaintance with classical languages or the newer humanist tradition. S. Eringa ("La renaissance et les rhétoriqueurs néerlandais." Diss. Amsterdam, 1920) concludes: "Her education was far from being complete. The humanist elements which one finds in her work have been inherited from the middle ages; she is incapable of comprehending the value of that Renaissance in art and letters which has left its imprint on four centuries of literature" (60; quoted from Roose 1963:333). One may

agree that her education was far from complete, but it is not really possible to judge her capabilities for appreciating a Renaissance which was not part of that education or her experience. The question, "Did Women Have a Renaissance?" (asked by Joan Kelly-Gadol in *Becoming Visible: Women in European History*, eds. Renate Bridenthal and Claudia Koonz. Boston: Houghton-Mifflin, 1977. 137-64), must also for Anna Bijns be answered in the negative.

20. Presumably this would have been to one of a number of hospices for the older women. The advent of Lutheranism, with its objections to the necessity of good works for salvation, "seems to have severely curbed this form of charity" in the course of the sixteenth century (Voet 436). It seems that Bijns' battle against the Reformation had implications for her own material existence.

21. The conjuction of printing (mid-fifteenth century) and the Reformation (after 1517) was a lethal one for the Roman Catholic church, which was quick to establish indices of forbidden books. The standard work on the subject is still Fr. H. Reusch, *Die Indices librorum prohibitorum des sechszehnten Jahrhunderts* (Tübingen, 1886). Apparently, the printer of Bijns's first book, Jacob van Lieshout, was later executed for the publication of heretical material (Aercke 1987:367).

22. See Bonnie S. Anderson and Judith P. Zinsser, *A History of Their Own. Women in Europe from Prehistory to the Present*, 2 vols. (New York: Harper and Row, 1988), 182.

23. Bijns seems to be referring to Luther's stunning repudiation of the peasant cause in his 1525 tract, "Against the Robbing and Murdering Hordes of Peasants" (*Luther's Works*, American Edition. Ed. Robert G. Schultz. Philadelphia: Fortress Press, 1967. Vol. 46, pp. 49-55).

24. Van Rossum is extensively discussed by Aercke (1987:377, note 19). The effect of van Rossum's plunderings on the popular imagination is manifested in numerous popular songs; five of these were printed in an Antwerp songbook of 1544. See H. Joldersma, "'Het Antwerps Liedboek:' A Critical Edition" (Diss., Princeton Univ., 1983): numbers 177, 182, 197, 210, 211.

25. Hendrik Pippinck, prior of the Franciscan Minorites in the Low Countries, and one of the most famous preachers of his time, wrote a lengthy preface to the 1567 book. In this preface, excerpted in the following, he clearly states that profits from Anna Bijns's third book will be used to begin restoration work on the Franciscan monastery in Antwerp, which had been burned and virtually destroyed by enraged anti-Catholics in 1566 (Roose 57-58):

"...Read these [profitable books] without fear; for they are the works of God's spirit, addressed to each of you for the furtherance of the Christian community. One such book I now present to you, my fellow believers; it is a small book, most artfully crafted by a godly and wise Roman Catholic maiden, Anna Bijns, residing in Antwerp and famed in distant lands. She has always persevered in the true faith and instructed the young with great responsibility; for more than fifty years (or thereabouts) she has diligently written against Luther's so venomous doctrine, as the two other books still read by many bear eloquent testimony. In these she most elegantly clarifies what sort of fruits are born from Luther's teachings, and from all the other sects of various stripes. She reveals what great damage and peril are visited upon towns, cities, and nations because false opinions and sects are allowed free reign. Now this third book, similarly excellent, has appeared; it, too, displays God's powerful might and his immeasurable grace, reveals the reasons why a nation comes to destruction and great desolation, but also shows the means through which God might be satisfied and his wrath be turned away from us. It includes many other eloquent arguments, and also fiery exhortations to all spiritual prelates as well as princes, rulers of nations, that they should keep watch (Ezekiel 3), for they are entrusted with this responsibility so that Christ's precious flock might be kept out of the clutches of the great myriad of their enemies (Acts 20), and that they might be preserved, each according to his station. Read this without fear; there is no peril in it, but rather benefit and abundant profit for the soul. And even though it be written by a maiden, do not therefore reject it; learned men have read it and approved. Furthermore, according to Joel's prophecy, the Spirit has been promised to all flesh (Joel 2): "Your sons and your daughters shall prophecy, even on my manservants and maidservants shall I pour out my spirit in those days," says Scripture, as also Peter relates in *Acts* 2. Thus do not dwell on the fact that a woman has authored this third book, but rather see the true Spirit, which has manifestly wrought his work through her and is still working today. Follow that Spirit, which you discern from her words, and you will be freed of all heretical tempest and remain steadfast in the true, upright, Roman Catholic faith, in victorious triumph against the enemy, hell, the world; which on the last day will bring you, fellow believers, to the right hand of the Father, where you shall praise the Lord without end. Amen." (B/vH 216-217; Joldersma trans.)

26. Of the *quattuor novissima* or "last things," namely death, judgment, hell, and heaven, which await all mortals at the end of their lives, medieval song placed by far the greatest emphasis on heaven. See J.A.N. Knuttel, *Het geestelijk Lied in de Nederlanden voor de Kerkhervorming* (Rotterdam: Brusse, 1906), 303.

27. It is no accident, for example, that it was the sixteenth century which crystallized the "Faust" figure into a man who sells his soul to the devil in order to overcome human limitations on space, time, and knowledge. The original German chapbook of 1587 was an explosive bestseller in all European languages; it was translated into Dutch in 1592.

28. The modern family began to emerge in the early-modern period. The historian Lawrence Stone describes its four key features: "intensified affective bonding of the nuclear core at the expense of neighbours and kin; a strong sense of individual autonomy and the right to personal freedom in the pursuit of happiness; a weakening of the association of sexual pleasure with sin and guilt; and a growing desire for physical privacy" (*The Family, Sex, and Marriage in England 1500-1800*. Abridged ed. New York: Harper, 1977. 22). It would be interesting to examine Bijns's texts (and possibly her life) in the light of these features. A few examples of the vast literary tradition of marriage satire, by no means adequately explored by scholars, are translated from the German in Steven Ozment, *When Fathers Ruled: Family Life in Reformation Europe* (Cambridge, MA: Harvard Univ. Press, 1983), 52-77. L. Dresen-Coenders ("De strijd om de broek. De verhouding man/vrouw in het begin van de moderne tijd (1450-1630)," *De Revisor* (4) 1977, 29-37) gives a brief overview of some of the more pertinent discussions internationally.

Translations by Hermina Joldersma[1]

Aubertus Le Mire's laudatory preface
to the 1646 Edition of Anna Bijns[2]

[For we know] that MARCUS TULLIUS[3] highly praised
CORNELIA,[4] mother of the Gracchi, and expressed similar
admiration for LAELIA, MUCIA, and LICINIA;[5] that LUCAN[6]
freely published the works of his wife POLLA ARGENTARIA;[7] that
BALTHASAR CASTIGLIONE[8] considered IPPOLITA[9] very highly,
and that FERRARIENSIS together with SCAEVOLA
SAMARTHANUS[10] sounded the praises of OLYMPIA
MORATA,[11] and of RUPEA OF POITIERS, far and wide. Similarly
it might be granted us to greatly praise ANNA BIJNS,[12] Maid and
School-Mistress of Antwerp, whose exceptional erudition (surpassing
that usual to the female sex), impeccable morals, and also Godly zeal
in the defense and protection of the Old Faith have gained
immortality. For she was another EUDOCIA[13] and PROBA
FALCONIA[14] in her battle, writing and publishing at the time of
LUTHER 16 learned books[15] in the Dutch tongue against his false
teachings, through which she kept many of the common folk safe in
the bosom of our Mother, the Holy Roman Catholic Church, and led
innumerable souls, who had almost gone astray, back to the path of
salvation, indeed, so aptly that ELIGIUS EUCHARIUS,[16] the famed
poet of Ghent, considered them worthy of faithful translation into
Latin.

Anna Bijns
"If sin be virtue, then Lutherans are saints"[17]

A.
Through wondrous folly my heart is disturbed
As I survey the whole world round;

There is not a thing that's not upside down,
And winds blow mindless folk about, yea,
As though there were no God, no hell.
Nary a one's a believer through and through
But all, it seems, incline to doubts.
Evil is named good, and what's now called sin,
Ere this had claim to title: good works.
Faulted is all that fights 'gainst flesh,
While pleasing the flesh is held great virtue;
Hence monks think the cowl too heavy a burden.
Alas, and has the Christian realm progressed
Through Luther's doctrine, sheer bursting with error?
The Gospel of Christ is now so construed
By foolish chumps, drunkards, hobbledehoys,
As fav'ring the flesh, one can learn well from this.
If sin be virtue, then Lutherans are saints!

B.

Would folk accord careful attention to this
Their seal of approval they'd stamp on my words.
If slander be virtue — here's a word to the wise —
All they would be saints, who to Luther do hold,
For speaking well of their neighbor, that they can't do.
Confessing our failings, is that now our sin?
And is it their virtue, to loudly proclaim
The extent of their sins, their fleshly wiles
That are all acquitted with one single sigh?
To eat meat on Friday, is that virtue now,
And do Christians sin, should they choose to abstain?
Then I will concur: they are prophets holy.
And if it be virtue, good deeds to neglect,
Thinking that faineancy earns heaven's reward,
Then surely is holy the day that they die.
If it be virtue, sowing tares in God's field,
So think I to myself, and proclaim many a time:
If sin be virtue, then Lutherans are saints!

C.

In Bacchus's temple to drink great draughts,
A virtue? to carouse, pig out, and loaf about
And through impurity to outstink sows?
Is it virtue to invent brazen lies,
Deride cardinals, bishops, popes,
Holler and rage against priests and monks
Leave the straight for the crooked way?
Upsetting lamps at the altar: virtue that be,
And in back alleys mumming with torches
Running 'round cowled, with flutes and with drums,
While madness of excess has gained sole possession?
They gamble their money hand over fist
And rob monasteries, churches, cathedrals:
If one could gain life eternal through this,
They'll soon rise to join seraphic choirs.
Is it a virtue, to insult upright preachers,
Despise saints and saintesses, the Mother of God?
If sin be virtue, then Lutherans are saints!

D.

Perverting God's word to approve fleshly lusts,
A virtue? to "interpret Scripture," as it's called
In order to justify any false whim?
A virtue to make mockery of statues holy,
To spurn icons, yea, even the Holy Cross;
While Venus, Cupid and similar scum
Hang naked in chambers most lecherously?
If this be virtue, I'm totally confused,
The breviary I'm used to must be written new.
No doubt here and there many are killed for this faith;
If honor were due them, as Martyrs for God
The old Church almanac might as well be torn up,
For in that old paper there are no Saints
Who do battle with faith and pervert the truth,
Use Scripture to erase all virtuous habit,
As these Lutheran skunks are now wont to do.

But I dare say loudly, to women, to men,
If sin be virtue, then Lutherans are saints!
                    Prince:
If indeed the Lutherans do remain proud
In their opinions, as they tend to do,
Remain piggish, impure, impertinent, stupid,
Remain dogg'dly in these virtues up to death's door,
Surely life eternal will be their reward;
In heaven, where Lucifer is the patron saint,
No purgatory for them, they'll zip up in a trice
To the highest throne; what a marvellous place!
With Arius,[18] Helvidius,[19] they'll be trusty chums,
With Huss[20] and with Wyclif,[21] those heretic louts.
There they'll have plenty of sulpher, of pitch,
There, together with all of the devilish hosts,
Ever and ever they'll sizzle and fry,
Till rats' piss douses the fires of hell,
As purgatory was pissed out; hear well, Lutheran chaps,
I'll say just once more, I'll make a wild guess:
If sin be virtue, then Lutherans are saints!

"Priests are as human as you and me"[22]

                    A.
Whether sacred or lay, whether peasant or prelate,
We're all of us mortal: poor, frail, sinful vessels,
Empty of virtue, though brimful of fault.   [Romans 3]
How can it then be that we hate one another,   [Psalms 13]
Drag through the mud, slander, deceive,
We, ourselves up to our ears in sin?
Now common folk think, dare voice strong opinion,
And that in the main about monks and priests;
The more these the truth do preach and proclaim
The more do these venomous asps at them gape.
Sure, priests were sometimes out to bamboozle,
After all they're not angels, but fallible men.

Take a look at yourselves, poor scabious sheep,
Be mindful: if they seem lamed, surely you're fully
                                                    crippled.
And if you quite like hearing clinks in your purse,
Do you wonder that pennies have value to priests?
I say, though it won't earn me great thanks,
Priests are as human as you and me.

B.

Fie, for shame, gossips, so quick to suspicion,   [Matthew 7]
You might well fear God's sternest punition
When he's ascended his judgement throne.   [Matthew 14]
Folk say, that clerics in benefices do trade,
Buying and selling; true, they do well
In noting such evil condition, but they've forgotten
How they themselves live by the sweat of the poor.
Only God knows, how sometimes their living they earn
Through lying, deceit, false account and false measure,
Or else through high finance or usurous loans.
Bankruptcy — as common a practice
Among the Dutch as among the French;
Five years of grace,[23] that's the guarantee given;
Of two obtained hardly one's repaid.
The same folk say that priests and monks err,
But they'd never think to cleanse their own minds.
Note your own weakness, and say resolutely:
Priests are as human as you and me.

C.

And if priests take to women, every now and again,
I don't say, mind you, that that isn't wrong,
But should their disease therefore be spread?   [Genesis 2]
You married men, understand me well,   [Ephesians 4]
Before the congregation you were joined to your wife,
                                                [I Corinthians 6]
And together you two have sworn to God,
That from one another you never would part.

Are you always to your partner true?
You too sometimes indulge a small fling,
Leaving your wife, squandering what's hers.
And if priests did have a sweetheart sometimes,
Well, the devil that plagues you, tempts them too,
Their flesh is as yours, purely conceived
But to all manner of misery inclined.
You'll feel this yourselves, if you judge well,
And remember, if you were ever to see
Priests accused of wrong, think to say:
Priests are as human as you and me.

D.

And if priests do sometimes laugh and sing,
In good company dance and spring
And if in joy they do excel,
One should understand such things,
And if one should see them bring out a glass
And even expect one with joyful mind.
Who was never joyful, is truly a beast,
Priests, too, must now and then gladden their hearts.
Be mindful of how you relish a feast,
Where Dame Venus's girls do merry make.
And if priests were to notice a pretty face
Are they then criminals straightaway?
And if they should prefer the best food,
Why, remember how tasty morsels appeal to you!
Ere you denounce priests, your own heart consider,
And if it's a haven for similar things,
Leave priests unjudged, and say with conviction:
Priests are as human as you and me.

Prince:

The falsehoods of gossips and liars
Will rarely another's shortcomings decrease,
But increase them grandly; let each be on guard.
If priests do wrong, should that trouble us?
They are Adam's children just like us,

Entirely made up out of flesh and of blood.
To the good one should want to turn all things,
And not the priest's office scoff and mock,
But do as Constantine did,[24] the wise,
Who used his mantle to cover its faults.
This would, with right, aid them to virtue.
Those who squander their time with slander,
Tarnish priests's reputations with lies,
Don't they effect more than they realize?
Listen here, you Lutheran disciples,
Who spy on God's stateholders this way,
Leave off your talk, you devilish artists,
Priests are as human as you and me.

"Steadfast of heart, I'm yours alone"[25]
A wife writes to her husband
To drive faithlessness far away

A.

May God bestow health and good fortune
On him I hold dearest under the sun,
The one whose being inspires this poem.
Words fail me utterly as I seek to pen
The way your love has pierced my heart.
The integrity of your visage has won my heart.
Do not believe, my sweet, that my esteem is fickle
For under heaven's dome it is you alone
Who's source of greatest pleasure for me, poor simple one.
All my relations I would forsake for you.
For me there's no spice in other friendships.
I pray, understand me: all of my passionate longing
Is for you, my love, night and day;
Steadfast of heart, I'm yours alone.

B.

My steadfast heart I've given you.
Troth I've pledged, and troth I'll keep;
My promise will not cool, it still burns hot,
Never yet has your love caused me regret;
If I've said otherwise, forgive me, put it out of mind,
'T was melancholy, cutting so deeply, which spoke.
I dare say little, for you know the truth,
Do not use me cruelly, let your wrath subside,
You are mine and I am yours in mutual affection.
My very blood is yours, I'd give it for you.
Never again will I dishonour my promise
Or cast a friendly glance on any man
Other than on you, my dearest; give thought to this:
Steadfast of heart, I'm yours alone.

C.

My passion in securing your love is such
That I would move heaven and earth.
Therefore farewell fear and dread, dear heart,
The pure love in my heart must come to light.
Ah, dearest, seek not the side of another;
My heart would grow heavy, all joy would flee.
None other than you can I bear by my side.
Grant me the fruits of purest love,
If other rumours were yet to reach my ears
Sighs would betoken my miserable estate.
My love for you will nevermore wane.
Know and confess my pure affection,
Let me lodge safe within your heart;
Steadfast of heart, I'm yours alone.

D.

And do not spurn my steadfast love;
I will never be sated with you,
There's nothing can harm me, with you by my side.
You always lighten my sorrow's burden.

Let me come to the aid of your steadfastness
Tread no strange paths, in my presence delight,
Thus harmony prospers and quarrels decline.
Speak freely with me, pour out your heart;
For surely in heart and in soul we are one.
Fie, faithlessness! flee from such knavery;
If you, my dearest, did ever disown me,
Even forsake me (this is a broad hint)
Now cease and desist, admit your fault;
Steadfast of heart, I'm yours alone.

E.

Beloved Prince, my sweetest flower,
My very health, my whole well-being,
I've told you all, my lofty heart.
If wounds you do sometimes inflict in my heart
They're healed by your solace before too long.
And did some chicaneries put troth to shame,
What's done, is done, lovingly I'll forgive.
Enough of quarrelling, my sweetest dear.
We will abide as we have abidden,
And live in serenity, thief of my heart.
Your heart's letter is for my pen alone,
Grant me my wish, choose no one else:
Then many a sorrow will be banished from me.
Steadfast of heart, I'm yours alone.

"When gone, a loved one's the source of great pain"[26]

A.

And were I to equal Charlemagne's might,
Be honored by all, surpassed by none,
And had I what treasure my heart could desire,
Prosperity, health, the noblest birth,
Affording me solace by day and by night
'T were all for naught, would I lack a friend,

For if a loved one's gone,[27] joy, too, is repelled.
My head would bow low
In such a plight.
Let those who have shared this lot attest:
A thousand spears do pierce the heart
Inflict great harm;
And blood wastes away
If a loved one's gone, which multiplies woe
For many, wailing, lamenting, in want of heart's ease.
A friend is absent, life's saltier than brine,
And my love has been absent for such a long time
That I've just cause to say, with sorrowful mien:
When gone, a loved one's the source of great pain.

B.

Were I to carouse, eat, drink and be merry,
And had I such joys as a mind's eye could see,
With violins, drums, with harps and with lutes,
Tinkling all hollow 't would sound in my ears
For all pleasure is but a stench to me.
No happiness from me flows forth
The lack of a loved one has locked up my heart
Joy's shut outside.
And heard I uttered
Even well-crafted words of sweet Rhetoric
Refrains, ballads, or other farces,
I'd stay locked in my cage.
No avail is flute's play,
Nor the sweet song of noble music good.
If love misses love, that love only it seeks,
For 't is evil, to miss a loved one for long.
And, missing love, the heart's faint with longing.
Hence on this occasion once more I'll repeat:
When gone, a loved one's the source of great pain.

C.

Forsooth, and were I to be an invited guest,
Where men and women make modestly merry
All in all it would leave me cold.
On the outside I might maintain a brave face
While inside my heart all solace spurns
When my dearest beloved is far from there.
Ah, the sorrow's too grievous when a loved one is gone.
Truly, a single day
Outspans a year
When my dearest beloved must absent be.
Daily the heart suffers fear, terror, dread,
For its most constant friend.
With passionate longing
It always seeks out the side of that friend.
When two hearts are both imprinted by love
And pull together at the same rope,
No greater joy can there be under heaven.
But the moment of parting brings venomous woe!
When gone, a loved one's the source of great pain.

D.

Sleepless nights breed, when a loved one's been gone,
As experience has taught me all too well;
Therefore the firmer my judgement dares be.
No food the world round holds flavour for him
Who pines for a loved one, he'll be hollow cheeked,
For there's no pleasure to be found in it,
All joy has been banished far away
To sigh and to tremble
His whole life's lot.
The mouth may be smiling, the soul inside grieves
When there's one who's been honored beyond the rest
And has been inscribed
Firm in one's heart.
If that one is gone the heart tears for love
And melancholy is locked fast inside.

Against this there's neither advice nor potion;
Or if something new seems to offer slight solace
It turns out impossible; and so I conclude:
When gone, a loved one's the source of great pain.
Prince:
To miss a loved one is no child's play
All who have tasted it, know this all too well,
No further do they dare probe its power,
No illness was ever so fierce or so cruel.
And were that the only grief in the world
It would still be a burden loathesome enough.
Far sooner would one give up friend and relation,
All prosperity wager,
Rant and lament,
Unhappy sighing's the song, where'er one be.
'T is a plague worse than any other around,
Never greater displeasure,
E'er bitter gnawing;
Verily, yesterday's solace has all been forgotten
As the heart has received full measure of mourning,
Not asking for food nor the power of wine.
Oh, I'll say it yet once, so it will be clearly known
Behooving no learned doctrine, I'll simply explain:
When gone, a loved one's the source of great pain.

"I've been wived: would I had died from the plague"[28]

A.
I've every right to complain, I've got good reason,
Alas! woe is me! for I've been wived![29]
Day and night I endure naught but nagging[30]
And yet I'm such a milksop, I haven't the courage
To make one retort to her endless cavilling.
If this devil's to be my companion much longer

I'll vomit my spleen out of sheerest rage.
For when that hussy airs out her wraps
I've got to help her smack and whack,
Surely I live in the parish of "Our Lady!"
Then she says: "Pookums, you're blubbering again;
'T was a pernicious spirit ever made me marry you."
Every morning she hollers: "Up, up, you oaf!
Hustle, hop to it, make me some gruel
And use lots of sugar, or you'll get a good drubbing!"
If I could I'd seek refuge in the hole of a mouse
Whenever she speaks; hence say I with passion:
I've been wived: would I had died from the plague!

B.

When she arises I must rush about
Making the bed, though I'd just as soon not;
Then she has me do dishes,
And pour out the pisspot, not to mention the ashes
That need to be swept out of the hearth;
And should I fail to sweep the floor
I'd rue the day I'd ever been born.
Alas, my wife's quick to reach for the rod,
When she scolds I quake in my boots;
For, the odd time I've dared give her tit for tat
Her fists ensure that I pay dearly.
Surely an ill-fated year brought me this bitch;
She makes me scour kettle and hook,
Chop the greens, stir the porridge,
Sweep the street, cart away mud,
Clean out the gutters: this all she demands.
Wherefore my daily lament is this:
I've been wived: would I had died from the plague!

C.

Evenings when by the fire I'm seated,
I twist thread to fill all of her spindles,
And she'd skin me alive if I tangled them.

The child cries: it's my job to hush it
Dandle it on my knee, sing "Tiere, liere;"
And when it's pooped I must straightaway
Rinse the worst chunks out of the diaper.
"Pee, little one, pee, pee," is my chant
Whenever it needs to poop or piddle.
I cool its porridge and spoonful by spoonful
Poke all in its mouth, there's no escape.
Yet my neighbor folks sympathize, it seems,
And though I've suffered every mishap, large or small,
It's with the good help of other people
That I've survived till now, that's cause for lament.
Alas, I have to turn a blind eye
Though she plays the common whore, else she'd strangle me.
I've been wived: would I had died from the plague!

D.
The little brat's cradle I rock to and fro
So the little bastard won't cry till it's blue;
For, if I did leave it cry, it wouldn't be long
Till her blows came raining down on my head.[31]
For, if the kid cries, I'm the one she'll blame.
For breakfast I often get served up a beating,
With a tumbler of blows[32] on the side.
I wipe mud clods off garments, if I don't want to be sorry,
Spruce up her clothes, and I'd do well to remember
To wipe her shoes and polish the soles to a shine.
When she entertains her lovers at our house
She makes me serve, though she should go to perdition
At table, and sends me for beer and for wine.
If I could feast as well as serve, I might not object,
But no, can't be done, nothing but bones to gnaw for me.
For others there's always a happy face
But she shows small pleasure in me;
I've been wived: would I had died from the plague!
Prince:
I haul water, bring it in, place it right in her hand,

Do all that she tells me, she'll brook no protest;
So I put the clothes in the water to soak,
Help her with the washing, and while they're bleaching
I draw water to sprinkle them some more.[33]
Then I cart them home, and woe, should I spill!
Then there are the child's diapers to dry
Otherwise I'd eat scratches and dine on fisticuffs.[34]
I've often got scars to show for my trouble,
She gave me two black eyes just the other day
Because I'd forgotten one of her orders;
And once she poured "chamber lye" out on me
Because I hadn't managed to catch the hen;
If I do anything to displease her
Straightaway she banishes me from her bed.
Small difference if the dog barks, or I speak,
Both are of equal interest to her;
I've been wived: would I had died from the plague!

"With childlike trust I come to Thee"[35]

A.

Wisdom unfathomable, Thou, eternal clarity,
Divine eyes plumbing the depth of all hearts,
Who notes our sins's multitude, and their severity,
And weighs them; O infallible truth,
Thou knowest our works before they do pass.
How dare I then show my face, as I know
How great the burden of my sin to be;
Yet there is nowhere I can hide from Thee,
Where'er I may hide, Thine eyes are watchful on me.
For Thou provest not only our sinful deeds,
But also every good work (and I have been remiss)
To test the reasons for our doing, the examiner Thou art.
How then shall I stand? I find myself beflecked
With hosts of evil desires, and the more my transgressions
                                                    wax

From Year to Year, the greater is my sorrow;
But as Thou waitest long,
Sparing the sinner in order to save him,
With childlike trust I come to Thee.

B.

I come before Thee, though I have tarried long,
As a criminal before his judge.
When I ponder Thy stern righteousness
Sheer terror causes my courage to fail;
Yet when I meditate on Thy mercy
So I call: Lord, loose Thou the bonds
Which have fettered me fast.
Come, aid me in battle, mightiest soldier,
And defend me, all the world round was never one weaker
And frailer than I to be found.
Hellish dogs have felled me with death's bite,
So I come to Thee as to a surgeon,
Needing advice, I display my wounds;
And full of sores I come to Thee
As the sick do seek a wise physician.
I show my frail mortality before Thy Godly face,
For in past times there's no ail Thou didst shun;
With childlike trust I come to Thee.

C.

A miserable beggar, penniless, poor,
I come before Thee, of virtue bared;
Dissipated have I the good gifts Thou hadst lent me,
Adversely squandered them; but since Thou has never
Ill-treated a beggar, weak and lame,
I am not misled in beseeching Thee,
One cannot increase the measure of Thy grace.
The pleading murderer Thou didst not condemn,[36]
The weeping sinneress Thou didst not chide.[37]
And though my sin far exceeds these,
In the light of Thy mercy it counts for no more

Than a droplet of water might to the wide sea.
And though Thy righteousness not one does spare,
Let mercy temper Thy judgement on me;
Let sheathed remain righteousness's sword.
Merciful Lord, break the rod in two
Though my love for Thee had begun to cool,
With childlike trust I come to Thee.

D.

A naughty child, I come to Thee,
As to a tender Father; it befits me
To fall before Thy feet, inclined to greatest sorrow.
While I have neither feared Thee nor adored
As I should my Father, I am most ashamed.
But mindful of how Thou cam'st into the world
Becoming a slave to set us free,
And that, out of love, Thou took'st on mortal flesh,
So I know well, Thou lavest the sinner,
Although here Thou chidest sometimes, it seems,
Saddening earth's moments, to gladden eternally.
Thus, merciful Father, deign not to disown me
Crucify flesh, mortality sever,
So that, as my life's journey reaches time's end
All of my sins will have been requited,
And the spirit might live, when the body does die
In the light of Thy love with unflagging zeal.
With childlike trust I come to Thee.

E.

Lord, I come to Thee as I would to a friend
Who knows me as untrue without measure.
I kiss the rod, which I deserve,
For I know myself as so frail of mind
That I justly deserved to be cursed
If Thy mercy did not to come to my aid.
How often did not Thy grace's light shine
On me, which I refused to let in

And, more, willfully blocked up any crack
(Indeed, virtue had taken its leave of me).
In darkness I wandered, I know not where
Entangling myself in my enemies's snares.
Hence I come before Thee, as to the one
Who can lighten my load; hear my sighing
Remove not Thy grace far from me.
Although my sins have earned Thy wrath,
So that I deserve Thy abomination,
With childlike trust I come to Thee.

F.

I come before Thee as a poor slave
Before my Lord, whom I have served
Most badly, and in my neglectfulness
Oft' angered; hence expiation I desire,
Requite my sin with liberal hand.
I've dawdled long ere serving Thee,
And yet Thou gavest great reward.
Wellnigh all my precious time
Lies waste in sin, and in the main
I've striven for world's honor, ease.
O Lord, beat not Thy poor small sheep,
But continue with father's sympathy.
Let "innocent" the verdict be: which overlooks
My great misdeeds, I beg of Thee, and wilt soon
Thy gracious eyes cast down on me.
Bottomless well, Thy grace ne'er runs dry,
And though I begin to age in sin,
With childlike trust I come to Thee.

NOTES to the Translations

1. As Aercke has noted (1985:232 and 1987:375), it is hardly possible to imitate Bijns' complicated and perfect rhyme schemes in translation; rather, it seems wiser to attempt an approximation of the natural flow of the original through free verse.

2. This laudation was probably taken from the second edition of *Elogia Belgica* (1609) by Aubertus Miraeus (1573-1640; Roose 63). It cleverly alligns Miraeus with all of the great men mentioned, even as it elevates Bijns by citing her as equal to Classical, Byzantine, and Renaissance writers. It also demonstrates that Bijns has kept strange company before being chosen as patroness of a modern feminist literary prize. The women listed here also share the fate of many female writers, in that their authorship is doubted or their work and their lives have been included only sporadically in the standard process of canonization. I have not been able to trace Rupea of Poitiers or the men who praised her. Source text of the laudation: B/vH xi.

3. Part of the work of Marcus Tullius or Cicero (106-43BC), author, orator, and Roman statesman, is a large collection of letters by him as well as others, which were published long after his death.

4. Cornelia (Roman matron of the second century BC, daughter of Scipio Africanus and wife of Ti. Sempronius Gracchus), wrote hortative letters to one of her twelve children, though her authorship of the two fragments which survive is in dispute. Two of her sons, Gaius Sempronius (153?-121 BC) and Tiberius Sempronius (136?-133 BC), were Roman political reformers also known as the "Gracchi." (*Oxford Companion to Classical Literature* 157).

5. Mentioned in Cicero's dialogue "Brutus s. de Claris Oratoribus" is Licina, one of two sisters thus named (daughters of L. Licinius Crassus, orator, consul BC 95), who "were distinguished for the purity and elegance with which they spoke the Latin language, an accomplishment which their mother Mucia and their grandmother Laelia equally possessed." *Dictionary of Greek and Roman Biography and Mythology*, ed. Wm. Smith. 3 vols. (New York: AMS Press, 1967.), Vol. 1, 724-725; Vol. 2, 782-783.

6. Lucan (Marcus Annaeus Lucanus, AD 39-65) was author of *Pharsalia*, an unfinished historical epic on the civil war between Pompey and Caesar.

7. Polla Argentaria married Lucan c. 60 and remained "a prominent and respected figure in Roman society long after his death" by suicide (*Penguin Companion to Classical, Oriental and African Literature*. Eds. D.M. Lang and D.R. Dudley. New York: McGraw-Hill, 1969. 107). Only Jöcher mentions that besides being erudite, noble and beautiful she also wrote good poetry and worked on her husband's *Pharsalia* after his death (Vol. 3, 1664).

8. Castiglione (1478-1529), Italian diplomat and writer, is most famous for the dialogues grouped together in *The Book of the Courtier* (ca. 1507, published 1528; tr. Sir Th. Hoby 1561). Part Three is a lengthy and spirited defense of women.

9. From a leading Ferrara family, Ippolita Torelli (1501?-1520) married Castiglione in 1516 when she was 15 and he 38, and died after the birth of their third child. Though much has been made of the affection expressed in their letters to each other (published by C. in 1534 as *Balth. Castilionii elegia, qua fingit Hyppolytam suam ad se ipso scribentem*), it is clear from Castiglione's correspondence with his mother about some twenty other possible partners, before finally settling on Ippolita, that dowry and social status were primary considerations (Erich Loos, *B. Castigliones "Libro del cortegiano." Studien zur Tugendauffassung des Cinquecento*. Frankfurt a/M: V. Klostermann, 1955. 45-46, 53). Jöcher claims that Ippolita's letters were actually written by her husband (Vol. 1, 1749-1750).

10. While the field of inquiry is narrowed by the fact that Morata's work was published in 1558, that Miraeus wrote his laudation in 1609, and that Morata was Protestant, I have not yet been able to identify either Ferrariensis or Scaevola Samarthanus.

11. Olympia Fulvia Morata (b. Ferrara 1526, d. Heidelberg 1555) was an Italian classical scholar. Educated by her father Peregrino Morato, she was able to speak Latin and Greek fluently by the age of twelve. She converted to Protestantism, and married a young German student of medicine and philosophy, Andreas Gründler, moving with him to Schweinfurt in

Bavaria. Her works ("scanty remains" of dialogues, letters, and Greek verse) were published by Celio Secundo Curio in 1558 with the title *O.F. Moratae Opera* and were reprinted several times. Her house in Schweinfurt bears a plaque with this inscription: "O famous woman residing in this house / Though cheap and poor it may be / Has by her simple dwelling there / Made its celebrity" (Jackson et al., vol. 8, 4; "Morata," *Encyclopedia Britannica* 1910 ed.; cf. Jöcher, vol. 3, 654).

12. Jöcher's accuracy may be tested in his entry on Bijns: "de Bins, oder Binsia (Anna), a learned maiden of the sixteenth century, who taught other girls and refused marriage for love of learning, died 1540"; he mentions only the Latin poems translated by Houckaert (vol. 1, 1097).

13. Meant is probably Eudocia (Eudoxia) Aelia (c.401-c.460), Byzantine empress who became Christian and married Theodosius II (408-450) in 421. Estranged from her husband, from 443 she lived permanently in Jerusalem, concerning herself mainly with church architecture and rebuilding. She has been called "the greatest private benefactor in Palestine...[S]he placed a six thousand-pound copper cross over the Church of the Ascension in Jerusalem, gave four hundred gold pieces to a monastery nearby, and built the church of St. Stephen, also in Jerusalem...It has been estimated that in all she spent in Palestine...a million and a half gold coins, two gold coins then being enough to keep one person for a year" (Deno J. Geanakoplos, *Interaction of the "Sibling" Byzantine and Western Cultures in the Middle Ages and Italian Renaissance (330-1600).* New Haven: Yale UP, 1976. 128.) She was also the first Byzantine princess to be known as an author of religious literature, though scholars differ widely in their opinion of what works she actually wrote and the literary value of her work (cf. e.g. "Eudocia Augusta," *Encyclopedia Britannica. Reallexikon für Antike und Christentum* [Stuttgart: Hiersemann, 1959-.] Vol. 6, 844-847. *Encyclopedic Dictionary of Religion* [Ed. P.K. Meagher et al. Washington, DC: Corpus Publications, 1977.]) Vol. 1, 1258. It is also reported that she was responsible for the murder of her (ex-) husband's emissary, sent to keep an eye on her in Jerusalem.

14. Proba (Faltonia Betitia), a Christian centoist of the fourth century, daughter of Petronius Probianus (consul, 310) and wife of Clodius Celsinus Adelphius (prefect after 351). Before her conversion to Christianity she wrote a *cento* (a composition constructed from words and lines taken

from other poets to express a content other than the original) on the conflict between Constantinus and Maxentius; after her conversion she wrote a similar *cento*, using hexameters, on the story of creation and redemption (Jackson et al., vol. 9, 262-263).

15. No counting of Bijns's (re)publications adds up to 16 separate books, as Roose remarks (54).

16. Latin name for Van [Vanden] Hoecke (also Eligius Houckaert), c. 1491-1547, priest, humanist, and teacher in Ghent.

17. B/vH 138-140.

18. Arius of Alexandria (c.260-336) denied that Christ was consubstantial with God but was rather created by him as a separate being; known as Arianism, this doctrine was officially rejected as heretical at the Council of Nicea in 325. Arius had been banished by Bishop Alexander but was recalled by Constantine in the latter's efforts to promote unity in church doctrine (Jackson et al., vol. 1, 284-285).

19. Helvidius (Rome, 366-384) argued against the perpetual virginity of the mother of Christ; his work is known only through Jerome's counterarguments. Helvidius proceeded on the assumption that Mary, subsequent to the virgin-birth of Christ, bore several other children in wedlock with Joseph, an argument opposed by those who held that Mary (and probably Joseph) remained virgins in perpetuity (Jackson et al., vol. 5, 219).

20. John Huss (c.1369-1415), professor at the University of Prague, amalgamated Wyclif's ideas on church reform with concerns for Czech nationalism and social reform. He was burned at the stake after having tried to defend his ideas before the Council of Constance (Jackson et al., vol. 5, 415-420).

21. John Wyclif (c.1324-1384), priest and professor of theology at Oxford University, advocated thorough church reform in many areas; his ideas influenced Huss and were later echoed in Luther's Reformation (Jackson et al., vol. 12, 454-467).

22. B/vH 42-44.

23. Bijns' word "quinckernel" ("quinquenelle") is cited, without reference to her specifically, as the main source for a term denoting a five-year grace period extended to debtors (*MNW* VI, 908-909).

24. Constantine (280-337) was the first Roman emperor to embrace Christianity after his reportedly dramatic conversion during a battle in 312; one of his concerns was to promote unity within the Christian church (Jackson et al., vol. 3, 249-253).

25. J/vH 64-65.

26. J/vH 22-24.

27. Bijns gives 16 variants of "lieve derven" throughout the poem. Significantly, "lieve" in all its forms designates neither erotic love ("minne"), nor Christian love ("caritate"), but specifically a non-sexual love between, for example, friends, or parent and child, or also between God and believer. It is also a non-gendered term, for the feminine noun "lieve" refers to goodness or friendship, while the neuter noun "lief" remains neuter in its designation of the beloved, whether male or female (*MNW* IV, 525-538; 570-575). Note also the ANNA BONAVENTURA acrostic in the last stanza. A great deal of attention to the identity of Bonaventura, who was held by some to have been Bijns's illicit lover, has failed to produce any satisfactory explanation (Roose 48-52).

28. Soens 319-322.

29. The original "verwyft" is a marvellous example of Bijns's ability to capitalize on lexical ambiguity, sometimes to such an extent that she is entirely original. While "verwyft" can simply mean "married" (Soens 319), it also has connotations of "effeminate" or "emasculated" (*MNW* IX, 346); Mak cites precisely the tagline of this poem (without naming Bijns) to translate it as "unhappily married, under a wife's thumb" (494). While both the Middle Dutch verb "wiven" and its archaic English equivalent "to wive" can be used intransitively or transitively to mean variously "to be married to a woman," or "to marry off (a woman)," the English verb includes the possibility of "to wed a man" or "to be or act as a wife." In the poem Bijns

seems to have incorporated also this last sense; the man's main complaint is that he has to do what is virtually matter of course for a woman, and by means of this role reversal Bijns satirizes neither the woman nor the man but rather the dreadful lot of a wife.

30. Positing a relationship to Middle Dutch "predike" (ML "predica") Soens (319) glosses "precaren" as "hearing sermons, being nagged at." Another possibility might be Middle Dutch "precarie" (*MNW* VI, 644-645), a document by which one had right to tenancy of property, usually belonging to a church, for a certain yearly sum; this tenancy had the quality of uncertain dependence on the property owner, as the agreement could be terminated at will (hence "precarious").

31. "Head" is an impoverished though accurate equivalent for "tuyten" (Middle Dutch "tute"), which generally designates an object ending in a point, especially as a spout. It also refers to a woman's hairstyle which ends in a point, such as a braid, and further can designate a woman of somewhat loose morals (*MNW* VIII, 780-781). Such ambiguity is unfortunately lost in translation.

32. "Muylenbier" seems to be Bijns's own word, playing on "muulbere" (mulberry), "muulpere" (a type of pear, but also a blow), "mule" (mouth, usually for animals) and "muul" (mule).

33. Clothes were bleached by being laid on grass in the sun, with frequent sprinklings.

34. The meal metaphor works better in the original: "crabben" is both "crab" and "scratches"; "vuystloock" (Bijns's own word) is a compound of "fist" with "alliums," either chives or garlic.

35. B/vH 403-406.

36. Both Matthew 27:44 and Mark 15:32 report that the two thieves crucified with Christ did not repent, but Luke 23:39-43 tells the story Bijns probably had in mind here.

37. Luke 7:37-50 relates that Christ forgave the sins of the woman who anointed him.

Bibliography

Primary Works

Bijns, Anna. *Refreinen*. Ed. L. Roose. Antwerp: De Nederlandsche
        Boekhandel, 1949.
_____. [B/vH]. *Refreinen van Anna Bijns*. Eds. A. Bogaers and W.L. van
        Helten. Rotterdam: J.H. Dunk, 1875.
_____. [J/vH]. *Nieuwe Refereinen van Anna Bijns*. Eds. W.J.A. Jonckbloet
        and W.L. van Helten. Groningen: Wolters, 1880.
_____. Soens, E. Ed. [Soens]. "Onuitgegeven Gedichten van Anna Bijns."
        Leuvensche Bijdragen (4) 1902. 199-368.

Translations

_____. Trans. Kristiaan P. Aercke. "Anna Bijns. Germanic Sappho." *Women
        Writers of the Renaissance and Reformation*. Ed. Katharina M.
        Wilson. Athens: Univ. of Georgia Press, 1987. 365-397. The
        following poems: "Dedication" (acrostichon on ANNA BIJNS);
        "'Tis a Waste to Cast Pearls Before Swine"; "Make Merry and
        Leap the Scythe"; "Unyoked is Best! Happy the Woman Without a
        Man"; "When Compared, Martin Rossom Comes Out Best"; "These
        Covet Happy Nights and Lose Their Happy Days"; "The Will I've
        Got, but No Force to See It Through"; "He Must Be Beautiful Who
        Created All This"; "Lord, If It All Deserts Me, Will You Stand By
        Me?"

Related Works

Aercke, Kristiaan P. "Anna Bijns." *An Encyclopedia of Continental Women
        Writers*. Ed. Katharina M. Wilson. 2 Vols. New York: Garland,
        1991. Vol. 1. 127-128.
_____. "Anna Bijns. Germanic Sappho." *Women Writers of the Renaissance
        and Reformation*. Ed. Katharina M. Wilson. Athens: Univ. of
        Georgia Press, 1987. 365-397.

_____. "Antwerp's Sharpest Tongue Against Luther." *Vox Benedictina* 2 (3) 1985. 224-238.

Basse, Maurits. *Het Aandeel der Vrouw in de Nederlandsche Letterkunde.* 2 vols. Ghent: Hoste, 1920.

Dorrestein, Renate. "How I Became a Writer." *Canadian Journal of Netherlandic Studies* 8 (i) 1988. 52-62.

Jackson, S.M. et al. Eds. *The New Schaff-Herzog Encyclopedia of Religious Knowledge.* 13 vols. Grand Rapids, MI: Baker Book House, 1959.

Jauss, Hans Robert. "The Alterity and Modernity of Medieval Literature." Trans. Timothy Bahti. *New Literary History* 10 (1979). 181-229.

Jöcher, Christian Gottlieb. *Allgemeines Gelehrten-Lexicon.* 11 vols. Leipzig: 1751. Rpt. Hildesheim: Olms, 1961.

Knuvelder, G.P.M. *Handboek tot de geschiedenis der Nederlandse letterkunde.* 6th ed. Vol. 1. Malmberg: Den Bosch, 1970.

Mak, J.J. *Rhetoricaal Glossarium.* Taalkundige Bijdragen van Noord en Zuid 12. Assem: Van Gorcum, 1959.

Marain, Elisabeth. "Het Roosterken." Unpublished radioplay. 1991.

Meijer, Reinder P. *Literature of the Low Countries.* The Hague: Nijhoff, 1978.

Meulenbelt, Anja. *Meer dan één engel. Over literatuur en seksenstrijd.* Amsterdam: Sara/van Gennep, 1989.

Mierlo, Jozef van. *De letterkunde van de middeleeuwen.* Vol. 2. 2nd edition. Part II of *Geschiedenis van de letterkunde der Nederlanden.* Ed. F. Baur et al. Brussels: Standaard, [1940].

[MNW] *Middelnederlandsch Woordenboek.* Eds. E. Verwijs and J. Verdam. 11 vols. The Hague: Nijhoff, 1885-1952.

Porteman, Karel. "In Memoriam Prof. dr. Lode Roose (1920-1991)." *Spiegel der Letteren* 33 (1991). 113.

Reimöller, Helma. "Approach to Anna Bijns: Social Role and Female Identity in the Late Middle Ages." Unpublished presentation. 26th International Congress on Medieval Studies (Kalamazoo MI, on May 9-12, 1991).

Roose, Lode. *Anna Bijns. Een rederijkster uit de hervormingstijd.* Ghent: Koninklijke Vlaamse Academie voor Taal- en Letterkunde, 1963.

Schneiderwirth, Matthäus P. *Anna Bijns. Eine flämische Lehrerin und Dichterin des 16. Jahrhunderts.* Paderborn: Schöningh, 1933.

Showalter, Elaine. "Feminist Criticism in the Wilderness." *The New Feminist Criticism.* Ed. E. Showalter. New York: Pantheon, 1985. 243-270.

Voet, Leon. *Antwerp: The Golden Age. The Rise and Glory of the Metropolis in the Sixteenth Century.* Antwerp: Mercatorfonds, 1973.

Waard, Elly de. *Anna Bijns.* Amsterdam: Anna Bijns Stichting, 1985.

Wiesner, Merry E. "Beyond Women and the Family: Towards a Gender Analysis of the Reformation." *Sixteenth Century Journal* 17 (1987). 311-321.

Anna Roemers Visscher and Maria Tesselschade Roemers Visscher

James A. Parente, Jr.

Anna Roemers Visscher (1583-1651) and Maria Tesselschade Roemers Visscher (1594-1649) have long held a major place in the literature of the Dutch Golden Age. They wrote poems, corresponded with the great writers of the early seventeenth century, participated in the meetings of the leading literary groups of their day, and were universally admired by their contemporaries for their learning, their wisdom, and their literary and artistic talent. They were the frequent recipients of the works of P.C. Hooft, G.A. Bredero, Constantijn Huygens, Jacob Cats, Joost van den Vondel, all luminaries of the Dutch Golden Age, and many others who likened them variously to the Muses, the Graces, numerous Greek and Roman goddesses, and more significantly, to virtuous men.[1]

The numerous panegyrics produced by their contemporaries stand in sharp contrast, however, to the relatively small number of poems that they composed. Very few of their writings were published during their lifetime, or even posthumously in the seventeenth century, and it was not until the 1800s that the works of these highly praised women were collected and read. Nineteenth-century scholars sympathetic to the promotion of female talent in the Golden Age uncritically accepted the hyperbolic plaudits showered on Anna

Roemers and Maria Tesselschade by their admirers and edited their surviving writings to legitimize their opinions.[2]

Because of the favor in which seventeenth-century male writers held the Visschers, their work, unlike that of many seventeenth-century Dutch women writers, has never truly been lost. Their names were conveniently preserved by their contemporaries, and their literary-historical fate tied to the shifting view of the Golden Age: they were "lost" only briefly in the eighteenth century just as many of the dominant seventeenth-century authors were forgotten when Enlightenment writers embraced the aesthetic ideals of French neoclassicism. The fact that these women authors have not required rediscovery by present-day feminist literary historians does not mean, however, that their writing should escape reevaluation. Nor does it mean that they have been spared the prejudices of male-dominated literary-historical scholarship. On the contrary, the preservation of these female writers has succeeded precisely because their writing and their lives allow for the maintenance of the patriarchal view that, at best, women's writing is an inferior female version of a male poetic voice.

The inclusion of a woman writer into a traditional national literary canon, i.e., the canons established in the mid-nineteenth century, usually resulted from the resemblance of their writings to the leading literary fashions of their day. To put it more plainly, they wrote as the important literary men wrote. The canonical place of the sixteenth-century poetess Anna Bijns, for example, is due, partly, to her use of the current Rederijker verse style. Similarly, Anna Roemers and Maria Tesselschade reaped the accolades of their contemporaries for their adherence to the neoclassical poetic forms of, among others, the humanist Daniel Heinsius and P.C. Hooft, or in Anna's case especially, to the homey versifying of Jacob Cats. But in the case of the Visscher women, there were additional reasons for their continued popularity: they were from Amsterdam, the locus of literary culture in the Netherlands; they were, for most of their lives, pious and obedient adherents of Calvinism; their father, Roemer Visscher, was a major figure in early seventeenth-century literary circles; they knew many of the authors who frequented their father's house; and they had been unusually well-educated. The reputations of these women writers was thus ensured since their social, educational, religious, and literary background corresponded to that possessed by their contemporaries. They had access to, and were active in, literary circles, but the social restrictions imposed on their sex, chiefly their exclusion from the Latin humanist world of contemporary men, prevented them from assuming a place alongside, rather than subservient to, the male literary establishment. As a consequence, their poetic writing remained exceptional because of its female source, yet clearly less accomplished because of the informality of their poetic education. The traditional literary-historical praise of Anna Roemers and Maria Tesselschade, therefore, must be carefully weighed, for it has served to uphold the patriarchal view that writing was primarily man's work.

The patriarchalism of Dutch literary historians toward Anna Roemers and Maria Tesselschade is most apparent in the distinctions commonly drawn between them.[3] Anna, the elder, is generally held to be more learned than her younger and more attractive sister; she had a greater knowledge of antiquity and of foreign languages; she was closer to her father (she prepared a new, posthumous edition of his emblem book, *Sinnepoppen*), and she had more responsibility for the maintenance of the household after their parents died; she was religious, disinterested in sex (i.e., she married late), and though more prolific than Maria, modest, even dull. Maria, on the other hand, was considered both learned (though not bookish like Anna) and beautiful; in addition to the usual female crafts of upper middle-class women of the time, embroidery, lace-making, and wine-glass (*roemer*) engraving, Maria excelled in singing, lute-playing, and dancing. Her mere presence and charming conversational skills enlivened the informal meetings of Dutch literati at the country castle of P.C. Hooft at Muiden; her early marriage attested to a lively interest in sexual matters, and her early widowhood made her the most desirable spouse for a learned man. Her apparent loyalty to her deceased husband made her even more attractive, and her late conversion to Catholicism, an unorthodox move in Calvinist Holland, showed her passionate, independent mind. In short, dowdy, owlish Anna was simply pious and learned; beautiful, witty Maria was a fiery, free-spirited, intelligent person who possessed a manly spirit in a desirable female form.

The physical beauty and recorded charms of Maria Tesselschade, immortalized by the seventeenth-century engraver Hendrik Goltzius and the impassioned words of Hooft, Huygens, and many others, ensured her continued popularity in Dutch literary history. To this day, they are many more publications devoted to Maria than to her sister, and she has almost always been included in collections about the Golden Age or women writers.[4] Such an imbalance has long required redress, for its perpetuation of the amorous and, at times erotic, adoration of Maria both unnecessarily obscures her sister's achievements, and tacitly continues the patriarchal suppression of the less appealing female voice. To be sure, neither Anna nor Maria thought of themselves first and foremost as writers and scholars. Writing was very much an avocation for them, as it was for their male contemporaries who, like Hooft and Huygens, turned to poetry for relaxation from their professional responsibilities. Both women were more devoted to their families and the management of their households than to the Muse, for they did not aspire to equality with their male friends, but were content to have garnered their respect. But this acknowledgment of their secondary status in seventeenth-century society does not exonerate the many literary historians who have continued to treat them in a patronizing way. The literary-historical image of Anna and Maria did not so much arise from their own writings but from later scholarship's embrace of the womanly and hence decidedly inferior role ascribed to them by their male contemporaries.

In this brief introduction, an attempt is made to disentangle Anna Roemers and Maria Tesselschade from their centuries-old literary-historical reputations. The character of their work and the nature of their individual poetic voices are considered apart from the opinions of their contemporaries. The translations that follow provide an overview of the different types of writing they practiced, and the prefaces place their work in the literary-historical context of the time.

Anna Roemers and Maria Tesselschade were privileged to have been born into a household in which late Renaissance art and poetry flourished. Their father, Roemer Visscher (1547-1620), a grain merchant, was also an established poet whose fame rested on his occasional verses (*Brabbeling* [Sputterings]) and his moralistic emblem book, *Sinnepoppen* (Meaningful Pictures, a play on the word for emblem, *zinnebeeld*). He had an extensive network of literary acquaintances ranging from the sixteenth-century reformer of the Dutch language, Hendrik Spiegel, to the young patrician poet, P.C. Hooft, and the racy satirist G.A. Bredero. Joost van den Vondel, the best known writer of the Dutch Golden Age, once remarked that Roemer's doorstep had been worn down by all the leading painters, artists, poets, and singers of the early seventeenth century.[5] In keeping with his cultivation of humane letters, Roemer Visscher provided an unusually broad education for his daughters: besides the customary female skills of music, painting and drawing, glass-engraving — an art in which both women later excelled — and calligraphy, it encompassed the study of French and Italian, and the composition of poetry. Visscher's program also included swimming in the family's suburban garden, an unusual practice for the time.

Within such a cultivated environment, it is no surprise that Anna and Maria would try their hand at poetry and be the frequent recipients of poems from many of Roemer's distinguished guests. Anna, who, in contrast to Maria, is generally thought to possess a good reading knowledge of Latin and ancient Greek, was praised by Daniel Heinsius, Jacob Cats, and many other lesser poets such as Jacob Zevecotius, for her learning and fine womanly character. Cats even dedicated his didactic poem *Maechden-plicht* (The Maiden's Duty, 1618), an idealization of womankind, to her, while Hooft sent her elegant letters about literary matters.[6] At the same time, Maria was worshipped by Bredero, who addressed his drama *Lucelle* and many amatory verses to her. In the meantime, Anna and Maria began work on a Dutch translation of the *Cents emblèmes chrestiens* (One Hundred Christian Emblems) of the French Protestant poetess Georgette de Montenay, a task in which Anna is believed to have played the major part. This work was never published during Anna's lifetime, but her translation activities were known to contemporary poets who encouraged her undertaking through verse.

   The majority of Anna's poems were composed early in her life between 1616 and 1623, a period stretching roughly from her occupation with the de Montenay translation to the appearance of several of her poems in the 1623 anthology, *Zeeusche Nachtegael*, a collection of writings by authors from the coastal province of Zeeland. During this time, Anna published the only book in which her name appeared, a new edition of her father's emblem collection *Sinnepoppen*, with additional verses by her. Anna's poems during this period were often responses to laudatory verses directed at her (see the poems to Heinsius and Cats below), but there were also some fine religious sonnets decrying the vanity of the world and man's inborn sinfulness. After her marriage in 1624 to Dominicus Boot van Wesel, Anna moved away from the familial house in Amsterdam, and consequently from the center of poetic activity. Her relatively few later poems were mostly written as acknowledgments to friends for gifts received, or as presents for acquaintances encountered on her travels to the southern Netherlands in the 1640s. Sometimes, as in her last poem to the rector of Leiden University, Anna used her poetry to request a personal favor, but for the most part, these later works remained truly occasional poems devoid of the self-analytical quality of her finest work. Anna's unique achievement as a poetess was her ability to transform the routines of her womanly existence into occasions for an unusually frank psychological investigation of the creative process and of the limitations imposed on her pursuit of the Muse by her sex.

   In many of her writings, Anna created a distinct poetic persona for herself. Mindful of her marginal status as a woman poet, she presented herself as a modest person of moderate talent with an inclination toward notoriety and praise. She acknowledged the superior talents of her male contemporaries, yet hoped that she might at least possess a small portion of their greatness. She complained that her womanly duties, especially the management of her father's house after her mother's death in 1619, kept her from honing her poetic skills, but at the same time, she remained well aware of the sinfulness of her artistic ambitions. She had the ability to laugh at herself, especially at her plump exterior, and she often expressed her delight that her domestic life was free from the professional and public responsibilities of her male friends. The image that emerges from her few verses is that of a self-reflective woman, wisely aware of the limits of her talents, yet driven by the quest for fame to cultivate the Muse. This last point should not be overlooked. Earlier critics preferred the shy, retiring Anna, for that role corresponded to their uninspired and unfounded characterization of her as the homely female scholar. But behind her protestations of modesty, a commonplace rhetorical device (*captatio benevolentiae*) lay an obvious play for her reader's indulgence to excuse the poetic forays of a woman.

Anna's self-deprecating persona reappeared in numerous places throughout her extensive oeuvre. The variety and scope of her writing is actually much broader than she seemed willing to admit. In addition to her translation of de Montenay and the edition of her father's emblem book, she composed almost one hundred poems in several forms, from sonnets, prayers, and inscriptions to mock epics about her constant war against Cupid and panegyrics of Dutch military victories; she also translated some psalms into Dutch. But the personal, indeed private tone, of many of her works indicates that poetic composition was more a meditative rather than a purely literary exercise. Her poetry, especially in her later years, became a function of her life, and her life, in turn, a function of her familial responsibilities. She rarely ventured beyond Amsterdam and the province of Holland, except for family reasons, as in the 1640s when her sons were studying at the Jesuit school in Brussels. She expressed few opinions about the tumultuous political and religious events that occurred during her lifetime, and appeared indifferent to the dogmatic distinctions between Catholics and Calvinists. Though a loyal supporter of the Dutch Republic, she disapproved of the continuing hostilities between the Northern Netherlands (United Provinces) and Catholic Spain, and, like many of her fellow countrymen in the 1640s, she longed for peace. Little is known about Anna between 1646, when she penned her last surviving poem, and her death in 1651, but her works attest to the appropriateness of the motto, borrowed from her father's emblem book, with which she sometimes characterized herself and her writing: "Ghenoegh is meer" ("Enough is more").[7]

Maria Tesselschade's world seems much more eventful than that of her sister. Her unusual name, Tesselschade, is itself the result of a business mishap of her father: shortly before her birth in 1594, Roemer Visscher had lost several merchant ships and sailors off the island of Texel (Tessel), the southernmost of the West Frisian islands, and he whimsically commemorated this misfortune by calling Maria "Tesselschade" (literally, "Texel's harm"). Such romantic origins, coupled with her physical beauty, contributed greatly to her subsequent allure, and her skill on the lute and her mellifluous voice appear to have enchanted all who knew her.

In contrast to her sister, Maria composed few poems; only 28 have survived along with approximately the same number of letters. Hardly any of her works were published during her lifetime, though some were included in later seventeenth-century anthologies. There is a much greater variety of subject matter, poetic form, and even languages (Maria wrote at least one poem in Italian) than in Anna's more extensive work. Maria wrote gallant, amatory verse (a fact usually suppressed by literary historians enamored of the image of Maria as the intellectual, otherworldly beauty[8]); songs in praise of music and nature (her untranslatable "Onderscheyt tusschen een wilde en een tamme zangster" ["The Difference Between a Wild and a Tame Songstress"] was a favorite with nineteenth-century Romantics);[9] religious lyrics on the Ascension and Maria Magdalene; several poems in praise of her male friends (Hooft; Huygens; Caspar Barlaeus) and other contemporaneous composers and lyricists; polemical verses against religious intolerance; a pastoral poem; and, most memorably, finely crafted epicedia (mourning poems) on the losses suffered by her friends and herself through death. In all of these verses she used a variety of forms, chiefly the sonnet and the madrigal, and she strove for the invention of complex conceits, favored arcane literary allusions and images, and engaged in elaborate wordplay.[10] As a result of her contact with the writers of the Muiden circle, and chiefly with its host P.C. Hooft, she studied Italian Renaissance lyricists, especially the contemporary mannerist Giambattista Marino, whose wordgames she imitated, and she began a translation of Torquato Tasso's epic *Gerusalemme liberata* (Jerusalem Delivered), of which only a few lines survive.

Maria's extensive literary activity, her participation in the meetings at Muiden and at Hooft's house in Amsterdam where writers gathered to continue the friendly criticism ("betuttelen") they had begun in their letters to one another, has tended to overshadow the circumstances of her private life. To the dismay, feigned or serious, of her admirers she married Allard Crombalgh, a naval officer, in 1623, and moved with him to his home in Alkmaar. Crombalgh had little interest in literature, and the poets of the Muiden circle wrote disdainfully of the apparent mismatch. But Maria's marriage was apparently very happy, and she worshipped her husband's memory after his untimely death in 1634 in her poems and letters. As a widow, she consistently repulsed the passionate and quasi-erotic advances of the learned humanist Caspar Barlaeus, and playfully responded to the flirtatious words of Hooft and Huygens during the brief periods in which they too were widowed. She was also an especially devoted mother, and she deeply mourned the early deaths of her children, all daughters: one child died as an infant; she lost another to smallpox in 1634, the same disease that took her husband from her a few days later; and the loss of her third daughter in 1647 precipitated the illness that led to her own death in 1649.

These personal tragedies in Maria's life gave rise to the few places in her writing where her own voice becomes apparent. Most of her poems appear impersonal and stylized when compared to those of her sister: Maria does not create a poetic persona, nor does she appear to reflect on her unusual status as a woman poet, or on her social role as a woman. Instead, as in her early "T'amo, mia vita" ("I Love You, My Life"), translated and discussed below, she is often engaged in a literary exercise in which she emulates the conceits and verbal puns of her contemporaries. In the case of personal loss, however, Maria excelled in the ability to transform emotional upheaval into metaphysical art. In her letters to Hooft after the death of his first wife, for example, she urged him to recall the moral-philosophical counsel of the Stoic philosophers not to indulge in grief. Writing, as she later tells Huygens in the epicedium written for his late wife, possesses therapeutic value and enables the aggrieved to overcome loss by harnessing the emotions through reason.[11] To be sure, this distanced philosophical response to personal sorrow appears contrived and stylized, but there is little doubt that Maria's identity was intimately connected to emotional control. The persona that she always took pains to project was that of a self-disciplined, rational woman devoted first to her family and then to the study of literature. In her hortatory epistles and poems to those overcome by emotion, be it grief or sexual passion, she displayed the extraordinary reserve and moral courage that earned her the epithet *sachte sedeles* ("mild moral lesson") from an enchanted Hooft.[12]

Maria's role as the lively spirit of the Muiden circle lasted from the mid-1620s until the dissolution of the group in 1647 with the death of Hooft. During that time, she was constantly cajoled by Hooft to travel from Alkmaar to Muiden to entertain his guests, an invitation which she, with her usual restraint, did not always accept. On many occasions, Hooft even lured guests to his castle with the promise that Maria would be there to sing.

There was much harmony among the frequent Muiden visitors, and Maria's steadfast resistance to the romantic advances of the widowers hardly ever disturbed the congenial atmosphere. Her conversion to Catholicism in 1641-1642, however, was quite another matter. Hooft and Barlaeus possessed an urbane, humanist preference for religious toleration and remained indifferent to her beliefs; Huygens, however, was deeply troubled and attempted to reconvert her through verse, letters, and long theological conversations. The controversy turned bitter when Maria accused Huygens of defending orthodoxy only to ingratiate himself further with the Stadhouder, Frederick Henry, an unjust charge that merely exacerbated the conflict. Their tempers gradually cooled, and after her death in 1649, Huygens remembered Maria in verse as a remarkable and truly exceptional woman.[13]

The motives for Maria's conversion to Roman Catholicism remain unclear. She strongly disapproved of the bloody, internecine conflict that the ravings of Calvinist preachers incited, and like many intellectuals in the 1640s she yearned for an end to the allegedly religious war against Catholic Spain. Perhaps like Hugo Grotius and Joost van den Vondel, who also turned to Rome in the late 1630s and early 1640s, Maria was attracted by the ideal of a universal Christian church free from the divisiveness of religious sectarianism, an ideal that bore little relation to the ecclesiastical and political ambitions of Counter-Reformation Rome. Huygens's response is also a mystery: as a member of the international Latin republic of letters he had many Catholic friends, and he appeared to respect their differences. In Maria's case, however, her independent action may have threatened his admiration and possibly even his love for her. Maria's intellectual and emotional freedom always dismayed those men who, like Barlaeus, were eager to transform her into an appropriate personal companion. Although her own poetic voice was often obscured by her eagerness to emulate the style of her male contemporaries, her personal experiences, and her reasoned response to them, betrayed the appropriateness of the motto that she, like Anna, chose for herself from her father's emblem book: "Elck zijn waerom" ["Each person has his own why"].[14]

In the translations of the poems that follow, no attempt is made to reproduce the rhymed couplets of the original texts. Such rhymes, though favored by many seventeenth-century English poets, would have necessitated too much recasting of Anna's and Maria's language. To modern ears culturally conditioned to regard Shakespearean blank verse as ideal, the preservation of rhymed couplets would appear artificial and distracting. Instead I have attempted to convey, as accurately as possible, the meaning and rhythm of the original in idiomatic English. The English translations are based on the editions of Anna Roemers and Maria Tesselschade compiled by Nicolaas Beets and J.A. Worp respectively, as cited in the bibliography.

NOTES to the Introduction

1. E.g., Huygens referred to both sisters as "Meyssjes, mannelick van sin" ("Maids of manly spirit") in a poem to them dated 7 September 1623 (Worp 32).

2. E.g., Scheltema 1808.

3. The most outrageous example of this type of criticism can be found in E. Gosse 1879.

4. Compare the list of critical literature on each author in the "Bibliography." Anna's poems have never been presented in as expansive a manner as Worp's edition of Maria's writings and her admiring contemporaries, nor have Anna's works ever been chosen for inclusion in an anthology of translated texts. See Bowring xi-xii. Most recently, in a special issue of the *Canadian Journal of Netherlandic Studies* (11[2] 1990) devoted to women writers, only Maria Tesselschade was included: F. Nichols, "Maria Tesselschade Roemer Visscher," (19-24).

5. Worp xix.

6. For an excellent discussion of these laudatory verses and Anna's reaction to them see Schenkeveld 1979/80.

7. Roemer Visscher, *Sinnepoppen*, ed. L. Brummel (The Hague: Martinus Nijhoff, 1949), 68.

8. When her amatory verse is discussed, it is usually understood, quite chastely, to refer to her husband. E.g., Brachin 22.

9. Gosse 261-62.

10. For an appraisal of her style, see Flinn 71-75.

11. The letter to Hooft and the epicedium for Huygens are discussed and translated below.

12. Vanderauwera 145.

13. Worp 343.

14. R. Visscher, *Sinnepoppen*, ed. L. Brummel 70.

Translations by James A. Parente, Jr.

Anna Roemers Visscher

To Daniel Heinsius (before 1615)

Anna Roemers and Maria Tesselschade were frequently
praised for their talents and learning by contemporaneous poets in
both Latin and Dutch. Although their admirers had varying degrees
of knowledge about the sisters' accomplishments, the main purpose
of the panegyrics was to provide an opportunity for the male poets to
extol the "paradox" of the learned woman. Daniel Heinsius (1580-
1655), the precocious professor of poetry at Leiden University, was
a frequent recipient, and dispenser, of the hyperbolic flattery that
humanist scholars customarily directed at each other. In his 1616
collection, *Nederduytsche Poemata*, edited by Heinsius's friend Petrus
Scriverius, a poem appeared in which Heinsius hailed Anna Roemers
as the tenth Muse. Anna, who probably had seen the poem in
manuscript before 1616, penned the following humble response. The
poem's uneven syntax and unaccomplished rhythms indicate that it
belongs among her earliest works.

With contempt, yea, with deepest contempt do I scorn
That which robs the most gifted men of their reason:
Foolish drunkenness. Yet with deceitful entreaties do I beg
For a sip of the liquid that other drunkards greedily swallow,
For a little bit on the sly. They are intoxicated
Not with French liquor nor with dry Rhine wine
But with the fountain of Pegasus.[1] O Goddesses, three times three,[2]
Dispensers of that precious drink, look favorably on me
That I might reply to the praise for which I am so unworthy.
Help me to escape the envy that always accompanies such honor,
Refusing to acknowledge this act as the custom of a courteous poet.
Think not, you Apollo,[3] to implant in your mind
That I dare deem myself as worthy as you find.

Sonnet to the Goddesses of Song (1619)

The seventeenth-century Dutch poet, Constantijn Huygens (1596-1687) became acquainted with Anna Roemers and Maria Tesselschade at a wedding feast in February 1619. On that occasion, Anna sent him a poem (which he subsequently lost) in response to his inclusion of her in his epithalamium for the newlyweds. Shortly thereafter Anna's mother died, an event that, as the following poem to the Muses betrays, deeply affected her attitude toward her art.

Alas, you guardians of my honorably sweet desires,
I must, alack, I must, driven by necessity
Abandon your company. Bitter death has brusquely
Snatched a person away to whom my heart and spirit were devoted.
O pleasing waters[4] that soothed me so lovingly
In self-contented sleep, now household worries,
Weightier than lead, have been dumped on my lap.
Whoever would have thought that when I kissed you last?
But you graces, I beg you, have pity on me;
With all your efforts bid that honored Constantine,
Your dear foster child, let me know the news,
Or at least remind me what songs you are humming
And what sweet, new events on Helicon are transpiring,
So that I may still think that I have not been forgotten.

Prayer on the Birthday of Our Lord Jesus Christ (1620)

Between 1616 and 1620, Anna Roemers composed numerous poems, chiefly sonnets, on the occasion of major Christian feasts, Christmas, Easter, and Pentecost. In these meditative works, Anna echoed the sentiments of the Reformed Church, in which she had been raised, by lamenting the sinfulness of human existence, the folly of earthly wisdom, and the hope for salvation through Jesus Christ. These religious verses display a world dominated by the devil and his agents who tirelessly seek to entrap mankind. The following poem of prayer restates Anna's familiar plea for humility as the best defence against the temptations of Satan.

Almighty Lord, O God, direct my thoughts now

Higher than before. I feel my soul yearning, yea encouraged,
To ascend out of the slough of earth, filth, and mud.
A child has just been born today, God united with man,
Who has come to wish us fallen people peace.
O wondrous mystery that no one can comprehend,
No matter how sharply their wits have been whetted
On worldly wisdom, nor how presumptuously they speculate,
They helplessly flounder in confusion therein.
Banish such thoughts far from me and humbly bend my heart
Toward that which your spirit has borne witness
So that my conduct might strengthen my dwelling places,
And your brightness shine in my lanterns.
Grant that I, earthly worm, might reverently worship
That which I can not yet understand.

Sonnet: Of a Woman Dressing Herself For a Wedding Feast (ca. 1619)

Anna Roemers's religious poetry also consisted of meditative verses on the familiar Baroque topos of the vanity of the world and the transitoriness of earthly existence. Anna frequently voiced such sentiments in the prose and verse comments she added to individual emblems in her father's collection *Sinnepoppen* (1614) that she began to reedit and enlarge in 1619. The following poem about a young girl's preparation for a wedding feast, was written by Anna about this time and provides a unique and personal reworking of the *vanitas* theme.

O benevolent God, how gently can you pull out
My unbridled senses that lustily are listing,
Yea, are nigh drowning in the world's pomp?
As I occupy myself with the adornment of my body,
Bind the devil fast, who yearns to swallow my soul.
How grateful shall I be, O Father, for your help?
With humbly bended knee, I shall confess my sins before you;
The steady beating of my heart will bear witness to my remorse.
But is it your will that for this wedding feast
I put on a festive gown? Then adorn my spirit

So that this body, outwardly decked out with ornament,
That, on the surface, appears both grand and beautiful,
Not be the dwelling place or hut wherein resides
A soul besmirched with all sorts of flaws.

To Johanna Coomans (1622)

In the summer of 1622, Anna Roemers travelled to the province of Zeeland where she was welcomed by the circle of local poets. During her sojourn there, the Zeeland poets began a collection of their writing, the *Zeeusche Nachtegael* (The Nightingale of Zeeland), published in 1623, to display their poetic gifts to a larger Dutch audience that had hitherto concentrated on the talented writers of the province of Holland, especially those of if its cultural centers, Leiden and Amsterdam. Anna had many friends in Zeeland, such as the famous Dutch poet Jacob Cats (1577-1660), and she befriended many others, chiefly Simon van Beaumont, the pensionary (chief legal official) of Middelburg, and the young poetess Johanna Coomans. The following verse was an inscription that Anna engraved onto a *roemer* (a wine-glass; the similarity between the Dutch word and Anna's name, Anna *Roemers*, was the occasion for much punning among her friends). Both Anna and Maria were famed for their glass inscriptions, and they delighted in decorating the *roemers* with personalized messages, such as the following:

Could I let you view my heart
Without suffering pain or smart
You would see more than you expect
How very deeply you've won my respect,
The smallest portion of which I cannot express
Nor write out fully on this glass.

To Pensionary Simon van Beaumont (1622)

Simon van Beaumont (b. 1573 or 1574), the pensionary of Middelburg, became a close friend of Anna's during her Zeeland sojourn, and he may have even been her host. During his student

years in Leiden in the 1590s, van Beaumont composed a series of
amatory sonnets in the Petrarchian manner and translated excerpts
from Vergil's *Eclogues*. Anna travelled to Zeeland in response to his
invitation, and he greeted her with many panegyrical verses. Anna
penned the following poem in response to Simon's surprise that,
though larger, he weighed less than she. In her reply, Anna creates
a self-satisfied poetic persona whose indifference to worldly ambitions
and turmoil grants her happiness and peace.

I have long warded off
The love that flesh and blood consumes.
Another's luck does not torment me,
For my own contents me so.
No high position have I held or sought,
Nor am I scorned for my low station.
I sleep peacefully through the night
And enjoy my food and drink with pleasure.
Do not be amazed, therefore,
That I weigh somewhat more than a man,
Who is constantly burdened with worry
About the welfare of his household
And the troubles of the commonweal
That he bears upon his shoulders.

To the Learned Gentleman Jacob Cats (1623)

Jacob Cats was an ardent admirer of Anna Roemers's writing
and of her modest, upright character. A chance meeting with her
inspired Cats to finish his didactic *Maechden-plicht* (1618) in which
she appeared as a fictional exemplum of the maidenly female ideal:
a chaste, emotionally self-disciplined woman, spiritually capable of
repulsing the temptations of the flesh. Cats dedicated this work to her,
an honor to which Anna responded with a poem in her usual, self-
deprecating manner. Anna wrote several more poems to Cats as well
as some moralistic verses about the emblems in his collection *Silenus
Alcibiadis* (1618). But the closest period of contact between them
occurred during Anna's Zeeland visit. Cats, a long-time resident of
Middelburg and its environs (like van Beaumont, he served as a

pensionary of Middelburg in the early 1620s) introduced Anna to the Zeeland circle of poets, whose mentor he had been for several years. Their affection for him is evidenced by the numerous poems dedicated to him in the *Zeeusche Nachtegael*. The following poem, one of Anna's most beautiful, first appeared in that anthology:

Yesterday when Phoebus released his exhausted horses from the yoke
And prepared to hide his shining golden head in the sea,
I thought about that which I had promised you.
I took pen, ink, and paper in hand and set down to write:
At first the book did not want to lie open;
The pen must have been worn, and the penknife dull,
For instead of the pen, it cut a deep wound in my hand.
The paper stained completely through; in the ink was neither gum
/nor luster;
A snuffer was not at hand to trim my darkly burning candle;
[Then] the sister of death[5] dragged me [off] to bed.
Thus, my learned friend, I was held back from writing,
To my advantage, as it happens, for dissatisfaction came flying
And, in a dream, set my lame, crippled, wooden verses before
/my eyes.
Bitter, pale Envy derided me: You think that you're Homer.
Black Slander cried out: Go away; if you want to put forward
Your silly verses, everyone will be quickly bored.
Good Sense then followed, saying: Keep your verses hidden,
So you won't be envied, slandered, or scorned.

Rebellion Against Cupid (1622)

The following poem, also printed in the *Zeeusche Nachtegael* was one of two amatory verses that Anna composed. Both poems relate Anna's contest with Cupid and her attempts, playfully expressed, to reject corporal desire. The first, *Ploeckhartie van Ionck-Vrou Anna Roemers met Cupido* (The Battle of Mistress Anna Roemers Against Cupid), in which Anna mocks Cupid's alleged invincibility, ends with her defeat at his hands. The second, which is translated below, follows in sequence to the former: the love-smitten Anna avers with great conviction that she will not fall prey to the foolish behavior customarily displayed by lovesick victims of Cupid. Early editors of Anna's work cite these two poems to demonstrate that Anna, though less worldly and charming than Maria Tesselschade, nonetheless possessed a beauty and wit that attracted many suitors and compelled her to deal with matters of the heart.

Although I have now been stung, you rascal, I shall refrain
From languishing and ranting as you have desired.
You shall not see your wish fulfilled, that I, besotted and dazed,
Shall commit the foolishnesses I have so often scorned.
Nor that I, fearful of pain, shall squeamishly conceal
My wounds so that they may fester and become fouled.
See me go forth and seek that very person
Who (experienced in the art) can treat me freely.
I shall not fear any pungent ointment or painful probing
Or bitter liquids that are capable of curing
My heart of this torment, that I, in my early years,
Feared so anxiously and avoided so diligently.
O you helmeted Maid, you most beauteous of the Goddesses,[6]
How could you have the heart to see me conquered so?
How could you have the heart to see her, your devoted servant,
So unworthily debased by a child — a child!
I burst with spite whenever this shameful bastard
Praises his mother's beauty and denigrates your own.
No, no, I do not value a body beautiful and sound
As dearly as a righteous temper in which virtue can be found.
Though his mother received the prize adjudged her by a shepherd,
Who only saw as far as his obscene lust and not a bit further,[7]
This fact is not important. In light of the outcome,
What was his reward? O unhappy man! Only misery and sorrow.
Who shall not want to root out wanton lust from his heart
When he sees the mountainous ruins of burnt out Troy?

Anna Roemers on Dutch Society and Politics

Much of Anna Roemer's poetry was written during tumultuous times in Dutch domestic and international politics, but there are few signs of these events in her works. Such reticence is not surprising in the limited domestic sphere that well-to-do, middle-class women like the Visschers, inhabited. However, in contrast to Maria Tesselschade, Anna did write a few works, such as the two poems that follow, inspired by contemporary social and political practices.

I. *Prayer for the Day of Prayer* (1622)

In 1621 hostilities resumed between Spain and the Dutch after the respite of the Twelve Years Truce. At critical moments in the ensuing campaigns, the Dutch government proclaimed public days of prayer and fasting on which the public was enjoined to implore God for special assistance. In 1622, the year in which Anna wrote the following poem (though it was not published until 1623 in the *Zeeusche Nachtegael*), there were three days of prayer. The first was held in June on the occasion of the Dutch military advance into Brabant; the second in September during the siege of the Dutch city of Bergen op Zoom by the Spanish; and the third was intended as a day of thanksgiving for the relief of that city. The sober but by no means desperate tone of the following suggests that it was written for either the first or second occasion, when the outcome of that year's Dutch military action still hung in the balance.

Anna's customarily humble poetic persona is coupled here with an unusually intense revelling in guilt and contrition. Such fervent sentiments did not prevent her from constructing an artfully crafted work with many wordplays (chiefly on the word "moed," courage; heart) and a clever introductory metaphor for atonement. Anna's notion of offering a contrite heart to God betrays her allegiance to the Reformed Church, for such a sacrifice contrasts with the traditional blood offerings of the Jews and the pagans, and more importantly to the Protestant mind, with the metaphorical blood offering of Christ during the Catholic mass.

O Almighty and Eternal God, who accepts an anxious spirit
And contrite heart as offerings (in place of the blood rattling
In the throats of slaughtered animals) as often as we set them aflame
In your honor on the altar of Faith. Look down! O look at us!
Do not allow your oppressed church to pass away so helplessly.
The smoke ascends into the air from many anxious sighs

That, though disheartened, take heart and seek refuge in your
/goodness.
Your grace so enheartens disheartened sinners about
To fall into the depths that they rise to heaven
And pray, and implore, and cry, and dare to demand your help
Without fearing to provoke you to anger.
We acknowledge our guilt! and fall in humility,
United in our sorrow, to the feet of your majesty.
We confess that there is not a single one among us
Who is not stuffed full of damnable sins
Committed by overstepping your laws and commandments.
Take pity on us, by the suffering of your son.
Let our proud and audacious enemies see
That you want to discipline but not forget us.
Be aggrieved that they so spitefully, haughtily, and scornfully
Mock the pain and pliants of our hearts.
Alas! Turn toward us, so that our bitter lamentations
Might turn into joy, and we might spread your praises through song.

II. *Letter and Sonnet to Pieter Roose (1642)*

Among the small number of poems that Anna wrote after her
marriage in 1624, two were addressed to Pieter Roose, chairman of
the Privy Council in the southern Netherlands from 1622 to 1653,
During the 1640s, Anna visted the southern Netherlands, chiefly
Brussels, Antwerp, and Leuven (Louvain), several times while her
sons were studying at the Jesuit school in Brussels. These visits gave
her the opportunity to encounter many renowned humanists from the
south, such as the Antwerp printer Balthasar Moretus and the Louvain
professor of Latin, Erycius Puteanus, for each of whom she wrote a
poem. Like many Dutch intellectuals in 1640s from North and South,
Anna yearned for an end to the war with Spain and for the peaceful
coexistence of all religious faiths. Such wishes were evident in her
poem for Puteanus, in her 1642 sonnet to Pieter Roose and, more
significantly, in her letter to Roose (one of her few surviving letters)
from the same year. The letter is also noteworthy for its
representation of the respect that Northern and Southern statesmen

shared for each other despite the continuation of the conflict between their governments.

A. *Excerpt from Letter to Pieter Roose*
    [After thanking Roose profusely for his friendship and many kindnesses, especially his help in securing neutral passage for her through the South, Anna continues]:
I was once invited to eat in the Hague, along with some of the most prominent gentlemen, at the home of Jacob Cats, a very close friend of mine, to whom I told that I had once toasted his health with Your Excellency. As soon as he heard this, he had a large *roemer* brought in, on which I had once scratched some words in his honor,[8] and, with great reverence and bared heads, they all drank to Your Excellency's health, wishing Your Excellency a long life and declaring themselves privately (having set aside their own, and your, public offices) Your Excellency's friends.
    In the middle of this cheerful meal, my heart became troubled, and I lamented to myself the misery of the beautiful Netherlands, devastated and oppressed by that hellish Fury, the accursed war. O divine peace! When will we see you again? Isn't there any Father Neyen to be found any more to stitch together the shattered hearts again?[9] Aren't there any olive branches growing toward each other? O my dear fatherland, to whom I am naturally bound, and you my worthy land of friends, whose many kindnesses compel me to grant it all the best. I wish (Oh!) that God might grant that my wish not remain a wish! — and that I might kiss the footsteps of the harbingers of peace!

B. *To the Right Noble Gentleman President Roose (1642)*
It was in vain, o Greeks, that the walls of Troy stood,
As long as Hector stood, yet should have been able to fall.[10]
It is in vain that the Hollander hopes that Brabant will be his
As long as Roose stands firm to his post.[11]
If Brabant had ten of him, she would defy the world,
Yea, even dare to expel the Turk from his seat.[12]
O marvelous man! Where does one find such a person
So foreign to self-interest, yet so selfish about the common good?

Your refusal pains me, yet, though pained, I must praise
That man so completely incapable of flattery or empty courtesies.
I beseech God that he take that which I have
Scratched on this glass with a diamond
And inscribe it with his finger on your heart,
So that your favor toward me may always remain.

To the Very Learned Gentleman Ewaldus Schrevelius, Rector of the
Most Illustrious School at Leiden (1646)
      Ewaldus Schrevelius (1576-1646) was professor of medicine
at Leiden University and twice served as its rector. In May 1646,
during Schrevelius's second rectorship, Anna's two sons matriculated
in the university, one to study law, the other, humanities. In the
following poem, probably Anna's last, she entrusts her two children
to Schrevelius's care. Here Anna also laments her absence from
Helicon, a complaint that she had voiced often, especially in the
1640s, when she apparently had little interest in, or opportunity for,
writing. The recurrence of this motif in a work by the 63-year-old
poetess conjures up an elegiac tone of talent spent by increasing age
and familial responsibilities. Despite her typically self-deprecating
posture, Anna's apologia was intended ironically to help secure her
an esteemed place among her fellow poets.

O learned, wise man, chosen by Pallas[13] from many
To impart your wisdom to young minds.
Glory of the Netherlands, Tribute to this city,
Light of the university, Leader on the path
Of all scholarship, I beseech for my sons
Your favor, your help, and your advice. I have come to live here
In this esteemed place, the Athens of the Netherlands,
For the sake of this dear pair of mine and nothing else.
O Phoebus, you who were once so devoted and gracious
That you kindly brought me to your expert sisters on Helicon,[14]
Continue to extend your favor to me.
Permit these two, my offspring, to be committed to you.
Permit this green youth, these quick-witted young men
To learn to sing many sweet tunes on Parnassus.[15]

My lyre is unstrung, my laurels wilted,
My voice hoarse and husky from thirst profound
Since I have not drunk for the longest time
The mind-purifying liquid that enkindles the spirits.[16]
But you, esteeméd gentleman, still known only to me
By that name that fleet-footed Fame
Proclaims throughout the world: Do not be vexed
That I presume to greet you and send you these trifles.
Though I try your patience with this clumsy fare,
Accept it not in anger, but as a token of a mother's care.[17]

Maria Tesselschade Roemers Visscher

T'amo, mia vita (I Love You, My Life)

    Like her sister Anna Roemers, Maria Tesselschade wrote few love poems. Those that survive contain the usual self-exploratory revelling in the sweet, but unwelcome, torments of love incited by Cupid's arrow. Such sentiments were commonplace among the Petrarchistic lyricists of the late sixteenth- and early seventeenth-century Netherlands, such as Jan van der Noot, Justus Harduwijn, and P.C. Hooft. The date of composition of the following poem is unknown, but many critics have speculated that Maria Tesselschade's amatory verses must have been written after she had fallen in love with Allard Crombalgh, whom she later married. The validity of this biographical reading, however, is undermined by the fact that the identity of the poetic speaker is clearly male. More importantly, the poem's complex reworking of several contemporaneous or near-contemporaneous texts suggest that its composition was more a literary exercise than a personal outpouring of emotion. The poem's title betrays its origin as an adaptation of a madrigal by the Italian poet Battista Guarini (1538-1612): it is the first line of Guarini's poem, "Parola di donna amante" ("The Speech of an Enamored Lady"). The second line of Tesselschade's poem is an adaptation from P.C. Hooft's sonnet "Mijn lief, mijn lief, mijn lief" ("My love, my love, my love"), published in his *Emblemata amatoria* (1611, Emblem Book of Love), a poem that is likewise indebted to Guarini for its inspiration.[18] What distinguishes Tesselschade's work from those of her models is her manneristic play with words beginning with "l" and especially with the word "love" ("lief") and its adjectival variations ("lieve" [dear]; "liefste" [dearest]).

My love, I love you. Thus spoke my dear life
As my lips parted from her dear lips.
No greater sweetness had ever been heard before
As when she gave me that which I took from her.
Preserve these sweet sounds, I bid you, dearest Cupid,
(You impish Lord of the Soul, you powerful little Miracle-Worker),
And implant them in my breast in such a way
That my pulse, spleen, heart, lungs, and liver beat to their rhythm.
Bid that my soul impart itself to my body,
And nourish it constantly with such dear life
Addressing it thus: My love, I love you, dearest mine.
Be my dear life, my love, be forever mine.

Answer to Vondel's Question From the Amsterdam Academy

Maria Tesselschade did not refrain from active engagement with polemical issues discussed by the intellectual élite of her day. The following work is the earliest surviving poem in which she addresses a controversial contemporary topic. In the late 1620s and early 1630s, the conservative Calvinist preachers (Counter-Remonstrants) in the province of Holland, chiefly Amsterdam and Leiden, organized a punitive campaign against the liberal Calvinists (Remonstrants), a group whose promulgation of religious toleration was strongly supported by many seventeenth-century Dutch writers, especially Joost van den Vondel (1587-1679) and Samuel Coster (1579-1665). The Counter-Remonstrants were repulsed by the tolerant attitude of the Amsterdam city council, where the Remonstrants prevailed, and they pursued every opportunity to prevent Remonstrants from establishing churches and a seminary. Rioting, the destruction of private and public Remonstrant buildings, and the desecration of churches were commonplace; on one occasion, Amsterdam officials called on the Stadhouder, Frederick Henry, for military assistance to restore order. In 1630, Vondel, a biting satirist

of Counter-Remonstrant dogmaticism, called on all Dutch poets who
loved freedom (i.e., the Remonstrants) to define the "best and worst
type of tongues," an allusion to the rabble-rousing rhetorical power
of the Counter-Remonstrant preachers. Vondel's call was published
as the poem "From the Amsterdam Academy to all Versifiers and
Poets of the United Netherlands, Lovers of Golden Freedom." Maria
Tesselschade's poem is a response to this work. She argues here in
an understated way for civil harmony: she is greatly disturbed by any
act of resistance that threatens the stability of the commonweal (e.g.,
the October 1628 refusal of several Counter-Remonstrant militia men
of Amsterdam to pledge an oath of allegiance to the new Remonstrant
captain appointed by the city, an incident referred to near the end of
the poem). The unity displayed by the coalition of Catholic and
Protestant nobles during the early years of the Dutch Revolt against
Spain, culminating in the Petition of Nobles (1566) presented to the
imperial regent, Margaret of Parma, daughter of Emperor Charles V,
serves here as an historical exemplum of the triumph of mutual
cooperation over sectarianism.

The best tongue that voices forged
Sang of praise to God and peace to man.
The tongue that silently best displayed its worth
Crowned the heads of Christ's apostles with fire.
The most malicious tongue on earth
Made man yearn for God's hidden wisdom.
The most corrupt tongue in heaven
Declared his power equal to the Lord's.[19]
God establishes his kingdoms in those men
Whose faith is manifested through deeds.
Illusion, like a phantom and erring spirit,
Leads whoever follows to darkness.
Holland's soft ground can no longer bear
The deception of righteous souls.
The Catholic nobles who signed the petition in Brussels
Sought freedom, along with others, from the emperor's daughter.
The mutineer who detests tranquillity and peace
The well-ordered state always discards.

Whenever a burgher storms the wall of another,
The city will not long endure.
There is no earthly God who is not bound by oath:
This is even more true for the town's militia.
If the preachers succeed in loosening this bond,
They will sever the cord that binds the seven arrows together.[20]

Maria Tesselschade and P.C. Hooft

Maria Tesselschade's long friendship with Hooft (1581-1647) is preserved in their correspondence with each other. As host of the Muiden circle, Hooft wrote often to Maria Tesselschade, inviting, or rather, cajoling her to entertain the gatherings with the delightful songs she performed on her lute, to decorate the great hall with flowery festoons — a skill in which Maria excelled — and, most importantly, to please him, his family, and their mutual friends with witty conversation. The letters also refer to literary matters: there are occasional requests for criticism about the poems they sent each other and passing mention of their work in progress. Roughly two-thirds of the surviving correspondence was penned by Hooft, and most of these letters are written in the urbane, learned style beloved of the humanists.

The contrast between the two epistolary voices is startling: where Maria's letters rarely contain more than the customary courtesies and the reason for writing, Hooft recasts simple communications into elegant missives, rife with mythological detail, poetic digressions, elaborate, manneristic figures of speech, and frequent lapses into Italian, French, and/or Latin. Rarely have the stark differences between the male humanist Latinate world and the private, pragmatic female sphere been made more plain. There are a few letters, however, where the stylized impersonal tone of the correspondents yields to the need to express intimate emotions. This is most evident in the following two letters where Hooft and Maria attempted to console themselves and each other about the loss of a close family member. The first letter, from July 1624, is Maria's response to Hooft's apologia for his heartfelt grief over the death of his first wife, Christina van Erp (1591-1624). Hooft confesses his unwillingness to forget his loss, and begs Tesselschade to understand his rejection of Stoic self-control, a philosophy that he had hitherto embraced, in this particular case. Maria responds with consolatory admonitions not to abandon reason and wisdom for self-indulgent mourning.

> Sir:
> Since I have been overcome by thoughts more powerful than those which politeness has been able to resist, I dare to wish that the virtues of our *patrona* [hostess] might live again in me (if you think me worthy) as much as they die out in Your Excellency. She enjoyed the earth longer than she deserved and has only just now been deservedly lifted up to heaven; she should have been taken from us sooner, for she has belonged at home there for a long time. I have heard of your grief with great regret and with much sorrow, though I still cannot believe it of you. Indeed, how could you, my lord, you who have had on hand a great supply of steadfast wisdom, how could you be made miserable by worldly necessity? I implore Your Excellency to respond to this difficulty of mine, and I shall remain Your Excellency's beholden servant and friend.
>   Tesselschade Roemers
> If it pleases Your Excellency to write, my brother will gladly deliver your letter with one of his wrapped around it.

The second letter, received by Hooft in June 1634, was written by Maria after the loss of her baby daughter, Tadea (Teetje), to smallpox and the death of her husband Allard a short time later.

> Sir:
> Experienced minds can imagine more vividly than my pen can express how much bitter fate, through a hard and senseless blow, has tested my endurance to the utmost on the touchstone of suffering (proof that one pain does not suffice for those whom God wants to test). For this reason I have resolved (so as not to present such an unpleasant image to Your Excellency) to carry this sorrow locked up in my heart, but your charming daughter Susanna[21] lured it out. The occasion of your nephew Sammer's departure presented itself, from which Your Excellency will be able to learn the character of the

illness, the swiftness of the death, and other details which I have forborne with a plaintive soul, heavy heart, and doleful spirit, but with dry eyes. No other thought occupies my mind in so sad a night of sorrow, bereft of the sunlight of my soul, as the memory of my beloved — alas — all-too-loving Allard, who has ascended to heaven, as on wings of love, after his Tadea; who, in preferring immortality to his mortal lot, has left behind for wretched me the company of his beloved other half, so that I shall always have his dear form to look at, as if into a mirror, in my mind's eye, reconciling myself to the Almighty's will, against which nothing can be done.

Hooft responded to the above on 15 June 1634 with a letter praising Maria's tearless, manly(!) self-control as a model for all heroes constrained to forbear the vicissitudes of fortune, and the wisdom with which she, in the tradition of Seneca, Plutarch, and Montaigne, has mastered her grief. Such appraisals contributed to the later literary-historical image of Maria as an unusually restrained, self-disciplined woman, whose detached, rational perception of the world was tempered only by her beauty. As Maria's letter makes plain, her manly heroism was more a figment of the heated imaginations of her male admirers than a reliable indication of her character.

The next letter (1 August 1636) gives a good impression of the tone that Hooft generally adopted toward Maria. She was a close personal friend of his, his two wives, and especially of his stepdaughter Susanna, who admired her greatly. The Hooft-Tesselschade correspondence is full of similar entreaties to enjoy the famous plums of Muiden, to accept fruit and preserves from the castle garden, or for the enchantress Tesselschade to work her magic and banish the damp, chilly weather and sour moods of Hooft and his guests.

My Lady,
The plums have begun all of a sudden to ripen at the same time and to call, "Tesseltje, Tesseltje, dearest mouth." Several songs of Belusar [Caspar Barlaeus] and others are calling, "Tesseltje, Tesseltje, dearest throat." They wish to be sung by her and desire too

that Your Excellency bring along Mistress Francisca to help.[22] When I tell them: Tesseltje is daydreaming; she doesn't have either pen or ink to answer a letter, they refuse to accept this and demand that I shake Your Excellency out of her dream. Arise, arise then: "Rosemund, do you heed neither playing nor singing?"[23] We await Your Excellency posthaste, along with Your daughter and Mistress Duarte and Her Excellency's husband. But send a note in advance about what we may expect. In the meantime, we'll look to the wind and sniff around those who come from Alkmaar and see whether they smell of your breath. God preserve Your Excellency on her trip and eternally in His grace with all those who are dear to her.

Maria Tesselschade and Caspar Barlaeus

After the death of her husband Allard in 1634, Maria was regarded as an ideal partner by many of the widowers and bachelors of the learned Muiden circle. Hooft flirted with Maria occasionally in their correspondence — a gallantry to which she did not respond, but her most serious wooer in the 1630s was the exceptionally learned and extremely prolific Leiden humanist Caspar Barlaeus. In his pursuit of the widow, Barlaeus was encouraged by Hooft and Constantijn Huygens, who also courted Maria in a playful way. His passion for her resulted in the composition of much amatory Latin verse, and the frequent exchange of racy letters and poems about her with Huygens (likewise all in Latin). Literary historians used to read the *Tessalica* verses of Barlaeus as heated outpourings of an impassioned spirit, but recent criticism has shown that he crafted his emotional outpourings in an extremely elaborate manner through his inventive reshaping of the language and motifs of Roman erotic love elegy (chiefly Ovid and Propertius), of his favorite Silver Age poet, Statius, and of the poetry of Claudian.[24]

As a woman, Maria had not had any formal training in the Latin humanist culture of the early seventeenth century. Some scholars have even wondered about her ability to read Latin. But as the following works make plain, Maria did attempt to participate in the study of contemporary Latin writing, and she most certainly had a basic reading knowledge of the language. Her preference for a Dutch translation of Barlaeus's *Oratio, de coeli admirandis* (Oration on the Wonders of the Heavens) in the poem that follows most likely arose out of convenience rather than necessity, for the complex subtleties of Barlaeus's Latin writing could only be fully appreciated by those few readers who were as learned as he.

To Professor Barlaeus,
When He Sent Me His Oration On the Wonders of Heaven

Tesselschade was never struck by the Thessalian art[25]
That can make the moon descend through sharp wits.
But you can bring the entire heaven onto earth
And hold it there with the wondrous power of the soul.
Were you to translate the secrets of these letters for me,
It would be clear to me what the light of the high heavens contains.

The following letter to Barlaeus from the spring of 1639 aptly reveals Maria's dedication to the study of literature and poetic composition. It also demonstrates Maria's familiarity with vernacular literature: here she uses Dutch emblem book imagery in as accomplished a way as Hooft or Barlaeus peppered their epistles to her with classical allusions.

Sir:
Better late than never I thank you for the grand book that you sent me. Although I cannot understand Latin well:
I shall see the shadow on a much prettier day
And with a healthier eye than that with which I regarded
/life.[26]
Now I should like to request of you, because of your generous and courteous learning, yet just as boldly because of the slight nobility of my mind so hungry for knowledge, that you kindly take the trouble to translate a poem of our stalwart Constantine into prose for me, or explicate it somewhat, so that I can transpose it accordingly into rhyme (even though this version will be of little value). *In magnis....*[27] I shall venture to attempt, if you lay the foundation, to set a memorial on top. The poem begins:

Coelo receptum sidus immenso sinu
Aeternitatis.....................
[O star received into heaven,
Into the boundless bosom of eternity...]

The light of this star pleases me insofar as I can see it through the dark cloud of my inexperience. I have an entire garland of fruit and leaves in readiness and feel like a guest of the fox and the crane.[28] May Your Excellency be so kind as to place the light of this star within my reach. I shall, in return, gladly trouble myself on your behalf and remain your friend.

                                                          Tesselschade

Maria Tesselschade and Constantijn Huygens[29]

For most of their long acquaintanceship, the relationship between Huygens and Maria was decidedly literary. Her preference for an obscure, mannered style was no doubt due in great part to her emulation of his sophisticated conceits, and it was Maria who urged Huygens to begin the study and translation of an equally complex poet, John Donne. They also shared a predilection for the elaborate verbal puns of the leading Italian Baroque poet, Giambattista Marino, though Maria rarely succeeded in reproducing the Italian's graceful, unhampered rhythms.

Before their friendship was darkened by their religious differences (see the introductory essay to this chapter), Huygens and his wife, Susanna van Baerle, enjoyed Maria's company at the gatherings in Hooft's Muiden castle. When Huygens's spouse died in 1637, Maria, who had lost both her husband and one of her daughters a few years before, penned the following epicedium to Hooft so that he might send it to the inconsolable Huygens to help him manage his grief.

To My Lord Hooft, On the Passing
Of Mistress Sulekom

She who like a beacon in the sea was laid low by sorrow,
Shorn of trunk and branch, and yet constrained to live,
Sends you this feeble support for your desolate heart

Drowning in a rolling sea of grief.

Tell Constant that he should trust the counsel of paper
Insofar as such pain can be expressed in writing.
He is staring into the radiance of love as an eagle into the sun;
Were he to entrust his sorrow to a book, he would not needs
/remember.

Paper was the weapon with which I warded off
The will to die ere heaven decreed it.
With paper I bade my enemy withdraw.

His own words will teach him to temper his pain,
For suffering set to meter has much less sting.
Press him on to express his sorrow in poetic song.

NOTES to the Translations

1. The fountain of Hippocrene, tended by the Muses on Mt. Helicon, from which all poetic inspiration derives. The winged horse Pegasus was said to have created this source by stomping on the summit of Mt. Helicon to stop its ascent to the heavens as it joyfully listened to poetry.

2. The nine Muses of Greek mythology, who, through their sacred springs, dispense poetic inspiration to poets.

3. Daniel Heinsius, whom Anna likens to Apollo, the Greek god of music and song.

4. The original reads "source." Anna is referring to the wells tended by the Muses on Mt. Helicon from which poetic inspiration flowed.

5. Somnus (sleep), the twin-sister of Mors (death).

6. Minerva, the Roman goddess of wisdom and patroness of the arts. In her other Cupid poem, Anna Roemers likewise calls on Minerva to assist her mentally in regaining rational control of her emotions. Minerva's

appearance in armor refers to her additional function as the patroness of warriors, who instilled courage and perseverance in their hearts.

7. Anna refers here to the Judgement of Paris that ultimately led to the Trojan war and the destruction of Troy. Paris, an estranged son of Priam, king of Troy, spent his early years as a shepherd on Mt. Ida. There he was chosen by Zeus to help settle a dispute between Hera, Athena, and Aphrodite about which of the three goddesses was the most beautiful. All three offered him bribes, but he chose Aphrodite, who, in return for this favor, promised him the fairest woman in Greece, Helen, the wife of the Spartan king. After Priam's acknowledgment of Paris as his rightful son, Paris travelled to Greece, seduced Helen, and brought her back to Troy, an act that led to a lengthy war against Greece and the eventual ruin of his native city.

8. In 1623, Cats was appointed pensionary of Dordrecht in the province of Holland. On that occasion, Anna presented him with a *roemer* upon which was engraved: "Sit cum Felino felicitas Senatui, pax populo Durdrechtano" ("May there be happiness for the Town Council with Cats and peace to the people of Dordrecht").

9. Father Joan Neyen was born a Protestant and later converted to Roman Catholicism. He became a Franciscan monk and was praised by adherents of both churches for his tireless efforts to bring about the truce between Spain and the Netherlands that was signed in 1609 and lasted 12 years.

10. The Fates had decreed that Troy would not fall as long as its most valiant warrior, Hector, a son of Priam, remained alive. Despite the protestations of his family, Hector responded to a challenge from the Greek warrior Achilles and was slain. Troy fell shortly thereafter.

11. Many of the major cities of Brabant, chiefly 's-Hertogenbosch and Breda, were captured and recaptured by the Dutch and Spanish during their long war. In the early 1640s, the Dutch controlled most of northern Brabant, but were unsuccessful in extending their rule further in that province. In the peace negotiations (1646-47), the Dutch republic retained portions of Flanders, Brabant and Limburg, a division of territory that greatly diminished the prestige of the South.

12. Constantinople, the center of the Turkish empire.

13. Pallas Athena, Greek name of the goddess of wisdom and the arts.

14. Phoebus Apollo was the stepbrother of the nine Muses who tended the fountains of poetic inspiration on Mt. Helicon (see note 2).

15. Another mountain haunt of Phoebus Apollo and the nine Muses.

16. The fountain of Hippocrene, the source of poetic inspiration (see note 1).

17. In this line Anna employs two stylistic figures, paronomasia and zeugma to creat an elegant close to her poem. The original line reads "Neem 't mij niet moejelijk maar moederlijken of." The paronomasia, where similar sounds are used to reinforce the contrast, appears with the two adjective/adverbs, "*moei*jelijk" and "*moe*derlijken." The zeugma, the conjoining of a word to two or more words in a context suited to only one, occurs because only "moeijelijk" makes the best sense with the verb.

18. The literary allusions behind the composition of this work have been analyzed by L. Strengholt, "Guarini, Tesselschade en Hooft in een netwerkje," *Tijdschrift voor Nederlandse taal- en letterkunde* 104 (1988), 131-40.

19. Maria establishes a hierarchy of good and evil speakers in these opening lines. She first refers to Christ, then the Holy Spirit, then, conversely, to the serpent in the Garden of Eden and finally to Lucifer.

20. The "seven arrows" refer to the original seven Northern provinces of the Low Countries who united against Spain in the 1560s.

21. Susanna Bartolotti, Hooft's stepdaughter, a close friend of Maria's.

22. Francisca Duarte, a resident of Alkmaar, who, along with her husband, frequently accompanied Maria to Muiden to join in the singing.

23. The opening line of Hooft's *Sang* (Song) written in 1621.

24. A. Van Gool, "Tessela — Thessala — Tesselschade," *Vondeljaarboek* 1949: 80-109.

25. Thessaly was the province in Greece where witches were thought to reside.

26. The "shadow" refers to a future translation of the work. Maria will regard it more favorably than she does its "life" (the source of the shadow), viz., the original Latin text.

27. "In magnis et voluisse sat est" ("It is also enough to have attempted great things"), a quote from Propertius 3.1.6. It may have been known to Maria as well from her father's emblem book where it is explicated in connection with an appropriate image. See Roemer Visscher, *Sinnepoppen*, ed. L. Brummel (The Hague: Martinus Nijhoff, 1949), 181.

28. The fox and the crane learned to share the booty they acquired together; the fable taught the lesson of gratitude. Maria may have known the story from Vondel's emblem collection *Warande der dieren* (1617), no. 13.

29. For a recent popular account of the Tesselschade-Huygens relationship, see Keesing 103-113.

Bibliography

Primary Works

't Hoge huis te Muiden: Teksten uit de Muiderkring. Ed. M.C.A. Van der
     Heijden. Utrecht/Antwerp: Het Spectrum, 1972.
Visscher, Anna Roemers. *Gedichten*. Ed. Nicolaas Beets. 2 vols. Utrecht,
     1881.
Visscher, Anna Roemers. *Gedichten van Anna Roemers Visscher, ter
     aanvulling van de uitgave harer gedichten door Nicolaas Beets*. Ed.
     Fr. Kossmann. The Hague: Martinus Nijhoff, 1925.
Visscher, Anna Roemers. *Letter-Juweel...in facsimile uitgegeven*. Ed. C.W.
     de Kruyter. Amsterdam: University Press Amsterdam, 1971.
Visscher, Maria Tesselschade Roemers. *Een onwaerdeerlycke vrouw:
     Brieven en verzen van en aan Maria Tesselschade*. Ed. J.A. Worp.
     The Hague: Martinus Nijhoff, 1918.

Related Works

I. *Anna Roemers Visscher*

Moltzer, H.E. *Anna Roemers Visscher*. Groningen: J. B. Wolters, 1879.
Schenkeveld, Maria A. "Anna Roemers Visscher, de tiende van de negen,
     de vierde van de drie." *Maatschappij der Nederlandse letterkunde
     te Leiden: Jaarboek* 1979/80. 3-14.

II. *Maria Tesselschade Roemers Visscher*

Bowring, John and Harry S. van Dyk, eds. *Batavian Anthology, Specimens
     of Dutch Poets*. London: Taylor and Hessey, 1824.
Brachin, Pierre. "Tesselschade, femme savante." *Études de littérature
     néerlandaise*. Groningen: Wolters, 1955. 9-30.
Flinn, John F. "La Préciosité dans la littérature néerlandaise: L'oeuvre de
     Maria Tesselschade." *Revue de littérature comparée* 40 (1966). 65-
     80.
Gosse, Edmund W. "A Dutch Poetess of the Seventeenth Century." *Studies
     in the Literature of Northern Europe*. London, 1879. 230-77.

Keesing, Elisabeth. *Het volk met lange rokken*. Amsterdam: Querido, 1987.

Nichols, Fred. "Maria Tesselschade Roemer Visscher (1593-1649)." *Canadian Journal of Netherlandic Studies* 11(2) 1990. 19-24.

Scheltema, Jacobus. Ed. *Anna en Maria Tesselschade, de dochters van Roemer Visscher*. Amsterdam, 1808.

Vanderauwera, Ria. "Maria Tesselschade." *Women Writers of the Seventeenth Century*. Ed. Katharina M. Wilson and Frank J. Warnke. Athens; London: Univ. of Georgia Press, 1989. 141-63.

Anna Maria van Schurman

Cornelia N. Moore

By all accounts, Anna Maria van Schurman (1607-1678) was an extraordinary woman: an accomplished artist in varous media, a renowned scholar who had mastered ten languages, and a sought-after correspondent for some of the most learned men and women of her time.[1] At age 61, she renounced worldly fame and joined the sectarian group around Jean de Labadie, and spent the last years of her life with his wandering flock in the Northern regions of Germany and the Netherlands. Extraordinary as her life may have been, it reflects the political, social, educational, and religious climate of the Dutch Republic of her time. In this essay, I will highlight Schurman's life and works against the background of life in the Dutch republic and to come to an understanding of this phenomenon of a woman who sought God in her learning and found Him in the Spirit; a search which formed the impetus and the foundation for her writing.

Anna Maria van Schurman was born in Cologne in 1607. Her city of birth reflects the political realities of the time. Her paternal grandparents, members of the Brabant nobility with protestant sympathies, had fled to Cologne from Antwerp where the political climate had become more and more repressive toward its protestant citizens. They found hospitality in the city on the Rhine, which had been a haven for many of the refugees from the Low Countries. While in Cologne their sons Johan and Frederik married the two sisters, Agnes and Eva von Harff, respectively, daughters of one of Rhineland's Protestant families. Anna Maria, fourth child and only daughter of Eva and Frederik, spent her first years in Cologne. The connections between Cologne and Antwerp were of long standing. Commercially, Cologne profited from the influx of wealthy merchants and well-trained artisans who flocked to it from the Low Countries as a result of the Spanish repression of the Reformation there. But as the seat of a bishopric, Cologne was subjected to close scrutiny; the city council walked a tightrope between its desire to accommodate the wealthy (albeit Protestant) newcomers and the necessity to placate the bishop. When Reformed services were banned in 1610, the Schurmans moved to the nearby castle Dreiborn, property of her mother's family. In 1613, they moved once more, this time to the newly founded Dutch Republic.

Politically, this was a timely move. In 1609, the Republic of the Seven United Provinces (i.e., the Northern Provinces of the Netherlands), had signed the "Twelve-Year Truce," in effect sealing their eventual independence from Spain and the German Empire, which was to be finalized in the Treaty of Westphalia (1648). Calvinism was the state religion and the economy was flourishing. In this confident — not to say, self-righteous — new country, many of the southern refugees found a new home. The Schurmans lived mostly in or near Utrecht, a quiet city with none of the hustle and bustle of the court in the Hague, the trade and commerce of Amsterdam, or the learned university activity of Leiden. In the former bishopric, the Dutch-Reformed canons now wielded power over the secularized — erstwhile diocesan — estates. Utrecht seemed ideally suited for a well-to-do pious family who wanted to live a quiet life.[2]

Anna Maria was sixteen when her father died. It is not clear what Frederik van Schurman's profession was. He probably had some court connections and, like so many others, lived mostly off the income of his own landed estates and those of his wife. He was able, at least, to move the whole family to Franeker when the Schurman boys went to school there and he was himself able to attend lectures there. According to his daughter's account in *Eucleria* (see below), he warned her against "the entangled sordid web of marriage" (Anna Maria did remain single). After his death, which occurred when Anna

Maria was sixteen, her life revolved around her brother Johan Godschalck (her two other brothers died young), her aging mother and two old aunts, and--when time permitted--her studies and the arts.

Social life may not have been as hectic in Utrecht as in the Hague or Amsterdam, but the family Schurman was certainly not reclusive. Utrecht is centrally located and not far removed from any of the towns mentioned above. The Italian Ludovico Guicciardini noted that one "may departe out of Utrecht in the morning and dine at whether you will of 26 walled towns and return again to supper at Utrecht in your owne house" (from *The Description of the Low Countreys* [London, 1593] as quoted by Marshall xix). The Schurmans were well-heeled and well-connected and their peerage added to their social cachet. They had connections with the Court of Orange as well as that of the Winterking Frederic of the Palatinate, who had found refuge in the Hague after the disastrous Bohemian campaign of 1618. Anna Maria kept up a lifelong friendship with Elizabeth of Bohemia (1618-1680), one of the Winterking's daughters and later Abbess of Herford. The poet, later state secretary, Jacob Cats, made Anna Maria's acquaintance when he came to consult with her father. Her Dutch acquaintances — men like Constantijn Huygens and Caspar Barlaeus — were, like the Schurmans, members of the upper bourgeoisie, *noblesse de robe* and aristocracy, who set the tone in the Dutch Republic, not only politically but also socially and artistically. In this social and political coterie, one knew one another, one took each other's daughters as brides, and one helped one another obtain coveted political positions or simply social introductions. Schurman's letters made references to dinners and gatherings attended by the socially and politically prominent

These patricians, who acted as patrons of the arts, in their spare time also tried their hand at various artistic media: writing poetry in various languages, painting and other crafts. The products of such leisure time diligence were to be given away as presents on social occasions. Thus Anna Maria knew, or knew of, most of the members of the Dutch upper class, made and received congratulatory and appreciatory poems and letters, gave and received artistic products in various media.

Anna Maria stood out in this circle because she possessed abundant natural talent in any artistic medium she tried her hand at, and also because she never did anything half-way. The few extant artistic pieces of, first, the precocious child, and, then, the young woman, show natural talent as well as a high degree of craftsmanship.[3] They are, however, "kunstkamer-kunst:" miniature portraits, little boxes, little statues, finely stitched embroidery, glass engravings: collector's items, intended to enrich the "curiosity cabinets" of friends and acquaintances, who in long appreciative poems and letters thanked her for these exquisite gifts and reciprocated with their own artistic products. To describe it as "kunstkamer-kunst" is not to belittle it; the designation tells us more about its social purpose than the quality (in Anna Maria's case always first-rate). Her contemporaries considered her a serious artist, and she was accepted as a member of the Utrecht painter's guild. Mostly occasional in nature, her poetry in Latin, Dutch, and French must be counted among these artistic endeavors, for example, a poem she wrote to celebrate the opening of Utrecht University in 1636. She was also the recipient of occasional poetry, and poems lauding her artistry abound.[4]

The combination of natural talent and intensive mastery of the medium, which had been visible in her artistic endeavors, was also the decisive factor in Schurman's learned studies. Her educated patrician class did value education. The Dutch Republic had a network of elementary schools where boys and girls were taught at least the rudiments of reading, writing and some arithmetic, primarily in Dutch, sometimes in French. Anna Maria did have a brush with this form of public education; she attended a so-called "French school" only for two months, because the company of the worldly little ladies ("joffertjes") was deemed not a good influence. It is not sure who made that observation — probably the same father who had selected Utrecht, who had attended the theological lectures of John Ames in Franeker, and who later warned his daughter against marriage. However, in her autobiographical *Eucleria* Anna Maria agrees wholeheartedly. This aversion to public education did not exclude her from education; most of the well-to-do received their education at home anyway, and Anna Maria learned reading, writing, arithmetic, French, Dutch and German at home. But she might not have received a more extensive education, had she not shown a precocious talent for absorbing the lessons which her older brothers were taught while she was playing in the same room. From her own account, we learn that her father, upon discovering her talent for learning, took an active part in her education.[5]

As Keesing points out, in her study of the women in the circle of Constantijn Huygens, most women in the Schurman circle had more than an elementary education.[6] Some of them, like the sisters Anna Roemer and Maria Tesselschade Visscher, daughters of an Amsterdam merchant, were accomplished poets; others spoke various languages. They took part in learned discussions and were coveted letter writers. Such learned endeavors lifted their own souls and alternately delighted and bemused those around them. The Dutch upper class did not deny its self-assured women their brains nor their studies.[7] It even doted on the learnedness acquired in private and valued it as an echo for its own learned dilettantism. Johan van Beverwijck, a Dordrecht doctor, published an annotated catalogue of the talented and learned women in his acquaintance, to show the "excellence of the female sex."[8] But when necessity demanded it, the pursuit of learning and the arts took a backseat to the other time-honored duties of women: the household and the family. Schurman's own study time was severely limited when she had to take care of her invalid mother and two old aunts. Women also did not have access to the university and could not attain the status of those learned men who, through their professions, could put their learning into practice.

The coterie of savants was in many ways similar to the social one. With her learnedness established and her modesty in place, Anna Maria could count first on the indulgence and then on the admiration of learned men and women, who were pleased to make her acquaintance, were willing to exchange information, and introduced her to others. As she became famous, her house was added to the scholarly roadmap as a destination for scholars and nobility, and many vied for a coveted invitation from the "learned maid." Christina of Sweden insisted on travelling to the Netherlands in 1651, just so she could visit the "Star of Utrecht." So did Queen Luise-Maria

Gonzaga, wife of the Polish King. Scholars like Justus Schottelius, Hofmann von Hofmannswaldau and Daniel Lohenstein also paid their respects. René Descartes was a frequent guest and learned correspondent, until Schurman's abhorrence of Cartesianism cooled the friendship. Anna Maria exhibited grace in welcoming such guests but generally lamented that such visits and correspondence took time away from more serious endeavors.

Religion provided the foundation for as well as the content of Schurman's works and again, the approach to religion by this daughter of Protestant refugees reflects the Dutch situation. Calvinism had provided the most visible impetus and rationale for the rebellion of the Northern Provinces against the Roman Catholic rulers, the Spanish Habsburgs. Having made its religious convictions the foundations for all its actions, Calvinism had put its stamp on Dutch thought as well as on Dutch life. However, as peace came the Dutch Reformed Church not only had to grope to define its own dogmas, but it also had to come to terms with having graduated from a church of martyrs to a state institution. Church actions in the seventeenth century manifested the desire to remain the national church, the church of all Dutch people (the "volkskerk"), while some of its leaders continued to demand that its parishioners live up to standards befitting the "chosen people" in all aspects of life and thought. The most influential proponent of this Calvinist *praxis pietatis* was Gisbertus Voetius, who saw the Bible as the foundation of all thought, knowledge and actions. First as a pastor and then as an Utrecht theologian, he argued vigorously against a church of "talkers, not doers" ("segghers, geen doenders;" Roldanus 36).[9] Voetius, president (*rector*) of the newly founded University of Utrecht, became Schurman's mentor and teacher of Greek and Hebrew. His influence made her not only turn more and more toward her studies, but also determined the nature of these studies, namely to search for greater knowledge of God's word, His Creation, and a lifestyle in accordance with that Word.

Religion, therefore, not only provided the foundation of her studies; it also provided the justification. Who could be against a pious maiden intent on using her learning in order to better understand the Bible, the Word of God, so as to glean from it a pious lifestyle? Voetius's mentorship of Schurman's budding scholarship reinforced this approach.[10] It also meant that she was privileged to hear his lectures at Utrecht University (albeit from behind a curtain) — something denied to other members of her sex — and he introduced her to many of his learned colleagues. Voetius's convictions were a natural progression of those held in the Schurman household.[11]

As Anna Maria continued her studies, she mastered twelve languages in addition to Dutch: French, German, English, Italian, Latin, Greek, Hebrew, Syrian, Arabian, Maurish, Chaldaean, and Ethiopean. (For Ethiopean she devised a grammar.) The choice of the classical languages was based on their supposed usefulness for Bible study. She spoke and wrote most of the modern languages fluently and was very well-read in them. Knowing languages was especially important to women, to whom universities were closed, since they provided independent access to sources of learning.

Schurman's scholarship was expressed primarily in two genres, the treatise and the letter. Her first two publications were (dry but well-written) treatises in Latin: eminently learned and logical debates on the merits of the chosen subject. The first treatise was titled *Amica dissertatio inter Annam Mariam Schurmanniam et Andr. Rivetum de capacitate ingenii muliebris ad scientias...* (1638). With this work she secured a place in the international debate regarding the intellectual capabilities of women. From its publication (prefaced by Spanheim, professor of theology in Leiden) onward, the *Dissertatio* was mentioned alongside Lucretia Marinella's *La Nobilita e l'Eccelenza delle Donne e i Diffetti e Mancamenti degli Uomini* (Venice, 1604) and Marie de Jars de Gournay's *De l'égalité des hommes et des femmes* (Paris, 1626). Anna Maria was familiar with both works. She disagreed with Marinella's contention that women are superior to men (*Opuscula* 92), Marie de Jars de Gournay's work evoked several admiring letters to its author, which in turn elicited an enthusiastic reply.[12] Actually, Schurman's argumentation is based on an entirely different foundation than that of either of these authors. Schurman argues that as a Christian, a woman should have the opportunity to seek a higher knowledge of God and His Creation.

Denying a woman this opportunity is to deny a Christian the chance to seek a higher knowledge of the Creator. It is clear that this argumentation is consistent with Schurman's (Voetius') overall *praxis pietatis*.

Schurman herself was aware that her dictum was quite revolutionary for her time. As she wrote to Johan van Beverwijck:

> I consider myself fortunate because I see how you favor my studies and how you approve of the way I lead my life. Nowadays there are quite a few people, who would not so easily agree with your opinion; indeed who would conclude that this more civilized adornment to our sex does not fit at all and that the access to this sanctum of Minerva is not open to us" (*Opuscula*, 185).

Rivet, as the recipient of her letters, echoed the opinions of his time. He did not share in Schurman's optimistism that all knowledge leads to an increased knowledge of God and the Creation, although he agreed with this goal in learning. He reiterated the premise that also the uneducated could sing the praises of God, lauded the value of homemaking, and derided the uselessness of learning things that could not be put into practice. Such arguments echoed the basic issue that Anna Maria had to come to terms with, that is, the question of leisure time for women and the appropriate way to spend it. [13]

It would appear that Anna Maria's logical debate with its lofty foundation for learning would be enough of a justification. As she put it, she had pitted her logic against custom. However, her arguments are not devoid of a few caveats and when we examine them, we find that social custom was very much evident in Schurman's defense of learning. Even if the justification is typically Schurman, the situation she describes had already been attained by herself and the other Dutch women of her class. She concedes that only those women whose social circumstances allow them leisure time should engage in learned studies, that is, those who have servants to do the housework, or those who are single and have fewer family obligations. Furthermore, in the 1636 text written for the inauguration of Utrecht University, Anna Maria shows that she is capable of a few preconceived notions herself. For example, her exhortation to other women not to waste their time in front of the mirror but to study is particularly ironic, because — except for herself — the doors of the academy she lauds were not open to women.

This treatise, Anna Maria's first modest claim to learning, was greeted with great approval. The congratulatory letter-mill churned mightily both in and outside the Dutch Republic: Cats, Huygens, Voetius, Spanheim, Gassendi, and others. Guillaume Colletet, a member of the French Academy translated the *Dissertatio* into French (Paris, 1646). The English translation entitled *The Learned Maid, A Logicall Excercise upon the Question. Whether a Maid may be a Scholar* (see below), was first published in 1659, and there were also Italian, German and Swedish translations.[14]   The treatise was quoted and used as a justification for women's learning in and outside of the Dutch Republic. More than thirty years later, Bathsua Makin, one of Schurman's learned correspondents, wrote an "Essay to Revive the Ancient Education of Gentlewomen," taking Schurman's *Dissertatio* as her example.[15]

The literary value of the treatise is questionable. It is a logical argument put into a consistent rhetorical framework and it intends to argue the topic as any other scientific topic worthy of discussion. Schurman's merit is that she treats the learned education of women as any other scientific topic would be argued, and that she does so with arguments that are founded on deep personal convictions about life and thought.

Schurman's second published treatise was *De Vitae Termino* (["On the Temporal Limits of our Life"]; Paris, 1639). It was submitted to Johan van Beverwijck, who had asked her to write an opinion on whether God has made a determination about the end of each human life. The treatise answered the question in the affirmative. Van Beverwijck had it published with a laudatory introduction by Cats. In her early thirties at the time of publication of these two works, Schurman had already acquired the reputation of a star in the scholarly firmament — albeit, in her own description, only a star of the sixth order (see *Eucleria* below).

Schurman's other medium was the letter. She had entered the world of scholarship by writing letters to famous men and women seeking advice and offering suggestions, almost exclusively on theological-philosophical matters. In his analysis of the letter form, Deissmann distinguishes between the letter and the epistle: a letter is a personal address intended for the addressee only; publishing is only an afterthought. The epistle is from the beginning intended for publication and therefore written with more than one potential reader in mind. The content of the epistle differs from the letter in that it tends to be more scholarly (194ff). Such distinctions do not take into account the kind of letter written by those for whom the hand-written word was usually the only medium, namely women. Schurman's writing blends Deissmann's two definitions. Her letters were not written with the printing press in mind, even if later, they proved eminently suitable for publication. They create the impression that they are written to one person; at the same time their content and style are appropriate for distribution and contain profound, learned discussions about mostly theological subjects. They lend themselves to copying and distribution, ready for a wider audience even if the printing press eludes them.

Schurman was urged to publish a collection of her letters by various well-meaning friends; *Opuscula Hebraea, Graecam, Gallica: Prosaica et metrica* appeared in Leiden in 1648, when Schurman was already famous.[16] She later stated in *Eucleria* that vanity drove her to consent to this publication, which now serves mostly as a testimonial to her accomplishment in various languages, her breadth of knowledge and her familiarity with the available literature (but it also contains thank-you notes for presents received and polite little billets accompanying the many art pieces bequeathed to others). Her style is exemplary and the letter form is brought to perfection. *Opuscula* also reveals the vast network of her learned and social connections, and gives the addressees a chance to bask in her glory. The Greek letters to Bathsua Makin and the Latin and Hebrew letters to Dorothea Moor serve to underscore a circle of learned women.

Then, at age 61, the well-recognized scholar, Schurman shocked her circle of friends and learned acquaintances by joining a group of followers of the French preacher Jean de Labadie. She had heard enthusiastic accounts about him from her brother Johan Godschalck who had heard him preach in Geneva. When de Labadie became a pastor in Zeeland, Schurman went there to hear him preach. De Labadie's detractors soon claimed that the views of this French interloper were separatist, mystical and chiliastic in nature and that he preached internal illumination. After having been expelled from the Wallonian Synod of the Reformed Church, de Labadie went to Amsterdam, and Schurman followed him there. Much as those around her decried this step, it was an appropriate conclusion to her desire to put life and faith on one footing, to exercise a *praxis pietatis*, and to move away from a church that, according to her, included many who were Christians "in name only." Following de Labadie was to return to the Church of martyrs of the previous century, whose stories had so riveted her as a child, and to move away from a church as a state institution that insisted on being all the people's church.[17] In one aspect, however, it represented a major turning point. Schurman came to reject the notion that learned study of the Scriptures will ultimately lead to a knowledge of God. Agreeing with de Labadie that knowledge alone will not suffice, she maintained that reading the Scriptures "in the light of the Holy Spirit" will render a far greater experience of God. Contrary to what her detractors said, Schurman did not reject all scholarship and aesthetics, but she considered them justified only when contributing to a Christian life. In this it remains consistent with what Schurman had put forth in her earlier treatise.

In spite of his expulsion, de Labadie was not a preacher for the fringes of society. His call to form a "household" was answered by members of the United Provinces' most influential families. For example, one of the mayors of Amsterdam provided him with accommodations in Amsterdam and the mayor's sister joined the "household." Although men and women of all walks of society joined, the wealthy upper class was most scandalized by the number of its *women* who went to Amsterdam to take part in the conventicle-like gatherings. Schurman's erstwhile friends and acquaintances exhorted her to see the errors of her ways.[18] The church felt slighted by the open criticism of its practices (Duker), the scholars by her rejection of their learned endeavors, and her friends by the rejection of their values. Constantijn Huygens wrote a poem, portraying her as sitting among "little-known ladies," and wondering why she would prefer to spend her time with persons below her intellectual stature. However, Schurman could still count on her influential connections to assure a new home for the little community when the hospitality in Amsterdam wore out.[19]

Although the regulations of the group reinforced some of the same stratifications which existed in the Christianity of its day (e.g., women were not allowed to speak out in gatherings),[20] it is clear from all accounts that Anna Maria van Schurman fulfilled a special role. She received visitors, she translated the works of de Labadie and his assistants. She kept up her correspondence, this time to give witness to her newly chosen lifestyle. One of her accounts, *Eucleria seu meliores partis electio*, starts as follows:

> It has become well known from the writings of some learned men, who erstwhile were well disposed toward me, that my new way of life does not please them. Neither is it a secret that some churchmen have serious preconceptions and have rendered a severe judgement against God's cause, for which I have declared myself openly. Therefore, I am pleased to have this opportunity, to add my testimony to those of the excellent witnesses of the truth, the faithful shepherds of our church, D. de la Badie, D. Yvon and D. Dulignon who rendered a declaration of their orthodoxy and stood up against the attacks of black slander... Even if I will hardly change the feelings of great men, I will at least affirm the hearts of the little children in Christ against all future prejudices. If any false impression...would linger in the mind of pious men, I will either cover this with the picture of sincere truth or at least juxtapose the true and the false.[21]

Eucleria offers an exquisite blend of the two genres practised, by Schurman, the treatise and the letter. It is different from the rest of her work in that it was, from the outset, meant for publication; a public defense as a printed document. However, the form it takes is still that of the extended letter, of the epistle; a personal account of a personal event intended for a larger audience. As rigid as the rules of the "household" could be, for Schurman they meant an emancipation, not to say a liberation. *Eucleria* was written at her own instigation; she no longer needed the goodwill of learned men. The first volume was written and published in 1673; the second volume, finished a few days before her death and dealing with the fate of the little community in the last years of Schurman's life, appeared posthumously in 1685. The fact that only the first volume appeared also in Dutch may suggest that Schurman had translated it from the Latin herself.

Schurman was a famous woman. On the one hand, *Eucleria* belittles that fame, declares it hollow and vain. On the other hand, it uses the same fame to give credence to its author. Learnedness is treated likewise. Never mind the rejection of learned scholarship as a saving grace, *Eucleria* is a learned account in Latin, prompted by the scholars who had written against its author. It employs all the tricks of the trade, is eminently logical, and quotes liberally from the Scriptures and classical sources. At the same time, it offers an intentionally personal account of a personal event, that uses a life story to show a woman's progression toward her choice of "the best part."

Schurman had come a long way since "The Learned Maid" and "The End of Life" and many difficult years had passed since the publication of *Opuscula*. After her mother's death, she had spent more than twenty years taking care of two aging sisters of her mother and often had found little time for her studies or art. But the many personal letters had further sharpened her quill. Then came *Eucleria*, which presents impassioned writing about a personally-felt subject in a flawless rhetorical setting. It is one long learned letter, a justification of a personal step, which demands to be taken seriously. It has often been said that women write autobiographically; learned account, impassioned plea and autobiographical detail have seldom been so convincingly blended as in *Eucleria*, which stands as one of the first pietistically inclined autobiographies.[22] But neither the learned accounts of the day, nor the subsequent biographies that gave witness to a newly found faith blend so effectively the learned treatise with the personal account. As such, *Eucleria* stands alone. Much as Schurman's life and oeuvre can be explained in terms of life in the Dutch Republic, her final masterpiece had not merely blended but had outgrown the traditions.

The phenomenon of a learned woman-turned-sectarian aroused the curiosity of her contemporaries as well as those of subsequent generations. Her Labadist leanings served as "evidence" of the unreliability of women — even those women (or especially those) endowed with brains.[23] Regardless, Schurman's defense of learning and her own reputed "learnedness" assured her a place in the catalogues of learned women designed to justify women's learning.[24] But whereas her modest defense of learning was soon outdated, her influence in forming the religious landscape of Northern Europe was far more profound. As Wallmann has pointed out, her correspondence with Johan Jakob Schütz and other Pietists had a profound effect on the shaping of many of the tenets of that Lutheran movement.[25]

In our time, Schurman is discussed in books such as the present anthology, designed to show the literary and/or religious contributions of women.[26] The primary sources, her manuscripts, letters and art work, are scattered in archives and collections.[27] Her works are still discussed mostly in terms of content and autobiographical justification and seldom for their intrinsic literary merit — perhaps because the genres she used (the treatise and the letter) have not received the literary attention they deserve. The fact that she wrote primarily in languages other than Dutch has made it even more difficult for her to enter Dutch literary histories. But she is undeniably a vital part of the literary and religious landscape of the United Provinces, and her works deserve to be studied further for their literary merit and for the picture they reveal about life and thought in the Dutch provinces of the time.

NOTES to the Introduction

1. See Anna M.H. Douma, *Anna Maria van Schurman en de studie der vrouw* (Amsterdam, 1924), introduction.

2. See, e.g., Cornelia W. Roldanus, *Zeventiende-eeuwsche geestesbloei* (Amsterdam: Van Kampen & Zoon, 1938), esp. pp. 331-41; David Maland, *Europe in the Seventeenth Century* (London: Macmillan, 1966); and Sherrin Marshall, *The Dutch Gentry 1500-1650* (New York: Greenwood Press, 1987).

3. The largest collection of Schurman's artistic endeavors is preserved in the Coopmanshus, Franeker (Netherlands). For a discussion of her art work, see Saskia de Bodt, *"...Op de Raempte off mette Brodse,"* *Nederlands borduurwerk uit de zeventiende eeuw* (Haarlem: H.J.W. Becht, 1987), and Katlijne van der Stighelen, *Anna Maria van Schurman (1607-1678) of 'Hoe hooge dat een maeght kan in de konsten stijgen'* (Louvain, 1987).

4. A Latin hymn written for the inauguration of Utrecht University (1636) is in *Opuscula*, 262-263. The Dutch hymn is in *Algemeene feestwijzer voor het tweede eeuwfeest der Utrechtse Hogeschool 1636-1836* (Utrecht: Bosch, 1836). For other occasional poetry by and for Schurman, see *Opuscula* (especially 321ff.).

5. See translation of *Eucleria*.

6. Elisabeth Keesing, *Het volk met lange rokken. Vrouwen rondom Constantijn Huyghens* (Amsterdam: Querido, 1987).

7. Foreign visitors often remarked upon the independent and self-assured demeanor of Dutch women. See Marshall xix-xx.

8. Johan van Beverwijck (1594-1647), physician in Dordrecht and Deputy to the States General, published *Van de VVtnementheyt des Vrouwelicken Geslachts* (Dordrecht, 1639 and 1643). He dedicated the second volume to Schurman despite her protests. He intended to show that throughout history women had excelled in the arts and sciences.

9. See also Wilhelm Goeters, *Die Vorbereitung des Pietismus in der reformierten Kirche der Niederlande bis zur labadistischen Krisis (1670)* (Leipzig, 1911; Amsterdam, 1974), and T. Brienen et al., *De nadere Reformatie en het Gereformeerde Pietisme* (The Hague: Boekencentrum 1989). Voetius' inaugural lecture was entitled "Oratio inauguralis de pietate cum scientia conjungenda" ("On joining piety with knowledge;" Utrecht, 1634).

10. One gains insight into her extensive library from two letters to Luffridus ab Osterwick (*Opuscula,* 224-228).

11. John Ames (Amesius), whose lectures Schurman's father had attended in Franeker, favored a *vivere deo* which resembled Voetius' *praxis pietatis*.

12. Letter to Rivet (October 1640) preserved in the Koninklijke Bibliotheek at The Hague (see *Opuscula*, 318-320).

13. See Cornelia N. Moore, "Books, Spindles and the Devil's Bench or What is the Point in Needlepoint?" *Chloe* 3 (1984), 319-328.

14. It was republished twice, with a slightly different title, in Leiden (1641, 1673). In the *Opuscula*, it appears with five other letters on the same subject between her and Rivet (1632-1638).

15. See Bathsua Makin, *Essay to Revive the Antient Education of Gentlewomen in Religion Manners, Arts and Tongues...* (London, 1673); rpt. with an introd. by Paula L. Barbour, The Augustan Reprint Society, Publication Nr 202 (Los Angeles: Williams Andrew Clark Memorial Library, 1980); Jean Brink, "Bathsua Makin," *The Huntingdon Library Quarterly* (1991) 315-28; and Frances Teague, "The identity of Bathsua Makin," *Biography: An Interdisciplinary Quarterly* 16 (1993) 1-17.

16. *Opuscula* contains 39 Latin letters to such scholars as Vorstius, Gassendi, Huygens, Heinsius, and Cats. Three complimentary letters in Hebrew are addressed to Rivet, Voetius and Dorothea Moor, a learned English lady living in Dublin. Of the five Greek letters, one is to Meletius, Archbishop of Ephesus, two to Johan van Beverwijck, two to Bathsua Makin, and one to Claude Saumaise (Salmasius), professor in Leiden.

Eighteen French letters address male and female friends, including Anne de Merveil, the unidentified Madame Coutel, Elisabeth of Bohemia, Marie de Gournay, Marie du Moulin, Princesse Anne de Rohan, and Madame de Saumaise, wife of Claudius Salmasius.

17. A Frenchman, de Labadie did not share the urgent desire of the Dutch clergy to maintain a "church of all the people" (*volkskerk*).

18. See Constantijn Huygens, *Heusche Vermaaning, aan de doorlugtige en wel-edele juffr. Anna Maria van Schurman, om haar selven te kennen, en af te wijcken van Jean de Labadie* (Amsterdam, 1670) and *Sedige en sielveroerende aenspraecke aen Juffr. Anna Maria van Schurman, om haer af te trecken van Jan de Labadie* (Amsterdam, 1670); Johann Gabriel Drechssler, *Eukleria Eukeatos seu Meliores Partis Electio rescissa* (Leipzig, 1673); and A.C. Duker, "Briefwisseling tusschen den Utrechtse Kerkeraad en Anna Maria van Schurman," *Archief voor Nederlandsche Kerkgeschiedenis* 2 (1887) 171-8.

19. The group first found a haven with Schurman's friend Elisabeth of Bohemia (Abbess of Herford), then in Altona, and finally in the Waltha-castle in Wieuwerd in the Province Frisia.

20. See Miriam de Baar, "'En onder 't hennerot het haantje zoekt te blijven:' De betrokkenheid van vrouwen bij het huisgezin van Jean de Labadie (1669-1732)," (*Jaarboek voor Vrouwengeschiedenis* 8 (1987) eds. Ulla Jansz. et al, 11-43. 31ff.

20. Her other works include adaptations of de Labadie's works in either German or Dutch, as well as *Korte Onderrichtinge*, an explanation of her own situation (Amsterdam, 1675).

22. E.g., Johanna Eleonore Petersen is said to have been influenced by *Eucleria* to write her own autobiography. See Cornelia N. Moore, "Johanna Eleonore Petersen," *Bitter Healing*, eds. Jeanine Blackwell and Susanne Zantop (Lincoln, Univ. of Nebraska Press, 1990), 51-78.

23. See Johann Heinrich Feustking, *Gynaecium Haeretico Fanaticum* (Frankfurt & Leipzig, 1704) 593-601.

24. See: Georg Philipp Hardörffer, *Frauenzimmer-Gesprächsspiele* (Nürnberg: 1644) Biiij; Georg Christian Lehms, *Deutschlands Galante Poetinnen* (Frankfurt/M., 1715) Intro. F5; Jean Woods and Maria Fürstenwald. *Women of the German Speaking Lands* (Stuttgart: Metzler, 1984) 111-2.

25. See also Johannes Wallmann, *Philipp Jakob Spener und die Anfänge des Pietismus* (Tübingen: Mohr, 1970; 1986) and *Der Pietismus: Die Kirche in ihrer Geschichte*, vol. 4 (Göttingen: Vandenhoeck & Ruprecht, 1990).

26. A.J. Schotel wrote the first full-length monograph on Schurman (1853); this was followed by Una Birch's biography (1909) and Anna M.H. Douma's dissertation on Schurman and women's education (published 1924). In her introduction and the various "Bijlagen," Douma also provides an excellent overview of the secondary literature until 1915, and lists Schurman's published and unpublished correspondence. Schotel, Birch, and Douma still provide the foundation of Schurman-scholarship. More recently, a long-existing lacuna has been filled by Katlijne van der Stighelen's work about Schurman's art. See also Bibliography.

27. Letters by and to Schurman are kept in the British Museum, the Koninklijke Bibliotheek in The Hague, the City Hall in Franeker, the Universiteitsbibliotheek in Utrecht, and the Universiteitsbibliotheek in Amsterdam. See also Douma (87), and van der Stighelen.

Translations by Clement Barksdale and Cornelia N. Moore

From *THE LEARNED MAID*[1]

[Foreword by] Fr[ederic] Spanhemius

The Low-Countries shew you a Virgin, excellent, not only in the learned Languages, but almost in all kinds of Literature; whose admirable wit and mind capable of all things, you may justly call the utmost Essay of Nature in this Sex. So largely hath the Divine bounty powred forth it self upon one person. If she hath a vast understanding piercing into all things, she hath also a skilful hand marvellously obedient to that guide, executing & expressing in all materialls whatsoever that commands. But these Gifts are far inferiour to those which she accounteth chief; Piety without Ostentation, Modesty beyond Example, and most Exemplary Holiness of Life and Conversation. And though she most deserveth Praise, yet (which is above all Praise) She desireth nothing less. *In Epist. ad Lect.*

TO THE HONOURABLE LADY, THE *LADY A. H.*

Madam, This *strange maid*, being now the second time, drest up in her *English Habit*, cometh to kiss your hand. She hopes you will admit her to your *Closet*, and speak a good word for her to your worthy *Friends*, and endear her to *Them* also. Her *Company* will be the more *delightfull*, because her *discourse* is very *rational*, and much tending to the *perfection* of that *Sexe*, where of you, *excellent Lady*, by your *Noble Virtues* are so great an *Ornament* and *Example*.

The Honourer of your Piety, more then of your Fortune;

C[lement] B[arksdale].

THE LEARNED *MAID*, A Logicall Exercise upon this Question. *Whether a* Maid *may be a Scholar?*

We hold the *Affirmative*, and will endeavour to make it good.

These *Pracognita* we permit: First on the part of the *Subject*, and then of the *Predicate*.

By a *Maid* or *Woman*, I understand her that is a *Christian*, and that not in Profession onely, but really and indeed.

By a *Scholar*, I mean one that is given to the study of *Letters*, that is, the knowledge of *Tongues* and *Histories*, all kinds of Learning, both superiour entitled *Faculties*; and inferiour, call'd *Philosophy*. We except onely *Scriptural Theology*, properly so named, as that which without Controversie belongs to all Christians.

When we enquire, *whether she may be*, we mean whether it be *convenient*, that is, expedient, fit, decent.

The *words* being thus distinguished, the *Things* are to be distinguished also.

For some *Maids* are *ingenious*, others *not so*: some are *rich*, some *poor*: some *engaged* in Domestick cares, others *at liberty*.

The studies of a *Scholar* are either *universal*, when we give our selves to all sorts of Learning: or *particular*, when we learn some one Language or Science, or one distinct Faculty.

Wherefore we make use of these Limitations:

First of the *Subject*; and first, that our *Maid* be endued at least with an indifferent good *wit*, and not unapt for learning. (*Of the erudition of* Maids *you may read* (in Liv.3. Plin.Epist.17.I.1. Athen. I.Plutarch.de educ. lib. Gord. I.16. de Negat. Fornar. ad Cas.)

Secondly, that she be provided of necessaries and not oppressed with want: which exception I therefore put in, because few are so happy to have Parents to bread them up in studies, and Teachers are chargeable.

Thirdly, that the condition of the Times, and her quality be such, that she may have spare houres from her general and speciall Calling, that is, from the Exercises of Piety and houshold Affairs. To which end will conduce, partly her immunity from cares and employments in her yonger years, partly in her elder age either celibate, or the Ministry of handmaids, which are wont to free the richer sort of Matrons also from Domestick troubles.

Fourthly, let her end be, not vain glory and ostentation, or unprofitable curiositie: but beside the salvation of her own soul; that both her self may be the more vertuous and the more happy, and that she may (if that chargely upon her) instruct and direct her Family, and also be usefull, as much as may be to her whole Sex.

Next, *Limitations* of the *Predicate, Scholarship*, or the study of *Letters* I so limit, that I clearly affirm all honest Discipline, or the whole Circle and Crown of liberal Arts and Sciences (as the proper and universal Good and Ornament of Mankind) to be convenient for the *Head* of our *Christian Maid*: yet so, that according to the Dignity and Nature of every Art or Science, and according to the capacity and condition of the Maid herself, all in their order, place and time succeed each other in the learning of them, or be commodiously conjoined. But especially let regard be had unto those Arts which have neerest alliance to *Theology* and the *Moral Virtues*, and are Principally subservient to them. In which number we reckon *Grammar; Logick, Rhetorick;* especially *Logick*, fitly called *The Key of all Sciences*: and then, *Physicks, Metaphysicks, History*, &c, and also the knowledge of Languages, chiefly of the *Hebrew* and *Greek*. All which may advance to the more facile and full understanding of *Holy Scripture*: to say nothing now of other Books. The rest, *i.e. Mathematicks* (to which is also referred *Musick*) *Poesie, Picture*, and the like, not illiberall Arts, may obtain the place of pretty Ornaments and ingenious Recreations.

Lastly, those studies which pertain to the practice of the Law, Military Discipline, Oratory in the Church, Court, University, as less proper and less necessary, we do not very much urge. And yet we in no wise yield that our *Maid* should be excluded from the Scholastick knowledge or Theory of those; especially, not from understanding the most noble Doctrine of the *Politicks* or Civil Government.

And when we say a Maid may be a Scholar, it is plain we do not affirm Learning to be a property, or a thing requisite, and precisely needfull to eternall salvation: no, nor as such a good thing which maketh to the very *Essence* of Happiness in this life: but as a mean and very usefull, conferring much to the integrity and perfection thereof: and as that, which by the contemplation of excellent things wich promote us to a higher degree in the Love of God, and everlasting

Therefore let our Thesis or Proposition be: A Maid *may be a Scholar.* For the confirmation whereof we bring these *Arguments*: 1. the part of the *Subject*:. 2. On the part of the *Predicate.*

1. Arguments, from the Property of the Subject.

Whosoever is naturally endu'd with the principles, or powers of the principles of all Arts and Sciences, may be a student in all Arts and Sciences: But Maids are naturally endued with the *Principles, &c.* Therefore, *&c The Proposition is thus proved.* They that may have the knowledge of *Conclusions* deduced from *Principles* may be Students, *&c.* But they that are naturally endued with the *Principles* may have the knowledge of *Conclusions* deduced from those *Principles.* Therefore, *&c. The Assertion* may be proved both from the property of the *form* of this Subject, or the rational foul: and from the very acts and effects themselves. For it is manifest that Maids doe *actually* learn any Arts and Sciences. Now, no *Acts* can be without their *Principles.*

II. Arguments. Again from the property of the Subject.

Whosoever hath naturally a *desire* of Arts and Sciences, may study the Arts and Sciences.

But a Maid hath naturally a *desire* of Arts and Sciences. Therefore, *&c.* The Reason of the *Major* is manifest: because Nature doth nothing in vain. *The Minor is thus confirmed.* That which is in the whole *Species* or kind, is in every *Individual* or particular person; in Maids also. But all Mankind have in them by Nature a desire of knowledge (*Artistot.Metaph.I.2.*) Therefore, &c.

III. Argument, from the externall Property, or Adjunct.

Whosoever is by God created with *a sublime countenance*, and erected toward Heaven, may (and ought) give himself to the contemplation and knowledge of sublime and heavenly things. But God hath created woman also with a sublime and erected countenance: *Os homini sublime*, &c. Therefore, &c.

IV. Argument.

Whosoever is in most *need* of solid and continuall employment, may conveniently give himself to learning: But woman is in most *need* of solid and continual employment: Therefore, &c. The *Major* is good, because nothing doth more exercise and intend all the nerves and powers of the mind: (and as the great *Erasmus* saith nothing takes so full possession of the fair Temple of a Virgins breast, as learning and study, whither, on all occasions she may rely for refuge. (*In his Epistle to* Budæus, *where he discourseth of the Institution of Sir* Tho. Moores *daughters.*)

The Minor is proved by these two reasons.

1. Whosoever through imbecillity and inconstancy of disposition or temper, and the innumerable snares of the world, is in most danger of *vanities*, is in most need of solid and perpetual employment. But woman, through the imbecillity and inconstancy, &c. Therefore, &c. The *Major* in this Syllogism is true; because contraries are best cured by contraries: and nothing doth more effectually oppose vanity, then serious and constant employment. The *Minor* we take to be without controversie: for hardly any, though Heroical Vertue can safely pass by the Sirens of the world and of youth unless it be busied about serious and solid things.

2. The second reason to prove the Assumption or Minor of the *IV. Argument* is this: They that abound with leisure have most

need of solid and continual employment: But women of higher rank, most part abound with leisure. Therefore: The Major of this syllogism is good, because leisure (or idlenesse) is of it self tedious, yea, burdensome, so that Divine *Nazianzen* justly said, *Tis the greatest pain to be out of action.* And because idleness is the Mother of wickedness: *Homines nihil agende male agere discunt.* Men by doing nothing learn to do ill.

V. Argument

They that have the happiness of a more quiet and free course of life, may with most convenience follow their studies: But Maids for the most part, have the happiness of a more quiet and free course of life: Therefore. The reason of the *Major* is evident: for nothing is so great a friend to studies as Tranquillity and Liberty. *The Minor is proved thus:* They which for the most part have their time to bestow upon themselves, and are exempt from publick cares and employments, have the happiness of a more quiet and free course of life: But Maids (especially during their celibate, or single life) most part have their time to bestow on themselves, &c. Therefore.

VI. Argument.

To whom is agreeable the study of the *principal Sciences*, to the same is also agreeable: the study of Sciences instrumental and subservient: But, to a Christian woman agrees the study of the Principal Sciences. Therefore: The *Major* is firm for this reason: To whom the *end* agrees, to the same is convenient also the lawfull *means*, whereby we are most easily brought unto that end: But the instrumental or subservient Sciences are the lawfull means, &c. Therefore. The *Minor* is true, because to a Christian woman agrees the study, or assiduous and serious Meditation of Gods Word, the knowledge of God, and contemplation of his most beautifull works, as being of most concernment to all Christians whatsoever.

VII. Argument.

The study of Letters is convenient for them, for whom it is more decent to find themselves both business and Recreation *at home* and in private, then abroad among others. But it is more decent for a Christian Maid to find her self both worke and recreation *at home* then abroad: therefore &c. The *Major* is most true: because studies have this prerogative, to give us a delightfull exercise, and to recreate us when we have no other company, whence in the Greek proverbe, *A wise man is self-sufficient.* The *Minor* is no less: because the Apostle requireth Women to be keepers at home, *Tit.2.5.* And moreover, Experience testifies; whose tongues, Ears, eyes often travail abroad, hunting after pleasures; their faith, diligence, and modesty too, is generally called into question.

VIII. Argument, from the Genus of the predicate, or, of Learning.

Arts and Sciences are convenient for those, to whom *all Virtue* in general is convenient for a Maid. Therefore: The *Major* is evident from the division of Virtue into *Intellectual* and *Moral*: under the former whereof, the Philosopher comprehendeth Arts and Sciences. The *Minor* hath no need of proof: for Virtue, as *Seneca* saith, chooseth her servants, neither by their State nor Sexe.

IX. Argument, from the end of Sciences.

Whatsoever *perfects* and *adorns* the intellect of Man, that is fit and decent for a Christian woman: But Arts and Sciences doe perfect and adorn the intellect. Therefore: The reason of the *Major* is, because all creatures tend unto their last and highest perfections as that which is most convenient for them. The *Minor* is plain, because Arts and Sciences are Habits, and by these Habits are the natural *powers* and faculties of the soul proved and perfected.

X. Argument.

The things that by their nature conduce to the greater *Love of God* and the exciting of his greater reverence in us, are convenient and fit for a Christian Woman: But Arts and Sciences by their nature conduce, *&c*. Therefore: The Verity of the *Major* is clearer then the Light. For the most perfect love and reverence of God becometh all mankind; so that none can here offend in the excess. The *Minor* is thus confirmed: That which exhibiteth and proposeth God and his works to be seen and known by us in a more eminent degree, naturally conduceth to the stirring up in us the greater love of God and reverence: But Arts and Sciences exhibite and propose God and his Works, *&c*. Therefore. The *Major* in this last syllogism is proved by this reason: Whatsoever is indeed most beautiful, most excellent and most perfect that, the more it is known, the more it is loved, and accounted more worthy of reverence or celebration: But God and his Works are indeed most beautifull, *&c*. Therefore. The *Minor* likewise may be proved from the end of effects of Sciences which do all confer somewhat to the more facile and more distinct knowledge of God and his Works.

XI. Argument.

That which armes us against *Hereties* and detecteth their fraud, is convenient for a Christian Woman: But Sciences arme us, *&c*, Therefore. The reason of the *Major* is evident: because no Christians in this common danger, ought to neglect their duetie. The *Minor* is proved, because sound Philosophy is as a hedge and fence (to use the words of *Clemens Alexandrinus*) *of the Lords Vineyard*, or of our Saviours Doctrine: Or, being compared with the Gospel, it is (in Saint *Basil's* similitude) like the *leaves* which are an *Ornament* and *Muniment* to the fruit. Indeed by right reason, that corrupt and false reason, upon which heresies mainly depend, may most easily be refuted.

XII. Argument

What teacheth *Prudence* without any detriment of Fame and Modesty, is convenient for a Christian Woman: But the studies of a good Learning teach Prudence, *&c.* Therefore: The *Major* is confessed: for no man is ignorant, that the Honour of the Female Sexe is most tender, and needeth nothing more then Prudence: and how hard a thing it is and full of hazard, to draw Prudence from use and Experience. The *Minor* is proved, because the Writings of Learned men doe offer us not onely excellent *Precepts*, but notable *Examples*, and do lead us as it were by the hand to Virtue.

XIII. Argument

That which makes to true *Magnanimitie*, is Convenient for a Christian Woman: But the study of Letters makes to true magnanimity. Therefore. I prove the *Major*; because, the more any one is by nature prone to the vice of pusillanimity, so much the more need there is of aid from the opposite Virtue. But a Woman is by Nature prone, *&c.* Therefore: The *Minor* is prov'd, because Learning erecteth the Mind and puts courage into the heart, and takes off the vizor from those things which are feared by the vulgar, or impotenly affected.

XIV. Argument.

That which affecteth and replenisheth the Mind with honest and ingenuous *delight*, is convenient for a Christian Woman: But, Learning doth so. Therefore. The reason of the *Major* is, because nothing is more agreeable to humane nature, then honest and ingenuous delight, which represents in Man a certain similitude of Divine gladness. Which *Artistotle* also highly extolleth. vii.*Eth.* xiii. *Pleasure* is by nature *a Divine thing* implanted in the hearts of Men.

The *Minor* is proved thus: Because there is no delight or pleasure (except that of Christians which is supernatural) either more worthy of an ingenuous soul, or greater then this, which ariseth from the study of Letters: as by examples and various reasons might easily be evinced.

XV. Arguments, from the Opposite.

Where *ignorance* and want of knowledge is not convenient, there the study of knowledge is convenient: But ignorance and want of knowledge is not convenient for a Christian Woman. Therefore. The *Minor* is confirmed thus: That which is of it self, not onely the cause of errour in the understanding, but of vice in the will or action not convenient for a Christian Woman: But ignorance and want of knowledge is of it self the cause of error, *&c.* Therefore, The *Major* of this syllogism is demonstrated; First, in respect of errour in the understanding; Because ignorance in the understanding (which is called the *Eye* of the soul, If the light that is in the be darkness [sic], how great is the darkness, Matt.VI) is nothing els but blindness, and darkness which is the cause of all errour. Secondly, in respect of vice in the Will or Action: because, Whatsoever make men proud, fierce, *&c.* that is the cause of Vice in the will or action: But ignorance and want of knowledge makes men proud, *&c.* Therefore. The *Major* is evident, the *Minor* is proved hence; because the less a man knowes himself, the more will he please himself and contemn others: And he who knowes not how much he is ignorant of, will be wise in his own conceit. And then (as to fierceness) nothing is more intractable than ignorance, as *Erasmus* upon much experience testifies: And that I may relate a Sentence of Divine *Plato* (VI. De Legibus): *Man well bred and instructed becomes the mildest and Gentlest of Creatures, but being ill brought up is the wildest of all the beasts of the Earth.* Addquod ingenuas &c. *Learning mollifies and sweetens a man and takes away roughness of manners and rusticity.* Lastly, the danger of ignorance, in respect of vice, may be shewn from the nature of vice and vertue. For whereas to every vertuous action is required such Exactness. that it must be conformable on every part to the rule of right reason; to the Nature of vice even the least *Inordination*, which followeth ignorance, may be sufficient. *Testimonies and Examples I doe here omit for brevity sake.*

XVI. *Refutation of the Adversaries.*

These Praecognita *are to be permitted.*

First, there are some of the *Adversaries,* who being as it were blinded by I know not what prejudices, do not limit our *Subject;* but think it followes from our *Thesis,* that there is no *choice* neither of Wits, nor of Conditions, to make the *predicate* agree unto it.

Others there are, who seem to acknowledge no other *end* of studies, then either Gain or vain Glory: which is the *prime error,* and shamefull enough: as if it were supervacaneous to Philosophize *for the avoiding of ignorance.*

And some there are lasty who deny not altogether that studies are convenient for a Maid, but only an *eminent degree* of Knowledge. Who are perhaps vexed with Emulation, or certainly with fear, least that should at any time come to pass. *Many scholars excell their Masters:* and that other saying of a very ancient Poet, *Vos etenim juvenes animos geritis Muliebres: Illa Virago Viri.* Those Men are spirited like Women, that Virgin like a Man.

XVII. *The Thesis of the Adversaries.*
A Christian Maid (or Woman) except she be perhaps divinely excited to it by some peculiar motion or instinct, may not conveniently give her self to the study of Letters.

I. *Argument. On the part of the Subject.*

Whosoever hath a *weak wit* may not give her self to the study of Letters: But Women are of weak wits. Therefore. They will prove the *Major*; because, to the study of Letters is required a wit firm and strong: unless we will labour in vain, or fall into the danger of a disease of the Intellect. *The* Minor, *they think, needeth no Proofe.*

We *answer* to the *Major*: that by our limitation such are exempted which by imbecillity of their wit are altogether unapt for studies; when we state it, that at least *indifferent good wits* are here required. Then, we say, not alwayes *heroical wits* are precisely necessary to studies: for the number even of learned Men, we see, is made up in good part, of those that are of the *middle* sort.

To the *Minor* we answer: It is not *absolutely* true, but *comparatively* onely in respect of the male Sex. For, though Women cannot be equalled for their wit with those more excellent Men (who are *Eagles in the Clouds*:) yet, the matter it self speaks thus much; Not a few are found of so good wit, that they may be admitted to studies, not without fruit. But

On the contrary we infer: They that are less able by dexterity of *wit*, may most conveniently addict themselves to studies: But women are less able by dexterity of wit. Therefore. We prove the *Major*, because studies do supply us with aids and helps for our weakness: Therefore.

II. Objection.

Whose mind is not *inclined* to studies, they are not fit to study; But the minds of Women are not inclined to studies. They prove the Major, because nothing is to be done *invita Minerva,* as we say, "*Against the hair.*" The Minor they will prove from use and custome; because very seldom do Women apply their mind to study.

We *answer* to the *Major.* It should be thus: *Whose mind,* after all means duely tried, *is not inclined to studies*: otherwise it is denied.

To the *Minor* we say, no man can rightly judge of our Inclination to studies, before he hath encouraged us by the best reasons and means to set upon them: and withall hath given us some *taste* of their sweetness, although in the mean time we do not want examples to evince the contrary to be true.

III. Objection

The studies of Learning are not convenient for those that are destitute of *means* necessary to their studies.   But Women are destitute of means. etc,   Therefore. The *Major* is without controversie.

They endeavour to prove the *Minor*, because there be   no Academies and Colledges, wherein they may exercise themselves. But we deny this consequence; for it sufficeth, that under the conduct of their *Parents*, or of some private Teacher, they may exercise themselves at home.

IV. Objection

Studies are not fitt for them whose labour misseth of its proper *End*. But the labour of Women misseth of its proper *End*. Therefore. The *Major* may be proved, because the *End* is that for which all things are done.   They prove the *Minor* by this, that Women are seldome or never preferred to publicke Offices, Politicall, Ecclesiasticall, or Academicall.

We *answer* to the *Major*: Women, in *speculative* Sciences are never frustrated of their *End*: and in the *Practicall* (now spoken of) though they attain not the *Primary*, or that publick *End*; yet doe they attain a *Secondary End*, as I may say, and more private.

V. Objection

To whom, for their Vocation, it is sufficient to know a *little*, to them is not convenient the *Encyclopady*, or a more sublime degree of knowledge. But it is sufficient to Women. etc Therefore. They prove the *Major*, because it is not convenient for any one to study things superfluous and impertinent to his Calling. The *Minor* they will prove; because forsooth the Vocation of a Maid, or Woman, is included in very narrow limits the termes of a private or Oeconomicall life.

Let the *Major* pass, we *answer* to the *Minor*. There is an ambiguity in the words; First, *Vocation*: for, if here they understand the Vocation of a private life, opposed to publick Offices, We say, by the fame reason the *Encyclopady* or a more sublime degree of Knowledge is denied all *men* too, that lead a private life: When yet, that most grave Sentence of *Plutarch* is pronounced of all men of what rank forever, without exception; *It becomes a perfect Man, to know what is to be known, and to doe what is to be done.* But if they understand a *special Vocation*, in order to a Family and Oeconomicall cares; We say, that the *universall* Calling which pertaineth chiefly to us all, either as Christians, or at least as men, is in no wise excluded by it. Yea, I may be bold to affirm, that a Virgin both may and ought especially to attend upon this *Universall* Calling, as being usually more free from the impediments of the former. She that is *unmarried careth for the things of the Lord*: I Cor.vii.34. Again, there is ambiguity in the words, *it is sufficient*, which is sufficiently taken away by what is above said in the *limitation* of the convenience and necessity of studies. Wherefore our *Thesis* stands firm: *A Christian Maid, or Woman, may conveniently give her self to Learning.*

Anna Marià Schurman to the Most noble Lady Moor[2]

Most Noble Lady,

Your Letters seemed unto me sweeter then Nectar; to which, because I am highly delighted in conferring with you, I had returned a more speedy Answer, had I not awaited for the Bearer my Brother's going that way toward *England*. He will declare unto you the manner of my Life, and open to your view the closet of my heart, (where you will finde your self to have a chief place.) Yet I cannot chuse but say something to the grave and serious Argument of your Epistle. You enquire, how I order and dispose of my affairs, that with least offence, I may especially in these calamitous times, pass through the troubles of this Life. Though I acknowledge your singular Modesty and Civility, that you esteem my Example not unworthy of your Imitation: yet I doubt not, if by Gods Grace, we might once enjoy happiness of living together in the same house, we may be able in so great a Conspiration of studies and affections, to excite each other unto Virtue. However, I will tell you in a word, not what I always attain to, but what mark I aim at, to come as near as I can. The compendious and fastest way is pointed out unto us by the Pole-Starre of Heavenly Truth. For it was excellently said, by that great Earle of *Mirandula: Philosophy seeks Truth; Theology finds it; Religion posesseth it.* But, that I may not goe from the purpose; we determine with the notable Philosopher *Epictetus* not amiss; *That Humane Affairs have two Handles:* yet not, as He, One convenient, the other inconvenient: but, Both most convenient, if they be well and orderly taken. Thus, Whatsoever pertaineth to a Virtuous and happy life, must either be referred to Divine Providence, or to our Dutie. As to the first, my business is, that in things out of our power, I may have one onely care, namely, to cast all my cares upon God: according to that Advice of the Apostle; *Cast ye all your care upon him, for he careth for you.* For indeed, here is the Originall of all our inquietude, that we use to roull in our minds too anxiously the events of things, which alone depend upon the pleasure of Almighty God.

Next, as to our Duty: it belongeth to us to moderate and govern those things onely which fall under our deliberation, both by our industry and prudence.

Nothing doth so much throw us out of the Castle of Tranquillitie, as evil Examples, and the falacious enticements of this World: That I may omit the tediousness and trouble, perpetually attending their Condition, who act as it were, upon the publicke Stage.) And for this Malady, I find no remedy more present and effectuall then the retirement of Studies. For, since the manners of Men are so corrupted, one can hardly raise so much heat in others for the prosecution of Virtue, as he shall abate of his own, for the most part, by frequent Conversation with the Men of this Age. But here, in our recesse, the vanities and deceits of the World, being farre removed, we judge of all things more rightly, and securely contemne the vanities that fill prophaner souls with admiration.

Here, sweetly passing away our time with the Muses, we erect our minds to higher matters, and without impediment runne the purse of Philosophy. Whereof you may reade more in the Printed Epistle enclosed. To which I have added my *Effigies* done in the Life with my own hand: that every way, so far as I can, I may make my selfe known unto you.

Farewell, the immortall Honour of our Sexe, and continue your Love to Her, who loves you most affectionately.

Utrecht, Cal. April MDCXLI.

From *EUCLERIA*[3]

I:...I will again pass up an account of my present life in favor of an account of my past, in so far as it will serve its purpose in this undertaking. I will not deny that from an early age on, I felt some sparks of sincere piety in my heart and those have remained easily identifiable throughout my life. Sometimes they were kindled and then they burst into little flames. For instance, I remember that, when I was only four years old, I was sitting at the side of a little brook with a maid who had been sent out to gather herbs. At her urging I recited the answer to the first question of the Heidelberg Catechism,[4] namely *that I am not unto myself but unto my faithful Savior Jesus Christ.* As I recited the answer, my heart was filled with such great and wonderful happiness and such deep feeling of love for Christ, that all the years that have since passed have not been able to erase the memory of that moment. And, to add one more instance, I remember that, when I was about 11 years old, I read the stories of the martyrs.[5] As I contemplated the examples of so many faithful servants of Christ and so many blood witnesses to His truth, my heart was filled with a burning desire to become a blood witness myself, and I wished with all my heart to exchange my pleasant life for such a wonderful death. Nothing has been more difficult for me to understand and more contrary to the Christian name, than the opinion of Erasmus as stated in his letter to Eckius,[6] in which he admitted openly that to be a bloodwitness surpassed the little hovel of his ambition and that he neither aspired to nor begrudged anyone else's martyrdom. Furthermore, to the best of my ability and knowledge, I have always striven honestly and without conceit for the true exercise of piety, although I will continue to stress how meager and crippled those endeavors have been. However much I have always favored piety — the princess of all virtues — hardly anyone has ever mentioned my piety as a reason for praising me. This could have been because my piety was not enough known to anyone, or because this virtue is not regarded highly enough. Therefore, I will now return to those exercises which have made me famous and happy in the eyes of all people. Through my truthful account I intend to lessen the value of such matters and point out whether they were harmful to my cause.

II: For such an account I have to delve into the first part of my life and I take this opportunity to express my filial gratitude to my parents. As much as they could, they strove not only to educate their children in the literature of man but also in piety. Because we lived in the country, my parents had us taught by an excellent home-teacher, with such progress, I have been told, that as a child of three, I could read and could recite portions of the Heidelberg Catechism by heart...In the year of our Lord 1618, when I was about eleven years old, it happened that my brothers (one was almost two years older than I and the other four years older) were examined by my father on the Latin and French exercises which he had previously assigned to them. Whenever they forgot something, I would give the correct answer, either by accident or with the help of Divine Providence, and that caused my father to think that maybe I, too, could be taught those languages successfully. When he saw that I followed his wishes eagerly (surely only because I wanted to please him), he guided my study from then on.

III: However, so that I would not be frightened off from the outset by tricky little points of grammar, he was careful to assign me the philosopher Seneca, whom I found very entertaining, to read and to explain, saying that an eagle catches no flies. He taught most of the basic grammar points afterwards with little games while we walked in the garden, so that I easily overcame the sorrow and the bitterness of all beginning studies. At the same time — so that this pleasant approach to a pagan author would not harm my Christian piety, which is averse to all wisdom of the flesh — he combined such reading with readings from the Scriptures.

IV: I consider it a divine blessing that from an early age, my parents, who always strove for what was honorable and fitting, scared me away from any authors who could have directed my thoughts away from chastity and maidenly purity. Thus, throughout my life, I have guarded myself against reading such books, especially works of poetry, Greek as well as Latin, as if they were poisonous drinks. Thus Homer and Virgil were the only authors whom I read extensively and with perseverance. They had been recommended by my father and they can be regarded without contradiction as the princes of poets. I chose to be very selective with modern writings. Some of it was dedicated to me by the authors, who were in many cases famous. That which dealt with secular material, I either did not read or just tasted a sampling. Nowadays, one meets only a few who deserve the kind of praise that has been given — and not without reason — to the French poet Bartassius,[7] namely that he never soiled his laurel wreath with a rotten leaf nor by even the slightest lewd verse.

V: A special advantage of my upbringing was that I spent little time — no longer than two months at age seven — at a French school. Therefore, I was not contaminated through playing with other children and by listening to their naughty talk, which could have made a deep impression on a tender mind. My parents were more intent on having me learn how to read and write and have lessons in voice and instruments with my brothers. They also wanted to make the serious studies more palatable by having me master various arts (for which I had a natural inclination). Such artistic additions to my studies were like a tasty sauce to a meal. My parents could hardly be chided for such intentions, as they kept me away from the idle company of "little ladies" and their preening ways. Had this not happened, I would certainly have picked up lifelong habits for which I had a natural disposition, although I had been born to better things. Certainly, it is hard to exercise a certain measure in things that please the world; the rarer and nobler the talent, the easier it is to use it unwisely.

VI: I will not deny that the gift of the intellect is a gift from God and that even the arts will have to recognize the Holy Spirit as their master, as it is written in Exod. 31 of Bezalel and Oholiab,[8] that they were talented and qualified to do many things. They used their talents meritoriously in the exterior and childlike religious services of the Jews. However, lately I have wondered, what to think of my own occupation with the arts. From an early age, my artistic talents were evident in many ways. For instance, when I was only a little six-year-old girl, I could make paper cut-outs of any piece of paper that fell into my hands with a pair of scissors, using no example. Almost none of my playmates, not even the ones who were older, could do likewise. About four years later, I learned in three hours how to embroider, and everyone was amazed, because a few weeks before I had learned how to draw flowers with a pencil. I don't dare to mention the various artistic media with which I passed the lonely time after my father's death without any teachers to guide me.

This would break all bounds of modesty and provide reasons for vanity rather than for true praise...

X: As I said before, I was so wrapped up in my studies and in the arts that I never missed playing with other children and other such trivial pursuits. I have to add that this also armed me against all worldly and useless society, which attempted to lure me in the following years. My mother took good care of me and my father taught me all the duties of piety and admonished me frequently. Thus he scared me away from the contamination of this century and from the company of worldly people. And, so that I would not entangle myself carelessly in the traps of this world, he especially admonished me seriously and passionately at the time of his death to avoid the unusually entangled and sordid web of marriage. I did not disregard this fatherly advice, because this is how the world sought to tie me to it.

XI: But oh, if I had only managed to stay away as faithfully from the vanities of human praise, as I have from the closer contact with worldly people. Many things have prevented me from doing so, and it would take too long to repeat them all. I will only sketch with a few strokes how I was dragged unto the stage of the world. This happened primarily when I was urged by lovers of learning, and especially by Mr. Voetius,[9] the most learned professor of Divinity, to spread the fame of the University of Utrecht through my poetry. Because if ever I served the vanity of learning, it was at a time in which I thought that one had to treat such sciences respectfully since they were the servants par-excellence of the Queen of Divinity. Indeed I believed that my own name recognition was to the benefit of the republic of science, which had to be treated seriously and which had to be spread as much as decency would allow. As a star of the sixth order among all other great luminaries, I added my little spark to this group of eminent scholars, this encyclopedia of sciences. But I confess that I was not too swayed by such thoughts. Because, although the well-known doctor and professor of divinity André Rivet,[10] with some other famous friends, had put much effort into making my name famous, I always tried to avoid fame as a heavy burden, because of an innate modesty and a sincere desire to remain hidden. I would have completely succeeded in this hiding and isolation, had not the excellent benevolence of men who were famous in the world rather than the adulation of the common people deterred me from that determination. I learned only too late how much all of this conflicts with Christian modesty and the renunciation of all creatures. I could not keep my ever-growing fame, which is still growing at this time, within bounds. And when I attempted to do as much, it raised the ire of the worldly divines, because I kept myself far from their company and their preaching, for which, as the proverb says, they spent altogether too much oil and labor. Not only did their comments lack even a dash of sound scholarship or of natural eloquence, but they also did not taste a bit like the oil which the Spirit of Christ pours out into the hearts of his disciples and which guards against the sadness of the pious listener. This, I tell you, was the reason why they thought that they had the right to despise me and my studies. As an act of revenge they thought they could sully my name through whisper campaigns and could lend a willing ear to the product of envy. They accomplished what they set out to do and thus relieved me somewhat of my fame, as from a heavy burden. This liberated me from the many untimely visits of my neighbors. But I wish that I could have dismissed the malevolence of the church people as easily as I was able to dismiss the goodwill of worldly people, no matter how famous, whom I did not hold to be servants of Christ, but rather to be traitors to His grace and glory, because they publicly preferred the world...

XII: Two or three things I will bring to light, which will bear witness how I strayed from the righteous path and how I served the world, although to others I seemed to be wise and happy. First of all, when my fame spread and preceded me everywhere, I thought I owed it to that fame to save others from the shame of being accused of lying when they spoke highly of me. Thus I kept my mind and my studies occupied with many different things and I will admit that often this happened for reasons of vanity. Secondly, I did not keep measure either in terms of time expenditure or in the number of sciences. I did not apply myself foremost to those things that honor God, or set a good example for my fellow man, or make my soul most pleasing to God. Thirdly, I followed my human inclinations and was drawn more to human than to divine things. I felt drawn to various arts and sciences and the pleasure that they gave me. Even if I did not always find pleasure in them, at least I sought that pleasure, all of which will be very apparent to any one who looks at my biography.

XIII: Looking back, I am amazed at the lack of measure which had aflicted me in my studies. I blushed when I happened to glance through my treatise to Mr. Andreas Rivet about the studies of a Christian woman. There you can find the following words: *"I clearly affirm all honest discipline, or the whole Circle and Crown of liberal Arts and Sciences (as the proper and universal Good and Ornament of Mankind) to be convenient for the head of our Christian Maid."* This shows that I then believed that I had to learn everything there is to know, and that I had to do so, as I quoted the words of the philosopher, in order to avoid ignorance. But how could I recommend to others, what I knew I did not have myself? These words make it clear to everyone how my thoughts at that time were far removed from the thoughts of our Savior: *"Only one thing is necessary..."*

XIV: Furthermore, even though I tried to maintain order and a proper equilibrium in my studies, the words from the same treatise show that I did not attain them:

> *But especially let regard be had unto those arts which have nearest allegiance to Theology and the Moral Virtues, an which are principally subservient to them. In which number we reckon Grammar; Logick, Rhetorick; especially Logick, fitly called the Key of all Sciences: and then Physics, Metaphysics, History, &c, and also the knowledge of languages, chiefly of the Hebrew and Greek. All of which may advance to more facile and full understanding of the Holy Scripture; to say nothing now of other books.*

This passage shows that I did make all other things subservient to the exercise of theology and that this subservience could be spread indefinitely, until one arrived at the milestone of pure theology. I thought it necessary to have so many different aids to understanding the Scriptures, that the exercises themselves easily surpassed the milestones of human life. And surely, if God's goodness had not determined otherwise, life would have failed me while I was trying.

XV: Let us look for instance, at the study of languages, which scholars call the vehicles of sciences, and to which I have devoted so many hours. I have found that language studies often held me back. And I ask you, for what purpose? So that, if asked, I could answer with Cato who learned Greek when he was 60 years old: "*so that I will die even more learned?*" Or if I were younger, "so that I could live more learned?" I did not study these languages to add laurels to my crown, but rather because I saw and regarded the Greek and the Hebrew languages as the basic languages of the Holy Scriptures and the other languages as the daughters or branches of Hebrew, and therefore pleasing and worthy of being recommended by learned men. I used to pride myself that I had to learn these by exhaustive labor, especially Syrian, Arabic, and Maurish because they have more roots from which derivations can be found in the Holy Scriptures. I thought that these languages would shed light upon the language of the Holy Scriptures and that I would find its most hidden meaning. But to be quite honest, is that not the same thing as to light torches before the sun, or to make an elephant out of a fly? Was this not, to put it lightly, playing around with very serious matter? There are probably few words left which remain a puzzle to learned translators or to those trained in the Hebrew language. What is most needed is a spiritual framework, and none of these endeavors contributed anything to that. Because the Holy Scriptures are read either in the light of the Holy Spirit or not at all. If they are not, minute grammatical explanations will not help you find its innermost and spiritual sense. But if you are taught by the Master, then the true, total and general sense of it will not depend on one little word or on one special root to clarify how everything fits together, since God and

His Spirit are the only undeceiving Explainers of the Holy
Scriptures...

NOTES to the Translations

1. Schurman's *Dissertatio de ingenii muliebris...* was translated into
English by Clement Barksdale (1609-1687), a clergyman. In 1659, when *The
Learned Maid or, Whether a MAID may be a Scholar? A LOGICK
EXERCISE Written in Latin by that incomparable Virgin Anna Maria
Schurman of Utrecht, with some Epistles to the famous Gassendus and others*
was published, Barksdale was a teacher in a private school at Hawlings in
Cottwold. He is best known for his *Memorials of Worthy Persons* (London,
1661). *The Learned Maid*, dedicated to a Lady A. H., shows his interest in
the education of women, as does his *Letter touching a Colledge of Maids or,
a Virgin-Society* (London, 1675), in which he proposes the establishment of
a school similar to a convent boarding school for young women. In addition
to the *Dissertatio, The Learned Maid* contains the English translation of the
original preface by Frederic Spanheim, professor of theology in Leiden,
who, among others, had urged Anna Maria to publish her treatise. Barksdale
also included letters to Spanheim, André Rivet, Petrus Gassendus (professor
of mathematics in Paris), Johan van Beverwijck (physician in Dordrecht and
deputy to the States General), Simon d'Ewes (English baronet and Member
of Parliament in 1645), and to Lady Dorothea Moor (a learned English
lady). I have chosen to translate the entire treatise as well as the letter to
Dorothea Moor. Although Barksdale writes that his 1659 publication was
"the second time" that Schurman was "drest up in her English habit," this
is the oldest extant English edition.

2. In the 1639 edition of *Van de Wtnementheyt des vrouwelicken
geslacht*, Johan van Beverwijck describes Dorothea Moor as "the widow of
an English nobleman, not yet twenty-seven years of age, adorned with all the
graces of body and soul. In a short time she learned Italian and French to
such an extent that she could read works written in both languages and spoke
French fluently. This encouraged her to study Latin, which she also
mastered soon. Not stopping there, she embarked on the study of Hebrew,
in which she progressed so far in a few months that she could read the Bible
in that language. In addition, she is so devout that, in between her studies,
she sets aside a special time each day to spend piously, reading and

meditating. A little while ago, she wrote a letter in Hebrew to the most learned maid that ever lived, who needs no further introduction here" (498-9). For a while, Dorothea Moore had lived with her husband in The Hague. At the time of Schurman's letter, she was living in Dublin. In the *Opuscula*, there is an additional letter to Dorothea Moor written in Hebrew (41-46 of the English edition).

3. These excerpts from the Second Chapter of *Eucleria* were selected to highlight Anna Maria's position toward scholarship before and after she joined the Labadists and her opinion on learning for women. In the original text, chapters are divided into sections marked with a Roman numeral (Translation by Cornelia N. Moore).

4. The first edition of this official catechism of the Reformed churches was entitled *Catechismus Oder Christlicher Unterricht, wie der in Kirchen und Schulen der Churfiirstlichen Pfalz getrieben wirdt* (Heidelberg, 1563). There are numerous later editions in various languages.

5. Schurman probably read Adriaen van Haemstede's *De geschiedenis ende de doodt der vromer Martelaren, die om de gethuyghenisse des Evangeliums Haer bloedt ghestort hebben, van den tyden Christi af tothen Jare MDLIX toe* ("The History and the death of the pious martyrs who shed their blood in the service of Scripture, from the time of Christ until the year 1559;" Amsterdam, 1559 and many later editions).

6. Erasmus' letter to Johann Eck (Basle, 15 May 1518) was in answer to a letter by Eck (2 February 1518) in which he had taken issue with various passages in Erasmus's edition of the New Testament. See *Opvs Epistolarum Des. Erasmi Roterodami*, ed. P.S. Allen (Oxford Univ. Press, 1933), 330ff.

7. Guillaume de Sallustre, Seigneur du Bartas (1544-1590), Huguenot poet in the service of Henri de Navarre. His most important work is *La Semaine*, an epic on the Creation. His *La seconde Semaine*, on the history of humanity, remained uncompleted.

8. Artisans engaged in the construction of the Temple.

9. Gisbertus Voetius (1589-1676), reformed pastor and theologian, professor in Utrecht, mentor of Schurman.

10. André Rivet (1572-1651), professor of theology in Leiden, educator of William II, and from 1646 onward curator of the illustrious school in Breda. His second wife, Maria Molinaea was also known to Schurman, as was his wife's niece, also called Maria Molinaea, the daughter of Petrus Molinaeus.

Bibliography

Primary Works

Schurman, Anna Maria van. *Amica dissertatio inter Anna Maria van S. et Andr. Rivetum.* Paris, 1638. Reprinted as *Dissertatio de ingenii muliebris ad doctrinam et meliores litteras aptitudine.* Leiden: Elzevier, 1641; 1673.

_____. *De Vitae Termino.* Leiden, 1639, 1651; Rotterdam, 1644.

_____. *Opuscula Hebraea, Graecam, Gallica: Prosaica et metrica.* Leiden, 1648; many subsequent editions.

_____. *Eucleria: seu meliores partis electio.* Altona, 1673 (vol. 1) and Amsterdam, 1685 (vol. 2).

_____. *Korte Onderrichtinge Rakende de Staat en de manier van leven der Personen die God t'samen vergadert en tot sijnen dienst vereenigt heeft door de bedieninge sijnes getrouwen dienstknechts Johannes de Labadie en sijner Broeders en Mede-Arbeiders Petrus Yvon en Petrus Dulignon* ("Short instruction concerning the state and the way of life of the persons whom God has gathered and has united in His service by the machinations of Johannes de Labadie and his Brothers and Fellow-servants Petrus Yvon and Petrus Dulignon"). Amsterdam, 1675.

Translations

_____. Trans. C[lement] B[arksdale]. *The Learned Maid, A Logicall Exercise upon the Question, Whether a Maid may be a Scholar.* London, 1659.

Related Works

Arnold, Gottfried. *Unpartheyische Kirchen- und Ketzen-Historie.* Frankfurt/M; 1729. 1198-1200.

Becker-Cantarino, Barbara. "Die 'gelehrte Frau' und die Institutionen und Organisationsformen der Gelehrsamkeit am Beispiel der Anna Maria van Schurman (1607-1678)." *Wolfenbütteler Barockforschungen* 14 (1987). 549-557.

Bijvoet, Maya. "Anna-Maria van Schurman." *An Encyclopedia of Continental Women Writers.* Ed. Katharina M. Wilson. New York; London: Garland, 1991. Vol 2. 1128-1129.

Birch, Una. *Anna Maria van Schurman, Artist, Scholar, Saint.* London, 1909.

Bovenschen, Sylvia. "Das Leben der Anna Maria Schürmann (sic), Paradigma eines Kulturtypus." *Die imaginierte Weiblichkeit.* Frankfurt, 1979. 84-91.

Brandes, Ute. "Studierstube, Dichterklub, Hofgesellschaft..." *Deutsche Literatur von Frauen.* Ed. Gisela Brinker-Gabler. München: Beck, 1988. 222-229.

Brienen, T., et al., eds. *De nadere Reformatie en het Gereformeerde Pietisme.* The Hague: Boekencentrum, 1989.

Douma, Anna M.H. *Anna Maria van Schurman en de studie der vrouw.* Amsterdam, 1924.

Irwin, Joyce. "Anna Maria van Schurman: From Feminism to Pietism." *Church History* 46 (1977). 48-62.

_____. "Anna Maria van Schurman: The Star of Utrecht (1607-1678)." *Female Scholars, A Tradition of Learned Women before 1800.* Ed. J. Brink. Montreal: Eden Press, 1980. 68-85.

Korte, Anne Marie. "Verandering en Continuiteit." *Mara, Tijdschrift voor Feminisme en Theologie* 1 (September 1987). 35-44.

Moore, Cornelia N. "Anna Maria van Schurman (1607-1678)." *Canadian Journal of Netherlandic Studies* XI (Fall 1990). 25-32.

Schotel, G.D.J. *Anna Maria van Schurman.* 's Hertogenbosch, 1853.

Voisine, J. "Un astre éclipsé: Anna Maria van Schurman (1607-1678)." *Etudes Germaniques* 27 (1972). 501-531.

Woods, Jean, and Maria Fürstenwald. *Women of the German Speaking Lands.* Stuttgart: Metzler, 1984. 111-2.

Maria Petijt

André Lefevere

Very little is known about the life of Maria Petijt (1623-1677): she was born in Hazebroek, a small town which then still belonged to the Low Countries, but is now situated in the North of France, and she lived a religious life in Flanders, first in Ghent and then in Mechelen. Her parents seem to have been relatively well to do, and because she was born in Hazebroek she must have grown up in a bilingual Dutch-speaking and French-speaking environment. Nothing much seems to have happened to her. In all likelihood her life was marked by only two conflicts. One occurred when her father, who was not very enthusiastic about her entering monastic life, tried to get her to come back home after her mother died, to run the household for him. The other, probably of more serious import to her, occurred when the nuns of the convent she had joined decided she could not stay because her eyesight was so poor that she could not participate in the liturgy in a meaningful and productive manner. The second conflict was also the more important one in its consequences. Since Maria Petijt was effectively prevented from "officially" becoming a nun, she decided to live the life of a religious in the less "official" manner in which it was lived by the begijnen ("beguines") in the Flanders of her time. These women lived in small communities, preserved a degree of independence that was greater than that enjoyed by nuns, and struck a balance between communal and individual pursuits. Their overriding pursuit was, of course, the ascent to God by means of the religious life. They tried to achieve that goal under the guidance of a religious counselor, very often a member of a religious order, who would be their confessor and help them with his advice.

Very little needs to be known about the rest of Maria Petijt's "outer life," to speak of it in the terms she would have used. It was not important to her, and her autobiography tells us all she must have wanted us to know about it. To her and the other mystics of the long and fertile Flemish tradition, the outer life was important only in as far as it allowed the "inner life" to unfold. The experiences of the inner life were the truly profound, essential experiences for Maria Petijt, the very experiences that made her life meaningful in her own eyes, in those of her fellow religious, and in those of her confessor and spiritual guide. The conflicts of the inner life were tumultuous indeed, and in the mind and soul of the mystic they acquired an importance that eclipsed everything else, inner or outer. But these conflicts could hardly be suspected, let alone seen, by anyone observing Maria Petijt's life from the outside. And here we touch on the real reason why she did not object to writing her autobiography when her spiritual guide asked her to do so. In writing her autobiography she does not primarily want to tell her readers about herself as a person, since her outer life is not important. She concentrates as much as she can on her inner life, or rather, the inner life of a soul striving after the mystic union with God, the Beloved, whom she speaks of almost exclusively in terms of Christ, and the struggle, despair, and fulfillment that are part of that life. She concentrates on the struggles of the soul because this is the relevant part of her life. In short, Maria Petijt writes her autobiography not as the story of a person, but as the story of a struggle.

In very practical terms, she needs to write down her inner struggle because she does not have occasion to meet with her spiritual guide and talk to him at short and regular intervals. The text, in other words, becomes a record of the struggle both for his benefit and, as importantly, hers. It was almost inevitable that, in telling the story of her soul, Maria Petijt would try to conform to the models she had been told to read, and that she would take over certain expressions and set phrases amounting to a kind of "mystical jargon" then in use among the initiated. One could even argue that the whole composition of the autobiography is tributary to much of what was current in the mystical literature of her time and of the century immediately preceding.

And this is the precise point at which we touch on the uniqueness of the text Maria Petijt produced. Even though it was not intended to concentrate on herself as a person, but rather on herself as a "struggling soul," Maria Petijt's autobiography provides us with perhaps the most direct and gripping description of the life of a person who has decided to follow the path shown by the brand of mysticism that came to fruition in the Low Countries, first in the work of Hadewych, and then in that of Ruusbroec. The difference between her text and those of her illustrious predecessors is, quite simply, that her text is not primarily intended to be didactic, but much rather confessional. Whereas Ruusbroec's treatises show the aspiring mystic how to proceed, Maria Petijt's autobiography shows, "from the inside," what happens to this particular aspiring mystic who has proceeded in the manner prescribed.

Maria Petijt's description of the life of a mystic is so direct and "unmediated," as Ruusbroec repeatedly put it, because her autobiography was not, originally, intended for publication. She wrote the text down at the request of her spiritual guide and confessor, the Carmelite friar Michael a Sancto Augustino, who decided to publish it after her death, for the edification of other pious women. In other words, what was written as the record of the struggle of one soul, would be published as an *exemplum* in the medieval Latin sense of the word, which survives in one meaning of the English word "exemplary." Maria Petijt's life becomes an example for other pious women to emulate: it warns of the suffering and despair they are likely to experience, but it also tells them that suffering and despair can be overcome, and that the mystic union can be achieved.

To achieve the transition from "record" to *exemplum*, Michael a Sancto Augustino added short paragraphs to most chapters, dulling edges here and making dogmatic points there, not least to forestall possible accusations of heresy that were often leveled at mystical writings, often written by women, which contained some passages that could be interpreted as "erotic." His additions are not found in any modern edition of Maria Petijt's work. He most probably added his comments because Maria Petijt most definitely lived in a "man's world." Mysticism was not exactly welcomed by the official Roman Catholic Church, certainly not after the Reformation, since the mystic union could easily be interpreted as an attempt to achieve the same direct relationship with God promised by both Lutheranism and Calvinism, though not in the same way. Moreover, mystics were often seen as "slightly beyond the bounds of the rational," they were just as often approached with distrust by theologians who did not look kindly on the possibility of the existence of "another way," something in the order of a "personal short cut" that would bring the soul and God together without their, the theologians' expert mediation.

Female mystics were almost automatically deemed to wander beyond the pales of the rational, since they were not only mystics, but women into the bargain. The fact that they were women implied that they had not received much formal education, which fact in turn implied that they would not be able to withstand the snares of the Evil One to anywhere near the same extent as the male theologians who had to sit in judgment on their work. It often happened, therefore, that spiritual guides, themselves convinced of the value of the work of one of the women under their guidance, would portray their charges as "inspired," with all the positive and negative connotations of the word, while insisting that little harm could be caused by their works since these works had not only been produced under the spiritual guide's close supervision, but also edited by him. Michael a Sancto Augustino may have particularly stressed this since it is believed that he also intended the publication of Maria Petijt's work to be the first step in the process that would lead to her eventual beatification. To that end he also translated passages of it into Latin, so that they could be submitted as evidence to the relevant committees of theologians in Rome.

Obviously Maria Petijt was much more than a "pious woman" of the kind she was supposed to "edify." Equally obviously, she never wandered beyond the pales of the rational. Rather, she lived through with great courage, and described with great power, the whole process of *vernietinghe*, the crucial concept in Dutch medieval mysticism and its Baroque avatar. Adumbrated in Hadewych and codified in the writings of Ruusbroec, the concept of "vernietinghe" requires the soul to become "niet," or nothing, but without implying the "annihilation" of that soul in any way. Rather, much in the way in which Maria Petijt talks of herself in her autobiography, the soul is supposed to empty itself of all that constitutes its "self," since that self, though created by God, also presents an obstacle to the great work God could achieve in and through the soul once it has emptied itself to the extent that it can absorb him fully into itself and act as his instrument on earth. Once the soul has fully absorbed God, God also fully absorbs it, in the *unio mystica*, making it his partner in eternity while the body that envelops the soul is still on earth. However — and this is also made abundantly clear in Maria Petijt's autobiography — there is no conflict between the mystical union and the practical work the person who has achieved it may be required to perform on earth for the salvation of his or her fellow men, nor should any such conflict be allowed to develop.

Since she had read Teresa of Avila and John of the Cross, who had both written within the orbit of the Carmelite order, Maria Petijt duly describes her experiences in terms of the "dark night of the soul." Her text becomes most interesting, however, when this kind of terminology proves insufficient for what she wants to convey. She then tends to dismiss it with a sovereign "&," inviting the reader to supply the requisite clichés or, more importantly, to follow her back to the wellsprings of Dutch mysticism in the terminology of Ruusbroec which she knew either from reading his works, or their extremely influential popularization in Thomas a Kempis's *Imitatio Christi*. These terms, like "inflow," and "unimaged," are not easy to translate, because they are so crucial to the experience and should therefore be rendered in an English form that remains as close as possible to the Dutch original, eschewing the obvious temptation of the facile Latinism.

Maria Petijt describes the development of the soul along the road of mysticism that leads to God beyond what she describes in an extremely daring phrase at the very end of these excerpts as "the darkness of faith." What we read is the vivid testimony of a woman of great feeling, immense courage, and independent spirit, who lived what the men who gave her guidance were usually satisfied to just teach. Hers is, with Hadewych's, the most original voice produced by Dutch mysticism. Her prose is so rhythmical and unobtrusively well-crafted that it has an incantatory effect on the reader. This effect is probably the single most characteristic feature of her style, and I have therefore tried to render it as closely as possible in the translation, breaking up Maria Petijt's beautifully constructed periods only when there was no other way.

Maria Petijt's work is referred to as the final flowering of Dutch mysticism. Needless to say, I do not have the space at my disposal to even begin to sketch the background to her writing here. Needless to add that is precisely why I have selected so generously from her work and kept this introduction to a bare minimum. Maria Petijt needs no mediator. Her words speak for themselves, and her voice is as compelling now as it was three hundred years ago.

Translations by André Lefevere

From *THE LIFE OF...MARIA A STA. THERESIA*

Chapter LXXI

Even though these noble and hidden souls are not held in esteem, or even acknowledged to possess any value, or any use whatsoever, yet they are the pillars of Christianity, who bear much more fruit in Holy Church in their lonely little cell by means of their incredible and unspeakably pure, powerful, and fiery prayer, than those who perform much outward labor and service in the Church without, as a rule, possessing such great internal purity and probity of love or, consequently, such great union with JESUS.

These best propitiate God for the sins of men; their prayer averts much evil and many punishments God threatened to send over the world; through their prayer many souls convert to a better life;

they obtain more grace for others so that they may please God more; the living and the dead sense the greatness of their love and their zeal, and the power of their prayer, even though the living commonly do not know from where this help comes to them, through whose endeavor they are spared much evil and guided to good, and how divine grace is increased in them; and behold: it is the endeavor of these lovely and lonely souls, arising from honest Christian love, that affords them the same love with their Beloved.

These are as honest mothers and fathers who would like to give birth to all men in Christ, to their salvation, and to many they do give birth indeed, through their burning love and their loving imprecations to their Mostbeloved, who is so close to them in intimacy; truly these should not be counted useless, infertile, and without love for their fellow man, even though one does not sense their fertility and the fruits of their love on the outside. It is there nevertheless, more so than people think; maybe I say so because of my own experience, since I am able to believe myself.

They keep all their riches and treasures, their virtues and their grace, and all their spiritual gains hidden under the ashes of silence, a deep humility, and a holy reserve; of this they make profession, that they may walk on firm ground.

Chapter LXXII

This spirit of reserve rules my soul with discernment and discretion in as much as it gives me freedom not to be discourteous, aloof, cross, and all too somber or silent with my fellow sisters when need or reason seem to call for it. For even though the Beloved wants me all to himself in all other occurrences and occasions, to give room to his grace and its penetration according to the direction it is supposed to take; even though he shows himself extremely jealous whenever I might spend my time on anything else, or engage in anything but devotion to him alone, with all my heart and all my soul turned toward him as is required by the honest, lonely, reserved life of a hermit.

Yet he does allow for some moderation in this among my little sisters, now and then. For instance, when I notice that one of them is engaged in some kind of struggle, or finds herself depressed, or sad, or in bad straits physically or spiritually. Even if I then felt myself very inclined and drawn toward God and silence, love would always tell me to call them to me, to give them strength through our conversation, to distract them and make them of good cheer. My spirit then bends itself very well to this, to entertain them with greater friendliness, affection, and attentiveness, and even to say something that may divert or amuse them and be a help to body and soul, together with spiritual sustenance, so that they may be better suited to prayer.

Except if I sense in my heart that it would please the Beloved more if they were to suffer through this in naked isolation; in that case I decide to leave them alone.

Chapter LXXXI

After the grace and the divine light had grown in my soul like this for a long time, as if to a perfect noon, it pleased God (perhaps through my fault and failure to work with the same grace as I should have, and to guard it as well as I could) that this inner clarity, which was so great, and those actions of the spirit, that had been so intimate, began to slowly diminish. These inflowings of divine grace did not stop immediately, but so softly and gradually that I hardly noticed until I had lost them completely and was left entirely to my naked nature, without feeling any more help or support from above, and it was utter night in my soul.

It happened almost as when the sun has reached its highest point at noon and slowly sinks, and evening falls because the sun goes under and the light vanishes by degrees without our noticing or sensing it until we find ourselves deprived of all light and placed in a sad darkness and night.

It was necessary that this feeling of being abandoned should come over me, that I might be tested and purified as gold is in the fire of the many different inner and outer tortures, temptations, struggles and sufferings I had to bear.

Even though I had been taught very well in my inner self about the previous state of grace, about perfect virtues, inner purity, the nakedness of all things that were not God, the pure, unadulterated love of God, the knowledge of my own *Nothingness*, and denial of my self, and more; yet to honestly acquire these I needed the occasion to apply this information and this divine influence in practice, since the knowledge thereof, the positive motivation toward it, the slow and steady practice, and the expression of the self are unequal in all kinds of moods, occasions, and encounters.

Chapter LXXXII

It is not very difficult, and of small perfection, to observe virtue, to be faithful to God, to cleave to him in love, to be reserved toward all creatures, and not to look for amusement or satisfaction except in God alone, when you are in a time of grace, when God receives the soul so well and treats her with such affection, overwhelming and overflowing her with spiritual luxuries and divine grace; all that takes care of itself, without pain or effort: gracious love makes all things light and grace spurs the soul on to all goodness and virtue through a sweet necessity.

These effusions of grace are very useful and profitable then, she makes great progress as long as God leaves her in that state and does not send her on to a more perfect one. But when God has disposed to lead her along more elevated and special roads, and when the time has come to place her in the dark night of the soul, in a taking away and withdrawing of all gracious help and inflowing of divine grace; even then something of the favors previously bestowed in grace clings to the soul unnoticed and keeps its affections so detached and ascetic that she cannot turn herself to any creature, or anything created with any enjoyment and satisfaction.

Therefore, when this divine grace is given to her, she must value it highly, thank God for it, receive it with humility, and guard it with faithful observation and cooperation.

Chapter LXXXIII

So it pleased the Beloved to lead me along a very hard and painful road for both my nature and my soul, and to place me in a very unhappy and desolate state of spirit, that I might indeed feel and experience how powerless I was and how impossible it was for me to do good, and that I might experience my nothingness, my brittleness, my wretchedness, and my being cast out, and that I might sink so low and be confirmed in a deep humility and knowing of my own self. And he used so many different means to achieve this that I could not escape in any other way than to be crushed and reduced to utter nothingness.

For the Beloved gave my nature blow after blow, wound after wound, so that it was as if forced to die utterly to itself, to wit in its love of self and other things it still clung to in a subtle way, and lived in, especially the gifts of God, even though I did not realize this before I came into that state of lack and despoilment of all things.

It was necessary, as I said before, that this state should come over me, in part to allow the divine virtues, Faith, Hope, and Love to work on me in a more perfect manner, and in part to allow all other Christian virtues to strike deeper roots in my soul because of these gales and tempests, in the same way as a tree strikes its roots deeper into the earth when it is bent and buffeted by the winds, this way and that.

Chapter LXXXIV

Before this I had enough knowledge in my intellect of all virtues, and enough motivation in my will toward them, but I did not have any particular occasion to put that knowledge and that motivation into practice. I also had knowledge of my own smallness and nothingness, but to base this knowledge in me as natural and essential it was necessary to have certain proofs and clear experiences of it. To experience this so clearly I had to be thrown or cast out into utter misery and wretchedness, and I had to be denuded and despoiled of all grace and the gracious effects of all virtues as if I had never had them. And what happened to me lasted a long time; it seems to me that that night of the soul and that deprivation of obvious grace lasted four or five years, though not usually with such great violence and extremity, since during that time I did experience some divine light and grace that gave me strength.

And when I experienced those, I thought the night of the soul and all inner suffering had come to an end, but I was deceived because I soon found myself in the middle of it again. It had come over me gradually, and become night inside me almost without my noticing; in the same way that sad and suffering state in me came to an end, and dawn broke gradually, very gradually, and the weather stayed steady, still, and calm.

The utter extremity of inner torture, oppression, anxiety, withering and desertion of spirit lasted about two years, and I did not receive any consolation from God, or very little, or from any man, nor any obvious comfort. Heaven seemed to be closed to me, and I did not feel even the smallest drop of dew or rain on the barren soil of my soul that seemed to wither and disappear in the drought.

Chapter LXXXVI

Very soon after this, the Beloved allowed unbearable pains of the body to come over me. Nobody understood what kinds of pains they were. Some thought they were not natural pains because natural remedies were of no help against them. Others said it had to be some devilry because they had never seen anybody experience this kind of pain and I had never borne such. I believe this was true: that the Beloved had given power to the Evil One to attack me and torture me in body and soul, internally and externally, with all kinds of suffering. For the inner withdrawal and desertion of spirit and the outer suffering both in the body, and caused by people happened together.

These pains were such that I would not be able to compare them to anything, except to a great torment and martyrdom. It seems to me that if the Beloved had not assisted me then with his grace without my knowing, I would have succumbed to pain or to despair.

It felt as if my body was run through and cut through with knives and swords from all sides. Sometimes all my inners seemed to be pulled out of my body with great cruelty. The sisters cried with pity when they saw me placed in such torment. They were unable to rest by day or night because of my wailing and sometimes screaming caused by the furious pains inflicted on me. Sometimes this fury would last for many an hour, so that they were forced to hold me down since I seemed to want to tear myself apart because I seemed crazy and out of my mind with pain.

After going through this pain for hours I was so exhausted in all my body as if I had had a long and serious illness. It was as if I had to take some refreshment to get my strength back so that I could go lie on the rack again. I did get some respite every day, as a rule, as if to catch my breath. This lasted for a few weeks, but I have forgotten how many. I think I shall never be able to forget this pain; and my love for suffering is still so small that my nature is still wary of it to this day.

To make this suffering hurt me all the more, the Beloved allowed some people to condemn me, as if it had been a sign of malediction, since (they thought) the Evil One had power over me to torture my body and tempt my soul with many, even strange temptations. This aggravated me all the more because some religious people said so, and also that I was the reason why God withheld his blessing from our house.

A religious person made life very difficult for me then and aggravated me by testing me and purposely gainsaying me in all manner of things, as I think, to test perfection of virtue and mortification in me. He therefore seemed to study me to find occasion to torture my nature and cause it to rebel, but alas, since that person had little or no knowledge of what I had to go through internally, of what the Beloved gave me to suffer, he treated me somewhat roughly, often hitting me blindly and giving me wound after wound. The worst then was that I had nobody I could open my heart to. And so I had to deal with these inner struggles and temptations myself, as well as I could, because my Spiritual Father was absent then for a long time.

Chapter XC

For a long time I felt locked in the narrowness of my nature as in a narrow, dark dungeon, pinioned and chained, as if bound with iron chains, without being able to stir my inner powers, to direct them toward God, or to use them for anything good: prayer and spiritual exercises aggravated me so that they filled me with loathing; indeed I dreaded the hour.

Yet no matter how great the aggravation, repulsion, and loathing I had of it, I never omitted anything, nor did I shorten the time; rather, I doubled it, to spite both the Evil One and my own nature, and not to deviate from the faithfulness that is required of those who want to become People of Prayer. Yet to sit there for an hour was like torment to me because it was as if I had to row against the current. Often I was unable to gather my thoughts and turn them toward God, not even for half a *Hail Mary*. It seemed as if there was an iron wall between God and my soul. Especially in the hour of prayer I found myself so far from my Beloved and so estranged from him as if he had been a thousand miles away from me. I am speaking here of feeling and experience; my will was never estranged from him at all.

I did not shirk great expenditure of labor in prayer to stay involved with God at that time, and to care about him; but in vain, since I often rose from prayer without being able to receive one good thought; all I did was seeking without finding. The Beloved had taken the gift of prayer away from me to such an extent that I did not know what prayer was, nor how I should prepare myself for it, not more than if I had never prayed before. It seemed to me that I had gained much when I had been able to obtain a quiet and peaceful heart: for my soul was like a sea where the waves and temptations held the upper hand. Beyond my nature I have always been quiet and confident in my heart, neither restless nor changeable. And then my prayer and loneliness were nothing but a jostle and commotion of manifold thoughts that led to nothing and took my soul away, I do not know where. I did not have many evil thoughts, but not many good ones either; I became so blunted and ignorant in the exercises of spiritual life that I could not speak of it to anyone, nor put it into practice, as if I had never experienced any of it before.

Chapter XCIX

I have been tortured for a few months by yet another kind of inner suffering, so great that I do not think I would be able to imagine a greater one. It was like an unbearable torment from hell that tortured me in my inner person as if I had been abandoned to the henchmen of hell, since everybody seemed to do his best to treat me in the most cruel way possible. I still remember how they sometimes, no, often, seemed to pull my heart apart with iron tongs. This caused such a deeply felt and unspeakable pain that I would have had to die of pain and torment if I had not been strengthened by the grace of God in a secret manner, without knowing how.

Sometimes I also felt like a body that is nothing but one wound from head to toe, and which is treated in a very rough and cruel manner by hands armed with iron. You may imagine what sorrow this must have caused me. This big wound was not really in my body, but it seemed so in what I felt. It was an invisible wound that seemed rather to be in my soul.

I sometimes felt as if suspended between heaven and earth, as if my throat had been throttled; as if hanging between two swords that seemed to pierce me whenever I wanted to move a limb to obtain some solace or relief.

I often felt as if placed on the rack, where I seemed to be stretched in all my limbs. The nerves of my whole body also seemed to pull against me. All that time I felt great oppression, pain, and sorrow. Speech gave out on me, as did breath, to some extent, because the body shared in the pain and suffering of the soul that was unspeakably great. When I was untied from that rack I was very tired and numbed in my strength, as if I had been engaged in a labor beyond it.

Chapter C

In this state of suffering described above I would usually be subjected to much inner and outer torment, and hard and difficult temptations that would hold me in a tight grip. I was attacked and overwhelmed from all sides, without being able to find any escape or help anywhere. For in this my greatest need I was deprived of my spiritual father, unable to receive any statement, support, or advice from him because he was far away, travelling through the province he administered for the order, and then to Rome.

I found myself left alone in this battle, not able to feel any support, comfort, or reinforcement from heaven or earth, God or man. Even if I had tried to find some comfort in created beings, I could not have found any since the Beloved allowed them to appear sad and bitter to me, and devoid of consolation, so that I would not come to rest in them, or be hampered by them. Rather, I had to suffer through that state disconsolate, to the very end, without any sweetening.

Even my fellow sisters were bitter toward me, and excessively so. I felt such opposition, revulsion, and horror from them as if they had been venomous beasts. I would have liked to have run away from there, had I been able to. I was wary of their presence. Yet in this state I had to converse with them and order their affairs. I do not mean to say that they were able to notice any of this in my behavior since I did not show anything outwardly, through the grace of God, except perhaps a sadder countenance sometimes, but that I did unknowingly, and without paying attention to it. This cost me great pains and great effort, since indeed they did not give me any cause for revulsion; rather it was the Evil One who touched my nature in this way, and stirred it up, so that it was all I could do to hold myself in check.

When I had offended against kindness in any way I sorely humiliated myself before the sisters, imploring their forgiveness and asking them to impose some penitence on me. Sometimes I would order them to kick me with their feet since I was not worthy to be in their company, much less to be their Superior whose task it should have been to guide them and edify them by setting a good example.

Sometimes I would order them to administer some disciplinary blows to me, on my arm or in my neck.

Chapter CIII

I have suffered yet another manner of desertion, darkness, drought, and insensitivity in all that pertains to the spirit, salvation, and religion, namely in the form of an immense temptation to leave this place and my spiritual father. The Evil One greatly tormented and oppressed me with a great revulsion toward both, filling me with many evil judgments and impressions, much contempt and bitterness of the heart. My nature turned itself upside down and shied away from him when I had to go to confession, or when I heard him somewhere, or became aware of his presence.

I was also sorely tempted to inflict some injury on myself in one way or another. Faint-hearted thoughts caused much despair because I had been incited to firmly believe that I had been rejected by God from now on and for all eternity; that there was no help, ointment, or remedy left for me; that it was all over and done with; that I could surely see I had to be among the number of the rejected. For the Evil One constantly incited me to so many wicked and evil deeds and inclinations that all passions and almost all sins seemed to live in the lower part of my nature, except the sin against purity, since the Beloved never allowed me to experience that temptation.

I seemed to sense that the Evil One was not away from me for a single second; he caused unspeakable spasms in me, and internal pains; I seemed to be suffering an insufferable torment from hell that seemed to close my heart, so that food could hardly pass through any more. He tried very hard to make me injure myself by not eating, but I overcame him by eating for the love of Jesus and Mary, to spend or consume my strength in their love and their service. I did it to spite him; I even had to express this with words sometimes, because everything was so estranged and without feeling inside; it seemed as if I did not mean what I said.

That inner torment would sometimes cause something like fury and rage in my nature, to the extent that I would have torn myself apart and destroyed myself. This forced me to flee to the crucifix and to embrace it with some trust; this would still the attacks of rage, but not the inner pains.

Chapter CV

When the state described above seemed to pass a little, and I found my inner strength somewhat more freely (as it seemed to me) I tried as hard as I could, even though it was against my will, to say a few Acts of Faith, Hope, and Love in God's presence. I also tried to invoke the saints, and to say some other prayers. But I did it in such a clumsy way that it seemed as if I did not mean it, so that I could hardly come up with a good thought, even after much pain and effort, or stay with it for the time of a Hail Mary. My brain, my memory, and my imagination were as twisted, scattered, unsteady, and changeable as wild birds that cannot be caught. From this I again learned the lesson to let go of myself, and to abandon myself in God, even though I experienced a harsh dying and a spiritual death to nature.

Whenever I had faithfully suffered through this state, or other similar ones, without turning my thoughts to finding any human or created comfort to sweeten my sorrows, even though my nature seemed to be somewhat inclined to this, I would experience a sweet peace of the heart in myself, a serenity of conscience, a spirit quiet, reserved, and lonely; nature tamed, mortified, and strengthened together with the soul, pious and prepared to go through all kinds of suffering, humiliation, contempt, accusations, oppression, backbiting, injustice, and more, for love of the Beloved.

I would also experience a willingness to suffer inner discomfort, to be abandoned by God, to be exposed to drought and darkness, to inner and outer torment. I would feel much inclined to these, and even find myself longing for them with an inner joy, for as in a sweet honeycomb I would taste in them the ability to speak these words from the heart, to which my spirit would bear witness: my Beloved you are all mine, and I am all yours; you alone are enough for me, you know my heart; the judgment of men and all their words cannot lessen me by a hair in your estimation.

Oh, how liberally does God repay with inner grace the soul who bears inner and outer suffering in faithful perfection, who does not allow nature to burst out in words or in her countenance, but keeps herself in check and subdues herself as much as she can.

Chapter CVI

And yet, after I had spent a long time in such a good, peaceful, and mortified mood; so humble, kind, patient, poor in spirit, resigned to all things and abandoned to the Beloved, clinging to him alone in naked faith, with a spirit pious and steadfast, in such full control of myself that nature would appear as if dead and I would think I would not have any trouble with myself anymore, and I would not even be able to live in my nature any longer, the Beloved would allow me to feel nature rising again when I least expected it, and doing violence to the spirit more than before, attacking it and assailing it with such a hard struggle, with such ardent and recalcitrant incitement to vices and passions that I did not know where to go or turn to escape.

I thought I saw myself as a ship in the middle of the sea, tossed by the waves from one side to the other, and sometimes completely covered by them. I felt myself to be a ship without a sail, or rudder, a vessel that cannot be brought under control, governed, or guided, since all the help I could muster appeared to be in vain. I therefore had to allow the little ship of my soul to float in the governance and grace of God, bearing the violence of the waves with a spirit resigned, or to anchor the ship when I could.

Sometimes when I was in such a state I thought I saw myself like a wild animal among hunting dogs that pursued my soul from all sides, pressing in on it and biting it ferociously, and I could not find a little hole to crawl into anywhere, to escape from their cruelty and violence. Indeed the violent and vicious inclinations, or the stirring up of unruly passions so strongly felt by a soul that is intent on God, seeks him in all honesty and purity, longs for him and aspires to perfection because she desires nothing more than to cling to God with all her power in an utter purity of the heart, are as cruel hunting dogs that seek to bite her and disturb her peaceful rest in her Beloved with their barking, their yelling, and the violence that descends on her.

The Beloved sometimes allowed these recalcitrant, strongly felt, and unconquered inclinations of nature to be much stronger than they were in my first conversion. For this the Evil One incited me to listlessness and faintness of heart because I felt a law so opposed to the law and the light of my intellect, or spirit, without being able to overcome it. For it is a kind of martyrdom for a soul who has tasted pure spirit to feel unconquered and unvirtuous inclinations, especially when they are rather powerful, so that she cannot really tear herself away from them, nor leave them unnoticed. I allowed myself to think that all I had achieved did not count for anything, that I was moving backward, and that nature began to live again, more than ever.

But I did not well infer the divine prudence in this, and the wondrous findings of his wisdom and goodness in treating a soul in this way to bring her to a clear and genuine understanding of her own self, of her own *nothingness*. These states of the soul, so changeable and opposite, point out to her, as with a finger, what she can do on her own, and that all the power she needs to do what she has to do comes from God alone.

Chapter CVII

The unconquered and recalcitrant inclinations I spoke of before, that I felt against my will, would impel me toward disobedience, irritability, pride, anger, or even sudden outbursts of rage, bitterness of the heart toward my fellow men, and toward spiteful and bad-tempered conversation with my fellow sisters. I would turn away from them and feel a stranger to them and to my spiritual father because I had been incited to contempt and distrust of his spirit, as well as disbelief of his teaching. I had been incited to close myself off from him, or even to leave him altogether. I sometimes felt such revulsion and contempt for him that hearing him, seeing him, or thinking of him would fill me with horror. Once I was so overcome by this struggle that I openly dismissed his Reverence, thanking him for the place I had lived in and the habit I had been wearing, and for the trouble his Reverence had taken with me for so many years; so firm was my resolve to leave him, the place, and the habit.

But his Reverence saw very well that I had come to the end of my endurance and that I had been overwhelmed by an exceptionally hard struggle, and he did all he could to put me at ease and to make me believe it was a struggle and a torment sent by the Evil One, to trap me and ensnare me in a corruption of the soul, as I would have been indeed if the Evil One had torn me away from my helmsman and the staff I could lean on, and had to lean on in that poor and overlonely state.

I had never seen my spiritual father in sadness, except for that time. For he realized the great peril I was in because the reluctance and revulsion I felt toward him then would rob me of the fruits of his teaching that should have brought me comfort and strength. My disbelief robbed me of all support and certainty and I could no longer follow his word in such a hard and dangerous struggle, nor take the risk of trusting his advice with peace of mind, as I had always done before.

It was strange to him to see me like this, so inflexible and somewhat obstinate, since I did not seem to be able to muster the will to simple and blind obedience, and to submit my intelligence, because the Evil One had instilled in me a strange distrust of him in whose word I had always felt such great faith and trust.

The Evil One knew very well that this was the crutch I leaned on, the pillar I clung to in the middle of the waves and the tempests, that he could not touch me to deceive me in anything and throw me down as long as I remained firmly anchored to this pillar of humble submissive obedience, and in the keeping of such a faithful guide. For this reason the Evil One labored so hard, with such lies and such deceit, and in so many ways to tear me away from my spiritual father, or at least to estrange me from him. But he did not succeed since my spiritual father's patience and discretion surrounded me and held me until this tempest passed and I could clearly see the lies of the Evil One and his deceit, and keep to my spiritual father, cling to the pillar of obedience, and gradually overcome all opposition through the grace of God.

Chapter CXIX

I appear moved to make mention at some length of nature's strong opposition and recalcitrance, which I felt in all our spiritual exercises by day and night, in getting up, in waking, in fasting, in prayer, &. It seemed at times that I had to drag the body on, or behind me, like an unwilling animal that does not want to follow. Sometimes I had to use such violence and force to get up at night, or in the morning, as if I had to pull an ox out of a pit. I had to use the last remnants of my strength, or else the body would have become my master. Sometimes I spoke to myself as follows: courage, my soul, fight with devotion; see that you overcome the body or you yourself will be overcome.

Because I had to force and brutalize myself in this way I felt such sadness and painful sorrow as if I had had a wounded body that would have been subjected to rough treatment. The Beloved let me taste the full bitterness of this each time, and I had to grit my teeth to the utmost, and my senses never felt any help of his grace. I seemed to be left utterly to myself; and yet he supported me with his loving and powerful hand beyond my senses, that I might not expire and be crushed under that heavy burden. For by the grace of God I do not think I did anything more or less than normal when in that state, nor did I fail in any way in my obedience to our Rule.

Chapter CXX

The same things happened when I had to go to my cell alone; my blood seemed to curdle and my whole nature shivered with horror and sadness, thinking how I could possibly pass the time there, in such desertion of spirit, in such great drought and dispersion of the soul, with so many temptations hard to resist, and such oppression of the heart.

Sometimes I found some courage, embracing both the bitter chalice and the cross, and resigning myself to a suffering to the end, without looking for sweetness or comfort anywhere else than in the naked will and pleasing of the Lord, but I would not be able to say how sharp, harsh, bitter, and sour that suffering seemed to me, nor how I felt it.

It seems to me that the state I was in then was in many ways similar to the state of the souls in purgatory, who are bereft of all comfort, solace, or sweetening in their pain. Wherever they turn, or go, all they feel is pain and unbearable sorrow with a constant screaming of love to be near God, since having to forego his countenance is their greatest torment. And it was the same with me: no matter where I turned, or did not turn, I found myself alone, like an outcast, bereft of all sensation of the presence of my Beloved to whom I addressed the laments of my loving in that sad loneliness, but he did not answer me in any way. And having to forego my Beloved made the cell and its loneliness so sad and unbearable.

Chapter CXXI

But behold, the Beloved is true, and he does not allow anyone to be tempted beyond his power. I can now say with David, the prophet, *he led me through fire and water and he brought me to coolness;* behold, the wounds are cured, the wounds are healed, the fruits have been born, the sorrows have been forgotten. And the fruits I have gathered in these painful and desolate states seem great to me indeed.

I find myself most advanced in the deep and thorough knowledge of my own nothingness; I feel how small I am and I distrust myself, and my trust in God is notably greater, my humility much deeper and more steady in its effects. Purity of heart and poverty of spirit have strongly increased. It seems to me that my spirit is more divested of all clinging to, or turning toward, or affection for anything created, including supernatural creatures, so that I can now have God as my goal much more plainly and essentially, that is according to his being and not his gifts.

Nature's subtle self-love and self-seeking has died off to a great extent; there is more of a risk and a giving up of myself to God; a more genuine or living faith, a purer love to God, a more steady fleeing of all things in which the Beloved is not purely sought, meant, found, and loved.

There is also a greater resignation under God and my superiors and less of a choice, or desire, or refusal where there is any sign of the will of the Beloved. I seem to feel a great ability for whatever use the Beloved, or obedience are likely to put me to, or not put me to. In a word, I feel total indifference: there is no need to choose, and I treat all things with equanimity, even though there is something like an inborn inclination to leave, deny, and abandon myself without finding rest or support anywhere.

Chapter CXXII

From that time onward the Beloved began to treat me in a more gracious, kind, and sweet manner. Even though the night of the soul & did not come to a total end, the Beloved would sometimes visit me suddenly for an hour, or half an hour, by showing his presence in me in some way. He did so to comfort me and to increase my strength, so that I would not let my courage sink too low out of despondence at having to do without his presence for too long. He seemed to feel sympathy for my sick, oppressed, and tormented nature. He seemed to take pity on all the sighs and lamentations of love addressed to him.

To comfort me then he made me understand that the state of the soul I have described above, which was one of suffering and desolation, was not punishment for any evil I had done, as I had sometimes surmised, that he was not angry with me, and that he had not abandoned me, or rejected me, even though the Evil One was trying to oppress me to bring me to smallness of spirit, but that all of this had sprung from unmeasured goodness and love, that he made us suffer because he wanted to be reconciled with the sins and unfaithfulness of some, and satisfied with them, and their sins are greater in the eyes of God than they know or think, &.

Through this I gained knowledge of the greatness of the sin that has to suffer such pain and punishment, for even though I would gain a kingdom by suffering like this for one day only, I would not want to do it; but I feel entirely prepared to do so if it will pay the debts incurred in the face of the Lord and vindicate the dishonor done to him; indeed, I count it as an honor and a favor altogether too great. The Beloved gave me to understand that this state of suffering and desertion needed to last a little longer, but not with the same intensity, and so it turned out to be, witness what follows.

Chapter CXXIII

The Beloved also ordered me to take great reserve and silence to heart, that I might bear a naked, comfortless, and perfect suffering, and not enjoy any sweetening, refreshment, or consolation in or from any creature, for the Beloved does not want to allow this in me. If he thought it necessary, the Beloved himself would come and comfort me, as he sometimes did after a heavy blow or in particularly crushing circumstances (although he did not do so often), because he wants to be my only consolation and satisfaction from now on, saying: *whoever still seeks something, or tastes something beyond me, is not able to taste me.* By this I felt impelled to even more thoroughly spurn and deny all that is not the Beloved, saying with Paul, the holy apostle: *I have considered all things excrement, that I might gain Christ.*

I have to faithfully persevere in this, without weakening, since that silence will be very needful and useful to me after this, in another manner, namely that the Beloved (as he shows himself to me) will be able to work in my soul without anyone knowing, or interfering with it. If I have not been deceived in what has been said to me in these matters, or in any information I have been given, the Beloved promises me much that is great, namely: to work many things in my soul and to enlighten it, to give himself to me, and to unite me with him.

Chapter CXXV

When the end of this previous state began to come near, I found myself neither in darkness nor in light, but as if in daybreak in between darkness and light, half in light and half in darkness, but in such a way that was not guided by this small light in what I had to do, or leave undone, according to God's will; I was guided only by the light of reason, which is dark, and yet somewhat sufficient to acquire the knowledge of what the Beloved wanted me to do, or leave undone, at one time or another.

I always felt my whole being very eager and able to oblige in this with joy in my heart, as one who could not find any life or satisfaction anywhere than in the Beloved alone, and in his most dearly beloved will, even though in this state this, too, comes to pass without one's feeling it, as it does not bring any taste or enjoyment to one's nature.

I do not know whether anyone will believe me in this; they will think that I do not understand myself well, or that I do not well explain the state of a soul so poor, deserted, and withered as mine was then, since it seems almost impossible, or highly contradictory, that a soul should be so turned away from divine influence, and deserted by it and by any impulse toward the good in its lower parts, while in its upper parts, which are totally spiritual, according to the soul's being and substance, it is habitually raised up toward God, or to what is divine, without (as I think) being in the least bent, or inclined toward any creature.

In the part of me that feels and experiences I seemed to be like infertile soil without water, which is left barren; it seemed to me that there were days when I did not feel a single inclination toward anything, nor could I gain any turning inward, or turning toward God in prayer, at least not of any duration; no matter how zealous I was, nor how earnestly I tried, I was not able, I thought, to stay with myself for the time of one Our Father; my inner powers were as if scattered, wandering here and there, without being able to remember, afterwards, where they had been wandering, or what had distracted them; but then again, at some time I was able to bring them back inside in unimaged loneliness.

The time of prayer passed with this running out and calling back in, and I was not able to gather any noticeable fruits of simplicity, silence of spirit, and coming closer to God--I mean, none that I could notice. I did not feel estranged from the Beloved, but rather with him, or close to him, although in the dark, without seeing him with the clear eye of faith. It was more as if someone would be together with his friend in a room in which the light would be blown out all of a sudden; he would therefore not think he would be separated from his friend, nor doubt his presence, even though he did not see him, but he would wait patiently for the light to be lit again, so that he could see his friend as he pleased. And yet, being in the dark, he would be able to speak to his friend and deal with him as before, even though this would not bring the same enjoyment and satisfaction. My soul deals with the Beloved in the same way, when he hides himself in the dark: she deals with him as if he were present, and even though she does not see him with the clear and illuminated eye of faith, she knows in naked faith that he is there.

Chapter CXXVI

Yet in this state I possessed a great inner peace, without being able to wish or want to be different, because I felt with too great a certainty that this was a special boon, or permission of the Lord, to guide me to a much deeper and more perfect knowledge of myself and my nothingness than I would have been able to achieve without his continuous assistance and particular help. Oh, how clear that knowledge was in me then, and how deeply felt.

This great inner peace and equanimity I enjoyed in that poor and sober state sprang from the unity of will I shared with the divine. I had achieved this by the grace of God through a persistent denying, turning away from, going beyond, and mortifying my own will, through a willing giving up and abandoning of myself in all that was pleasing to God, through never wittingly and willingly giving a place in my heart to any desires, wishes, or preferences in things temporal or eternal, both in spirit and in nature, except for the most dearly beloved will of God.

I accustomed myself to taking my only rest and satisfaction in this, even though this cost my nature many a death, since the Beloved put many a bitter portion before me, through which my taste became as if lost, or found little distinction between bitter or sweet, poverty or pre-eminence, as if it did not lust after anything, not even in what touches the spirit.

Even if it had been left to the freedom of my will to prefer, to desire, and to wish, I do not think I would have been able to, because my will seemed dead and reduced to nothing, or at least utterly denuded of all imperfect desires and of all willing of my own. Since I was united with the divine will in this way, all things and inner states were just as pleasing to me, and as one. Oh what a good exchange has he made who gives his will to the Beloved in this way! What spiritual gain accrues from this losing of his own will in the will of the Beloved! For the little he gives he receives so much.

Chapter CXXVII

From now on day began to break through more and more in my soul: the Beloved began to let a few rays of light shine in it to drive out the dark mists that seemed to cover the intellect, so that it would be able to understand the divine truths more easily, and to live in him through a faith that was purer and more clear; to which end he made some perfect virtues known to me in his grace, and made me pursue them, sweetly inciting my will and affection to practice them faithfully. Principal among them was the virtue of humility with all that pertains to it, its qualities and abilities, and the practice thereof with ease and satisfaction in all occasions that befell me, as is told in what follows.

The principal effects and products this new grace and mercy fostered in my soul were that they led me very deep into myself, in a special manner, where they taught me, and showed me by means of a clear light the secret and hidden ways of deepest humility, and of reducing my self, even to nothingness. They also showed me the light of discernment that allowed me to recognize the subtle ruses, deceitful thoughts, and self-searching impulses of nature, which it expresses, or affects, or mixes in most of its outward behavior, and in all it does or leaves undone, always fleeing whatever may humble or diminish its self. Its inborn and deeply rooted pride turns it into a sworn enemy of true humility, and it sets itself against this divine or Christian virtue with all the power and powers it can muster within itself, since it considers this virtue its direct opposite.

For this reason I considered it a very particular grace that the Beloved had opened my eyes so that I could recognize these deceits and falsehoods, and flee from them once I had come to know them. This light seemed very useful, even necessary to me, that I might pursue the spiritual death of nature with steadfast courage in all things, and everywhere. For a person who walks with her eyes open in the full light of day is not likely to stumble easily.

Chapter CXXIX

These are the features and states of the soul which the spirit of humility, described above, began to impress on me and work in me: it began to ground true humility in a foundation that went deeper and deeper in me, through a very thorough and clear knowledge of my own *Nothingness*. I also felt that I was excessively small, so that it now appears to me that my dwelling was placed in an excessively deep valley, as in an essential humiliation, contempt, distrust, and annihilation of myself.

In previous years I seemed to have gradually walked upward in clarification of inner purity, in knowledge of God, in exaltation of the spirit, and in ascensions of the soul, all through a fiery and burning love, and other contemplations; now I seemed to be walking down, and sinking downward, not in creatures, in the senses, or in nature, but always through more knowledge of greater annihilation, deeper sinking into, and more thorough knowledge of my own unworthiness. Therefore I would sometimes say to the Beloved with heartfelt intention, and from the inner recesses of my heart: Beloved, reduce me to nothing, I am not worthy to live, to be counted among the number of your creatures, and together with them to enjoy your general benefactions, acts of grace, and benedictions, not even the benefaction of being served, fed, and cared for in the body together with creatures that lack reason, and yet I would not dare to compare myself to them because I have often dishonored God, the utmost good, and made him angry, as they have not.

Out of this humble knowledge flows an unconquerable peace, since such humble thoughts can never be disturbed anymore; on the contrary: they feed one's inner peace, mixed with a sweetness and tenderness of divine love through which the soul is utterly refreshed, restored, and reinvigorated, so that it is able to suffer much, and to bear many blows with a joyful heart &, such as experience often made me taste that true humility, or a humble spirit, flows like a sweet sauce over all crosses and all suffering that come over us inwardly or outwardly.

It sweetens those elements of nature that are bitter and distasteful to itself; it alleviates all difficulties and burdens; it transforms all things into inner rest, peace, and satisfaction of the heart.

Chapter CXXX

I think that a person who has reached this degree of humility will not be saddened, perturbed, distressed, or tormented by anything, or by whatever may happen to himself or another, nor will his soul be oppressed; rather it will be able to preserve equanimity, serenity, and inner peace without any disturbance. All torments of men or evil spirits cannot touch this soul. Why? because she is so small, she is able to crawl through everything, and slide away with quiet skill from all that might sadden her, oppress her, or impose suffering or torment on her, like small fish who are able to skillfully crawl through the meshes when they are caught in the net, so that they can save themselves and not lose their freedom in swimming. Oh, what treasure does a soul acquire who has reached this state! A treasure nobody can take from her because the peace she possesses cannot be overcome.

Even if she sees that people hate her, persecute her, ridicule her, hold her in contempt, insult her, speak ill of her, lie to her &,

even if she is addressed by some people who owe her respect in an impolite, gruff, irreverent, disrespectful and insulting manner, she does not torment herself in this, but with a sweet turning inward and sinking downward in her own smallness she lightly loses it in God, thinking people are right indeed to hate me, to persecute me, to spurn me &, and some are right not to respect me as they should, for what is there in me that can bring them to love me and to be loyal to me, or kind, and polite, to have a good opinion of me, and so on?

Moreover, she does not feel any bitterness toward anyone, nor does she turn away from anyone because she believes from the bottom of her heart that no injustice is done to her, and that is why she is not able to complain about anybody, nor does she know anybody to complain about, or accuse, or judge more imperfect than herself. And when she sees that they have come to themselves, or to knowledge, and admit their guilt & she will forgive them with good grace, without remembering the evil that went before and that they did to her. She is kind to them, and gentle, as if they had never wronged her in any way; she behaves toward them as if they were her best friends, she excuses their faults and makes amends for them as best she can, not seeing the evil and lack of virtue that are in them; she thinks God allowed it to be so for her greater good, and in this way she puts all things to right without losing peace over anything.

Chapter CXXXI

The same holds when she feels herself in poverty of spirit, as if abandoned by God, when it seems to her that her divine Beloved does not want anything to do with her anymore, nor to engage in any intimacy with her as he did before, but seems to behave toward her in such a strange manner as if he had cast her out and rejected her from his countenance; for then she also thinks God is right indeed, and he has good reason to abandon me like this &, for what is there in me that could please God, or make me worthy of his love and his favors? I have often abused his gifts of grace, and ignored them &, and so I praise him and thank him because he is just. It is too much even for him to suffer me among the number of creatures that stand before his real presence. Far be it from her to wait, or to desire that God may come to her, or come over her; no, she has sunk below all this already, and she is most satisfied with her *nothingness*.

I felt as if insatiable in this belittling of myself, in this sinking downward, in this descent into the abyss, the more I sank into my *nothingness* and made my dwelling in that emptiness, the more I felt the inclination to sink deeper and deeper still, always. Oh what a great gift of grace this was, and the Beloved gave it to me! It seemed much greater to me, much more profitable for me, and of greater value than all the enlightenment I ever received from God, and all the divine works he ever wrought in my soul. This grace, this humble foundation put me on paths so certain to guide me to God that there could not be any afterthoughts, nor any shadow of falsehood or deceit.

It seemed to me that the same humility laid the foundation in me of such deep-rooted, steadfast, and perfect virtues, as if it had produced a congregation of all virtues, and given birth to them in me, so that it seemed as if my whole humanity was as if preserved in them, even though I did not always remain in them to such a degree of perfection, to my sorrow, since much time and practice had to be expended before those virtues became as if essential, or natural in me.

But as long as I was in that state of humble spirit no vices nor love of self, seeking of self, pleasing of self, or respect of self could find a place in me; during that time the soul is as if unsinful, and no evil seems to be able to touch her. The spirit of humility made the foundation of my being so pure, so refined and unmixed, so attuned to God, so quiet, so clear and so overmuch at peace, so removed from all creatures & that if I had had to die before I could have said an Our Father I could not have better prepared or disposed myself, since I felt always prepared to separate from my body at once; there seemed to be no part left for me down here to cling to with any affection, or to desire.

Chapter CXXXII

Even though I stayed in this deep valley of humility in which I had sunk, small, fully at peace, beyond all claim or expectation of being visited, entertained, or lovingly caressed by the Beloved, he suddenly let a clear ray of divine light shine and sparkle inside my soul, as if from a clear sun that pulled my soul up to God with all its glorious love, ever higher and sweeter, as if it had been touched a little by an ascending fire of burning love that made me climb firmly toward God.

This was no wonder, since it is very typical of this state of utmost humility, like what you see happening to the dew that usually tends to fall most in deep valleys and when day draws near, when the sun begins to shoot its rays at the earth it pulls that dew up into the air, far above the earth; so too the dew of divine grace tends to fall most in empty and humble souls that are sometimes pulled up by the divine sun, above themselves and above all things that are here below.

This divine ray gave me some insight, that I might see and know some properties and conditions pertaining to the *Nothing*, or to a soul that has been brought to nothing: what is it that assists the soul in being honestly reduced to nothing, what is it that delays this process, and what is it that runs contrary to it; but I do not see how I could express this insight as clearly as it was given to me; I understood and saw that honest *Nothing* is receptive to God alone; that the aim of all my endeavors had to be to acquire it to perfection and to remain steadfast in it, because God can only live unhindered in a soul that has been reduced to nothing, and work his most beloved pleasure in and through her.

This *Nothing* consisted, it seemed to me, of a total spiritual death, both in the inner and the outer being, at all times, without ever allowing for any life, or feeling any natural love or inclination for whatever is created and not God. *Nothing* leaves all things untouched in God, losing them in him and reducing them to nothing; its inner foundation must be utterly empty of these, without caring for them and without any images of them our thinking might cling to beyond God because it is arrested by them. It comes to me that I have written at greater length about this in previous years, in the states of the soul I was in then, and there is therefore little point in repeating it all again here.

It was necessary for the Beloved to renew that knowledge and information in me, since that light had all but vanished completely because of the inner darkness I had to suffer for so long.

Chapter CXXXIII

I was given more inner teaching: I had to practice staying in the humble state described above, humiliating myself, making myself smaller, and reducing myself to nothing in a more unimaged and nobler manner, in greater simplicity and loneliness, and with greater ardor, which made me lose myself at once and forget myself and all other things outside myself, as if immediately devoured by the unmeasured greatness of God, like a small spark that is thrown in a great fire and seen no more.

I was happy in this state of being lost and devoured; I would have been satisfied if I had been allowed to stay in it for ever, since being in such a state I would not be able to sin; because the part that feels and is sensual has all its powers taken away from it then, and whatever they can freely achieve, in utter subjection to the spirit, which is in utter subjection to God.

There is then a great, ardent, and deep silence in the inner and outer being and in the powers of feeling and reason, especially at the time of prayer; this inner silence is a sweet rest or sleep of love in God, perhaps similar to that the loving Bride enjoyed when the Beloved ordered all creatures not to wake his Bride from that sweet sleep of love until she herself would want them to. This resting in God & came to me most often after I had suffered through some hard labor, or painful and difficult struggle, &; the whole being was restored by this, strengthened, and nourished.

Chapter CXXXIX

Once, when I was in prayer, I was shown a great number of religious people and people dedicated to God, and they were moving away from God. The Beloved seemed to rouse me to pray for them, or better: the spirit of God itself prayed in me and through me with unspeakable sighs that God's goodness might keep them back with a strong hand and tie them closer to him than before.

This spirit brought with it a very tender and loving love to God, with a thirst for the salvation of all men, that God, the good supreme and most deserving of love, might be loved, honored, praised, and glorified by them for all eternity. The loss of a soul inflicts great sadness on me, because it wounds my heart in tender love that God will be hated and reviled by that soul for all eternity. This arises from a reverent knowledge of God's more than infinite honor; I would have wanted to die for every soul.

The Beloved also made me pray for all those who inflicted torment, suffering, and persecution on me; for those who held us in contempt and spoke ill of us, for those who were our opponents and subverted our good intentions; for those who showed themselves to us in dissembling, with two faces; I felt as sweetly and lovingly inclined to all those as I felt toward my best friends; I prayed to the Beloved that he would not count it for them as sin, but repay them with blessings and gifts of grace.

More in particular a person was shown to me in spirit who had inflicted much suffering on me, because she had been incited to do so by the Evil One; this happened in such a vivid way as if she had been present there with her body. Love seemed to move me to pray for her, that she might desist, through God's unmeasured mercy, and come to a blessed end.

It seemed to me that it was very pleasing to the Beloved that I had forgiven from the heart, and that I had prayed for those who inflict evil on us, persecute us, and hate us; that I wished them all manner of good, without any grudge, as I wished it for myself. The Beloved gave me to understand that such prayers are answered much sooner because they spring from an honest foundation of love.

And so we must love our enemies, according to the teaching of Jesus Christ. The Beloved gives me the same tender love and the same goodness of heart toward my enemies as toward my best friends; indeed, even more toward my enemies because I feel a tender compassion for them in all they do that displeases God. When I am with them, or when they meet me somewhere, I have no memory of the suffering they inflict, or inflicted on us.

Chapter CXLIII

I can say very little about the state I was in during the whole octave of Pentecost. I felt as if I were filled with God, and as if I were standing in his presence always; indeed, I dare say without having to be without him for a single second, to the extent that resting, breathing, and living in God seemed to have become my nature, in a way that could be clearly felt, as if face to face, without difficulty or labor, only with a quiet attentiveness to keep the spirit unmixed, pure, cut off, and separated from the lowest part, without allowing the same to participate in any way.

Only the spirit was allowed with the Beloved; the slightest intrusion of the sensual part seemed to upset everything and to cause such coarse mediatedness that it became as if night inside, and God could no more be seen.

The spirit was then apparently far removed from the lowermost part, as if they could no longer have anything in common: whenever a distracted thought would come by, or some stirring in the lowermost part, to assail the spirit in its silence and rest, it appeared as if very far away from me, and I had nothing but a blurred memory, or vision of it, as of something that did not touch me, or could not touch me; and so the spirit stayed steadfast and untouchable in its turning toward God in an unimaged way; the spirit was able to gently avoid all opposition of the lowermost part, skillfully gathering itself or pulling itself inward as in a small dot, deeper in the ground, without opposing any resistance, just turning its attention and awareness away from it.

The Beloved also gave me the gift of grace that I seemed very steadfastly filled, illuminated, and as if possessed by some divine light and clarity, which produced in me a miraculous purity of the heart that consists of emptying it of all creatures, and of my own self.

Chapter CLIV

One Christmas Day I found myself placed in the unity of God's undivided being; I could not stay with my thoughts on anything, or achieve anything with my inner powers, than to stand and stay in this unity; I seemed to want to trouble myself because I found myself so devoid of any deeply felt action of love, amazement, humility, knowledge, or awareness of the great mystery Holy Church teaches us, thinking instead that it is good to wonder at this with reverent love, and to adore it, since it is a mystery of mysteries full of the food of love, &.

As I was thinking about this there came into me a knowledge that gave me comfort, as follows: if you have God, and if you are taken into God, or the unity of God in this way, you have love and you are in love, since God is love itself; you therefore have a love much more noble in its being; you do not have this or that, but you have the *All*; no parts, but the whole. I did not seem to be able to know anything, or bring anything into my mind, nor did there seem to be anything except this divine unity.

Once it was given to me to see the Beloved Mother, to honor her, to love and adore her as if swallowed, overshadowed, surrounded by the unity of the divine being. It seemed to me that the blessed in heaven look at each other and love each other in this way.

I also sometimes seem to see the Evil One, full of hatred and envy because God so ennobles this little worm of the earth, lifts it up and makes it divine; and scoffing at him the Beloved said that God lifted up the small one, and that he, the Evil One, had lost this beauty and nobility through his pride. I also scoffed at him because of a temptation he had once infused in me, when I was in the previous deserted and suffering state of soul, telling me: what a nice God you have, who you try to serve so faithfully, who is so hard on you, and who has forgotten, rejected, and deserted you, &; if you want to serve me I shall give you many delights, &; was that not a coarse and evil temptation by such a cunning devil?

Chapter CXLV

Once when I had been to Holy Communion, God gave me the gift of grace to teach me and have me experience through faith a little of a profound finding, or meeting, and enjoyment of his unimaged being, in a way that seemed very different to me from what I had known or understood until then.

This profound enjoyment I am talking about is not dependent on, or subject to any illumination of any divine light that enters your being and grows stronger or weaker, darker or lighter; rather it is accompanied by a steadfast, simple, unimaged, and essential divine light, without your noticing, or knowing that it is a light, because it is so simple, silent, and subtle in itself.

The effects it produces are these: it possesses and fulfills the inner and outer senses, the highest and the lowest powers, and all affections of the soul; and it pulls them together, or unites them all at once, as in a mass; and so it fashions a simple vision of that unchangeable, simple, unimaged, divine being, and remains caught in it with a very simple breathing in it, as in sweet air. This breathing in God happens out of God's own essence, it is not the soul's own doing, not mixed with its own intent or intelligent discernment.

This simple breathing in God is the essential enjoyment I am talking of; it should not be called an ardent contemplation and enjoyment of God, but a simple and essential one, since the ardent one is linked with a turning inward, a being estranged and removed from all things, &; but this way is very different: it is not turned inward, but also not turned outward; it is simple; it is strong and not weak, as is the ardent one; it also has more freedom, and dominion over all things because the senses and other powers do not oppose it, nor prevent it from steadfastly clinging to, contemplating, and enjoying God, since they are so united and commingled with the spirit, because they share one and the same goal with it.

Even if the body is busy with simple work, &, the senses remain so cut off from it, and so denuded that they do not seem to draw any forms or images toward themselves; and it is also as if the creatures they deal with, hear, see, taste, and feel, are in some way swallowed up in God, and changed.

Chapter CXLVI

In this state the soul is not pulled upward above the senses, nor pulled inward under them; it is with freedom in the middle of all things, not noticing, nor experiencing with any intellectual discernment that might arrest it at any point, anything but the unity of God in all things, and above all things.

Once you are placed in this state it does not appear to be permissible for you to intentionally practice any virtue, nor to notice them with discernment, not even the love of God, not only not in actuality, but also not to have it in your thoughts as an image, because this most simple enjoyment of God is then subjected to mediatedness, and pulled out of its loneliness into multiplicity.

Not that she is indeed devoid of practicing the love of God, nor of practicing virtue when the time requires it, or when circumstances demand it, since she could not remain for a while in that simple enjoyment of God except if all virtues were an essential part of her, and at their highest degree of perfection, and as if changed into nature, at least for that time; but she forgets the virtues as she forgets other creatures, to be more intent on the supreme good alone, and more attentive to it; she also forgets love and yet she truly loves indeed, without noticing or knowing, since that noticing or knowing would be a seeing, or knowing beyond God alone; for that is the most refined simplicity, where that unimaged *One* is the soul's only goal.

Chapter CXLVII

The loneliness of the spirit I wrote about before was only internal, in a space in the soul, in separation from the lowermost part and from other creatures: by not noticing them I discovered a lonely desert in my inner being, and I felt inclined to silence, both in my inner and my outer being, to be able to all the more freely enjoy this loneliness, this inner space, &.

But the state I am writing about now does not have such choice or such intent, it is more indifferent and freer toward all things in which there is any sign of God's holy will; she is much freer, disentangled, the fear of losing God or her peace does not occupy such a great space in her mind, because her loneliness follows her everywhere, and not ardently, but simply.

The spirit is not lifted up here either, nor does it sink down, as in other states and exercises; but the soul seems to live in God, to breathe, to rest, &, in the middle of all things, in equanimity without disturbance; she does not have to turn herself away from anything, nor flee from anything; for God's loneliness seems to meet her indifferently above all things.

Oh good *Jesus*, who generously gave us insight into this truth, be good enough to help us to steadfastly practice it for the love and glory of your name.

The spirit seems to be driven even further to a broader explanation of what is written above, namely that the spirit becomes so generous, wise, learned, and magnanimous in this, that she would even laugh at the gifts of God that are given to the senses, as if they were child's play, or milk, what is proper to children because they are still weak and unable to digest solid food.

In this state the soul would not even want to look at these things, since she has been weaned off the breasts given to suckling babes, and is more inclined toward more pious food; I understand these gifts given to the senses to be sweet comfort, visitation, union as felt by the senses, the influx of love and its passions as felt by the senses, tender submissions, &, for the spirit sees and understands well that all those states are lower, and less perfect, because they are subject to many changes of the senses and their clinging to worldly things; that those souls usually vacillate in their exercises: now of good cheer, then cast down; now joyful, then somber; now at rest, then not at rest; now fiery, passionate, and strong, then flaccid, weak, and sick, as the flood of grace ebbs and flows, especially when they involve their heart, or affection a little in this, with pleasure and enjoyment of nature.

If, I say, they do not let these things in them go away unnoticed, as if they were not there, without wishing for them or not wishing for them, without wanting or preferring anything, having only that unchangeable, unimaged being of God as the only aim of their soul; or, for those who have not progressed to the extent that they cling firmly to God's will and pleasure only, without mixing their own will, their own satisfaction, lust, delight, and advantage in with it, they will not allow the flood to flow under them, coming and going as God pleases.

Chapter CXLIX

Six years ago I was allowed to see a small ray of the beauty of the divine being inside my soul; from this small ray and this vision I proceeded to knowledge of the wondrous and unspeakable joy, delight, and supreme happiness the blessed enjoy in the contemplation of that divine being so utterly beautiful, so utterly delightful, and so utterly worthy of love. And I became so thirsty to be able to enjoy it together with them, face to face, utterly denuded of the darkness of faith and all the darkness dealing with creatures sometimes brings with it, that nothing in this life could please me more through the longing and the desire to be unbound and allowed to go and enjoy the divine being to the full.

I saw clearly what the Holy Prophet David says, that *God is dressed in light, as in a garment*; I greatly wondered how it was possible that a soul who had received this gift of grace only once, one small ray of the knowledge of God, as it was given to me then, could turn her face away for even a single second from that most beautiful being to turn herself for a while toward creatures that attract her attention, to notice them, and cling to them.

Because of this I fell all the more in love with that unique, supreme good, that utterly beautiful being so utterly worthy of love, that Majesty of God; I became much more intent on pleasing the pure and all-seeing eyes of God with a tender, amorous, and jealous love for him, because he is who he is.

Bibliography

Primary Works

Petijt, Maria. Ed. Michael a Sancto Augustino. *Het leven van de weerdighe moeder Maria a Sta. Theresia.* 1683-1684. 4 vols.

_____. Trans. Michael a Sancto Augustino. *Vita venerabilis matris Mariae a Sta Teresia.* Ms. Collegio S. Alberto, Rome, Post. III.

_____. Ed. J.R.A. Merlier. *Het leven van Maria Petijt (1623-1677), haar autobiografie* Gent: Faculteit Letteren en Wijsbegeerte, Rijksuniversiteit te Gent, n.d.

_____. Ed., trans. L. van den Bossche. "De la vie 'Marie-forme' au mariage mystique." *Etudes Carmélitaines* 16 (1931). 236-250 and 17 (1932). 279-294.

Translations

_____. Trans. Th. McGinnis. *Union With Our Lady. Marian Writings of the Venerable Maria Petyt of St. Teresa.* New York: Paulist Press, 1954.

Related Works

Bossche, L. van den. "Le grand silence du Carmel. La vocation de Marie de Sainte-Thérèse." *Etudes Carmélitaines* 20 (1935). 233-247.

Deblaere, Albert. *De mystieke schrijfster Maria Petyt (1623-1677).* Ghent: Koninklijke Vlaamse Academie, 1963.

_____. "Leven 'in de grond.' De leerschool van een Vlaamse mystieke."
Bijdragen. Tijdschrift voor filosofie en theologie 25 (2-3) 1964. 211-228.

Merlier, J. "Het leven van Maria Petyt (1623-1677). Het probleem van de eerste druk." *Ons Geestelijk Erf* 1975. 29-41.

Elizabeth Wolff & Agatha Deken

Jeanne Hageman

Sara Burgerhart, by Elizabeth (Betje) Wolff and Agatha (Aagje) Deken, is one of the finest examples of the Dutch bourgeois epistolary novel of the eighteenth century. Upon its publication in 1782, it was an immediate success; proof of its lasting popularity and appeal is the fact that it remains in print today.

Simply enough, *Sara Burgerhart* is the story of a 17-year old orphan who is living with her overly devout and old-fashioned aunt, an elderly spinster who does her best to force the young girl to conform to her sober and strict moral code. Sara's guardian, Abraham Blankaart, is a liberal-minded bachelor friend who resides in France for business purposes; much to her aunt's chagrin, he continuously encourages Sara to become an independent, free-thinking young woman. When life becomes unbearable at her aunt's house, Sara flees to the refuge of a boarding house, run by a kindly widow who acts like a surrogate mother to Sara. All of this occurs in the first 100 of the total 350 pages. The remainder of the book details Sara's passage into womanhood, with its dangers, distractions, and culmination in marriage and subsequently happy married life.[1] Why, then, if the story is so simple, so banal, has this book enjoyed such success? So much so even that it is the only eighteenth-century Dutch novel still in print today (Roosenschoon 36)? What interest can it possibly hold for today's readers? In their Introduction to the first edition, the authors argue that their novel contains "no misdeeds...no exaggerated virtues...in the whole book, there is not one single duel fought" (12). Yet, while certain aspects of the letters may seem quaint or outdated to the modern reader, many of the issues dealt with remain as pertinent today as when the novel was first published.

Let us first look briefly at the biography of the authors and the context in which they wrote. Although an exhaustive history of the eighteenth-century novel and of the Dutch middle-class that *Sara Burgerhart* addressed is beyond the scope of this chapter, certain aspects bear clarification. The eighteenth century, the Age of Enlightenment, was a period of discovery and invention throughout Europe. Educated people began to question openly the very institutions upon which society was built, reject ancient traditions and replace these with ideas based on science and reason. In literature and in society at large, the relatively new "genre" of "the novel" was gaining increasing acceptance. In fact, the eighteenth century is still often considered the era in which the novel as we know it today came into existence (Simons 13). In Holland, novels began, as constituents of a developing genre, to reflect more and more the values of the increasingly powerful Dutch mercantile and middle class. While still condemned by some, novels were not considered, by many authors and readers, simply a leisure time distraction. The Englishman Richardson had first popularized the concept that the novel could be used successfully to teach moral lessons (Naber 184) and this idea spread quickly to France and Holland.

As elsewhere in Western Europe, Holland — and its middle class in particular — experienced the eighteenth century as a period of economic prosperity. Colonial trade flourished and the wealthy merchant class could afford the luxuries which previously had been reserved for the nobility. In his introduction to *Sara Burgerhart* (viii), Knappert describes the era as follows:

> "The tea rooms of the patrician residences reflected calmly in the water of the Amstel and Vecht, where white swans floated. Lavishly adorned carpet knights in lightly powdered wigs, their three-cornered hats under their arms, wearing red cloth vests with little

swords wrapped up in silk, minced across the
polished floor on their way into the cool sitting room
where they bowed with coquettish elegance to young
ladies with tall hairdos wearing dresses with square
necklines who were sitting at tables with mosaic
inlay, playing cards and chatting" (my translation).

New wealth and the leisure time that came with it allowed
many in the middle-class to provide their children with new
opportunities for education and travel. Yet it was this very education
which made it possible for children to begin questioning the values
that had enabled their parents to prosper, seeking to change a society
which they felt was too rigidly structured and whose rules were
grounded in tradition rather than in reason. A conflict between the
two generations, parents and children, was inevitable. It was this era
which Elizabeth Wolff and Agatha Deken described in their novel;
they knew it very well, having grown up with the constraints and
prejudices against which they would rebel.

Elizabeth Bekker was born in 1738 in Vlissingen (Zeeland),
the youngest of five children. Her mother sent her to a French school
and insisted that Elizabeth receive lessons in music, drawing and
English.[2] When Elizabeth was 13, her mother died and from then on,
she enjoyed a great deal of freedom, more, at least, than was
customary for a young girl of the time. She showed an early passion
for literature and studied theology and philosophy on her own. At the
age of 21, she married a 52-year old clergyman and went to live with
him in Beemster, in northern Holland. This was not a love match, but
Elizabeth respected her husband, who, in turn, allowed her much
freedom. Yet, her liberal beliefs and the fact that she wrote did not
earn her favor with her husband's conservative Protestant
congregation (Gielen 112).

Indeed, Elizabeth, or Betje as she was known, had begun to
write even before her marriage: original poems and short stories,
while she also translated from the German, English and French,
including works by Diderot, Maupertius, and Pope (Vieu-Kuik 27-
33). In 1776, she began a correspondence with the spinster Aagje
Deken. Born in 1741 in Amstelsteen and raised in an Amsterdam

orphanage, Aagje earned a living as a companion to elderly women, and, though not so well educated as Wolff, she, too, greatly enjoyed literature. Following the death of Wolff's husband in 1777, the two women entered upon a domestic as well as literary joint venture, which was to last until Elizabeth Wolff's death in 1804 (Aagje did not survive her loyal companion by more than ten days). Among several works which the two women created together, *Sara Burgerhart* is generally considered the best.

By the mid-1700s, the epistolary novel had become a dominant form of the genre throughout Europe. Elizabeth Wolff was familiar with Richardson's work (e.g., *Pamela*, 1740-41; *Clarissa*, 1747-48; and *Charles Grandison*, 1753-54) as well as with Rousseau's *Nouvelle Héloise* (1761).[3] Historically, *Sara Burgerhart* is noteworthy as the first Dutch epistolary novel; some even maintain that it was the first truly original Dutch novel of any kind. Prior to its publication, the novels that were popular in Holland were either translations of English, French, or German originals or close copies with such titles as *Dutch Pamela* or *Young Grandison*. Clearly, Wolff and Deken were well aware of the fact that they were entering into a new realm, for they wrote in the Introduction to the first edition that most of their compatriots felt that "no native writers can create interesting works" (10). Acknowledging that it was necessary to write novels in Dutch for the Dutch people, they proposed to do precisely that:

> Fully aware of these notions, we hope to see that day [when original novels will be written in Dutch], and at the same time, we have undertaken to publish an original Dutch novel. A novel aimed at the average Dutch person's life. We will paint Dutch characters for you, people who can really be found in our country.

As if to avoid any possibility of error, the title page states clearly: "not translated." The emphasis on the book's originality is seen by some as almost a publicity stunt on the part of the authors

(Buijnsters 10). Still, the immediate success of *Sara Burgerhart* proved the authors's point: well written and interesting novels could and should be written by Dutch authors. However, the fact that this novel was the first of its kind in Holland does not sufficiently explain its continued popularity. In order to understand this, we must re-examine more closely the content of the novel.

For the authors of *Sara Burgerhart*, the novel is first and foremost a lesson about morality. In many ways it is a typically middle-class morality, which envisages a happy marriage as its ultimate goal. Yet, it would be wrong to consider the proposed ethical principles completely typical for the age. Instead, the authors offer an enlightened morality which considers reason and knowledge far superior to blind faith. Although marriage may well be the ultimate goal, the path suggested by the authors is far from traditional.[4] Children are to be treated with respect and their opinions taken seriously, and they should, above all, marry for love, for it is by this means that they will be assured a happy home life.

Sara is portrayed as totally justified in fleeing her overly devout aunt's house so that she can live the life of a "normal," carefree 17-year old girl. Notice that she does not run away in order to embark upon a life of sin, but rather so that she might enjoy the finer aspects of an enlightened household. This is carefully described in the Widow Spilgoed's letter to Sara:

> My house is at your service. It is fairly large, very pleasant and has a pretty little garden with a summer house where we hold our little concerts, because we love music, and I hear that you do also. We read many tasteful works in different languages. I have three servants and try to make the lives of all my ladies as pleasant as possible (27).[5]

At the same time, Sara is portrayed quite realistically: she is far from perfect and makes mistakes of her own in the process of discovering what she wants from life. While she is basically a good child, she is free spirited at times and does not always heed the advice of older, wiser people in her environment. It is this head-strong behavior that causes Sara to be almost raped by "Mr. R," who has been able to take advantage of Sara's naiveté.[6]

It is this careful attention to realism, both physical-circumstantial (the people themselves, as well as the setting) and psychological, which provides, perhaps, the key to explaining the novel's continued popularity. It is almost as if the reader is looking into a mirror (Simons 16-7). With a few minor exceptions, the characters are so carefully described and developed that, by the end of the novel, the reader knows a great deal not only about their present life but also about their past.

The authors's adept manipulation of the epistolary form allows them to really provide the reader with a complete character, while at the same time maintaining the illusion of immediateness. On the one hand, we find letters which are interrupted either due to the lateness of the hour or to an unexpected visit, which provides a feeling of "writing to the moment;" and at the same time, characters are more than happy to write, when asked to do so, about previous events (Buijnsters 13). In many instances, the reader is also provided with the several sides there are to a story, and is left to make his or her own judgement. For example, Sara writes to Abraham Blankaart, her guardian, after she has run away from her aunt — but so does the aunt. And "Mr. R" describes in detail his plans for Sara's abduction; later, we can read Sara's account of the incident in a letter to her fiancé Hendrick.

The authors also introduce various epistolary techniques and styles in order to hold the reader's interest, while maintaining the distinct character traits of each individual. In keeping with their enlightened education, the girls, Sara, Letje, and Anna, exchange letters containing poems and songs in French, Dutch and English. While the men tend to avoid poetry, they demonstrate good breeding by their ability to cite pertinent verses from various classical works.[7] Aunt Suzanna and her pious friends quote verses from the Bible, showing not only their religious zeal but also their total lack of understanding of enlightened thinking.

If it were only a study of eighteenth-century society and morality, *Sara Burgerhart* might not easily hold the modern reader's interest. It is therefore also important to mention the fact that, throughout the novel, bigotry and prejudice are repeatedly condemned. While I have already mentioned the authors's treatment of Aunt Suzanna and her cronies, many other striking examples could be cited which would illustrate just how far ahead of their time these two women were. For example, they dared to criticize the idea that inter-faith marriages were somehow unnatural, an idea that persists to this day. When Hendrick Edeling's father forbids him to marry Sara because she is a member of the Dutch Reformed Church and not a Lutheran, Hendrick enlists the help of his brother and uncle, both of whom are sympathetic to his plight. In addition, Sara's guardian writes to Hendrick's father with an impassioned plea for religious tolerance. Using both reason and the Bible to strengthen his case, he writes to the father, "Are you then the Pope, or are you a father? Can you ever be mistaken, or are you infallible?" (159) When the father finally cedes, he admits that his original decision had been based on tradition rather than reason: "It is difficult for a man who has followed his master for so long to say he is wrong; and even more difficult when he must say it to his very own children" (274). Wolff and Deken further criticize pedantry in their treatment of Cornelia Hartog, the 30-year-old spinster who also lives with the Widow Spilgoed and who attempts to show off her education at any occasion. Although Hartog writes only two letters, she often appears in letters by others as a subject of conversation.[8] In her own conversation, she insists on quoting famous authors and philosophers; in the end, she is unable to find happiness because of her education and attitude.

While certain aspects of *Sara Burgerhart* can perhaps be interpreted from a feminist point of view, Cornelia Hartog provides a good example of the limits which the authors placed on a woman's emancipation. Women are encouraged to be independent in many areas, but there must be limits to their independence. While they should be allowed to interact with young men, it must be under the watchful eye of an adult, and such contacts should serve only to allow them to make the wisest decision in their choice of a husband. As Sara's abduction proves, even a little too much freedom can have catastrophic results. Girls should be educated, but at the same time, they must avoid becoming too educated, as this might prevent them from attaining the ultimate goal, that of marriage and family. This type of education is aimed at turning them into pleasant conversationalists and good mothers who will in turn be able to educate their own children. The idea that there may be options other than marriage is never considered by either the women or men in the novel. Even Abraham Blankaart, the confirmed bachelor, regrets his own unmarried state, therefore taking it upon himself to spare Willem Willis his own fate by facilitating the latter's marriage.

Sara Burgerhart is far more interesting than many other epistolary novels. On one level, it provides us with a detailed, realistic description of the eighteenth-century Dutch middle-class, which is certainly of importance from a historical standpoint. But more importantly, it deals with real issues, real emotions and real people. The reader can identify with the different characters' thoughts and emotions. The generation gap, the uncertainties of puberty, first love, and betrayal, and ideas and problems of this kind transcend the centuries. Elizabeth Wolff and Agatha Deken's thoughtful and realistic portrayal of such emotions has allowed their *Sara Burgerhart* to endure the test of time.

NOTES to the Introduction

1. While the letters themselves end shortly after Sara's marriage, the authors have been kind enough to supply the curious reader with an epilogue which assures us that even ten years later, Sara "is living happily with her honest husband and is already the mother of five good children..." (351).

2. Although Dutch was spoken in the home and at work, it was considered vulgar by the better educated. French was the language of the upper classes and was considered the hallmark of a good education.

3. It is unclear whether she read Richardson in English or in Dutch translation. His work was readily available in Dutch long before *Sara Burgerhart* was written; *Clarissa*, for example, was translated by Johannes Stinstra between 1752 and 1755 (Buijnsters 7).

4. Sara realizes very quickly that her aunt, Suzanna Hofland, is being duped by a shameless charlatan, the preacher Brother Benjamin, who eventually runs off with her life savings. The aunt's blind devotion is in fact her downfall.

5. The idea of an enlightened household is reiterated much later; in Letter 159, Sara describes her own future household (310).

6. "Mr. R" is a libertine and the only aristocrat in the novel. When his evil is uncovered at the end of the novel and he is forced to flee, we witness, again, the triumph of bourgeois values.

7. An exception to this occurs in Cornelius Edeling's letter which describes in detail the marriage of Sara and Hendrick Edeling (Letter 160). A copy of the bridal poem is enclosed with the letter (316-18).

8. One of Cornelia Hartog's two letters is an anonymous poison pen letter to Sara's guardian, for she is jealous of Hendrick's love for Sara (Gielen 119).

Translations by Jeanne Hageman and Kristiaan Aercke

10TH LETTER

[Miss Sara Burgerhart to Miss Aletta de Brunier][1]

Douce et tendre Amie![2]
Je suis enragée at the old shrew — my aunt;[3] I don't want to stay another week; it's as if I'm living in Hell. My aunt has many of her Master Satan's characteristics; and Brecht deserves a fine pension in his hellish kingdom.[4] Oh well! Someone is knocking; I won't answer and I won't open the door either. Hush! I hear her hobbling down the stairs, grumbling. Have a nice trip down. *Ma chère*, I must describe a scene to you that will not disappoint you.

Wednesday morning, she was raving like a madwoman because I was playing a few new arias. (Just like a shrew, isn't it?) She was being helped out by that savage old maid, who dared tell me that she too was tremendously offended.[5] Just then someone rang. Brecht, who is the perfect type of a round-bellied old woman, waddled to the door, and Auntie gave me a nasty slap on the ear because I kept playing. "Madam, Mister Benjamin is here." "Well good gracious, let our brother in then." In comes brother, a lazy sot of a fellow, in a purple frock (you have to wonder how such a crass butcher's apprentice learned to wear a frock). "Welcome, dear brother. How is everything going with you?" "It could be better, but my head, my head." "That's too bad, but you do ask a lot of yourself." "Yes, it's my duty; and how are you, sister? You seem a bit upset." "Yes, I am in fact; it's not always easy going, brother." (To Brecht:) "Oh girl, isn't there still something to eat? Then brother would stay here and eat with us." (To me:) "Say, dear little Sara," (I couldn't bear that, *dear little Sara*, when my cheek still burned from her slap), "hurry up and go make some thin pancakes; dear brother loves them so." I closed my keyboard and said, "All right, Auntie." I went into the kitchen and made them right away; but as I was baking I ate them all up myself. That's the first trick I've played on her; I rarely get to enjoy myself.

I have to do everything here because Brecht is a clumsy creature and snuffs an awful lot. I went to set the table while Brecht bungled about the house. Brecht eats with us, because, you see, Letje, she's *dear Sister Brecht*. Tartuffe would say something good, but this fellow prayed (for that's what they call that whining) for over fifteen minutes. What he whines about seems to be more the mumbled complaints of an ungrateful cow than the sighs of an uplifted heart rendering praise to God.

A l'ordinaire, I get my food served on my plate. Two little scoops of vegetables with a shred of cold meat from the previous day. I spread my napkin before my chest: "If I'm to be served my food like a child, then I must also be careful not to spill on myself." "Oh good gracious, as if you were a child!", said the gourmet, as he licked the butter off his finger and thumb from the cutlet in *robe de chambre*.[6] "That would be pleasant!", said Auntie. "Very pleasant," said sister Brecht. Then I got a bit more of the spinach that they scraped together and a piece of cutlet. At the same time, the saintly sister and brother had something to drink. I never get wine; Auntie says that it isn't good for me, and that could be true, because I am young and strong. "Come on, little Sara, clear the table; Brecht is a bit tired; the drudge is getting on in years." I did as I was told and brought the dessert out. "Where are the pancakes, Sara?" "They're in my stomach, Auntie." Snap, I flung off my napkin (unfortunately hitting the brother's silly wig), and went to my room to wait out the storm. You know, I'm fairly quick, which served me well then. Click, the door was locked. In the evening, up came the savage with a piece of bread and a glass of sour beer, and added "that I could never justify having played such a joke on so pious a person." "Get out of my room, scram" I said, and slammed the door shut. I ate the bread (it was good on top of the pancakes). I threw out the beer, and instead drank a bit out of my carafe, went to bed early and slept like a log. Upon arising, I got a slice of bread with a bowl of tea, that looked like dishwater. Auntie went out and didn't want me to show my face. That's where we are right now. It's possible that I'll give you this letter myself, maybe not: I don't know how this will all end.

I'll be there soon. The letter from the dear widow has strengthened my resolve. I would already have joined you, but I'm waiting for a letter and it doesn't arrive. Before I leave this house, I will write to her one more time, you know who I mean, ... but I suppose I can just as well do that when I'm with you.

Yes, dear miss, you are perfectly correct! One must only do good and live happily. Do you know what? Fine people can't be depended upon. Actually (in case you don't believe it), some of them are such pious souls that if the heads of these good people were as well organized as their hearts, they would be pure and holy...well, in short, Letje, Solomon, the wise King Solomon, is my man: one must treasure the good of one's life and one's work— but so be it, and that's the end of it.

It's getting dark and I don't get any light in my room; therefore, I can't write any longer. What will happen when I come downstairs? First, I will say good evening to Auntie, and, if she's bearable, go sit by her and knit; if not, I'll go into the sitting room;

the lamp will be burning in the entryway. I'll open my keyboard and play what I feel like playing. My compliments to the widow Spilgoed, and tell her as much as you judge necessary if you receive this before I can embrace you myself. Good night, dear soul.

Tout à toi,[7]
S. Burgerhart

11TH LETTER

[Miss Sara Burgerhart to Mr. Abraham Blankaart]

Honorable Sir, very worthy Guardian!

The stone has been cast: I've run away from there and I think it my duty to report everything to you. I arrived here at my new lodgings yesterday afternoon; I will tell you everything.

I often wonder if Auntie did not pester me so much these last weeks, to push me to this all the sooner. The following events led me to bring all of this to an even earlier end. In a French store, where I was buying a pair of gloves, I met one of my girlfriends from school, a certain Letje Brunier. The dear girl's father was Mr. Philips Brunier, a respected commission merchant in Germany and Italy. I am sending her letter along with this one, as well as a letter from the widow with whom she is living so that you will know everything that I know. Now the story.

Yesterday noon, Auntie went out for lunch. I got dressed and gathered up some things to take with me: some linens, as well as the jewels that you gave me before you went to France, even though I have never worn them, and a little bit of money (because she gives me nothing — not a cent). Brecht had the guts to ask me, "Where are *you* going?" "That's none of *your* business." "Then *you* can as well stay home." "If *you* think you can, just try to stop me." I can get angry but not quarrelsome and seeing that Brecht was putting her talents to good use, I changed tactics. "Brecht," I said, "If Auntie gave you those orders, then I will have to ask her to explain her reasons when she gets home. What is there to eat?" "Left-overs," she said. "Good, because I'm hungry, but first we shall drink to Auntie's health. Dear girl, go get a bottle of wine. Surely you have the key." "I do not, Miss Sara" (now that I mentioned the booze, I was suddenly addressed like this!). "You are lying, Brecht; if Auntie says anything about it, I will pay her for the wine." "Your aunt always keeps the key, but if Missy won't tell on me, I can still manage to get in." "Me, tell on you! Well, I would have to be quite crazy; go get it then and quickly." She left. I had noticed for quite some time that sister Brecht was tippling. Therefore, I appealed to her weakness. She had been in the cellar only a moment when I locked the door behind her and turned the bolts. Then I left the house, closing the front door behind me. What happened to the sister after that I don't know.

I left a note on Auntie's table so that she wouldn't worry. She has bugged me so terribly. She will likely remember this and I don't need to torture her, now that I'm out of her control, isn't that so, Sir!

How I long for a letter from you! I received the music. Oh, you're such a good man. If only I could tell you face to face how much I respect you, how happy I am that I am

Your humble servant and pupil,
Sara Burgerhart

P.S. I'm enclosing my address, too.

[After Sara's departure, Brother Benjamin takes it upon himself to write Sara's guardian to tell his side of the story.]

24TH LETTER

[Brother Benjamin to Mr. Abraham Blankaart]

Dear Sir

You have disturbed us, our people, and our way of life, and though the sisters would bear all of this with only quiet murmurs, so I feel forced to do the right thing for them, the good cause and myself, because I am their edifyer and the guardian of their house. Even though you are a great lord, I will show you that I am no foolish dog on the walls of our domestic Zion. You will see from my bark that I am no intruder, no busybody, but instead that I have a justified calling. It's true, my father had me learn to be a butcher; he was a man of this world, a cobbler, but my mother was in the church's service, because she was one of the church cleaning women, and if my father had not forbidden it, she would have had me pursue my studies; but he always asked "if she was raving mad." The means were lacking and I had a lot of spirit and strength, but much more calling for spiritual than for butcher's work. With my unconquerable aversion to all bodily labor, I heard my calling to another function. I obeyed. I taught the catechism to the children and the women of my neighborhood for a bite of food, because he who labors is worthy of his reward. The news of my talents spread quickly; the great people of this world gladly traded their worldly goods for my illuminations, even though their numbers were not large. This is how I became acquainted with the devout Mistress Hofland, whom you pursue like another Saul.[8] I spend many a happy hour with her. Now you know who I am; but you are an Atheist, an Arminian, a Socinian.[9] Yes, you are, I may well say, a Deist. You are a proponent of all godlessness, you defend a wanton miscreant, yes you do, yes you do. You also know that Mistress Hofland, like a true daughter of Gaius, tithes, yet you deny her her money; so that you are a church robber; yes you are. So, has little Sara not cost three hundred guilders? Well, now you once again show your worldly heart. It is true, we have kept the child in a truly sober Christian state, we clothed her modestly; I know better than you, just how much she cost every year on food and clothing — one hundred rixdollars! — but how many times has the dear Mistress not sighed over the sins of that wanton child, how many tears has she not cried, how many prayers has she not prayed for her poor soul, and how often has she not been sick from all these worries! Are all this time and care then worth nothing? Or do you think that you can have it all for nothing? No, you will, you must pay for it. But that's how you people are; you people can calculate and figure in earthly terms, but you people are blind when it comes to matters spiritual. Mistress Hofland shall have her money, I will force you, I — fear me ... In this god forsaken city there are still thousands of us. Woe, woe on he who would raise a finger against us!... We are zealous in defense of the pious, and our hate is holy. This warning carries great weight when it comes from the heart of a man such as

Your true friend,
Benjamin

33RD LETTER

[Miss Suzanna Hofland to Miss Cornelia Slimpslamp]

Dear Sister!
I want to thank you again for the blessings. Your little cookies are delicious and the home-grown grapes were very welcome. Dear Brother was also very talkative, and I have never heard our Brecht answer quite so candidly. The poor maiden, she has also her share of our folk's oppression, so that, if I may say, she has begun to drink to excess.[10] I'm really sorry that I did not make Satan have his way with our Sara. I should not have tried to rely only on my own feeble strength but should have used some more holy ruses. I know now that dear Brother had a deeper understanding of it than I. Why, yesterday he was making such an exquisite comparison between my neighbor the star-gazer and the Antichrist. It's as if he places himself above everything else, just like the Antichrist, when he is up

there standing on that thing that he put up on his house. Indeed! But I can't remember it all, or even understand it. In the application, he made it all pertinent to Sara. Brecht, the poor old drudge, cried, she was so impressed.

I'll now finally get to the point I wanted to write to you about. Well, Brecht saw Sara with a wild young gentleman. She thought that he was an actor, and she was dressed with even more levity than Pieternel's doll, the one you wrote to me about once. Her hairdo was at least a yard high, her skirt was all beribboned (Yes, I too wore such a devil's outfit in my unsaved state), you've never seen something like it in your life. You shouldn't live this way. She had white silk stockings on. Think, sister, white silk stockings, and expensive shoes and there was a bunch of rubbish and rags hanging from her watch fob. She was going about arm in arm with this man like the whore from Babylon. She whispered something to him, Brecht saw it clearly, and then he looked at the maid and laughed out loud, it was scandalous. Listen, Nell, I sometimes have a heavy heart over her, but Brother knows how to put my mind at ease. He asks me, shouldn't you have something to keep you humble, dear Suzanna? Isn't it better to have a heavy heart over your sins rather than to fall into Arminian tendencies? Or that your soul would be handed over to the devil like stolen goods because of your own righteousness? And then everything becomes so light for me to bear, so light, oh yes, so light.

But sister, you have advised me so often in times of emotional problems, and Solomon said, "Two are better than one." My dear, what should I do? Brother Benjamin wants me to sue Blankaart, if he doesn't pay me every last penny per the conditions agreed with her mother. All of her things are still here, all her clothes and other stuff of her mother, who was a gorgeous woman, and all of the family silver; but to get our hands on that; how will that go? Blankaart is a sad creature to have to deal with. Oh yes, he would bring me scandal. The infernal creature doesn't deserve so much stuff, she'll only use it to further corrupt herself anyway. To have to give it all up to them, is hard for a person to do. But I have to say that it was all my sister's property [...] Our salutations, and please send me your answer, will you?

Suzanna Hofland

[This very negative description of Sara's life since she left her aunt's house is contrasted sharply in the letters which Sara writes to her friends. As we see, she is not ready to sacrifice herself to anyone but the right man.]

40TH LETTER

[Miss Sara Burgerhart to Mr. Willem Willis]

My dear Willem![11]
Has the man become a child? Should I be displeased? And for what reasons? Because a good, proper young man, with whom I often find companionship, whose mother and sister are my most respected friends, finally, in the most fitting way, asks me if I do not have feelings for him. Really, that's all horrible stuff. Don't you fear that I will tell you, in a very theatrical manner:

"Moi, je suis femme, je ne pardonne jamais!"[12]

Really, Willem, I didn't think that you were so silly or that I was such a prude, but one of the two must surely be true. I shall tell you once and for all that you are the guilty one and not I. Do you understand, my friend? I will write to you like I would write to a young man whom I respect because he is worthy of the esteem of people who are much better than a nineteen year old girl can possibly be. I further trust that you will not abuse my sincerity.

Believe me when I say that until yesterday I had never thought that you looked upon me as anything more than a friend. My relations with you were nothing less than sisterly, and I have regretted a thousand times over that you were not my brother, even at the expense of half my inheritance. I accepted all of your courtesies for just that, courtesies, and, to put things as plainly as they are, I didn't wonder at all why you kept us company when I was at your mother's; rather, I thought, I had a right to it. What girl, so happy and so carefree, would not think this? But now that you have told me what you told me, told me without frills and with such touching countenance, I must take a new course of action because I could never forgive myself if I would allow an honest man who loves me to have great expectations built on idle hopes which would lower me to the despicable level of a coquette. It distresses me that your affection should have fallen upon the only stubborn girl who could possibly disappoint you in these matters. How can I help it? I don't know what love is and I haven't the slightest desire to learn about such a capricious business because I am completely happy with my present situation. From this I'm sure you can see that you have every possible reason to greet this person in as friendly a manner as ever, like someone you meet now and again, which brings me to my point: you would surely be unfair if you did not hold this person as dear as your heart demands.

Well Willem, well Willem, will you too start telling nasty satires about women? Who has told you that we always prefer silly fops rather than courteous young men? Some or other venomous, grumpy, old suitor, I suppose, who would be all too happy to shove the sins of his youth on to a sex, which is respected by the best men. May I just for once tell you how it really is? We girls are, for the most part, brought up in a very childish fashion. It seems that people think about the state of our souls like orthodox Muslims would. Our posture, our complexion, our poise receive all the attention. We are taught the art of pleasing, and for this reason we are given dancing and music teachers, for this reason we must learn French, and how to play card games, etc. I confess that a girl must not be sillier than I am now to realize, before she is old and ugly, that all of these pretty skills are no more than window-dressing and that she is capable of thinking as well as her brother Peter, as her cousin John, or as her Uncle Gerard. There are more such girls than it is generally believed. So what shall we do then, poor souls, when we see that our prospective husbands and masters are so exalted intellectually that they idolize us because of these petty skills and what's more (because they themselves want it), readily absolve us from everything that has merit according to reason. It is also true that many of you awful fancycocks are really unpleasant little men, and why should we choose boring mopes to keep us company before we have to? Remember this lesson and act accordingly. Then you will always be my favorite Willem.

My feelings for you are based on your good and honest character, and you have my friendship because of the thousands of good qualities that I have noticed in you as a son and brother. Be happy with that, because I assure you that there is nothing more there for you. Forget me and try to make yourself worthy of the love of a woman who would be far better for you than I ever could be. If you send her to me to ask for assurances about you, I will give reasons to satisfy her completely about you. I will be much obliged to you if you can overcome the pain that you might possibly feel when you take leave of me. I am,

Your true friend,
S.B.

91ST LETTER

[Mr. R to Mr. G]

Dear friend John![13]

How often must I tell you, you clumsy lout, that everything works on my nerves, and you most of all with your damned monkey business, quackery and silly invitations, with a few of our little darlings. What can I do, poor devil; why think, if not about the prettiest lass who ever had half the world in an uproar at the wink of her beautiful eyes? Crazy, yes, totally mad I am about her, and I have to play the role of the hypocrite in order to ever get near enough to her so I can whisper, "I love you." Women, women, what of this isn't your fault! Now we will settle our accounts, my proud little girl. For that "I don't use snuff and I never accept presents," I'll get my

revenge.[14] This is the first time that my ego, which is surely a
worthy match for yours, has ever been beaten, and by such a lovely
hand. Am I not a handsome man? Can't I prattle and chat with those
little fools? Reason with those little know-it-alls? Do I ever shock a
woman who is worthy of respect with the slightest ambiguous word?
Do I ever blurt out something which would cause anyone to blush
(even if only for decency's sake)? There must be an end to all this.
I don't usually live this way. But what sort of end? Do you ask
yourself that, my libertine friend? I, a man of good birth, of means;
and she, a bourgeoise with only a few cents to her name. You are an
absolute idiot, or you want to draw me out. Marriage? Are you
completely crazy? I will, I think, never go to such a desperate
extreme. *Freedom stimulates love.* This, as you know, is my motto.
As my mistress, she will be the *Sultan's favorite*, but my wife! For
shame! There you have it. That alone would suffice for *un homme de
mon goût* to find her unbearable.[15] You can marry her in four
months or so. I think I will be able to love her for about that long.
And you will be able to arouse my flagging desires then by making
it a bit more difficult for me to carry them out. You know very well
that "a libertine does not deserve an honest wife."

Now, you have seen her once, but I will blow you from the
face of the earth if you see her again in the next six months. O love,
love! What a rogue I may be when it comes to women but I will not
attempt to arouse my passion, which has for its goal only my own
satisfaction, with your blessed name. Crazy prejudice! It's a case of
the pot calling the kettle black, nothing more. What is it that my
Hartog says?[16] *Happiness is virtue.* You know, Jan, if she were not
so ugly, I would give her a kiss sometime for that little moral rule.
Let us be consistent in our heathen beliefs and not serve the devil for
naught.

Well, my carriage is waiting. I'm going to pick her up. The
lady, since she lives under my roof, I have also invited through her.
Oh, I know quite well that that one doesn't go out to such parties.
And the foolish girl who was there too. It all goes along with the
show. I already know how I must handle her! She will bend for me

since she doesn't fear me. It's possible that I will make remarkable progress in the next five hours.

[At this point R stops writing and goes off to meet Sara. After the outing, he finishes the letter.]

I am furious; I want to raise a ruckus with the whole world. I yell at Philip like I am drunk, and I would like to have you here in order to give you a good drubbing. Oh you despicable slave of my pleasures, who grovels for a pretty frock and a decent meal! What is there left to do, you ask with your air of a spendthrift beggar. Shut up and listen.

I ride off to her, full of elation. I am very politely led into the sitting-room by the widow. She tells me, "that she will indeed accept my polite invitation, for she thought that the Tragedy should be excellent, just reading it had inspired her greatly."[17] Where are you, Rembrandt, great painter of the passions that rage on our face! Paint it as quickly as you can. The blood rushed to my face, I felt a tingling in my brain. Such a shock...such a disappointment...She didn't notice. It was over in a flash. I pulled myself together, and, bringing my hand to my lips, I bowed respectfully, thanking her for the honor offered to me. Just then, the very sister of the three Graces floated in the room, full of happiness, full of life, full of spirit, her hair tastefully styled, and dressed with noble simplicity. I helped the three ladies into the carriage and when I was in, her valet jumped up next to mine. My loge was the only empty one left, so all eyes were on us. The widow is no longer young, but she is still, truthfully, a very pretty woman. My little girl? Well, you've seen her. And that silly girl is not ugly either.

Confound it, Jan, I had to be on guard. The widow...I don't know for sure, but I think that she, almost unnoticed, was observing all my movements. I honestly didn't dare use any of these tricks we usually use at first to explore the field. There was nothing to do but play the bad cards I'd been dealt as best as I could. I would call myself an idiot if I would not have been able to fool the widow, even if she had caught wind of something. I spoke mostly to her and in the way I always speak to proper women. We rode back in my carriage

and when I helped my charming lady out, I squeezed her hand but I
got no answer. Can one bear that? I took my leave politely in the
sitting room, humbly begging the ladies to accept my compliments.
Do you know Hein Edeling? But where would such a jackal as you
have ever met such a stiff character as he (although he is truly an
honest fellow, so I hear). It seems that he's the widow's friend....
Shut up, I tell you. I don't want to hear about it! Let him dare! Not
to worry. If it were Satan himself who wanted to marry her, that
cursed magician couldn't take her away from me. I have hopes, Jan.
And now what? I only have to find a way to get her. But can I really
avoid another disappointment? *Fortune helps the strong.* There, ten
more ducats, dog. Come by tomorrow morning, as soon as you've
read this, and bring the letter with you, or I will leave you on your
own.

R.

NOTES to the Translation

1. Sara describes her life with her aunt in a letter to a friend from
school. Her aunt, a devout, old-fashioned woman is being duped by Brother
Benjamin, a charlatan preacher with a habit of visiting around dinner time.

2. "Dear sweet friend." Like Elizabeth Wolff herself, Sara was
educated in a French school, and she uses numerous French phrases in her
letters. These phrases are supposed to prove that she has received a good,
enlightened education.

3. I am outraged.

4. Brecht is Aunt Suzanna's maid and housekeeper.

5. I have translated as "savage" Wolff's use of the word
"Hottentot," the name of a native people of southern Africa.

6. A breaded cutlet or chop.

7. Sincerely yours.

8. Samuel 1:9-31 tells the story of Saul, a man driven by jealousy to seek out David to kill him. But after having seen his sons die in battle, he commits suicide.

9. Benjamin refers to two religious sects of the time. In 16th-century Poland, Fausto Sozzini had created a church based on a form of Christian humanism; to escape persecution, he fled to Holland and established his church in Zevenburgen. Jacobus Arminius founded his church in the early 1600s; a number of his tenets were later incorporated into the Wesleyan Methodist Church (*Grote Winkler Prins Encyclopedie.* 25 Vols. Amsterdam: Elsevier, 1982. Vols. 2 and 20).

10. In an earlier letter to Mr. Blankaart, Aunt Suzanna describes that, upon her return home, she found Brecht drunk in the cellar. She pretends that the poor maid was so upset by Sara's action that she has taken to drink, even though Sara says this has been going on for some time.

11. Willem Willis is the brother of Anna Willis, one of Sara's girlfriends.

12. As for me, I am a woman, I never forgive.

13. Mr. R, who is never identified, is the villain who attempts to seduce Sara. Mr. G. is R's faithful servant and partner in crime.

14. This same incident is told from Sara's point of view in the previous letter.

15. A man of my taste.

16. Mr. R refers to an earlier incident. "Hartog" is Cornelia Hartog, a woman who also lives with the widow.

17. Mr. R has invited the women to accompany him to the theater.

Bibliography

Primary Works

Wolff, Elizabeth and Agatha Deken. *De Historie van Mejuffrouw Sara Burgerhart*. 20th ed. Amsterdam: Wereldbibliotheek, 1974.

Anthologies

Van Vloten, J. Ed. *Het Leven en de uitgelezen verzen van Elizabeth Wolff-Bekker*. Schiedam: Roelants, 1866.
Vieu-Kuik, H.J. Ed. *Keur uit het werk van Betje Wolff en Aagje Deken*. Zutphen: Thieme et Cie., 1969. 27-33.

Related Works

Buijnsters, P.J. *Sara Burgerhart en de ontwikkeling van de Nederlandse roman in de 18e eeuw*. Groningen: Wolters-Noordhoff, 1971.
Gielen, Jos. *Belangrijke Letterkundige Werken*. 13th ed. Vol. 2. Purmerend: Musses, 1976. 112-121.
Knappert, L. Ed. "Introduction." *De Historie van Mejuffrouw Sara Burgerhart*. 2 vols. Amsterdam: Schreuders, 1906. vii-xxv.
Naber, Johanna. *Betje Wolff en Aagje Deken*. Amsterdam: Meulenhof, 1913.
Roosenschoon, Wies. *Leven en Werk van Betje Wolff en Aagje Deken*. Beemster: Historisch Genootschap J.A. Leeghwater, 1986. 35-41.
Simons, Piet. *Wij beginnen te sympathiseren*. Leiden: Sikthoff, 1970. 9-25.

Anna Louisa Geertruida
Bosboom-Toussaint

Augustinus P. Dierick

A.L.G. Bosboom-Toussaint (1812-1886), the greatest Dutch author of narrative prose in the nineteenth century according to G.W. Huygens (83), is a transitional figure in whose development the history of Dutch literature between the 1830s and 1870s can be demonstrated admirably. After writing, in the 1830s, a series of large and detailed historical novels, meticulously researched, Bosboom-Toussaint came to shed the overpowering influence of English Romanticism, above all of Walter Scott, and graduated to a psychologically more modern and subtle type of novel, exemplified especially in *Majoor Frans* (1874, "Major Frans"), thereby repeating essentially what was happening in Dutch literature between the same dates.

Truitje Toussaint was born in Alkmaar in 1812, from Huguenot stock. From her eighth year on she was educated by her grandparents in Harlingen. In 1830 she returned to Alkmaar and studied for a teacher's certificate; upon completion of her studies she obtained a teaching post in Hoorn as governess (1833), after which she once again returned to Alkmaar. Because of her early publications, especially the historical novel *De graaf van Devonshire* (1839, "The Duke of Devonshire"), she established contact with the influential circle of literary critics and historians around the newly-founded journal *De Gids* ("The Guide"), since 1837 under the editorship of E.J. Potgieter, and became betrothed to the brilliant but frivolous critic, historian and editor Reinier Bakhuizen van den Brink (1810-1865). This engagement was called off, however, when the latter had to flee Holland because of debts. In 1851 she married the well-known painter Johannes Bosboom. The couple established itself in The Hague, where the author died in 1886.

Truitje Toussaint was fortunate enough to have a father whose readings extended not only to the European classics (among the French: Racine, Voltaire, Victor Hugo, De Lamartine, and Alexandre Dumas; among the Germans: Schiller, Goethe and Jean Paul; among the English: Byron and Walter Scott), but whose library must have contained a fair amount of important Dutch literature, since a number of influences of contemporaneous Dutch authors can be traced in the daughter's works. But it is by virtue of her own talents rather than of fortune that the young lady was able to embark upon a career which in her time, but above all for her sex, was most unusual and, undoubtedly, frought with difficulties and obstacles. She must have struck her contemporaries by her intelligence, her solid education, and most of all by her obvious powers of imagination and her understanding of the human psyche, judging by the help and support she received from colleagues, in an environment which fostered no such aspirations for a woman. It was these assets she complemented, following the promptings of her critics, with extensive research, before writing the historical novels which constitute her main literary reputation.

The whole of Europe was swept up in a frenzy over the historical novel ever since Walter Scott had revived the genre and modernized it by applying methods of research only recently acquired in the periods of the Enlightenment and Romanticism. To be sure, in Holland in the seventeenth and eighteenth centuries history had already been an important topic for novel-writing, and the genre of the romance had been popular. In the so-called "French period" (1795-1818), the interest in the country's own past increased even further, undoubtedly inspired by the need to provide a nationalist counterweight to French domination, witness *Het leven van Maurits Lijnslager* ("The Life of Maurits Lijnslager") by Adriaan Loosjes

(1761-1818). That nationalism and patriotism were indeed more decisive criteria than historical accuracy in the writing of such novels can be seen both in Loosjes's work and in the rhetorical poem *De Hollandsche Natie* (1812, "The Dutch Nation") by J.F. Helmers, and the long poem *De overwintering der Hollanders op Nova Zembla in de jaren 1596 en 1597* (1819, "Depiction of the Survival during Winter of the Dutch on Novaya Zemlya in the years 1596 and 1597") by the immensely popular Hendrik Tollens. But Scott provided the formula which would revolutionize the genre and make it for a while the "dominant prose genre" of the time (Meyer 206).

That formula can be defined as having three main components (de Gier ix-x): first, a story with much suspense, centered around a secondary character in the proximity of a true historical figure, complete with all the elements of the old adventure novel (intrigues, obstacles, secrets, rescues, imprisonment, etc.), and combined with a broad depiction of the lower social classes and the important element of humor; secondly, a large dose of local color, primarily evident in elaborate descriptions of dress, landscape, interiors and customs, and based on careful research. Though it runs counter to the former component, in slowing down the action, precisely the latter element held the greatest attention of the nineteenth-century audience, while for the modern reader it presents perhaps the most important impediment. The third component, which by contrast could be considered a more modern aspect, is the absence of any obvious moral message; Scott leaves it to the reader to draw his own conclusions, and does not stand in the way of his/her enjoyment of the story.

This formula finds an early application in Holland, though without much depth, in the novels of Jacob van Lennep, author of the *Nederlandsche Legenden* ("Dutch Legends"). Van Lennep had published a *Verhandeling over het belangrijke van Hollands grond en oudheden voor gevoel en verbeelding* ("Treatise about the Importance of the Dutch Soil and Antiquities for Sentiment and Imagination") in 1827, in which he suggested a large number of possible themes for historical novels, primarily concerning the Middle Ages. Some critics, like W.A.P. Smit, have seen in van Lennep's treatise the single most important element in the reception of Scott in Holland; but de Gier (xi) argues that its influence was rather limited, and that a number of authors had already on their own discovered Scott and cultivated the genre. At least Aarnout Drost, however, can be said to be a true disciple of van Lennep's, and hence of Scott's, though in one respect he departs from Scott's practice. Drost's main work, the novel *Hermingard van de Eikenterpen* (1832, "Hermingard of the Eikenterpen") shows a clear moral and religious viewpoint: its treatment of Christianity's struggles during the fourth century carries a message which obviously is the result of the author's personal convictions, that of an evangelical Christianity which is opposed to Christianity seeking secular power.

Bosboom-Toussaint's own early works were not primarily conceived as imitations of Dutch practice of the historical novel. Her very first effort, the novelle *Almagro* (1837), inspired by an episode from Schiller's drama *Die Räuber*, showed, rather, the direct influence of Scott and the English Romantics. A subsequent collection of stories, *De echtgenoten van Turin* (1839, "The Spouses of Turin"), similarly contains many romantic elements, though there is a first halting attempt to ground the characters in a more or less consistent psychology. Much more important is her first major novel, *De graaf van Devonshire* (1839, "The Duke of Devonshire"), in which she begins to distance herself from Scott and his imitators.

The crucially important preface to this novel outlines the theoretical standpoint which from now on will inform her practice of the genre. It is not her intention, she states there, to write a "historical novel, not in the sense, at least as I understand it, as Walter Scott has executed it." Whereas Scott attempted to describe the customs and morals of the bygone centuries, and introduced "romantic" elements only to create more interest, Bosboom-Toussaint argues that she is concerned mainly with the *characters* and their emotions; historical accuracy, which results from research, is for her merely a means not to sin against veracity and local color. First and foremost for Bosboom-Toussaint comes the subject itself, which is essentially a character's personal drama resulting from historical circumstances, and which must "inspire" her, catch her imagination, because it invites analysis and explanation: the subject is, in a certain sense, a "riddle" to be solved by the author. Thus, whereas J.M.C. Bouvy can call Scott's method "historical-descriptive" (44), it is Bosboom-Toussaint's goal to arrive at an *interpretation* of history (48). Since historical events and circumstances primarily invite an interpretation of history's impact on selected characters, it is not surprising to find that in those cases where tradition is incomplete, Bosboom-Toussaint claims the liberty to invent and fill in the "empty spaces." Despite this claim to artistic liberty, however, the author is in practice apt to cling very closely to historical details and in fact to shower the reader to such an extent with her knowledge (sometimes quoting original sources in their entirety), that at times she becomes rather tedious. This is certainly the case in both *De Engelschen te Rome* (1839, "The English in Rome") and *Lord Edward Glenhouse* (1840).

Two factors account for a significant shift in Bosboom-Toussaint's production after 1840. There is first of all the criticism to which E.J. Potgieter subjected *De graaf van Devonshire*. Potgieter and Bakhuizen van den Brink were in the process of attempting to narrow the European movement of Romanticism, in order to create a specifically Dutch Romanticism. The criteria for this change were laid down especially and specifically in Bakhuizen van den Brink's review of Jakob van Lennep jr.'s novel *De Roos van Dekama* (1836, "The Rose of Dekama"). The historical novel was to serve a national purpose: its subject ought, in their minds, to come primarily from the glorious period of the Dutch Golden Age, the seventeenth century, and was to trace modern political institutions and existing situations back to their origins in this period. Since it was felt that such literature would bolster national pride, a clear didactic purpose was attached to the genre of the historical novel. A vision or idea was to underlie the novel which would give it both depth and unity. To fulfill these requirements, a thorough study of historical sources must be undertaken, local color and even language would play a major role, as well as the thoughts and imagination of the characters. A final criterion would have to be the elegant, varied and lively representation of the events and characters. On a number of accounts, *De graaf van Devonshire* obviously failed to live up to these criteria. A second factor influencing Bosboom-Toussaint's career at this time was the increasingly important role which her thinking about Protestantism came to play. Through her contacts with the circle of Heilo (Hasebroek, Nicolaas Beets, Willem de Clercq), she made the ideas of the so-called *Reveil* her own. This movement, initiated by the poet Willem Bilderdijk, and carried on by such disciples as Isaac Da Costa, was intended to counter the rationalistic and superficial type of religion predominant in Holland at this time and was designed to lead to a deeper, more committed form of Christianity. It appealed to Bosboom-Toussaint, whose unorthodox-liberal outlook, inherited from her father, could not fit into the more rigid, rule-oriented and rather intolerant Protestantism of her time.

The first product of these two factors is the novel *Het Huis Lauernesse* (1840, "The House of Lauernesse"). The subject ought to have pleased the editors of *De Gids*, since it deals with the time of the Dutch Reformation and describes the process whereby the *Jonkvrouw* of the Utrecht castle Lauernesse, under the influence of the preacher Paul van Mansfeld, abandons the Catholic Church, thereby sparking a violent conflict with her fiancé, Aernoud Reiniersz, an imperial officer. The fact that the novel was nevertheless not reviewed in *De Gids* was due not to its method (the scholarship for this novel was exemplary, and, in the words of Knuvelder, "prepared according to the recipe of Bakhuizen and Potgieter" [248]), but rather because of the obvious tolerance shown toward both Catholic and Protestant figures. Bosboom-Toussaint's "humanistic Christianity" (Knuvelder 249), the result of her acquaintance with the ideas of the *Reveil*, shows particularly in the author's treatment of the vicar of the bishopric of Utrecht, a quasi-Erasmian figure. Apart from the change in locale — the Netherlands rather than England — and the evidence of a more extensive research, the main principles laid down by Bosboom-Toussaint in the preface of *De graaf van Devonshire* are upheld in this novel: the emphasis is on the effects of the Reformation on individual characters and groups, whose psychology is investigated and shown in reaction to historic events. Unfortunately, as in her previous novels, there are still many excursions, meditations and reflections which retard the flow of the novel, and too many bald facts which prevent the present-day reader from being charmed by the story; moreover, the psychology of the characters is often wooden, static and schematic.

A work much more successful in shedding these negative elements is the novel *Eene kroon voor Karel den Stouten* (1841, "A Crown for Charles the Bold"), recently reissued in the Netherlands by J. de Gier (1989). From de Gier's extensive introduction we get the impression that the one major criticism that can be levelled at the novel, its excessive historical detail, may in fact be attributable not so much to the author herself, but to the "help" which the author received from the editors of *De Gids* in the writing process. A certain overzealousness and conscientiousness do at times stand in the way of the narrative flow — a problem not unique of course to Bosboom-Toussaint but inherent in the genre itself.

The novel deals with a crucial, and, according to a number of historians, tragic episode in the history of the Netherlands. Charles the Bold, the ambitious ruler of what was (as the story emphasizes repeatedly) the most progressive and wealthiest region in Europe, the Burgundian territories, seeks to unify his scattered empire, separated especially by Alsace and Lorraine, through the marriage of his daughter, Mary of Burgundy, with a number of suitors in turn, among them Nicolas of Calabria. He also attempts to obtain from the German Emperor, Frederick III, a royal crown or an imperial "Vicarage" which would allow him to become a member of the Electoral College, and thus establish himself as an equal to his greatest and most imposing rival, the French king Louis XI. Frederick III, a weak ruler, sees in a treaty with Charles, strengthened by a marriage between Mary and his son Maximilian, the possibility of keeping his unruly and restless vassals in check. In these ambitions Charles is thwarted during the conference in Trier in the autumn of 1473; while the thrones have already been installed and his goal is within his grasp, he overreaches himself in making new demands, and the Emperor, already overwhelmed and disturbed by the Burgundian display of pomp, departs overnight. This debacle sets the stage for Charles's gradual decline and his ultimate tragic failure, which is prompted especially by his attempts to acquire Alsace, for which he must wage a series of military campaigns against Lorraine, Cologne and Switzerland. While battling Rene II of Lorraine, on the fifth of January 1477, Charles's army is routed, partly because of treachery, and Charles himself disappears with his horse through the ice; his corpse is found a few days later, torn to pieces by wolves.

I have selected a number of passages from this novel for translation which demonstrate some typical aspects of Bosboom-Toussaint's technique. As the novel opens, the focus is not on the protagonist, Charles the Bold, but on his daughter and one of her suitors. We are thus immediately drawn into a *personal* conflict rather than an abstract political one, though it becomes clear very soon that political and personal goals cannot be separated. Typical is also the fact that characters are introduced first by a description of their external appearance: clothes and trappings, and physical beauty are of the utmost importance. Bosboom-Toussaint, wittingly or unwittingly, follows two established procedures here: her insistence on the elaboration of local color is inspired directly by Scott; and her choice of a medieval subject also suggests this kind of treatment, since medieval literature consistently stresses the role of external features and dress in order to define status and role of the protagonist. For example, in the second translated passage, Charles's appearance and entourage are described in great, perhaps even somewhat excessive detail. Bosboom-Toussaint wanted to make clear to the reader that Charles's strategy was to overwhelm Frederick by a grandiose display of his already considerable wealth and power. By doing so, he also makes the tragic mistake which will lead to ruin and disaster. In addition, Bosboom-Toussaint deliberately tried to suit her language to the "elevated" subject, which on a number of occasions leads her to use archaic syntactical constructions and expressions (which cannot always be rendered effectively in translation). Furthermore, the lower classes are strikingly absent as "actors" in this political drama: the end of the second passage suggests that the author (unlike Scott) was not very interested in the crowd as such. Finally, it is worthwhile drawing attention to the extremely sensitive portrait, despite its brevity, of the female protagonist in the opening passage: the adolescent Mary is depicted in a fashion which, one feels, could only have been achieved by a woman. This raises the central question of the "female voice" in these novels, to which we will return later.

The positive and negative comments prompted by *Eene kroon voor Karel den Stouten* are equally relevant for Bosboom-Toussaint's next major work, the monumental trilogy known as the Leycester-Cycle. It consists of *Leycester in Nederland* (1846, "Leycester in the Netherlands"), which deals with the activities of Queen Elisabeth's ambassador to the Netherlands during his first sojourn (December 1585 to the end of of 1586); *De vrouwen uit het Leycestersche tijdvak* (1850, "The Women of the Leycester Era"); and *Gideon Florensz* (1855), which deal with the second sojourn of Leycester in Holland. To prepare for this rather daunting work, the author had spent several years researching the subject, with the intention of rendering history as closely as possible to the truth. True to her principles, and despite the rigorous research of the historical facts, the psychology of her characters is nevertheless clearly intended to be the more important element of the novels. But since we are dealing with a "recreation" of a reality for which few sources and little documentation were available, this cannot but mean a great deal of liberty and invention on the part of the author: a contradiction of principles from which there is no real escape, and one of which the author herself was aware from the start.

Bosboom-Toussaint was so fascinated with Leycester (a necessary condition for her art, as we have seen), because he could stand for the kind of enlightened, tolerant Christian for whom the *Reveil* had provided the idealized model. In the figure of Gideon Florensz, moreover, she re-created the character of Paul Mansfeld in *Het Huis Lauernesse*; both preachers are concerned above all with a Christianity which is a matter of the heart rather than of orthodoxy. That the cycle is nevertheless not necessarily "her greatest achievement" (de Vooys-Stuyveling 113), is the fault of two problems that dominate all of Bosboom-Toussaint's historical novels. First, as we have indicated, a dichotomy — or perhaps even a contradiction — exists between the principle of historical veracity (which concerns the novel as a work of history) and the original inspiration and final aim of the author, which was to re-create with imagination and suggestion (which concerns the novel as a work of art). When these two aims do not coincide, the work remains ambivalent, the didactic and merely factual parts of the novel do not fuse with the imaginary episodes and characters. This problem exists for most historical novels, but in the case of Bosboom-Toussaint, it strikes the reader as particularly acute. The second problem, also valid for most of her historical novels, concerns the difficulty of bringing the psychologically deficient characters to life — a difficulty aggravated by a prose style which, in the rhetorical tradition of Bilderdijk and Potgieter, leads to considerable obstacles for the modern reader. In fact, only *De vrouwen uit het Leycestersche tijdvak* is free from both weaknesses. One has the feeling that precisely because of the lack of authentic documentary material the author was able to give her imagination free reign, with much more interesting results than in the other two volumes. No doubt also, it is because here the focus is on the fate of individual women rather than on the more abstract course of history, that the book holds greater attraction.

A more pronounced focus on the female psyche and women's fate stood the author in good stead also in her next important novel, *Mejonkvrouwe de Mauléon* (1847, "My Lady of Mauléon"), which Knuvelder calls "a masterpiece" (257). Once again, the source was a foreign work: Voltaire's *Le Siècle de Louis XIV*. This time the author's intention was not so much to give a picture of an historical period, but to describe the emotionally charged youthful love between Bossuet and Yolande Desvieux. This love was to have led to marriage, but Bossuet's obvious talents caused those able to further his career to destine him for the Church. In view of this higher mission, Yolande sets Bossuet free, but in spirit she remains faithful to him. Bossuet, in turn, makes possible Yolande's purchase of the castle of Mauléon, where he often visits her. Yolande remains independent and seemingly uninterested in other young men, with the result that her behavior arouses suspicion in her social circles. In certain ways, the novel reminds one of the earlier works of Bosboom-Toussaint — especially for its intrigues, mysterious events, and mysterious characters (such as a very young priest who is associated both with Bossuet and Yolande and whose origins are never revealed). All these elements contribute to the fascination with which the reader follows the story; the language, moreover, is much more supple, and the psychology of the characters much more convincing than in the previous novels. Especially Yolande's self-sacrificing attitude as a foil to Bossuet's basic egotism gives the novel its feel of veracity, even though in this case the novel is largely a product of the imagination, not of historical fact.

In Yolande Desvieux the author created a figure which can be called an immediate predecessor to the character of Francis Mordaunt, the female protagonist of Bosboom-Toussaint's last major novel, *Majoor Frans* (1874). With this work Bosboom-Toussaint can be said to stand on the threshold of the modern Dutch psychological novel; and whereas her historical novels are still of significance from a generic point of view as well as from the point of view of Dutch literary history, *Majoor Frans* has an intrinsic interest which explains its frequent reappearance in various kinds of popular editions and in a number of translations. If there is one novel by Bosboom-Toussaint which can still be called alive and well today, it is this one, and this is due above all to the wonderful way the free and independent, high-spirited and slightly outrageous young woman Francis dominates the action and holds the reader's attention. Another reason for the novel's success is its analytical strength: the character and circumstances of the *freule* are only gradually revealed, either through passages narrated by the main characters or by the interaction between the male protagonist, Jonker Leopold van Zonshoven, and his cousin Francis. This allows, even forces, the reader to identify with the male protagonist, whose main goal in this novel is to discover whether Francis is a suitable partner for marriage, as stipulated in the will of his aunt.

Leopold's mission is a delicate one: though he is under no legal obligation to marry Francis in order to inherit a million guilders, he feels morally obliged because of the wrong done to Francis's family; at the same time, he cannot appear to be acting out of greed or appear to want to force the young woman. He has been informed of Francis's idiosyncracies, which the reader gradually comes to recognize as the "symptoms" of an emancipated young woman. The moral outrage and the often vicious gossip concerning Francis at first put Leopold on guard, but it is to the young man's credit that he does not let himself be scared away, and faithfully pursues his road. Once he encounters Francis, Leopold's mind is quickly made up. What develops is partly a comedy, partly a tragedy — the age-old battle of the sexes, in fact, conducted with considerable psychological subtlety. Leopold is a tolerant, almost liberated male, whose efforts to "convert" Francis into a more traditional female do not tend in the direction of domination but of modification. Francis's struggle to maintain her freedom are partly still in the tradition of the Enlightenment comedy, and in certain episodes she is made the target of the author's own irony. Nevertheless, Leopold, and, we feel, Bosboom-Toussaint, would like to preserve most of Francis's admirable morality and straightforwardness and sacrifice only those aspects of her character which are the result of her bitter experiences and of a certain amount of exaggeration. In this respect the resolution of the conflict (which does not come about easily, and involves a number of peripeteias) is almost in the nature of an Hegelian *Aufhebung*, in which the original dichotomies have been overcome, though not eliminated.

The novel is composed in the form of a series of letters by Leopold to his friend Willem Verheyst, a lawyer who has accepted a post in the Dutch Indies. This convention is a mere excuse to tie the action's development to a chronological scheme in which Leopold's discovery of Francis's character and background runs parallel with the reader's own process of discovery. The reader thereby remains as much in suspense, and as uninformed, as Leopold. Bosboom-Toussaint again increased the tension in the novel by introducing certain "mysterious" events — a leftover from her earlier historical novels in the tradition of Scott — and traits in her characters which become understandable only in the light of later revelations. These revelations mostly take the form of narratives by the several characters, though sometimes also letters are introduced. Because of these narratives, the whole novel has a rather episodic structure, but this looseness is counterbalanced by the quite modern psychology of the novel, and above all by the unifying force of Francis, a truly remarkable creation.

This brings us to an interesting parallel between two so seemingly different texts as *Eene kroon voor Karel den Stouten* and

Majoor Frans. In both novels the female protagonists are presented as lively, somewhat independent characters: both were children whose fathers would rather have liked to have sons and who were raised therefore in a rather unorthodox fashion. Although Mary of Burgundy is a pawn in Charles's political games and the victim of her father's ruthlessness (his basic flaw) — as the climax of the novel, a (fictional) encounter between herself and Maximilian in Trier, makes clear — , she is also very much a character in the round who gradually gains the admiration of the reader. In a similar way, Francis is the victim of many a manipulation, from which she liberates herself with the help of Leopold, after a suitable amount of soul-searching. Women as victims of a male world, therefore? Perhaps in the world of Charles the Bold, but definitely not in that of *Majoor Frans*, although Francis's early experiences do point in that direction; but then, perhaps Leopold, in his depth of understanding and the commitment of his love, is really an exception. By contrast, we feel that the author attributes not only to these women but to most women in her novels an enormous vitality, the (sometimes merely dormant) capacity to love and sacrifice.

And yet, there is something about *Majoor Frans* which is not present in Bosboom-Toussaint's historical novels. De Gier suggests that in *Eene kroon voor Karel den Stouten*, with its historical protagonist, the author's freedom to manipulate the facts was extremely limited. This observation seems basic, but it must be developed. For it is the generic difference between the two novels that accounts for the essential difference between the characters of Mary and Francis. The historical novel has rules which must be followed lest the genre as such be destroyed; it requires a greater degree of "objectivity," even if only illusionary, than any other type of novel. This accounts, for example, for the positing of the historical novel as the "ideal," "classical" and "artistic" novel in late nineteenth-century Germany (Freytag, Spielhagen). Consequently, the "female voice" is perhaps less heard in this type of novel than in any other. This suggests a number of extremely interesting problems, which cannot be pursued here: did women in the nineteenth century choose to write historical or quasi-historical novels because the generic rules allowed them to hide behind a mask of "scientific" objectivity, and thus to adopt, as it were, the conventions of their male counterparts and establish themselves as bona-fide authors? Do women-novelists subconsciously adopt male conventions as such? Does the choice of genre tell us something about the woman author herself? And with specific reference to *Majoor Frans*, does the "taming" of the rebellious woman and the "successful" socialization process make a statement about the author? These are questions to which specific texts alone cannot provide adequate answers. Only by placing such texts, and their makers, in a larger context such as the present one, can one hope to begin to understand the question, the precondition for an eventual answer.

Translations by Augustinus P. Dierick

From *EENE KROON VOOR KAREL DEN STOUTEN*[1]
("A Crown for Charles the Bold")

[In the first chapter, the author introduces Mary of Burgundy, daughter of Charles the Bold and a crucial pawn in his political strategies, in conversation with Nicolas of Calabria, one of many young men to whom she has been promised in marriage.]

..."Sure and certain! I am the most wretched knight in Christendom! No Saracen or heathen has a destiny as sad as mine is now. Alas, from now on I will suffer without end or succor." The young man who uttered these complaints in a somber, passionate voice, united in his appearance so many advantages, that a listener would find it hard to believe in his lamentable state. His clothing was more than splendid, it was princely. Over a light breast harness of the finest Milanese steel, generously inlaid with jewels, he wore a short skirt of fiery red scarlet, completely shot through with golden embroidery, and trimmed with sable fur. The leggings were of pure white velvet, tight-fitting on the legs, and gathered above the knees with colourful ribbons decorated with jewels. The shoes, very pointed, were of gold cloth, with solid gold points. The hilt of the cross-sword was of the same metal. He was decorated with the venerable order of the Golden Fleece, and on the gloves he wore a coat of arms which showed a double ducal crown. Just as he was not, judging from his dress, deprived by fortune, so he was not by nature. If he drew profit from his clothing, he did not need it in order to rivalize with the most attractive and best-shaped. The jet-black eyes could compete with the shine of diamonds, and the splendor of his dark curls, which fell down playfully around his well-formed neck, the interest of his features, and the manly brown complexion, which he owed to a hardened life or southerly blood, would have made any splendor of dress superfluous in the eyes of many a woman. The place where, and the person to whom the knight uttered this complaint seemed to justify it as little as did his appearance: for it was in the ducal Hôtel de Mons, and for the ears of Mary of Burgundy, that he uttered it.

Most of all the exclamation must create amazement if one knows him as Nicolas of Calabria, Duke of Lorraine; if one knows that written marriage vows had been exchanged between this prince and the only daughter of Charles the Bold; a fact which certainly made him enviable in the eyes of all unmarried sons of princes. With none of the many to whom the Duke of Burgundy had promised the precious hand had he meant it so seriously as precisely with this Calabrian prince; he had awarded him publicly all the rights of a blood relative, and had shown him all the affection of a father-in-law. The young man had fought in his battles, at his side; he had shared his confidence and had been witness of how he had outwitted and confused all his rivals, while granting him favors never granted others. He had been allowed to spend a month in Mons, where at that time the young princess held court, and the few restrictions which were imposed on his frequenting the princess strenghtened his sweetest hope more than any written assurance.

And indeed, Nicolas could be considered a suitable son-in-law for Duke Charles: John of Calabria, the prince's father, had been a friend and ally until his death; the Duchy of Lorraine, of which he was now already the proprietor, and which unfortunately enough separated the Duchy of Burgundy from the territory of Charles's other states, would, through this alliance, fall to his house; a union which had always formed a part of his plans; the young prince, as sole heir on the male side of the House of Anjou would also come into the possession of the beautiful Provence, apart from what his godfather René would leave him in claims on the Kingdoms of Sicily and Naples, Catalonia and Jerusalem. What a beautiful prospect for a conqueror, those rights which he would have to enforce with the power of weapons! And it is a certainty that no ruler let himself be caught more readily by such bait as the ruler of Burgundy; moreover, the young prince was brave, quick in decisions and actions, and full of enterprise; qualities which would make him attractive to a father-in-law who found his own character traits in him; and yet not so excellent in great military virtues or brilliant qualities that he, for whom the choice was so difficult, was not protected from jealousy or rivalry; for whatever the young Duke of Lorraine might eventually become, right now he was neither powerful nor independent enough to go beside him as an equal, an equality which this most proud of all rulers could not have tolerated even from his own son.

The sincerity of Charles was therefore almost beyond suspicion, and yet, the complaint had escaped from the lips of the youth, a complaint of disappointment! The boldest hope with which politics had ever built up the imagination was allowed to blossom only one summer long; it was October and...the Duke had demanded the marriage vows to his daughter to be withdrawn, to give hope elsewhere. Politics had bound, politics had separated; but what this bond or separation had broken or severed, for this there was no protective clause; that was not part of the calculations. Separated! it was easy for him, the Duke of Burgundy, to talk; for him, whose only passion was the lust for power, that sun which does not leave stars or moon visible when it shines; could he know, or think, what that word meant for this youth, who so suddenly saw the most illustrious plan of his life scrapped; whose beautiful future was darkened with one move; whom one had allowed to frequent a world of greatness and love, and whom one suddenly now cast out, without mercy or apology; whom one now coolly told that it had been a dream; whom one had allowed to drink the cup of hope until intoxication, and from whom one now mercilessly snatched away the chalice as if deprivation was to be an easy affair; to whom one had granted the seductive proof of confidence, without thinking whether he would be able to stand it; and he *could* not, he had collapsed under it.

Nicolas of Calabria had not seen in the hand of Mary only the sceptre of her territories; he had also looked at her fine fingers, and they had touched him more deeply than anyone creature could reach; he had not only counted the pearls on her ducal crown; he had also espied the pearls between her lips as she smiled the sweet smile of confidence; and *their* shine had delighted him more than the qualities of those other pearls. He had not only paid attention to the lilies in her coat of arms; he had also noted the lilies on her throat, and her whiteness had no less struck him than the golden glow of the first. He had not only seen a monarch on a broad throne which he could share, but he had also seen a child playing around it, among flowers and birds; he had seen a growing young woman with a happy lust for life, and innocent playfulness running with light-footed gait; he had been her companion on trips and walks, the subject of her teasing or daring jokes, in which the bewitching coquetry of a woman shone through, and nothing yet of the reticent shyness of a virgin. That had been dangerous for him! That had done more than ignite his imagination in dreams of ambition which only heat the head; it had set the heart aflame! That glow of the head he could cool down with the sword of vengeance in his hand, or fortune could compensate for the interrupted dreams of power and wealth, and a daughter of a king could replace the daughter of an Archduke; the hand of Anna of France was his, if he would accept it;...but the flame in his heart would continue to burn, seething and torturing his whole life long; no steel could bring coolness, unless it be a murderous one; the wound of his heart would not let itself be soothed by compensation; love would not let itself be bartered by an exchange. A ducal seat, a throne could give back to the Duke of Lorraine what had been taken from him; but Nicolas of Calabria could not love anyone among all the women of the world but Mary!

To complaints similar to these the young prince continued to give vent, within hearing of the beautiful heiress, on that afternoon in October in which we encountered him. And she herself? The young lady whom one gave away and took back; whom one dangled before the eyes of every royal son of Europe in turn, like a beautiful plaything, only to be put aside when one had stared oneself blind on it; to whom one announced that she belonged to this one, only to tell her the next day that she had no bridegroom, without worrying about what she herself could feel; whom one made exchange rings and marriage vows without investigating whether she made another exchange also, or whether she gave away something else than a piece of parchment with writings on it; she — ...but we shall see. Now she sat opposite her complaining lover and listened silently, while her little hands played involuntarily a childish game with the little silver bells on the bonnet of a little dwarf who knelt at her feet. Whoever did not know her as the most fascinating female figure of her time, because of the many and important interests which attached to her person, would nevertheless have awarded her the prize of attractiveness, as she sat there in that dress of white damask silk; a pure splendour which suited the childlike simplicity of her features and bearing. Neither her shape nor her beauty were fully formed yet; she still had the fragile slenderness of that age in which the growth of the body increases at the expense of its flowering; her cheeks did not have that fresh blush of childhood any more, and not yet that other blush which colours it with such an attractive pink bloom; her eyes did not even sparkle yet with that bright shine which passion would make glitter in them; nor with that softer scintillation which emotion could lay in them. But their beautiful colour, the cleverness which they already expressed, the dark eyebrows which arched over them, promised what they could become one day, when the soul had spoken. The precious little shirt of silver lace could cover a fuller neck, but never a whiter one; and a more delicate foot had never hidden itself in such red velvet, embroidered with pearls; a longer veil of Brabant lace had never hung down from so splendid a hairdo, and no cape of blue satin, shot through with gold, had ever with envious jealousy hidden the beauty of shinier locks and softer forehead.

But although her eyes were dull rather than sparkling, although only a languishing blush threw a single rose-petal among the lilies of her neck, there was nevertheless nothing which testified to the truth of a slander which the slanderer himself [Louis XI] would have liked to be true: she was *not* weak and languishing; her health even seemed robust, and she had not been enfeebled in the lukewarm atmosphere of women's quarters, nor had she been led to melancholy by a stationary life in a cell behind colorful cross-windows and among silk carpets. Charles the Bold, who perhaps had wished for a son, had nevertheless not wanted a weak maiden for a daughter, and he himself, with his sharp eye which was able to cast a glance at everything, had made sure of that part of her education to which she owed her force and strength. On his travels to Flanders he had taken her with him, as much as this was possible. We see her in Ghent, in the middle of the revolt which greeted his rule. He gave her life variety and enjoyment through changes of location; now the joyful industriousness of a harbor delighted her in Sluys, which offered safety to ships of all nations in turn; then again, in Bruges, she looked down from the grandiose ducal palace on the colourful bustle of merchants who looked like princes, and of tradesmen more impressive and powerful than noblemen, and yet bent under the sword and disciplining staff of her father; then again she folded her hands respectfully in Brussels, while viewing the stately processions in which so much splendor, so much external piety went side by side, and trained her young mind in the recognition of the banners of the guilds and those of the spiritual brotherhoods. Then again, at the hunting lodge of Hesdin, she followed the splendid falcon hunts of her father, learned to name the famous birds of prey, and delighted in their conquest more loudly and sincerely than if her warrior lord had added a new territory to her future inheritance; not to mention at what she had assisted in the way of tournaments, teeming with jolly noblewomen and princely knights, the court celebrations at which the selected splendors of the assembled nobility of France, Holland, Flanders and England applauded in astonishment and admiration.

As little, therefore, as her youth was sad or singular, so little there was now also of pain or languishing meditation in her face, even though she was witness and object of a suffering and a passion which described themselves in such somber colours. While she carelessly leaned back against the high back of a seating bench, upholstered with gold cloth, she looked at the offended prince with more astonishment than compassion; like someone who tries to understand in order to pity; and when he, perhaps for the third time, began a repetition of his complaints, she interrupted him with this word:

"You know, I find it strange, noble lord and cousin! that you do not tell me anything of the feats of armour and great knightly deeds of my noble lord the Duke of Normandy and Artois, to which you were witness, and to which I hope you contributed..."

[The following scene describes the entry of Charles the Bold into Trier, where he is about to have the fatal meeting with the Emperor Frederick III; here Charles's hopes for a royal crown are dashed by his own overreaching and impetuous attitude.]

...On the morning of that day grey Trier, which had a memory dating back to Roman times, had dressed up like an old coquette who expects her last conquest; everything which had been prepared for her decoration she was now wearing to excess; because Charles the Bold was now close by, and the Emperor with the Archduke and all their retinue had left the city to join them, the impatience of the crowd, which had thronged together by the thousands in every spot where there was a likelihood, or even only a probability to see the procession, mounted with every minute. The inhabitants of Trier, and of half of Germany and all the surrounding regions, stood there with bated breath, with necks stretched, with tense features, and with hearts pounding with expectation; then they heard that John of Baden, Archbishop of Trier, and his brother the Margrave Christoffel had left through the gate to receive the illustrious visitors. Now there could only be a few moments left between expectation and receiving — finally — a deep sigh of anticipation went through the whole crowd — finally the men at arms of the Emperor showed themselves with the imperial banners and the standard of the Holy Roman Empire, the double eagle, with the coat of arms of the House of Austria in the middle; beside them, in narrow columns, went six hundred Burgundian men, in light armor and uniformly dressed in red; both were more an escort than part of

the procession, which really only opened with a hundred Burgundian
youths of excellent beauty, adorned with almost feminine care and
refinement, with long blond locks which fell to their shoulders; they
were unarmed and carried standards on which shone the lion of
Burgundy and the red cross of St. Andrew.

They by themselves already commanded the admiration and
the shouts of joy of the crowd. Immediately following them there
were the twelve battle trumpeters of the Duke, and his fluteplayers,
as well as six minstrels with their king, and the musicians of his court
orchestra, which caressed the ears of the people of Trier no less than
they had earlier called forth the astonishment of the inhabitants of Aix
la Chapelle. The venerable Bishop-Confessor, surrounded by his
clergy and all the laymen who belonged to the service of the chapel,
went beside them with dignified steps. The Great Master of the
House, carrying the large banner which is never folded, followed
with the page boys entrusted to his governance, the children from the
most respected houses of Burgundy and Flanders; the first Carver,
with the other high officials of the Duke's table, the Upper Court
Steward and his subalterns, the High Lord Chamberlain, splendidly
accompanied, and many others passed by before the staring eyes of
the spectators, who were led from astonishment to astonishment at the
sight of all that splendor of dress, the equipment of the horses, the
treasures of gold and jewels, in furs and silk, in velvet and gold cloth
which made of all their previous notions of splendor and wealth mere
childish and innocent fairytales. And yet they could have saved their
jubilation for a yet more significant spectacle. They ought to have
waited until the groups of heralds and bearers of coats of arms had
gone by, each of whom held carried in his hand the banner, wore in
the clothing the colours, and carried on the uniform the coats of arms
of one of the estates of the Duke; the bearers of the coats of arms
with their crowns of gilded silver, without embellishment or precious
stone except for the sapphire, the symbol of purity of their service;
they ought truly to have waited; for only then did they get to see what
surpassed everything put together: Charles the Bold himself,
completely dressed in armor, as is fitting for such a warrior prince,
but a harness more richly decorated, and of a higher value than the
whole dress of gold cloth of the Emperor, although the wide,

loose-fitting sleeves of that dress were decorated with pearls. Over his equipment he wore a ducal coat of gold cloth, lined with the finest fur, and on which diamonds and jewels of the highest value formed figures in flowers and borders. The jewel which gathered this piece of clothing at the right shoulder was known and famous by name at all the courts in Christendom. It was not strange that he had chosen the "Lamp of Flanders" to cast its shine on his stately procession. Similar jewels, of which one has researched and written down the history, also held the fiery red plumes on top of the helmet together, and others, in the form of flintstones, sparkled in the sign of the Order of the Golden Fleece; but more yet than by the splendor of the clothing, on which the eye could stare itself blind, and in which admiration could find saturation, he distinguished himself from all those around him, especially from the Emperor, by his proud and haughty bearing, his well-shaped figure which betrayed his unusual muscle power and a fresh health, and above all by the lively glow of that expressive dark eye, through which every glance became commanding and demanded respect; by his unyielding willpower, and the tenacity, which was blind to every obstacle, marked on a forehead which frowned slightly with impatience, but which could not be grooved by care; by that bold undauntedness in the features of his dark-brown face that could glow with pugnacity or anger, but could never pale out of fear. This was indeed the most regal warrior, and the ruler most capable of bearing arms, that had ever waved a ruler's staff together with a sword — oh! the Emperor, Emperor Frederick might wear the most venerable crown in the world, he might dress his limbs in a stately gown of gold cloth, might wear Charlemagne's sparkling coat around his shoulders, he appeared, in comparison with the former, no more than a dressed-up old greybeard, and the other appeared to be the real ruler, in the disguise of a soldier in a coat of mail. Charles might ride on Frederick's left side as his subordinate; he may, when meeting him, have descended from his horse, as was his duty as a vassal, and bend one knee to the ground; the Emperor may have raised him up with authority and may have embraced him like a father — a superiority not expressible in words, but felt by all present, remained on the side of the noble Duke.

The impression which the unprecedented display of pomp of the latter and all his retinue had made on the company of the Emperor expressed itself in a deep dejection. If up till now we have made little mention of them, although they proceeded at the same time, in the same numbers, along with the condescending Burgundians, it is because we do not dare make constant comparisons which would have to be to their disadvantage. They had in any case made these comparisons themselves on first encountering the strangers. On this day, the nobility of Germany paid with bitter disappointment and shame for its arrogance to measure itself with the display-loving knighthood of the wealthiest and most luxurious nation of the known world. If they had not set so much store by rivalry, they would have escaped ridicule, together with exhaustion; and in this, too, the old Duke had been right: if they had dressed themselves in armour, the mocking smile which Charles and his men, on seeing an array they considered shabby, tried with difficulty to conceal would have changed into esteem; the Duke of Burgundy, a warrior at heart, would have recognized underneath the steel the value of the soldiers which he was forced to underestimate under the silk.

They were after all the best and most noble of the Empire, those who surrounded the Emperor: Ludwig and Albert, Dukes of Bavaria; Charles, Margrave of Baden; Eberhard, Duke of Wurtemberg; the Duke of Vernemburg; the Duke of Catzen-Ellenbogen, Lord of Darmstadt; and others such; also high clerics, the only ones who could compete in appearance with Charles's courtiers: the Archbishop of Mentz, Adolph of Nassau; George of Baden, Bishop of Metz; but the pearl of the whole court, the hope of his house, was the Archduke Maximilian, a graceful youth in whose bright eyes there sparkled intelligence and astuteness, just as charming affability smiled at one from his youthful face. In his robe of purple damask silk with silver embroidery, which he wore with noble dignity, he looked as suited his years and rank, without excessive desire for pomp, and without artificial simplicity. Yet another person one saw in the ranks of the Austrian lords, who was a complete stranger, and who yet drew the attention of many: a young Turkish prince, brother of Sultan Mahomed, who had softened his imprisonment among the Christians by taking over their religion.

Whereas his national dress made him be noticed, his slightly melancholy appearance drew interest.

Of the Burgundian Duke, so proud of his power and of his dominions, it need hardly be said that he had himself accompanied by all that was high and powerful in his states; that he showed off with all his princes who had their table at his court. He was most closely surrounded by Duke John of Cleve, Louis de Chateau-Guyon, of the House of Orange, the Sire d'Arguel, Philippe de Croy, the Duke of Chimay, the Duke of Nassau, one of the sons of the Connetable of St. Paul, Antoni, the Bastard of Burgundy, Guy de Brumeux, the Sire d'Himbrecourt; both Charles's blood relatives, the Bishop of Liège and Utrecht, Louis of Bourbon and David of Burgundy, representatives of the clergy of his states; from most of his towns he was accompanied by burghers and noblemen, and even chastised Liège had sent her proud sons to help heighten the victory pomp with their bowed heads.

But whatever treasures of rank and merit he had collected around him, one wasn't there, one he had lost whose value he had not sufficiently treasured, and whom he had for that reason lost. Philippe de Commines no longer was with him, was now already in the service of his envious rival, Louis XI, to the detriment of Charles's present interests, which he could have served with his advice and farsightedness, but to still greater detriment for his memory, for that man later took up the pen of the historian, and wielded it with great prejudice against the master he had abandoned, with the skill of someone who must justify himself for this abandonment; and posterity has believed him and must continue to believe him, and see flaws, clearly and unvarnished, which by a softer nuance could easily have been excused as virtues.

We cannot here discuss further Philippe's grievances; but we could not see his place empty without giving vent to the grievance we have against both him and his lord. Against Charles, because he was too conceited and opinionated to honor a man who could serve him in a fashion other than with sword and silent obedience; and against Commines, because he, taking counsel with nothing but his cool, calculating self-interest, at a time when he ought to have remained at the side of his ruler, had torn asunder the bonds which ought to have tied him to the latter, if not because of devotion, then because of habit, of loyalty, because of *that* devotion which must grow together with a man's strength. He ought not to have forgotten Charles the master of his youth; the heart ought also to have had a voice in a man of his culture, not only his intellect! Not so much that he parted company with the Duke of Burgundy when the latter's ambitions threatened to drive him to his destruction, but that he could take leave of the Duke of Charolais when he might have needed him the most, that certainly is to be condemned in him.

No matter how great Charles's anger may have been at the announcement of this treachery, at this moment he certainly did not think of that, but rather, how he could court his imperial ally without giving up any of his own authority; and Frederick...?

Whatever *he* might think of this pompous display of wealth, with which he saw himself crushed by a man who came to him as his inferior, he shut his thought within his soul, and showed the proud vassal a sincere and courteous face in front of both their united nations. A single consideration, which of course had to surface in Frederick's soul, was, moreover, well suited to make him see everything with a softer glance. The rich ruler would be the father-in-law of his son: that marriage would bring all those treasures into the House of Austria; it had to give him a secret satisfaction to see such splendid proofs of their existence; a father is not easily annoyed by the large dowry of his daughter-in-law; and Maximilian? Oh, with the confident hope of youth he already saw everything with the eyes of a future proprietor...

...And now it would be time to describe, what impression the sight of all this made on the spectators, and with what gestures or by means of what exclamations they expressed it; but we leave the shouting, staring, astonished crowd for what it has been through the ages, and will remain...

From *MAJOOR FRANS*[2]

[In a letter, Squire Leopold van Zonshoven informs his friend Willem Verheyst, a lawyer, about a conversation at a social gathering where Francis, the *freule* [honorable miss] Mordaunt, was first mentioned to him.]

...The past of that young lady must have been very obscure and strange, if there is any truth in the stories being told about her here. I know very well, one has to attribute a lot to gossip, and the narrow-minded interpretations of a small town, but still...judge for yourself. Among the ladies to whom I was introduced there was one, a cute little young widow with pitchblack eyes and lively facial features, who was presented to me as a distant cousin of the Roselaers, and of whom I was sorry at first that she wasn't called Francis Mordaunt and the chosen niece of Aunt Sophie. But when, as by coincidence, she was brought to the subject of the von Zwenkens, by my friend Overberg, I was very happy that I could remain a complete stranger to her. I even felt a sense of hatred and bitterness towards her, so without mercy did she attack poor Francis.

"Yes, they had been good acquaintances in the time her grandfather was the commander of the garrison, and she had frequented the house of the colonel, but friendship, no friendship there had never existed between her and that young girl; for that she was too bizarre and unmannered. Imagine, Squire, she once turned up at our place for a young people's party, of which it was known there would be music and dancing, so unlady-like as possible, with a dark dress of merino wool, high up to the neck, with a turned-down collar and a silk shawl, like an adolescent boy, and her shoes! *bottines de roulier!*[3] On my word of honor, I believe there were nails in them; no non-commissioned officer would have had the gall to enter a salon with such boots on..."

"Ignorance of the circumstances, perhaps...," I excused her.

"Not at all! She had been asked eight days ahead of time. During that time one *can* prepare one's clothing, I should think. Besides, she was not *au dépourvu*,[4] that became quite clear two days later, at a very simple ladies' party, where, around ten o'clock, as we returned home escorted by our servants, she appeared *en grande toilette*, and with a décolleté as if she had to go to a dance, *éblouissante* because of her *parure*,[5] and with costly diamonds in her hair. Now I ask you, wasn't that to *railler* us all,[6] and insult us mortally?"

"It seems to me that she wanted to honor her friends more than their cavaliers."

"The truth is, she makes very little effort towards the gentlemen," an old-fashionedly dressed skinny old maid, who should have been the last to rush to the defense of a sex which had obviously neglected her, broke in.

"And these surely reciprocated her nonchalance?" I asked. "She probably remained a wallflower, sitting next to the ladies of a certain age?"

"Because she wanted it herself," the little widow spoke again. "Whatever she looked like, she was sure she could get a dancing partner. All the young officers are obliged to court the daughter, niece or granddaughter of their colonel. Moreover, Francis Mordaunt is very well versed in the art of attracting by repulsion. Despite her bizarre nature and her caprices, she was never short of cavaliers. Hardly had she entered a room somewhere, or she knew how to draw attention to herself. The gentlemen surrounded her, she was flattered, courted..."

"Yes, courted, that's quite possible, but not esteemed, that's for sure!" the old spinster interrupted again. "It was usually to draw some risqué witticism from her, or such remarks for which she has become famous."

"The truth is, that everyone had a good time at her biting repartees."

"Which the ladies feared," one of the gentlemen spoke half in jest, half reproachfully, "because they were as a rule as true as they were sharp."

"As a rule she chose gentlemen as the *point de mire* of her railings."[7]

"How strange then, that the ladies defend her so little," I couldn't help remarking.

"That is *not* strange, Squire! The peculiarities by which she managed to cause a stir are precisely those which we cannot stand in our own sex. In all her victories we saw defeats; the good tone perished in the process."

"And how did the party end for Miss Mordaunt in that curious dancing costume?" I broke in, for I was less interested in a *combat d'esprit*[8] with this precious little widow than in a more complete character sketch of Francis, even though it was coloured somewhat by a touch of gossip.

"Just as she wanted it to end, I think. She was neglected a little bit that evening, and that seems to have been her goal, because she did nothing to ward it off: on the contrary, she declared her decision not to dance in so loud and so strange a voice to the hostess herself, that there could be no further question of asking her."

"She was clever enough for that," the old spinster now interrupted. "She took the initiative not to be left sitting in embarrassment, in case no dancing partner came to ask her."

"The truth is, it takes more moral courage than our gentlemen possess as a rule, to take a lady by the hand who has chosen such a get-up," continued the widow.

"The custom not to spare us seems to be contagious here," an officer whispered to me, who had been introduced to me as Captain Sanders. I nodded in silence, because I wanted to listen as Mrs. X continued:

"At last, as the cotillon was called, she *had* to participate, and the unfortunate leader of the dance had to sacrifice himself. Lieutenant Willibald, the adjutant of her grandfather, was forced to drag her along. He took his courage *en deux mains*,[9] and, after some resistance, which seemed to be meant seriously, she let herself be taken along, but she did nothing to make his task any easier; on the contrary, she was so recalcitrant, so inattentive and gauche, that every so often there was some confusion and her cavalier had the greatest trouble to correct her mistakes and distractions. The courteous gentleman was pitied by everyone, all the more since one knew that he had in fact sacrificed himself out of duty, since he was engaged with a most lovely girl, who had to stay home because of a bereavement in the family."

"Pardon me, Madam! Allow me to say that your presentation has ended up somewhat incorrect," Captain Sanders, with whom because of his serious and intelligent appearance I was impressed immediately, now broke in.

"Permit me to rectify a few things, because I am a friend of Lieutenant Willibald, and I know that it would disturb him if this sketch were to be presented as the truth. It was absolutely no *corvée*[10] to lead Miss Mordaunt to the dance, in whatever costume she chose to show herself, because he liked her well enough to overlook some little bizarreness...Yes, I dare say, if he had had his choice, his most lovely future bride, a very young, stiff doll brought up a bourgeoise, would never have become his wife; but the circumstances forced him, and Miss Mordaunt seems to have done her part, to let him marry into fortune."

I thanked the captain in my heart that he took up the glove in such a courteous fashion for the truth against that false little tongue, and I would have liked to thank him openly and shaken his hand, but I had to be careful and hide my interest, if I wanted to hear more.

"And did Miss Mordaunt get married later on?" I asked, and tried to let the question fall from my lips as indifferently as possible.

"Of course not!" the skinny old spinster cried with a triumphant smile. "She has, as far as I know (and one knows a fair bit in these circles) never had a serious pretender."

"Well, that's very strange, isn't it? A young lady who seems to have so many attractions," I remarked.

"That's not at all strange," the little widow retorted in a coquette and sentimental tone. "To attract admirers and flatterers of the moment around one is not difficult for her; but a woman only gains serious affection and respect through the heart, and nobody has ever been able to take Francis Mordaunt *au sérieux, n'en deplaise à* the captain,[11] because she has no heart: she has never loved anything but horses and dogs..."

[Leopold encounters Francis during a ride in the woods, his carriage having gotten stuck in the sand.]

..."Major Frans," the coachman in his overly loud and penetrating voice exclaimed, unable, in his anger and surprise, to contain himself. It was she herself! It was Francis Mordaunt who so mercilessly mocked our embarrassment. I could not have been prepared for such a reception on her part. As she stood there, a few feet above me, but still quite close, I could observe her well, and I can't say that appearances reconciled me with her personality which had already caused so many unpleasant experiences. That was not her fault, but it *was* her fault that she had got herself up in such a silly fashion that one hesitated at first sight whether one were dealing with a man or a woman. She had her riding dress tied up in a fashion which made one think of the trousers of the Zouaves,[12] and with it she had thrown a wide *vareuse*[13] with long, shaggy hair over the narrow jacket of her riding dress, very efficient to be sure, but little suited to show her graceful figure, in case she really possessed one. Her head was covered by a grey *flambard* hat with the buckles coming down; the blue or green veil which usually gives such a masculine headcovering, if the ladies consent to wear it with their riding costume, some feminine distinction, was missing; only a few feathers, which had been loosely attached to it by a green silk ribbon, gave it an air as if the wearer had wanted to imitate the wild hunter of the fairy tale, and to crown the whole thing, she had tied a red kerchief over the top of the hat and tied it under her chin. As far as this unsettling costume left me the possibility to judge her appearance, she must be fine and slim rather than coarse and stout, and her appearance was altogether in contrast with the picture I had dreamed of her. The idea had taken hold of me that she would resemble the actress Ristori in the character of Medea,[14] with pitchblack curly hair and sharp expressive features. Of her hair nothing could be seen because of the turned-down borders of the flambard hat, but as far as I could judge from the portion of her face that was not overshadowed by that graceless covering, she was blond, with fine features and a roman nose; it required more goodwill than I felt at this moment to receive a pleasant impression of this face under her explosive laughter and the awful red silk scarf, tied on as if she had a toothache, which surrounded it. I felt teased by it, and, little in the mood to show any politeness for a woman who so obviously forgot her self-respect, I called to her: "Listen, you there! You who make such fun of your fellow man's miseries! You would do better to show us how to continue our way."

"There is no way to continue, that, it seems to me, is easy to see. Whoever comes into the forest other than to go riding makes a stupid mistake. That's all."

"And you?"

"Me?" She laughed again. "I've jumped with my horse across a dry ditch over there between the bushes, and so I got onto the heath. Do the same, if you like, but with horse and carriage it won't be so easy! Where did you want to go anyway?"

"To the house De Werve."

"To De Werve!" she repeated, and deigned finally to descend from her horse and to come to the edge of the ditch, from where I stood talking to her.

"What's your business in the manor, sir?" she now asked in a completely different tone, no longer the bantering, frank tone of *somebody* who does not have to spare *anybody*.

"A visit to general von Zwenken and the *freule* Mordaunt, his granddaughter."

"The general no longer expects visitors, and what you want to say to his granddaughter you can say to me. I am Miss Mordaunt."

"I can hardly believe it, but if it is true, I request of the *freule* to show me a less unsuitable place for an interview than this one; what I would like to say cannot be shouted across a dry ditch and within hearing distance of a coachman."

"Then drive with your carriage to the toll, there you can find the way back to the village and the manor, if the visit is necessary."

"So that you can send me away at the gate, major!" I said to myself; "no, the occasion is now, and I won't let it slip away!"

I gave the coachman orders to drive back (he did not have to be told twice), placed the sturdy walking stick with which I had equipped myself as best as I could into the soft, mossy ground, and came to the other side, without quite knowing how; for a moment I saw stars before my eyes; if I had had the bad luck of missing my jump, and had ended up in the mud, I would again have cut a ridiculous figure with Francis, who would without mercy have mocked my misfortune. I risked a lot, but it had to be done. The motto of my ancestors appeared to be prophetic: boldness had been crowned by success.

"Bravo! Well done!" Francis called with her full alto voice, which for the first time did not strike me as hard and provoking, and she clapped her hands with a jollity and roguishness which well suited her.

Once onto the field, I had only a few steps to do, and only to jump across a dry furrow and I was with her. I took off my hat, she saluted with her riding crop.

"That's a comical adventure, sir," she said, again smiling.

"If you are still intent on ending up at De Werve, you must walk across the meadow."

"Is it a long walk?"

"No, it's much shorter than by carriage; but since you do not know the way across the heath, you risk getting lost."

"You forget that I have the right to count on your company during the walk."

"A right! A right! you're just like the others to take your rights from a casual word that has escaped me."

"The *freule* Mordaunt had promised me an interview; is it strange that I take her at her word, and grasp at the first opportunity?"

"Well all right, I do know my way across these grounds. I had wanted to ride back, but my horse has lost a shoe, and I had left it with the forester over there," she pointed to a farm house that lay a little lower, and as if hidden between fir and spruce trees, "he'll bring it to the blacksmith in the village, and so I was just wandering around a bit; we can be at the manor in half an hour, if we are attentive and always keep to the left; but I would first like to know if you really must go there; the general does not at all appreciate guests, that I can assure."

"I'm not going to ask for hospitality. I just wanted to pay him a visit and get acquainted with him, because I'm going to be in the neighborhood for a while, and I remembered that I'm related through my mother to the family of the von Zwenkens."

"So much the worse for you: on De Werve they're not particularly subject to fondness for family."

"I've heard of that; but I am not a Roselaer, I'm a van Zonshoven, miss. Leopold van Zonshoven."

"I've never heard that my grandfather had relations with gentlemen by that name. But if you are *not* a Roselaer, there's less harm, and because of the strange fact that someone is at all interested in our family, you'll perhaps be succesful with the general. Surely you come on business?"

"In that case I would have sent a solicitor or notary, and make sure that Miss Mordaunt would not get mixed up in it."

"That would be wrong," she answered seriously, "the general is far in his seventies, and has had much sorrow in his life. I don't want to hide from you that he's in deep trouble, and that I, as often as I can, try to prevent people from bothering him."

"But by avoiding what is annoying, one hasn't solved the problem yet, I should think," I answered, while looking at her with a certain directness. Deep, dark blue eyes met my own gaze.

"You're telling *me*," she said with a deep sigh, while she directed her telling blue eyes downward, and a sign of pain came into her face.

"But still I do all I can, even if it is not all I would like to, and therefore, I repeat, if there is anything unpleasant in your visit, better tell me frankly right away; possibly I can find a solution to it."

"I can only tell you that I would like to support wholeheartedly your attempts to spare the general any trouble."

"That speaks for your heart; but if you think that way, I hesitate to recognize you as a member of the family, because it goes completely against our traditions."

"That's quite possible, but you can confidently call me cousin, because there are exceptions, and I hope to prove to you that I am one."

"If that is true, you will be welcome at De Werve, exceptionally, also, because usually we do no longer admit new faces."

"That's a pity. It seems to me, it can't be your desire to live in such strict isolation."

"Precisely my desire!" she interrupted with a certain arrogance. "I have enough experience of people to not be particularly keen on having contact with them."

"So young still and already such a misanthropic view of the world," I remarked.

"I'm not that young anymore: I'm twenty-six, cousin, and there are campaign years among them, as my grandfather would say, which count double. You can talk to me as if I were a woman of forty. I have experience."

"I would be ill advised to take you at your word; something like that the ladies only say to be contradicted."

"The ladies!" she cried out with scorn. "I ask you very seriously, cousin, not to count me among those beings which are generally designated as 'the ladies'."

"Under what rubric must I place you then, cousin? The truth is that I didn't at first sight know for what I should take you."

"It's true," she said smilingly, "for someone who doesn't know me I really must look a little strange...But say, what did you take me for? I like sincerity; *that* at least separates me from 'the ladies'."

"Well then, I shall be sincere (the words of Gremio: *He will kill her in her own humor* were constantly on my mind).[15] I took you at first for..." (*courtoisie* began to play tricks on me: the harsh word would not come out).

"For the apparition of the Black Hunter?" she asked smilingly.

"An apparition? Absolutely not! that's too ethereal. I took you for a sad realist...for a forester with a toothache."

She seemed hurt for a moment and bit her lip; her cheeks glowed.

"That's strong language," she said finally, and looked at me with a glance as if an arrow would shoot out of her eyes.

"You wanted sincerity and said that you could stand it," I replied.

"You're right, and you will find that I spoke the truth. Let's shake hands on it, cousin, there's my hand. I believe we'll be friends."

"I hope so, cousin! But don't be halfway generous. Let me really shake your hand, not your rough riding gloves."

"You're a dandy," she said, shaking her head; "but you'll have your wish: here." And a fine, white hand lay in mine which I held a minute longer than was strictly necessary; she didn't seem to notice it.

"But call me Francis, I will call you Leo. This calling each other cousin is such a nuisance," she said in a generous tone.

"With pleasure." I once again pressed her hand, which only now liberated itself, while she continued with a mixture of roguishness and seriousness that suited her, "but the coachman must have told you that he recognized Major Frans."

"That's only too true; and you, Francis, don't you find it most insulting that they dare call you that?"

"Oh, no, I don't pay attention to it; I know they've given me that nickname. I'm neither better nor worse for it. I know very well that they consider me a Cossack or a cavalry officer in this neighborhood, because I ride a horse more easily than those city prigs, and that they stare at me everywhere as if I'm a circus wonder, because I take the liberty to dress according to my own convenience, and not according to their taste."

"But a woman must be somewhat concerned for the effect she makes on others."

"I wouldn't know why, if the others don't concern her!"

"The first duty of a woman to herself, it seems to me, is to make herself attractive."

"The 'ladies' try to convince their men of that, for whom they don't want to be anything but *objets de luxe*, so that they will grant them everything the excesses of fashion and luxury demand."

"I fear that there are such, and too many of them; but are all those to be condemned, who like to appear in a favorable light? Doesn't self-respect demand, be one man or woman, that one should take care of one's appearance, and can't one show taste even in the most simple things, if one *has* taste?"

She blushed a little.

"So you believe that I don't have taste at all, because I equipped myself against this blustering spring day with a *vareuse*," she asked somewhat insulted.

"I know better than to judge you by a single piece of clothing; I only spoke of the ensemble; and because a woman who is completely indifferent to her appearance is an abnormality, I must get a poor opinion of the taste of a lady who accepts wrapping her face in an ugly red cloth."

"Which gives her the appearance of a forester with a toothache," she repeated quickly and boldly. "Well, if that is the offense, it can soon be eliminated; if only the wind does not take too much liberty now with my *flambard*."

Thus saying, she had unknotted the cloth and at the same time removed the pin which held up her riding habit. The stately train suited the fine, slim figure. No longer hindered by the surly *foulard*,[16] I could for the first time admire the ensemble of her face.

No, in truth she was not ugly, even though she had done everything to look quite uncomfortable. Her traits were irregular and sharp, to be sure, but not at all rough or coarse; there was an expression of pride and firmness in this face, which testified to independence and character, but was far removed from meanness and sensuality. Only a faint blush coloured the paleness of those cheeks, which were a little lean and hollow. You could tell that she had been through combat and suffering, without her vivacity and cheerfulness of spirit having suffered too much in the process. The big blue eyes had a certain openness which inspired confidence; that they could sparkle out of indignation, or glow with enthusiasm, I had already noticed.

As she walked beside me, I noted that she was shorter than I had first thought, seen from above; but there was true grit in this feminine figure, that couldn't be denied, although it wasn't precisely the bold he-woman I had imagined I would meet, judging by the information of others, and the heroic nickname which didn't seem to annoy her at all. It wasn't the moment to ask how she had gotten it; I was already satisfied that I had scored a victory over her which did not seem without significance. That she had made certain concessions showed that she was not quite so indifferent about what impression she made on others as she wanted me to believe. Yet I had to admit that she had been correct in hitching up her riding habit, even though it was in a somewhat unelegant fashion, because it now prevented her from walking through the loose sand, and kept getting stuck on a branch or a bush. Once she even stumbled because of it, and would have fallen if I had not quickly grabbed her arm to help her up.

"There you have the result of all the coquetry you're preaching to me!" she said laughingly. "My own method was much better in practice. Wait a minute, I have it." She took the train over her arm and wasn't worried by the fact that there didn't emerge a coquette *jupon* with a neat *plissés*[17] or embroidered panels, such as our ladies are not loath to display, but a plain blue little *merinos*[18] which looked rather discolored.

I offered my arm against a possible *recidive*[19] of the accident.

"Thank you, cousin," she said somewhat bitingly, "I can walk by myself, as I am used to. I'm not one of those helpless creatures as you men like them, who always let themselves be supported and guided."

"I will have you know that it is *you* who is being my guide; why would I not be allowed to be your support in turn?"

"You must be a lawyer, that you can always respond so skillfully."

"I will tell you what I am, if you take my arm: *une fois ne fait pas la loi*,[20] at most it is because of my being sociable."

"No, this time you will not have your way, Leo. It's just as cosy each to his own, and if I *am* your guide, I should know what is best, walking on these grounds. I can listen to you just as well."

"Excuse me, then I will postpone my confidential announcements till later."

"Oh, all right," she said drily. "I'm not so curious; and what if I made a mistake in choosing the path, if your story became too interesting and demanded too much of my attention?"

"I agree with you," I answered in the same tone of voice, "that we musn't get lost, because I really must get to De Werve."

"I gladly believe you; the trip hasn't been an easy one," she noted with a mixture of bitchiness and roguishness.

"On the contrary; I couldn't have anticipated making the acquaintance so quickly and in such a suprising fashion, with my cousin, Francis."

"Make the acquaintance, make the acquaintance," she repeated almost growlingly; "one doesn't get to know me just like that, at the first encounter; and as far as the surprise is concerned, if you call it a pleasant one, I don't see where your vaunted sincerity has disappeared to."

"It is, where it always is, and it forces me to have you know that one can also speak of a surprise when it is far from pleasant; and I readily confess, if you are keen to hear it, that your malicious pleasure in my accident left a not quite comfortable impression on me."

"That is a happy circumstance for me; then there is a chance that I might turn out better than expected."

If she was looking for a compliment, it wasn't the moment for me to let myself be caught; I walked on silently beside her.

Suddenly she stopped and spoke to me with generous vivacity: "Forgive me, Leo! that I so mercilessly laughed at you. Please believe me that it didn't concern your person, but...what shall I say, I always enjoy it so much when I see one of the so-called lords of creation making a fool of himself, that I had to laugh out loud, even though the anger of the one so mocked could make me pay dearly for it."

"Of course it is not for that that I hold a rancor against you, Francis!" I said seriously. "But what hurts me for your as well as for my sake, is the bitterness against all of us, which speaks so clearly out of your behaviour, and of which that *Schadenfreude*[21] about my misadventure is only the expression."

"Can I help it if I see men as they are? They call themselves our lords and masters; they would love to be that, even though most of them don't succeed; and why not? Because they are above all slaves of their own weaknesses, passions and instincts; most of them are so bitterly mean-spirited and simple that one can wind them around one's finger, if one took the trouble of finding out their weaknesses and to flatter them. Those, on the other hand, whom they call powerful and clever, are so hard-hearted, so selfish, so unreliable, that a woman would do better to smash her heart against a rock, rather than to dare approach the cliff against which her heart will break apart."

"That is a harsh judgment, Miss Mordaunt! And it seems to me that you do not yet have the right to pronounce it with such determination."

"It comes from Major Frans, who has had ample opportunity to observe gentlemen and their game."

"Could it also be that Major Frans has let herself at one time be blinded too easily by shining uniforms; that upon later closer observation disillusionment followed, when it appeared that under the uniform one didn't find what the exterior promised; with the result that now the military and the civil are both weighed in the same scales, and found to be too light?"

"You're mistaken, that isn't how it went. Major Frans didn't have the opportunity to be impressed by fancy uniforms; he was, as it were, raised on ammunition bread, and has seen pass by him all the ranks from corporal to field marshall, so that he knows precisely what is hidden below the braids and embroideries; he also is not quite unacquainted with civilians, and has been able to observe smokings and decorated breasts in ample variety, to arrive at a final balance sheet, and the conclusion is this: that discipline is probably the best way to draw out whatever good there is in a man, while evil is at least kept within certain boundaries. A *preservative* which so-called bourgeois freedom lacks. For the rest, one ought not to say that military discipline lowers a person; on the contrary, it keeps erect what cannot stand on its own, whereas the servility which rules bureaucracy throws one into the dust, and spoils the character, if indeed character there was."

"The description isn't very flattering for either categories. It seems that Major Frans has difficulty acknowledging the superiority of our sex."

"She thinks that first there has to *be* superiority, before superiority can be acknowledged."

"Miss Mordaunt must be very highly placed, to make such exorbitant demands on others."

"She would, it seems to me, be very lowly placed indeed, if she didn't make any higher demands than the pitiful mediocrity with which people usually content themselves."

"Not a favorable prospect for your future spouse, miss!"

"My future spouse!"

She laughed out loud, but there was something shrill and smarting in that laugh.

"I can see, dear Leopold, that you've fallen from the skies. Rest assured: nobody will suffer from my excessive demands...I won't marry."

"You can't say that yet. The circumstances could so conspire that..."

"That I would take a husband in order to pacify them," she interrupted, speaking with indignation. "Listen, Leo! You know nothing about me; and what you possibly *think* you know will have been whispered to you through rumour and gossip. That's why I can't blame you for speaking like this. But I beg of you not to think so low of me that you think me capable of sacrificing my name and my person for material gains, from whomsoever. That would be the last straw! A *mariage de raison*,[22] the most immoral contract there can be! Any day, who in the world considers it folly? Who in the world would consider it a shame? Well now, I do. Major Frans! Even though I am the only one with these feelings, I insist on them, and nothing or nobody can make me abandon them. I do not barter with my freedom, with my hand. I will be the lady of De Werve one day, and I want to remain a free woman."[23]

Lady of De Werve! Poor Francis, I had but to say the one word, to take away her illusions. Lady of De Werve she could never be, unless she gave me the hand which she held up so high, beyond all reach. Lady of De Werve! Only with my permission could she be that. But it was not at all the time yet to speak to her in so determined a fashion. I took a sidestep which nevertheless went in the direction of my goal.

"Many a proud young lady who thought like you, Francis." I spoke, "and who would never have given in to the search for gain, nevertheless let herself be pried away from her strength by considerations of a different kind precisely on those who pride themselves at being free women, gossip and lies sharpen their arrows... "

"And against those she would have to take a man, like a shield, to hide behind it!" she cried out with vehemence "No, Leopold van Zonshoven, once you have gotten to know Francis Mordaunt, you will know that she is not afraid of those arrows, even if she feared them, she would not be a coward enough to hide against them in that way. I have in any case heard them whizzing around my ears long enough to know what power they have; and that is why I know that a shield would not even protect: it would merely show a double target, and rather than a second, a careless target who would attempt to expose himself to them with the heroism of a Don Quixote, I would receive them all alone in my breast: they can't harm me any more anyway," she ended with a contemptuous shrug of her shoulders. Not only pride and willpower, but also proud self-confidence spoke out of these words, which were apparently more than words; I could read that in her glance, had I not understood it from the firm, soulful tone of her voice, which touched me deeply. I felt that she must have gone through deep and narrow roads to be able to talk like this; I was about to put into my voice something which would show commiseration, when she suddenly spoke again, with a lightness which was a little artificial: "but there is no danger that someone will lead me into such a temptation: the race of Don Quixotes and Knights of the Round Table has been lost in our century, and nobody will get the idea to ask Major Frans to marry him; and that is very fortunate, because the general would like to see me what he calls 'established' before his death; the good man doesn't realize that there can be no thought of that; he would console himself to all sacrifices, enter into every compromise to convince me; and that would only give unrest and conflict without a good solution; because my decision is made."

This statement promised little good for the success of my journey, and she wasn't a little miss of 19 years, who says "no" when she means "yes;" but she nevertheless gave me, without knowing or wishing it, hints and information which I could make use of. *Un homme averti en vaut deux;*[24] and I had understood that I would have to proceed with the utmost care before I could dare to attempt in earnest to dislodge her from that firm decision, but it wouldn't hurt to fire a wild shot. I had unintentionally gotten a few paces ahead of her, turned around suddenly and stood before her, while I said: "And if I had come to De Werve with the express purpose of making you such a proposal?"

"What do you mean by that?" she asked, frowning; "a proposal? What kind of proposal?"

"Well, that of which you spoke, and which you consider so unlikely that someone would hit upon."

"A marriage proposal, and by you?" she asked, with as much bitterness as surprise, "that's not true! Say that it's not true," she cried with vehemence.

"But suppose for a moment that it were true, what would you answer?"

"I will not even entertain that assumption; you please me as a cousin, as a curiosity, but if I were to believe that you came as a barrister in such a bad business, I would simply leave you standing in the middle of the heath. You would then have to see how you got to De Werve; and that's my answer." And as if she had started to execute this intention, she ran quickly ahead, but not so fast that I didn't catch up with her with a few paces.

"An answer more direct than polite, as was to be expected from Miss Mordaunt," I resumed; "but I, in turn, must tell you that if I had my mind made up to get to De Werve, with whatever proposal — despite my warrior cousin, I would not let this *detail* bother me. I am stubborn, too, when I want to reach my goal, and I would not give it up, even if I had to walk around all day in the loose sand; but rest assured, I am not a flatterer, there is enough old courtesy in my blood not to hurt a lady (excuse me if I use that word) in her most tender and highest rights: hence I would not be foolish enough to make such a proposal in such a brusque manner, and above all not before I had gained the conviction that it would at least be taken into consideration."

"Well, if the case were to present itself, you have been warned, but if I am to take this to be nothing but a purposeless joke, I must tell you that I had expected better from you than a pleasantry in which I can find neither wit nor invention."

That was more than a *coup d'éventail*;[25] that was a firm slap with the riding crop...

[Having gotten to know Leopold a little better, Francis tells him about the advantages and disadvantages of her peculiar "education."]

..."They say that my education has been neglected, but in a certain sense that's not true. I have not at all grown up wildly, but precisely that direction has been lacking of which I had most need, because I have grown up as a boy! As you have already heard, my mother survived my birth by only a few days: *she* at least is not guilty of anything undertaken against me. Rolf's sister, a victim of a despicable seduction and an unwed mother, but otherwise a solid, honest farm girl, became my wetnurse. Her child had died, and all that was in her heart in the way of motherly love was transferred to me. I was her child. She did not understand it otherwise. She also stayed with me till her death, when I was already no longer a child. But her love was nevertheless a different one from what she would have shown towards her own child. Our women from the farming classes tend not to be weak mothers; yet she was that to me. She gave in to everything I wanted, and her argument for that giving in was always that there was nobody else in the world but she to love me. That was an exaggeration, because grandfather, who at the time lived in, the same house with my Father, loved me, although it was all too true that Sir John Mordaunt concerned himself very little with the little girl. The truth is that he had wished for a son, not only because of his name, but also because his future fortune depended on that. He had had a son, baptized Francis like myself, on whose existence he had built great expectations, but who only lived for half a year. Twelve months after this loss, over which my father could never console himself, a daughter was born to him, which was greeted by him with so little satisfaction that the mother herself was painfully touched by it. After all I have experienced later, I must assume that sadness over the wounding disappointment his coolness caused her, has soured the last hours of her life, if not hastened her death. Be that as it may, Sir John Mordaunt wanted nothing to do with the little child, until one day nurse, who could not stomach this indifference, carried me to him to show what a strong, sturdy child I was, and how much the force and health of the girl had the upper hand over the languishing boy, who had not been able to live seven months. "Truly, it could be a boy!" papa is said to have exclaimed, according to the story of Rolf, who was present. And from that day on, Sir John began to occupy himself with me, that is to say, to give a specific direction to my education, which has made me what I am now, and which could have made me into something far worse, if not intervening persons and circumstances had somewhat modified the effects of his unusual educational methods. Under the pretext of hygiene and English custom, they let me wear until my seventh year a wide and comfortable costume which my nurse called a boy's suit, but which was extremely appropriate for allowing me to do all kinds of physical exercises. The minute I could walk, I already got a gymnastic teacher; I was hardened against hot and cold, like a young Spartan. Rolf was ordered to teach me exercises when I could only carry a child's gun. Nor did he neglect giving me lessons in fencing, and I didn't lack the opportunity to practice myself in that noble art, since all the young officers who came to visit us found pleasure in it; or did so out of friendliness against my father, in order to measure themselves against me. For a true or pretended victory against them I was most brilliantly rewarded by Sir John. I was allowed to indulge in every whim, as long as they were wild, brutal and boyish caprices. I don't know when they began to give me my nickname of the "little major," nor even why; I presume it was Rolf who thought it up in order to give me proof of his deep admiration and at the same time to distinguish me from grandfather, who had ascended to the rank of major; but I do know that papa liked the title and never let the opportunity slip by to use it, and I clearly remember how astonished I was when an officer, probably a newcomer, addressed me as Miss Francis. I know that I took it rather badly, and that I angrily pronounced an English curse which I had heard Sir John use several times. I also know that papa lifted me off the ground then and kissed me while smiling. It was the first time that he showed me his fatherly affection in this way. Is it my fault that I considered that uncouth word a beautiful one, and didn't neglect to resort to it, and more of the kind, when I wanted to have my way or wanted to put some emphasis in my expression? They always laughed about it, and I was kissed and applauded for it... how could it have been different!"

"It is even surprising that the bad habit has not remained with you!"

"Long enough, to tell you the truth; and even now I'm not quite sure that in a fit of temper... Still, I must credit nurse that she reacted to it in her own way by telling me that cursing is sinful; for as soon as I could somewhat grasp the meaning of that word, she had inspired a healthy dislike for it in me. "But is father allowed to sin?" I asked. "Oh, for gentlemen it's a different matter." "Well, I don't want to be a girl then!" — There usually followed then a conversation wherein the honest woman preached morality in her way. It always ended with my being angry that I wasn't a gentleman and the regret of only being a girl has truly spoilt my carefree years as a child. And the fury with which I destroyed white muslin dresses and graceful little hats, which my nurse ordered me at certain times to wear on her own authority, proved clearly that there was very little of the character of a girl in me."

"It was there all right, Francis! I am sure of it. But one has forced nature and..."

"It's true that I never got anything but boys' toys: drums, whips, tin soldiers, and when grandfather once got the idea to give me a doll, it was immediately thrown away with the deepest contempt. The pattern had been set; papa could relax. To children's parties I wasn't allowed to go; little misses didn't come into our house; I grew up in a circle of adults, officers, amateurs of the hunt and of horse-riding — an exercise of which I could speak from experience — and of women one noticed precious little more than the servants and the nurse. When it came to learning, I received my teachers at home, and when nurse declared herself no longer able to govern the wild, capricious and unmannered child, I got...a governor! He was a clever man, who possessed a lot of knowledge, but a low character; a useful person, as they say, and one who really also let himself be used to tailor me for the role which they wanted me to play in the mystification on a grand scale they were planning. It was later revealed to me that Sir John had kept the death of his child in

England a secret, just as the birth of his daughter; that he wanted the latter to take the place of the former on the other side of the Channel, and that he prepared for the possibility of having me appear in certain circles. The isolation in which they kept me, the education they gave me, were intended to isolate me from persons of my sex, to inspire disgust in me for their life's task, and a certain resentment against the position which we were allotted in society, whilst my tendency towards independence was fed and flattered, and they tried to give to my mind certain peculiarities which they called bold, masculine formation, although I later observed these highly praised characteristics far less in most men than in some women. I profited from that education, but not in the way which was the most useful for their purposes, because I hated all deceit and untruth, and considered it treachery and cowardice, while it was my pleasure to show myself the way I was, bold and open to everyone..."

[After many complications, intrigues, and several dramatic changes in their relationship, Francis and Leopold are finally reconciled.]

...when I arrived downstairs I heard from Frits that the *freule* was getting dressed and would go out riding. And indeed I saw the young Pauwels draw up with her graceful riding horse, and a few moments later the amazon arrived herself, dressed as I had seen her the first time, but now she wore a charming little hat with a dark-blue veil, which suited her extremely well.

"Sacrifice your ride for once," I asked her with a certain vigor, under which I tried to hide my uncertainty, without succeeding very well.

She looked at me with a somewhat sly astonishment, grew pale and was silent, while she played with her riding crop.

"Surely you can ride an hour later," I added, a little more insistent.

"No, because I have a long circuit, I even have to hurry, if I want to complete it before dinner."

"Then you will have to postpone your long ride till tomorrow, Francis," I said seriously. "It's for the first time that we can get out quietly together since your grandfather's illness; don't refuse me this." And the glance with which I looked at her must, despite myself, have expressed something of the hope and fear which animated me, because I saw her hesitating, as she answered me with forced regret: "You always like to disturb my plans."

"Not arbitrarily, Francis, believe me; but I have a good reason: I will perhaps not be able to demand it of you tomorrow."

"Well, that sounds threatening," she replied, with an attempt at a smile which didn't succeed very well. "Well now, if it's like that," and she threw her riding crop away with that unwillingness with which an officer takes off his sabre to give himself up a prisoner; "but you will have to wait till I have put on another dress, because going for a walk with you in a riding habit doesn't go very well."

Thereupon she gave orders to take Tancred to the stable and went into the house.

If she were animated by the usual female passion for tormenting, I ran the danger of waiting a long time. A coquette would certainly not have missed the opportunity to punish the imprudent who obstructed her in her intentions; but it showed that she was above such narrow-minded lady-like manners, for she came back very soon and had only changed the annoying riding habit for a short, light dress that was less obstructive for the walk. Her little hat and the jacket she had kept, and she came quickly and determinedly up to me, as she asked:

"And where are we going now?"

"But...I would say to the forest."

"You're right; it's lovely there now; we can walk up to the round-point and rest there."

Thus we went a stretch up the great avenue which led to the forest, in silence, precisely because we had so much to tell each other.

I was determined to speak, but not quite at one with myself how I would like to start, when she began:

"I can sacrifice my ride, Leo! but not the duties which are connected with it."

"Believe me, Francis! that I will never be in your way if we're dealing with your duties; on the contrary, you can count on me to support and strengthen you."

"I don't need help in that. I only need to go my own way."

"That sounds strong, Francis! because I have led you from your road this time. But it had to be, because I have to talk to you undisturbed. I can't stay here any longer; all sorts of interests call me back to The Hague."

"I've seen it coming, Leo!"

"Are you sorry?"

"I should say no, to answer that silly question in a silly way."

"But I shall come back, if you approve."

"No, Leo, I do not approve, and it would even have been better if you had gone when I first advised you to do so."

"I don't understand. Have I been a nuisance?"

"You know you haven't; you know I have much to thank you for; but it's precisely because of that. You stood by my side in dark days; you have shared all manner of sorrow and trouble; moreover, we have squabbled so pleasantly, in a word, you have spoilt me. Loneliness will now lie more heavily on me than before."

"Not for long, because I'm only going in order to come back soon."

She didn't answer, but kept on walking slowly and silently beside me.

"What do you want me to bring back for you from The Hague?" I asked, not to let the subject slip.

"You have already given me a souvenir, Leo! and I'm very grateful for it. You can see that I'm already using it; that's enough, I don't need any more."

"Not even an elegant summer dress, Francis? You've told me that yours is in a bad way."

"I have no business getting dressed up now, Leo! Understand that."

"All right! If you don't want to help me, I shall know myself what to do."

"What are you planning? You really make me curious," she said with some agitation in her voice, which she couldn't control.

"I will order a trousseau for you."

"A trousseau! Why a trousseau!" she cried out, laughing loudly. "It seems my clever cousin Leopold too has his hour of saying *folies*, or even of doing them."

"Or do you prefer a *corbeille de mariage*?"[26]

"Have you lost your senses, Leo? a *corbeille de mariage*! For God's sake, for whom?"

"It seems to me for nobody other than my lovely, obstinate cousin, Francis Mordaunt!"

"That's not a very nice pleasantry, Squire! You know that your cousin Francis will not marry."

"Listen, Francis! When you spoke of that decision once to me, when we walked on the heath, I had no reason to try to make you give it up. I felt nothing but the interest which forced me to get to know you, and I knew nothing about you to try seriously to advise you against your decision. But now you know yourself that everything has become different between us. I have used great frankness with you to point out such flaws as could harm your noble character. You have taken that attention for what it was: proof of my intense interest, and you have rewarded it with your full confidence. But you must understand yourself, that I could not have allowed myself to frequent you so long and in this fashion, if there had not been a firm determination in me to ask you to be my wife."

"That really sounds like a declaration *bout portant*,[27] and since I could not have expected such a sudden outburst, I will take it for what it seems: a *raillerie*.[28] I know you like to tease me a little, and to amuse yourself with my repartees, and that is fortunate for you, otherwise you would run the danger of being rejected outright."

I understood that she had come to the battle armed to the teeth; she was cool, sharp, hautain in her answer; but in the voice, which wanted to be so indifferent and joking, there vibrated an emotion which she tried to deny by turning her face away.

"To tell you the truth, Francis! I don't believe in your rejection at all. You want to misunderstand me, because you're in a mood to torture me and to defend yourself to the utmost against the voice of your heart; but you cannot have been so mistaken in mine or you know that I now speak in complete earnest. "

"Well, then, Leo!" she interrupted with a deep sigh. "If you want to be serious, I must remind you of my earlier warning not to speak to me of such wishes; it cannot, it must not be!"

"But why? Have I been so mistaken when I thought that I was not completely indifferent to you? I had expected something better from you, I thought that you felt something for me."

She nodded with her face turned away and was silent, but suddenly I heard something like a stifled sob.

"Are you perhaps no longer free?" I asked softly, and, myself deeply touched, took her hand and placed myself before her to be able to look into her eyes.

"Free! Certainly I am free," she cried out bitterly. "I have done my share to remain free!" — and turning away from me quickly "but I have always told you, I must retain my independence. I have to."

"Oh, I understand you, Francis!" I said, despite myself also with bitterness now. "You have not yet given up certain illusions; you're waiting for your Lord William; you have promised yourself and ..."

"Lord William? Lord William who has never loved me!" she cried out passionately. "Lord William who has wounded me with his conceited compassion, who has broken my heart, who has led me to wildness and folly by his provident wisdom; Lord William who now must be a well-behaved man of sixty. Leo, Leo! You who love me, know it, don't torture yourself with being jealous of Lord William. Would I have confessed everything so freely if I had not overcome all of that long ago?"

"Then your distaste of marriage, that desire to remain free is only a feminine caprice, a last resistance of Major Frans, who will not give herself up a prisoner, and then I will counter that obstinacy with all my will-power and tenacity."

"Do not hurt me with your tenacity, Leo! for you could only torture me without my fighting back. Even if you were to break my heart, and you can, I confess, you could not overcome any resistance."

"Then I want to know that invisible force which strengthens you against me!" I cried out, wild with anger and pain.

"Oh, Leo, you know of what painful duties I am the slave. Why initiate yourself further into the depths of misery and despair in which I almost drown, with which I will have to struggle all my life."

"I want to know, Francis! to share them with you, to bear them with you. Fighting together, we shall conquer, I am sure of that!" I called out passionately; and, overwhelmed by the most tender compassion, I put my arms around her and clasped her to my breast. She consoled herself with this tender violence without resistance, as if weary and at the end of her fight, she let her head rest against my shoulder...

[A chance encounter with a Mrs. Jool at this point casts, a serious suspicion on Francis: Leopold believes for a moment that Francis has an illegitimate child. This mistake he is able to rectify without Francis knowing it. The mystery of her "duties" is solved: Francis pays Mrs. Jool for the care of a child born out of wedlock from a former lover and a peasant girl. Leopold commits himself to taking over the charge of the child, but Francis fears that there will be gossip. Leopold persists:]

..."I'm not afraid of a few barbs."

"It's bad enough that Mrs. Jool has seen us together today and has spied on us."

"She will notice tomorrow that she doesn't have to spy on us when we show ourselves together in public."

"No, no, Leo! that can't, that mustn't be," she cried, turning her head away with vehemence, "who knows what silly gossip she has already spread, after that encounter with us."

"If we simply make the gossip into truth, it isn't silly gossip any more."

"To make it into truth! You don't know what you're saying."

"Very well; she thought we were lovers; was she so far from the truth, Francis?" I asked softly, but seriously, and taking her hand, which she left me, "she will probably tell people that we are fiancéd, and does it harm us so much if we prove that she didn't make a mistake?"

"He still comes back to it, still, even though he knows everything!" Francis spoke half loud, as to herself.

"Who would I be, Francis, if I now retreated?"

"But I tell you, you're not taking account of all the burdens and objections which would rest on you," she said with some impatience; "De Werve with Rolf, whom we cannot set aside, my grandfather with all his needs and his negligible income. How can we afford all that? I know," she added in a changed voice, "you're going to The Hague to reconcile yourself with your uncle, the minister, as the general has advised you; I know why...But don't, don't do it for me, Leo! because you once called it cowardice!"

"If ever I reconcile myself with my uncle, Francis, it will be because the wish to forgive suits us; but never, you can count on it, to hunt after honors or favors through reconciliation."

"I thank you for that word, Leo! I thank you for all that you have been for me. Oh, I knew you are as proud as you are firm, but because of that — let your mind speak — is it not better *not* to start something one can't follow through anyway? Remain my friend, as you have been up to now, but..."

"You speak like one who herself has no passion, nor understands it in others," I interrupted. "I'm not like Willibald, I cannot remain your friend if I cannot be your lover. I can no longer sit quietly by your side and prevent myself from kissing your fine white hand which you leave so coolly and carelessly in mine (I suited the action to the word). I love you, Francis! passionately; I have repressed expressions of passion with a self-control of which you cannot form a picture; but now that I have uttered it, there has to be a decision, I have to leave you forever, or I have to become your husband, and that is what I want, Francis! with a firmness of will that considers all your problems as negligible."

"Leo, Leo!" she cried, getting up, as if she wanted to escape from me; but without turning away, "do not speak to me like that, not in the tone of violence that carries one away, not with that glow in your eyes; nobody has ever spoken to me like that; nobody has ever loved me so passionately; you bring me beside myself; you lead me into temptation, but I have to resist you! For I cannot choose your unhappiness, even if it costs me so much," her voice vibrated with a violent emotion, a deep red flushed her cheeks, and her eyes reflected something of that glow which made mine sparkle.

I took both her hands in mine and spoke with firmness: "If the separation hurts you, Francis, let's not separate!"

"It is intoxicating, Leo! The...the...possibility that I... that I still can be happy," she stammered.

"Enough, Francis! you're mine. I will not let you go. Put your hand in mine for life."

"For life!" she repeated firmly and determinedly, but with fluttering lips; she grew pale, so pale that I jumped up to support her. She was close to fainting.

"Leo! I'm yours. I entrust myself to you; I love you as I have never, never loved," she stammered, as I held her in my arms.

"Finally!" I cheered, and pressed the first kiss of love on her lips.

NOTES to the Translation

1. This novel was chosen for translation because it was recently published again, which suggests that it is still alive and somehow accessible to the modern reader. The selected passages give an impression of the weaknesses and strengths of Bosboom-Toussaint's method; since they are descriptive rather than narrative, they are, to be sure, not fully representative, but can, on the other hand, be easily understood without elaborate introduction and commentary.

2. The specific passages of this accessible novel were chosen because they demonstrate most effectively the main issue under discussion: the roles of men and women, the "battle of the sexes" and Bosboom-Toussaint's fine depiction of the psyche of both sexes.

3. Carter's boots.

4. Without means.

5. Blinding; a set of jewels.

6. To make fools of people.

7. Target.

8. Battle of wits.

9. In both hands.

10. Unpleasant task.

11. Even if the captain disapproves.

12. Volunteer papal troops who wear baggy kneepants.

13. Sweater.

14. Adelaide Ristori (1822-1906), celebrated Italian actress of classical roles.

15. In English in the original.

16. Scarf.

17. Underskirt with pleating.

18. Woollen skirt.

19. Recurrence.

20. Actually, "une fois ne fait pas coutume:" once does not a habit make.

21. Pleasure in someone's misfortune.

22. Marriage of convenience.

23. Untranslatable pun: Francis wants to be the "Vrijvrouwe" (châtelaine) of De Werve, while remaining a "vrije vrouw" (free woman).

24. A warned man counts for two.

25. A slap with a fan.

26. Gift of the bridegroom to his bride.

27. Almost in the face.

28. A joke.

Bibliography

Primary works

Bosboom-Toussaint, A.L.G. *Almagro* (1837).
_____. *De graaf van Devonshire*. Amsterdam: Otto, 1839.
_____. *De Engelschen te Rome*. (1839).
_____. *Het Huis Lauernesse*. Rotterdam: Bolle, 1840.
_____. *Lord Edward Glenhouse*. (1840).
_____. *Eene kroon voor Karel den Stouten*. Amsterdam: van Kampen, 1841.
_____. *Leycester in Nederland*. Amsterdam: Beyerinck, 1846.
_____. *Mejonkvrouwe de Mauléon*. Rotterdam: Bolle, 1847.
_____. *De vrouwen uit het Leycestersche tijdvak*. Rotterdam: Bolle, 1850.
_____. *Gideon Florensz*. Amsterdam: Gebr. Kraay, 1855.
_____. *De Delftsche Wonderdokter*. Amsterdam: Kirberger, 1870.
_____. *Majoor Frans*. Rotterdam: Bolle, 1874.
_____. *Romantische Werken* ([incomplete] collected works, 25 vols.) Arnhem, 1880-1888.

Modern Editions

_____. *Majoor Frans.* Ed., introd. Marijke Stapert-Eggen. Utrecht: L. J.
Veen B.V., 1977 [3rd. ed. 1980].
_____. *Eene kroon voor Karel den Stouten.* Ed., introd. J. de Gier. Utrecht:
Jan Perfect, 1989.

Related Works

Berg, W. van den, and P. van Zonneveld. *Nederlandse literatuur van de
negentiende eeuw.* Utrecht: HES, 1986.
Bouvy, J.M.C. *Idee en werkwijze van Mevrouw Bosboom-Toussaint.*
Rotterdam; Leiden: De Voorpost, 1935.
Busken-Huet, Conrad. "Mevrouw Bosboom-Toussaint." *Litterarische
Fantasiën en Kritieken.* Vol. 2. Haarlem: Funke, 1878-79. 73-96.
Erens, Frans. "Over Mevrouw Bosboom-Toussaint." *De Gids* III (1912).
492-506.
Huygens, G.W. "A.L.G. Bosboom-Toussaint (1812-1886)." *'t Is vol van
Schatten.* Catalogue of Dutch literature of the Letterkundig
Museum, The Hague. Vol. 2. Amsterdam, 1986. 83-85.
Kalff, G. "Anna Louisa Geertruida Toussaint." *Geschiedenis der
Nederlandsche Letterkunde.* Vol. 7. Groningen: Wolters-Noordhoff,
1912. 287-299, 520-527.
Knuvelder, G. "A.L.G. Bosboom-Toussaint (1812-1886)." *Handboek tot de
geschiedenis der Nederlandse letterkunde.* Vol. 3. Den Bosch:
Malmberg, 1973 (7th ed.). 345-359.
Meyer, Reinder P. *Literature of the Low Countries.* Assen: Van Gorcum &
Co, 1971.
Potgieter, E.J. "De Graaf van Devonshire." "Boekbeoordelingen," *De Gids*
1883. 650-664.
Reeser, J.B.G.H. "De wordingsgeschiedenis van *Eene kroon voor Karel den
Stouten.*" *Levende Talen* 1958. 465-479.
Smit, W.A.P. "Een literaire uitdaging in 1827 of drie romans over Karel de
Stoute." *Levende Talen* 1957. 9-20.
Vooys, C.G.N. de. "Onzuiverheid van taal bij mevrouw
Bosboom-Toussaint." *De nieuwe taalgids* 39 (1946). 59-61.
_____, and G. Stuyveling. *Schets van de Nederlandse Letterkunde.*
Groningen: Wolters-Noordhoff, 1980.

Henriëtte Roland Holst-van der Schalk

Gary Lee Baker

On December 24, 1869, a daughter was born to Anna Ida van der Schalk (née van der Hoeven) and her husband, a practicing lawyer, Mr. Theodoor Willem van der Schalk. Henriëtte Goverdine Anna was the second child of three. Henriëtte Roland Holst-van der Schalk enjoyed the life of a person born into the upper middle-class. She was raised, in part by nannies, in the town of Noordwijk-Binnen on the Lindenhof near the city of Leiden, not far from the sea and dunes. In spite of her class, a sense of social justice and fairness was awakened early in the young Henriëtte. Her uncle Jacques told stories about his exploits correcting injustices in Rembang, Indonesia, as colonial Resident for the Dutch government. Another uncle published a liberal newspaper and talked to her about international politics.[1] Her mother's wealth stemmed mostly from the family's gin factory in Schiedam — where the young Henriëtte was first confronted with the poor conditions of the Dutch working class. She also saw the unfortunate children in the Schiedam orphanage directed by her uncle.

In 1884, Henriëtte was sent to the Oosterwolde boarding school near Arnhem. Her education, which was typical of the time for her gender and class, included music, dance, foreign literature, religion, biology, Dutch history, Dutch language, geography, arithmetic, and physics. She was not immediately popular at school and soon earned the reputation of being a "pedant." Later, she admitted to having been, at school as well as at home, "alienated from reality and wrapped up in romantic dreams" (22). At Oosterwolde, Henriëtte demonstrated her nascent talent for writing poetry as well as an incipient social posture that was directed against authority. She surprised her classmates with a poem honoring Petrus Augustus De Génestet (d. 1861), who was buried in nearby Rozendaal. The assignment of writing and subsequently reciting the poem had been a practical joke, but she claimed that "this is exactly what I had imagined being at school with other girls would be like" (23). On another occasion, she was assigned to write a composition on the basis of her faith, in which she failed to mention the authorities of the Bible, the church and the leaders of the community. Unable to answer her teacher directly when confronted with this "error," she explained in her autobiography: "I had little feeling for that" (28). For the most part, she viewed her Oosterwolde experience and her education negatively: she acquired conventions and learned about conformity, but procured little to help her thrive philosophically, spiritually, and intellectually. The curriculum lacked important subjects such as philosophy, mathematics, and economics, which, however, did not hinder her poetic development in the least. In fact, some of her earliest creations (1884) originate from her days at Oosterwolde.[2] In October 1888, she went to Liège in Belgium, to spend time abroad like most girls of her social standing; in Liège she learned French, and studied music and contemporary culture. In spite of her formalized education and bourgeois family life, the two aspects that were to influence and guide her convictions, emotions, principles, and actions throughout her life were early awakened: poetry, and the idealism and sense of justice that were to lead her to Socialism.

On her return to Noordwijk, her career as writer and socialist commenced, for it was during these days at home that she encountered artists and poets and read the literature that inspired and sharpened her poetic expression and political awareness. Although not interested in "going out," as was expected of women of her age and social position, she did spend a few years at home leading the life of a young lady waiting for what was supposed to be her life's greatest reward: a husband. Yet, these were not wasted years. At age 21, she visited Albert and Kitty Verwey in their "Villa Nova" in Noordwijk. Though her father considered holding company with Verwey, "undesirable," he allowed it nonetheless. The impression the Verweys made on Henriëtte can be compared to that made by a divine manifestation on a mystic. Poetic impulses conquered their space in her soul and forced their way to expression: "the days were full of restlessness and the nights full of dreams" (57). At this time, Henriëtte's father took her to see the atelier of the famous painter Jan Toorop; she came away from the visit greatly inspired and wrote a sonnet cycle, which she sent to Toorop who sent it on to Verwey. Henriëtte herself considered this work the best she had done up to that point. She then visited Verwey, read her latest poems to him, and received his critique; he advised her to account for every word and to test each word to be sure it expressed what she wished to say. At this point in her life the lack of exposure to Dutch poetry made itself felt. One of her greatest laments about her Oosterwolde education was precisely about the lack of Dutch literary studies; knowing so little about Dutch poetry, she felt inferior to Verwey and his colleagues. Thus she began studying the classics, especially Hooft (1581-1647) and Vondel (1587-1679) (61). She frequented Verwey's home more and more and she noticed that her father was actually proud that someone from *De Nieuwe Gids* ("The New Guide") movement valued his daughter's work.[3] But in 1892, precisely when her poetic expression and her knowledge of Dutch poetry expanded and matured, she lost both her father and younger sister. Though these deaths (by drowning) were devastating, they stimulated Henriëtte's creatively. She underwent a great transition, as the "magic wand of poesy" assumed the expression of her "feelings and thoughts, sorrows and joys, desires and expectations" in poetry (54).

Upon Verwey's suggestion, she sent selected poems to Willem Kloos, then editor of the *Nieuwe Gids*, who accepted them for publication; thus her work finally reached those best apprised of the scene in Dutch literature. For example, Herman Gorter, eager to meet with the young poetess, skated (!) in February 1893 from Haarlem to the Verwey's to meet Henriëtte—hence, the beginning of a relationship that crossed the fields of politics and poetry and endured until Gorter's death in 1927. He advised her to read Dante and

Spinoza, claiming that reaching the level of great poetry required "reflection, wisdom and virtue" as well as good form (67). Again, her deficient background and training in philosophy hindered her understanding of Spinoza, but she had an easier task with Dante, who became the more important and lasting influence on her work, especially where her thoughts on love and the spirit are concerned. However she admitted to herself that Gorter's advice to read texts by these men was indirectly responsible for a temporary obstruction in her poetic development. She first met her future husband, the painter R.N. Roland Holst, at one of the weekly Sunday meetings at the Verwey's. Their courtship had the initial and beneficial effect of steering Henriëtte away from the influences of Gorter, whom she nonetheless admired and whose judgment she valued. She continued to read Dante, especially the *Commedia*. After the wedding on January 16, 1896 the Roland Holsts moved to Graveland. Married life, however, calmed her poetic spirit to such an extent that she feared, mistakenly, that it had left her.

Her husband worked at the time for a cultural publication, *De Kroniek* ("The Chronicle"), and became acquainted with P. L. Tak, an important member of new S.D.A.P. ("Social Democratic Workers Party," founded in 1894). Both the S.D.A.P. and *De Kroniek* consistently sided with the workers in the erupting labor conflicts in the Netherlands. Through her acquaintance with Tak, her reading of William Morris (1834-1896), and her visits to the textile factories owned by her husband's family, Roland Holst, as we will from now on refer to her, according to custom, began to develop a closer solidarity with the working class: "It was as if the scales had fallen away from my eyes" (95). Her new perception of society and capitalism was to end her poetic stagnation. She now realized that capitalism not only ruined the workers' lives but also, generally, made the world an "ugly" place; she blamed it for socially destroying the artist by destroying nature, old cities, and all sense of communal existence.

At this crucial transition, Gorter again recommended a book to her: *Das Kapital*, by Karl Marx. Bemoaning anew her lack of knowledge of economics and philosophy, she nonetheless came to an understanding of this book and especially of its economic aspects. The principal message she harvested from her reading was that the working class had to fight against its oppressors and struggle for its own power. She soon translated these feelings of anticipation and solidarity for the cause of the oppressed into public commitment. She, her husband, and Herman Gorter attended the S.D.A.P. Congress in April 1897, where they all became members. Thus began for her a life of demonstrating in the streets and composing propaganda songs for the cause of working class people.[4] Roland Holst was one of very few women who attended meetings of the S.D.A.P. and took part in the propaganda and political agitation of the party. Her life gained new resolve where she could unleash feelings of solidarity and compassion for the underprivileged. Her sense of justice, and perhaps a sense of guilt for the good life she had always led, found release and expression in her S.D.A.P. activity. Eventually, she was asked, together with Gorter, to help edit *De Nieuwe Tijd* ("The New Age"), a monthly which maintained a Marxist posture but was mainly interested in informing S.D.A.P. members about national and international events and in promoting socialist opinions. Its message to S.D.A.P. leadership was that, first of all, workers needed to be educated and had to be made aware that class interests had priority over personal ones and that long-lasting achievements were preferable to ephemeral ones.

Even though wages had gone up in the last years of the 19th century, civil unrest and the number of strikes increased. The first test of action for the S.D.A.P. came in January 1903 when disgruntled railroad workers began a strike which resulted in what Roland Holst described as "the most dramatic episode in the history of the Dutch working class movement" (106).[5] But it failed, and although Roland Holst felt great discontentment about its politics, she did not abandon the cause of socialism. In August 1904 she attended the International Socialist Congress in Amsterdam;[6] her most lasting memory of this Congress was the "general spiritual atmosphere, that harmonized so wonderfully well with the sunny summer days" (119). During these years she felt a positive sense of solidarity with her cause so intensely, that she produced her most optimistic material about socialism, revolution, and life in general, with the collections

De Nieuwe Geboort (1903, "The New Birth") and *Opwaartsche Wegen* (1907, "Upward Roads").

During the years 1904-1908, Roland Holst witnessed growing discord in the S.D.A.P., especially between the party leaders Troelstra and Gorter. In trying to reconcile disputing factions, she grew tired of petty political power struggles which she found sad and boring. Later she claimed that if it had not been for her enthusiasm for the Russian situation, she would have abandoned party politics much earlier than she actually did. Indeed, she created her first play, *De Opstandelingen* (1910, "The Rebels") to describe the "heroic courage, the solidarity, and the willingness to sacrifice" demonstrated by the Russian peasants (128). She perceived a great contrast between the life-threatening struggles in Russia and the party squabbles at home, and in order not to see her ideals reduced to trivial politicking, she spent the winter of 1908-1909 in London with her husband. Upon her return, discord in the S.D.A.P. came to a head when 500 members, among them Gorter, formed the "Social-Democratic Party" (S.D.P.) around the weekly *De Tribune* (1907, "The Tribune") whose editors had been young radicals within the S.D.A.P. Roland Holst remained in the S.D.A.P., co-editing *Het Weekblad* ("The Weekly") which was an attempt at creating more discussion within the party. In an artistic sense, these were fruitful years, because she expressed her feelings about these negative events in *Thomas More* (1912-1913), her most influential play, and in a poetry collection called *De Vrouw in 't woud* (1912, "The Woman in the Wood"). At the 1909 S.D.A.P. Congress, the supporters of *De Tribune* were officially shut out of the party; Roland Holst felt trapped between the two rivalling party factions, and, having lost all desire to continue working, she resigned in 1910 as editor of the party weekly. In 1911, she gave up party membership; thereafter she took several trips and became involved in her own work in order to forget the negative S.D.A.P. experiences. In the winter of 1913, she finished *Het Feest der Gedachtenis* (1915, "The Feast of Memorial") which was dedicated to her mother and wrote several essays on the working class and its position in society.

The First World War was a difficult period even for the neutral Netherlands. War politics deepened the split between the

S.D.A.P. which supported Germany, and the S.D.P., which stood by the Entente. A crucial event for Roland Holst in this time was her participation, as the only representative from the Netherlands, in the International Socialists Conference in Zimmerwald, Switzerland, where she met Lenin and Trotsky. She viewed this conference as a truly utopian impulse in a world of turmoil and strife: socialists from all warring nations met in peace and ignored national boundaries. Their principal message to the international working class was that all should work for peace. As such they condemned the war and the nationalism, that started it. French and German socialists even signed a pact obliging them to work for peace in their respective homelands. The experience of the conference was so moving and important to Roland Holst that she included the complete text of the conference resolution in her autobiography, which was published 34 years later (266-271).

In May 1915, prior to the Zimmerwald conference, Roland Holst founded her own political organization, the "Revolutionary Socialist Union." This was her attempt to remain within an organized socialist group but outside party politics that depressed her so much. In 1916, on the advice of the German socialist Karl Radek and with the greater ideals of socialism in heart and mind, she allowed her group (with 200 members) to merge with Gorter's small but influential S.D.P. Out of this fusion emerged the Dutch Communist Party (1918-1919).[7]

While the First World War raged on, Roland Holst closely followed events in czarist Russia. She harbored great hope for the development of socialism in Russia. The initial desires of the revolutionary government to feed its people, give land to the peasants and make peace, were in line with the proposals made at Zimmerwald. Such discontent as existed in the Netherlands, Roland Holst claimed, was "hardly heroic" when compared to the sacrifices made in the Russian revolution (172). In the Netherlands, food was the first concern of the working poor, rather than political demands or noble goals. November 1918 marked the end of the War and much unrest in Germany, beginning with uprisings in Kiel, the Dutch exile of the Kaiser, and leading to the establishment of the Weimar republic. In the same month, D.J. Wijnkoop (formerly of *De Tribune*) and Roland Holst organized a small meeting of workers to be followed by a demonstration. But as the marchers proceeded past army barracks, shots were fired and several workers killed or wounded. This incident, coupled with the obvious ineffectiveness of the "Federation of Revolutionary-Socialist Intellectuals," signaled the beginning of a particularly reactionary period in Dutch history.

Roland Holst continued to support the cause of socialism despite all its failures. Western communist parties, under the direction of the Soviet politbureau, formed an organization called the "West-European Bureau," for which Roland Holst performed tasks in Paris and Strasbourg. While attending a conference in Berlin in the early winter of 1921, she was invited to participate in the Comintern congress in June. She aspired to witness the historical event of the realization of socialism, but was already disillusioned at the border of the budding Soviet Union, when she observed a guard stabbing with his bayonet, shouting "Bourgeois, not good not good." What disturbed her was the exaggerated class antagonism and the idea that young soldiers were trained to hate in this manner (198). Upon her arrival in Moscow she spoke at the women's conference, she became acquainted with Lenin's wife, and eventually met with Trotsky again. One of the main goals of the conference was to inform representatives about the New Economic Policy (NEP) of the revolutionary government. As such the thrust of party activity was propaganda work. The workers had to be convinced that communism was the best thing for them and that capitalism was evil and a system of tyranny. Apart from the problem of low industrial productivity, there was the threat of mass starvation of the population living on the Volga river. Roland Holst learned of things that discouraged her in her support of the Comintern, not the least of which was her observation that the women's movement became less and less popular as a part of the revolution (207). It was due to unsavory tactics and political unfairness, so she claimed, that "the 'Comintern' quickly lost its influence on honest communists" (207). She counted herself among the "honest" communists who supported Trotsky. In fact, the poem *Heldensage* (1927, "Hero's Saga") deals with Trotsky and his socialist struggles; in this piece she denounced violent revolution as a viable method of change. Her sojourn in the Soviet Union was "a great disillusionment" (214). Though her husband wished her to abandon the Communist party since it was a continual source of misery, Roland Holst remained convinced of the humanistic tradition of socialism and fulfilled her Moscow promise to help the starving millions on the Volga river. She devoted the winter of 1921-22 to fundraising for this cause, because "one thing goes above every political persuasion and that is love of humankind" (215). Although Roland Holst, in the course of the decade, continued lecturing in support of communism as a member of the party, "it became constantly more difficult for me to defend communism in public meetings and I often had the feeling that I was not speaking about 'what lay at the bottom of my heart'..." (216).

In 1926, she spoke, together with the Indonesian revolutionary Mohammed Matta, on colonial policies at the meeting for the "International Women's Association for Freedom and Peace" in Gland, France. On this occasion, she rediscovered something that she had lost while working for the communist party (with which she broke in November 1927): a spirit of "something lasting" (220). At another conference she met the Swiss-German Leonhard Ragaz, a leading proponent of a religiously motivated socialism. She subsequently devoted herself completely to this brand of socialism, giving lectures at a worker's community in Bentveld and publishing in the religious-socialist weekly *Tijd en Taak* ("Time and Task;" Schaap 17). The positive spirit of Gland she found again in Ragaz and his followers, to whom she offered her testimony in the hope that the young enthusiasts would avoid her own political mistakes. She seems to have viewed her struggles in national and international politics as fruitless, although one cannot say she had no effect on the development of the socialist movement. Besides there is no evidence that she ever abandoned her belief in the possibility of a society in which humankind exists without fear of losing the necessities of life and with the greatest moral, communal, and material integrity. Due to a demanding, and to a certain extent, self-imposed workload, years of illness and physical breakdowns followed; she was now in her late fifties. On a trip to Italy, she was loathe to discover that the fascist government refused her entry to the country because of her work for socialism. In 1931 she was named an Honorary Member of the Royal

Flemish Academy for Language and Literature. Clearly, she had become an internationally known figure. Although she remained relatively inactive politically, she published many dramatic, poetic, and prose works (more than half of her oeuvre appeared between 1928 and 1952. During the Second World War, she lived in several places; in 1943, she moved to a secluded property in the tranquil countryside near Zundert. During the Nazi occupation, she had poems published illegally, and she also assisted with the illegal newspaper *De Vonk* ("The Spark"). After the war, she helped establish the "Friends of India" club: avidly following the struggle for independence of the Indian people, she considered Gandhi a figure of peace and justice. She wrote a biography of Gandhi and also devoted a poetic cycle to him: *Wordingen* (1949, "Creations").[8] In 1947, she was awarded an honorary doctorate by the University of Amsterdam. Henriëtte Roland Holst-van der Schalk died in a nursing home in Amsterdam on November 21, 1952, one month short of her 83rd birthday.

Her poetry is of a prophetic or even jeremiadic kind that juxtaposes intense disconsolation for the state of humankind with an unswerving hopefulness for a future humanistic community. The feeling that her poetry evokes and the central themes thereof are transition, transcendence, decline, and disaster contiguous with utopian renewal. She lived with her spirit and desire solidly behind the abolishment of the wretchedness of the human condition, never losing sight of a goal which was a community based on love for all people(s). One finds in the development of her ideas an interest, sense of responsibility, and passionate love for fellow human beings. Whether manifest in Marxist doctrine or as the basis of religious socialism, it remained the type of love that she considered a *levenswet*, or law of life. A sense of anticipation and hopeful expectation runs conspicuously through Roland Holst's poetic expression, indicating that possible salvation from the iniquities of modern society is at hand but presently out of reach. The underlying tension in her poetry is a perception of a society sorely in need of change and a status quo that resists change by all means. The good spirit of which she speaks in her early poem "Ideals" is precisely this desire for innovation and change. The metaphor of awakening and gaining an advantaged perspective on both the life outside (object) and inner life (subject) is the key to her utopian vision and serves as another important theme in her poetry. Here the individual and collective enter into a gesture of rapprochement, indicating at least a possibility of reconciliation. These are moments when inner truth is projected outward and rejoined by the same truth in society.

Two distinguishable notions of history surface in Roland Holst's poetry. The first evolves from her enthusiastic participation in the activities of the various socialist and communist parties to which she belonged and supported up to 1927. With such personal commitments, the individual as an agent of history dominated Roland Holst's view thereof. Remedies for social injustice are to be found on earth, in organized action, and not in the cosmos, beyond our view and comprehension. The individual can control historical development which for that reason proceeds slowly but maintains a reforming nature, as it is spurred on by progressive people. Change is brought about by individuals who suffer material and spiritual deprivation impugned on them by the controlling class: the satiated bourgeoisie. Her poem "Poet and Proletariat" reminds the reader that history is usually made at the expense of the forgotten working class; hence the poet's task is to celebrate workers and provide the voice denied them by the historical narratives of the ruling class. Worker and poet share the desire for change; but it is the worker's hand "that alone is power" to bring about that change.

Her other view of history emerged when she became less active in political struggle. In the poem "In Days of Pain" (1946) three companions of a dismal existence — "hunger, cold and darkness" — are followed by the Grim Reaper. Here Roland Holst suggests that history is apocalyptic; it does not really develop and exists as a vast area of suffering due to the three figures mentioned, which she describes as "primordial demons" and part of human experience. Basically, she sees history as a record of human misery; after all, by 1946 Roland Holst had witnessed two world wars (including Nazi occupation), economic disaster of every sort, political turmoil, and personal tragedies of death and illness. She also realized that socialism did not develop in the fashion that she, and possibly her friends and foes in the socialist and communist movement, had expected or hoped; for example, her poem "Is this Socialism?" expresses intense disappointment with Stalinism. But to counter negativity, Roland Holst impels her readers to persevere until the arrival of salvation. As such, history will remain an area of acute suffering for humankind until a swift, immediate messianic intervention will save it from the iniquities of the status quo and transform the suffering human condition into some form of utopian community.

Roland Holst constructs many symbols in her poetry; wind, sails, the sea, and waves occur frequently. These items can be viewed as autobiographical elements since she grew up a mere half hour's walk from the sea, but she uses them to represent her notion of history as well. Wind is a symbol of change as it moves stagnate air; it is latent motion forward, motion that cannot be seen but felt and that becomes manifest in those who feel it. Thus one can either resist the change or follow it, as history suggests. Wind is especially relevant in "Your Damp Atmosphere Weighs On Us," where it allows the sail and the ship to move freight and people on a course to new destinations. Ships and sails are images of hope of better things to come, instruments that will transport us to new shores of existence and hence utopian communities. Sea, waves, and water all carry ships, and represent thus positive symbols in Roland Holst's poetry. The waves, moved by the wind, provide several images that connote progress and development of history as well as the inner self. The wave is an isolated phenomenon like an individual in society; yet many waves make up the sea just as many individuals make up society. Thus the motion of the wave in the sea depicts harmonious movement between the particular and the whole, i.e., the individual and the collective. Although this in itself is not utopian, it has great potential for improving the human condition as it stands. Roland Holst reached, perhaps, her spiritual zenith as a witness of workers' solidarity during the railroad strike of 1903. This type of solidarity manifest objectively in society seldom reveals itself. Other evidence of harmonious movement toward a common, selfless goal can be detected in the later Zimmerwald and Ragaz meetings. The movement of waves simulates that of history, such as in "Nothing Was Ever In

Vain:" "There are the retreats/and unavoidable reversals,/for all progress is ephemeral/and is followed by depression."

This motion or development takes place within the individual as well, as we see in "Everything Is Dark And Dim." Each advance of a wave brings change because it gradually eats away at the solid surface of congealed and stagnated middle class values, economic relationships, and notions of democratic government, all of which Roland Holst sought to change in her own feelings and actions. By the same token, wave-like motion from within eats away at what has congealed inside one's soul. All these symbols of the sea constitute a megasymbol that represents Roland Holst's poetic expression of transition, decline, and renewal.

Her resistance to organized actions manifested itself relatively early in her poetry, long before she actually ceased joining demonstrations, giving speeches, and attending conferences. In "Dream and Action" she addressed the difficulty of translating dreams into the reality of actions and how such a transition tarnishes the true essence of the dream. Analogous to the inadequacy of language to express human experience, is the inadequate action in expressing the absolute dream that entails the salvation of the oppressed and ultimately of all humankind. In fact, dream and action prove for Roland Holst to be unreconcilable and diametrically opposed aspects of existence. In "The Answer," too, the poetic subject rejects the call of a "friend" to rejoin the political struggle — which may refer to Roland Holst's reaction to the petty politics and intrigue that took place in 1908 in the S.D.A.P. as well as her disappointment with the 1903 railroad strike. The theme of irreconcilable dreams and actions remains a motif in her poetry until the end. She never ceased engaging in activity to help alleviate people's suffering. Yet, in her poetry, she continually advanced the notion that her dreams for humankind could never be realized in the actions she performed for it.

Roland Holst engenders utopian life as it once existed and will exist in the future but which is not part of the present. These utopias are strongly associated with women, while the contemporary situation, so sorely in need of change, is represented as a male phenomenon. The utopian vision of the "Homecoming" is inspired by the ultimate reconciliation of all individuals: women returning home arrive in a great community that is based on their love and tranquillity. This poem counters the situation of women in "Courageous Women" where *male* unity is depicted as exclusionary, i.e., centering around struggle against others. Camaraderie of this type excludes women and creates strife. In "Homecoming," men are introduced into the community established by women only late in the poem and then mostly to assist the women; hence, the homecoming, itself a concept of future, is truly a women's utopia. On the other end of time is "The Mother" with whom "the world begins." Here Roland Holst reminds us that we originate in the woman and with a mother's love, and that, even though forgotten, these facts are undeniable and real. A mother's love, which lives on in her children, could, again, be the basis of a utopian community. Whereas "Homecoming" describes a utopia that awaits us in the future, "The Mother" describes a neglected utopian possibility based in our origins; the latter is lost to be regained, the former is possible but must be obtained. The possibility of a humanistic community is there but it is neglected and misunderstood in the here and now, because we are unable to allow the emotion that makes this community possible to well up in us and control our actions: Love.

Thus, Roland Holst divides the world not into camps, parties, nations, movements, interests, or sexes, or even geographical entities, but into emotions or affects. Already in her early poem "Confidence" she proclaims love as "life's law." Some affects remain allied with love, such as kindness, hope, courage, joy, while others counter its influence on life. The mother is the root of life and the origin of the type of love that is required for a human community without strife. Thus, love represents a feminine alternative to reality as it is. In her sonnet "Apparent and Real Knowledge," "harmony with all things" is "the truest knowledge" because it is knowledge of the essence of all things as well as the self that can relate to them. But the emotion that makes this knowledge possible is love, an idea manifest in the "Homecoming" poem. Knowledge as we know it in labeling, categorizing, and in "what appears to be sound" is superficial knowledge that fragments the world. Love laces up this type of instrumental knowledge of the world and instead finds unison with inherent essence. In "Credo" she writes that "all revealed truth turns to power"; thus, realities perceived as truth congeal to ideologies that are used as instruments of control over others. The affects associated with this type of knowledge and desire for power are hatred, contempt, vanity, greed, pride, and self-interest. Of course, the affects that are prevalent in the world today are negative and they bury love in the economic, political, and social systems in which we choose to live. Roland Holst never abandons her cause of Love for all; in "Songs of Praise XI," the penultimate poem of her final collection, she calls on the poets of the future to "set free the slumbering powers/of love and courage, joy and trust."

Throughout her long career as a poet, form remained a crucial aspect of Roland Holst's poetry. Although she used the sonnet form and tercets in her early work, thereafter she employed meter, rhythm, and rhyme in all conceivable combinations and with varying effect. Even in her early sonnets she departed from the traditional forms of meter and rhyme (leaving only the fourteen line-structure intact). Form is, nonetheless, her gift to the reader. The sense of resolution and gratification that one can experience from reading her rhymed and rhythmical poetry suggests that she is a "reader's poet," a "public poet." She cannot be accused of being artistically conservative and cliché, because of the global concerns and the utopian, radical substance of her work. Indeed, she wrote for the community, to be read by and for the collective, and she packaged her utopian message in an appealing form. One could argue here that she should have used the essay form to convey her messages instead of the relatively subjective medium of poetry. In fact, Roland Holst wrote many essays, gave many lectures, published monographs, and wrote books in which her concerns for society are clearly laid out. But she viewed herself as a poet — and much of her poetry has an essayistic, journalistic, even philosophical quality.

Obviously, Roland Holst was not a proponent of "art for art's sake," meaning "art free from every social function, which has turned itself away from the knowledge of nature, society and the human being with a gesture of disdain" (*Poëzie en maatschappelijke vernieuwing* 30). Roland Holst advanced and lived the idea that poetry must be embedded in the society in which it is produced in order to be great. By the same token she did not advocate art for purely political purposes. The danger of serving ideology in poetry lies in the fact that writing for the interests of a particular group reduces poetic expression to those particular interests, against the interests of humankind and culture on the whole (ibid. 76). Two types of poetry address society directly: the propagandistic and the dynamic types. Although she did not disclaim the former — political propaganda aims at awakening the will and directing action — she claimed the latter to be true poetry: dynamic poetry seeks to ignite the flame of holy passion, awaken the fiery conviction which is the mother of action. Political propaganda leads to immediate willingness for action-in-struggle, of which the balled fist is an age-old symbol. Dynamic poetry leads to the intensification of inner tensions (ibid. 80-1).

Roland Holst, in brief, is a poet who desired to see artistic expression within social engagement, political agitation within cultural monuments, and artists as socially aware yet true to their craft. She referred to rhythm as the truly democratic aspect of a poem's form because it speaks to all recipients of the verse in the same manner. Roland Holst, in analogy to rhythm, is herself a democratic poet in that she, too, speaks to all in the same way (ibid. 20). Even though the working class was often the focus of her concerns, Henriëtte Roland Holst-van der Schalk advocated the improvement of its lot out of concern for the *entire* human community.

NOTES to the Introduction

The author gratefully acknowledges the generous funding received from the Denison University Research foundation, which enabled him to carry out research for this chapter in the Netherlands.

1. Most of the biographical information in this Introduction is culled from Henriëtte Roland Holst-van der Schalk, *Het vuur brandde voort: Levensherinneringen* (only direct quotations are indicated with page numbers).

2. These texts can be found in Henriëtte Roland Holst-van der Schalk, *Jeugdwerk 1884-1892.*

3. *De Nieuwe Gids* was the journal for and by the Dutch literary avant-garde.

4. Henriëtte Roland Holst translated the "International" anthem of the communist movement. Her translation is still used in the Netherlands today. See Prins 44.

5. The strike lasted from January 31 to April 10 and was unique for its unprecedented sense of unity; the railroad workers demonstrated in solidarity with striking dockers who had refused to work with nonunion colleagues loading railroad cars, and the railroad workers in turn refused to unload cargo loaded by nonunion dockers. Led by the S.D.A.P. and the N.A.S. ("National Labor Secretariat"), workers increased their demands for improved working conditions but were countered with laws that made strikes by train and streetcar workers illegal. Due to faulty communications between P.J. Troelstra, the representative of the S.D.A.P. in the House of Representatives and the strike leadership, two different messages were communicated to their common constituency, one of compromise, the other of continued action. In the end the strike fell apart, with few achievements to show for the effort.

6. On that occasion she met two major figures in the socialist movement of the time: Katarina Breschkofskaja, whom she called "the grandmother of the revolution" and Karl Kautsky, who asked her to write for his journal *Neue Zeit*, on which the Dutch *Nieuwe Tijd* had been based (de Lange 41). On her various trips to Berlin to visit Kautsky between 1904 and 1910, she met other leading figures of the German workers' movement, namely Clara Zetkin and Rosa Luxemburg.

7. J. Bosmans, "Het maatschappelijk-politieke leven in Nederland 1918-1940," *Geschiedenis van het moderne Nederland: Politieke, economische en sociale ontwikkelingen* (De Haan: Houten, 1988), 411. In 1935, the name was changed to "Communistische Partij van Nederland."

8. Henriëtte Roland Holst-van der Schalk, "Leiders: Gandhi," *Wordingen* (Rotterdam, 1949), 187-193 and 210-211.

Translations by Gary Baker and Judy Cochran

From *JEUGDWERK 1884-1892* ("Youth Work")

"Ideals"

If you have an ideal to govern
Your life and give it true worth,
A good spirit will guide you;
If you seek beauty and truth,
You will find an ideal here on earth,
And know how wonderfully good
Is a life serene and pure.
If you have never sought or prized an ideal,
You cannot know its wondrous worth.

If you have an ideal, it will impel
You to shun evil and follow virtue;
It will strengthen you in fear and sorrow
While tempering your grief and pleasure.
You need only think of your ideal
To regain hope, strength, and courage.
If God has not granted you this joy,
You cannot know its wondrous worth.

"Poesie"[1]

The sky is blue and smiling,
    All nature is on holiday,
One small white cloud
    Is floating overhead.

Where does it come from, what is its goal?
    What is it doing, alone in space?
We have barely glimpsed it
    Before it evaporates or passes by.

In the same way, in our hearts
    A thought may arise,
A thought, a glimmer
    That fades like a dream.

It dies, like the sigh
    Exhaled by the plaintive wave,
And how quickly we forget
    This passing thought.

Be careful not to scorn it,
    Nor dismiss it with a smile,
For what it may engender,
    Oh! who can tell?

The white cloud that passed by,
    The voice one hardly hears,
Were sent to us by God,
    It was God who traced their way.

"Tristesse"[2]

The other night, I was thinking how cruel life is,
How heavy our burdens, how vain our efforts.
— When suddenly, out of nowhere, over nothing,
I began to cry, my head in my hands.

Those who saw me looked on uncomprehending,
Saying: What a big baby! Come now, stop crying.
— And I fell silent. — How could I make them understand
I was weeping for my dreams of happiness — all lost?

"I was a child"

I'm perforce more wise, and that means, sadder.

When I was a child...without a past,
I dreamed a love-dream, like every woman.
I did not know what life would bring,
But my dream was hazy-blue and beautiful
I was a child...a long time ago.

I was dreaming sweetly...When my hero came,
His eyes were true and his voice low.
I asked nothing more; my heart yielded to him
Seeking his heart in return...But these dreams are old.

I was a child...The world spoke and I obeyed
wise words, full of cold reason.
By the time my heart was bound in marriage

And I became a woman...I was no longer young.

Now I am a woman...the days of my youth are fading
Slowly, for they have not yet vanished;
Life has brought me joy and pleasure,
And I am happy...but something is lost.

From *SONNETTEN EN VERZEN...* ("Sonnets and Verses...")

"My Soul's Awakening"

The full days are arriving with poise,
With long strides, like tall white-clad women
From fairy tales: their hands hold flowers
And radiance surrounds their golden hair.
The days lie open as secrets
Shared between friends who have longed to tell
Yet hidden their longing until their trust
Had grown and each to the other dared open his soul.
The days are like flowers, broken only
By nights wide-open as gardens flooded in moonlight,
And through all this I walk with shining gaze
Toward life. Then, it seems that I am standing
On the topmost dune, and far away
I glimpse what I have long desired.

"Writing a Poem"

What I pour into a poem
Are the changing moods of my heart
From the time I was very young,
Veiled beneath my face and clear
Only to my mind's eye, which scrutinizes
Every word to see if memory imparts truth.

How difficult it is to shape oneself
On paper, when thought turned inward
May produce nothing but astonished fear to learn
That what they have found has nothing in common
With what they expected or desired to find;
For each day takes something from us
While leaving something in return:
Throughout these changes we endure,
And if our silent, pondering gaze glides
Over those days of long ago, we see
How a piece of the old self clings to each
Like the tufts of wooly fleece hanging
From the spines of the hawthorn hedge —
Because these things are as I say,
I do not fear the murmur of this voice
Whispering of a self from long ago:
In such exchange shall I find strength
To seek the right and fitting words
That bring truth to all I see.
Just as the strong blows of the axe
Ring out through the wood, their steady
Rhythm resounding in the stillness,
So shall I tell of my heart's moods
Beneath the veil of my face; the force
Of my mind's eye bends to my will.

"Confidence"

People are lost in doubt,
The face of their God has not withstood time,
So I have come to comfort them with songs
Of timelessness and abundance.
I bring courage to the fearful,
A clear voice speaking calmly
Because my heart does not cling
To clouds, but sees through them.

I was born with the confidence
To penetrate to the core of all things,
But something kept me from my work.
As I grew, I put all that aside:
Everything became clear, my doubts gave way
So that I saw life's law was love.

"Apparent and Real Knowledge"

Naming and ordering bring peace of mind.
Some call it "knowledge" and are soothed;
Hearts that have found no comfort
Have turned to what appears to be sound.
Their words are systematically allied,
Confined to the limits we can see;
For they hope to erase the mysterious wind
That cloaks knowledge yet permeates the world.

Systems, human categories, all lack
The force to cut to the essential core,
Of this my heart is sure.
Only, — like a sun just risen, —
Is a feeling of harmony with all things
The truest knowledge known to human beings.

"Credo"

I believe in *truth* that exists
In the essential purity of all things,
Whose essence is absolute.
It is we, as alien and remote from them
As diverse as the height and form of mountains,
Who misread their meaning.
Just as the countryside blossoms in mist,
The essential exists under dense layers

Of appearances as untouched
And beguiling as the sleeping princess
Awaiting the prince from a mighty kingdom,
Who will arrive and break the spell.
In that prince's spirit I see
The glory of generations,
For I believe truth lies
In the minds of those who seek it
And from the depths of the soul
The *essential* reaches us through thought.
This capacity has long comprised
Man's *essence*, forever separating
him from the unreasoning beast. —
He who is true to his own nature has merit:
Our lives deserve praise if we use
Them to splinter the tree that stands
Between us and the garden of *knowledge*:
Thus will our spirit live as long as it may
Wander, despite fear and doubt, and tranquilly
Reflect on the truth of things revealed to it.
Just as, in Dante's teaching, highest authority
Appeared on earth as pope and emperor to form
One power, the worldly side
And the spiritual allied — two separate
Voices joined in a common utterance —
So limitlessness and thought express
The dual being we profess.
And since the one follows the many,
The individual reflects the common end
Like the wave that rides the sea,
And every human being contains
A spirit behind his material face:
Our senses bear the imprint of ideas,
Our earthly thoughts perform the deed.
All life is revealed twofold:
Clarity comes to him who understands, —
Knowledge of limitlessness is the given

Which enabled the human spirit to rise
From utter dependency to proclaim laws,
And by increasing laws to aspire
To even greater freedom,
For all revealed truth turns to power:
Thus all men will strive until
Their sense of truth revealed on earth
Has merged with spirit on equal base.
Knowledge of spirit in the world
Eludes us, keeping beyond our reach,
But the way to it does exist.
Just as a forest pond preserves
All the trees its mirror reflects,
So truth leaves its imprint
In the spirit, welcomed
And acknowledged without question.
No one asks if dawn brings day:
Truth is a day carrying its own
Light and law,
Silencing feeble, erring notions
Like a fearful, light-shy brood
Hiding from the rising sun.
He who understands his nature
No longer bows to fickle doubts
Nor suffers faltering in himself;
He who finds invisible truth
Feels it to be steadfast
As seafarers' unseen winds.
He who perceives truth in his thoughts
Seeks it as his greatest joy
And tries to give it concrete form.
This is the essence
Of those who praised
And followed truth;
Crystallizing their thoughts
And bringing them to bear on life,
They created a generation of heroes

Whose voice and gaze, gestures and gait
Appeared more intense and thus more real
Than those of men who merely walk the earth:
Truth made their lives blossom
And with them came a new generation
Of human beings less men than gods:
Its exemplars are Dante and Homer.

From *DE NIEUWE GEBOORT* ("The New Birth")

"Poet and Proletariat"

Bearer of pain, belabored being striding
Through history, shouldering the heavy yoke,
Age-old victim, sacrificed for the world's
Happiness, condemned to endless suffering,

Powerless and stooped you marched
Until time had lost all meaning,
You looked up from long misery
And sighing deeply croaked "here lies my lot."

Since then you have not swerved
From your upward striving as the dawn-light
Plays on your lips, long white with suffering,
As it colors them with its holy sign.

Give me your hand, for there alone is power,
In your ascent lies the world's sole hope,
We come to rescue you, the best part
Of our freight, from our sinking barge.

Let this be a prelude to the bond
Between us, for we, too, have fled
An old world and offer you
The precious fruit of our voice.

Let us be comrades, and the beautiful
Hymn to our strength, chosen
For our glory, will belong to you
And long lend splendor to your struggle.

Though you will not reap the fruits of our struggle
Nor will its blessings fall on us,
The sweetness and joy of our vision
Will make possible the harshness of our work,

In our hearts hope will swell,
The burden of impotence and suffering
Will be cast off like a constraining robe,
In that time which fills our silent dreams.

From this union the song and image
Of our courage will arise as easily
As the sun creates whole worlds
Free of fear and pain.

"Your Damp Atmosphere Weighs On Us"

Your damp atmosphere weighs on us,
Holland, we suffer but defy death,
We fill our lungs greedily
With purer air from a far greater

Empire where our bodies move freely,
Where reality is as vast
As your dreams, and with full gust
We blow this air into your stagnant seas.

One day there will arise a wind
Whose beautiful, blissful waves
Will overrun the borders that confine you:
Holland, what a future you will see,

What feelings of liberation will move you
When this fraternal life begins.

"They Say Ten Thousand Slaves"

They say ten thousand slaves built one
Of Pharaoh's pyramids in forty years,
Dragging stone blocks and stacking them:
Many perished from this ponderous work.

We build, not from dead loam and stone
But from human will and learning,
Harnessing both toward an end
To be achieved when not one of the present

Builders will be alive. How many young
And old have disappeared, heaving through hot
Loose sand loads too heavy for them.
Quietly they died, without a murmur others
Fill their ranks and the high walls rise:
Let us in silence remember them.

From *OPWAARTSCHE WEGEN* ("Upwards Roads")

"Courageous Women"

Outside in the bright, eventful world
Men accomplished brilliant deeds,
They filled the hours with victory,
Like beacons, they drew every gaze.

Standing in the limelight, they heard
Their comrades' war cries as the enemy fled;

Hope rose up on wings of glistening green
Brushing their cheeks as it climbed.

At the happy end they stood, forming a chain,
Conscious of the power their union proclaimed:
Many were anticipating the end of the day
As one looks at a mountain bathed in sunset's splendor.

As for the women, how were their days spent?
What went on behind the scenes, what filled
The empty hours when they lay awake?
What did they see on those sleepless nights?

The children grew pale, the house felt empty,
Dame Worry moved in, would not stir from the hearth;
Men found in battle the reward of their struggle:
How easy the lot of those whose lives are shared.

What became of the women behind the walls?
How did their hearts endure?
Restlessness burned deep holes in their flesh:
They didn't weep, they tried to persist.

They forged through time like a ship toward the horizon,
Their hearts racing ahead to that ephemeral line,
Sometimes uncertainty invaded them,
Sometimes despair froze their hearts.

Often a small sail of hope arose
On the distant horizon, it drew near
Then drifted away, leaving them alone
As before, struggling against the tide.

Then it was as if the waters
Closed above their brooding heads,

And they swallowed in a gulp
Endless misery's bitter drink.

Now, like frightened animals after a long chase,
They show relief, and their lips
So long tight with suppressed grief,
Convulse and laugh in pain.

Their gaze is as black
As windows nibbled on by fire:
Take their warm hands with respect
And tell them morning has come.

Promise them they will bear children
Who will bring peace without fail
Because their mothers were brave
Because their hearts did not weaken.

"The Mother"

The world begins with the mother, who appears
In our hearts at our first moment of consciousness,
Loyal through the days and nights that pass,
She has the warmth of an open heart,
A generous caress, a kind voice and gaze,
Bringing the peace of home to all.
To her clings an aura
Unchanging and misted,
In intimacy no other holds:
Her voice promises the shining
Softness of the most tender caresses.
Her smile is like a moonlit night.
Mother possesses the unbounded power
To reach back before memory began,
Every thread leads us to her.
Youth arises, thinking itself free,

Imagining it can conquer all things;
Youth strays unnoticed from love's source.
However, one day late or soon
Youth will return.
Without estrangement, without question,
The child's soul seeks again its Mother,
Pressing against life's warm fleece.
Not one tuft of her love has been lost;
She was always close by waiting,
Ready as for a child new-born.

Severance from a mother can not last:
How can it when her heart is all-knowing?

With the years a child's love grows wiser
Ever sweeter as ripening fruit,
Because the heart needs love's refreshment
All the more as life presses on.
Less strong becomes life's hold
Over this first intimacy;
Though love seems lost,
Undisturbed remain the blessings
Of nature's ultimate benevolence.

Mother stands at the heart of all things,
No illusions remain between her and you.

When the constant grinding of the years
Has worn away what is most familiar, most dear,
Like the waves that erode the weary shores,
Life flows from her still figure like the tide
And her eyes close in hazy sleep,
As when over meadows the twilight falls,
The sharpness of our senses decreases,
Our souls fade in tender sunset-red,
Then our final happiness comes, our greatest love,
Who lingers in the hearts of her children.

Her children look on shyly
At what dwindles in the bay of memory,
Drenched in shining radiance;
A new light rises on the rim of evening:
Filial love, so used to asking, now begins to give,
The mother becomes the child in her children's hearts,
What a perfect and beautiful wreath!

From *DE VROUW IN 'T WOUD* ("The Woman in the Wood")

"Dream and Action"

The lands drop away more and more abruptly,
As time carries us in its long strokes,
We no longer see the slippery mooring post
And sharp stones cut our feet;
Both highland and lowland have vanished
And we are wrapped in everlasting peace.

We see the land that was Today
Become the Past stretched out behind us,
No longer hidden by chance
Its outline becomes clearer;
We read a sentence in the pages of our life
Which in writing them, we had not uncovered.

We grasp now what our eyes,
Blinded by pain and shame, could not decipher,
Why the kind of life, which we had given
All our mature strength, has betrayed us,
Why we marched off defeated
In the midst of the battle.

This is the great and just law of order,
What is required of us and what must be done,
Tasks are dealt to the great masses
To assuage their desire, joy, and healing,
Granting comfort and sweetness to some,
Like a wreath crowning their heads.

We who live in the soft embrace
Of a dream world's coasts,
Waiting until society brands us
With her sign, quietly waiting
Until the pounding waves of unconsciousness
Wash into our hands the shell of beauty, —

We may well listen to the fall of the ax
That comes to us from the nearby wood,
Where an army of cutters hews out a route
And through the darkness breaks a path of light,
We may whisper excitedly to one another
That through the trees light is appearing.

And sometimes we may raise dream-drenched eyes
To their armies when they arrive enveloped
In the uproar of battle, at the place where beauty's
Sweet, golden voice surprises their great hearts,
And makes us aware for a brief moment
That not everything in life is strife.

As they longingly sink down next to us,
To drink from the noble draught of color and sound,
To drink in gulps from the magic potion,
To still their age-old thirst
Beside the sparkle of beauty to which we bow
Morning and evening without giving thanks,

Waiting until our hands put within their reach
Imagination's colorful carpet of leaves and flowers,
Where, without understanding its design,
Their inexperienced feet move gropingly,
Waiting for our rhythms to guide them
To the glorious shores of beautiful dreams.

When they have enjoyed what we have to give
And go heartened, with a greeting joyous
As the sea to the land, they leave
For us an array of beautiful gifts,
The shining threads spun by our dream-thoughts
From their quiet courage, might and virtue.

They stayed in our house only as guests
Who come and go, not as children
Who feel the intimacy of home
And all things recognize and touch.
For them follows a long fast
After the brief pleasures of sights and sounds.

Just as they dare not linger long
In the golden light of our dreamlands,
But must hasten once again to the task
That needs all their mature strength, —
So must we remain where hatchets
Do not crash and trees fall by their hand.

This was the error that restricted us,
This the wound from which our hearts bled
So that we joined their fighting ranks
Because their bravery fiercely moved us,
And the beautiful dream that had seduced us
Remained our final, most cherished goal.

Because Dream and Action cannot be one,
Together they make the world richer,

For on a single patch of ground cannot grow
These two extremes of the heart's territory.
Whoever wishes to preserve beauty's flame must watch
Out for the sharp wind, which blows from action's realm.

Whoever wants a life of action
Must wrap up and hide his dream. —
Will the time come when, like milk and cream,
Dream and action will mingle in a single whiteness?
Will humankind's journey ever lead where
Their waters flow together in a single stream?

This I know not, but I do know that whoever mixes
Them in his cup prepares a drink
Sour with disappointment, bitter as grief
— An acrid drink whose taste remains —
I know whoever wants to contribute to humankind
Must choose between reality and dreams.

I do not regret that my lightly-clad feet
Once trod the stony land of deeds,
Nor that, far from Beauty's bright face,
I slaved laboriously in twilit fields:
I won the right to greet those who chose to act,
With the untarnished name of comrade.

I do not regret this, but I have learned
To keep within the borders of my lot,
Like a child who no longer grasps
At the dancing light with fingers the flame once burned.
I have learned to avoid the fields where battle stirs
Incessantly calling to my repressed desire.

O sweet measure! the Heart that can accept you
Finds the best medicine for its pain.
Not to want to drink of every wine,
Not to grasp for every fruit on earth,

This is the wisdom which has kept human beings
From being overcome by Existence.

"The Answer"

You ask if I am going to take a step
Closer to hear the great battle's din,
You put your arm around my shoulder,
Letting that light nudge guide me to my friends.

Surprised disappointment knots your brow
That I resist the pressure of your voice
While your arm continues to question trust,
Over-shadowed by loneliness.

Then you ask scoffingly if all the high flames
On the parapet of my soul are dead,
And you try to revive the hot embers
Of hours gone by in my lowered head.

O friend, let your hand slip from my shoulder,
Resheath the sword of your admonition,
For you do not know how, since those days,
My heart has sought the valley of peace;

How arduous its struggle, how fierce
Its pursuit, and how merciless words
And all that bore the harshness
Of a warrior's gear.

How I desire a serene, secure life
Where the days follow their course calmly,
Whispering through silently trembling lips
But only with subdued song.

How I long to hear the water's murmur
As the clouds sail overhead, running through fields
Of flowers, and the hum of the swarms of diligent bees
That come for honey to the high heath,

And the soothing rustle of wise trees
Settling the unrest that leads
The soul beyond unquiet streams
Into silver valleys of tranquillity.

Perhaps when my heart has rested there
On the cool turf of musings,
Desire will stir in me once again
At the sound of the battle call.

Perhaps — in times as yet unborn,
On whose face the veil remains,
But now I only desire days that glide by
Like the shadow that glides over the dial

On which the golden sun kisses the hours,
As they drop off to sleep, caressing
The garden where summer pleasures linger
From dawn's first glistening until evening rest.

Therefore, let your hand slip from my shoulder
And rake no more at the dead coals of my hearth,
For my heart grows greyer and older
The longer it stares at fading dreams.

Your pleading and warnings are powerless to move me,
For they are tinged with the blossoms of desire;
Nothing intrigues me like twilit pathways
And the dreamy scent of the silent muse.

From *HET FEEST DER GEDACHTENIS*
("The Feast of Memorial")

"The Homecoming"

In evening's sky rose a small white cloud,
Crescent of the new-born moon, when
The women gathered to return, down
Through the pure air to the world's glen.

They descended the foot-paths,
Without haste, without impatience,
Their hearts refreshed by the great peace
That comes to the world with twilight.

Not as we mortals descend from mountains,
Knowing that strife and turmoil await
To divide and torment the heart once more,
Forcing it to don its armor of power,

Of hardness, of hate, of misgiving; —
They went full of deep tranquillity,
Knowing that love awaited them below,
Confidently they smiled and did not hurry.

The air glowed softly like a seashell
Shining with mother of pearl: blue,
Grey-white, and pale rose. On the far side
Of the sky reposed the golden-striped clouds.

Along the slopes their choir sang softly:
The young women, in turn, in unison,
Sang the violet song of Love's desire,
Of Love's splendor, all along their way.

And when they paused, the matrons raised
Their song; in deep, ripe tones
They praised the World, singing
With love of the beauties of Life.

When they drew near the mountain's base,
They saw about their heads wide rings
Of circling swallows and clustering lilacs,
A sweet honey-smell wafted toward them.

Birds and fragrance greeted them joyfully,
Like all hill-dwellers, they found delight
In the pleasant valleys, hearts buoyed
By their senses' sweet caress.

Jubilant children ran to greet them,
Arms overflowing with buttercups
And daisies, which they showered
Like rain upon the women.

While mothers bent down to kiss
Their children, the clear air sparkled
With gold as their voices echoed
In resounding waves.

Humankind had preserved the golden tongues
Of all hearts, united in one voice,
And above this glorious gathering
The bells were heard to chime.

Out of the oneness of humankind, the perfect bliss
Of a single life tied to all lives;
They rang out the supreme joy
Of harmony in oneself and the Universe.

And while these pleasant sounds continued,
A group of men approached the women,

Eager to give a joyful welcome
To their dear ones returning from the celebration.

Joyous hurrahs resounded over and over again,
The companions dispersed with haste,
Accompanied by soft words and laughter;
Many pairs of boys and girls embraced,

Plunging into the sweet-smelling foliage;
Many matrons with mild, solid mouths
Felt the strong grip of a long-trusted
Friend: the old magic

Rushed through their hearts, some whom life had bent
Walked with the help of silver-haired men,
Others, leaning on laughing youths
Whose energy brought back to old eyes

Their own tender years.
Not one of those thousands
Who descended the mountain was alone:
All found their part of common pleasure.

Not one was alone. Like one great household,
Humankind existed. Each house, every heart
Had open doors. Each bore the cares
Of the other on strong, devoted arms,

Each radiated happiness to all.
Sorrow withered and disappeared,
The common joy grew every day through sharing,
Human beings became crystals of sparkling

Delight — all as one. In great halls
The companions met for the evening meal,
Enjoying friendly conversation, love's
Cordial, and the earth's good fruit.

From twilit gardens came beautiful music,
Bringing to lovers loving greeting,
Soothing mourners' downcast mood
With the caress of a magic wing.

There was not one among them
Who could envision music growing
From a source other than love. Evening's glow
Faded, night raised her unshakeable walls

All around. From the mulberry-deep darkness
Blinking everywhere were silver lights,
The bright, open faces of comrades
Bending delightedly to hear one another.

Women's eyes still held a glimpse of pensiveness
For the sorrowful world that passes,
Like travelers from distant lands
To whom a certain unfamiliarity clings.

Gradually through youthful joys
And the mild laughter of beloved comrades,
Melancholy vanished, and the well-spring
Of happiness flowed again: the beautiful day

Gathered her children into her womb.
Then our somber world of grief and discontent
Drank once more from oblivion's cup, her true tomb,
Oblivion swallowed her up.

While daylight lay swallowed up by night,
The other side of earth turned toward the sun,
Morning cries are heard there,
There glows the brazen light of dawn,

There blows the morning wind, wherein
New generations of women have arisen

To spread their great desire, the holy breath
Of their love over the mountains' empire.

From *VERZONKEN GRENZEN* ("Sunken Borders")

"The Gentle Powers Will Surely Prevail"

The gentle powers will surely prevail
In the end — I hear this like an inner voice.
If it kept still all light would fail,
All warmth would stiffen inside me.

The powers that hold love captive
Will be overcome as love moves forward,
Then the great rapture
We see in our hearts as we listen

To the murmur of tender acts,
Just as in small shells we hear the sea.
Love gives meaning to life, to the planets,
To humans and animals. Nothing can prevent
Our ascent toward love. This is certain:
Everything rises toward perfect love.

"The Mother Of Life Is Death"

The mother of life is death,
But self-sacrifice is the mother
Of ascension: thus heaven's
Unfathomable law is revealed.

And if humankind was vexed by this law,
The course of human striving would be lost
In darkness; but where it is inscribed in deeds,
Human endeavor brings a new dawn.

This is certainly the highest splendor
That radiates from the face of death:
Dying lifts humankind upward.

And certainly with laughing measure
Those who die enter your dark valleys,
Knowing death to be a happy event.

From *TUSSCHEN TWEE WERELDEN* ("In Between Two Worlds")

"For Our Dearly Departed"
In Memory of Rosa Luxemburg

The stagnant waters have closed
Over the pale head, spread out in gloom;
The stagnant waters of eternity
Already engulf the living.

She always lived in you, o eternity,
She carried you in her womb.
Death cannot reach her; death
For her was neither failure nor abyss.

Vulgar people full of delusions
Tried to hurt her with their hatred:
They did nothing but create
New splendor, nourishing the idea
That now enters the world as her Image

To liberate the world from greed, —
Only the heart, which in the dark hours
Felt the torment of all creatures,
Will bloom again in the meadows of eternity.

This was her end: the brief, sharp pain,
The cruel unconsciousness,
And then magnificence: sinking and repose
In star-studded clouds, in eternal being.

She is all around us, everywhere;
She sings aloud in the great heroes' choir,
We hear her in the whispering
Arising from the peaceful, twilit vale.

"There Is Not Much Room On Earth For Kindness Now"

There is not much room on earth for kindness now,
For violence has spread all around;
Hatred has fired shots, words have become blades;
Hearts have collapsed in this frozen sphere.

Over there in the deep caves' gloom
Love patiently awaits her blessed hour,
Doubt has not veiled her clear gaze;
The smile on her lips remains pure.

The day will come when the golden powers
Will radiate over the fields of life, —
But these are days when the heart must still
Its yearning as the hero his pain.

From *HELDENSAGE* ("Hero's Saga")

"In Praise Of Courage"

Courage is old, far older than mankind.
It is part of life itself, for life
Is struggle. Wherever there were battles,
The fire of courage filled the warriors.
Courage and strife, like wave and surf, are one.

Courage has pulled humankind upward;
Courage has, allied with will and hope,
Undone the chains of human bondage, —
Has day by day filed down the iron bars
Of necessity; — courage
Always renewed the struggle, emboldened the blood
That fear might have bent or called to turn "back":
Courage pushed its foot forward, arched its back,
Raised its voice in triumph...
O distant fathers, we bring you thanks,
For what you did along nature's way
To steel our hearts for this hour.
This hour, this moment, what is it
In the endless becoming, whose beginning
Out of the deepest depths of time
Shimmers; each time must the shining end
Move further away? For us, the living,
This hour begins a new chorus
In the play of the centuries, a prelude
To the new dance of grief and glory.
In this hour we deliver a new race. Courage
Will be needed. Inscribed in pain, in blood,
The law of centuries was born:
This is nature's way. Out of the pain of birth,
Out of the pangs of birth, we appeal to you:
"O courage, o courage, help us."

To the woman in childbirth a day and night
Seem endless. But many battles
Will be needed for the birth of a new race:
During this time she who gives birth must stand
The pain. At times the pangs will lessen:
She will lie down, breathless from the painful
Work, weak and lifeless, whispering brokenly
"When," her inquiring look dark
With bewilderment...
                                  O courage, glorious power,
God-within-us, always singing, always laughing,
Always aware of the long-awaited blessing,
Even when the way goes wrong,
You feel, in the shards of pain,
The magnificence of our far-off goal, —
Show us the entrance to your kingdom,
Teach us to inhabit your fortress.
You are the noble breath that blows over us
From the bloody days and dark nights
Of the distant past — let your essence
Penetrate our thoughts so that words
Grow out of our empty talk — control
Our pretensions, curb our gestures,
Help heal our feelings,
Our thoughts, our words...
Swell, o courage, like the fruit of our womb,
Know our heart, drive out our pale
Beseeching: engrave our deeds with your sign
So they will bear witness to you...Let us know
Death as the pit in which sink
And arise all living things,
So your noble tranquillity will not forsake us
When Death looms up cold and grey.

"Nothing Was Ever In Vain"

Nothing was ever in vain, nothing is ever lost:
Everything becomes part of life's stream,
Intention, thought, dream and deed, —
Where all are reborn
Other than they were, each one different,
But the old is not renewed in one swoop,
Nor do all the colors and sounds
Of a new day awaken at once.

There are the retreats
And unavoidable reversals,
For all progress is ephemeral
And is followed by depression.

One must not ignore
The haste and sanctity,
The fruitful impatience of Life's
Stream that opened new paths

Before the new foundation was laid...
Now some of its waters return
While others flow onward...the waves
Washing over new shores will bathe the All.

Just as in the first dawn of earliest spring
Winter's bleakness may retreat,
A softer blue shines round heaven's crown,
Mild laughter breaks out on Earth's grim face.

Then sullenly they pull themselves together,
He who is merciless rules again,
Though Spring will not betray our hope:
A herald announces her coming.

Thus yesterday's great Light, though not entire
Truth, was not all glumness either:
Splendor and humiliation together
Form truth, both play their part.

From *VERWORVENHEDEN* ("Achievements")

"Everything Is Dark And Dim"

Everything is dark and dim
In a world without magic...
Does not a single spark
Of the old splendor remain?
The inner realm has been lost,
The way there is closed off...
No roe leaps forward anymore,
No deer ambles through the woods...
Gone is all I love
To hear and see.

When will the walls that keep me
From my own place be gone?
When will spring open the portals
And colorful crowds press in,
Like my heart sees in dreams?
Shall I never hear the singing
Rise up from realms below,
The sweet murmur of that lay?

Desire alone has power
To unearth the buried grandeur.
But what great desire's wand
Can split the barren stone
And let the bright stream

Of songs rush over me,
This water for which I thirst?
What great desire, what deep sorrow?
I do not know, I cannot tell.

"Darkness Has Enclosed Me In Its Walls"

Darkness has enclosed me in its walls,
Protecting me. With motherly hand
Stillness caresses my eyes. Like the wanderer
Returning to his land, I turn inward to my being.

How much have I sacrificed for deeds!
How I have wearied myself on distant journeys,
How long and bitterly have I fought my deepest being,
How often have I betrayed myself!

Now I must struggle to find myself again,
For I have lost touch with my inner fortress.
Birds find, upon returning, their former nests
By themselves, but it is dangerous for us to stray

Far from our hearts. Yet there burns in me a spark
Of glee, a tiny light in the black hedgerows —
A little flicker of joy in me glows
For one certainty, which the year has granted me...

I HAVE LEFT ILLUSION BEHIND ME
LIKE A CHAIN AND GO CLAD
IN LIGHT GARMENTS LIKE A CHILD
THROUGH MORNING STREETS

Humility, from which I had turned away
In my long, dark, haughty night, —
Has returned, I have recovered from illusion,
Which denies the mystery of Life.

Just like groups of broad-winged chords
Spring from an unknown scale, —
Or the laboriously studied words
Of a majestic epic in a foreign tongue,

So are you, o Life. Sometimes we feel welling
Up in us something like a glorious secret,
Which recedes like floodwaters,
Leaving us alone with your vast silence.

"The Envoy"

He appeared driven, as if from a mist,
And was himself fog-grey
When I found him sitting in evening's shimmer
By my hearth fire. He looked mild and wise

Instead of happy, not sad, but resigned.
The trace of a smile wrinkled his mouth
As he said, "Now I shall not leave here,
Until the Master who sent me comes."

"Who is your master," I asked. The name died
On his grey lips, which formed the word
But could not speak,
And I felt my gaze wander beyond him

To one greater. Timidly I asked: "When
Will your Master come?" — I saw his hands
Move to sign: "These things
Are not known to me." Then all was

As before, and I thought that if
He could teach me one thing,
I would wait peacefully for the high
Master who had sent him. So I spoke

Thus: "Friend, if I am to be your friend,
Tell me one thing, o tell me,
How do I wait for him without anxiety,
How may I see him approach without fear?

Many who think he is coming
Close their eyes and hold their ears
To muffle the beat of his wings,
But I want to meet him face to face,

As is right, with calm,
Reverence, fear and trust."
Then, full of shame, I cast my eyes down and listened
To the even tones of his voice divulge this truth:

"Sweep your house clean of all vanity;
Whatever is vain cannot exist before him;
Let a strong wind blow through your room,
And in peace you will see him draw near."

From *VERNIEUWINGEN* ("Renewals")

"The Thought That Thousands Of Years Ago"

The thought that thousands of years ago
A silent power was born on earth,
Appearing with quiet strides,
Like a loving woman, who goes softly, —
Whose sole weapons are prayers
And pleas, and yet submits
To the crueler sex, — who was the first
To bring peace and mildness to men, —

The gift of Mediators who proclaimed
The unity of all that lives, in his essence
Radiating the divine spirit, —

Thus were we taught to read life's meaning,
To know in whose essence we are joined, —
Yet we evaded that which caused us dread.

There was in us a drop of the spirit
Of love that enveloped all creation,
Down to the innocent animal,
In love's festival.

That drop softened the rigid order,
Warming the cold and emptiness:
Our purest power came from a region
We did not recognize, it came from God.

Power to overcome injustice,
To celebrate right, to join together
The lonely, the helpless, the weak.

Power to restore to the blind their sight,
Give health to the infirm, — and awaken Evil
To the knowledge the Law has been broken.

"O Socialism..."

O socialism, you must learn once again
To yield to inner strength,
To feel at home in other spheres
Than those in which your great work was done.

Now you must reflect on your beginnings,
When you were only a thought,

Find again the tone and gestures
Of your term as outcast on earth.

You must turn inward to your origins
And contemplate the source of your essence,
Drink of it, forgetting all else.

You must fill your tired lungs
With purer air than that of these hot,
Noisy cities: then you will recover.

From *TUSSCHEN TIJD EN EEUWIGHEID*
("Between Time and Eternity")

"I Think, A Long Time Ago, We Learned"

I think, a long time ago, we learned
To leave behind selfish striving,
Yet long ago, we gave up the best
To provide a kiss for the monster's growth:

The joy of the common human struggle,
Hunger and yearning will again lead
To love, free of selfish desire.
Only then will new times come.

I think, for a long time, we shall be lonely,
Feeling ourselves far from God, forsaken,
We'll stagger through bare passages,
Groping, in quivering, dimly shining light.

I think this, because I hold it all
In my soul. This is how God made me:

Humanity's grief prevents my sleep,
Its guilt is a bitter gust sweeping through me.

"The Harvest"

These are the days of harvest!
The strong sun scorches the fields:
Rarely do plants, humans and animals
Feel its glow so fiercely in our Holland.

It blanched the stalks,
While the grain was still growing:
Ripe are rye and oats,
Come gather them quickly.
The hour demands heroes!
The peasant folk have raised
The old, familiar banner.

The banner of work waves
Now over the fields of Holland:
The bow of strength is drawn
To the breaking point.
Before the rooster greets the day,
The men's struggle begins:
The fields are completely soaked
With their sweat.

Yet no sign of paling or reluctance
Taints the red of their courage,
Nor does this thought cripple them:
"This grain, nourished by sun, earth,
Rain and the sweat of our bodies, —
Does it exist in vain?
Who will buy it? At what price?"

Not one of them asks. Not one wavers.
Questions weaken and doubt ages us.
The hand trembles slightly, then falters.
Daily worries banished, they neither
Question nor stumble: work and know,
Deep, deep inside you, what is wise and good.

There is a law, too high for words.
To have violated it makes
Cities' inhabitants powerless,
They are restless and fragile.
But the farmers have not broken it:
Therefore eternal security sings
Through their blood and bones.

Days of harvest are days of fever.
Across all the teeming fields
The marksman sun shoots off his rays;
Swings hour for hour a burning torch.
And hour for hour the troop perseveres
Unconscious of hero's deed:
Not one wavers.

Whether the sun scorches and burns,
Whether uncertain today and menacing tomorrow:
The harvest is retrieved.

From *UIT DE DIEPTE* ("De Profundis")

"In Days of Pain"

Satanic powers that inhabit humans
Set fiercely upon humankind,
Three mauling primordial demons

Whom you know well:
Hunger, cold and darkness.
Afterward, trotting along
On bony legs comes the Grim Reaper,
Scythe sharpened for stabbing.
He slices to the right, he slices to the left,
Hunger, darkness and cold, —
He gathers young and old,
Passing not a single hamlet.
Gleaning before and behind him —
His scythe sharper than a sword —
He harvests the great and the simple,
We hear the scattered grain fall.
Hunger, cold, darkness:
Were not dead but merely hidden
In the far corners of the world,
Waiting for their day and hour
To spring from the shadows upon us,
When the Grim Reaper with scythe sharpened
Has grasped humanity by the throat;
— O hunger, cold, darkness, —
Holds fast until the debt is paid,
Until cosmic powers have forgiven
And restored the balance we violated,
Until God's high meaning is revealed.
(24 January 1942)

"It Has Been One Year Now"

It has been one year now since the great day,
When courage rode through the grey streets;
Without a single cry, a single howl,
Life regained its glorious meaning,
And suffering in sparkling beauty stood.

The men with coarse skin
Strew love's flowers, flaming sparks
Of the spirit's light throughout the dim universe;
We were drunk with elation:
Flashes of future, shining with hope, shone on us.

It has been one year now, — o seemingly dead,
A bright new flame of action has shot up;
Courage stormed in from distant shores
Where it had been waiting, and its glittering seed
Burst through the crust, where for years it had reposed;

Only then will the inhumanely treated
Feel the warm, friendly clasp
Of their brothers' hands, and know once again
The human bond that will revive their forgotten
Dreams, giving rise to sunny lands of tenderness.
(25 February 1942)

From *IN DE WEBBE DER TIJDEN* ("In the Web of Time")

"The Web of Time"

The web of time
Has been woven
From the suffering
And trials of the living.

The year has gone by,
The months, the days,
As though their lazy
Hand could not wait

Until autumn red
Brought quick retreat;
Now everyone cries:
"Freedom is dead."

"Rebirth"

Alone, the last hand has let go,
Past houses, past streets,
You fall; you fall
Past people and peoples
In the whirlpools
Of the speechless —
Where the word-roses
No longer bloom, my love,
Because all our senses
Are subdued.

All is sinking
In ink-black darkness.
Anxiety, distress...
Men would cry out
(If their voices had not failed)
Like the child separated from its mother.
Isn't every birth a wonder?
The beginning of each new self?

This one too. From very far,
Beyond the bounds of time,
Two sea gulls spiral upward,
Silvery-white, majestic birds.
Somewhere, in the falling night,
A spray of light begins,
The waters rise,
And distant gates are opened:
New birth ensues —

The World's Eternal Heart
Beats softly within the newborn child.

From *WORDINGEN* ("Creations")

"Humankind's Origin II"

Silently...in the beginning
Filled by time,
Is concealed-revealed
A new ungirdling,

A new animal is born
Amongst the other creatures,
The only one
Who has an upright gait,
The only one who laughs from pleasure,
Weeps from pain,
Arranges symbols,
Gives things names.

Driven up
Out of the cosmos' depths,
Man stands and walks,
Woven into existence,
Bathed in swelling streams
Of cosmic life.
Man belongs to nature;
Nor is he exempt from universal laws,
All flow through him.
But in humans, laws meet another face,
Full of flickering liberty,
Like the child stepping from obscurity
Into rays of sunlight.

"Christ Jesus VII"

Christ Jesus, my eyes had turned from Thee;
My hands had pushed away Thy cross:
I saw gleaming horizons of freedom,
Other bridges spanning salvation's way.

The mighty have too long burdened Thee
With their pride and will to power.
In this sea of blood Thy grace is lost,
And Thy smile greets us no more.

Christ Jesus, Thou, and He who made Thee,
Have become an all but forgotten legend
From an old book: When we turn its pages,
An echo comes to us from a deep cavern,
No more...and yet...and yet...

O, Christ Jesus, can hopes of brotherhood
Grow in hearts that no longer know the Father,
Can men be praised if they no longer
Kneel in humility? They have long forgotten

How to pray. In God, they hate the Master,
Neglecting faith as slavery's vice.
Beautiful is the pride of sparse hedgerows
Growing in the gardens of life.

Beautiful was the exuberance of brave youths,
Taking many fields in storm.
Those they seized thought: "now will come
The times of glory"...Yet the crystal
Of their joy fell to pieces...
                    O darkest times!
As if an invisible hand continues to hold
Humankind firmly: it floats above the rim
Of the abyss...if it lets go, our time

Will end...These people with their hopes
And works and jubilant expectation
Are sinking.
      Can a new day arise out of darkness?
Have we not shunned the highest law?

These people grew from different roots,
They set their own goals;
They, and I with them, rose up,
Full of our own will:

"Humans are the measure of all things."
They saw themselves at life's center,
They fell into gross negligence,
Imagining they fought to better existence

For themselves and others, to forge on earth
Salvation's way, their tides of brotherhood
Streaming forth over the earth. In this struggle
They know lies highest worth...But are they,

And are we, truly brotherly people?
Doesn't selfishness invade our hearts?
Pride and envy's yellow? Speak, do our desires
And actions achieve their rightful end?

Christ Jesus, I too was blind,
Blind faith in human beings seduced me.
I belonged to those who wanted truth
To bind us to a doctrine, class, or party.

Nor did I understand that the strongest streams
Of will and deed become lost in the sands,
I knew not that human hands
Betray their highest dreams;

That all is exposed
Along the path to fulfillment;
By the time the morning glow
Reaches us, its purest light has died.

Thus, we must learn to curb
Our stubborn will, restrain our pride,
So we may kneel beside the tranquil
Waters, wherein dreams the face of God.

How many of us have forgotten,
Just as in my delusions I forgot
Thy sorrowful countenance
Christ Jesus, we ignored Thy help,
Pushed away Thy hand...And yet...and yet...

And yet, Christ Jesus, these must be closer
To Thee than the hypocrites in priest's robe;
They are still brothers in poverty,
Shirking evil, wanting to expel
Indignity, oppression...Late or soon
They will once again make their way to the Father.

Greed has not yet set deep within them
Its poisonous sting...Look, their faces
Do not yet wear masks, their eyes mirror the light
Of innocence in children's eyes; no murder is seen there.

Had they not the right to think of themselves,
Since their masters thought only of private gain?
O how wonderful it is to give oneself away,
But one must first be free...

          Thou mighty comrade
Of the disinherited and deprived,
Were they their own masters? O, Jesus,
Were they not strangers to themselves,

Is it not true they wanted all
To see joy, justice and brotherhood
On earth? Or is this illusion?
Have we misunderstood Thy teachings,
Does Thy essence not impel our struggle?

Christ Jesus, I know that the waters dry up
That feed not the Fountain in Life's heart;
I see the earth red with the blood of strife
And darkness fall over all our flags,

As over those we loved without measure,
Upheld with blind passion,
Followed, defended...
                    Silence, sorrowful songs
Of what was once famous, all end here...

Christ Jesus, my eyes had turned from Thee,
My heart no longer fed at Thy source.
My blood stirred to a different measure,
Another ocean filled my ears...

"Tribulations VI"

Is this Socialism? Its face no longer holds
Any shining dreams, it radiates no grace,
Nor freedom, nor beauty.
What is left of you,
My beloved Socialism? All your magic
Is gone. You are ugly, crude, uncivil;
You are often treacherous and stupid...
O I fear it will be a long time to come
Before the earth basks again
In your fair smile.
Paralyzed your breath, your great heart chilled,
Your amiably flowing water

Is now a frozen brook...
Your gaze is petrifying.

O, if we could only see
A shred of your starry robe
Fluttering, a shimmer of your morning glow,
We would not be so disheartened,
We would take your stagnating soul in our hands,
Bearing it proudly along the way
With singing.

"Songs of Praise XI"

Poets of tomorrow, rise up:
Let your songs like hunting horns resound,
Leading men in whooshing gallop
High over mountains, through deep ravines,
To the heart of humanity's place,
Make them a sun that radiates light
In great bands all around.
Set free the slumbering powers
Of love and courage, joy and trust,
Help hearts through the dead hours,
Fill all eyes with the beloved blue
Of flowers that people seldom see,
Sing of the *Self*! Sing of *Ourselves*:
Hold up the image, not of Ourselves in dreams,
Hidden in illusion's mists and recognized
By those who come after, saying: "They were mistaken,"
Not Ourselves as we go gloating our colors,
Lost in the superficial beauty
Of the rainbow's arc above the earth.
Sing of Ourselves, you of pure nature,
Sing our praises in pure tones,
Catching the thousands of sparks
From our incomplete present, here and now,

Created by incomplete people,
Who have not yet felt God's peace
Enter their hearts, nor beheld
His face bending over them,
Who struggle alone against doubt,
Discouragement, and unrest,
For they miss the essence:
Faith gives doubt wings
And perfect light makes sadness blithe.

Poets! Sing of those who thought
That God, like a wilted flower,
Or weed, had to disappear from life,
Who had learned to despise God,
But were sent, like their ancestors,
To increase His renown.
With smiles they accepted the sacrifice,
With manliness, without pride,
Testifying at their final hour:
"Thankful for life, I willingly die."
God has been merciful to them,
Minding the cargo before the flag.

Sing, poets, a song for those who kept silent,
Knowing a word, a single word,
Might bring freedom, repose, the joyous
Reunion of mother, father and child,
But rather than betray their highest selves,
They chose to toil in the streaming rain,
Hungry, numb with cold, heeding a cry
In the night and finding at dawn
The lifeless body of their dearest friend,
Yet they remained steadfast and true.

Poets of tomorrow! Sing a hymn of praise
To the strong, courageous women,
Who survived the years of tribulation,

The times of want, the roughness;
Sing of the women who, when the final walls
Of love and peace were lost,
While day after day the battle of all
Against all was raging, —
When it seemed that God had lost
Our world and Satan raised his flag
On earth forever — walked through the morning
Streets, faces bright,
Restoring sun to the somber day.
Smiling they entered
Where a lonely man kept watch through the night;
She knew "there is nothing to be done here
But listen calmly to the long lament;"
Afterward, she offered comfort,
Cooked porridge for the old mother,
Gave the children warm food
And mended their clothes.
When she left, everything was nice and clean,
The old woman looked at her gratefully:
"God reward you, child." The blood rose
Warmly in her heart, and moved by gratitude,
She held the frail hand.
"I expect, mother, this speaks for itself."
With a smile, she disappeared...
O, if only it were evening, so that she might let
The tears flow, hidden by night,
Her heart ached so...And she thought:
"How distant those years seem,
And yet how like yesterday,
When he called me silly names"...
She heard his voice, she saw his face,
His grave eyes bright with happiness:
Again and again she asked for strength,
Again and again God provided more,
On her path sparks of rapture fell,
Her gaze reflected an inner grace,

But her existence remained lonely;
No one knew the rich treasure within her,
A page in her remains unwritten for good...

And build a monument to her,
Poets, let her fill your verse,
As she was in her hope-filled youth,
Describe her loyalty in acts both great and small,
What she never suspected nor considered virtue.
O poets of tomorrow, please remember
Our generation's bitter struggle:
Although little was achieved and ended,
Instill it with the look of love,
Create an image of its essence,
Ennobling our suffering
By a glimpse of beauty; remember in love
All those faces from long ago
And you will be our more-knowing comrade.

NOTES to the Translation

1. Translated from the French by Judy Cochran.

2. Translated from the French by Judy Cochran.

Bibliography

Primary Works

Roland Holst van der Schalk, Henriëtte. *Sonnetten en Verzen in terzinen geschreven.* Rotterdam: Brusse, 1895.
_____. *Socialisme en Litteratuur.* Amsterdam: Poutsma, 1899.
_____. *De Nieuwe Geboort.* Rotterdam: Brusse, 1903.
_____. *Opwaartsche Wegen.* Rotterdam: Brusse, 1907.
_____. *De Opstandelingen. Een lyrisch treurspel in drie bedrijven.* Amsterdam: Maatschappij voor goede en goedkoope lectuur, 1910.
_____. *De Vrouw in 't woud.* Rotterdam: Brusse, 1912.
_____. *Thomas More.* Rotterdam: Brusse, 1913.
_____. *De maatschappelijke ontwikkeling en de bevrijding der vrouw.* Rotterdam: Brusse, 1914.
_____. *Het Feest der Gedachtenis.* Rotterdam: Brusse, 1915.
_____. *De revolutionaire massa-aktie.* Rotterdam: Brusse, 1918.
_____. *Verzonken Grenzen.* Rotterdam: Brusse, 1918.
_____. *Tusschen twee werelden.* Rotterdam: Brusse, 1923.
_____. *Heldensage: een gedicht.* Amsterdam: Querido, 1927.
_____. *Verworvenheden.* Maastricht: n.p., 1927.
_____. *Vernieuwingen.* Rotterdam: Brusse, 1929.
_____. *De krisis der westersche kultuur.* Arnhem: Van Loghum Slaterhus, 1933.
_____. *Tusschen tijd en eeuwigheid.* Rotterdam: Brusse, 1934.
_____. *Poezie en maatschappelijke vernieuwing.* Religieus-Socialistische vragen 5.2. Arnhem: Van Loghum Slaterhus, 1935.
_____. *Uit de Diepte.* Haarlem: De Gulden Pers, 1946.
_____. *In de webbe der tijden.* Rotterdam: Brusse, 1947.
_____. *Het vuur brandde voort: Levensherinneringen.* Amsterdam: Van Ditmar, 1949.
_____. *Wordingen.* Rotterdam: Brusse, 1949.

Anthologies

Schaap, H. Ed. *Het leed der mensheid laat mij vaak niet slapen.* Leiden: Martinus Nijhoff, 1984.

Stuiveling, Garmt. Ed. *Bloemlezing*. Rotterdam: Brusse, 1951.
_____. Ed. *Jeugdwerk 1884-1892*. Amsterdam: Meulenhoff, 1969.

Related Works

Albarda, M. K. *Inleiding tot de poëzie van H. Roland Holst*. Amsterdam: De Arbeiderspers, 1935.
Boogman, J. C., et al. *Geschiedenis van het moderne Nederland*. Houten: De Haan, 1988.
Cosman, Carol, et al. Eds. *The Penguin Book of Women Poets*. New York: Viking, 1979. 221-222.
Greshoff, J. *Over Henriëtte Roland Holst*. Rotterdam: Brusse, 1934.
Kempen van, Yves, et al. "Henriëtte Roland Holst's bijdrage aan een socialistische estetika." *Materialistische Literatuurtheorie*. Sunschrift 68. Nijmegen: Socialistische uitgeverij, 1973. 102-126.
Lange, Daniel de. "Henriëtte Roland Holst." *Herman Gorter en Henriëtte Roland Holst in hun tijd*. The Hague: ANDO, 1977. 35-49.
Miskotte, P.J. "Het lyrisch werk van mevrouw Roland Holst." *Christelijke Letterkundige Studiën* 4. Amsterdam: Holland, 1927. 75-141.
Praag, J.P. van. *Henriëtte Roland Holst: Wezen en werk*. Amsterdam: Contact, 1946.
Prins, Johanna. "Henriëtte Roland Holst-van der Schalk (1869-1952)." *Canadian Journal of Netherlandic Studies* 11 (2) 1990. 43-45.
Simons, Wim. *Henriëtte Roland Holst: Ontmoetingen*. Bruges: Desclée De Brouwer, 1969.
Weevers, Th. *Poetry of the Netherlands in its European Context 1170-1930*. London: Athlone Press, 1960. 203-207.

Hella S. Haasse

Jolanda Vanderwal Taylor

As one of the Netherlands' premier female contemporary writers, perhaps one of the Netherlands' premier writers, Hella Haasse is unusual in two respects. While she has populated her writing with a number of strong female characters, she eschews "feminism" as a label and has a fundamentally ambivalent relationship to Dutch feminism. There is no doubt that her work has found an appreciative reading audience in wide circles; when the Anna Bijnsprijs, the Dutch literary prize for "female voices in letters" was founded, she let it be known that she disagreed with the assumptions upon which the prize was based. Nevertheless, she was nominated for the prize.[1] The quality of her work has been officially recognized and marked by the awarding of the Constantijn Huygens prize in 1981, the P.C. Hooft prize in 1984, and an honorary doctorate from the State University in Utrecht in 1988. When Haasse received the P.C. Hooftprijs, the most prestigious literary prize in the Netherlands, the case for her recognition was somewhat unusual; most authors to whom this prize had been awarded before Haasse received it were cited for a major work they had published in the previous three years, Haasse, on the other hand, was awarded the prize for her entire *oeuvre*. Her works have been translated into French, German, Indonesian, Italian, Romanian, Slovenian, Spanish, Swedish, Welsh, and — recently — English.[2]

Secondly, Hella Haasse's works which are commonly assigned to the genre of "historical fiction" reveal a complex and unusual relationship of the author and her authority and the issue of fictionality. Dirk van Ginkel expresses common knowledge about her work when he states: "History and Haasse are two peas in a pod"[3] — but the meaning assigned to history is by no means uncomplicated. One of the more interesting theoretical concerns addressed in Hella Haasse's fictional works is how this expert in what we call historical fiction — a term which is, in her case,   an oversimplification — fictionalizes the historical and historicizes the fictional. One might well speculate on whether a fundamental ambivalence toward historical fiction (based on an imperfect understanding of the genre) taken together with the fact that Hella Haasse is a woman may have contributed toward diminishing the respect which she ought to enjoy.

Hella Serafia Haasse was born in Batavia (now in Indonesia) on February 2, 1918. Her mother was a concert pianist, her father chief inspector of finance employed by the government of the Dutch East Indies.   The Haasse family (Hella's brother Willem Hendrik Johannes was born on October 4, 1921) went to the Netherlands for a furlough in 1920, then returned to Surabaya in 1922, where Hella attended kindergarten and primary school. It is worthy of note that in her autobiographical book *Zelfportret als legkaart* (Selfportrait as Jigsaw Puzzle)[4], she cites as an early experience of alienation the fact that she was the only non-Roman Catholic child of her age in her primary school. Her parents had chosen this school for its proximity to their home rather than for reasons of religious commitment. Since she came from a non-Roman Catholic home, the nuns were scrupulous about not imposing any religious activities on the young Hella.   As a child, she was naturally unaware of the abstract considerations which determined her exclusion from certain events and understood her condition only as that of an outsider. Indeed, one of the more prominent and well-developed themes in Haasse's work later centers on questions concerning the relationship of the individual to the society in which she finds herself, and the issue of personal identity as it relates to the identity of the culture at large. One of Haasse's strongest skills as a novelist is characterization, and she handles outsiders and those whose wishes conflict with societal expectations with insight, sensitivity and finesse.

Although readers do well to resist the temptation to attribute to such early reminiscences more significance than they are due, I mention this anecdote because it provides a very personal introduction of one of Haasse's most notable themes, namely the question of how individuals find their places in society, how the role of the individual may alter with maturity, and what strategies are available to improve the "fit" between societal expectations of an individual's roles and said individual's proclivities and desires.[5] If little Hella's feeling excluded in Catholic school is hardly an unusual or particularly terrible event, it was an experience of alienation which she remembered clearly much later. What may be telling here is that the relatively subtle slight of an inability to be just like her peers is recounted. Later, in 1948 she would publish the story *Oeroeg*, which raised questions about the relationships between the colonial and indigenous populations who resided in Indonesia at that time. Haasse's strength has always been her eye for detail — for the keenly observed pivotal and poignant moment in a relationship. Her work more strongly emphasizes the impact of political problems and duties on individuals than the significance of politics in the broader sense. It is her strength to bring abstractions to the forefront by embodying them in concrete and strikingly individual guises.

In 1924, Hella's mother fell ill and was sent to a sanitarium in Davos, Switzerland. The children made the voyage to Europe with her and lived in the Netherlands while awaiting her recovery. While her brother Willem lived with their grandparents, Hella was housed in a residential school nearby. It would be natural to note that the young Hella was lonely during this time; what is noteworthy and fortuitous was her response to her solitude. She mentions that she found her comfort in writing and inventing texts of various genres of fiction. By 1928, her mother had recovered and the family was reunited in the Dutch East Indies. Hella remained there until she returned to the Netherlands for her education at the university. By Haasse's description, her family life was peaceful, productive and pleasant, a life which encouraged the children to devote themselves to their own projects and develop interests of their own just as they saw their parents doing. By Haasse's description, all members of the family were assumed to have their individual interests and hobbies, and their parallel activities were respected as an integral part of family life; it was during her secondary school years that Hella began to develop a passion for the Middle Ages and to collect materials for her celebrated historical novel *Het woud der verwachting* (In a Dark Wood Wandering).

Haasse moved to the Netherlands after completing secondary school, where she attended the University of Amsterdam as a student of Scandinavian Languages and Letters from 1938 until 1940. She reports[6] that she decided to quit the program after becoming physically ill during a lecture on Germanic sagas, although her distaste was directed toward the misappropriation of the material by the Nazis rather than toward the material itself. Ms. Haasse's family had been planning to follow her to the Netherlands in 1940, but were unable to do so because of the Second World War. Both her parents were placed in Japanese concentration camps in the Dutch East Indies, and the family was not reunited until 1946.

In 1940, Haasse applied for admission to the Amsterdam Academy of Dramatic Art and was accepted as a student of acting; she completed the program in three years, in the midst of the war. She managed to support herself by acting for a brief period while somehow avoiding the requirement instituted on January 22, 1942 that all employed artists be members of the Nederlandse Kultuurkamer (a professional organization organized by the Nazi government). Following her marriage on February 18, 1944 to Jan van Lelyveld, it was no longer necessary for her to support herself financially by her craft. She did not wish to continue her career as an actress while also being a married woman; Hella Haasse took up the role of homemaker, and managed to find time to write. During and after the War, she wrote cabaret texts (1942-1947) and continued to write poetry. Her transition to a prose writer may be dated to sometime in 1944. At first, she wrote shorter pieces; the story *Oeroeg*, which first put her name on the literary map, was published in 1948. Her first major historical novel, *Het woud der verwachting*, was published in 1949. This novel provided a hint of the work to come — both for its consistent quality and for its genre and thematic material which have maintained a significant position within Haasse's *oeuvre* ever since.

Two clusters of themes require particular mention at this point as being centrally important to Haasse's entire work. The first might be called interdependence, a question posed in various guises about the relationships which exist between individuals, other individuals, and society. The second theme is that of the mystery or puzzle which is a significant element of every Haasse story. Frequently, the conundrum is intimately related to issues of the place of the individual character within society. In the autobiographical *Persoonsbewijs* (Identity Card), Haasse stated: "In almost everything I have written, some sort of quest occurs. It may be an inner exploration, or a quest in the outside world; sometimes the two occur together [...] It usually becomes clear that the main characters will have to go through a metamorphosis, will have to change into a 'subsequent' form of themselves in order to plumb the depths of the truth, and then to endure in the new set of circumstances."[7] She has also provided in *Persoonsbewijs* a clue to her interest in the patterning of individual lives within the context of society:

> Music has always been extraordinarily important to me because of my mother, not just because of the beauty of its sound, but particularly because of the miracles of composition — its flowing complexity, its polyphony. Nothing is as deeply satisfying to me as recognizing 'patterns,' structures of motifs and themes, in reality."[8]

The protagonist of Haasse's *Het woud der verwachting*, is an individual whose development is pursued within the context of a society whose preconceived role for him does not fit his personality and talents; he develops more or less in spite of this society. The novel's main character is Charles of Orléans, the medieval French poet and nobleman. By no means, though, is he alone as main character: he is surrounded by his extended family, the members of the court, and indeed the whole of political France with its intrigues and its place in the whirl of international politics. Haasse presents this wealth of material in the form of a succession of third-person narratives. Each of these large segments of the novel places one character at its center. After a substantial Prologue, the first chapter presents his father, the second his mother. The final chapter in the novel's section "the First Book" is entitled "Burgundians and Armagnacs," and portrays in detail the various machinations among those noble families who wield considerable power (though not enough power, in their opinion). This third chapter demonstrates how unsuited Charles is constitutionally to the task which his high birth sets upon his shoulders in the society he inhabits. In Book Two, Charles is sent into exile and undergoes its attendant personal transformations prior to his being brought back to the court.

   Het woud der verwachting is historical fiction closely based on historical studies and actual poetry written by Charles of Orléans,[9] but with an omniscient narrator who does not hesitate to ascribe motivations and emotions in extensive detail to her many characters: the work is an interesting and substantial "good read." Haasse has stated that her approach to writing this work had been to build the characters of the primary figures upon carefully collected historical material which elaborates upon established facts, and choosing the more logical alternative when several possible puzzles of motivation present themselves. But those places where she interpreted more freely were — unsurprisingly — also those where she felt most strongly about the issues, and where she was most likely to be working through her own concerns within the context of the engagement with the fictional world.[10] Haasse later called it a youthful work: "The perspective is that of a nineteenth-century novelist who is omnipresent and omniscient."[11] As we will see, her approach to the historical novel has changed substantially since the 1940s.

   As I have already mentioned, this novel thematically raises the tragic aspects which underpin the question of the interdependence of individuals within a society: Charles is expected to live within the parameters set by the social order even though he is unable to fulfill either those expectations or his own personal potential. In addition, it seems that this very society is threatened by his lack of interest in and skill at the duties considered normal for one of his station — such as avenging his father's death. When he is literally imprisoned (by society's standards), his confinement in fact constitutes a liberation for him — an opportunity to indulge his desires and advance his talents as a poet. Until that which society views as catastrophic occurs, he is imprisoned by social expectations of the historical and political role he is to play. Paradoxically, Charles the poet is liberated by the failure of Charles the nobleman. However, Haasse reminds us that his liberation is only partial; society does exact a toll. Charles is

> a human being, who has however already been so conditioned by his circumstances that he [...] will never be able to escape from the straightjacket of duties and responsibility — even his poems remain primarily courtly and formal, despite their lyrical glow.[12]

De scharlaken stad (The Scarlet City), Haasse's second historical novel, is set in sixteenth-century Rome. The theme of interdependence encountered in *Het woud der verwachting* is even more central to an understanding of this work. Not only is the dependence of the main character on his (mysterious) place within society a main theme of the novel, but this dependence is additionally mirrored in the structure of the work: the essential unity of perspective found in *Het woud der verwachting* is here replaced by a multiplicity of interlocking perspectives, each of which is represented by one or more separate chapters. Each chapter concentrates on a specific person, with a specific set of knowledge about and a personal perspective on life in Rome and — sometimes — a shred of information which has some bearing on the central puzzle of the story. By reading fragments from the lives of these different persons, the reader attempts to piece together the segments of the mystery at the center of the novel. The main character, known as Giovanni Borgia (he is considered to be some sort of relation to either Cesare or Lucrezia Borgia) is literally searching for his identity. Giovanni Borgia knows neither what he can do or be in life nor what he should do, unless he first knows who he is — an understanding which for him lies in knowing the identity of his parents. While Borgia is trying to solve his personal conundrum, the reader of the novel is treated to a wonderful image of the interdependence of many lives in Rome, of the dependence of the entire city on the vicissitudes of international politics, and of the dependence of individual residents of Rome on the status of Rome in the world and the foreign policy community in turn. The cast of characters includes Michelangelo Buonarroti, who is worried about finishing his time-consuming commissions, Francesco Guicciardini and his correspondent, Niccolò Machiavelli (well-known as author of *The Prince*), and Tullia d'Aragona, a high-class courtesan whose ambitious mother is concerned for her future after Tullia becomes enamored with Giovanni Borgia and forgets to behave in a properly professional manner toward her other guests.

In her later novel *De meermin* (The Mermaid), Haasse again takes both her fundamental interest in the notion of interdependence and her love of mystery to new heights. Sera, the main character in this work, learns to recognize that shifting knowledge leads to changing interpretations of the "facts" we think we know, and that our "knowledge" of both events and their meaning are subject to constant re-interpretation and reassessment. Positions and notions about truth must therefore be held provisionally, because new information may become available at any time and change one's perspective on what one thought one knew. In addition, Haasse uses such an occasion of discovery to raise the notion of collective guilt; the "facts" and personal alliances which the main character is learning to reinterpret are related to possible crimes committed during a time of war: a fruitful fictional stage for secrets, danger, excitement, and a time which illustrates a heightened need to make well-considered (moral) choices.

Sera — wife, mother, daughter-in-law, poet — lives through a single day in which she appears to make some progress in coming to an understanding of the various relationships in her life (i.e., those with her children, her husband, her in-laws, other artists, the world of poetry, and the strong ties created by events in the past). In doing so, she takes a significant step toward understanding herself better; she is herself redefined along with the provisional "facts" which constitute her world.

The day begins for the heroine of *De meermin* with the discovery that a beloved stone statuette of a mermaid has fallen from its perch on the façade of the house and shattered on the doorstep. It is an event which unsettles the two families residing in the house: Sera, her husband Leonard, and their children, who live upstairs, as well as Leonard's parents, who live on the ground floor. For Leonard's parents, the broken mermaid upsets breakfast: the maid hurries about trying to simultaneously set in motion the predictable order of the day by making tea, and also to deal with the intrusion of accident and disorder by sweeping up the mess. This tableau is associated with the arrival of a death notice which is (more or less) good news for Leonard's father, Mr. Doornstam. The note which arrives signals the end of an era; the man who has just died had been the contact between Doornstam and an illegitimate son to whom he had secretly been giving financial assistance. For Doornstam, the past returns only to release him from its grip — or so he thinks.

For Doornstam junior, Leonard, the mermaid is likely to be associated with his legal practice: he has been temporarily advising a client of his senior partner's on the legal and social embarrassment of a woman whose body has been discovered buried in a well. The body was found after the land had been sold to a developer — and, of course, rumors are running wild. Leonard's client is just now returning from a journey. The conversation between Leonard and his partner Hazekamp upon the return of the latter is telling; Hazekamp insists that his client has no reason for concern, first, he says, "she has nothing to do with it," and second, because the statute of limitations on this crime (if it was indeed a crime) has expired. He takes a purely legalistic approach which suggests to the reader that Hazekamp could perhaps be in the know. Leonard's approach is strongly ethical, and he questions many actions of the resistance movement during the Nazi occupation of the Netherlands.

That the fall of the mermaid is probably more significant to Sera than to anyone else is appropriate, as she is the novel's protagonist. However, the disruptions that the statuette's fall occasions are more subtle. There are practical consequences — it upsets Sera's daughter Digna, who becomes more unmanageable than she already was. More importantly, the mermaid is thematically

associated with Sera, who has written a long poem about a diver.
Sera has her living room decorated in blues and greens, so that — as
the narrator points out — it resembles an aquarium. The mermaid of
the novel's title is thus identified with this period in Sera's life. The
diver of Sera's poem is out of his/her element: he descends to a place
in which he does not naturally belong in an attempt to bring things to
the surface (if only to the surface of consciousness as a visitor to
hidden places). In contrast, the broken mermaid of the novel's title
is a creature of the water whose half-human status is intended to
remind the reader of the tendency of things in the material world to
break — or an image of the notion that things in the world go awry.
The novel's other mermaid-like creature (the corpse in the well) has
to be pulled up out of the water — moved from her state of
hiddenness (although some of the novel's characters would have
preferred that she had never been discovered at all). Sera's diver
bobs for hidden treasure, looking for the unknown — as we learn in
this novel, this diving is seen to be symbolic for Sera's search for her
own identity (indeed, the search for the artist in general). And when
Sera is trying to understand the world around her, the narrator thinks
in water-imagery. Toward the end of the novel, Sera comes to
believe that she is about to figure out the constellations of
relationships between some of her acquaintances:

> Roduman and Hazekamp looked at each other. Sera
> caught that look, what she saw, or thought she saw,
> took her breath away. Time stood still; during a
> second which seemed to last an eternity, they became
> a fossilized group [...] [Sera] was right on the edge
> of discovering something. But the image moved, the
> way reflections vibrate as soon as a rock falls into the
> water. They raised their glasses and drank.[13]

Sera is about to see the truth — either below the surface of the
water or reflected in the surface of the water — but the moment
passes, the water ripples, and the image has temporarily disappeared.
But the reader need not despair; by the end of the novel Sera will
have connected all the pieces. She will have teased out all the strands

of the lives in this circle of friends, and she will have discovered how and where their ultimate connection with each other resides.

As it turns out, the connection between each of these people — the single piece of the puzzle which makes everything make sense (at least from Sera's point of view), is ultimately retrieved from events during the Nazi occupation — a time which is "hidden" in the depths of history. It turns out that Hazekamp was an agent known in Resistance circles as "Deepwater" (his name nicely in keeping with Sera's metaphors for life), and that the corpse in the well was a young woman who died during the occupation under suspicious circumstances — possibly killed at "Deepwater's" behest. It also becomes clear that Deemster — Leonard's unacknowledged half-brother — thinks his father refused to recognize him because he was a collaborator. Everything fits together when you know what happened during the occupation. Sera not only dredges up all the pieces, she fits them together and recognizes the responsibility her family bears. Oddly their responsibility — the only direct "crime" against humanity committed by a family member of hers — is the impregnating of the servant girl, an event actually unrelated to the war. Sera appropriately resolves to expiate the real familial burden of guilt by caring for the troubled daughter of her husband's half-brother.

Hella Haasse's use of the Second World War as an instrument for the examination of personal history, collective guilt, and the relation of memory to the "facts" which underlie one's view of the world should not be surprising; it is merely the most broadly autobiographical examination of these themes in the context of history — in this case, the history of her own time. In *Persoonsbewijs*[14], Hella Haasse refers to the war as a life-changing experience: "A completely new inner territory opened up. In many respects, the years between 1940 and 1945 were the most important years of my life." In large measure, though, Haasse has chosen to pursue these themes in the context of the historical novel. Moreover, she has chosen to pursue what for her have increasingly become central questions about the value of "facts" and of their ability to change the way the world is viewed — the historicity of her fictions — in the context of times and histories far removed from the span of her own life and experience. Her mature work may be seen as a movement away from the conventions of omniscient narration and toward one in which authority is shared between an author and the texts of the historical record, or between an author and the fictional characters she creates. The thoroughness of her historical research remains a common theme, but Hella Haasse's later and more mature work reflects upon the use of those materials in a radically different way. It is as if she takes the narrative conventions she uses to move the reader through the fictionally recreated societies of *Het woud der verwachting* and *Een scharlaken stad* and turns them to the task of creating a history in the midst of fiction.

It is in the interests of looking at Haasse's mature work (which is, at present, untranslated into English) in terms of this interdependence of the historical and the fictional that we will briefly turn our attention to two of Haasse's later novels set in the same time period (the eighteenth century) with a female and male protagonist. We will attempt to investigate the unusual relationship of issues of historicity and fictionality in Haasse's fiction and show how this complex of issues is related to her construction of female and male historical characters. While *Een gevaarlijke verhouding of Berg-en-Daalse Brieven* (1976, A Dangerous Liaison or Letters from Hill-and-Vale) may seem a straightforward "epistolary novel" in its form, Haasse challenges the normal parameters of the genre. The text is constituted of an exchange of letters written between the Marquise de Merteuil (the fictional character of Choderlos de Laclos' *Les Liaisons dangereuses*, 1782), and the present-day Haasse as author, who violates the explicit historical conventions of the epistolary novel by "corresponding" with her main character. Within the context of the letters, she describes both the Marquise de Merteuil's social "power" as a woman and the severely limited sphere of its influence. The mechanism of fictionalization in this novel exerts the same instrumental power as the Marquise's correspondence. After the "real" (that is, Laclos' fictional) Marquise's correspondence falls into the wrong hands and her "authority" as a collaborator in the seduction and ruin of other women is made known, she is made a social outcast by the trail of correspondence which functions as the proof as well as the currency of her authority. The relationship between Haasse the character and de Merteuil in Haasse's novel is fraught with a similar promise of autonomy and authority which also proves illusory; while de Merteuil expresses her hope that she might be able to escape her dismal situation through fiction, Haasse exerts her authorial power and asserts that the Marquise will "remain" fictional. However, the fact that the author and character correspond with each other suggests that the character has a different epistemological status for the author (and the reader) than in the common dialogues between character and character in the more traditional epistolary novel.

Ms. Haasse plants clues for the careful reader at the beginning of *Een gevaarlijke verhouding of Daal- en Bergse Brieven* that there is something unusual about the ontological status of one of the correspondents when letter number 1 "To the Marquise de Merteuil" begins as follows:

> Madame, you came to mind[15] in the Daal- en Bergse Laan [Avenue of Hill and Vale] in southern the Hague, near where I live. I was standing there, facing the woods of Pex, the blurred brown and green of young foliage, and imagined, amidst that thicket, instead of tennis courts, soccer fields, pony stables, and restaurant, a small country house, late eighteenth century [...] How is it, I thought to myself, that here, amidst the edges of the dunes [...] one doesn't find the remains of a country estate, while after all, the area is replete with the memories of small and large rural estates from the days when rich residents of the Hague had a 'second home' built here?[16]
>
> The air I breathe when I walk there contains something — I imagine — that must promote what Goethe called "the inclination to spin a yarn."[17] [...] I thought I saw white walls shimmering [...] the Daalberg Estate, I thought, and simultaneously: Valmont! And because of that one word "Valmont,"

you, madam, were present there, almost physically.[18]

The contemporary correspondent has imagined the presence of her foil out of the *possibility* that there might have once been a building bearing a name that, translated, would remind one of the fictional character. Valmont, was, of course, Madame de Merteuil's lover, a significant character in de Laclos' novel. The writer thus, with an attention to detail typical of Haasse, picks up more or less where de Laclos left off, since at the end of *Les liaisons dangereuses*, in letter 175, de Laclos mentions the direction in which Madame de Merteuil's may have fled: "It is thought that she went in the direction of Holland." The fictional status of not only the character, but even of the domicile becomes increasingly explicit in the course of the passage *even though* the language Haasse chooses closely echoes that of the beginning of *Schaduwbeeld of het geheim van Appeltern* (Shadow Image or The Secret of Appeltern), where the description is of a historical building.

   Schaduwbeeld begins, as does *Een gevaarlijke verhouding*, with the narrator posted in front of the house which will become central to the tale she is about to tell.

   I was standing on the dike near Appeltern, not far from the locks, my back to the river Maas, which flowed peacefully between its green banks. In front of me the road descended toward a dense thicket. The treetops rustled in the wind, billowing clouds sailed through the air like giant ships. The land smelled of grass and manure, and a vague scent of sludge blew across from the river. The magnificent landscape was bathed in noonday light [...] I took the newspaper clipping from my coat pocket. I was familiar with Appeltern from eighteenth century depictions...[19]

The descriptive prose, with its emphasis on light and the colors of vegetation, is remarkably similar. In both cases, she imagines a building — where in *Een gevaarlijke verhouding*, she muses on the possibility that a building might once have existed, in *Schaduwbeeld* she recalls an eighteenth-century etching or drawing showing the castle, thus appealing to its historical existence.

These quotations also illustrate Haasse's notions about history — that it is not lost, but remains connected to the present. But the contemporary correspondent in the epistolary novel has apparently not invented her correspondent single-handedly. In letter two, de Merteuil in turn invents Haasse: after lamenting her loneliness and her lack of appropriate correspondents, she, too, comments on the quality of the light in The Hague:

> In my opinion, the clarity is not necessarily safe; one might be tempted to see more than really exists. In a moment of weakness (constant solitude can tempt one to foolish play) I attempted to imagine a correspondent from a period of time which is yet to come. I could imagine a woman who is entirely my opposite in appearance and circumstances, but who resembles me in the quality of her intelligence.[20]

Thus, the fictional character de Merteuil has also imagined *her* correspondent, thereby playfully inverting the expectations of historical fiction even as the genre is invoked.

As Haasse mentions,[21] Madame de Merteuil is frequently considered almost the most evil female character in literature. Haasse approaches her with some sympathy, perhaps toying with the interpretation that her bad reputation may be attributed to the judgment of male readers responding to a characterization of Madame de Merteuil by a male author in a time when women were not supposed to wield power or authority, and allowing herself to feel "a certain academic amazement for the manner in which this woman managed to exert such power with limited means."[22] However, in the course of the correspondence it becomes increasingly clear that Haasse can not accept de Merteuil's philosophy of life, as she comes to view her as not only a pre-Revolutionary French beneficiary of class privilege, but so consistent in her thoughts and opinions as only one steeped in and entirely (criminally) uncritical of "Reason" could be:

> You embody absolute egotism. Not because of inherent or cultivated malice or misanthropy, but rather because you are so in the thrall of a need for independence and Reason that you constantly remain conscious of your own individual ability to create meaning. To you, cogito ergo sum, I know that I exist because I am capable of thought, means: I will make sure that what I think of will come to pass, and also: the thoughts of others, all that takes place beyond my consciousness, does not exist as far as I am concerned.[23]

Madame de Merteuil's vice is that she ruins an innocent woman with the help of her male accomplice, her (former) lover Valmont. She asks him to seduce the victim, then leave her. When the correspondence between Valmont and Madame de Merteuil becomes public, and particularly the *one* scurrilous letter which she so imprudently penned in her own hand, she loses the considerable social power she had collected over the years, and she is exiled, a broken, ill and lonely woman.

The problem, of course, is that the actions which de Merteuil justifies as based on Reason are dangerous and callous machinations from the point of view of a twentieth century author/character. Haasse chides de Merteuil that her commitment to abstract consistency, though perhaps innovative in the eighteenth century, is less impressive from a contemporary point of view, particularly since, in her opinion, women now have other modes of behavior open to them than they did in de Merteuil's day. The discussion between de Merteuil and the fictional twentieth century character, as mentioned above, becomes a discourse on the function of fiction and the role of women in society.

Haasse's fictionalization of a male protagonist and *his* reconstruction from letters and documents in *Schaduwbeeld* (1989) pursues a course which outlines a different relationship between gender, power and "history." The novel's main character Joan Derk Van der Capellen is a "patriot," a proponent of democracy during the reign of Willem V (1751-1795) who, unlike the Marquise, *has* access to the public sphere — at least in theory. Van der Capellen's marginalization, both in the sense of "history" and of his behavior as a character in the novel, is the vehicle through which Haasse explores the relationships of power and texts yet again; Joan Derk Van der Capellen had only a marginal claim to nobility; his lack of pedigree was used against him and, since he (the historical figure) was frequently prohibited from appearing in "de Staten" (the governmental body of the nobility in the province), he took as his weapon the written word, pursuing authority by way of anonymous discourse. He attempted to influence public opinion by publishing pamphlets, the existence of which then becomes one of the preconditions for his appearance two centuries later as the protagonist of a semi-fictional text by Hella Haasse; Haasse calls it a "chronicle." The great volume of extant letters to and from friends, and occasionally enemies, and the pamphlets attributed to Van der Capellen are carefully arranged by Haasse to allow the reader to know the character as she has come to know him. Haasse does express regret that the topics in most of the documents she had at her disposal are political rather than personal, and yet, as an exceptionally careful reader, she has managed to find hints to his character and personal life, which subsequently guided her in her choice and structuring of the order of documents in her work. The presentation of Van der Cappelen here is explicitly non-determinate. Historians have alternately interpreted Van der Cappelen as a misunderstood, noble character, and (alternately) as an egotistical, self-important whiner. Haasse's work does not exclude the material which would support either view, but rather presents it side by side. In addition, her tradition of careful and voracious reading is not limited to the documents related directly to the history of Van der Capellen, but extends to many other documents of the time as well. Thus, when the author admits to having "filled in holes" in the representation "from her imagination,"[24] one must understand this correctly: her supplements are not pure imagination, but carefully constructed from or by analogy to other sources, so that they may boast at the very least of historical verisimilitude.[25]

Whereas Madame de Merteuil is ruined when her letters are read by the wrong audience, Van der Cappellen's texts first (in the historical sense) become an important method for the promotion of his ideas and secondly (for the sake of fictionalized history), at least fall into the "right" hands: those of a twentieth-century female author who knows how to *read* and consume a text, to construct characters whose "historical" position is rewritten in terms of the invisible (the Marquise's correspondence and Van der Capellen's authority [or lack thereof] in "de Staten") and the visible (Van der Capellen's pamphlets and the Marquise's social position) as seen through the lens of the modern author and her authority whose "historical" investigations are a device to address power and gender by means other than explicitly feminist discourse.

In *Les liaisons dangereuses*, the Marquise de Merteuil, normally excluded from the public sphere as a woman, creates her own space in the private sphere, gaining influence in the world — one might even say: she enters the public sphere — at the point where the private intersects with the public, by means of not just the written word, but particularly by means of the word written in her own hand. The fact that she writes the fateful document in her own hand becomes her downfall, as it precludes the possibility of plausible denial. At the end of his novel, de Laclos sends the Marquise de Merteuil, who has gained substantial social influence by writing her letters, back to the *very* private sphere — a secluded house somewhere "in the direction of Holland" where her only interlocutor is an uninvited author from another age — who considers herself much more liberated, and imposes her presence on the lonely refugee. Joan Derk Van der Capellen, however, is also excluded from the "public sphere," which in his case is the ruling class of noblemen to which he felt he belonged by right. He, too, brought his influence to bear by anonymous writings, though his anonymity was essentially preserved.

In closing, let us return to the questions of method or form. Hella Haasse proves to have an extraordinary talent for "consuming" texts: the historical and literary texts which form the basis or the starting point, and sometimes the meat of her novels. It is certain, and certainly appropriate, that Haasse reads voraciously when preparing to write a historical novel, and that even the fictional *Een gevaarlijke verhouding* uses, consumes in a sense, the *Liaisons dangereuses* as penned by Laclos as well as a substantial body of historical, philosophical and literary texts of his time. An arduous task? Perhaps. Haasse speaks of her research with such delight that one concludes it is much more closely related to appetite or desire than to duty. She once described the genesis of *Schaduwbeeld* as one in which her appetite was whetted when she began reading the archival materials with which she had been provided, as if her appetite had been induced by the presence of sense stimuli. Just as a normal human being is induced to eat by a complex of stimuli (scents, colors, textures, temperature), so Hella Haasse is tempted to do research, and subsequently write, by a boxful of archival material.

Of course we must recognize that there are various methods of consuming such historical material. *Schaduwbeeld* presents the reader with not only letters to and from Joan Derk Van der Capellen, his friends and enemies, which present a discontinuous narrative. These letters are placed in the context of a historical narrative, which in turn is interrupted and enhanced by chapters on the activities of contemporaries, such as John Adams, John Wilkes, Beaumarchais, Willem V, and so on. The discontinuity serves to simultaneously present, and make comprehensible, a wealth of facts and perspectives to the reader, and to resist a simplistically positivistic view of history.

In this brief consideration of Hella Haasse's work, we may conclude that her good writing does indeed involve voracious and careful reading, and that such an observation holds true over the entire span of her written work. While her solid scholarship distinguishes her, her ability as a great writer lies in something more than that. It lies in her ability to elaborate lovingly upon of the detail that makes good fiction and good history, and in her ability to interest her reading public in whatever material she chooses — be it entirely her own invention, or based on history — and to simultaneously subvert the simple expectations which might allow one to easily dismiss "historical fiction" as a genre. Like the diver of Sera's poem in *De meermin,* Haasse is able to descend into the darkness of history and to return with an artifact whose chief surprise is its familiarity.

NOTES to the Introduction

1. Renate Dorrestein: "Hella Haasse: 'De vrouw als redster van de wereld? Bah, wat een enge gedachte!' " *Opzij*, januari 1987, 23.

2. *Het woud der verwachting* was published as *In a Dark Wood Wandering* in 1989 by Academy Chicago Publishers in a translation by Lewis C. Kaplan, revised and edited by Anita Miller. (Also: London: Hutcheon, 1990). *De scharlaken stad* was published as *The Scarlet City* in 1990 by Academy Chicago Publishers in a translation by Anita Miller. In progress: *A Newer Testament*, a translation of *Een nieuwer testament*, tranlated by Anita Miller, to be published by Academy Chicago Publishers.

3. De Haagsche Post, April, 1990.

4. Hella S. Haasse, *Zelfportret als legkaart*. Amsterdam: De Bezige Bij, 1954.

5. Of course, I would not have been able to mention this anecdote if Haasse had not herself mentioned it in *Zelfportret als legkaart*, 26-27.

6. Hella S. Haasse, *Persoonsbewijs*, Bruges: Desclée-De Brouwer, 1967. 27-28.

7. Hella S. Haasse, *Persoonsbewijs*, Bruges: Desclée-De Brouwer, 1967. 65-66.

8. Hella S. Haasse, *Persoonsbewijs*, Bruges: Desclée-De Brouwer, 1967. 37.

9. Note that the Dutch edition of this novel provides a bibliography of works in Dutch, English, French and German.

10. Hella S. Haasse, *Persoonsbewijs*, Bruges: Desclée-De Brouwer, 1967. 59.

11. Johan J. Diepstraten, ed., *Hella S. Haasse: Een interview*. The Hague: BZZTôH, 1984. 83.

12. Hella S. Haasse, *Persoonsbewijs*, Bruges: Desclée-De Brouwer, 1967. 60.

13. Hella S. Haasse, *De meermin*. Amsterdam: Querido, 1962, I am quoting from the Salamander edition, 175-176.

14. Hella S. Haasse, *Persoonsbewijs*, Bruges: Desclée-De Brouwer, 1967. 43

15. Literally: "into my mind."

16. Hella S. Haasse, *Een gevaarlijke verhouding of Daal-en-Bergse brieven*, 1976. I am quoting from the 2nd. ed., in the Salamander series, Amsterdam: Querido, 1982. 5.

17. Haasse quotes Goethe in German: "Lust zu Fabulieren."

18. Hella S. Haasse, *Een gevaarlijke verhouding of Daal-en-Bergse brieven*, Amsterdam: Querido, 1982. 6.

19. Hella S. Haasse, *Schaduwbeeld of Het geheim van Appeltern*. Amsterdam: Querido, 1989. 9.

20. Hella S. Haasse, *Een gevaarlijke verhouding of Daal-en-Bergse brieven*, Amsterdam: Querido, 1982. 44.

21. Johan J. Diepstraten,ed., *Hella S. Haasse: Een interview*. The Hague: BZZTôH, 1984. 89.

22. Johan J. Diepstraten, ed., *Hella S. Haasse: Een interview*. The Hague: BZZTôH, 1984. 89-90.

23. Hella S. Haasse, *Een gevaarlijke verhouding of Daal-en-Bergse brieven*, Amsterdam: Querido, 1982. 8.

24. Hella S. Haasse, *Schaduwbeeld of Het geheim van Appeltern*. Amsterdam: Querido, 1989. 463 (in the postscript.)

25. *Elsevier* "Een rampzalige stoelgang", Wammes Bos, 10 februari 1990: "'...although she does base her work on verifiable historical material.'"

Translations by Lewis C. Kaplan and Anita Miller

From the Prologue to *In a Dark Wood Wandering:
A Novel of the Middle Ages*.

Revised and edited by Anita Miller from an English translation from the Dutch by Lewis C. Kaplan. Chicago: Academy Chicago Publishers. English translation copyright 1989 by Edith Kaplan, Kalman Kaplan and Anita Miller. Reprinted by permission of the publisher.

Valentine, Duchess of Orléans, lay in her green-curtained bed of state, listening to the bells of Saint-Pol. The church was not far from the royal palace — only a stone's throw away. The pealing of the bells swelled into a heavy sea of cheerless sound; Valentine folded her hands over the green coverlet. The christening procession of her fourth son, Charles, had left the palace.

The people of Paris, crowded behind the wooden barriers set up to protect the procession, strained to see Charles VI, the godfather of the royal child, and the King's brother Louis, the father, preceded by torchbearers, noblemen, high dignitaries of the Church and clergy. Following Charles and Louis were their uncles: Philippe, Duke of Burgundy, and the Dukes of Berry and Bourbon.

The King walked faster than the solemnity of the occasion dictated; the agitated movements of his head and his aimless, wandering stare betrayed his unfortunate mental condition even to the uninitiated. But the spectators' attention was riveted on Louis the Duke of Orléans, because of his smile and splendid clothes, and on Isabeau the Queen, surrounded by princesses and royal kinswomen and followed by many ladies-in-waiting. In the midst of the women's crowns, veils, pointed headdresses and trailing, ermine-trimmed mantles, the infant Charles d'Orléans was carried to church for the first time.

Valentine's weary body lay beneath the coverlet. She stared at the women busying themselves at the hearth, at the open cupboard filled with platters and tankards, the torches set along the walls in their iron brackets, the green wall hangings of the ducal lying-in chamber. Before the hearthfire stood the cradle on small wooden wheels in which Charles had slept from the moment that, washed, rubbed with honey and wrapped in linen cloth, he had been entrusted to the care of his nurse, Jeanne la Brune. Women hurried back and forth from the adjoining room, filling the platters on the sideboard with sweets and fruit, bringing green cushions for the benches along the walls. The torches gave off a stupefying smell of resin; their heat, together with the heat of the hearthfire, was almost unbearable in the tightly-closed room. The Duchess broke into a sweat.

Her body had been worn out by four confinements in four years' time. But more exhausting still, perhaps, was the pace of court life — an uninterrupted series of dances, masquerades and banquets. On Valentine Visconti, exhaustion worked like a poison. At her father's court in Pavia, she had loved the small elegant gatherings frequented by poets and scholars, the debates and word games, the music played in her own chambers. Gian Galeazzo Visconti, although denounced as a tyrant and a sorcerer, had a more acute eye for learning and the fine arts than the pretentious inhabitants of Saint-Pol.

The glitter of the torch flames, reflected in the gold and silver plate on the sideboard, hurt her eyes. She closed them and sank away instantly into a deep pool of exhaustion, a darkness without rest, riddled with the voices and stifled laughter of the women. It seemed to her that the walls of Saint-Pol vibrated with sound like the walls of a gigantic beehive. The entire enormous palace, with its complex

structure which linked halls, chambers, towers, bastions, inner
courtyards, annexes, stables and gardens, enclosed her like a
honeycomb of cells, buzzing with bees. She was aware all at the same
time of members of the household running up and down the stairs and
through the corridors; of the continuous uproar in and around the
kitchens, larders and wine cellars where the christening meal and the
banquet were being prepared; of the stamping of hooves and the
jingle of weapons and armor in the guardrooms; of the chirping and
twittering of birds in the great indoor aviary; of the roaring of
lions — the King's menagerie — in their winter quarters. And more
disturbing than all this was the ceaseless cacophony of the bells. She
murmured prayers and endeavored to lose herself in thoughts of the
ceremony nearby in the church of Saint-Pol, where even now her son
was receiving baptism over the basin hung with gold brocade. She
thought of her brother-in-law the King who, as godfather, had to hold
the child in his right arm throughout the christening. She had been
told that he was pleased at the birth and the planned festivities.

For the first time in months, he had left the castle of Creil
where he was confined, to show himself to the public. His relatives,
warned by physicians, watched him anxiously, fearing a sudden
renewed outburst of madness. Valentine felt a heartrending pity for
the King, of whom she was as fond as he was of her. The news two
years earlier of an unexpected eruption of his illness had upset her no
less — although she reacted in a different way — than it had upset the
Queen. Despite her displays of desperate grief, Isabeau believed — or
professed to believe — that recovery was possible; Valentine, on the
other hand, perhaps because of her swifter Southern intuition, knew
that the germ of madness, always present in the King's childlike,
capricious nature, had now put down roots that were ineradicable. To
some degree, Valentine shared the view that a madman was little
more than a dangerous animal; but the thought of her brother-in-law
imprisoned in the barred balcony high above the walls of Creil,
gazing down from his cage at the nobles of his retinue who were
playing ball in the dry moat below, filled her with horror and
compassion. Although she knew that Isabeau's grief was sincere, she
could not remain blind to the avidity with which the Queen had taken

over the administration of the court, and the Duke of Burgundy the control of affairs of state.

She had little faith in the physician Guillaume de Harselly, however capable he might be. She no longer believed that illness could be banished by confession and exorcism. The previous winter she had found another physician's recommendation for a cure even less beneficial; the King should be kept away from the Council and all state business; he should be diverted with various amusements. As a result, Saint-Pol became a madhouse where the music was never silenced, where the uproar of balls and drinking bouts never stopped; where Isabeau, evening after evening, on the arm of Louis d'Orléans, led the rows of celebrants in their multi-colored finery, and the King, actually somewhat recovered, clapped his hands in time with the music and looked on eagerly at each new entertainment.

The torchlight pricked Valentine's closed eyes; the heat of the lying-in chamber made her think of the endless nights spent under the canopy of tapestries and fading flowers at the side of the King, who enjoyed having her near him and would not allow her to withdraw. As she looked down from the raised platform upon the crowd in the overflowing hall, it often seemed to her that she was in a purgatory more cruel and terrifying than the one the Church had taught her to fear. The statues in the niches of the cathedral, the spewing monsters, the devils and gargoyles which looked down upon Paris, grimacing, from the exterior of Notre Dame, had come to life in the grotesquely-masked dancers illuminated in the torchlight: in the women whose high headdresses were decorated with horns and rolls of stuffed cloth, in the men whose wide pleated sleeves looked like the wings of bats and who wore sharply pointed shoes like the beaks of alien beasts.

Valentine moved her head restlessly on the pillows. The rush of milk made her feverish. The normal cure for this, the feeding of her child, was denied to her: that was taken care of by the wet nurse who sat by the hearthfire, a cloth folded over her breasts. A chamberwoman threw some logs on the fire; the flames leapt high in the recesses of the hearth.

Flames had put a premature end to the wild masquerade which Isabeau had held in January to celebrate the marriage of her friend and confidante, the widow of the Sire de Hainceville. The celebration of a second marriage offered abundant opportunity for unbridled pleasures, jokes full of double entendres, reckless debauchery. An endless train of guests danced hand in hand through the hall. And the King, infected by the general atmosphere of wild elation, allowed himself to be seduced into joining a game of dressing-up invented by some noblemen who wanted to terrorize the women for sport.

In a side room they had their naked bodies sewn into garments of thin leather smeared with pitch and then strewn with feathers; they put on feather headdresses to make themselves look like savages. So attired, they leapt shouting among the dancers who dispersed in panic in every direction, to the onlookers' delight. The Duchess of Berry, the very young wife of the Duke's uncle, sat beside Valentine under the canopy. She recognized the King by his build and laughed uncontrollably at his antics, which were wilder and more excited than those of the others. Louis d'Orléans entered the hall, drunk, with a lighted torch in his hand, accompanied by some friends; the savages rushed over to him and began, crowded together, to dance around him. The shouts of the bystanders drowned out the music. A scuffle broke out, in the course of which the feathered headdresses caught fire.

In nightmares, Valentine still heard the screams of the living torches, hopelessly doomed in their tight garments; they ran in circles, frantically clawing at themselves, or rolled howling over the floor. Isabeau, who knew that the King was one of the dancers, collapsed at the sight of the flames. But the young Duchess de Berry, tears of laughter still on her cheeks, wrapped the train of her dress around the King and was able to smother the fire. The others burned half an hour longer, but they did not die for several days.

Valentine moaned aloud and threw her hands over her face. This caused a stir among the women near the door. Someone came quickly to the bed; it was the Dame de Maucouvent, who looked after Valentine's oldest son Louis.

"Madame," she said, curtseying low, "the procession is returning from the church."

The Duchess opened her eyes — she was still overcome by the memory of that hellish night which had caused the King to have another, and prolonged, relapse. She gazed for a time at the trustworthy, somewhat faded face of the Dame de Maucouvent. "Help me," Valentine said at last, holding out her arms.

The woman helped her to sit up, wiped the perspiration from her face and spread the deeply scalloped sleeves of her upper garment over the coverlet. The pealing of the bells began to subside.

The Dame de Maucouvent put a silver dish filled with sweetmeats and spices on Valentine's lap. Custom dictated that the mother of a new-born child quit her bed during the King's visit to offer him refreshment with her own hand. The women took the lids from the jugs on the sideboard; a fragrance of warm hippocras filled the chamber. The voices of arriving guests could be heard in the antechamber; pages opened the door to the lying-in room and the King entered quickly, walking between rows of torchbearers and curtseying women.

Valentine, who had not seen him since the early spring, was so shocked and horrified by his altered appearance that she forgot her manners and remained sitting in bed. She watched him approaching her, slovenly in his rich clothing, his eyes distended with nervous mirth. Behind him, on the threshold of the chamber and in the anteroom, stood the royal kinsmen and the court. The baptized child began to wail.

Hastily the women pulled back the coverlet and Valentine, supported by the Dame de Maucouvent, set her feet on the floor.

"Sire," Valentine whispered, lifting the dish toward him. She was blinded by a sudden dizziness; two ladies of the court held her firmly under the arms while the King, dawdling like a child, poked among the delicacies in the dish.

"Take this, Sire, it is a deer," Valentine said softly, almost in tears to see him staring uncertainly at the sugar beast in his hand. Over his shoulder she caught the Queen's eye, cold and full of suspicion. Louis, Valentine's husband, leaned against the doorpost, toying with his embroidered gloves; he held them before his face to conceal a yawn. The King clutched the piece of candy and raised his eyes for the first time to Valentine's face.

"A deer?" he asked, motioning for the dish to be removed. "A deer? Yes, surely, a deer. You are right, Madame my sister-in-

law, Valentine, dear Valentine. A deer. You know of course that a
deer brings me luck? You know the story, don't you?"

His eyes strayed about the room. No one said anything.

"I'll tell you what happened to me," the King continued in a
confidential tone, walking along with Valentine who was being led
back to bed. "I was already crowned, although I was still only a boy.
I was hunting in the forest of Senlis..."

The Queen, the Dukes of Burgundy, Berry, Bourbon and
Orléans, the prince and princesses of the royal House and all the
counts and barons and their ladies, as well as the women who carried
the infant Charles, followed the King into the lying-in chamber. They
accepted some of the hippocras and candied fruit offered by the
Duchess's women and exchanged knowing looks. It was not for the
first time that the King talked in front of them about this youthful
experience, which held great significance for him.

"Know then, Valentine," said the King. He bent over his
sister-in-law and took one of her cold hands in his. "At a crossroad
I came upon a deer. I did not shoot it. It let itself be taken by hand.
It was like the deer of Saint Hubert, but instead of a cross it wore a
collar of gilded copper — what do you say to that? — and on it was
written in Latin..." He placed the spread fingers of his left hand over
his mouth and looked with glistening eyes at Valentine, who smiled
sadly at him. "On it was...well, what was written there?...In Latin?"
he asked suddenly, with an impatient stamp of his foot.

One of the nobles stepped forward and bowed. "*Caesar hoc
mihi donavit*, Sire," he murmured, sinking onto one knee beside the
bed. His long red sleeves trailed behind him on the carpet.

"That was it! 'Caesar has given me this collar'," continued
the King, speaking so quickly that he stammered. "That is to say, the
deer was more than a thousand years old. Think of it, Valentine! Was
that a good omen or not? Well?" He tugged at the hand which he still
clutched tightly.

"It was a good omen, Sire," the Duchess said in a flat voice.
She was constantly aware of Isabeau's eyes; the Queen stood near the
bed, staring at her husband.

"I thought so too — no, I'm sure of it!" the King said loudly.
"I dreamed of a hart on the eve of the battle of Roosebeke. And

didn't I win a glorious victory there? Who dares to deny that? I was twelve years old then, no older. But you should have seen that battlefield...Ten thousand dead, ten thousand, all because of *me*." He struck his chest, panting with excitement. "*I* won it; it was I who gave the signal for the assault. When I finally had the flag hoisted again, the sun broke through the clouds for the first time in five days...Wasn't it so? Wasn't it so?...Mountjoye for the King of France!" he cried hoarsely, stepping down from the platform on which the bed stood.

Isabeau made a movement toward him, but he stepped back, looking at her with anger and fear.

"Who is this woman, anyway?" he said to the courtiers standing near him. "What does she want from me? She is always bothering me. She wants to *touch* me. Send her away!"

Valentine's lips parted in terror. What she had heard whispered these past few months was true...that the King did not recognize his wife and refused to see her. It was true. Isabeau turned white, but her mouth remained pulled down in an expression of contempt. She stood in the middle of the lying-in chamber, broad and heavy in her ermine-lined mantle, the train held up by two ladies of the court. On her head she wore an extraordinarily tall crowned hat, under which her face looked small and full, with almost lashless eyes, round cheeks and well-shaped lips. On her breast above the square deeply-cut bodice, jeweled stars trembled with her heavy breathing.

Valentine's cheeks burned with shame at the insult inflicted on the Queen; she nodded to her women. The platter with the candied fruit was passed around once more. Although the child was now in its cradle, it did not stop crying. It was carried into an adjoining room.

The King showed no sign of quitting the chamber. He allowed a chair to be brought to him and sat down next to Valentine at whom he stared fixedly without speaking. The court, which could not leave before the King gave the signal for departure, stood in a half-circle around the bed. The Duchess found this wall of bodies, of faces wearing formal smiles, immensely oppressive. She could not sit upright because of the roaring in her ears, which rose and fell at regular intervals. Although no one betrayed impatience by word or look, she knew only too well what thoughts were hidden behind those courteous masks.

The King's affinity for his sister-in-law was no secret; from the moment she had arrived as Louis' bride in Melun to celebrate her marriage — Louis then was still Duke of Touraine — Charles had openly manifested signs of the greatest affection for her. He had paid all the costs of the wedding fetes, had issued orders that the municipal fountain should gush milk and rosewater as it had at the Queen's formal entry into the country some years earlier, and had heaped gifts upon Valentine. But the affection which, before the King became ill, had been a mark of favor that increased the respect of the court for Monseigneur d'Orléans and his wife, evoked a different response when it was evinced by a madman. The contrast between the King's almost morbid fondness for his sister-in-law and the aversion he showed for Isabeau, was glaring. Indignation, derision, perverse enjoyment of someone else's discomfiture — all these feelings undoubtedly existed behind those polite smiles.

Isabeau had sat down too; she turned to whisper to Louis d'Orléans, who stood behind her. The Duke of Burgundy finally decided to put an end to this painful waiting. He took off his hat and approached the bed. He had been Charles' guardian and the real ruler of France in the first years of the kingship. Now he had completely regained the power which had been threatened when the King, full-grown, had chosen other advisors. He bent down and spoke to Charles as though he were speaking to a child, with his stern impenetrable face close to the King's.

"Sire, my King, it is time."

"So soon?" the King asked impatiently. He had taken off his rings and set them on the edge of Valentine's bed. Now he picked them up one by one and dropped them into the Duchess's lap. "For the child--from his godfather," he said with a smothered laugh as he arose. "Valentine, dear Valentine, don't forget to come and visit me tomorrow, or the day after tomorrow."

He kissed her on both cheeks, stroking the damp braids on either side of her forehead. The Duke of Burgundy drew him away. The King looked back. "Be sure to remember," he muttered. The courtiers stepped aside to make way for him. Isabeau took leave of her sister-in-law, but her kiss was no more than a fleeting touch with pursed lips; her eyes remained cold. The ladies-in-waiting picked up the Queen's train.

The old Duke of Bourbon, Charles' uncle on his mother's side, took Isabeau's hand and led her out of the room; the court followed. Even before the anteroom door had closed, Valentine fell backward upon the pillows. The heat in the lying-in chamber was unbearable, but custom forbade anyone to let in fresh air before the mother had taken her first walk to church. Not the Dame de Maucouvent nor any of the other women could unlace the Duchess's bodice to make her breathing easier because Louis d'Orléans, who had stayed behind in the room, came and sat on the edge of the bed. The women withdrew to the hearthfire.

"Well, my darling," said Louis, smiling. He stooped to pick up his wife's handkerchief from the floor. "Our brother the King has been quite generous today." He took the rings which lay scattered over the bed and looked at them carefully, one by one; finally, he slipped one onto his index finger. "How are you feeling today? You look tired."

"I am tired," answered the Duchess. She did not open her eyes.

There was a brief silence. Louis looked down at his wife's face, which had an ivory tint in the green reflection of the bedcurtains. In a sudden rush of warmth and pity, he reached for her hand which lay weakly, half-open, on the coverlet. She turned her head slightly toward him and her narrow lips curved into a smile—a gentle smile, not without melancholy.

"Maître Darien brought me our new son's horoscope this morning," Louis went on. "He says the child was born under a lucky star."

Valentine's smile deepened. Her husband rose to his feet.

"Adieu, Valentine." He pressed her cold fingers. "You should sleep well now." He stepped easily from the dais, tossed his right sleeve over his shoulder, saluted the women and left the room.

The Duchess beckoned. The Dame de Maucouvent came quickly forward and removed the heavy crown from her head.

Louis d'Orléans went directly to the armory, a room adjacent to the library. That portion of the palace of Saint-Pol which he and his household occupied was no less sumptuous and was, in fact, more elegantly furnished than the apartments of the royal family. The armory reflected, in a small way, the opulence with which the Duke liked to surround himself. A Flemish tapestry depicting the crowning of Our Lady covered two walls with the colors of semiprecious stones: dull green, rust red and the dark yellow of old amber. Facing the arched window hung racks of Louis' weapon collection: daggers with wrought-gold sheaths, swords from Lyon, Saracen blades, the hilts engraved with heraldic devices and set with gems, the scabbards covered with gold and enamel.

Three men stood talking before the fire; they turned when Louis entered. They were Marshal Boucicaut and Messires Mahieu de Moras and Jean de Bueil, noblemen of the Duke's retinue with whom he was on very friendly terms. They bowed and came toward him.

"Well, gentlemen," Louis said; he flung his gloves onto a chest. "You were able to see the King today."

De Bueil strode to a table where there were some tankards and goblets of chased silver — part of Valentine's dowry — and at a nod from the Duke poured out wine.

"The King is undoubtedly mad," said de Moras, fixing his eyes upon Louis with a trace of a smile on his heavily scarred face. "To whom do you want us to drink, Monseigneur?"

"To the King — that goes without saying." Louis sat down and raised the goblet to his lips with both hands. "I don't want you to misinterpret my words — not for anything."

"Monseigneur of Burgundy is not present," said Jean de Bueil with a significant look. Louis frowned.

"I've noticed that seems to make little difference," he remarked, sipping the wine slowly. "My uncle hears everything, even things which I never said and which I never had any intention of saying. Things which I don't even *think*," he added. "For Monseigneur of Burgundy, Satan himself couldn't be any more evil than I." He began to laugh and set the beaker down.

"It's a good thing that he can't hear you speak so lightly of the Enemy," said de Moras. "I doubt that would help your reputation much — in the inns and the marketplace..."

"I've heard it said that men suspect you of sorcery, my lord," said Jean de Bueil; at Louis' nod he refilled the goblets. "You have brought astrologers from Lombardy..."

Louis interrupted him with a gesture. "I know that. Don't they say too that my father-in-law, the Lord of Milan, has signed a pact with the Devil? The learned gentlemen of the Sorbonne are behind this; they hate me so much that they would even learn sorcery if with that they could cause me to vanish from the earth. My father-in-law is anything but pious, and perhaps he does know more about the Devil than is good for him. But I vastly prefer him to the bellowing clerics who can only expel wind."

Marshal Boucicaut looked up quickly. "Monseigneur," he said earnestly, "talk like that can give rise to misunderstanding. Everyone who knows you knows that you are a devout Christian."

"You are not abreast of the times," Louis said sarcastically. "If you were, you would know that things are not what they appear to be. Do you know what the common people call the chapel of Orléans? 'The Monument to Misrule'... *my* misrule, do you understand? Building it was the penalty I paid for my sins. And don't forget above all that this spring I set fire to the King — to say nothing of the six noble gentlemen who did not come off as well as he did."

"You can mock, Monseigneur," said Boucicaut coolly, "because you know that with us your words are in safekeeping. But you must remember as well as I do how the people behaved the day after the unfortunate accident."

"They came by the hundreds to Saint-Pol to see the King himself and to curse us," Louis said, the ironic smile still on his lips. "They would have torn the Duchess and me to pieces if a single hair on his head had been scorched. The people think a great deal of the King."

"They would think as much of you if only they knew you," Jean de Bueil said staunchly. Louis stood up.

"You ought to concern yourself with reaching a good understanding with the people of Paris, my lord," Boucicaut said in a low voice. "You will become regent if the King dies."

Louis turned quickly and stared at the three men, his hands on his hips. "*If* the King dies, indeed," he said finally. "May God grant the King a long and healthy life."

He walked to a window and stood looking out, his back to the others. Beneath the windows in this part of the palace was an enclosed garden with a marble fountain in the middle, surrounded by galleries. The trees, to which a single half-shrivelled red leaf still clung here and there, loomed mournfully through the autumn mist. The turrets and battlements of the palace walls were barely visible on the other side of the courtyard. The Duke turned. The three young noblemen still stood near the table.

"You're right, Messires. I joke too much," Louis said. "And I must certainly not make jokes about such worthy gentlemen as the doctors of the Sorbonne. And now enough of these things."

He took a lute from one of the tables and handed it to Jean de Bueil. "Play that song of Bernard de Ventadour's," he said, sitting down. In a clear voice de Bueil began to sing:

> Quan la doss aura venta
> Deves vostre pais
> M'es veiare que senta
> Odor de Paradis...

Two servants entered the room; the arms of Orléans were embroidered on the cloth over their breasts. One of them began to light the torches along the wall; the other approached the Duke and stood hesitantly before him because Louis sat listening to the song with closed eyes. Jean de Bueil ended the couplet with a flourish of chords; the Duke of Orléans opened his eyes and asked, "Why have you stopped, de Bueil?" Then he noticed the servant. "Well?" he asked impatiently.

The man slipped onto one knee and whispered something. The peevish expression vanished from Louis' face; he smiled at the servant absently, absorbed in thought. Finally he snapped his fingers as a sign that the man could go and rose, stretching, as though to shake off every trace of lassitude. "Forgive me, gentlemen," he said. "I am needed elsewhere." He saluted them and walked swiftly to disappear behind a tapestry where the servant held a hidden door open for him.

De Bueil took up the lute again and softly played the melody of the song he had just sung. "Things are allotted queerly in this world," he remarked, without looking up from the strings. "The King is a child who plays with sugar candy. And Monseigneur d'Orléans deserves a better plaything than a ducal crown. We are not the only ones who think so."

Boucicaut frowned and rose to leave. "But it's to be hoped that everyone who thinks so is sensible enough to keep quiet about it for the time being," he said curtly. De Moras was about to follow him; he turned toward the young man with the lute.

"Don't worry about it, de Bueil," he said. "No man escapes his destiny."

Chapter 1 of *The Scarlet City: A Novel of 16th-Century Italy.*

Chicago: Academy Chicago Publishers. English translation copyright 1990 by Anita Miller. Used by permission of the publisher.

Borgia am I; two, perhaps three times a Borgia. To others, my lineage is a riddle; to me, it's a secret — no, more than a secret — a source of torment. In Italy, for a quarter of a century, no name has had a more evil sound than Borgia; if I didn't already know this, I would discover it anew every day. Anyone who wants to curse wholeheartedly says Borgia! Anyone who wants to sum up the wretchedness of these times, the corruption in Rome, the decline of Italy, spits out his bitterness: Borgia! Deceit, decadence, fornication, black arts, murder and manslaughter, incest: Borgia! Quarrels and dissension, endless discord among towns and principalities, invasions by rapacious foreigners in North and South, hatred, avarice, failure, hunger, disaster, pestilence and approaching doom: Borgia! To grasp fully all the connotations of the word Borgia, I had to come back to Italy.

God knows that in France — at least during the last years of my stay there — I was proud of my name. If the court secretly slandered me and my lineage behind my back, I wasn't aware of it. The King was well-disposed toward me: after all, I was considered to be a protege of the House of Este of Ferrara, and in those days France had no better friend and ally in Italy than Alfonso d'Este, Lucrezia's husband.

Equally important to me was the good will of another blood relative: Luisa — or Louise as she was called there — Cesare's daughter by his French marriage. Since I still believed then that Cesare was *my* father too, I set great value on the influence of this woman whom I thought was my half-sister.

Luisa was four or five years younger than I; we shared the same mixed feelings toward our lineage. On the one hand, pride, inborn Spanish pride in the fact that we both belonged to a race that had dared to challenge kings and emperors; but on the other hand, a secret gnawing doubt, a sense of shame which neither she nor I could put into words and which we both tried to hide behind a great show of arrogant self-confidence. This was easier for me than for Luisa, because she was cursed outwardly as well: sickly, thin, her face disfigured by scars...living proof of the truth of the rumors circulating about Cesare before his marriage to Charlotte d'Albret. By now everyone knows that he suffered from the illness that the Italians call the French disease — a high price to pay, in my opinion, for the pleasures of love. He poisoned Luisa's blood with it — and, they say, the blood of most of his bastards. I suppose I should consider myself fortunate that I've been spared physical infirmities. *My* suffering is invisible: my soul has been poisoned.

So in France I could — in spite of certain earlier events — still maintain my self-respect. When I came to the court of Francis I, Cesare had been dead for more than ten years. People seldom talked about the last period of his life in Navarre, and never — in my presence — his inglorious end. If his name came up, it was usually in connection with current Italian politics: compared to my other countrymen who supported the French cause, Cesare appeared in a favorable light: he, at least, had shown himself to be *hardi homme* — a man of courage.

At those times I was always struck at how strongly his name, his personality, still held the imagination. Even then Cesare was more than a memory; he was a legend. In him good and evil had assumed dimensions that went beyond the powers of human judgment. In speech and in writing he was always referred to by his French titles; it was not forgotten either that his escutcheon bore the lilies of Valois and that his daughter Luisa was married to one of the greatest lords of the kingdom.

All this tempered any possible negative connotations of the Borgia name. In addition, I had been presented at the French court by Alfonso d'Este himself, and further, I wasn't officially called Borgia, but Duke of Nepi and Camerino. An imposing title, but a hollow one, nothing more than a string of names, because the possessions and the rights that went with them had been taken from me when Julius the Borgia-hater became pope; he returned the territories to the former owners — the Varano and the Colonna. For my fine titles, worthy of a prince of the blood, I have Pope Alexander to thank, the father of Cesare and Lucrezia. As the bastard of the illegitimate son of a former vicar of Christ on earth, I could in a certain sense consider myself to be a member of a dynasty.

In my first years at the French court, I lived in the customary style. I had a permanent place among other young nobles in the King's retinue. I held an honorary post and received an annuity. But the office and the salary were purely symbolic. Most of my companions served the King for the honor of it; they had solid backgrounds: money, castles, lands — and they bore ancient illustrious French names — their escutcheons were unblemished. I was poor, a foreigner. I had no fortune, no income beyond the handful of ducats doled out to me each year in the King's name, and gifts sent by Lucrezia. After her death in 1519, I received nothing more from Ferrara.

I kept a horse, a valet and a groom; beyond that all I possessed was a trunk with clothes, books and a few valuables. I rode in the royal hunt, sat at the banquet tables, indulged in my share of diplomatic intrigue and amorous adventure, like everybody else. In the halls and parks of Chaumont, Poissy, Chambord and Fontainebleau, life whirled past in a kind of happy intoxication. It was all a game — we knew that. We played against each other with courtly flourishes: move, countermove, attack and retreat...as much in love affairs as in the unending struggle for rank and precedence in the King's good graces. But all this was carried on with ceremonious restraint; the intrigues and maneuvers were like the movements in a ballet, executed with compliments and bows and well-chosen words. To be deeply serious or openly passionate was considered tasteless. At first my mixed Spanish and Italian blood played me false; eventually I managed to adapt.

I never forgot that the world extended beyond palace walls and the borders of a royal park. How could I? I carried the memory of my youth, of the early years with Cesare in the Romagna and at the Castel Sant'Angelo, of isolation in the Castle of Bari and the long period of wandering after that. I remembered events and faces — at night, especially. My childhood passed before me — a furious cavalcade lit by torches; most of it was lost in blood-red smoke, but sometimes a glaring light played upon an image that I recognized: the angel Michael on the Citadel of Rome silhouetted against an angry sunset...a series of flags hanging from the ledge outside the great hall of the Castle of Camerino...a landscape filled with heaps of rubble, scorched black and still smoking, seen from the window of a palanquin...hollow-eyed heads on pikes, grinning above a city gate...

Faces of the men and women of Cesare's retinue: his mother, Madonna Vannozza, stout, faded, with a shadowed upper lip, but regal in bearing and gesture; the shy, quick-tempered Gioffredo, his youngest brother, who was comfortable only with children and animals; his fortress-builder and engineer Messer Leonardo da Vinci, that man with the penetrating eyes, who could use a lead marker to create landscapes and figures from mildewed blotches on a damp wall; Micheletto, Cesare's advisor and right hand; Agapito, his secretary — and finally, the children, my playmates: Camilla, Carlotta and of course Rodrigo, the confidant and bosom friend of my youth.

I was five or six years old then. I knew that we were in danger, but the how and the why were beyond me. Much later it all became clear to me. In the silence of the night, in antechambers and alcoves of French royal palaces, lying sleepless next to tossing, snoring French nobles with whom I had to share a bed, I had plenty of time to connect the facts I had learned over the years with my memories — the shreds and fragments of what I had heard and seen as a child.

* * *

There are reasons why I want to write all this down here: the adventures of my youth, my life in the French court and the experiences which I've had since then and still have every day. A man who feels himself threatened and spied upon from all sides, who knows that he can't confide in anyone and that there's no security anywhere, has to keep his own counsel. To speak one's thoughts, even to whisper them, is out of the question. The Vatican galleries are as crowded as the streets on market day; the walls have eyes and ears here and anyway, only fools, prisoners or madmen talk to themselves out loud. My writing doesn't attract any attention; it looks to be part of my work. Nearly every day I stand at a desk in the papal library, covering sheet after sheet with words: drafting letters and speeches to oblige the lesser diplomats of His Holiness Clement VII. Papal scribe: a curious occupation for one who was brought up as a nobleman, who has fought for France in Navarre and before Pavia.

They probably think here that I aspire to the purple — or at least to a red hat. Considering my lineage, anything is possible, I suppose. Of course there's nobody in the court of Rome who would dream of asking me openly what my intentions are. No one dares — at this stage — to show himself either for or against me. My name creates space, a no-man's-land between me and the others. *Borgia* — it's like the warning sign on the door of a plague-stricken house. They keep their distance; I still can't quite tell why. All I have are my suspicions, because whatever might be planned against me remains cloaked in darkness for the moment. I'm left in peace because they think I'm in the good graces of His Holiness's favorites. But I know perfectly well that I have to make good use of this quiet time, this respite. Uncertainty makes one vulnerable...Now, first of all, I have to find out why people are avoiding me. The poison is hidden in the name: Borgia. They don't know who I am, what I want, what connections I have, what friends and relatives I protect, what enemies I can hurt. They know less than I do, and what do I know myself?

I'm not certain of the exact day and year of my birth, any more than I know who my father and mother were. There must be records of my birth in Ferrara, but I haven't seen them. I'm roughly twenty-eight years old, my name is Giovanni Borgia, or — to employ the Spanish title which is mine by right — Don Juan de Borja y Llancol. When I was still a child, I thought Cesare was my father, probably because no one said he wasn't, and because I lived in his immediate entourage with two of his other bastard children, Camilla and Carlotta. Later, Lucrezia's son Rodrigo joined us; we knew that Cesare had taken pity on him because Alfonso d'Este refused to have the boy at his court in Ferrara; he didn't want to be reminded of his wife's previous marriage.

Cesare took the four of us everywhere with him; we had a secure place in his retinue with the women appointed to look after us. I spent the first years of my life in palanquins and coaches, in tents, in halls of newly captured or hastily abandoned castles in the Romagna. I no longer remember names. Later I heard about Imola and Forli, Cesena, Senigallia — I've probably been there, too.

I remember Camerino only because when Cesare took possession of it, I played a role in the solemn ceremony that was performed there. The previous owners of the castle and estates, the Lords Varano, had been murdered or driven away by Cesare; Pope Alexander issued a bull that made me, the male heir of the Borgia family, Duke of Camerino. At the same time, I received also the castle and lands of neighboring Nepi, which had belonged to the Colonna family — almost half of the Romagna. At that time I was scarcely — if at all — aware of the great honor which had befallen me.

I sat in front of Cesare on his horse; surrounded by soldiers, we rode through the steep and narrow streets of the town. Cesare's standard was flying from the damaged tower of the castle. *Duca! Duca!* the people cried, packed together in the alleyways and on the roofs of the houses. Cesare's armored hand lay on my knee.

In a gloomy hall filled with armed men he held me under the armpits and lifted me up high.

"Behold the new Lord of Camerino, the first Duke, by the grace of Pope Alexander!"

He pushed a heavy ring, too wide for it, onto my finger, and told me to make a fist. So for the first — and up to now the last — time in my life, with Cesare's seal which was also mine, I sealed official documents as Duke of Camerino. Coins were struck with my head on them. When I was in France I still had one of those coins, a silver carline with the legend: *Joannes Bor. Dux Camerini*. But I seem to have lost it somewhere.

In the following year, Pope Alexander — whom I took to be my grandfather — died. With him went Cesare's power in the Romagna and also my dukedom, forever.

* * *

When I came back to Rome two months ago, I didn't recognize the Vatican. The rooms where Pope Clement usually lived were unfamiliar to me. When I went looking for the Borgia apartments, I found only closed doors. The section of the palace where Alexander had lived and where Cesare had spent time now and then, is no longer used. I've heard that no one has entered there since the days of Pope Julius. I haven't requested admittance yet — if only to avoid giving away a long-cherished, secret desire.

Sometimes, standing in the Belvedere court, I look up at the open galleries which circle the outsides of the apartments. The ground floor rooms belonged to Alexander; the floor above was fitted out for Cesare. Whenever he put up at the Vatican for a while, Rodrigo and I lived in a house in the Ponte quarter where two Spanish cardinals looked after us as our guardians.

Of our many visits to the Vatican — Alexander couldn't seem to see enough of us when we were in his neighborhood — all I remember are the papal apartments.

In a room with brightly painted walls which sparkled with gilt
and sky-blue enamel, was a fat old man leaning comfortably back
against the cushions of a state chair. He permitted us to kiss the ring
on his forefinger, and his hand, which was broad, soft and always
very warm. Then he bent forward and squeezed us against him,
breathing heavily with emotion; his velvet cape smelled of stale
incense and musk.

"Are you here again, my boys, my fine, handsome boys, my
falcons, my cubs...You, Rodrigo, from my beautiful Lucrezia, and
you, Giovanni, Giannino *mio*, my little dukes; I'll make you rich and
powerful, you'll rule Italy like kings, Borgia kings!"

He kissed us and petted us, put his hand in blessing on our
heads, groped in a dish of preserved fruit next to him and scattered
sweets over us. Sometimes he threw a ducat, a jewel or something
similar between us and watched us romp and scuffle for it. With
applause and shouts he urged us on until Rodrigo and I, excited,
overheated, paying no attention to our surroundings, rolled through
the chamber, dragging carpets with us, knocking over candlesticks.
Those present — shadows in the background, prelates, nobles, a
handful of servants — smiled and clapped, echoing Alexander's
childlike pleasure in our rough-housing. But Cesare, who usually
came with us on our visits to his father, didn't look at us or give any
sign of enjoyment.

Now, after all these years, I know that his unwavering dark
look was not for us, but for Alexander. Whenever I think of Cesare,
I see him with that expression on his face — a look at once mocking,
contemptuous and wryly amused: the sourly indulgent smile of one
whose patience has been tested for all too long a time.

These visits to the Vatican must have taken place in the last
months before Alexander's death — that would have been in the
summer of 1503. I was about six years old then. The summonses
calling us to the papal palace which usually came every day from
Alexander or Cesare, suddenly stopped. After that our guardians the
cardinals barely showed themselves in the house in the Ponte, cool
and dark as a tomb, where Rodrigo and I were believed safe from the
fevers which rose from the marshes in August.

Finally our nurses came, crying, wailing, repeating rumors about poison: Pope Alexander dying, Cesare seriously ill, the Vatican in an uproar, Rome a place where those who support Borgia will go down to perdition...The servants' agitation spread to us too. While the doors were being bolted, shutters nailed over the ground floor windows, Rodrigo and I crept away to crouch in deadly terror inside the darkness of the bedcurtains, listening to sounds inside and outside the house: muffled voices close by or resounding in the distant galleries; quick footsteps beneath us, above us; chests and pieces of furniture being dragged over the floor; horses snorting in the courtyard.

When the curtains were suddenly thrust roughly apart, we expected to see the dreaded assassin. But by the light of the candles which the women hurried to hold high, we saw Don Michelle Corolla, called Micheletto, Cesare's captain, friend and confidant, the head of his bodyguard, his constant companion and frequent deputy: a Venetian with such dark skin and eyes that he was always taken for a Spaniard. We had learned to respect him; he seemed to us to be a part of Cesare himself, as inseparable from him as his shadow, but a shadow of flesh and blood, a replica, a creature emanating from Cesare, obeying his unspoken will.

The chamber was full of people, servingmen and women taking down tapestries from the walls, throwing linen and silver into chests; from the open door came the tumult of armed men striding through corridors and across landings.

Surrounded by Micheletto's men, we hurried on horseback through an unfamiliar nocturnal Rome. The newly risen moon shone yellow and swollen through the shimmering haze of heat which, day and night, hangs over the town in August. With a clatter of hooves, creaking and bumping of wagons, with cries, curses and a great hubbub, the procession squeezed through a labyrinth of narrow streets. Black clouds of dust swirled high behind us between houses and churches and the steep, windowless walls of palaces.

Later, I woke in a strange bed. Rows of Borgia bulls in parallel lines, climbed the stiff shiny cloth of the bedcurtains. Next to me, as usual, Rodrigo slept peacefully. I turned my head toward the light. By an open window, in the cool dawn breeze, stood Cesare's mother, Madonna Vannozza. I called her by the name which we sometimes heard Cesare use: *matrema*, little mother. She came to me, her black garments rustling, so quickly and angrily that it seemed as though she had been waiting for me to wake.

"Be still, you'll wake Rodrigo. Lie down."

She pushed me ungently back onto the pillows. I could never understand why she loved Rodrigo and not me.

"Is there danger, *matrema*?"

"Yes, danger to *Borgias*," she said, stressing the last word.

She stood half-turned away, looking at me over her shoulder while she tucked stray wisps of hair under her kerchief. Her eyelids were swollen, there were deep lines at the corners of her mouth. What I remember most clearly about Vannozza are her eyes and mouth: the sparks in her black pupils, alternately glowing and dying, the shadows on either side of her broad fleshy upper lip with its faint moustache, which gave her face a look of bitter pride. Her harsh, probing stare frightened me.

She always treated me roughly, resentfully. She spoke to me only if it were unavoidable, and then with perceptible antipathy. This attitude of hers, for which I can now easily find an explanation, filled me then with anxiety and insecurity. Of all the time which I spent in Vannozza's company, that early morning hour of the day after Alexander's death remains the most vivid in my memory. Silent and unmoving, she stood with her back to me at the open window, while the sun rose in the hazy sky and the bells of Rome pealed, alternately and together. The daylight brought the heat; a faint swampy smell rose from the town. From a distance came a sound that I could not identify. It must have been going on since I woke, but I had not been conscious of it earlier. Not the sound of the sea or the wind, which rises and falls; this was a continuous rustling murmur like falling rain or the splashing of a brook.

"What is that outside, *matrema*?"

Even before Vannozza replied, I sensed that there was a connection between the distant noise and her air of motionless, tense listening.

"Shouting and screaming in San Pietro's square. They must have come from Rome by the thousands last night when they heard the news."

"Why are they shouting, *matrema*?"

"You don't remember much of what you're told. What did Fra Baccio say in the story when the stranger asked him when Rome was at its most cheerful? — When a pope dies."

"Where are we now?"

"In my house in the Borgo. Be quiet now, lie down. Don't let me hear from you again."

The harshness of her voice frightened me more than her severity. I broke into a sweat. I did not dare to stir, or to push aside the covers. Rodrigo was sleeping and I felt that the woman at the window was aware of my every movement, although she did not look at me.

The bed in which I lay was her bed; I was suddenly certain of this. I recognized the scent which rose from the pillows as Vannozza's, but mixed with another, stale smell, fleeting but still persistent: an odor from the past, an odor of musk and incense, a strange faint animal smell, both exciting and repulsive. The linen was clean, aired in the sunlight and stored with perfume, but neither fresh air nor all the oils of Araby could dispel from its folds that scent of dead lust. Without knowing why, I felt oppressed to the point of suffocation in that bed. I sank slowly into mattress and bolster as into treacherous quicksand; under the brocade coverlet, I lay bewitched, condemned to immobility.

Wherever I looked, above me, before me and on both sides of me, I saw, in an endless procession on the bedcurtains, gleaming gold on a scarlet background, the Borgia bulls climbing toward a hidden goal.

* * *

I am describing these events as they arise in my memory and as I experienced them as a child, when I could not understand the reasons behind them — although much that was important must have been discussed by the adults around me. When, as a young man, I wandered about Naples, and later before I left for France, when I stayed for a short while with Lucrezia in Ferrara, I heard things. I know now why Micheletto rushed us headlong to the Borgo. The chests carried by packhorses and mules on that nocturnal procession contained, apart from our possessions, gold, silver and valuables from the pontifical treasury, taken from the Vatican at Cesare's command by Micheletto with a dagger in his fist, as soon as it was known that Alexander was dead.

Cesare himself, weakened by poison or an intestinal illness — no one knew the truth — took action from his bed to forestall popular uprisings and attacks by the Colonna, the Orsini and other lords whom he had driven out of the Romagna. His soldiers took over the Borgo, which was fortified. I remember that Gioffredo, Cesare's youngest brother, and his wife Sancia of Aragon, that man-crazed, unpredictable shrew, had fled from their palace on the other side of the Tiber to Vannozza's house, in deadly terror of the vengeful crowds which raged and threatened before their door day and night.

We didn't see sun, moon or stars in those days. Behind closed window shutters and bolted doors, we awaited the outcome of Cesare's negotiations with the Spanish and French envoys, and with the College of Cardinals. Vannozza, her vigilant eyes upon us, told her rosary quickly and loudly; Sancia started quarrels or sat yawning. Gioffredo bit his nails in silence. Rodrigo, Camilla, Carlotta and I amused ourselves as well as we could, throwing a ball or playing with Sancia's lapdog in the stifling, darkened chambers. Visitors were incessantly announced and admitted: messengers from Cesare in the Vatican, Micheletto, the Spanish cardinals. Over our heads disputes raged, accusations, arguments, bursts of fury. We heard it as we played, without listening to it. All that I remember is the account of Alexander's deathbed and burial, probably because particular details made an impression on me: the blue-black swollen body, already decaying, which no one wanted to touch and which had been dragged by the feet to San Pietro's where it was forced into the coffin with blows of the fist; the black dog — Alexander's soul or the Devil in disguise? — which roamed restlessly through the basilica as long as the corpse remained above ground.

At the beginning of September, we left Rome in an endless procession: armed men — on foot, on horseback — protected the column of wagons and the sedan chair carried by halberdiers, in which Cesare, too weak to ride, lay hidden behind black curtains. We were on our way to the Castle of Nepi, which was still my property and thus a haven for Cesare.

We didn't stay at Nepi long. Before the chests were unpacked, they were tied once again on the backs of the pack animals. That return to Rome was sheer flight; even at the time I realized that. The vindictive barons followed us to Rome. For safety's sake, Cesare put up at the palaces of friendly cardinals, sometimes here, sometimes there. We children scarcely had time to get used to the strange beds, had hardly learned to find our way through the series of unfamiliar rooms, before the signal was given once more for departure. To our questions, Vannozza gave the surly, off-hand response that our lives would be in danger from the Colonna, the Orsini, Varano and other Borgia-haters if we stayed in that particular place an instant longer.

I remember this time of confusion and uncertainty as being endless, but in reality it lasted only a few weeks. One morning we were awakened before sunrise, wrapped in cloaks and brought outside. This time no sedan chair was waiting. Horsemen carried us before them on their saddles. In the glimmer of torchlight I saw Cesare mounting; he had to be supported by grooms. We went through Rome at a quick trot. The rider who held me shouted something at a comrade over my head. I heard, "Ostia...ships...sea..." But before I could grasp the significance of these words, an uproar broke out in the troop. The battle cry of the Orsini reverberated between the houses; fighting was already at fever pitch in the vanguard.

It didn't last long. Our column dashed back at full speed by another route, this time over the Tiber Bridge into the Borgo, where the Vatican buildings and the basilica rose darkly against the sky tinted yellow by the dawn. There were threatening shouts behind us — life or death! — and the pounding of horses' hooves, while we pushed our way into a forecourt of the papal palace. I was pulled from the horse, half-carried, half-dragged between armed men rushing forward shoulder to shoulder through galleries and halls where the frightened screams of Carlotta and Camilla raised infinite echoes.

Suddenly we found ourselves under an open sky. I almost cried out when, accidentally, I was held away over a parapet; I looked down on the roofs of Rome. But after I had been swung around on the shoulder of the man who was carrying me, I saw, at the end of a narrow uncovered passage, the outlines of the Castel Sant'Angelo and the angel on its highest battlement glittering in the sunlight. I realized that we were fleeing through the corridor which connects the Vatican with the Castel.

I know now that Cesare thought he would be safe there, inaccessible to his enemies, under the protection of Pope Pius, Alexander's successor, a timid sick old man who — out of self-interest, incidentally — spread his mantle over us Borgia. In actuality, Cesare sat in the Angel Castle like a mouse in a trap. We hadn't been there five days when Pius died...following an operation, it was said. With his going, Cesare lost his last base of support; now all he had to depend on were his own cunning and sagacity. Of what followed, Cesare's bitter struggle for self-preservation, I was — then, at any rate — unaware.

The apartments in the Castel Sant'Angelo where we lived with Vannozza were low-ceilinged, dark and chilly, situated around a semicircular garden. On roof cornices and doors, and on the walls of the well in the garden, Alexander Borgia's arms were painted: crossed keys crowned with the papal tiara and the Borgia bull. We played there every day amid the symbols of Borgia power. It scarcely occurred to us that this power had been destroyed. We seldom saw Cesare. He remained secluded in the section of the fortress where he had taken up residence, writing letters, receiving trusted friends, negotiating with messengers sent from the Vatican and foreign countries.

Vannozza sat sullenly for hours, not speaking, at a window overlooking the garden. Now she would pray, now she would rub the beads of her rosary between thumb and forefinger. She was often overcome by fits of rage and despair; she called us to her and punished even the most minor infraction with blows and kicks, or she cried, lamenting, for help to a long series of saints, ordering us to pray too. Sometimes she burst into complaints; then she chose to heap pity on Rodrigo,her pet: my boy, my child, *duchetto mio*, what will become of you? Your father is murdered, your relatives are our enemies, your mother can't take you in, our family is going down in ruins, our power is broken, we're lost.

At other times she allowed herself to be carried away by less comprehensible feelings. Her eyes closed, her head thrown back, rocking back and forth as though she were in pain, she whispered accusations, entreaties, curses...these toneless whispers had nothing to do with us. When she behaved like that, she was truly alarming. We didn't understand the sense of what she was muttering; her words were as enigmatic as the words of a sybil. Later, much later, I remembered this oracular talk and realized that it wasn't gibberish. I could have been spared much uncertainty and doubt if I had been able to forget Vannozza's dark mumbling. When we lived in Bari, in the formal elegant court of our foster mother Isabella, my youth was disturbed by the suspicions roused by the courtiers' behavior: odd glances, stray words picked up by chance, conversations quickly broken off when I approached...I asked Rodrigo then what he thought Vannozza had been saying. But Rodrigo couldn't remember anything about our stay in the Castel Sant'Angelo. That's understandable: he was two years younger than I.

Our sojourn in the Castle of Rome was suddenly interrupted. That didn't upset us; we had become quite accustomed to unannounced journeys and house-movings. We were brought to take leave of Cesare. He was lying on a couch, his legs crossed. I looked at him with curiosity. I hadn't seen him since we had come to the Castel Sant'Angelo. In his eyes, his face, his behavior, I sought an explanation of Vannozza's mysterious complaints. Peeling, raw patches — the result of his recent illness — stood out sharply against his sallow skin, already disfigured by old scars. He had grown thin; at intervals a restless light flickered in his eyes. I found this odd: an unwavering, lackluster dark stare had always been characteristic of Cesare. I believe that others had noticed this too.

It didn't surprise me to hear it said later that Cesare had the evil eye. Many — and especially those who had reason to fear him — must have believed that with that stare he could read their most secret thoughts and feelings.

When I saw Cesare for the last time in his murky apartment in the Angel Castle, that magic power seemed to have left his eyes. As always, he had perfect control over his body and the expression on his face. He lay on his side, propped up on his left elbow, letting a perfumed ball roll back and forth — an habitual gesture — on the palm of his hand. Behind him two prelates from his retinue sat at a table playing cards. We stayed only a short while; I no longer remember what was said. Vannozza wailed softly and whispered into his ear; but when she tried to embrace him, he thrust her away. He raised his hand in farewell, his eyes resting for a moment, absent, indifferent, filled with secret disquiet, first on Rodrigo, then on me. "Take them away now," he said finally, with a shrug.

That night we left the Castel Sant'Angelo by a secret door; our departure had to remain hidden from Cesare's enemies in the Vatican. The two little girls remained behind in Rome under Vannozza's care, but Rodrigo and I travelled quickly, with our guardians the cardinals, southward to Naples.

* * *

I ask myself who is that man with the insolent face who roams about the Chancellery for a while every day and then chooses apparently to dawdle near my reading desk? He's there now too, extravagantly decked out, like an actor, and literally drenched in musk. He might superficially be taken for a nobleman, but his face, posture and manner give him away. A newly rich flunky, an artist, a favorite, or even Ganymede to a powerful man here at the court? It's obvious that he considers himself a man of great consequence. He walks back and forth like a strutting peacock, poisoning the air with his perfume. He knows everyone, greeting people left and right; he has a really adroit and rather amusing way of indicating, with a nod, a gesture, a bow, how high — or low — a value he sets on the person in question. A conceited comedian and undoubtedly an adventurer. He betrays himself by the way in which, obsequious, humble, with a thousand and one bows, he approaches the dignitaries who pass through here on the way to the audience chamber of His Holiness.

Yesterday the most powerful man in the court, Monsignore Schomberg, the Archbishop of Capua, visited the Chancellery with his retinue. On these occasions anyone who has the opportunity comes forward and salutes. My friend in the peacock blue literally flung himself at Monsignore's feet, pouring forth a bewilderingly eloquent stream of flattery and praise; after that he proceeded to act as though he belonged to the august company.

Whatever he might be — parasite, buffoon, adventurer — it's obvious that some people find it in their interest to cultivate him as a friend. Glances and comments are exchanged as soon as he turns his back, but if I'm not mistaken, everyone is actually afraid of him. I'd like to know who he is. He's different from the others. In that respect we're alike, he and I. With this difference: that *he's* a familiar figure at court. No one can allow himself the luxury of snubbing him. What concerns *me is* that in the two months of my stay here I haven't held a conversation with anyone beyond strictly necessary exchanges. I must admit that I've consciously kept my distance. It's not in my nature to rush into intimacies. I feel that my comings and goings are being closely watched — but again, I don't know by whom and why, although I have my suspicions.

Before I came to Rome I tried of course to get a feeling for the current situation and relationships at court and to find out the names of the most influential people. I thought that that kind of knowledge would be useful to me. But as it happened the opposite was true. The French court is structured on unvarying principles: everyone has a fixed place there and belongs to a clearly defined circle. The rules of the game are complicated, but they're always strictly maintained, under all circumstances. Here, I feel as though I were living inside a chameleon. Things are continually changing: titles, benefices, appointments, new parties, come and go with mysterious rapidity. One must adjust constantly: he who was powerful yesterday appears today to be out of favor, and vice versa. And there's no way of predicting which way the wind will blow.

The papal household is a tangled mass of functionaries, spiritual and secular, all with their own retinues, relatives, friends, favorites, servants and hangers-on. I have gradually learned to recognize the most important cardinals; the Monsignori, numerous as they are, at least distinguish themselves from the multitude. But the rest: prelates, lords-in-waiting, secretaries, masters of ceremony, valets, officers of the watch and other people with more or less clearly defined duties...From sunup to sunset they all swarm through the Vatican's series of rooms. Half of Rome seems to have free access here.

They say it's busier here than ever, not so much because of the Holy Year — one consequence of the Battle of Pavia is that far fewer pilgrims have been coming to Rome from the provinces — but because of the continual arrival of legations. A day doesn't pass without meetings with ambassadors from Venice, Milan, Florence, Ferrara. Official and unofficial representatives of France and Spain are trusted guests. The events at Pavia have caused great confusion, because nobody knows where they stand now. The defeat of the French was completely unexpected here. It seems that Pope Clement was half-dead from fear. No wonder, if the truth is that this time he had counted upon a victory for King Francis without leaving himself a loophole.

It's beginning to be realized in Rome that the Emperor holds Italy in his power. The defenses of cities and principalities are in a sad state, according to reports from the ambassadors who are continually arriving and departing. The Imperial troops have suffered few losses and have not yet been disbanded. Who would dare to deny that this is an extremely dangerous situation? The Emperor has given repeated assurances that he has only the best intentions, that he wants peace and nothing but peace. As far as I can judge, there's no one in Rome naïve enough to believe these pronouncements. It's being said openly that the Emperor plans to come to Italy to teach His Holiness a lesson. It may be true that the Emperor received the news of the victory at Pavia with humility and prayers of thanksgiving. But his thoughts, his deepest desires, are known to no living soul. All princes are ambitious and as a general rule a prince doesn't become more self-effacing after a victory. Anyway, one thing is certain: his advisors and more especially his agents here in Rome are trying to spur him to further action. At the moment a joke is circulating about the Pope: His Holiness, they say, must now rely for the first time upon the authority conferred through papal dignity.

On the subject of the spiritual prestige which His Holiness should possess as God's representative, I prefer to be silent. I'm not qualified to judge matters of faith. Every day wiser men than I take it upon themselves to speak and write about these things. Apparently the Pope wishes to be considered a temporal authority--only as such, then, should he be judged. Clement has neither troops nor money; no one supports him with enthusiasm. It's difficult to believe that only three years ago the selection of this Pope was greeted with shouts of joy. The Ecclesiastic State is lacerated by party strife: Rome, more than any other city, is polluted with the evil of political dissension.

At the court, two conflicting points of view are embodied in His Holiness's two most influential advisors — the real rulers here: on the one hand, the Datary Giberti, a childhood friend and favorite of the Pope, an avowed partisan of France, and on the other, the Archbishop of Capua — a Fleming or German named Schomberg — who exerts his influence on the side of the Emperor. The Pope stands between them: he turns first to one, then to the other. This waffling and wavering seems to have infected His Holiness's entire entourage. Add to this, mutual distrust, fear of treachery, general insecurity. The situation is discussed incessantly: meetings, conferences and audiences follow one after another, but it all comes to nothing.

Still, there must be capable and sharp-witted men enough in Rome. Left and right I hear gloomy predictions from insiders, or from those who pretend to be insiders. In this court I have yet to find one man whom I would wish to follow, one group which I would be willing to join. I'm following a wait-and-see policy. On this turbulent sea, fraught with currents and cross-currents, I'm an inexperienced helmsman. I must know more, see more and hear more, before I risk deciding on a course. Anyone like me, without money and without protection, who has to rely on his own resources, can't be too careful.

It was by a stroke of luck that I came to Rome. Most of my comrades, friends from France, were killed, wounded or taken prisoner at Pavia. Now I don't know what direction to take. When I was in France, I had a clearly defined goal: I wanted to make a career for myself in the King's army. I believe that I have all the necessary qualifications for military service: courage, skill, adaptability. My men respected me and I knew how to obey my superiors. After the disturbance in Navarre, I was given a permanent appointment in the Bayard cavalry as a reward for my services. I want to continue on this path. I don't have friends or relatives, I'm free of obligations — that can surely only help me in the military profession.

As I stand behind my reading desk in the Chancellery, it looks as though I must forget these plans for the time being. Strange as it seems to me even now, I'm a speechwriter; I perform a function which is usually reserved only for scholars or aspiring scholars. I gained this post through the influence of Bishop Aleandro, who was papal nuncio at the French court for a considerable time. He knew that I speak French and Spanish, have some Latin and a passable handwriting. Presumably the pious man wasn't able to think quickly of a more suitable occupation for me.

However it happened, here I am then, commissioned by one of the secretaries of His Holiness's secretary to frame a speech which will be read by the *podesta* in the square of some hamlet or other: "Good people, the taxes have been raised again, the cost of bread has gone up once more..." Because of these and similar regulations here and there, the starving, plague-ridden populace seems to have arrived at the conclusion that His Holiness is the Devil incarnate. This puts my work in a peculiar light. What am I doing here among these clerks? Few laymen practice this profession; those who do, consider it an honorary post: they scoop up the annuity and take a monk into service to do the work. If I saw a chance to spend my time in a better way, I would follow their example.

Does the man in peacock blue, that walking scent-bottle, belong in that category? I don't know. On further reflection, I have decided that he is less of a shallow braggart than I thought he was at first. He's not stupid. That boisterous affability, that overbearing geniality, is a show, a display, designed to mask the fact that he's constantly watching and listening. He has an obsessive desire for information. He considers me, too, his prey. I've noticed that. Whenever I look up, I see his eyes fastened on me: a flashing, arrogant stare which troubles me. An honorable man doesn't stare at someone like that. I have to know who he is and what he's up to.

* * *

Borgia, Borgia. Under the vaulted ceilings of the Vatican, my name has taken on another sound for me. Never have I felt such an incessant, overwhelming need to call back memories of my youth. What possesses me, to return again and again to a past that holds nothing for me but confusion and upheaval?

In France I was able to get rid of my constant secret uncertainty for the first time. Once I entered King Francis's household, I felt freed from ghosts and shadows. The men accepted me because I was a good rider, hunter and fighter; the women were amused by my Southern gallantry. Why did I need to be anyone but myself? I shook off my uneasiness the way a snake slips out of its withered old skin. Perhaps Luisa helped to bring back my childhood belief that Cesare was my father. Occasionally after a dreamfilled night the old doubt stirred; but I knew how to fight it off. I was no longer oppressed by thoughts of my lineage. I believed that once and for all I had lost the feeling that I had to drag the Borgia name with me always, as a galley slave drags his chain. I was used to living with the dregs of uneasiness buried deep within me.

Knowing it was there — and probably for good reason — made me dress and behave more formally. I noticed the same tendency in Luisa: she led an exemplary life at the frivolous court; proud reserve was her armor. We were both trying to emulate the stiff dignity of the Spaniards, a style which suited us better than French elegance or the Italian grand manner. Speaking of this, I remember something that happened when I was fighting in the Pyrenees for King Francis. That was in '21. The Spaniards were occupying Navarre. We were

marching to win back the territory under the command of the Duke
of Navarre. In the main the army was made up of Gascons, Basques
and Navarese; I belonged to the King's men-at-arms. After some
skirmishes near the city of Pamplona, my men found a wounded
Spaniard among the bushes by the side of the road.

I spoke to him in his own tongue — asked him his name,
where he came from. He listened attentively, measured me from head
to toe with a sharp look.

"You're a Spanish nobleman, as I am," he said finally. "Why
are you fighting on the wrong side?"

I took this remark as a compliment. At that time, under the
influence of Alfonso d'Este and my friends in France, I was opposed
to Spanish policy. In addition, I knew even then that the Borgia
family was permanently out of favor in Spain. In spite of all that, I
decided after that encounter to model myself on the example of the
hidalgo: the best part of the Borgia heritage which had — I
found—fallen to me. The Spaniard was later ransomed. I remember
his name: he was called Ignacio de Loyola.

* * *

A constant interaction existed between my new-found self-
respect and the soldier's life I was leading. The journeys and
marches, filled with hardship, over the southern and southeastern
borders of France, the sieges and battles, the companionship of
experienced soldiers, steeled my body against discomfort of every
kind, my mind against feelings that I thought I had banished to its
most profound depths. I couldn't guess that they had flourished there.
Now that I'm breathing the air of Rome, they're sprouting up, a
poisonous growth. The man I was during that life of action under the
open sky — riding, fighting, free, unfettered — no longer exists. When
I put aside my cuirass and coat of mail, I gave up my identity as a
knight. The speechwriter in court dress, who sees only the rooms and
galleries and adjacent symmetrical inner gardens of the papal palace,
is a stranger whom I don't like to identify with. Who and what am I
here? I shall know that when I find out how others see me.

I haven't been able to present myself at court as Duke of Camerino. Aleandro told me tactfully that doing that would get me into considerable trouble. Apparently the present holder of the title, Giovanni Maria Varano, is in Rome now. But even if he weren't, there isn't a living soul here who would acknowledge my claim. To tell the truth, even *I* don't believe that I can assert a claim to the dukedom. Varano is the legitimate heir of a family that has been settled in Camerino since before living memory — naturally he's the legal owner of the lands and the title. What have I ever been, but a usurper? If I were to mention the gratuitous role which I had unwittingly filled as a little child, I'd only make myself ridiculous.

In this environment the name of Borgia has more significance than I can quite grasp just now. People don't see *me* as a man in myself; all they see is — a Borgia. If I knew what facts, rumors, myths and invented or half-forgotten mischief I'm identified with, I could at least take a stand, defend myself. But there is silence all around me. There's plenty of courteous bowing, gracious saluting, a readiness to let me share in superficial conversations, but no one takes me into his confidence, there aren't any efforts to draw me into the intrigues of any cliques. Of course, on the other hand, I've also been spared the feeble jokes which newcomers here are sometimes subjected to. Every day in the Belvedere garden, a new courtier tumbles into a branch-covered pit, dug and filled with muck for that purpose. Up to now, no one has dared invite me to take a stroll like that, with a surprise at the end.

Bibliography

Primary Works

Haasse, Hella S. *Oeroeg*. Amsterdam: Vereeniging ter Bevordering van de Belangen des Boekhandels, 1948.
_____. *Het woud der verwachting. Het leven van Charles van Orléans*. Amsterdam: Querido, 1949.

_____. *De scharlaken stad*. Amsterdam: Querido, 1952.
_____. *Cider voor arme mensen*. Amsterdam: Querido, 1960.
_____. *De meermin*. Amsterdam: Querido, 1962.
_____. *Een draad in het donker; een toneelspel in drie bedrijven.* Amsterdam: Querido, 1963.
_____. *Een nieuwer testament*. Amsterdam: Querido, 1966.
_____. *De tuinen van Bomarzo*. Amsterdam: Querido, 1968.
_____. *Huurders en onderhuurders; een fictie*. Amsterdam: Querido, 1971.
_____. *Een gevaarlijke verhouding of Daal-en-Bergse brieven*. Amsterdam: Querido, 1976.
_____. *Mevrouw Bentinck; of Onverenigbaarheid van karakter; een ware geschiedenis*. Amsterdam: Querido, 1978.
_____. *De groten der aarde; of Bentinck tegen Bentinck*. Amsterdam: Querido, 1981.
_____. *De wegen der verbeelding*. Amsterdam: Querido, 1983.
_____. *Berichten van het blauwe huis*. Amsterdam: Querido, 1986.
_____. *Schaduwbeeld of Het geheim van Appeltern. Kroniek van een leven.* Amsterdam: Querido, 1989.
_____. *De heren van de thee*. Amsterdam: Querido, 1992.

Translations

_____. *In a Dark Wood Wandering. A Novel of the Middle Ages*. Revised and edited by Anita Miller from an English translation from the Dutch by Lewis C. Kaplan. Chicago: Academy Chicago Publishers, 1989.
_____. *The Scarlet City. A Novel of 16th-Century Italy*. Translated by Anita Miller. Chicago: Academy Chicago Publishers, 1990.

Note: Ms. Miller is working on a translation of *Een nieuwer testament*.

Non-fiction

_____. *Zelfportret als legkaart*. Amsterdam: De Bezige Bij, 1954.
_____. *Dat weet ik zelf niet*. Amsterdam: Vereeniging ter Bevordering van de Belangen des Boekhandels, 1959.
_____. *Leestekens*. Amsterdam: Querido, 1965.

_____. *Persoonsbewijs.* Bruges, Utrecht: Desclée-De Brouwer, 1967.

_____. *Zelfstandig, bijvoeglijk. Zeven essays over schrijvers, schrijfsters en hun personages.* Amsterdam: Querido, 1972.

_____. *Bladspiegel. Een keuze uit de essays.* Amsterdam: Querido, 1985.

_____. *Naar haar eigen beeld.* Leiden; Antwerp: Nijhoff, 1988.

Related works

Diepstraten, Johan. *Hella S. Haasse; een interview.* With extensive bibliographies of works by Hella S. Haasse (by Charlotte de Cloet) and of secondary literature (by Aloys van den Berk). The Hague: BZZTôH, 1984.

Goedgebuure, Jaap. "Verhaal en waarheid in Hella Haasse's historische romans." *Nederlandse literatuur 1960-1988.* Amsterdam: De Arbeiderspers, 1989.

Michielsen, John. "Hella Haasse." *Canadian Journal of Netherlandic Studies* XI (ii) 1990. 46-50.

Popelier, Ed. *Hella Haasse.* Nijmegen: Gottmer, 1977.

Vermij, Lucie Th. *Women Writers from The Netherlands and Flanders.* Trans. Greta Kilburn. Amsterdam: International Feminist Book Fair Press: 1992. 10-14; 27; 28.

Wouters, Gerti. "Hella S. Haasse. Emancipatiestrijdster of feministe tegen wil en dank?" *Ons Erfdeel* 33 (1) 1990. 75-82.

Hella Haasse's books are routinely reviewed in major Dutch and Belgian newspapers and magazines, such as *Algemeen Dagblad, Elsevier, De Gelderlander, De Groene Amsterdammer, De Haagse Post, Haarlems Dagblad, NRC Handelsblad, Nieuwsblad van het Noorden, Provinciale Zeeuwse Courant, De Standaard, De Tijd, Trouw, De Volkskrant,* and *Vrij Nederland.* Reviews and articles about her works also appear in literary journals such as *Bzzlletin, Dietsche warande en belfort, Spiegel der Letteren, Tirade,* and *De Vlaamse Gids.*

Marga Minco

Johan Pieter Snapper

The story that I chose to translate for this anthology was originally published as "Terugkeer" (1965, "Return"). It is one of a number of novels and short stories dealing with the Jewish plight in the Netherlands during World War II, all of which are based on the personal experiences of Marga Minco (born 1920). The first of these, *Bitter Herbs*, one of the most successful post-war Dutch novels, has appeared in over thirty editions and has been published in English, German, French, Spanish, Norwegian, Swedish, Welsh, and Hungarian translations.[1] In 22 separate but related stories, all narrated in the first person singular, the autobiographical novel soberly chronicles the experiences of Selma (as Marga Minco was called at the time), the youngest daughter of a Jewish family during the Second World War. It spans from the city-wide evacuation of Breda (the city where the narrator lived) during the first few days of the invasion of the Netherlands by Nazi Germany in 1940 to Selma's solitary return five years later. It depicts the anti-semitism of the local Catholic church, expressed by the children in the village who piously blamed the Jews for having crucified Jesus Christ. It also describes how two years later every Jew had to wear the yellow star of David, that — in a twist of Nazi sadism — was made in multiples of millions by the Jews in the Polish ghettos and distributed by the local Jewish councils. In the same year the Germans summoned Selma and her siblings to newly instituted labor camps for Jews. By the end of that year there were 37 such camps in the Netherlands, crammed full with approximately 7000 Jews. To mask all evil intents, the physicals were officially administered by the Jewish Council, and at first even carried out by Jewish physicians. These camps represented the first phase of the expatriation into concentration camps. 1942 also introduced the first razzias in Amsterdam, ostensibly to punish only Jews who refused to wear the star or who lived in other than specially designated areas. The offenders were sent to the concentration camp of Mauthausen, Austria.

In this novel Minco also describes her parents' compulsory evacuation to a Jewish ghetto in Amsterdam; how they were allowed to take only as much baggage as they could carry, after which their home with all their possessions was sealed off. In the figure of a neighbor girl, presumably sent to cash in on the family's misfortune by offering to take personal items for "safekeeping," Minco portrays another subtle, yet shocking example of prevalent antisemitic behavior.[2] After having joined her parents in Amsterdam, Selma witnessed whole streets being forcibly purged of Jews, including her own house. In separate incidents, her aunt, her parents, and her brother were among those carried off, but the narrator escaped, a fact that filled her with guilt and remorse for the rest of her life. She spent the remaining years of the war in hiding, having frequently changed not only her living quarters, but also her name and appearance. The novel ends with Selma's return after the war to visit her demented uncle, the only other family member to survive the holocaust, because he was married to a gentile. He spent the remaining months of his guilt-laden life by taking daily walks to the tram stop, in the vain hope of meeting a brother who would never return.

The story "The Day My Sister Married" might well have been incorporated into *Bitter Herbs*. It deals with the marriage of Selma's sister Bettie in 1942. The story focuses on a pervasive theme in Minco's oeuvre: the collective pretense that everything was normal, like before the war, and a persistent refusal to accept the gravity of the situation even while being forced to leave their homes for the last time, as in "The Return." In *Bitter Herbs* the Minco family managed this despite such ominous signs as the presence of the hated yellow star on everyone's coat, the premature withering of the bridal bouquet of star-shaped flowers, and the screech of a cat on their wedding day, sounding like a human scream. Written as a recollection, this powerful story also reveals that the newlyweds were deported and killed shortly after their wedding.

Another piece in Minco's narrative puzzle is provided by the story "My Mother's Village," an account of Selma's odyssey to the village of her mother's birth, in the hope of saving her parents who were detained in the labor camp of Westerborg and were about to be shipped off to a concentration camp. On the train ride to the village, she saw the camp in the distance. At the home of the local pastor Selma hoped to obtain a surrogate baptismal certificate for her mother. But the preacher and the righteous elders could in all good conscience not produce a false document and Selma had to go home empty-handed. Her parents's unsigned postcard, presumably thrown from the fateful train en route to Sobibor, their final destination, concludes the story with understated tragic irony: "We are en route to the border. Mother is fine. The train is very full."[3]

The ordeals that Minco experienced during her years in hiding are movingly described in the novel *The Glass Bridge*. This story deals with the narrator's painful quest to accept her new identity, which had belonged to a girl who had died early in the war. In order to do so, she visits the village of her namesake in Belgium, a journey that also renders her with answers to other unresolved questions. The novel provides a vivid insight into Minco's uprooted life as an underground refugee.

In several other works Minco concentrates on the familiar problem of survival, also dominant in "The Return." She approaches this post-war stress from a variety of perspectives. In the story "The Address" Minco describes how the familiar figure of the surviving daughter of a Jewish family visited the address where her family belongings were stored for safekeeping in order to reclaim them after the war. Barely suppressing her hostility, the lady of the house refused to let her in, but on a second visit, while the woman was absent, the narrator entered the house and found that all their precious belongings had been fully integrated into their new surroundings, as if they had always belonged there. No longer willing to reclaim the now estranged personal objects, she decided to leave empty-handed. Such subtle forms of post-war anti-semitism take a different twist in the untranslated story "Je mag van geluk spreken" ("Consider Yourself Lucky"). Here the narrator recalls how she returned to the city of her childhood, where she met someone she vaguely remembered from the past. The woman had little to say except to comment coldly on the fact that the narrator had survived the war. With similar detachment she inquired about the other members of the family, wryly adding: "You can consider yourself lucky."

In the powerful novel *An Empty House* there are two sole surviving daughters of two Jewish families. The principal character, Sepha, meets Yona while hitchhiking. It soon becomes clear that Yona functions as Sepha's alter-ego. They are both prisoners of the past, having lost their families and their homes. Each has great difficulty dealing with the present because the past continues to govern it. Minco reflects this theme also in her style, by frequently, and often abruptly, switching the past and the present, employing the present tense for flashbacks and recollections and the past tense for the present. This forces the reader, like the characters in question, to work through a perplexing maze of time layers. Returning from the countryside, the two young women are on their way to Amsterdam to begin a new life. But neither is properly prepared for this move. Too much has happened. Their outlook on life and their view of others as well as themselves have turned them into strangers. For Yona, who is unable to shake the past, there is no future and therefore no hope. She takes her life by jumping from a speeding train. Sepha chooses a different direction. Against all apparent odds, she reluctantly opts for another, albeit uncertain, future, not unlike the Goldstijns in "The Return."

The story "The Return" readily reflects many familiar motifs inherent in the other stories by Marga Minco. Dominant among them is the role Minco ascribes to the streets that the weary principals must travel (an image often extended to the bus, or more often, to the precarious train). In "The Return" we learn of Mr. and Mrs. Goldstijn's escorted walk from their home in Amsterdam to the train station, which in turn led to an underground destination. During their years in hiding we also see them watching the road through a peep hole in the attic window of the farm. On the one hand this daily activity served to kill time. On the other, the road also represented their only link to the outside world, to the past, and to the future. It is always that way for Minco's personages. We next observe the Goldstijns shortly after Holland had been liberated, taking to the streets of a town that harbored them for two and a half years without their ever having seen it. The reader subsequently walks the streets of Amsterdam with them, as it were, crossing bridges and visiting old familiar places. In this story, as elsewhere, the Minconian street functions as a metaphor for the wayward course of the persecuted, whose arbitrary itinerary often defies both meaning and logic. For most of the silent personages on the periphery in the stories the streets end in a dead-end, Hitler's so-called final solution. For the Jewish survivors the roads lead to a fate that is equally tragic, turning the homebound travelers into strangers, separated from their families and their environment, and ultimately even alienated from themselves. This state of being totally lost in a world in which they are perpetually on the move, having no longer a place to call their own, is the setting of most of Minco's stories, including "The Return."[4] Consequently, the Minconian image of the house is crucial to the proper understanding of her work. As the temporary shelter for the dispossessed, it encapsulates the tragedy of a whole people in the Netherlands during the 1940s and beyond.[5]

The houses in Minco's stories cry out that there is something seriously wrong not only with the Nazis and their antisemitism, but with (Dutch) society as a whole. This is most evident in her depiction of the homesteads which the families had to abandon, and, in some cases, to which they were forbidden to return, as our story shows. But even in the accounts where they do manage to reclaim their old home, they often find it either empty or uninhabitable, or both, as in *An Empty House*. Something is also wrong with the temporary dwellings along the treacherous Minconian highways. In these unfamiliar quarters, often dark and cramped, and surrounded by wary strangers, the Minconian Jew ponders her/his fate. These are the precarious shelters of the lucky ones who managed to elude the camps that housed all the rest. In one way or another, nearly all of Minco's houses mirror the holocaust, even the houses of the gentiles with whom the characters come in contact, especially after the war. One such house dominates the story "The Address," which refused to return the appropriated Jewish possessions after the Netherlands was liberated. But perhaps the ultimate structural reflector of the Jewish tragedy is the house that belonged exclusively to the whole family of Israel, the synagogue. As in *Bitter Herbs* and "The Day My Sister Married," so also here, not even the house of God could withstand the ravages of genocide. In "The Return" it has been turned into a warehouse and the Rabbi's spacious home into a business enterprise. In the post-war world to which Minco's characters return there is no place for vacant houses or empty temples. For the returning Jews of Amsterdam and elsewhere, their very cultural identity has been purged from the city, as if it had never existed.

"The Return" is unique in that it is an account of the survival not of a child, but of the parents. This complex story concentrates on the agony of Mr. and Mrs. Goldstijn, who are "orphaned" by the extermination of their children, thereby reflecting the totality of familial grief experienced by Minco's survivors. As is frequently the case in her work, the narrative covers several wrangling time periods that correspond in function and style to the places they conjure up.[6] The four periods in "The Return" — the happy days before the war, the hiding place during the war, the homeless months right after the war, and the resettlement in a new place not far from Amsterdam are all connected by painful roads and represented by houses that could never be claimed as their own, at least not for long. Unlike Minco's earlier work in this regard, each of these stations seems to beg the unanswerable question of the "why" of their plight. This is especially the case with Mr. Goldstijn's wandering within the intertwining mazes of time and place in which he seems unable to find his way out. Although the story begins eight years after the war, with the couple still living in a house and city that they cannot call their own, the numerous flashbacks to earlier periods dominate the present. We see the man surveying the streets of Amsterdam where they used to live, visiting familiar places and buildings, like the park and the old synagogue, and above all the family home, now occupied by strangers. Everything is irreversibly altered. As he crosses the proverbial Minconian bridge, the old man studies his old house from rooftop to the doorstep — like Sepha in the novel *An Empty House* — and concludes that he himself is the real stranger in the old familiar street — a realization that underscores Minco's oft-repeated theme that the present and the future after the war are even more difficult for the Jews than the years of hiding during the war.[7] Goldstijn knows this and he suspects his wife does too: "Didn't she want to let on that she suspected the same? That it wasn't really over. That, in fact, it had only just begun for them."

Mr. Goldstijn's search for the happy past was as futile as his wife's concern whether there were enough bedrooms in their new house for the children, of course. Again, they both knew this, though they could not talk about it. (They had lost their trust in words long ago, partly out of fear of utterances too painful to express or to hear, and partly because words had acquired double meanings, or lost their meaning altogether. So they relied on their eyes to express their feelings). Goldstijn's search for old points of reference is ultimately much more than a reconnaissance of familiar places, it is a desperate search for meaning, for answers. In no other narrative is Minco as unambiguous about this as in this story, although the question is always present in her work. Everything that the Goldstijns experience is part of their compulsive inquiry into the reason for the holocaust. Such is the function of the children motif, for instance. It serves as a symbol for a lost future that gains in importance through the accumulation of the other references to children. Take the children of the previous neighbor or the unfriendly childless couple that took their place, the purple-faced boy playing a badly out of tune trumpet, the cheering children on the farmer's cart, the girl in the park offering a mudpie, even the ducklings swimming behind their mother in the canal near their old home — they all serve to amplify their anguished outcry for their own children. Without their progeny, as without their temple, the Goldstijns are adrift, lost in their own city. A similar function is represented by the travel motif. It, too, emphasizes the painful realization that the wandering parents have nowhere to go in time or place. Doomed to live as permanent aliens in an environment that they cannot accept — or worse, that does not accept them — the Minconian search for a concrete past assumes gigantic existential proportions. Even the casual question "Are you looking for somebody?" by one of the workers at the temple-turned-warehouse reflects part of Goldstijn's pervasive struggle with his own identity, not unlike Stella's in *The Glass Bridge*. With the aid of false identification papers Rosa and he had assumed the identities of others for the duration of the war. Now, after the war, when they may once again bear their own names, they are learning that it is not possible to become their old selves again. This is the crucial point of Goldstijn's visit to his old home, where he confronts the fact that his name has been replaced by three unfamiliar nameplates. While he studies his house from top to bottom he finds out that he is no longer the man who used to live there, but someone else, although he does not know who. It is a conclusion that reverberates throughout the narrative.

The answer to his own question eludes him. The people he meets have little to say, so he avoids them. His closest friend Alex, with whom he could always discuss everything, had not returned from the camps. So he wants to turn to the Scriptures that were so important to him more than ten years ago. Maybe the Judaic laws of old offered a clue: "Perhaps the Talmud contained a text that [...] would lead to the answer to the why that won't leave him alone and that he felt might never leave him alone." But Mr. Goldstijn knows better. The awesome question that confounds all of civilization will always go begging for Minco's survivors.

The remaining question: how to continue living without the answer, is certainly one of the most pervasive practical problems in Minco's stories, including those that seem to have nothing to do with the war.[8] To illustrate this dilemma, Minco frequently introduces the image of the bridge. There are two principal bridges that the Goldstijns choose to cross when visiting Amsterdam, one that leads to their old house with all the personal memories and one that leads into the park where they used to spend so much time with their little children Jacques and Stella.[9] The function of both bridges in this story is to link a meaningless present with an almost idyllic past. As we have seen, the one leading to his house is the most difficult to cross for Mr. Goldstijn; it leads him further into the no-man's-land of his very existence. That is the reason why he has been avoiding it.

The arched bridge in the park also represents an attempt at retrieving a past, if only in his imagination. But he knows that it is a futile exercise, that the happy past is forever gone.

Since the bridge is a vivid childhood memory for Minco herself, it also appears in several of her other works, including the short story "De stoep" (The Front Steps) and of course in the novel *The Glass Bridge*. One of the bridges in *The Glass Bridge* actually refers to the same bridge near the house on the Singel mentioned in "The Return." But the one that is indelibly etched on her memory, the titular "glass bridge" actually refers to the bridge of her childhood in a park in Breda. Like the others, it functions as a link between an empty present and a past that was still full of promise. At the same time the bridge is a metaphor of a life that has been shaped by experience and that incorporates all of its baffling ambiguities. In several flashbacks Stella, the only survivor of her family, recalls the times she and her father traversed the arched bridge. One specific occasion stands out, however. As the two hesitantly approached the slippery ice-covered bridge and started to cross it, only Stella continued and slid down on the other side, while her father suddenly stopped. She could still see him. With his hand clutched around the railing, his eyes filled with tears, he did not follow her. Even many years later Stella still does not understand the reason for his hesitation. But the physical setting of this particular recollection suggests that it was an alarming omen of things to come. Behind the silhouette of her father Stella recalls the image of a broken tree protruding from the ice below, its black branches forming a disturbing backdrop to the heavyhearted father. Clearly the recollection is no longer only that of an idealized past. Rather, it serves as a prophetic profile of the future. That is why this memory continues to haunt Stella throughout the story. She herself wrestles with it as if it were a parable of their family history. It does not provide ultimate answers; at most perhaps an intimation of life's sinister fate. But even that little insight seems to elude Mr. Goldstijn in "The Return," at least until the final scene in the story.

The most important bridge in *An Empty House* is not set in a park, but right in the middle of Amsterdam, like the one on the Singel in "The Return." Yet it ultimately resembles the park bridge more. After Sepha learns that her friend Yona has committed suicide, she visits her house for the last time. She examines the living quarters, including the personal possessions, as if looking for a key to Yona's inner life — and perhaps also her own. As she leaves, she stops on the bridge near Yona's flat, turns around and from a distance examines the house also from the outside, scanning it from top to bottom, like Mr. Goldstijn in "The Return." These dramatic moments are perhaps the most important time in Sepha's life. Minco suggests that during this brief juncture, Sepha chooses an alternate course from her counterpart. She takes leave not only from her friend, but also from a life consumed by a dark past, in favor of a future that may hold some light. The novel ends with her joining her husband: "But I was turned round by Mark. With his arm around my shoulders he pulled me away into a side-street where it was dark and where, at that very moment, the street lights went on" (151).

From the vantage points of the bridges the story "The Return" seems to approximate the last narrative most closely, for there appears to be a partial resolution of Goldstijn's conflict. It happens on the very park bridge he has crossed dozens of times before. Here he unexpectedly meets his wife one day. Though startled, the two begin to communicate cautiously for the first time in years, signifying the possibility of a new, if fragile life. Unbeknown to him, Rosa, too, has been scouting out the old city by herself. But after a brief dialogue in which he does most of the questioning and she provides him with straightforward answers, he learns that her reconnaissance differs from his; that is, her "bridge" symbolizes an attempt to step out of the painful past into the present, no matter how difficult. Unlike her husband, Rosa explores the city not to compare it to what it used to be, but to get to know it in its present form, "because we came back. Because everything simply goes on." Goldstijn knows what she means and he senses that she has somehow progressed further than he. He takes her arm and in an expression of solidarity like that of Sepha and Mark in *An Empty House*, they walk across the bridge together in the direction of a bus that will bring them home. It is a limited step, but it is the most that Minco's characters can hope for.

The view from the bridge is misleading, however. It is not the way the story ends at all. The conclusion of the story takes away the fragile hope that the Goldstijns had just begun to harbor. In one of Minco's most ironic tours de force the titular "Return" refers not merely to the return of two straggling Jewish refugees, but also to the return of the enemy, who seems to have the last word after all. As changed as the life of the Goldstijns has become, the enemy has come back in stubbornly unaltered form. Like an echo of the old Nazis who first uprooted the family more than ten years ago, the new neighbor has begun to disturb their peace all over again. Deep into the night, the hissing sounds of the hated Horst Wessel song with its unforgettable lyrics of Nazi solidarity, "die Fahne hoch, die Reihen fest geschlossen, S.A. marchiert" haunts them once more.[10]

The fact that this should happen shortly after Mr. Goldstijn has begun to accept the present, and at precisely the point that he resolves to establish friendly relations with the whistling newcomer lends yet another twist to the ironic ending of the story. The ignominious rallying cry of yesteryear emanating from the shed below takes on a prophetic dimension. The past that Goldstijn has been struggling with for years has come back and is once again squeezing its iron grip. While Goldstijn looks at his watch to see what time it is, Minco reiterates that the horrible past, permanently carved on the streets with their returning travelers and on the houses with their displaced inhabitants lives on in the present. No matter what Goldstijn's watch says, the hands of Minco's clock show that the past and present are in collusion, and that in a profound sense, it is both earlier and therefore also later than it seems. In the final analysis, "The Return," is Marga Minco's most pessimistic view of history.

NOTES to the Introduction

1. If English titles are used, these refer to the published translations of Minco's texts.

2. In keeping with an almost childlike naiveté on the part of the narrator, Minco does not engage in overt judgements, especially in her most autobiographical work, in which she even avoids the word "German." Her sober, matter-of-fact style feeds the subtlety of the underlying indictment of friend and foe alike.

3. The irony of the upbeat letter under the most dire circumstances is typical for Minco. In "The Day My Sister Married," for instance, she remembers receiving a postcard from her uncle briefly before he and his entire famile were deported. It contained his customary greetings: "We sincerely hope that everything is in accordance with your wishes."

4. The theme of moving from one place to another is based on Minco's own life. Even before she was forced to move underground, where she repeatedly had to change hiding places, she and her family had lived in numerous different houses. In "The Return" there is also an ironic employment of this motif in the reference to the moving van that had brought the new neighbors into their life, and that rekindled one of the most anxiety-filled recollections of the war.

5. A powerful example of the temporal tenacity of the holocaust is Minco's *De val* (1983; translated as *The Fall* [1990]). In this gripping novel the heroine's struggle with the past is resolved with her own death some 40 years later.

6. For a more elaborate discussion of the interaction between time and space in Minco's work, see my article "The Work of Marga Minco: A Wrangle of Time and Space" (Snapper 1992[2]).

7. The bridge functions as an important metaphor in Minco's work, suggesting a crucial link between possible directions that are open to the character in question. Minco develops this motif in *An Empty House* and in the titular novel *A Glass Bridge* (See Snapper 1992[2]).

8. For a discussion of Minco's other work, see my article "De twee gezichten van Marga Minco" (The Two Faces of Marga Minco) (Snapper 1992).

9. Stella is also the name of the heroine in *The Glass Bridge*. It is no coincidence that the name of so many of Minco's fictional characters begin with the letter S. The author, whose own name originally was Sara, later Selma, hereby intentionally establishes a close relationship between the fictional characters and herself, as she told me in an interview in 1991. The name Marga (Marga Faes van Hoorn), incidentally, is the name she last assumed during the war, and which she decided to keep as her permanent name.

10. This was the party song of the N.S.D.A.P. (the National Socialist Democratic Workers Party), which, after the party had gained power in 1933, became the second official national anthem, to be sung alongside the better known "Deutschland über alles." The lyrics Goldstijn cites are "With banners raised and solidly united the S.A. [storm troops] march onward." Horst Wessel (1907-1930) was the propagandist for the Nazis.

Translation by Johan Pieter Snapper

"THE RETURN"

He could not get to sleep. He had been awake for hours. It was warm. He carefully pushed the blankets aside, making sure Rosa did not notice anything. She slept with her arm on the cover. A reddish arm. He had warned her not to stay out in the sun too long. That always made her laugh. "My skin isn't as delicate as yours." During their time in hiding they had hardly seen the sun. They stayed in a tiny attic-room on a farm, with only one small window, up high in the wall, made intransparent with white chalk. It was carefully blacked out in the evening. A few times a day he climbed on a chair to look outside. With his fingernail he had scratched a small peephole in the chalk, about the size of a penny. You could look out over the barn yard to a stretch of country road, a wide curve, lined with poplars.

"A woman is passing by," he told Rosa. "She is about 30. A boy on a bicycle. With big ears. A haycart. They are going to milk the cows. Two kids on a vegetable crate." It had become a routine game. You could kill time with it. Sometimes he would stand motionless at his lookout, with baited breath. A dark DKW screeched around the curve. A truck full of soldiers appeared, a whole column. The walls shook. Once two soldiers entered the yard, to refill their canteens. He did not move and did not say a word. Rosa, seated with a book on her lap, looked up at him. She held the page she meant to turn over between her fingers. It lasted about five minutes, but days later they could still see it in each other's eyes.

A big fly buzzed over the bed, just above his head. He did not want to swat at it, afraid of waking Rosa. Now the fly was sitting on the screen. He saw the dark speck crawl over the mesh and fly away, when a ray of light came in from below. It must have come from the neighbor's yard, from the shed. He heard footsteps, a door squeaked, something was being moved. The man often worked in the shed. Probably a handyman, someone with a hobby. What exactly he was doing, he did not know. They had been neighbors only for a short time. Rosa was sorry that the former neighbors had left. She liked the little children, who played in the yard and whom she called inside when the weather turned bad. When the new occupants arrived the first thing she said was: "They don't have any children." The moving van came from The Hague. City folk. People from the big city don't bother with their neighbors. They are not used to it. Rosa stirred for a second. The big bright spot in the room bothered him. But when he closed the curtain, it became too stuffy.

The day it was safe to go outside again it had been stifling hot in their hiding place. The window wouldn't open. They heard the farmer's wife running through the hallway, up the steps, calling. Suddenly, she stood in the middle of the room. "Come outside," she yelled, "come out, come outside!" Rosa dropped a cup on the floor. She covered her face with her hands. "It can't be true," she said. "What can't be true? What is it?" he asked. He was cold and trembling. "The Germans are capitulating. I just heard. It really is true. Come outside with me, hurry!" Of course they knew of the advance of the allied troops. They knew it could be all over any day.

But now that it had finally happened, he was shocked. What to do next? He wanted to go outside, and yet he didn't want to. They walked down the street with small stiff steps. The war was over; you could tell by the flags hanging out of the windows and the people wearing orange and red, white, and blue. A boy came by, playing a trumpet that was completely out of tune. His face was purple. A farmer's cart filled with cheering children followed them. As they shivered in the warm sun, they walked arm in arm along the road to the village, their eyes blinking.

"Here we go," he said, outside again. "We can come and go as we please." He listened to his own voice. It felt as if he hadn't spoken out loud in years.

"Where are we going?" asked Rosa.

"Just for a walk."

"Let's have a look at the village. Have we ever been here?"

"Not as far as I know."

"The scenery is supposed to be beautiful."

"Yes, so it seems."

They had lived here two and a half years without seeing any of it. They arrived one winter evening, after a long train ride. They felt uncomfortable in the train compartment with their false ID's and their silent companions. They were the only people to get off at the small station. He had not been able to make out the name of the town. It had still been a half hour walk to the farm, over dark country roads. They had to hold each other by the hand.

"It's just like we're on vacation," said Rosa. She had become thin. Her skin was pallid. Broad gray streaks ran through her dark hair. Her shoulders hunched forward. He had never noticed that about her before.

They passed by an office supply store. Rosa stopped. Someone had constructed a pyramid of paper string on a faded piece of cardboard. It was decorated with little orange flags and surrounded by pictures of the Royal Family. But she looked at the postcards in the front. Faded cards from long before the war, displaying an unreal tranquility.

"Look how beautiful it is around here." She stretched to look at the postcards in the top row.

"Why don't you buy some."

"Shall I buy a little packet? How many are there in a packet?"

"About a dozen, I think."

"To send, you mean."

He did not answer.

"To whom, to whom would we send them?"

"It is for you. A keepsake."

While she was in the store he waited in front of the window. He saw his reflection in the glass. An old man, in an ill-fitting suit. It had become far too big for him. A man with thin hair, bags under his eyes, tired of doing nothing, of waiting. He stretched and took a deep breath. His head stuck out a little farther from the roomy collar. He pulled his shoulders back, stretched his arms downwards, and planted his feet solidly on the ground, until he felt his whole body tense up and his bones creak.

"Are you doing exercises?" Rosa came out of the store.

"A little, yes. I need it. It has been a long time."

"Two and a half years."

"It feels like three times that long."

She put the packet of postcards in her purse. "But it's all over now, isn't it?" Her hand touched his sleeve slightly.

"Come, let's sit down in a terrace café somewhere, in the sun."

"If they have something to drink."

"Here they still might. Surrogate coffee and surrogate lemonade, it doesn't matter. It's the thought that counts."

"Yes, it is legal again, isn't it?"

They walked slowly, in search of an outdoor café. He felt as if there was something he had known for a long time, that he was certain of now, but that had not yet dawned on Rosa. Or was she just pretending? Didn't she want to let on that she suspected the same? That it wasn't really over. That, in fact, it had only just begun for them.

The fly sat still somewhere. Maybe on the side of the bed. Downstairs the light was still on. There was a scraping noise, as if someone were using a file. He was right: the time ahead was more difficult to cope with than the years in hiding. The days they didn't dare to talk to each other, when they were hesitant to use certain words. Many words now had a double meaning for them. The neighbor dropped something on the tile floor. Of course he had a workbench in the shed. Who knows, his wife probably did not like him to spend his days puttering, and that was why he did it at night, while she was asleep.

They had stayed in the village a few more weeks. They could not find transportation back to their own home that readily. Instead, they moved into another room on the farm, where the people did everything to make them feel more comfortable. But he was more in a hurry to get away than Rosa. Every day he went into the village to see if it was possible to make a telephone call yet, or if the mail was operating again, or if he could send a telegram. The man at the window said the same thing every time: "Sir, you'll have to be patient just a little longer. They are working very hard to get everything going again." He clasped his hands behind his head and stretched. Rosa was restless in her sleep. Shouldn't he get up to close the curtain?

When they returned to their home town, three families were occupying their house. They had to stay with relatives. A house was hard to find. Everyone tried to help. They had a choice between temporary housing until something more permanent became available, or a house in a town near-by. They chose the latter. It was a small house. In the beginning Rosa had occasionally asked about sleeping arrangements for when the children came back. He did not know what to say. She looked at him for a long time.

"Just you wait," she said, "one day they'll suddenly stand in front of us. Jacques was never as strong as Stella, but he'll rely on his wits. And there is no doubt about Stella, she's in great physical shape."

He did not dare look at her while she spoke. He knew she didn't believe her own words. She said it for him, both to delude herself and to ease some of the tension between them, or simply to say the names once again, as in the old days. He always watched when Stella played in a tennis tournament. In the summer before mobilization she had beaten a famous English player. "That girl is fantastic," the man next to him in the stands had said. "She is my

daughter." "Then I must congratulate you." That same summer
Jacques had passed his exams and had gone to study economics in
Rotterdam.

They did not come back. Neither did the other relatives. The
letters from the Red Cross said so indisputably. Still, they had gone
to look at the lists that had been posted at the office. With his finger
he traced the columns. To him it was only a question of recognition,
to discover familiar names, even if they were on the list of those who
wouldn't come back. Nothing was left of the sizable Jewish
community in their hometown. The small number of young people
who had survived had illegally moved to Palestine. But the void
created by their absence provided such a strong pull that he was
unable to resist it. He went there regularly by bus. He told Rosa he
had to take care of business. Of course he had to start thinking about
his business again. Vriens, who had kept things running during the
occupation, had already visited him a few times. When he heard
everything was going just fine, he felt more or less superfluous. In
the old days he would never have considered leaving matters to
others; he wanted to be involved in everything; nothing happened
without his knowledge. But now he hesitated as he stepped off the
bus. Should he go to his office? Occasionally he did, but most of the
time he walked the other way. He was searching for points of
reference, houses, streets, stores. One day he visited the old
synagogue. It had been turned into a warehouse. And the house next
door, where the rabbi used to live, was now a business establishment.

He remembered the Shabbat mornings, the men in their high
hats shaking hands at the entrance, the muffled voices in the foyer.
He was standing at his bench with the tallith around his shoulders,
and his hands were resting on the wooden ledge in front of him. He
smelled the leathery, sweet scent and looked up, to Rosa and the
other women behind the partition. At the front steps a van stopped.
A man in overalls walked to the main entrance, which opened only
on special occasions, when there was a huppah or when the chief
rabbi was visiting. The door flew back and slammed against the wall,
its hinges screeching. Another man carried a pile of boxes from the
van. He looked past them inside. Worktables designed for packing

were placed in the empty hall. The back wall, where once the holy ark had stood, was now covered with scaffolding. He walked to the side entrance. Crates were piled against the wall. That wall bordered the rabbi's garden. Sometimes, when he had to be in the conference room behind the synagogue, he could hear the rabbi's children playing in the garden. Stella had often been with them. When she sat on the swing he could see her face over the wall. She would call out to him and he would wait until she ascended again. With her head forward and her hair flying in the wind, they would wave to each other. He entered the lobby and asked one of the men:

"What kind of business is this anyway?"

"A paper wholesaler. Van Resema."

"Has it been here long?"

"Long? No, not really, a few years. There used to be a Jewish church here."

"Oh, yes."

"Are you looking for somebody?"

He said no and walked on, along the street beneath the big tower, where the wind was always blowing, past Samsom's dry-goods store, now a bicycle repairshop, and Meier's drugstore, also taken over by somebody else. He went in and asked for a roll of peppermints. A thin woman in a white apron waited on him. He slowly took out his wallet. He wanted to ask the woman something. She held out her hand. Suddenly he was having trouble sorting out his coins. Pretending he had something in his eyes, he simply handed her a guilder. While she made change, she turned to somebody who had come up behind her and now stood next to her behind the counter. He walked across the square where the dairy market used to be. The butter hall was now used as a rehearsal room for the local marching band, so he had been told. They had managed to keep most of the instruments out of German hands and now wanted to perform again as soon as possible. And why not? Now and then he ran into acquaintances. At first he stopped to talk to them. But the conversations varied little. Later he tried to avoid them.

"Hey, Mr. Goldstijn, you're back!"

Then he would say yes.

"How are you?"

He would say he was fine.

"And your wife and children?"

He would say his wife was fine too. The children. He shook his head. A momentary silence. Then they would ask about the other relatives from the town. Again he shook his head.

"Do you still live on the Singel?"

He told them he no longer lived in town, but in D., where they were quite comfortable. And then they would give their regards to Rosa.

Around the corner was the post office, where he used to pick up his mail on Sunday mornings. And across the bridge was the Singel. After initial visits with neighbors, he had avoided this bridge. Now he crossed it, walked along the embankment and looked at the house where he had lived for more than twenty years. Lace curtains in front of the windows, potted plants, a flower box. The wood had been painted brown. It used to be white, he thought, but he wasn't sure. It left him cold. He turned toward the water, where a duck was swimming now, followed by five little ducklings. As he leaned against a tree, he looked at the house again. He scanned it from porch to gable and felt he was somebody else, not the man who used to live there. Who had witnessed the birth of his children behind those windows, had seen them grow, had hummed along with their jazz records, danced at parties with his daughter's girlfriends. Was he that same man? Better not stay too long, it would draw attention. At the end of the Singel he crossed the road. He walked back along the houses. He passed the house of his friend Alex and did not understand: of this house he recognized everything. The green stained glass in the upper windows, the enamel plate with the house number of which the 8 was still so badly damaged that it looked more like a 3. The copper knob of the bell. The cracks in the concrete threshold. On the door of his former house he saw three nameplates: two near the bell. The top one said: W. Witgans. Below it a card: ring 3x. Doorman was the name of the other occupant. The third had attached his nameplate above the mailbox: L. Spijking. He knew none of them.

On the day he had closed the door behind him for the last time, he said to Rosa: we'll be back in a year, maybe sooner. Rosa had left the house the way she did when they would leave for a week or so. She checked everything: if the stove and the main faucet had been turned off, whether the window in the hallway was properly latched. In the kitchen she stopped in front of the cabinet with a package of rusks in her hand, until he called her and she put it back into the bin. Without looking back they and their companion had walked along the Singel, to the station.

Several times he had also visited the café on the market square, which he used to frequent with Alex. Nothing had changed. Only the beer smell was more pungent, he thought. The waiter who brought his coffee acted if he had been gone no more than a month. He asked about his wife and children, where they had been hiding, how business was going. It was the same everywhere. But he continued wandering through town as if he were looking for something, as if he expected to meet someone one day who would come up to him and tell him something completely different, something he would understand. He paused by the house where one of Rosa's sisters used to live. A corner house on a boulevard across a meadow. She had been a librarian and never married. A funny woman with whom he liked to talk. The front yard was neglected. It was full of plants and stacks of brick, with grass and weeds sprouting up between them.

Saturday mornings he walked home with Alex. They discussed the service, the texts the cantor had used, how he had sung that morning. They had gone to the same school and continued living in the same town. They had consulted each other on business matters, and helped each other with financial problems. With Alex he would have been able to talk about it, all the things that were left unsaid between Rosa and himself, the subject they intentionally avoided. But maybe it had been recorded somewhere in just a few words. Perhaps the Talmud contained a text that alluded to it and which in turn would lead to the answer to the why that won't leave him alone and that he felt might never let go of him.

One morning he had gone by bus to the city park, to the small restaurant by the pond. When the children were little they had often sat down here. Stella and Jacques always immediately ran to the playground. It was chilly, the sky was gray. There were only a few children on the grounds. They were playing in the sandbox. A mother with a woollen scarf around her head sat on the concrete edge smoking a cigarette. The cold did not seem to bother the toddlers. They were eagerly filling their little buckets, made mudpies, and built a small mound, as his children had done, as he himself had once done, under the watchful eye of his mother.

"Mr. Goldstijn! How are you! So long since I last saw you!"

A tall man with a goatee came toward him. He did not recognize him. But he did not let on. He pointed to the seat across from him and offered coffee. While they were talking he realized that this was Mr. Visser, the music teacher, who had taught Stella and Jacques to play the piano.

"I thought about you just last week! What a coincidence!"

"Yes, that is a coincidence."

"I happened to hear, you see, that you no longer live on the Singel."

"No, we don't. We now live in D."

"Not such a bad place, very quiet."

They usually said "not such a bad place," and he sensed a certain chauvinism in that. It irked him.

"You remember coming to our house when the students gave a recital? Your son was very talented. He was my best student."

He nodded and said he remembered.

"We still live in the same house." Mr. Visser tapped his bony fingers on the table. "When I returned I was rather surprised to find my wife still living there."

"How so? Had you been gone?"

"Yes, you didn't know? One year in the concentration camp of Vught and a year in Buchenwald." He laughed. Red blotches had appeared on his gaunt cheeks. "So it goes." He stirred his coffee. His gray beard touched the edge of his cup. That emaciated face, that beard. No wonder he hadn't recognized him immediately. They drank their coffee, without another word. He sensed a similarity between this silence and the one at home. After a while he said:

"Are you teaching again?"

"Definitely. I am starting a music school here. I have always wanted to do that."

"How was it, there?"

Mr. Visser looked past him. "I think about it as little as possible. At least I try not to. It's not so easy."

He got up.

"I'd better be off."

He watched the skinny man as he left with somewhat shaky steps, as if his nervous system had been damaged. The sun broke through and lit up the table. When he went outside a child was standing in the entrance with both hands full of sand.

"Would you like a mudpie?"

He was expected to accept.

"Thank you very much," he said.

With the moist sand in the palm of his hand he walked past the pond, along the path with the benches. On the arched bridge he spotted a woman. It was too late to turn around. He prepared to answer the questions. She walked toward him.

"I thought you were at the office."

"Rosa, what are you doing here?"

"I could ask you the same thing."

He let the sand run through his fingers, rubbed his hands on his coat and took her by the arm.

"Have you been here before?"

"A few times. But never for very long. I always had to go back one bus earlier than you."

"Have you been everywhere?"

She nodded. "And I met quite a few people who knew me."

"What did you talk to them about?"

"I don't talk to them all that much. Of course they ask all kinds of questions. They want to know everything in detail."

"I know what you mean. Would you like to live here again?"

They walked across the little bridge. He gently nudged her going up and braced her going down. She wore a black winter coat with a big collar. Black used to make her look young.

"No. We live quite well out there, don't you think? And we can go back every now and then, if we want."

"Do you feel the need to see everything again?"

"Sometimes. Then I go to the Singel, through the inner city streets. I look at the houses and stop in front of shops."

"And then you imagine how it used to be?"

"I try to see how it looks today."

"Why? To compare?"

"Because we came back. Because everything simply goes on."

Had she somehow progressed further than he, or did it just seem like that? Strange how they had never run into each other before. He wanted to say something about the dismantled synagogue, about her sister's house and about Mr. Visser, who had been in several camps, but instead he said:

"You are right. Shall we take the bus back together?"

"Yes, let's do that."

They left the park and walked toward the bus stop. When somebody greeted them with the intention to stop, they simply answered the greeting and walked on.

He looked at his watch. It was almost half past one. What kept the neighbor in the shed all this time? They really should not keep such a distance from everybody, especially from their neighbors. The woman actually seemed quite nice to him. Why not chat with them sometime? Over a garden wall words come easy enough. And there is always some pretext: the weather, the plants, the new lawn mower he had ordered, the condition of the tomatoes, many of which had now sprung up, too many for the two of them. It would be a shame to have to throw them out. Food and drink. Everything is available again. Nature takes its course, things come up from the ground, return to it, and sprout again.

It was quiet now down below. The light was still burning. Could he have gone to bed forgetting to turn it off? He raised his head and listened if the man was still there. He heard something. He sat up straight, his hands on the cover.

"Rosa," he whispered, "Rosa, did you hear that?"

Now he could hear it clearly. The neighbor was whistling. He whistled something that at one time had haunted him every day. A few lines he knew: "Die Fahne hoch, die Reihen fest geschlossen, S.A marschiert." Strange how one remembers such words. The whistling sounded muffled, almost hissing, as if it was not supposed to be heard by anyone. Why would that man whistle the Horst Wessel song in the middle of the night? He was getting warm, sweat appeared on his forehead, on his neck, on his back. Did he whistle it because it simply happened to come to mind? But who would remember this particular song? The war had been over for eight years. He could be no older than his mid-thirties. An ex-Nazi, only recently released? Eight years. Then he must have been in for something serious, or maybe he had held a high function, or betrayed somebody. Could be. But people often do the strangest things when left to themselves. Thinking nobody sees or hears them, they pull faces in front of the mirror, stick out their tongue, conduct an invisible orchestra, say words they would normally not dare use, and whistle songs nobody wants to hear again, but whose melody lingers on. Quite possibly the man did not even realize what he was whistling. Why immediately think the worst?

He looked over to his wife. He was glad she had not awakened. He lay down, pulling the cover up over him. He no longer felt warm. He had to try to fall asleep. Tomorrow he would think it over one more time. He was getting excited over nothing. Tomorrow he would work things out and then it would become clear that his first reaction had been wrong. But what did it matter whether he was right or wrong? It would not change anything.

In the yard the light finally went out. The whistling continued a little while longer.

Bibliography

Primary Works

Minco, Marga. "Een voetbad." *Mandril* 3/5, (March 1951). Reprinted in Marga Minco, *Verzamelde verhalen*. Amsterdam: Bert Bakker. 1982.

_____. "De troeven van Gejus." *Mandril* 3/9, (July 1951). Reprinted in Marga Minco, *Verzamelde verhalen*. Amsterdam: Bert Bakker. 1982.

_____. "Een verhoor." *Mandril* 3/11, (September 1951). Reprinted in Marga Minco, *Verzamelde verhalen*. Amsterdam: Bert Bakker. 1982.

_____. "Meneer Frits." First published under the title "De andere kant" *Vandaag*. Utrecht: Bruna. April 1954. Reprinted in Marga Minco, *Verzamelde verhalen*. Amsterdam: Bert Bakker. 1982.

_____. "Vlinders vangen op Skyros." *Het Parool*, (11 December 1954). Reprinted in Marga Minco, *Verzamelde verhalen*. Amsterdam: Bert Bakker. 1982.

_____. "Rose schuimpjes." *Haarlems Dagblad*, (8 September 1955). Reprinted in Marga Minco, *Verzamelde verhalen*. Amsterdam: Bert Bakker. 1982.

_____. *De verdwenen ambtsketen*. A television play for children, first aired 1955.

_____. "De man die zijn vrouw liet schrikken." *Haarlems Dagblad* (1 February 1956). Reprinted in Marga Minco, *Verzamelde verhalen*. Amsterdam: Bert Bakker. 1982.

_____. "Bomen." *Maatstaf* 5/2, (May 1957). Reprinted in Marga Minco, *Verzamelde verhalen*. Amsterdam: Bert Bakker. 1982.

_____. "Het adres." In: Marga Minco, Ingeborg Rutgers, Auke Jelsma, *Drie bekroonde novellen*. Amsterdam: De Mutator N.V. 1957. Reprinted in Marga Minco, *Verzamelde verhalen*. Amsterdam: Bert Bakker. 1982.

_____. "The Address." Trans. Jeannette K. Ringold. *TriQuarterly* 61 (1984). And in: *Fiction of the Eighties*. Evanston: TriQuarterly. 1990. 243-247.

_____. "Iets anders." *Maatstaf* 5/8, (November 1957). Reprinted in Marga Minco, *Verzamelde verhalen*. Amsterdam: Bert Bakker. 1982.

_____. "Something Different." Trans. Elisabeth Eybers. *Short Story International* 1/8. (June 1964).

_____. *Het bittere kruid*. Een kleine kroniek. Met tekeningen van Herman Dijkstra. Den Haag: Bert Bakker, Daamen N.V. 1957.

_____. "De tekening." *Maatstaf* 7/6, (September 1959). Reprinted in Marga Minco, *Verzamelde verhalen*. Amsterdam: Bert Bakker. 1982.

_____. "In het voorbijgaan." In: *De andere kant*. Den Haag: Bert Bakker, Daamen N.V. 1959. Reprinted in Marga Minco, *Verzamelde verhalen*. Amsterdam: Bert Bakker. 1982.

_____. "De dochters van de majoor." In: *De andere kant*. Den Haag: Bert Bakker, Daamen N.V. 1959. Reprinted in Marga Minco, *Verzamelde verhalen*. Amsterdam: Bert Bakker. 1982.

_____. "De vriend." In: *De andere kant*. Den Haag: Bert Bakker, Daamen N.V. 1959. Reprinted in Marga Minco, *Verzamelde verhalen*. Amsterdam: Bert Bakker. 1982.

_____. "The Friend." Trans. Anne Pool. *Trends*. 2/4. (Scotland: Paisly. 1979).

_____. "De andere kant." In: *De andere kant*. Den Haag: Bert Bakker, Daamen N.V. 1959. Reprinted in Marga Minco, *Verzamelde verhalen*. Amsterdam: Bert Bakker. 1982.

_____. "Alleen de boeken." *Ruimte*, driemaandelijks cahier,12. (June 1961). Reprinted in Marga Minco, *Verzamelde verhalen*. Amsterdam: Bert Bakker. 1982.

_____. *Tegenvoeters*. With Bert Voeten. Amsterdam: Het Corps Typographique van het Instituut voor Kunstnijverheidsonderwijs. 1961.

_____. "Het dorp van mijn moeder." *Vandaag* 7. Utrecht: Boekenweek, March 1961. Reprinted in Marga Minco, *Verzamelde verhalen*. Amsterdam: Bert Bakker. 1982.

_____. "My Mother's Village." Trans. Elisabeth Eybers. *Jewish Affairs* (Johannesburg: 11/16/61). Republished in *De andere kant*. Amsterdam: Bert Bakker. 1979.

_____. *Kijk 'ns in de la*. Een leesboek voor jongens en meisjes van zes tot tien jaar. Amsterdam: de bezige bij. 1963.

_____. *Moderne joodse verhalen*. Ed. and Intro. Marga Minco. Amsterdam: Polak & Van Gennep. 1964.

_____. *Terugkeer*. Amsterdam: Uitgave Cefina JMW. 1965. Reprinted in Marga Minco, *Verzamelde verhalen*. Amsterdam: Bert Bakker. 1982.

_____. *Het huis hiernaast*. Amsterdam: Meulenhoff. 1965.

_____. *Een leeg huis*. Amsterdam: Bert Bakker. 1966.

_____. *An Empty House*. Trans. Margaret Clegg. London: Peter Owen, 1990.

_____. "De Mexicaanse hond." First published under the title "Radio" in *Maatstaf* 15/1, (April 1967). Reprinted in Marga Minco, *Verzamelde verhalen*. Amsterdam: Bert Bakker. 1982.

_____. *De trapeze*, 6. with Mies Bouhuys. Original stories for the elementary school. Groningen: Wolters-Noordhoff. 1968.

_____. "De stoep." *Avenue* 11 (1969). Reprinted in Marga Minco, *Verzamelde verhalen*. Amsterdam: Bert Bakker. 1982.

_____. *De hutkoffer*. Television play, first aired 1970.

_____. "De dag dat mijn zuster trouwde." Den Haag: Bert Bakker. 1970. Reprinted in Marga Minco, *Verzamelde verhalen*. Amsterdam: Bert Bakker. 1982.

_____. "The Day My Sister Married." Trans. Jeannette K. Ringold. *TriQuarterly* 61 (1984).

_____. "Het scherm." *Tirade* 17/190, (October 1973). Reprinted in Marga Minco, *Verzamelde verhalen*. Amsterdam: Bert Bakker. 1982.

_____. "Om zeven uur." In: *Verhaal nog es wat...2*. Antwerp/Amsterdam: Standaard Uitgeverij/P.N. van Kampen en Zoon. 1974. Reprinted in Marga Minco, *Verzamelde verhalen*. Amsterdam: Bert Bakker. 1982.

_____. "Van geluk spreken." In: *Je mag van geluk spreken*. Utrecht: Bulkboek. 1975. Reprinted in Marga Minco, *Verzamelde verhalen*. Amsterdam: Bert Bakker. 1982.

_____. *Daniël de Barrios*. Television play, first aired 1975.

_____. "Israel op het eerste gezicht." *Holands diep* 2/13, (19 June 1976). Reprinted in Marga Minco, *Verzamelde verhalen*. Amsterdam: Bert Bakker. 1982.

_____. *Maart*. Utrecht/Amsterdam: Het spectrum. 1979.

_____. "Gina's pijn." First published under the title "Het wegebben van pijn" in *Nederlands Tijdschrift voor Geneeskunde* 125/44, (31 October 1981). Reprinted in Marga Minco, *Verzamelde verhalen*. Amsterdam: Bert Bakker. 1982.

_____. *De val*. Amsterdam: Bert Bakker. 1983.

_____. *The Fall*. Trans. Jeannette K. Ringold. London: Peter Owen, 1990.

_____. *Ik herinner me Maria Roselier*. Amsterdam: CPNB. 1986.

_____. *De glazen brug*. Amsterdam: Bert Bakker. 1986.

_____. *The Glass Bridge*. Trans. Stacey Knecht. London: Peter Owen, 1988.

_____. "De bol en de bolero." *Entr'acte*. May/June 1990.

_____. *De zon is maar een zeepbel*. Twaalf Droomverslagen. Bibliophile edition. Woubrugge: Avalon Pers. 1990.
_____. *Aan de Dinkel*. Bibliophile edition. Alphen a/d Rijn. April 1990.
_____. *Een leeg huis*. A drama. Arnhem: theater van het Oosten. 1992.
_____. *Breda*. 's-Hertogenbosch: Het Noordbrabants genootschap. 1992.

Related Works

Betlem, Trix. Interview of Marga Minco. *Revue* (6-24-67).

Hoven, A. van den. "*Het bittere kruid* by Marga Minco. Paradise Lost: Paradise Regained." *Canadian Journal of Netherlandic Studies* 8, ii-9,i (Fall 1987-Spring 1988) 92-96.

Kroon, Dirk, ed. *Over Marga Minco*. Den Haag: BZZToH. 1982.

Middeldorp. A. *Over het proza van Marga Minco*. Amsterdam: Wetenschappelijke Uitgeverij. 1981.

Peene, Bert. *Marga Minco. De val en De glazen brug*. Apeldoorn: Walva-Boek. 1987.

_____. *Marga Minco. Eeen leeg huis*. Apeldoorn: Walva-Boek/Van Walraven. 1985.

Snapper, Johan P. "Twee gezichten van Marga Minco,". *Neerlandica Extra Muros* XXX.2 (1992).

_____. "The Work of Marga Minco: A Wrangle of Time and Space." *The Low Countries and Beyond*. Ed. Robert S. Kirsner. Publications of the American Association for Netherlandic Studies 5. Lanham: University Press of America. 1992.

Vanderwal Taylor, Jolanda. "Bitter Herbs, Empty Houses, Traps, and False Identities: The (Post)-War World of Marga Minco (1920—)." *Canadian Journal of Netherlandic Studies* XI,ii 1990.

Anne Frank

Laureen Nussbaum

On May 11, 1944, after almost two years of hiding in the secret back quarters of an Amsterdam canal house, Anne Frank wrote to her imaginary friend Kitty: "You have known for quite a while now, that it is my fondest wish to become a journalist and eventually a famous writer. It remains to be seen, whether I can ever make good on these grandiose ambitions (or delusions!) but so far, I have plenty of topics. In any case, once the war is over, I want to publish a book under the title "Het Achterhuis" ("The Back Quarters"). Who knows, whether I can bring it off, but it can be based on my diary..." It was the posthumous publication of this epistolary diary that has made Anne Frank probably the best known Dutch writer in the world.

Anne (Anneliese Marie) Frank was born June 12, 1929 in Frankfurt am Main, Germany, the second and youngest child of an upper-middle class family. Her grandparents were bankers and manufacturers, her parents, Edith and Otto Frank, culture-loving, well-assimilated Germans of Jewish descent. At the time Anne was born, Otto's father had long since died and Otto, together with his younger brother Herbert and his brother-in-law Erich Elias, ran what was left of the family bank after the staggering inflation of the early 1920s. In subsequent years, during the Great Depression, the partners scattered: Herbert went to Paris and the Eliases to Basel, where Erich opened the Swiss branch of *Opekta*, manufacturers and distributors of pectin. Otto finally closed the family bank in the spring of 1933, just after the Nazis had assumed power in Germany, and soon thereafter, he moved his family to Amsterdam.[1] For years, Otto Frank had maintained business relations in Amsterdam, which he had frequently visited in the twenties. There, thanks to Elias, Frank was able to establish a Dutch branch of *Opekta*, which provided the family a reasonable standard of living, especially after Hermann Van Pels joined the business and added a new line in the form of spices, necessary for the production of sausages (*DAF* 6-10). Anne and her sister Margot, who was 3 years her elder, grew up in a brand new neighborhood of three- to four-story apartment buildings at the southern edge of Amsterdam, where many Jewish refugee families from Germany had settled starting in 1933. Thus, there were numerous neighbors who shared their fate and, typically, parents would compare notes in German. The children, however, soon adapted themselves completely to their Dutch surroundings, especially those who had come as young as Anne, who was to receive all her schooling in the new country.[2]

In the years 1938-39, after Hitler's troops had marched into Austria and Czechoslovakia, war clouds gathered over Europe, but the Franks, like thousands of other refugees, hoped that the Netherlands could maintain its neutrality just as it had during World War I. Otto concentrated on consolidating his business, Edith took care of the family, which from 1939 also included Edith's elderly mother.[3] In addition, Edith got involved in the liberal Jewish congregation, founded by refugee families in Amsterdam (*DAF* 16ff). Margot received some religious instruction within the framework of this congregation.[4] Anne, according to her very close friend and schoolmate Hannah Pick-Goslar — Lies Goosens — the Diary, followed her father's inclinations and "wasn't religious at all" (in Lindwer 15). Both girls went to public elementary schools in the neighborhood and in the fall of 1938, Margot moved on to an academically demanding high school, the *Gemeentelijk Lyceum voor Meisjes*. Anne was by no means as excellent a student as her sister, but one of her teachers recalls that she "was able to *experience* more than other children,...she heard more, the soundless things too, and sometimes she heard things whose very existence we have almost forgotten..." (in Schnabel 42). Another teacher remembers that Anne was in her element when the children wrote plays and put them on: "Of course she was full of ideas for the scripts, but since she also had no shyness and liked imitating other people, the big parts fell to her. She was rather small among her schoolmates, but when she played the queen or the princess she suddenly seemed a good bit taller than the others. It was really strange to see that" (in Schnabel 43 ff). Hannah Pick-Goslar recalls that Anne was writing diaries long before her thirteenth birthday, that she would even make entries during breaks in school, very secretively, so that nobody could get a glimpse of what she was jotting down. She was very popular with boys as well as with girls, an opinionated little girl..."always the center of attention at our parties. At school, too, Anne was always the center." Hannah continues, "I remember that my mother, who liked her very much, used to say: 'God knows everything, but Anne knows everything better'" (in Lindwer 16f). By the spring of 1940, Anne was a lively fifth grader, well liked and well adjusted to life in what was called the "river district" of Amsterdam.[5] Then, May 10, disaster struck. Within five days, Hitler's troops occupied the Netherlands. Very few people could escape to England, everybody else had to submit to the occupational regime of the Nazis with its discriminatory laws against Jews. Anne was still able to finish her elementary grades in the Montessori school (Niersstraat), which is now named for her. But in the fall of 1941, all youngsters from Jewish families had to attend separate Jewish schools — just one of many new restrictions that regulated Jewish life. By May 1942, all Jews had to wear the invidious yellow star with *JOOD* ("Jew") on it, and on July 5, just as the school year ended, thousands of Jewish men and women between ages 16-40 were called up to report for forced labor. Margot Frank was among them.[6]

At this point, Otto Frank was already in the process of preparing a hiding place for both his family and that of Van Pels in the backrooms and attic of the partners' business premises at 263 Prinsengracht. The summons for Margot caused them all to cut short their preparations and go immediately into hiding. Anne had just turned 13 a few weeks earlier and her most treasured birthday present had been a diary in a red and white checkered cover (*DAF* 59).[7] It was to be her steady companion and a great source of comfort as she experienced accelerated puberty in the hothouse atmosphere of the hide-out. Forewarned by what had happened to Jewish firms in Germany, Otto Frank had made sure that *Opekta* was no longer officially in his hands. Trusted non-Jewish business associates and the office personnel ran the firm for him and Van Pels. Henceforth, these same people took care of the two hiding families, who were soon joined by a Jewish dentist.[8] They provided for all the needs of eight persons as well as they possibly could under very trying circumstances. Many details of their loving care are known from entries in Anne's "Diary." Miep Gies, the firm's executive secretary, was the main lifeline for the hiders. She was also the one who salvaged Anne's diaries — the original checkered book and its more modest successors — after her charges had been betrayed and arrested on August 4, 1944 (*DAF* 21 and 62). The last cattle train from the Netherlands with destination Auschwitz, Poland departed on September 3, 1944 from camp Westerbork. The eight hiders from 263 Prinsengracht were among the 1,019 Jews of this last shipment (*DAF* 50ff).

Liberated in Auschwitz by Soviet troops, Otto Frank already knew that his wife had died from exhaustion in that notorious death camp. When he returned via Odessa and Marseille to Amsterdam in early June, 1945 he was anticipating being reunited with his two daughters, who, together with other young women, had been sent from Auschwitz to camp Bergen-Belsen in North West Germany. Since the latter was not an extermination camp, Otto had great hopes for their survival. But by the time the girls arrived there, around November 1st, 1944 the place was so overcrowded and hygiene and food supplies were at such a dismal low that typhoid fever soon spread like wildfire and killed tens of thousands (*DAF* 52ff).[9] As survivors trickled back from Bergen-Belsen, Otto would ask them about his girls only to learn, after weeks of agony, from women who had known his daughters, that in March both girls had succumbed, first Margot and shortly afterwards Anne. Eventually, Otto had to resign himself to the bitter fact that of the eight deported hiders, he was the only survivor. It was then that Miep, who together with her husband had lovingly taken him in, handed Otto his daughter's diaries and loose sheets of note paper, which she had kept locked away in hopes of returning them to Anne (*DAF* 62).

At first, Otto Frank had no intentions of publishing his daughter's diaries. Understandably, he was deeply moved by her entries and decided to copy what he deemed the "essential" passages in order to share them with relatives and friends. For the benefit of his mother and other close relatives in Basel, who did not read Dutch, he translated his excerpts into German. Subsequently, he went about typing a more complete transcript, partly basing himself on Anne's original diaries, partly on her own revisions and on her vignettes of life in the "back quarters." This typescript, corrected for language errors by some of Otto's Dutch friends, was allowed to circulate among a somewhat wider circle of acquaintances, which included Dr. Kurt Baschwitz, also a German refugee, at that time lecturer and later professor of journalism and psychology of mass media at Amsterdam City University (*DAF* 63ff). Baschwitz was deeply impressed by the typescript of Anne's journal. In a letter to one of his daughters, dated February 10, 1946 he commented:

> "It is the most moving document of our time I know, also from a literary standpoint a surprising masterpiece. It deals with the inner experiences of a maturing girl, her impressions in the close confinement together with her father, whom she adores, her mother, with whom she runs into conflicts, her sister, in whom she discovers a friend, with the other family sharing the hide-out, and with their son, with whom she is beginning to fall in love. I think it ought to appear in print."[10]

Others shared this sentiment, particularly the eminent Dutch historian Jan Romein, who, after reading the typescript, published an article in the daily *Het Parool* (April 3, 1946) in which he praised Anne's writing not only for its documentary value but also for the way she handles the language, for her insight into human nature, for her sense of humor and her empathy.[11] On the strength and persuasiveness of this article, several publishers expressed interest in Anne's "Diary" and before long, the Amsterdam publishing house Contact secured the rights.

Thus, Anne Frank's *Het Achterhuis: Dagboekbrieven 12 Juni 1942-1 Augustus 1944* ("The Back Quarters: Diary-letters June 12, 1942-August 1, 1944") first appeared in June 1947 with an introduction by Annie Romein-Verschoor.[12] Comparing Anne's "Diary" to *The Journal of a Young Artist*, also an autobiographical work by a very young woman (Marie Bashkirtseff) which had shaken up Paris in the 1880s,[13] Romein-Verschoor points out that Anne's text happily lacks the self-consciousness that marks the reflections of the earlier, very ambitious child prodigy. While granting Anne Frank "the one important characteristic of a great writer: an open mind, untouched by complacency and prejudice," Romein-Verschoor emphasizes the young author's "direct, non-literary and therefore often excellent" descriptions that have a natural purity devoid of extraneous admixtures (v-ix). But in fact she overstated the natural, non-literary quality of Anne's "Diary." Its textual history is as complicated as Anne Frank's short biography is straightforward. In 1986, that history was made accessible to the general public, when at long last the critical edition of *De Dagboeken van Anne Frank* ("The Diaries of Anne Frank") was published under the auspices of the Netherlands Institute for War Documentation.[14]

In a radio broadcast from London (via the clandestine Dutch station *Radio Oranje*) on March 28, 1944, Gerrit Bolkestein, the Education Secretary of the Dutch cabinet in exile, announced that after the war, diaries and letters written in the occupied Netherlands would be collected as first-hand documentation. Few people realize that soon after this broadcast, Anne very consciously started rewriting her diary on loose sheets of paper with an eye to post-war publication. "At last," she writes on May 20 of that year, "after considerable deliberations, I started working on my 'Achterhuis.' In my mind, I have already finished it as far as I can, but in reality it won't get done all that fast if, indeed, it will ever get finished" (*DAF*

653). As pointed out, Otto Frank had picked and chosen from Anne's extant diary versions when assembling the typescript on which the original (1947) Dutch edition and the subsequent translations into dozens of languages would be based. He had added some of the vignettes she had written separately about life in the back quarters,[15] made several rearrangements and corrections while omitting some passages which he deemed either too irrelevant or too personal to include. In other words, Otto Frank had edited his daughter's "Diary," to which he had, of course, a perfect right; a prefatory note to this effect, however, would have saved him many future problems. To make matters worse, the Dutch publishing house labored under some constraints regarding the length of the book. Moreover, they rather prudishly insisted that some of Anne's references to her own maturing body be left out. Since the publishers of the German and English translations went back to Otto Frank's typescript and did not feel compelled to exclude certain entries or passages, these versions are actually more complete than the original Dutch.[16] All this led to a great deal of confusion, which is meticulously explained and sorted out in the critical edition (*DAF* 59-77).

The publication of *Het Achterhuis* gave Otto Frank a great sense of satisfaction. He had been able to fulfill his daughter's most cherished wish and, as the Dutch reviews were unanimously favorable, he was sure that he had done the right thing (*DAF* 71). When the American edition, graced with a preface by Eleanor Roosevelt, was published in 1952, *The New York Times Book Review* carried a glowing review by Meyer Levin, which aroused widespread interest in the book. According to Levin,

> "Anne Frank's diary is too tenderly intimate a book to be frozen with the label 'classic,' and yet no lesser designation serves. For little Anne Frank, spirited, moody, witty, self-doubting, succeeded in communicating in virtually perfect or classic form the drama of puberty... Because the diary was not written in retrospect, it contains the trembling life of every moment — Anne Frank's voice becomes the voice of six million vanished Jewish souls. It is difficult to say

in which respect the book is more 'important,' but
one forgets the double significance of this document
in experiencing it as an intimate whole, for one feels
the presence of this child-becoming-woman as
warmly as though she was snuggled on a near-by
sofa... Surely she will be universally loved, for this
wise and wonderful young girl brings back a poignant
delight in the infinite human spirit (*NYTBR* June 15,
1952).

From the beginning, Meyer Levin championed the idea that
Anne Frank's "Diary" should be made into a play and a film. With
Otto Frank's blessing, he tried his hand at a play script and felt
deeply hurt when, eventually, Frank gave the rights to Frances
Goodrich-Hackett and Albert Hackett. A most painful lawsuit
followed and Levin remained obsessed with the affair for 20 years,
claiming that his version of the play had been rejected because it was
deemed too Jewish. He maintained that in the name of a more
universalist appeal the Hacketts and their supporters had not been true
to Anne's intentions, since they had left out significant passages in
which Anne tried to come to grips with the fate of the Jews.[17]
Several American reviewers of *DAF* appear to be sympathetic to
Meyer Levin's point of view.[18] Undoubtedly, the Goodrich-Hackett
dramatization of *The Diary of Anne Frank* was an overwhelming stage
success. It premiered in New York, on October 5, 1955, with Susan
Strasberg as Anne and Joseph Schildkraut as Otto Frank and won
various awards including the 1955 Pulitzer Prize for drama.[19] When
in 1957 a film based on *The Diary* proved equally successful, Anne
Frank's story conquered the world.[20]

That same year, the Anne Frank Foundation was established.
It was charged with the upkeep of the house at 263 Prinsengracht,
especially its back quarters, and with the dissemination of Anne's
ideals of religious tolerance and interracial cooperation. About half a
million visitors file through the premises every year. Moreover,
schools and streets are named for her all over the world. For
countless people, Anne Frank has become a symbol of the six million
Jews murdered by the Nazis, not a symbol in an abstract sense, but

somebody very real and endearing, because of her youth and the directness of her words (compare *DAF* 74ff). What made her story so powerful is the fact that it brought home the genocide of European Jewry. Small wonder then, that from 1957 on Neo-Nazis and revisionist historians from Scandinavia via Germany to Austria and from France via Britain to the U.S.A. had a vested interest in attacking the authenticity of Anne Frank's "Diary." Otto Frank's editorial changes and omissions, the deviations from the Dutch edition in the German as well as the English translation, and finally the public dispute between Otto Frank and Meyer Levin, all were grist for the mills of the detractors. They claimed that Anne's father with the help of professional writers had forged the "Diary." In 1959, Otto Frank, Miep and Jan Gies, and others closely involved appeared in court to prove that *The Diary of Anne Frank* was not a hoax. (*DAF* 84-101) New attacks on the authenticity of *The Diary* were launched again and again until August 1980, when Otto Frank died at the age of 91. The Dutch Institute for War Documentation, to which Otto Frank had wisely willed Anne's original handwritten diaries, loose sheets and stories, sought to lay to rest all further speculations. It was decided to subject these original text materials to a document examination and a handwriting identification by the State Forensic Laboratory and to publish the results of these probes together with a complete, critical edition of *The Diary of Anne Frank. DAF* contains an extensive summary of the forensic report, from which the "Afterword" concludes without a reasonable shade of doubt that both the original and the revised version of *The Diary* were written by Anne Frank between the years 1942-44 (102-67). The Critical Edition includes the manuscript materials, as far as they are extant, printed in parallel with the previously published text of *The Diary*, thus providing the reader an opportunity to compare versions and to see a more complete Anne emerge from the pages, an Anne who matured over a period of two years both as a person and as a writer.

The original diary with the red and white checkered cover, Anne's most cherished birthday present, opens with a full page picture of herself and spans the period from June 12 until December 5, 1942. The early entries in this book (version **a**) are juvenilia of a zestful teenager, telling about her thirteenth birthday and her ping-pong club and focusing on her girl friends and admirers as well as on school events. On June 15-16, Anne gives a thumbnail sketch of each of her classmates. Suddenly, she realizes that she had better tell her own life story, which she does succinctly on the next page, so as to lay the foundation for her diary (*DAF* 187ff). Once the Frank family had gone into hiding, Anne's life changed drastically. After her account of the day they left home and moved into the secret back quarters, she appears rather overwhelmed by her new experiences. Quite understandably, Anne found it difficult to sort out her very mixed feelings, so at first she left large gaps to be filled in later. Then, after about ten weeks in hiding, there is a marked shift toward introspection. Henceforth, the diary is going to take an important place in Anne's new life. On September 21 she decides to write her entries in the form of letters (*DAF* 237), addressing them to a variety of girls, mostly characters from her favorite series of juvenile books by Cissy Van Marxfeldt. Kitty is just one of these characters.[21] A week later Anne begins to fill some of the empty spaces in her diary, e.g. with small annotated photographs of herself and her closest kin and a very large one of her beloved father preceded by a charming letter from him (*DAF* 190f, 225). She reflects about her looks and about her earlier entries, is dissatisfied with what she wrote before and explains somewhat apologetically:

> "...I see things differently now but I cannot very well tear pages out of my diary, and I hope nobody will reproach me later for poor penmanship in those days, since that is not what it was. Rather, I just did not feel like writing into my diary because I found it quite hard to do so" (*DAF* 192).

Subsequent entries dealing with life in the back quarters include occasional squabbles between the hiding families and tensions between Anne and her mother. There is the schoolwork, which Anne takes quite seriously so as not to fall behind, great appreciation for what their helpers are doing for the hiders, and deep worries about their many friends and acquaintances who could not go into hiding and are now being sent to Poland. Anne also indulges in a curious daydream: she and her darling father somehow make it to Switzerland and then share a room at their relatives' home. He gives her enough money to go and buy herself a new wardrobe, which she does immediately with Bernd, her cousin. A shopping list is attached. A week later she fantasizes that she is attending eighth grade in Switzerland. She quickly picks up French and German and is popular in school. One of her new friends is Kitty. Bernd teaches her figure skating and the two of them become very successful ice skating partners and are eventually filmed. She sketches the movie scenes, which also include her father (*DAF* 269-71 and 283).

When in the spring of 1944 Anne revised her diary with an eye to possible publication, she omitted much of what she had entered in her first journal and tightened the rest as she rewrote it on loose sheets of paper (version **b**). The first entry now is dated June 20, 1942. Anne, putting herself in her state of mind of two weeks before she went into hiding, explains why, despite all her popularity, she feels lonely and in need of a true friend to whom she can direct her outpourings. That friend she decides to call Kitty and after a terse version of her original autobiographical sketch, she proceeds immediately to write her first "Dear Kitty" epistle (*DAF* 180ff). In just four letters she summarizes both her school and her social life of the spring of 1942 and ends with a beautiful transition: an evening stroll with her father, during which he broaches to her the subject of hiding and all the drastic changes which that move will entail.

After an entry about the July 3 graduation exercises in the Jewish Theater — soon to be the round-up place for tens of thousands of Amsterdam Jews — Anne gives a gripping description of her consternation when Margot received her call to report for a labor camp, and of the family's quick decision to go into hiding right then and there. Otto Frank made only very minor changes in this captivating account for the printed version of the *Diary* (version **c**), but he substituted the conversational term "*onderduiken*" ("to duck under [water]") for the rather stilted "*schuilen*" ("to take shelter"). Moreover, in this entry (as, indeed, throughout **c**), he systematically replaced people's real names by pseudonyms, most of which Anne had devised herself for eventual publication.[22]

In revising her original diary (version **a**) Anne cut out the Swiss daydreams and other entries, which in retrospect she may have deemed somewhat frivolous, and set about consolidating and focusing her writing with amazing insight and skill. Anne's new version was apparently too sparse for her father, for he reinstated some early entries, e.g. Anne's description of her thirteenth birthday (*DAF* 177ff) and a passage of October 3, 1942 in which Anne reports her father's admonition to show more forbearance toward her mother (*DAF* 266).[23] The fascinating process of revising can only be followed in *DAF* until December 5, 1942. Then there is a year's gap since Anne's original second journal has never been found (*DAF* 61ff). Hence, for that period, we have only her revised manuscript **b** on loose sheets and Anne's vignettes about life in the back quarters, the vast majority of which were written during that same year. Anne had assigned some of them to both her version **b** of the "Diary" and her very special "Book of Tales," while others were to appear only in the latter.[24] Otto Frank augmented Anne's version **b** by including some of the vignettes Anne had not intended for the Diary (see Note 15). In doing so, he extended Anne's attempt to sketch a complete and at times humorous picture of the hiders' daily life under steadily worsening circumstances. Food is getting scarcer and scarcer, clothing worn and outgrown, and resources to provide for both via the black market are drying up. In the course of 1943, the Netherlands are "cleansed" of all Jews (*DAF* 351). The Allies bomb some selective targets in and around Amsterdam, but their counter offensive is progressing much too slowly for the hiders, although they take heart from the capitulation of Italy (*DAF* 403). Burglars enter the premises at the Prinsengracht and there are very real fears of betrayal. Cooped up under these dismal conditions, Anne continues her studies, her readings and her writings and her valiant efforts to make sense of life and to become her own person.

The new diary, a black notebook, which Anne started December 22, 1943 has been preserved (*DAF* 59, 122, and 427); so from that date there exist again three versions — the original (**a**),

Anne's rewriting (b) and the amalgamated version her father published (c) — but only until March 29, 1944. Sadly, Anne had not gotten beyond that date with her revisions by August 4, the fateful day the hide-out was raided by the authorities (see *DAF* 61ff).

On Christmas eve 1943, Anne draws up a balance sheet of her one and a half years in hiding: there is on the one hand her gratitude for still being alive and on the other her despondency at being cheated out of a normal adolescence. In her original version she writes how she is longing to do the things other teenagers do: "*fietsen, dansen, flirten*" ("to bike, to dance, to flirt") but in her sterner revised version she apparently changed that into "*fietsen, dansen, fluiten*" ("to bike, to dance, to whistle") — if indeed, her usually very regular and legible handwriting has not been misread (*DAF* 431). But there cannot be any doubt that when revising her black notebook during the late spring and early summer of 1944, only a few months after she had originally filled it with her outpourings, Anne had become very critical of her infatuation with Peter Van Daan and of her repeated *de profundis* calls on God and on the memory of her beloved grandmother. In the **b** manuscript she eliminates most of her more effusive entries of that emotional period, their essence having been sublimated in two of her tales of fiction.[25] Otto Frank reinstated the bulk of those eliminations.[26] Did he think that this mixed version made better reading in connection with the unrevised last part of Anne's "Diary?" Or did he want to preserve a stormy stage in the development of his beloved little Anne rather than allow her to present herself as the more objective and self-contained young writer she had become at such a precocious age? One can only speculate.

As it is, the middle part of Anne's "Diary," i.e., the year 1943, stands out for the balanced expository quality of her revised version. By contrast, the mixed version **c** of late December 1943 through March 1944 and the unrevised text of the last four months tell the reader a great deal about her roller coaster emotions during that fateful period of hope and despair both in her most intimate life and with regard to the progress of the war, on which her chance of survival depended. Some of the most famous Anne Frank passages

are from these last seven months, including the one expressing her
faith in the intrinsic goodness of human beings, which is now written
in her handwriting on the outside wall of her former elementary
school.[27] While that last period will be well represented by a number
of excerpts, one cannot help but miss Anne's keen, artistic
discernment, which she had used so scrupulously in the process of
rewriting.[28] Her very last entry of August 1, 1944 is therefore by no
means a climax or a well-rounded coda, but just another variation on
one of her main themes, signed with her full name, as she was wont
to do with her unrevised letters.

Because of space limitations, no samples of Anne Frank's
fairy tales and short stories will be included. They are very well
written and of great sensitivity, with an appeal to young teenagers.
The Diary, however, has captivated a world-wide readership of all
ages since it deals with the struggle for survival and growth under
dismal circumstances. Moreover, it offers a rare glimpse into the
development of a most promising woman writer whose life, like that
of the millions for whom she stands, was snuffed out so tragically and
wantonly.

This author has felt a deepening sense of admiration, as she
pored over *The Diary*, an admiration for Anne's exceptional honesty
and directness, for her genuine spirituality, and for her cheerful
readiness to work seriously and assiduously, both on herself and on
her writing.

NOTES to the Introduction

1. *De Dagboeken van Anne Frank* ("The Critical Edition"), 1-5.
Since by and large the English translation of the Critical Edition is proving
less than satisfactory, the present author has made her own translations for
this essay. References to the corresponding pages of the English version of
the Critical Edition will be made throughout and marked as *DAF*, for the
convenience of the reader.

2. The present author grew up in similar circumstances in the same neighborhood, was acquainted with the Franks, and shared many of their experiences. She was even aware of the fact that Otto Frank was more involved in the upbringing of his daughters than any other refugee father she knew in those years.

3. Grandmother Holländer died in January 1942. Anne was particularly fond of her and often mentions her lovingly in her *Diary* (e.g., *DAF* 190, 435, 447, 508).

4. The present author bicycled with Margot to the same Wednesday afternoon classes.

5. In the "river district," i.e., the then new part of South Amsterdam, all streets and squares were named after Dutch rivers and waterways. Traditionally, neighborhoods in Dutch towns are named after rivers, painters, poets, composers, explorers, statesmen, etc., which can be quite helpful in finding a particular street.

6. *DAF* 18, and Anne's "Diary" entry for July 8, 1942 *DAF* 208 ff. For a more comprehensive historical overview, see chapters 2 and 3 in Jacob Presser, *Ondergang: De vervolging en verdelging van het Nederlands Jodendom 1940-1945* (The Hague: Staatsdrukkerij, 1965). This study is also available in English (see bibliography).

7. See also Anne's first "Diary" entries of June 12 and June 14, 1942 (*DAF* 177ff).

8. The Van Pels family included a son, Peter, almost a year younger than Margot. Dentist Friedrich Pfeffer moved in November 17, 1942 and shared Anne's little room thereafter (*DAF* 16 and 303ff).

9. For more details, see Lindwer. The six women interviewed in this book, including "Lies" to whose plight Anne had devoted her diary entry of November 27, 1943 all survived the ordeal of several concentration camps and had been in contact with Anne in Westerbork, Auschwitz and/or Bergen-Belsen. Lindwer made a gripping television documentary of the interviews. An English translation of Lindwer's book, by Alison Meersschaert, has recently been published (see bibliography).

10. My translation. A longer excerpt of this letter appears in *DAF* 64.

11. A translation of Romein's article is reprinted in full in *DAF* 67ff.

12. She was the wife of Jan Romein and herself a historian.

13. Bashkirtseff, the daughter of a wealthy and noble Russian family, spent most of her formative years in Western Europe and wrote her journal in French. It was translated into English by Mary S. Serrano (New York: Dutton, 1919).

14. The Hague: Staatsuitgeverij; Amsterdam: Bert Bakker, 1986. The English edition (Doubleday, 1989), mentioned in Note 1, and referred to throughout, is a translation of this critical edition.

15. Such as the struggle for "The Best Little Table" (*DAF* 367ff); "The Communal Duty of the Day: Potato Peeling" (*DAF* 395ff), and some descriptions of the daily hiding routine like "As the Clock Strikes Half Past Eight..." (*DAF* 401ff).

16. The German version was published in 1950 by Lambert Schneider in Heidelberg, and the English version, *The Diary of a Young Girl*, in 1952 by Doubleday in London and New York (trans. by B.M. Mooyaart-Doubleday). Both of these versions have an entry for August 3, 1943 in which Anne describes humorously how the back quarters were infested with cat fleas and the hiders, stiff after a year's confinement, lacked the agility to catch them, and another entry for April 15, 1944 dealing with a great commotion, since Peter had forgotten to unbolt the front door, so that the office staff had to break their way into the building. Both entries are missing in the original Dutch edition. A passage dealing with Anne's desire before she went into hiding to touch her girlfriend's breasts is cut out of the Dutch version but can be read in German and English at the end of a long entry dated January 5, 1944. There are a few more omissions in the Dutch edition.

17. Otto Frank's side of the controversy is explained in chapter 6 ("The Play") of *DAF*, while Meyer Levin poignantly recounts his disappointment and distress in the autobiographical book, *The Obsession* (1973).

18. See e.g., Ruth Wisse in the *New York Times Book Review* (July 2, 1989); Judith Thurman in *The New Yorker* 65 (December 18, 1989), 116-20; and Robert S. Wistrich in the *Times Literary Supplement* (April 13, 1990), 393.

19. For more details see *The Diary of Anne Frank*, dramatized by Frances Goodrich and Albert Hackett, Acting Edition (New York: Dramatists Play Service Inc., 1958).

20. *DAF* speaks of 15 to 16 million copies of the *Diary* in more than three dozen languages. An excellent source of secondary materials on Anne Frank's impact is D. Poupard and J.E. Person, eds. *Twentieth-Century Literary Criticism* 17 (1985), 98-122. After a short overview of Anne Frank's life and works, there are excerpts of some 20 topical articles, essays and reviews by scholars and writers from different countries, starting with Jan Romein's tribute of 1946, followed by Annie Romein-Verschoor's and Eleanor Roosevelt's introductions and Meyer-Levin's review, all mentioned above. The collection includes excerpts from Ann Birstein's and Alfred Kazin's sensitive introduction to *The Works of Anne Frank* (1959). (Besides the "Diary," this Doubleday edition contains some of the fables, reminiscences, essays and short stories written by Anne Frank while in hiding.) Furthermore, there are selections from essays by Lies Goslar Pick (=Hannah Pick-Goslar) and by Otto Frank, excerpts from a polemic by the psychologist Bruno Bettelheim and from a Freudian literary analysis of the "Diary" by John Berryman. The compilation closes with extracts from Stefan Kanfer's most appreciative review of Anne's "Tales from the Secret Annex" published in 1983 followed by an additional annotated bibliography.

21. The series carried the name of its heroine, *Joop Ter Heul*, and is referred to several times in Anne's diary (e.g., *DAF* 240, 260, and 267). Mirjam Pressler, the German translator of the Critical Edition, first established this connection (*DAF* 223 note).

22. *DAF* 60ff. The first names of Anne, Margot, Peter and Miep were kept, but for example Van Pels became Van Daan, Jan Gies became Henk Van Santen, and the dentist's name was changed from Pfeffer to Dussel.

23. But Otto Frank did omit much of Anne's defiant reaction to this admonition. There are many such examples of editing, prompted by paternal solicitude or vanity! As to the latter: Otto eliminated Anne's repeated remarks in both versions dealing with the poor Dutch of her elders, and with her offer that in return for his help with French and other school subjects she would work with him to improve his Dutch (e.g., *DAF* 233 and 246).

24. The Dutch edition of *Anne Frank's Tales from the Secret Annex* (op. cit.) shows on its cover the meticulous "Table of Contents" that Anne had lovingly written for her *Verhaaltjes, en gebeurtenissen uit het Achterhuis* (Amsterdam: Bert Bakker, 1986). The book contains not only vignettes but also fantasies, fables, short stories and the first chapters of an unfinished novel, entitled "Cady's Life."

25. "The Guardian Angel," dated February 22, 1944 deals with the solace a young girl finds in the living memory of her beloved grandmother. "Happiness," dated March 12, 1944 describes a very meaningful first relationship between a lonesome girl and an equally friendless boy (*Anne Frank's Tales from the Secret Annex*, 42-44 and 141-45).

26. E.g. *DAF* 489-96, 499-501, 505-14, 540-56. On the other hand, he cut out a rather feminist entry from the unrevised last part of Anne's "Diary" (*DAF* 678).

27. See the end of Anne's entry for July 15, 1944 (*DAF* 694).

28. See Judith Thurman's *New Yorker* review of *DAF* mentioned above. Thurman gives Anne high marks for her meticulous revisions and calls her a "strong, fluent and truthful writer...with a gift for detachment like the young Jane Austen's" (117).

Translation by B.M. Mooyaart-Doubleday, annotated by Laureen Nussbaum[1]

From *ANNE FRANK, THE DIARY OF A YOUNG GIRL,*

by Anne Frank. Copyright 1952 by Otto H. Frank. Used by permission of Doubleday, a division of Bantam Doubleday Dell Publishing Group, Inc.

Saturday, June 20, 1942

I haven't written for a few days, because I wanted first of all to think about my diary. It's an odd idea for someone like me to keep a diary; not only because I have never done so before, but because it seems to me that neither I — nor for that matter anyone else — will be interested in the unbosomings *[outpourings]* of a thirteen-year-old schoolgirl. Still, what does that matter? I want to write, but more than that, I want to bring out all kinds of things that lie buried deep in my heart.

There is a saying that "paper is more patient than man;" it came back to me on one of my slightly melancholy days, while I sat chin in hand, feeling too bored and limp even to make up my mind whether to go out or stay at home. Yes, there is no doubt that paper is patient and as I don't intend to show this cardboard-covered notebook, bearing the proud name of "diary," to anyone, unless I find a real friend, boy or girl, probably nobody cares. And now I come to the root of the matter, the reason for my starting a diary: it is that I have no such real friend.

Let me put it more clearly, since no one will believe that a girl of thirteen feels herself quite alone in the world, nor is it so. I have darling parents and a sister of sixteen. I know about thirty people whom one might call friends — I have strings of boy friends *[admirers]*, anxious to catch a glimpse of me and who, failing that, peep at me through mirrors in class. I have relations, aunts and uncles, who are darlings too, a good home, no — I don't seem to lack

anything, save "the" friend. But it's the same with all my friends, just
fun and joking, nothing more. I can never bring myself to talk of
anything outside the common round. We don't seem to be able to get
any closer, that is the root of the trouble. Perhaps I lack confidence
[a way of sharing trust] but anyway, there it is, a stubborn fact and
I don't seem to be able to do anything about it.

Hence, this diary. In order to enhance in my mind's eye the
picture of the friend for whom I have waited so long, I don't want to
set down a series of bald facts in a diary like most people do, but
want this diary itself to be my friend, and I shall call my friend Kitty
[...]

Sunday morning, July 5, 1942

Dear Kitty,

Our examination results were announced in the Jewish
Theater last Friday. I couldn't have hoped for better. My report is not
at all bad, I had one *vix satis*, a five *[D]* for algebra, two sixes *[C's]*,
and the rest were all sevens or eights *[B/C's or B's]*. They were
certainly pleased at home, although over the question of marks my
parents are quite different from most. They don't care a bit whether
my reports are good or bad as long as I'm well and happy, and not
too cheeky: then the rest will come by itself. I am just the opposite.
I don't want to be a bad pupil *[poor student]*; I should really have
stayed in the seventh form in the Montessori School, but was accepted
for the Jewish Secondary. When all the Jewish children had to go to
Jewish schools, the headmaster took Lies and me conditionally after
a bit of persuasion. He relied on us to do our best and I don't want
to let him down. My sister Margot has her report too, brilliant as
usual. [...] Daddy has been at home a lot lately, as there is nothing
for him to do at business *[in the office]*, it must be rotten to feel so
superfluous. Mr. Koophuis has taken over Travies and Mr. Kraler the
firm Kolen & Co. When we walked across our little square together
a few days ago, Daddy began to talk of us going into hiding. I asked
him why on earth he was beginning to talk of that already. "Yes,
Anne," he said, "you know that we have been taking food, clothes,

furniture to other people for more than a year now. We don't want our belongings to be seized by the Germans, but we certainly don't want to fall into their clutches ourselves. So we shall disappear of our own accord and not wait until they come and fetch us."

"But, Daddy, when would it be?" He spoke so seriously that I grew very anxious.

"Don't you worry about it, we shall arrange everything. Make the most of your carefree young life while you can." That was all. Oh, may the fulfillment of these somber words remain far distant yet!

Yours, Anne

Wednesday, July 8, 1942

Dear Kitty,

Years seem to have passed between Sunday and now. So much has happened, it is just as if the whole world had turned upside down. But I am still alive, Kitty, and that is the main thing, Daddy says.

Yes, I'm still alive, indeed, but don't ask where or how. You wouldn't understand a word, so I will begin by telling you what happened on Sunday afternoon. At three o'clock [...] someone rang the front doorbell. [...] A bit later, Margot appeared at the kitchen door looking very excited. "The S.S. [German political police] have sent a call-up notice for Daddy," she whispered. "Mummy has gone to see Mr. Van Daan already." (Van Daan is a friend who works with Daddy in the business.) It was a great shock to me, a call-up; everyone knows what that means. I picture concentration camps and lonely cells — should we allow him to be doomed to this? "Of course he won't go," declared Margot, while we waited together. "Mummy has gone to the Van Daans to discuss whether we should move into our hiding place tomorrow. The Van Daans are going with us, so we shall be seven in all." Silence. [...] in our bedroom, Margot told me that the call-up was not for Daddy but for her. I was more frightened than ever and began to cry. Margot is sixteen; would they really take girls of that age away alone? But thank goodness she won't go,

Mummy had said so herself; that must be what Daddy meant when he talked about us going into hiding.

Into hiding — where would we go, in a town or the country, in a house or a cottage, when, how, where...?

These were questions I was not allowed to ask, but I couldn't get them out of my mind. Margot and I began to pack some of our most vital belongings into a school satchel. The first thing I put in was this diary, then hair curlers, handkerchiefs, schoolbooks, a comb, old letters. [...]

At five o'clock Daddy finally arrived, and we phoned Mr. Koophuis to ask if he could come around in the evening. Van Daan went and fetched Miep. Miep has been in the business with Daddy since 1933 and has become a close friend, likewise her brand-new husband, Henk. Miep came and took some shoes, dresses, coats, underwear, and stockings away in her bag, promising to return in the evening. Then silence fell on the house; not one of us felt like eating anything, it was still hot and everything was very strange. [...] I was dog-tired and although I knew that it would be my last night in my own bed, I fell asleep immediately and didn't wake up until Mummy called me at five-thirty the next morning. Luckily it was not so hot as Sunday; warm rain fell steadily all day. We put on heaps of clothes as if we were going to the North Pole, the sole reason being to take clothes with us. No Jew in our situation would have dreamed of going out with a suitcase full of clothing. I had on two vests, three pairs of pants *[panties]*, a dress, on top of that a skirt, jacket, summer coat, two pairs of stockings, lace-up shoes, woolly cap, scarf and still more; I was nearly stifled before we started, but no one inquired about that.

Margot filled her satchel with schoolbooks, fetched her bicycle, and rode off behind Miep, into the unknown, as far as I was concerned. [...] At seven-thirty the door closed behind us. Moortje, my little cat, was the only creature to whom I said farewell. She would have a good home with the neighbors. [...]

Yours, Anne

Thursday, July 9, 1942

Dear Kitty,

So we walked in the pouring rain, Daddy, Mummy, and I, each with a school satchel and shopping bag filled to the brim with all kinds of things [...].

We got sympathetic looks from people on their way to work. You could see by their faces how sorry they were they couldn't offer us a lift; the gaudy yellow star spoke for itself.

Only when we were on the road *[in the street]* did Mummy and Daddy begin to tell me bits and pieces about the plan. For months as many of our goods and chattels and necessities of life as possible had been sent away [...]. The plan had had to be speeded up ten days because of the call-up, so our quarters would not be so well organized, but we had to make the best of it. The hiding place itself would be in the building where Daddy has his office. It will be hard for outsiders to understand, but I shall explain [...]. Daddy didn't have many people working for him: Mr. Kraler, Koophuis, Miep, and Elli Vossen, a twenty-three-year-old typist, who all knew of our arrival.

[The warehouse crew had not been told anything. Anne proceeds with a precise description of the premises; the warehouse on the street level, the offices one flight up. From there in the middle of the house, another flight of stairs takes you to a little corridor, which has two doors, one leading to more storage space in the front of the building, the other to the back quarters, the "Secret Annexe."]

No one would ever guess that there would be so many rooms hidden behind that plain gray door. There's a little step in front of that door and then you are inside. [...] On the left a tiny passage brings you into a room which was to become the Frank family's bed-sitting-room, next door a smaller room, study and bedroom for the two young ladies of the family. On the right a little room without windows containing the washbasin and a small W.C. compartment [...]. If you go up the next flight of stairs and open the door, you are simply amazed that there could be such a big light room in such an old house by the canal. There is a gas stove in this room (thanks to the fact that it was used as a laboratory) and a sink. This is now the kitchen [and also the bedroom] for the Van Daan couple, besides being general living and dining room [...].

A tiny little corridor room will become Peter Van Daan's apartment. Then [...] there is a large attic. So there you are, I've introduced you to the whole of our beautiful "Secret Annexe."

Yours, Anne

Saturday, July 11, 1942

Dear Kitty,

[...] I expect you will be interested to hear what it feels like to "disappear;" well, all I can say is that I don't know myself yet. I don't think that I shall ever feel really at home in this house, but that does not mean that I loathe it here, it is more like being on vacation in a very peculiar boardinghouse. Rather mad idea, perhaps, but that is how it strikes me. The "Secret Annexe" is an ideal hiding place. Although it leans to one side and is damp, you'd never find such a comfortable hiding place anywhere in Amsterdam, no, perhaps not even in the whole of Holland. Our little room looked very bare at first with nothing on the walls; but thanks to Daddy who had brought my film-star collection and picture postcards on beforehand, and with the aid of paste pot and brush, I have transformed the walls into one gigantic picture. This makes it look much more cheerful, and, when the Van Daans come, we'll get some wood from the attic, and make a few little cupboards for the walls and other odds and ends to make it look more lively.

[...] The four of us went down to the private office yesterday evening and turned on the *{English}* radio. I was so terribly frightened that someone might hear it that I simply begged Daddy to come upstairs with me. Mummy understood how I felt and came too. We are very nervous in other ways, too, that the neighbors might hear us or see something going on. We made curtains straight away on the first day. Really one can hardly call them curtains, they are just light, loose strips of material, all different shapes, quality, and pattern, which Daddy and I sewed together in a most unprofessional way. These works of art are fixed in position with drawing pins *[thumbtacks]*, not to come down until we emerge from here.

There are some large business premises on the right of us, and on the left a furniture workshop; there is no one there after working hours but even so, sounds could travel through the walls. We have forbidden Margot to cough at night, although she has a bad cold, and make her swallow large doses of codeine. I am looking for*ward to* Tuesday when the Van Daans arrive; it will be much more fun and not so quiet. It is the silence that frightens me so in the evenings and at night. I wish like anything that one of our protectors could sleep here at night. I can't tell you how oppressive it is *never* to be able to go outdoors, also I'm very afraid that we shall be discovered and be shot. That is not exactly a pleasant prospect. We have to whisper and tread lightly during the day, otherwise the people in the warehouse might hear us.

Someone is calling me.

Yours, Anne

Friday, August 21, 1942

Dear Kitty,

The entrance to our hiding place has now been properly concealed. Mr.Kraler thought it would be better to put a cupboard in front of our door [...], but of course it had to be a movable cupboard that can open like a door.

Mr. Vossen made the whole thing. We had already let him into the secret and he can't do enough to help. [...]

I'm not working much at present; I'm giving myself holidays until September. Then Daddy is going to give me lessons; it's shocking how much I have forgotten already. There is little change in our life here. Mr. Van Daan and I usually manage to upset each other; it's just the opposite with Margot whom he likes very much. Mummy sometimes treats me just like a baby, which I can't bear. Otherwise things are going better. I still don't like Peter any *[better]*, he is so boring; he flops lazily on his bed half the time, does a bit of carpentry, and then goes back for another snooze. What a fool! [...]

Yours, Anne

Monday, September 28, 1942

Dear Kitty,

[...] Somehow or other, we got onto the subject of Pim's (Daddy's nickname) extreme modesty *[selflessness]*. Even the most stupid people have to admit this about Daddy. Suddenly Mrs. Van Daan says, "I too, have an unassuming nature, more so than my husband." Did you ever!

[A full-fledged brawl develops.]

Mrs. Van Daan was scarlet by this time. Mummy calm and cool as a cucumber. People who blush get so hot and excited, it is quite a handicap in such a situation. [...] Mrs. Van Daan: "But, Mrs. Frank, I don't understand you; I'm so very modest and retiring, how can you think of calling me anything else?" Mummy: "I did not say you were exactly forward, but no one could say you had a retiring disposition." Mrs. Van Daan: "Let us get this matter cleared up, once and for all. I'd like to know in what way I am pushing? I know one thing, if I didn't look after myself *{around here}*, I'd soon be starving."

This absurd remark in self-defense just made Mummy rock with laughter. That irritated Mrs. Van Daan, who added a string of German-Dutch, Dutch-German expressions, until she became completely tongue-tied; then she rose from her chair and was about to leave the room.

Suddenly her eye fell on me. [...] I was shaking my head sorrowfully — not on purpose, but quite involuntarily, for I had been following the conversation so closely.

Mrs. Van Daan turned round and began to reel off a lot of harsh German, common, and ill-mannered, just like a coarse, red-faced fishwife — it was a marvelous sight. If I could draw, I'd have liked to catch her like this; it was a scream, such a stupid, foolish little person! [...]

Yours, Anne

Thursday, October 1, 1942

Dear Kitty,

[...] Now and then Peter comes out of his shell and can be quite funny. We have one thing in common, from which everyone usually gets a lot of amusement: we both love dressing up. He appeared in one of Mrs. Van Daan's very narrow dresses and I put on his suit. He wore a hat and I a cap. The grownups were doubled up with laughter and we enjoyed ourselves as much as they did. [...]

Yours, Anne

Friday, October 9, 1942

Dear Kitty,

I've only got dismal and depressing news for you today. Our many Jewish friends are being taken away by the dozen. These people are treated by the Gestapo [German secret police] without a shred of decency, being loaded into cattle trucks and sent to Westerbork, the big Jewish camp in Drente [a Dutch province]. Westerbork sounds terrible: only one washing cubicle for a hundred people and not nearly enough lavatories. There is no separate accommodation. Men, women, and children all sleep together. One hears of frightful immorality because of this; and a lot of the women, and even girls, who stay there any length of time, are expecting babies.

It is impossible to escape; most of the people in the camp are branded as inmates by their shaven heads and many also by their Jewish appearance *[features]*.

If it is as bad as this in Holland, whatever will it be like in the distant and barbarous regions they are sent to? We assume that most of them are murdered. The English radio speaks of their being gassed.

Perhaps that is the quickest way to die. I feel terribly upset. [...]

Yours, Anne

Saturday, November 7, 1942

Dear Kitty,

Mummy is frightfully irritable, and that always seems to herald unpleasantness for me. Is it just chance that Daddy and Mummy never rebuke Margot [...]?

[...] It's obvious that Mummy would stick up for Margot; she and Margot always do back each other up. I'm so used to that that I'm utterly indifferent to both Mummy's jawing and Margot's moods.

I love them; but only because they are Mummy and Margot. With Daddy it's different. If he holds Margot up as an example *[If he favors Margot]*, approves of what she does, praises and caresses her, then something gnaws at me inside, because I adore Daddy. He is the one I look up to. I don't love anyone in the world but him.

[...] I'm not jealous of Margot, never have been. I don't envy her good looks *[intelligence]* and her beauty. It is only that I long for Daddy's real love: not only as his child, but for me — Anne, myself *[the person I am]*.

I cling to Daddy because it is only through him that I am able to retain the remnant of family feeling. Daddy doesn't understand that I need to give vent to my feelings over Mummy sometimes. He doesn't want to talk about it; he simply avoids anything which might lead to remarks about Mummy's failings. Just the same, Mummy and her failings are something I find harder to bear than anything else. [...] I can't always be drawing attention to her untidiness, her sarcasm, and her lack of sweetness, neither can I believe that I'm always in the wrong. [...]

Sometimes I believe that God wants to try me, both now and later on; I must become good through my own efforts, without examples and without good advice. Then later on I shall be all the stronger. [...]

My treatment varies so much. *[There is no consistency in the way I am being treated].* One day Anne is so sensible and is allowed to know everything; and the next day I hear that Anne is just a silly little goat, who doesn't know anything at all and imagines that she's learned a wonderful lot from books. I'm not the baby and the spoiled darling any more, to be laughed at, whatever she does. I have my own views, plans, and ideas, though I can't put them into words yet. Oh, so many things bubble up inside me as I lie in bed, having to put up with people I'm fed up with, who always misinterpret my intentions. That's why in the end I always come back to my diary. That is where I start and finish, because Kitty is always patient. I'll promise her that I shall persevere, in spite of everything, and find my own way through it all, and swallow my tears. I only wish I could see the results already or occasionally receive encouragement from someone who loves me [...]

Yours, Anne

Monday, November 9, 1942

Dear Kitty,
Yesterday was Peter's birthday, he was sixteen. He had some nice presents.
[...] The biggest surprise came from Mr. Van Daan when, at one o'clock, he announced that the British had landed in Tunis, Algiers, Casablanca, and Oran. [...] There is certainly reason for optimism. Stalingrad, the Russian town which they've already been defending for three months, still hasn't fallen into German hands. [...]

Yours, Anne

Tuesday, November 10, 1942

Dear Kitty,
Great news — we want to take in an eighth person. Yes, really! We've always thought that there was quite enough room and food for one more. We were only afraid of giving Koophuis and Kraler more trouble. But now that the appalling stories we hear about the Jews are getting even worse, Daddy got hold of *[sounded out]* the two people who had to decide, and they thought it was an excellent plan. "It is just as dangerous for seven as for eight," they said and quite rightly. When this was settled, we ran through our circle of

friends, trying to think of a single person who would fit in well with
our "family." [...] We chose a dentist called Albert Dussel, whose
wife was fortunate enough to be out of the country when war broke
out. He is known to be quiet, and [...] a congenial person. Miep
knows him too, so she will be able to make arrangements for him to
join us. If he comes, he will have to sleep in my room instead of
Margot, who will use the camp bed [in our parents' room].

Yours, Anne

Thursday, November 19, 1942

Dear Kitty,

Dussel is a very nice man, just as we all had imagined. Of
course he thought it was alright to share my little room.

Quite honestly I'm not so keen that a stranger should use my
things, but one must be prepared to make some sacrifices for a good
cause, so I shall make my little offering with a good will. "If we can
save someone, then everything else is of secondary importance," says
Daddy, and he is absolutely right. [...]

Dussel has told us a lot about the outside world, which we
have missed for so long now. He had very sad news. Countless
friends and acquaintances have gone to a terrible fate. Evening after
evening the green and gray army lorries trundle past. The Germans
ring at every front door to inquire if there are any Jews living in the
house.

[...] Often they go around with lists, and only ring when they
know they can get a good haul. [...] In the evening when it's dark,
I often see rows of good, innocent people accompanied by crying
children, walking on and on, in {the} charge of a couple of these
chaps, bullied and knocked about until they almost drop. No one is
spared — old people, babies, expectant mothers, the sick — each and
all join in the march of death.

[...] I feel wicked [bad] sleeping in a warm bed, while my
dearest friends have been knocked down or have fallen into a gutter
somewhere out in the cold night. I get frightened when I think of
close friends who have now been delivered into the hands [are now

at the mercy] of the cruelest brutes that walk the earth. And all because they are Jews!

Yours, Anne

Saturday, November 28, 1942

Dear Kitty,

[...] It was always said about Mr. Dussel that he could get on wonderfully with children and that he loved them all. Now he shows himself in his true colors; a stodgy, old-fashioned disciplinarian, and preacher of long, drawn-out sermons on manners. As I have the unusual good fortune(!) to share my bedroom — alas, a small one — with His Lordship, and as I'm generally considered to be the most badly behaved of the three young people, I have a lot to put up with [...].

Honestly, you needn't think it's easy to be the "badly brought-up" central figure of a hypercritical family in hiding *[censorious family of hiders]*. When I lie in bed at night and think over the many sins and shortcomings attributed to me, I get so confused by it all that I either laugh or cry: it depends what sort of mood I am in. [...]

Yours, Anne

Thursday, December 10, 1942

Dear Kitty,

[...] Dussel has opened his dental practice. For the fun of it, I must tell you about his first patient *[consultation]*. [...] Mrs. Van Daan was the first to face the ordeal. She went and sat on a chair in the middle of the room. Dussel began to unpack his case in an awfully important way, asked for some eau de cologne as a disinfectant and vaseline to take the place of wax.

He looked in Mrs. Van Daan's mouth and found two teeth which, when touched, just made her crumple up as if she was going to pass out, uttering incoherent cries of pain. After a lengthy examination (in Mrs. Van Daan's case *[perception]* lasting in actual

fact not more than two minutes) Dussel began to scrape away at one
of the holes. But, no fear — it was out of the question — the patient
flung her arms and legs about wildly in all directions until at one
point Dussel let go of the scraper — that remained stuck in Mrs. Van
Daan's tooth.

     Then the fat was really in the fire! She cried (as far as it was
possible with such an instrument in one's mouth), tried to pull the
thing our of her mouth, and only succeeded in pushing it further in.
Mr. Dussel stood with his hands against his sides calmly watching the
little comedy *[scene]*. The rest of the audience lost all control and
roared with laughter. It was rotten of us, because I for one am quite
sure that I should have screamed even louder. After much turning,
kicking, screaming, and calling out, she got the instrument free at
last, and Mr. Dussel went on with his work, as if nothing had
happened!

     This he did so quickly that Mrs. Van Daan didn't have time
to start any fresh tricks. But he'd never had so much help in all his
life before. Two assistants are pretty useful: Van Daan and I
performed our duties well. The whole scene looked like a picture
from the Middle Ages entitled "A Quack at Work." [...]

                                                          Yours, Anne

                                              Friday, February 5, 1943

Dear Kitty,
     [...] Margot and Peter aren't a bit what you would call
"young," they are both so staid and quiet. I show up terribly against
them and am always hearing, "You don't find Margot and Peter doing
that — why don't you follow their example?" I simply loathe it. I
might tell you I don't want to be in the least like Margot. She is
much too soft and passive for my liking and allows everyone to talk
her around, and gives in about everything. I want to be a stronger
character! [...]
     The atmosphere at table is usually strained, though luckily the
outbursts are sometimes checked by "the soup eaters"! The "soup

eaters" are the people from the office who come in and are served with a cup of soup. [...]

Yours, Anne

Saturday, March 27, 1943

Dear Kitty,

[...] Rauter, one of the German big shots [the highest S.S. and police chief in the Netherlands], has made a speech. "All Jews must be out of the German-occupied *[Germanic]* countries before July 1. Between April 1 and May 1 the province of Utrecht must be cleaned out (as if Jews were cockroaches). Between May 1 and June 1 the provinces of North and South Holland." These wretched people are sent to filthy slaughterhouses like a herd of sick, neglected cattle. [...]

Yours, Anne

Friday, April 2, 1943

Dear Kitty,

Oh dear: I've got another terrible black mark against my name. I was lying in bed yesterday evening waiting for Daddy to come and say my prayers with me, and wish me good night, when Mummy came into my room, sat on my bed and asked very nicely: "Anne, Daddy can't come yet, shall I say your prayers with you tonight?" "No, Mummy," I answered.

Mummy got up, paused by my bed for a moment, and walked slowly towards the door. Suddenly she turned around, and with a distorted look on her face said, "I don't want to be cross, love cannot be forced." There were tears in her eyes as she left the room.

I lay still in bed, feeling at once that I had been horrible to push her away so rudely. But I knew too that I couldn't have answered differently. *{To pray with her in spite of myself would have been sheer hypocrisy.}* It simply wouldn't work. I felt sorry for Mummy; very, very sorry, because I had seen for the first time in my life that she minds my coldness. I saw the look of sorrow on her face when she spoke of love not being *[which cannot be]* forced. It is hard to speak the truth, and yet it is the truth: she herself has pushed me away, her tactless remarks and her crude jokes, which I don't find at all funny *[about things that are no joking matter to me]*, have now made me insensitive to any love from her side. Just as I shrink at her hard words, so did her heart when she realized that the love between us was gone. She cried half the night and hardly slept at all. [...]

They expect me to apologize; but this is something I can't apologize for because I spoke the truth and Mummy will have to know it sooner or later anyway. [...]

Yours, Anne

Tuesday, April 27, 1943

Dear Kitty,

Such quarrels that the whole house thunders! Mummy and I, the Van Daans and Daddy, Mummy and Mrs. Van Daan, everyone is angry with everyone else. Nice atmosphere, isn't it? Anne's usual list of failings has been brought out again and fully ventilated. [...]

Yours, Anne

Sunday, July 11, 1943

Dear Kitty,

[...] Elli gives Margot and me a lot of office work; it makes us both feel quite important and is a great help to her. Anyone can file away correspondence and write in the sales book, but we take special pains.

Miep is just like a pack mule, she fetches and carries so much. Almost every day she manages to get hold of some vegetables for us and brings everything in shopping bags on her bicycle. We always long for Saturdays when our books come. Just like little children receiving a present.

Ordinary people simply don't know what books mean to us, shut up here *[in our confinement]*. Reading, learning, and the radio are our amusements *[only diversions]*.

Yours, Anne

Monday, July 19, 1943

Dear Kitty,

North Amsterdam was very heavily bombed on Sunday. The destruction seems to be terrible. Whole streets lie in ruins, and it will take a long time before all the people are dug out. Up till now there are two hundred dead and countless wounded; the hospitals are crammed. You hear of children lost in the smoldering ruins, looking for their parents. I shudder when I recall the dull droning rumble in the distance, which for us marked the approaching destruction.

Yours, Anne

Monday, July 26, 1943

Dear Kitty,

[...] Wonderful news, such as we have not heard for months, perhaps in all the war years. "Mussolini has resigned, the King of Italy has taken over the government." We jumped for joy. After the terrible day [of bombardments] yesterday, at last something good again and — hope. Hope for it to end, hope for peace. [...]

Yours, Anne

Tuesday, August 10, 1943

Dear Kitty,

New idea. I talk more to myself than to others at mealtimes, which is to be recommended for two reasons. Firstly, because everyone is happy if I don't chatter the whole time, and secondly, I needn't get annoyed about other people's opinions *[judgment]*. I don't think my opinions are stupid and the others do; so it is better to keep them to myself. I do just the same if I have to eat something that I simply can't stand. I put my plate in front of me and pretend it is something delicious, look at it as little as possible, and before I know where I am, it is gone. When I get up in the morning, also a very unpleasant process, I jump out of bed thinking to myself: "You'll be back in a second," go to the window, take down the blackout, sniff at the crack of the window until I feel a bit of fresh air, and I'm awake. The bed is turned down *[aired]* as quickly as possible and then the temptation is removed. Do you know what Mummy calls this sort of thing? "The Art of Living" — that's an odd expression. *[Don't you think that is a droll expression?]* [...]

Yours, Anne

Friday, October 29, 1943

Dear Kitty,

There have been resounding rows again between Mr. and Mrs. Van Daan. It came about like this: as I have already told you, the Van Daans are at the end of their money. One day, some time ago now, Koophuis spoke about a furrier with whom he was on good terms; this gave Van Daan the idea of selling his wife's fur coat. It's a fur coat made from rabbit skins, and she has worn it seventeen years. He got 325 florins for it — an enormous sum. However, Mrs. Van Daan wanted to keep the money to buy new clothes after the war, and it took some doing before Mr. Van Daan made it clear to her that the money was urgently needed for the household.

The yells and screams, stamping and abuse — you can't possibly imagine it! It was frightening. My family stood at the bottom of the stairs, holding their breath, ready if necessary to drag them apart! All this shouting and weeping and nervous tension are so unsettling and such a strain [...].

[...] My nerves often get the better of me: it is especially on Sundays that I feel rotten. The atmosphere is so oppressive, and sleepy and as heavy as lead. You don't hear a single bird singing outside, and a deadly close silence hangs everywhere, catching hold of me as if it will drag me down deep into an underworld.

At such times Daddy, Mummy, and Margot leave me cold. I wander from one room to another, downstairs and up again, feeling like a songbird whose wings have been clipped *[brutally plucked out]* and who is hurling himself *[fluttering]* in utter darkness against the bars of his *{narrow}* cage. "Go outside, laugh, and take a breath of fresh air," a voice cries within me, but I don't even feel a response any more; I go and lie on the divan and sleep, to make the time pass more quickly, and the stillness and the terrible fear, because there is no way of killing them.

Yours, Anne

Monday evening, November 8, 1943

Dear Kitty,

If you were to read my pile of letters one after another, you would certainly be struck by the many different moods in which they are written. It annoys me that I am so dependent on the atmosphere *[moods]* here, but I'm certainly not the only one — we all find it the same. [...] At the moment, as you've probably noticed, I'm going through a spell of being depressed. I really couldn't tell you why it is, but I believe it's just because I'm a coward, and that's what I keep bumping up against.

This evening, while Elli was still here, there was a long, loud, penetrating ring at the door. I turned white at once, got a tummy-ache and heart palpitations, all from fear. At night, when I'm in bed, I see myself alone in a dungeon, without Mummy and Daddy. Sometimes I wander by the roadside or our "Secret Annexe" is on fire, or they come to take us away at night. I see everything as if it is actually taking place, and this gives me the feeling that it may all happen to me very soon! Miep often says she envies us for possessing such tranquillity *[for our time out]* here. That may be true, but she is not thinking about all our fears. I simply can't imagine that the world will ever be normal for us again. I do talk about "after the war," but then it is only a castle in the air, something that will never really happen. If I think back to our old house *[home]*, my girl friends, the fun at school, it is just as if another person lived *[experienced]* it all, not me.

I see the eight of us with our "Secret Annexe" as if we were a little piece of blue heaven *[patch of blue sky]*, surrounded by heavy black rain clouds. The round, clearly defined spot where we stand is still safe, but the clouds gather more closely about us and the circle which separates us from the approaching danger closes more and more tightly. Now we are so surrounded by danger and darkness that we bump against each other, as we search desperately for a means of escape. We all look down below, where people are fighting each other, we look above, where it is quiet and beautiful, and meanwhile we are cut off by the great dark mass, which will not let us go upwards, but which stands before us as an impenetrable wall; it tries to crush us, but cannot do so yet. I can only cry and implore: "Oh, if only the black circle could recede and open the way for us!"

Yours, Anne

Saturday, November 27, 1943

Dear Kitty,

Yesterday evening, before I fell asleep, who should suddenly appear before my eyes but Lies!

I saw her in front of me, clothed in rags, her face thin and worn. Her eyes were very big and she looked so sadly and reproachfully at me that I could read in her eyes: "Oh, Anne, why have you deserted me? Help, oh, help me, rescue me from this hell!"

And I cannot help her, I can only look on, how others suffer and die, and can only pray to God to send her back to us.

I just saw Lies, no one else, and now I understand. I misjudged her and was too young to understand her difficulties. [...] It was horrid of me to treat her as I did, and now she looked at me, oh so helplessly, with her pale face and imploring eyes. If only I could help her!

Oh, God, that I should have all I could wish for and that she should be seized by such terrible fate. I am not more virtuous than she *[She was at least as religious as I am]*, she, too, wanted to do what is right, why should I be chosen to live and she probably to die? What was the difference between us? Why are we so far from each other now?

Quite honestly, I haven't thought about her for months, yes, almost for a year. Not completely forgotten her, but still I had never thought about her like this, until I saw her before me in all her misery. [...]

Good Lord, defend *[support]* her, so that at least she is not alone. Oh, if only You could tell her that I think lovingly of her and with sympathy *[compassion]*, perhaps that would give her greater endurance.

I must not go on thinking about it, because I don't get any further. I only keep seeing her great big eyes, and cannot free myself from them. I wonder if Lies has real faith in herself *[is really religious on her own terms]*, and not only *[by]* what has been thrust upon her?

I don't even know, I never took the trouble to ask her!

Lies, Lies, if only I could take you away *{from where you are now}*, if only I could let you share all the things I enjoy. It is too late now, I can't help, or repair the wrong I have done. But I shall never forget her again and I shall always pray for her.

Yours, Anne

Friday, December 24, 1943

Dear Kitty,

I have previously written about how much we *[all of us]* are affected by atmospheres *[moods]* here, and I think that in my own case this trouble is getting much worse lately.

[...] Today, for example, Mrs. Koophuis comes and tells us about her daughter Corry's hockey club, canoe trips, theatrical performances, and friends. I don't think I'm jealous of Corry, but I couldn't help feeling a great longing to have lots of fun myself for once, and to laugh until my tummy aches. Especially at this time of the year with all the holidays for Christmas and the New Year, and we are stuck here like outcasts. Still, I really ought not to write this, because it seems ungrateful and I've certainly been exaggerating. But still, whatever you think of me, I can't keep everything to myself, so I'll remind you of my opening words — "Paper is patient."

When someone comes in from outside, with the wind in their clothes and the cold on their faces, then I could bury my head in the blankets to stop myself thinking: "When will we *{again}* be granted the privilege of smelling fresh air?" And because I must not bury my head in the blankets, but the reverse — I must keep my head high and be brave, these thoughts will come *{all the same}*, not once, but oh, countless times. Believe me, if you have been shut up *[confined]* for a year and a half, it can get too much for you some days. In spite of all justice *[fairness]* and thankfulness, you can't crush *[repress]* your feelings. Cycling, dancing, whistling, looking out into the world, feeling young, to know that I'm free — that's what I long for; still, I mustn't show it, because I sometimes think *[for just think]* if all eight of us began to pity ourselves, or went about with discontented faces, where would that lead us? [...]

Yours, Anne

Sunday, January 2, 1944

Dear Kitty,

This morning when I had nothing to do I turned over some of the pages of my diary and several times I came across letters dealing with the subject "Mummy" in such a hotheaded way that I was quite shocked [...].

[...] I used to be furious with Mummy, and still am sometimes. It's true that she doesn't understand me, but I don't understand her either. She did love me *[very much]* and *[hence]* she was tender, but as she landed in so many unpleasant situations through me, and was nervous and irritable because of other worries and difficulties, it is certainly understandable that she snapped at me.

I took it much too seriously, was offended, and was rude and aggravating to Mummy, which, in turn, made her unhappy. So it was really a matter of unpleasantness and misery rebounding all the time. It wasn't nice for either of us, but it is passing.

I just didn't want to see all this, and pitied myself very much; but that, too, is understandable. Those violent outbursts on paper were only giving vent to anger which in a normal life could have been worked off by stamping my feet a couple of times in a locked room, or calling Mummy names behind her back.

The period when I caused Mummy to shed tears *[of tearfully condemning Mummy]* is over. I have grown wiser and Mummy's nerves are not so much on edge. I usually keep my mouth shut if I get annoyed, and so does she, so we appear to get on much better together. *{Yet,}* I can't really love Mummy in a dependent childlike way *[with the devotion of a child]* — I just don't have that feeling.

I soothe my conscience now with the thought that it is better for hard words to be on paper than that Mummy should carry them in her heart.

Yours, Anne

Thursday, January 6, 1944

Dear Kitty,

My longing to talk to someone became so intense that somehow or other I took it into my head to choose Peter.

Sometimes *[In the past]* if I've been upstairs into Peter's room during the day, it always struck me as very snug, but because Peter is so retiring and would never turn anyone out who became a nuisance, I never dared stay long [...]. I tried to think of an excuse to stay in his room and get him talking, without it being too noticeable *[obvious]*, and my chance came yesterday. Peter has a *{sudden}* mania for crossword puzzles *[at the moment]* and hardly does anything else. I helped him with them and we soon sat opposite each other at his little table [...].

[...] When I lay in bed and thought over the whole situation, I found it far from encouraging, and the idea that I should beg for Peter's patronage *[favors]* was simply repellent. [...yet] I have made up my mind to go and sit with Peter more often and to get him talking somehow or other.

[...] Don't think I'm in love with Peter — not a bit of it! If the Van Daans had had a daughter instead of a son, I should have tried to make friends with her too. [...]

Yours, Anne

Wednesday, January 12, 1944

Dear Kitty,

[...] I have a craze for dancing and ballet at the moment, and practice dance steps every evening diligently. I have made a supermodern dance frock from a light blue petticoat edged with lace [...]. I tried in vain to convert my gym shoes into real ballet shoes. My stiff limbs are well on the way to becoming supple again like they used to be. [...]

Yours, Anne

Saturday, January 15, 1944

Dear Kitty,

There is no point in telling you every time the exact details of our rows and arguments. Let it suffice to tell you that we have divided up a great many things, such as butter and meat, and that we fry our own potatoes. [...]

Mummy's birthday is rapidly approaching. [...] Mummy has expressed the wish — one which cannot come true just now — not to *{have to}* see the Van Daans for a fortnight.

I keep asking myself, whether one would have trouble in the long run, whoever one shared the house with *{whether in the long run one should not get into arguments with anybody one shares the house with for such a long period of time}*. Or did we strike it extra unlucky? Are most people so selfish and stingy then? I think it's all to the good to have learned a bit about human beings *{here}*, but now

I think I've learned enough. [...] I also believe that if I stay here for very long I shall grow into a dried-up *[old]* beanstalk. And I did so want to grow into a real young woman *[to be just a real teenager]*!

Yours, Anne

Friday, January 28, 1944

Dear Kitty,

[...] One favorite subject of Koophuis's and Henk's is that of people in hiding and in the underground movement. [...] There are a great number of organizations [...], which forge identity cards, supply money to people "underground" *[to hiders]*, find hiding places for people and work for young men in hiding, and it is amazing how much noble, unselfish work these people are doing, risking their own lives to help and save others. Our helpers are a very good example. They have pulled us through up till now and we hope they will bring us safely to dry land. Otherwise, they will have to share the same fate as all the many others who are being searched for *[have to share the fate of all those who are being hunted]*. Never have we heard *one* word of *[referring to]* the burden which we certainly must be to them, never has *one* of them complained of all the trouble we give.

They all come upstairs every day, talk to the men about business and politics, to the women about food and war time difficulties *[burdens]*, and about newspapers and books with the children. They put on the brightest possible faces *[try to look as cheerful as possible]*, bring flowers and presents for birthdays and bank holidays, are always ready to help and do all they can. That is something we must never forget; although others may show heroism in the war or against the Germans, our helpers display heroism in their cheerfulness and affection. [...]

Yours, Anne

Saturday, February 12, 1944

Dear Kitty,

The sun is shining, the sky is a deep blue, there is a lovely
breeze and I'm longing — so longing — for everything. To talk, for
freedom, for friends, to be alone. And I do so long... to cry! I feel
as if I'm going to burst, and I know that it would get better with
crying; but I can't, I'm restless, I go from one room to the other,
breathe through the crack of a closed window, feel my heart beating,
as if it is saying, "Can't you satisfy my longings at last?"

I believe that it's spring within me, I feel that spring is
awakening, I feel it in my whole body and soul. It is an effort to
behave normally, I feel utterly confused, don't know what to read,
what to write, what to do, I only know that I am longing...!

Yours, Anne

Wednesday, February 23, 1944

Dear Kitty,

[...] Nearly every morning I go to the attic where Peter works
to blow the stuffy air out of my lungs. From my favorite spot on the
floor I look up at the blue sky and the bare chestnut tree, on whose
branches little raindrops shine, appearing like silver, and at the sea
gulls and the other birds as they glide on the wind *[at the bare
chestnut tree with glistening little raindrops along its branches, at the
gulls and the other birds, that seem to be made out of silver as they
skim by]*.

He stood with his head against a thick beam, and I sat down.
We breathed the fresh air, looked outside, and both felt that the spell
should not be broken by words. We remained like this *[kept looking
outside]* for a long time, and when he had to go up to the loft to chop
wood, I knew that he was a nice fellow *[is a great guy]*. [...] I
watched him from where I stood, he was obviously doing his best *{to
chop well in order}* to show off his strength. But I looked out of the
open window too, over a large area of Amsterdam, over all the roofs
and on to the horizon, which was such a pale blue that it was hard to

see the dividing line. "As long as this exists," I thought, "and I may live to see it, this sunshine, the cloudless skies, while this lasts, I cannot be unhappy."

The best remedy for those who are afraid, lonely, or unhappy is to go outside, somewhere where they can be quite alone with the heavens [the sky], nature, and God. Because only then does one feel that all is as it should be and that God wishes to see people happy, amidst the simple beauty of nature. [...]

Oh, who knows, perhaps it won't be long before I can share this overwhelming feeling of bliss with someone who feels the way I do about it.

Yours, Anne

Sunday, March 12, 1944

Dear Kitty,

I can't seem to sit still lately; I run upstairs and down and then back again. I love talking to Peter, but I'm always afraid of being a nuisance. He has told me a bit about the past, about his parents and about himself. It's not half enough though and I ask myself why it is that I always long for more. He used to think I was unbearable: and I returned the compliment; now I have changed my opinion, has he changed his [does that mean he must have changed his] too?

I think so; still it doesn't necessarily mean that we shall become great friends, although as far as I am concerned it would make the time here [the hiding experience] much more bearable. [...]

Margot is very sweet and would like me to trust her [to be my confidante], but still I can't tell her everything. She's a darling, she's good and pretty, but she lacks the nonchalance for conducting deep discussions; she takes me so seriously, much too seriously, and then thinks about her queer little sister for a long time afterwards, looks searchingly at me, at every word I say and keeps on thinking: "Is this just a joke or does she really mean it?" I think that's because we are together the whole day long and that if I trusted someone completely, then I shouldn't want them hanging around me *[That is what you get, if you are constantly together; I could not possibly have my confidante around me]* all the time.

When shall I finally untangle my thoughts, when shall I find peace and rest within myself again?

Yours, Anne

Thursday, March 16, 1944

Dear Kitty,

The weather is lovely, superb, I can't describe it; I'm going up to the attic in a minute.

Now I know why I'm so much more restless than Peter. He has his own room where he can work, dream, think, and sleep. I am shoved about from one corner to another. I hardly spend any time in my "double" room *[I am hardly ever by myself in the room I share]*, and yet that is something I long for so much. That is the reason too why I so frequently escape to the attic. There, and with you, I can be myself for a while, just a little while. [...]

But, still, the brightest spot of all is that at least I can write down my thoughts and feelings, otherwise I would be absolutely stifled *[completely suffocate]*! I wonder what Peter thinks about all these things? I keep hoping that I can talk about it to him *[we can discuss them]* one day. [...]

Yours, Anne

Wednesday, March 29, 1944

Dear Kitty,

Bolkestein, an M.P. *[Last night, secretary Bolkestein]* was speaking on the Dutch News from London, and he said that they ought to *[will]* make a collection of diaries and letters after the war. Of course, they all made a rush at my diary immediately. Just imagine how interesting it would be if I were to publish a romance *[novel]* of the "Secret Annexe." The title alone would be enough to make people think it was a detective story.

But seriously [...], although I tell you a lot [...], you only know very little of our lives [...] and I would need to keep on writing the whole day if I were to tell you everything in detail. People have to line up for vegetables and all kinds of other things; doctors are unable to visit the sick, because if they turn their backs on their cars for a moment, they are stolen; burglaries and thefts abound [...]. No one dares to leave his house [unoccupied] for five minutes, because if you go, your things go too. [...] Electric clocks in the streets are dismantled, public telephones are pulled to pieces — down to the last thread *[are disassembled to the last wire]*. Morale among the population can't be good, the weekly rations are not enough to last for two days [...]. The invasion is a long time in coming, and the men have to go to Germany. The children are ill or undernourished, everyone is wearing old clothes and old shoes *[miserable clothes and shoes]*.

There's one good thing in the midst of it all, which is that as the food gets worse and the measures against the people more severe, so sabotage against the authorities steadily increases. The people in the food *{rationing}* offices, the police, officials, they all either work with their fellow citizens and help them or they tell tales on them *[denounce them]* and have them sent to prison. Fortunately, only a small percentage of Dutch people are on the wrong side.

Yours, Anne

Tuesday, April 4, 1944

Dear Kitty,

For a long time I haven't had any idea of what I was working for any more; the end of the war is so terribly far away, so unreal, like a fairy tale. [...]

[Then one night Anne went through a catharsis.]

And now it's all over. I must work, so as not to be a fool, to get on, to become a journalist, because that's what I want! I know that I *can* write, a couple of my stories are good, my descriptions of the "Secret Annexe" are humorous, there's a lot in my diary that speaks, but — whether I have real talent remains to be seen.

[...] I'm the best and the sharpest critic of my own work. I know myself what is and what is not well written. Anyone who doesn't write doesn't know how wonderful it is [...].

I want to get on; I can't imagine that I would have to lead the same sort of life as Mummy or Mrs. Van Daan and all the women who do their work and are then forgotten. I must have something besides a husband and children, something that I can devote myself to!

I want to go on living even after my death! And therefore I am grateful to God for giving me this gift, this possibility of developing myself and of writing, of expressing all that is within me.

I can shake off everything if I write *[By writing I unburden myself]*, my sorrows disappear, my courage is reborn. [...]

So I go on again with fresh courage; I think I shall succeed, because I want to write!

Yours, Anne

Tuesday, April 11, 1944

Dear Kitty,

My head throbs, I honestly don't know where to begin. [...]

Peter heard two loud bangs on the landing, ran downstairs, and saw there was a large plank out of the left half of the door *{to the warehouse}*. He dashed upstairs, warned the "Home Guard" of the family, and the four of them proceeded downstairs. When they entered the warehouse, the burglars were in the act of enlarging the hole. Without further thought Van Daan shouted: "Police!"

A few hurried steps outside, and the burglars had fled. In order to avoid the hole being noticed by the police, the plank was *{again}* put against it, but a good hard kick sent it flying to the ground. The men were perplexed at such impudence, and both Van Daan and Peter felt *{an impulse to}* murder welling up within them; Van Daan beat *{forcefully}* on the ground with a chopper, and all was quiet again. Once more they wanted to put the plank in front of the hole. Disturbance! A married couple outside shone a torch *[flashlight]* through the opening, lighting up the whole warehouse. "Hell!" muttered one of the men, and now they switched over from their role of police to that of burglars. The four of them sneaked upstairs, Peter quickly opened the doors and windows of the kitchen and private office, flung the telephone on the floor, and finally the four of them landed behind the swinging cupboard. [...]

The married couple with the torch would probably have warned the police: it was Sunday evening, Easter Sunday, no one at the office Easter Monday, so none of us could budge until Tuesday morning. Think of it *[Imagine]*, waiting in such fear for two nights and a day! No one had anything to suggest *[We refrained from imagining anything]*, so we simply sat there in pitch-darkness [...], talked in whispers, and at every creak one heard "Sh! Sh!"

It turned half past ten, eleven, but not a sound; Daddy and Van Daan joined us in turns.Then a quarter past eleven, a bustle and noise downstairs. Everyone's breath was audible, otherwise no one moved. Footsteps in the house, in the private office, kitchen, then...on our staircase. No one breathed audibly now, footsteps on our staircase, then a rattling of the swinging cupboard. This moment is indescribable. "Now we are lost!" I said, and could see us all being taken away by the Gestapo that very night. Twice they rattled at the cupboard, then there was nothing *[then something dropped]*, the footsteps withdrew, we were saved so far. A shiver seemed to pass from one to another, I heard someone's teeth chattering, no one said a word.

There was not another sound in the house, but a light was burning on our landing, right in front of the cupboard. Could that be because it was a secret cupboard *[there was something mysterious about the cupboard]*? Perhaps the police had forgotten the light. Would someone come back to put it out? Tongues loosened, there was no one in the house any longer, perhaps there was someone on guard outside.

Next we did three things: we went over again *[made guesses as to]* what we supposed had happened, we trembled with fear, and we had to go to the lavatory. The buckets were in the attic, so all we had was Peter's tin wastepaper basket. [...]

Talk, whisper, fear, stink, flatulation *[flatulence]* and always someone on the pot; then try to go to sleep. However, by half past two I was so tired that I knew no more until half past three. I awoke [...and] prepared myself for the return of the police, then we'd have to say that we were in hiding; they would either be good Dutch people, then we'd be saved, or N.S.B.-ers [Dutch National Socialists], then we'd have to bribe them.

"In that case, destroy *[get rid of]* the radio," sighed Mrs. Van Daan. "Yes, in the stove!" replied her husband. "If they find us, then let them find the radio as well!"

"Then they will find Anne's diary," added Daddy. "Burn it then," suggested the most terrified member of the party. This, and when the police rattled the cupboard door, were my worst moments. "Not my diary; if my diary goes, I go with it!" But luckily Daddy didn't answer.

[...] They wanted to call Koophuis at seven o'clock and get him to send someone around. Then they wrote down everything they wanted to tell Koophuis over the phone. The risk that the [...] guard at the door, or in the warehouse might hear the telephone was very great, but the danger of the police returning was even greater. [...]

Everything went according to plan. Koophuis was phoned [...]. Then we sat around the table again and waited for Henk or the police.

Peter had fallen asleep and Van Daan and I were lying on the floor, when we heard loud footsteps downstairs. I got up quietly: "That's Henk."

"No, no, it's the police," some of the others said.

Someone knocked at the door, Miep whistled. [...] Of course, Henk and Miep were greeted with shouts and tears. Henk mended the hole in the door with some planks, and soon went off again to inform the police of the burglary. Miep had also found a letter *[note]* under the warehouse door from the night watchman Slagter, who had noticed the *[open]* hole and *[had]* warned the police, whom he would also visit. *[Henk would also visit him.]*

[...] At eleven o'clock we sat round the table with Henk, who was back by that time, and slowly things began to be more normal and cozy again. Henk's story was as follows:

Mr. Slagter was asleep, but his wife told Henk that her husband had found *[noticed]* the hole in our door when he was doing his tour round the canals, and that he had called a policeman, who had gone through the building with him. He would be coming to see Kraler on Tuesday and would tell him more then. At the police station they knew nothing of the burglary yet, but the policeman had made a note of it at once and would come and look around on Tuesday *[but they made a note of it right away and would also send somebody by on Tuesday]*. On the way back Henk happened to meet *[stop by]* our greengrocer at *[around]* the corner and told him that the house had been broken into. "I know that," he said quite coolly *[laconically]*. "I was passing last evening with my wife and saw the hole in the door. My wife wanted to walk on, but I just had a look in with my torch; then the thieves cleared at once. To be on the safe side, I didn't ring up the police, as with you *[since in your case]* I didn't think it was the thing to do. I don't know anything, but I guess a lot."

Henk thanked him and went on. The man obviously guesses that we're here, because he always brings the potatoes during the lunch hour. Such a nice man *[great fellow]*! [...]

None of us has ever been in such danger as that night. God truly protected us; just think of it — the police at our secret cupboard, the light on right in front of it, and still we remained undiscovered.

If the invasion comes, and bombs with it, then it is each man for himself, but in this case the fear was also for *[extended to]* our good, innocent protectors. "We are saved, go on saving us!" That is all we can say.

This affair has brought quite a number of changes with it. [The house rules will be even stricter.] Kraler reproached us for our carelessness. Henk, too, said that in a case like that we must never go downstairs. We have been pointedly reminded that we are in hiding, that we are Jews in chains, chained to one spot, without any rights but with a thousand duties. We Jews mustn't show our feelings *[mustn't act upon our emotions]*, must be brave and strong, must accept all inconveniences and not grumble, must do what is within our power and trust in God. Sometime this terrible war will be over. Surely the time will come when we are people again, and not just Jews.

Who has inflicted this upon us? Who has made us Jews different from all other people? Who has allowed us to suffer so terribly up till now? It is God that has made us as we are, but it will be God, too, who will raise us up again. If we bear all this suffering and if there are still Jews left, when it is over, then Jews, instead of being doomed, will be held up as an example. Who knows, it might even be our religion from which the world and all peoples learn *{what is}* good, and for that reason and that reason only do we *{also}* have to suffer [...]. We can never become just Netherlanders, or just English, or representatives of any country for that matter, *{in addition}* we will always remain Jews, but we want to, too.

Be brave! Let us remain aware of our task and not grumble, a solution will come, God has never deserted our people. Right through the ages there have been Jews, through all the ages they have had to suffer, but it has made them strong too; the weak fall, but the strong will remain and never go under!

During that night I really felt that I had to die, I waited for the police, I was prepared, as the soldier is on the battlefield. I was eager to lay down my life for this country, but now, now *{that}* I've been saved again, now my first wish after this war is that I may become Dutch! I love the Dutch, I love this country, I love the language and want to work here. And even if I have to write to the Queen myself *[herself]*, I will not give up until I have reached my goal.

I am becoming still more independent of my parents, young as I am, I face life with more courage than Mummy [...]. I know that I am a woman, a woman with inward strength and plenty of courage. If God lets me live, I shall attain more than Mummy ever has done, I shall not remain insignificant, I shall work in the world and for mankind!

And now I know that first and foremost I shall require courage and cheerfulness!

Yours, Anne

Wednesday, May 3, 1944

Dear Kitty,

[...] As you can easily imagine we often ask ourselves here despairingly: "What, oh, what is the use of the war? Why can't people live peacefully together? Why all this destruction?"

The question is very understandable, but no one has found a satisfactory answer to it so far. [...]

I have often been downcast, but never in despair; I regard our hiding as a dangerous adventure [...]; I am still in the midst of it and can't grumble the whole day long. I have been given a lot, a happy nature *[disposition]*, a great deal of cheerfulness and strength. Every day I feel that I am developing inwardly *[my inner growth]*, that the liberation is drawing nearer and how beautiful nature is, how good the people are about me, how interesting this adventure is! Why, then, should I be in despair?

Yours, Anne

Monday, May 22, 1944

Dear Kitty,

[...] To our great horror and regret we hear that the attitude of a great many people towards us Jews has changed. We hear that there is anti-Semitism now in circles that never thought of it before. This news has affected us all very, very deeply. [...] The Christians blame the Jews for giving secrets away *[blurting out things]* to the Germans, for betraying their helpers [...].

This is all true, but one must always look at these things from both sides. Would Christians behave differently in our place? The Germans have a means of making people talk. Can a person, entirely at their mercy, whether Jew or Christian, always remain silent? *[Can anybody,whether Jew or Christian, keep silent when forced by German methods?]* Everyone knows that is practically impossible. Why, then, should people demand the impossible of the Jews?

It's being murmured in underground circles that the German Jews who emigrated to Holland and who are now in Poland may not be allowed to return here; they once had the right of asylum in Holland, but when Hitler has gone they will have to go back to Germany again.

[All this comes as a great shock to Anne, who had not experienced any anti-Semitism in the Netherlands and who had put great stock in the decency of the Dutch.]

I love Holland. I [...] had hoped that it might become my fatherland, and I still hope it will!

Yours, Anne

Thursday, May 25, 1944

Dear Kitty,

[...] This morning our vegetable man was picked up for having two Jews in his house. It's a great blow for us, not only [for....] those poor Jews [....], but it's terrible for the man himself.

[...] This man is a great loss to us too. The girls [Miep and Elli] can't and are not allowed to *[mustn't]* haul along our share of potatoes, so the only thing to do is to eat less. [...] We are going to be hungry, but anything is better than *[no privations are as bad as]* being discovered.

Yours, Anne

Friday, May 26, 1944

Dear Kitty,

[...] I feel so miserable, I haven't felt like this for months, even after the burglary I didn't feel so utterly broken [...]. The vegetable man, the Jewish question, which is being discussed minutely *[at length]* over the whole house, the invasion delay, the bad food, the strain, the miserable atmosphere, my disappointment in Peter [...].

[...] The affair of the vegetable man has made {*all of*} us more nervous *[fearful]*. You hear "shh, shh," from all sides again, and we're being quieter over everything *[everything is done in a more hushed way]*. The police forced the door there, so they could do it to us too! If one day we too should...no, I mustn't write it, but I can't put the question out of my mind today. On the contrary, all the fear I've already been through seems to face me again in all its frightfulness.

[...] Again and again I ask myself, would it not have been better for all of us if we had not gone into hiding, and if we were dead now and not going through all this misery, especially as we shouldn't be running our protectors into danger *[imperil our protectors]* any more. But we all recoil from these thoughts too, for we still love life; we haven't yet forgotten the voice of nature, we still hope, hope about *[for]* everything. I hope something will happen soon now, shooting if need be — nothing can crush us *more* than this restlessness *[anxiety]*. [...]

Yours, Anne

Tuesday, June 6, 1944

Dear Kitty,

"This is D-Day," came the announcement over the English news [...].

According to German news, English parachute troops have landed on the French coast [...].

English broadcast in German, Dutch, French and other languages at ten o'clock: "The invasion has begun!" [...]

Great commotion in the "Secret Annexe"! [...] Could we be granted victory this year, 1944? We don't know yet, but hope is revived within us *[is revitalizing us]*; it gives us fresh courage, and makes us strong again. [...] Now more than ever we must clench our teeth and not cry out. France, Russia, Italy and Germany, too, can all cry out and give vent to their misery, but we haven't the right to do that yet!

Oh, Kitty, the best part of the invasion is that I have the feeling that friends are approaching. [...] Perhaps, Margot says, I may yet be able to go back to school in September or October.

Yours, Anne

Tuesday, June 13, 1944

Dear Kitty,

Another birthday has gone by, so now I'm fifteen. I received quite a lot of presents. [...]

There's still excellent news of the invasion, in spite of wretched weather, countless gales, heavy rains, and high seas. [...]

Yours, Anne

Thursday, July 6, 1944

Dear Kitty,

It strikes fear to my heart when Peter talks of later *{possibly}* being a criminal, or of gambling *[speculating]*; although it's meant as a joke, of course, it gives me the feeling that he is afraid of his own weakness *{of character}*. Again and again I hear from both Margot and Peter: "Yes, if I was as strong and plucky as you are, if I always stuck to what I wanted, if I had such a persistent energy, yes then...!"

[...] Quite honestly, I can't imagine how anyone can say: "I'm weak," and then remain so. After all, if you know it, why not fight against it, why not try to train your character? The answer was: "Because it is so much easier not to!" This reply rather discouraged me. Easy? [...]

How can I make it clear to him that what appears easy and attractive will drag him down [...]?

[...] I can't understand people who don't like *{to}* work, yet that isn't the case with Peter; he just hasn't got a fixed goal to aim at *[a sense of purpose]*, and he thinks he's too stupid and too inferior to achieve anything. [...] He has no religion, scoffs at Jesus Christ, and swears, using the name of God; although I'm not orthodox either, it hurts me every time [...]. It isn't the fear of God but the upholding of one's own honor and conscience. How noble and good everyone could be if, every evening before falling asleep, they were to recall to their minds the events of the whole day and consider exactly what has been good and bad *{in their own conduct}*. Then, without realizing it *[automatically]*, you try to improve yourself [...]; of course, you achieve quite a lot in the course of time. Anyone can do this, it costs nothing and is certainly very helpful. [...]

Yours, Anne

Saturday, July 15, 1944

Dear Kitty,

[...] It's really a wonder *[great miracle]*, that I haven't dropped all my ideals *[given up on all of my expectations]*, because they seem so absurd and impossible to carry out. Yet I keep *[cling to]* them, because in spite of everything I still believe that people are really good at heart. I simply cannot build up my hopes on a foundation consisting of confusion, misery, and death. I see the world gradually being turned into a wilderness, I hear the ever approaching thunder, which will destroy us too, I can feel *{empathy with}* the sufferings of millions *{of people}* and yet, if I look up in the heavens *[sky]*, I think that it will all come right, that this cruelty too will end, and that peace and tranquillity will return again *{to the world}*.

In the meantime, I must uphold my ideals *[ideas]*, for perhaps the time will come when I shall be able to carry them out *[in times to come, they can be carried out]* .

Yours, Anne

Friday, July 21, 1944

Dear Kitty,

Now I am getting really hopeful, now things are going well at last. Yes, really, they are going well! Super news! An attempt has been made on Hitler's life and not even by Jewish communists or English capitalists [...], but by a proud *[pure-bred Aryan]* German general [...]. The Führer's life was saved by Divine Providence [...].

[...] I don't want to anticipate the glorious events too soon. Still [...] I can't help it; the prospect that I may be sitting on school benches next October makes me feel far too cheerful to be logical! Oh, dearie me, hadn't I just told you that I didn't want to be too hopeful *[to rush to conclusions]*? Forgive me, they have not given me the name "little bundle of contradictions" all for nothing!

Yours, Anne

Tuesday, August 1, 1944

Dear Kitty,

"Little bundle of contradictions." That's how I ended my last letter and that's how I'm going to begin this one. "A little bundle of contradictions," can you tell me exactly what that is? What does contradiction mean? Like so many words, it can mean two things, contradiction from without and contradiction from within.

The first is the ordinary "not giving in easily, always knowing best, getting in the last word," *enfin*, all the unpleasant qualities for which I'm renowned. The second nobody knows about, that's my own secret.

I've already told you before that I have, as it were, a dual personality. One half embodies my exuberant cheerfulness, making fun of everything, my high-spiritedness, and above all, the way I take everything light*{ly}*. This includes not taking offense at a flirtation, a kiss, an embrace, a dirty *[off color]* joke. This side is usually lying in wait and pushes away the other which is much better *[more beautiful]*, deeper and purer. You must realize that no one knows Anne's better *[more beautiful]* side and that's why most people find me so insufferable.

Certainly, I'm a giddy clown for one afternoon, but then everyone's had enough of me for another month. [...] My lighter superficial side will always be too quick for the deeper side of me and that's why it will always win. You can't imagine how often I've already tried to push this Anne away, to cripple her, to hide her, because after all, she's only half of what's called Anne: but it doesn't work and I know, too, why it doesn't work.

I'm awfully scared that everyone who knows me as I always am will discover that I have another side, a finer and better side. I'm afraid they'll laugh at me, think I'm ridiculous and sentimental, not take me seriously. [...]

Therefore, the nice Anne is never present in company, has not appeared one single time so far, but almost always predominates when we are alone *[I'm by myself]*. I know exactly how I'd like to be [...]. But, alas, I'm only like that for myself. [...] I am guided by the pure Anne within, but outside I'm nothing but a frolicsome little goat who's broken loose.

A voice sobs within me: "There you are, that's what's become of you: you're uncharitable, you look supercilious and peevish *[negative opinions, mocking or disturbed faces]*, people {who} dislike you, and all {that} because you won't listen to the advice given {to} you by your own better half." Oh, I would like to listen, but it doesn't work; if I'm quiet and serious, everyone thinks it's a new comedy and then I have to get out of it by turning it into a joke *[to save the situation with a little joke]*, not to mention my own family, who are sure to think I'm ill, make me swallow pills for headaches and nerves, feel my neck and my head to see whether I'm running a temperature, ask if I'm constipated and criticize me for being in a bad mood. I can't keep that up: if I'm watched to that extent, I start by getting snappy, then unhappy, and finally twist my heart round again, so that the bad is on the outside and the good is on the inside and keep on trying to find a way of becoming what I would so {very much} like to be, and what I could be, if...there weren't any other people living in the world.

Yours, Anne *[Anne M. Frank]*

NOTE to the Translation

1. Translation by B.M. Mooyaart-Doubleday (New York: Doubleday, 1952), with the permission of the publisher who holds the English language rights to Anne's *Diary*.

The present author was not granted Doubleday's permission to use her own new translations of considerable excerpts (a labor of love especially performed for the present anthology) both from Anne Frank's *Het Achterhuis* and from *De Dagboeken van Anne Frank* ("The Critical Edition"). The Doubleday-version features some very beautiful passages, notably in the entry for November 8, 1943 and in that for April 11, 1944 which do justice to Anne's use of language. But by and large, the Doubleday translation tends to be too literal, which makes for awkward reading, and quite often it is downright wrong.

Some passages could simply not be used because they do not convey what Anne has written. As an example can serve the witty play on words which closes her letter of November 28, 1942 — the flip side of her final entry for August 1, 1944. Anne writes: "Then I fall asleep with the weird feeling that I want to be different from what I am or that I am different from the way I want to be, may be also that I behave differently from the way I want to or from the way I am. Oh dear, now I am confusing you, too; forgive me, but I do not like to cross things out and to throw away a sheet of paper is prohibited in times of extreme paper shortage." Anne certainly confused the Doubleday translator, whose version of the first sentence makes no sense at all: "Then I fall asleep with the stupid feeling of wishing to be different from what I am or from what I want to be; perhaps to behave differently from the way I want to behave, or do behave." For obvious reasons, this garbled passage was not included in the present anthology. Another example: in her letter of July 15, 1944 Anne reviews her relationship with her parents, stating that her father is the only one who has confidence in her and who gives her the feeling that she is a sensible person. Yet she feels she cannot share her innermost thoughts with him, because he does not confide to her what is on his mind. The Doubleday translation reads: "...Daddy's the only one who has always taken me into his confidence..." only to continue a few sentences later that she cannot confide in her Dad, because he has told her so little about himself. So, here is another passage that could not be used. Yet, it is frustrating to keep excluding text samples because the translation does not do justice to the writer's intent. To forestall this, closer translations in italics between italicized square brackets are introduced where the Doubleday-version simply would not do, and words they have skipped altogether are rendered in italics between italicized braces.

Two examples will serve as an illustration. The penultimate paragraph of Anne's letter of January 2, 1944, which deals with her feelings toward her mother, reads in the Doubleday-version: "The period when I caused Mummy to shed tears is over. I have grown wiser and Mummy's nerves are not so much on edge..." Instead, the passage should read: "The period of tearfully condemning mother is over. I have grown wiser and mother's nerves are not so much on edge..." In the present excerpts, the reader will have to contend with "The period when I caused Mummy to shed tears *[of tearfully condemning Mummy]* is over. I have grown wiser..."

Again, the last paragraph in Anne's last entry, reads in the Doubleday-version: "A voice sobs within me: 'There you are, that's what's become of you: you're uncharitable, you look supercilious and peevish, people dislike you, and all because you won't listen to the advice given you by your own better half.'" More accurately, this passage should read: "A voice is sobbing within me: 'There you are, that's what has become of you: negative opinions, mocking and disturbed faces, people disliking you, and all of that only because you won't listen to the good advice from your own better half.'" Instead, the reader of these excerpts will be faced with: "A voice sobs within me: 'There you are, that's what's become of you: you're uncharitable, you look supercilious and peevish *[negative opinions, mocking or disturbed faces]*, people *{who}* dislike you, and all *{of that}* because you won't listen to the advice given *{to}* you by your own better half.'"

These parenthetic additions will make the reading somewhat cumbersome and the present author and editor apologize for them, but we feel that they are necessary to do justice to the text that Anne really wrote. The few instances where italicized brackets surround a word or two of plain text indicate that Doubleday added these words to the original. These instances will not pose any problem nor will, we trust, the few editorial remarks rendered in the usual fashion in plain brackets and plain text. They are meant to tide the reader over between text passages, where Anne's original wording would have been too detailed for the present purpose.

According to a letter from the president of the ANNE FRANK-Fonds in Basel, Switzerland, dated February 10, 1992 a new edition of the *Diary of Anne Frank* is soon to be published by Doubleday, an edition which will also take versions of Anne's entries into account that have so far only been published in the *Critical Edition*. We were barred from using specimens of the *b* version for the present anthology. It is to be hoped that Doubleday will thoroughly revise and improve their translation of all the "Diary" texts in fairness to the writer Anne Frank, who, unlike what the Doubleday-version would have us believe, e.g. very consciously replaced "Daddy" and "Mummy" by "father" and "mother," and who made sure to write the equivalent of "many" or "a great deal" instead of colloquial expressions like "a whole lot." In addition, many a British term ought to be replaced by standard American words (such as "flashlight" for "torch"). Since the "Diary" in the less than satisfactory Doubleday-edition of 1952 has already had such an impact as a human document on the English-speaking world, how much more will the new edition have to offer, if it does also justice to Anne Frank, the *writer*.

Bibliography

Primary Works

Frank, Anne. *Het Achterhuis: Dagboekbrieven 12 Juni 1942-1 Augustus 1944*. Introd. Annie Romein-Verschoor. Amsterdam: Contact, 1947.

_____. *De Dagboeken van Anne Frank* ("Critical Edition"). Eds. David Barnouw & Gerrold van der Stroom. The Hague: Staatsuitgeverij; Amsterdam: Bert Bakker, 1986.

_____. *Het Achterhuis*. Ed. Mirja Pressler. Amsterdam: Bert Bakker, 1991.

Translations

_____. *The Diary of a Young Girl*. Trans. B.M. Mooyaart-Doubleday; introd. Eleanor Roosevelt. New York: Doubleday, 1952.

_____. *The Works of Anne Frank*. Trans. B.M. Mooyaart and Michel Mok; introd. Ann Birstein and Alfred Kazin. New York: Doubleday, 1959.

_____. *Anne Frank's Tales from the Secret Annex*. Trans. Michel Mok and Ralph Manheim. New York: Washington Square Press, 1983.

_____. *The Diary of Anne Frank: The Critical Edition*. Eds. David Barnouw and Gerrold van der Stroom; trans. Arnold J. Pomerans and B.M. Mooyaart-Doubleday. New York: Doubleday, 1989.

Related Works

Anne Frank Foundation. *Anne Frank in the World/De Wereld van Anne Frank*. Bi-ling. ed. Amsterdam: Bert Bakker, 1985.

Gies, Miep, and Alison Leslie Gold. *Anne Frank Remembered*. New York: Simon & Schuster, 1987.

Levin, Meyer. *The Obsession*. New York: Simon & Schuster, 1973.

Lindwer, Willy. *The Last Seven Months of Anne Frank*. Trans. Alison Meersschaert. New York: Pantheon Press, 1991.

Poupard, Dennis, and James E. Person jr., eds. "Anne Frank. 1929-1945." *Twentieth-Century Literary Criticism* 17. Detroit, MI.: Gale Research Co., 1985. 98-122.

Presser, Jacob. *The Destruction of the Dutch Jews*. 2 vols. New York: Dutton, 1969.

Roth, Philip. *The Ghost Writer*. New York: Farrar et al., 1979.

Schloss, Eva, with Evelyn Julia Kent. *Eva's Story: A Survivor's Tale by the Step-Sister of Anne Frank*. New York: St. Martin's Press, 1988.

Schnabel, Ernst. *Anne Frank: A Portrait in Courage*. Trans. R. and C. Winston. New York: Harbrace Paperback, 1958.

Steenmeyer, Anna G. Ed., with Otto Frank and Henri van Praag. *A Tribute to Anne Frank*. New York: Doubleday, 1971.

Thurman, Judith. "Not Even a Nice Girl." *The New Yorker* 65 (December 18, 1989). 116-20.

Monika van Paemel

Basil Kingstone

Monika van Paemel was born in 1945 in the village of Poesele in East Flanders. Her childhood was dreadful; her father wanted a son and her mother didn't want any children at all. In the words of her husband:

> Her parents never had much influence on her. A mother who rejected her even before birth — that is of course a fundamental trauma. A birth which dragged on for three days. A doctor who was criminally incompetent. A forceps was improvised on the spot. The newborn baby was put aside with a bleeding head wound, they thought nothing could be done about it anyway. An aunt who had herself just lost a baby, took pity on her and she stayed with this aunt's family for the first few years of her life[...] And then she was taken away from the aunt by her grandmother, the head of the clan.[1]

At the age of nine Monika contracted a brain disease from which it took her four years to recover, the first two being spent in hospital and the next two with foster parents. During this time she was educated privately, read a lot and wrote her first poetry. At fourteen she was well enough to go to a Catholic boarding school in Turnhout. She took commercial studies, but she wanted to be a journalist and writer.

In 1963 she married Theo Butzen, an electronic engineer; in 1985,[2] they had two daughters and lived in a rebuilt house on the Leie River.

Van Paemel has written poetry and short stories, essays and feminist criticism; in 1982 and 1983 she was co-editor of the annual volume of essays selected from reviews, *Kritisch Akkoord*. She has worked a great deal for radio and tv; her first radio assignment was to go to Vinkt, very near her birthplace, and record the memories of the survivors of the Nazi atrocities committed in that village in 1940. (We translate an extract about this below). She is well known, among other things, for her radio show on which women phoned in and discussed their problems. Indeed, she has been active in the women's movement for years. Carlos Alleene was presumably expressing the common perception when he called her the number one feminist among Flemish women authors (Alleene 158). What kind of feminist she is, however, needs to be defined; we will return to this later.

Her feminist and literary interests coincided in the figure of Belle van Zuylen. She translated some of Belle's letters, wrote a book about her (*Leven op afstand*), founded a Werkgroep Belle van Zuylen and became its secretary, organized a conference on her at Zuylen in 1974, and has remained concerned to see that all Belle's works and letters are translated into Dutch.

Two honors came to Monika van Paemel in 1988. Firstly, she was chosen president of the Flemish section of the PEN Club, and in that position she campaigned vigorously for author's lending rights, i.e. the introduction of a modest fee for borrowing a library book, the fee to go to the author. Secondly, her novella *De eerste steen* (The First Stone) was commissioned as the 1988 Flemish "Boekenweekprijs," that is to say, the free volume given away by bookstores to customers who buy books of a certain value during the annual week-long promotion. It is an honor to add to the prizes won by her novels.

It is with these that we shall concern ourselves here. They are: *Amazone met het blauwe voorhoofd* (Blue-fronted Parrot, 1971); *De confrontatie* (The Confrontation, 1974); *Marguerite* (1976); and *De vermaledijde vaders* (The Accursed Fathers, 1985); and *De eerste steer* (The First Stone, 1992).

Amazone has a narrator who alternately recalls scenes from her early childhood on a farm and reflects on her present situation. If the past was delightful, the present has depressing elements: she lives alone with her two children, and has a lover whom she sees briefly in one season of the year. Her comments on her present situation, her reflections on life, take the form of imaginary letters, incidents in which she finds symbolic meaning, and most notably the story of the parrot of the title, preceded by a long quotation from an encyclopedia, which we translate below.

We already see here van Paemel's basic storytelling principle: not a linear narration, but what she herself calls, in her interview with Carlos Alleene, "a piling up of stories" (Alleene 165). She gives him two reasons for not writing a linear narration. Firstly, we are constantly bombarded with information and unable to form a coherent picture out of it; in the nineteenth century, when we knew less, we did not have that problem. Secondly, a linear narrative seems authoritarian, and she does not wish to impose her vision on us. Conversely, we are warned in *Amazone* not to want to understand the book; we should rather listen to the author as an equal and co-create the book with her.

As the book piles up stories, so lyrical passages pile up images, and the opening page piles up memories: the narrator's uncle's horse defecating as it pulls her along in a cart; feeling her breasts grow; and her desire for a young German named Dietrich the moment she saw him. This young man is the addressee of the (perhaps unwritten) diary or (perhaps interior) monologue that we read. It alternates between memories and present events and reflections. The time frame is supplied by a cycle of seasons, spring to winter, which represents the cycle of love: "Spring meeting, summer reunion, fall longing" (68). And winter separation and gloom — a gloom so deep that the narrator says she goes on living only out of cowardice. She lives in permanent fear and writes to exorcize it. She writes also to correspond with the man she loves; or so the reader assumes, but this isn't certain. He cannot answer, and she says to him "more and more you become a story I'm making up, or have made up." But then, "without a goodly dose of self-deception this life wouldn't be tolerable" (80, 85).

This is only one side of her personality, however, and only one of her reactions to the world. For she also sees social injustice, the insane destructive things done by political leaders, by men of certain social classes, men with power. She also suffers because of the habit men have of trying to make a woman conform to a socially ordained pattern and to the image they find it convenient to have of her. The parrot of the title symbolizes her lifelong fight against these things. It is interesting that male animals (tomcats, the parrot) fight on her side against male humanity, and consequently they are perhaps the only male company she can put up with. Certainly she identifies with them. As a child she objected to being coddled like a pet. And when asked why she insisted on playing boys' games, she replied, "Because I'm a girl."

De confrontatie is the only novel of van Paemel's not to win a prize. It was written at Elsevier's request in a few months, to cash in on the success of *Amazone*. One may easily conclude that it must be less good, and that the problem is the experimental form. We would deny the first statement, but one could find the form perplexing; we may call it transitional. The narrator (who in this book is more specifically presented as its author) continues the musings of *Amazone*. There are, as in *Amazone*, echoes of her daily life with her two daughters. The seasons continue to reflect emotions, though they no longer provide the shape of the work. New notes are heard, however: the fact that she has published a book, and — more clearly than in *Amazone* — the fight against depression. Whereas the first novel contrasted a happy past and present gloom, this one has some pleasant days and gritty memories.

To wage the fight against depression, the author-persona not only keeps a diary, as the narrator of *Amazone* did; she invents two characters to accompany herself, two women who have been friends since their schooldays: Zoë (=life), who goes to places and meets people, and Miriam (=bitterness), who only at the end agrees to leave her apartment, and who writes a never-sent letter to a perhaps imaginary man. The reader might conclude that the women are meant to be respectively a writer and a wife and mother, since a married woman writer has to balance these two activities, and indeed van Paemel spoke of that to Alleene (163). But those are not the two women's roles; all of that is reserved to the diarist. Rather the two characters represent two possible strategies one can adopt when life hurts. Miriam defends what she thinks is her essential self by cutting off contact with life; Zoë goes out and takes the risk of establishing relationships with people, arguing that in order to live as you wish, you have to live. One may feel that neither woman is a fully realized character, but this is acceptable: they are like the figures in some Rodin sculptures who are only half freed from the marble. What is perhaps a weakness is that in the series of dialogues, monologues, letters, and reminiscences (no doubt thought rather than spoken or written) that combine with the diary to make up the novel, Zoë has a considerably larger part than Miriam.

Description of reality plays a greater part in *De confrontatie* than in *Amazone*. Two long sequences form an interlude in the middle; first Zoë describes a week's vacation in the Ardennes, and then she tells a "folk tale" for Miriam, spun around some things she saw on that vacation: a mill, a woman standing motionless by it guarding goats, and a boy in the village who looked at her with desire. It is a model of how fiction is woven from fact, and no doubt also an exercise and self-encouragement to write on the part of the author-persona. The vacation in the Ardennes is a pretty reality, but Zoë also brings herself face to face with an ugly one, namely the experience of her childhood. We have seen that van Paemel's own childhood was appalling. An abused childhood contains dreadful moments but may also have pleasant ones in between. We have said that in *Amazone*, as is understandable, the narrator tells us her pleasant memories of life as a little girl in the country. In *De confrontatie* the process of facing the other memories begins.

The task of describing the childhood traumas is given to Zoë—
again, she seems the more fully used character. We give below an
extract from this sequence. It continues with examples of her
grandmother's domination over the entire family, and culminates in
the harrowing page where Francis, the lad next door, takes her
pregnant cat from her, puts it in a sack, stomps on it, and to make
doubly sure it is dead, drowns it. This incident is perhaps
foreshadowed by the one in which Santa Claus comes to the house
with his helper Black Peter (according to Netherlandic custom, Santa
Claus rewards good children but also has his helper punish the bad
ones), both men are blind drunk, and Peter bundles a boy into a sack
and beats him with a bicycle chain.

Thus we see van Paemel starting to relive the memories of
her terrible childhood. Perhaps even to face them. A person may
keep these things from herself for many years, but she must finally
face them in order to be free of them and become herself.

Marguerite marks a further step in that direction. The story
told here, however, is not yet the central one, of her relations with
her parents; such brief hints about that as we are given imply a
history of child abuse. Her mother, as in *De confrontatie*, is a
fleeting figure called simply SHE, who rejects her and flops about all
day in her bathrobe. Her father is dismissed as a lifelong child who
is frightened of everything and lashes out in his fear, which implies
that he hits his daughter. For the moment, however, van Paemel
concentrates on her grandmother.[3]

As the reader will gather from the extract we give below, the
narrator's feelings towards her grandmother are powerful and
ambivalent. On the one hand, she hates the woman who found fault
with everything she ever did or said, had no patience with her love
of nature, and opposed her wish to become a writer. On the other
hand, she understands that her grandmother saw they had something
in common—"She was different, as I was different" (54)—and set
out to mold her into a woman capable of standing on her own two
feet. This harsh education, however, was traumatic. Grandmother
became a ghost that has to be exorcized. Let us quote a passage
where we can feel that the terrifying power of this woman is still
active in the narrative present, even though she is dead:

> She makes me and she destroys me. She takes away
> all my illusions and gives me dignity. She rejects me
> and hurts me and consoles me, all in the same
> movement. She torments me with my stupidity, she
> teases me with what I know. She knows better about
> everything and I can't stand it. Sometimes she
> shakes me awake, very roughly. But she won't let
> me alone. And it's always been that way. (52)

Matters are brought to a head by the sight, in a museum in
Arles — a city that inspires in the narrator the same mixture of strong
emotions, appreciation and fear, as her grandmother did and
does — of an old portrait that looks exactly like her. The time has
come to face this obsessive superego and deal with it. And so she
talks it out, or "writes it out."

Part of the confrontation is achieved by considering what
forces formed the grandmother, by seeing her as a woman living in
a particular age and society. She had four surviving sons and many
children who died in infancy. After years spent in childbearing, she
devoted more years to mothering the four weak sons and a weak
husband. "Never marry a man who calls you mother," she tells the
narrator. True, in later years, she takes over her husband's
construction business and makes a success of it. But by then the
pattern of furious contempt for men is set in her. It is a frozen
helpless revolt. The narrator comments:

> I think of my grandmother, I don't want to become
> like her, when all you know for certain is what you
> don't want to be (118).

By becoming a writer, the narrator can hopefully move on from the
position of a previous generation of women.

Much about this figure remains unsaid; as van Paemel herself
remarks, in one of this book's rare authorial intrusions, she had to
decide what to leave out. For example, if the narrator's father is a
frightened weakling, could it be that his powerful mother made him
that way? And if she chose his wife — all her sons, we read, shit their

pants at the thought of proposing marriage — is she responsible for the appalling choice? But the exorcism of the parents is a much bigger subject, and so it was held over until the next novel.

De vermaledijde vaders, however, is not solely about a girl's relationship with her parents. It is about the life of a narrator called Pam, from her birth through to old age; it is about wars; and it is about the history of Flanders. All these threads are interwoven constantly, so that even more than in her shorter works, this 423-page novel — her masterpiece, she says, in the sense that it is the work you have to do in order to be promoted from journeyman to master — is "a piling-up of stories." An interviewer from the Flemish weekly magazine *Knack* (March 6, 1987, 25-31) asked van Paemel whether it was a settling of accounts with her youth, a farewell to it, a feminist tract, or an anti-militaristic message. Hopefully, she replied, it was all of these things.

In so far as the novel is an account of Flanders under Nazi occupation (Pam is born just after the war, but her father joined the SS and fought on the Eastern Front), critics also frequently compared *De vermaledijde vaders* with Hugo Claus' *Het verdriet van België*, which had appeared the previous year. But, as van Paemel pointed out with some irritation, her own book was five years in the writing, and so she had not read Claus' novel before completing her own. She preferred the comparison of her work with that of Louis-Paul Boon, whom she admired.

In so far as it is a book about her father, it is about all men. But the author pointed out, in the interview with *Knack*, that it is not against them:

> That's all nonsense, of course. The book is directed against a certain type of man, who always thinks in terms of power structures and threatens you with destruction. That type I call the masters. They have to be straightened out, because the smallest child can see that otherwise everything turns out badly for all of us.

We use the word "masters" here to translate *de heren*. In the extract below we translate it as "gentlemen," but always there is that double meaning. Respectable men, men in power, act like masters, with the results we see all around us. In particular, they start wars. The message has not changed since *Amazone*.

In a sense this call for a massive change of male attitude is the most radical position a feminist could take. Yet some feminists have felt that van Paemel isn't radical, or even that she isn't a feminist. For example, she has a husband and two children. As she remarked in an interview with *De Stern* (November 2, 1976), the "Rode Vrouwen" (Red Women) of Amsterdam used to make fun of her for wearing a bra and make-up. She herself does not think feminism is a question of lifestyle, or of demonstrating about Vietnam or any other question, and advises feminists not to join a political party, for they will be a minority in it. The first wave of feminists made that mistake, she said; the second wave, of the late 1960s, knew better. They, like her, know that it is the whole body of masculine attitudes that has to be changed, and that that will take generations. Feminism is bound to be socialist, but a socialism that just cuts the cake differently is still patriarchal. A woman who succeeds in life may merely become "a second Mrs. Thatcher"[4] only concerned to protect her gains.

She says also that all writing is by definition committed, but that she has no time for commitment as a literary fashion. She does not write in order to promote a feminist position about a contemporary political problem. Such problems are transitory. She writes because she has to. By this she does not mean that writing is a therapy:

> I can't write things out of me and say "Good, it's all
> in the book, I've gotten rid of it." [...] Writing is a
> necessity for me. It helps me to live.

It does this by ensuring that the facts she tells will not make her bitter in her relations with other people.

Even without any predetermined program, *De vermaledijde vaders* calls in question the whole body of masculine attitudes. The work is in five parts. Van Paemel says (also in the *Knack* interview) that the first part is about Flanders, the country that everybody wants to keep from existing; the second part is about human relationships in which everybody wants to win; the third part is about "sex and the godmother (protectress)," and the fourth part is about destruction and resistance to it. (The opening pages of the fourth part are translated below). Thus she covers four seasons, and four stages of life. She had to write these four parts in order to write the fifth, in which her character has won through to a stage where she can be herself, and which is also about the importance of the culture one is born in.

Van Paemel's description might imply that the different themes of the novel are set out separately. They are not: they are all present in every part, indeed in every passage. In the extract we give below, for instance, the narrator's personal memories and imaginings intertwine with the account of the atrocities. The novel also constantly juxtaposes a variety of styles to suit the proliferation of characters. Thus the second part introduces two more women who are victims of male society: Elisabeth and her childhood friend, two different personalities, each with her own style. One finds also a variety of genres: fragments of essays, journalistic reportage, lyric passages, as accents standing out against the narrator's nervous modernistic style with its ellipses and sentences sometimes consisting only of one noun or noun-phrase.

These techniques, together with the non-linear narration, force the reader to react and think for himself: both to co-create the text, and to question his own opinions about the questions raised. The novel's publication, it has been said, was "one of the literary events of the 80's;"[5] its impact will be lasting.

As was the case before *De vermaledijde vaders*, Monika van Paemel's readers had to wait a long time for her latest novel, *De eerste steen*. She suggested in the above-quoted interview with *Knack* (which she gave just before visiting Israel) that her next novel might be about the Jews; she admired the sense of humour which enabled them to survive. And that is indeed the subject. The novel also reflects the tragic suicide of van Paemel's daughter. What it does not seem to be is a development of the 1988 *Boekenweekprijs* short story of the same name, which was about a misunderstood child.

The novel is about the impressions and memories of a Flemish woman named May whose personal tragedies have led her to come to Israel. She is staying in a damp little basement in Jerusalem with a Dutch Jewess named Hagar and a large group of Hagar's friends. It does not seem to be the healing experience she needs. Between these strong personalities and the cramped quarters, May feels hemmed in. Israel itself, which the group show May around, likewise aroused in her an overwhelming mixture of feelings, as our extract below shows.

Impressions of the places visited, May's reflections on the people and places, and her memories of Flanders all mingle in her mind. The remarks that van Paemel made to Carlos Alleene about non-linear narration, which we quoted earlier, apply more strongly here than ever; the reader feels keenly that constant bombardment of information which, as she said in that interview, we must endure. Her technique is taken farther than ever. Unlike *De vermaledijde vaders*, where the blocks of experience are of considerable size and the whole narration is visibly moving forward through the narrator's life, *De eerste steen* has little sense of temporal progression and the switches from present to past are frequent and abrupt.

May is constantly in two places at once. She makes free associations between something she or a friend is saying or doing now in Israel and a past event in Flanders. As May says, the past runs through the present like zebra stripes (22). She wishes it didn't. The good moments (she thinks of childhood songs) torment her because they cannot return; the bad ones will not go away. She feels unable to escape the traumas of her past: "May could not go back, she could not go on, and it was her damned duty to stay alive." The suicide of her daughter is but the most recent tragedy in a long series of "*faits accomplis* that make life unbearable if you think about it too long."

To break out of this impasse, like many others, May has come to Jerusalem. But the Israelis do not necessarily welcome people like her with open arms, for they have problems of their own.

Whether they escaped the Holocaust or were born later, in Europe or in the United States or Israel, they live in fear, either of past experiences or of the Palestinians. It is a State miraculously reborn, and a tropical paradise, but the place has been affected by religious ideals turned sour.

Add that these women also have fears particular to women: of men, and of breast cancer and menopause and all the ills that female flesh, especially, is subject to, and we will perhaps think that May is not likely to find the solution to her problems in this country. Nor does she: there is no happy ending. Indeed, it is hard to speak of an ending at all. The novel goes on till it stops, and we may feel it could have stopped, like life itself, earlier or later. However, we have cause to think May will learn to live with herself and with life, and we think so because of the importance in this novel of women as a group. Men and war occur in the novel, but they are not the enemy; indeed the idea of having an enemy is seen as wrong, the suffering individual has enough of a fight on her hands as it is. The group of women, quarrelsome though they are, provide May with support. They are indeed survivors. It is as if, now that van Paemel has faced and exorcised her individual childhood traumas through her fiction, she is free to give due prominence in it to the comfort that can be derived from the solidarity of women.

Her earlier novels echo in this one. For example, there are many memories of Constant and his wife Poldine, who are in the construction business in Antwerp and clearly correspond to Marguerite and her husband, the grandparents in *Marguerite*. There is even a parrot, who of course is an *amazone met een blauw voorhoofd*. These echoes reinforce the impression already created by the recurrence of May's memories, that existence is cyclical. For writers who cannot believe in a happy ending, this cycle is a common second-best consolation. Other topics in the book recur, and certain events also symbolize this theme. Thus when May visits Nazareth, the spot where Christ was born looks to her like a grave. A gloomy reversal, we may think, of the usual statement that out of death comes life. But then Christ did die, and was born again. At present van Paemel can give her readers this much to hang on to.

NOTES to the Introduction

We are grateful to Meulenhoff, Amsterdam, for their permission to translate extracts from the works of Monika van Paemel for this book.

1. In *Writing in Holland and Flanders* 40 (Autumn 1982) 33.

2. For most of the facts about Monika van Paemel's life, and all references to interviews with her (except Carlos Alleene's) and critical reviews of her work in newspapers and magazines, I am indebted to the "Archief en Museum voor het Vlaamse Cultuurleven" in Antwerp, which kindly allowed me access to their voluminous and valuable press cutting file on her. This file also contains the text of the radio program she prepared about the atrocities at Vinkt.

3. We are justified in equating the author and the narrator for a moment by statements Monika van Paemel has made, to the effect that her grandmother was really like that and that she herself saw the portrait, which did look like the old lady. However, she gives the grandmother she portrays the numerous progeny of the other one, who had twelve children and was "a sniveling creature." The portrait, which appears on the cover of the novel, is of one Marguerite Luchard and was painted in 1834 by Claude Jullien.

4. Margaret Thatcher, British Prime Minister in the 1980s, had a reputation for heartlessness. She once remarked: "What has feminism ever done for me?"

5. Janssens et al., 201.

Translations by Basil Kingstone

From *Amazone met het blauwe voorhoofd*[1]

"Blue-fronted parrot, Amazona aestriva.   Also called Red-Shouldered Parrot.   Central Brazil.   Amazones, Amazona, Blunt-tailed Parrots.

Amazon parrots (Amazona): overall length 26-47 cm. Plumage mostly green, marks of different colours on the head (mostly on the forehead) and on the shoulders (cf. the names of the subspecies), often red marks on the tail or a red wing mark. 26 species, 52 subspecies, including the Red-Shouldered Parrot (Amazona aestriva), often called the Blue-Fronted Parrot by dealers.

Being adapted for forest life, parrots can climb well; their flight, however, is somewhat heavy, and on open ground they waddle around clumsily. In their environment climbing is the most important skill; flight is of secondary importance. Parrots kept as pets give up flight entirely after a while, and even in large spaces they climb or run for long distances.

In their homeland parrots, like the great Aras, are kept in villages and allowed to roam free. European dealers continue to import parrots in large quantities. The birds are usually already tame when they are brought here and can already say a few words.

Unfortunately most of these parrots are condemned to live for decades without a mate, in a cage that is almost always too small.

The years of loneliness turn these birds, so cheerful and lively in their natural home, into the dull creatures we constantly see in the homes of bird 'lovers.' They sit sleepily on their perch all day and pay scant attention to what is going on around them. You will derive more pleasure from your feathered pet if he has enough room to move about, and also a mate." (From Bernhard Grzimek: *Enzyklopädie des Tierreiches* ["Encyclopedia of the Animal Kingdom"]. Zurich: Kindler Verlag, 1969. vol. 8 [Birds, 2], p. 327 ff.)

My Brazilian friend, my colorful rebel. One evening they brought you in your copper cupola, your trellised cage. It was dark and cold. And for you with your sun colors, your red vibrating eyes, it had been a day of misery and senseless commotion. The old woman who had taken care of you had passed away, her time was up, and the distant childless niece who was preparing to have her come and live with her didn't like you. For her you were just a creature. A fiery male. But in fact, my little friend, let's admit that women were all fond of you. How seductively you could fluff up your feathers, make enticing noises, or surprise them with your jet-black tongue. On men you never bestowed one friendly word. Your crest stood straight up in dislike, and how many of them did you greet in your sweet tones with affectionate nicknames like nasty man, swine, nigger and rubbish-head (especially pastors). You got into the house through a misunderstanding. They thought you were stuffed, an exotic decoration, but you sure as hell weren't dead. You stared at the electric light, at first frightened but then fearless. Oooh! you said, and then you presented yourself. Pretty Polly. A name we buried with the previous woman in your life. From now on you were Koko. Now I'm a bit sorry about that. Too late, as always. Once somebody is gone for good, when it's over, you suddenly see all the little mean things you did to them. But then it's too late. So regret is an unnecessary and uncomfortable feeling. But I refuse to bury feelings. I have earned regret and mistrust amply. The fact that I was stupid is no excuse. I know people like the back of my hand, so I should never have handed you over to them. Defiant little creature, you fought an unequal battle, your neck hairs straight out, your head pushed forward, you couldn't make it but you fought to the death rather than give in. And our romance, you knew exactly what my footsteps sounded like when I came home, you rocked impatiently against the cage door, called me affectionate names, climbed all the way up the wicker bars and snuggled your little head against me. You made wonderfully realistic kissing sounds. In the mornings you climbed up the slipped-off coverlet and into my bed. I felt your sharp claws through the blanket but I stayed asleep. You murmured in contentment, hello little Koko, cautiously tugged my hair, and then when I unexpectedly opened my eyes you went Oooh! in delight.

Nobody could ever sing such an intense Oooh! as you did and nobody ever will. It came from your whole body, all the way from your toes right up to your eyes, Oooh! But then flirting was in your blood. You ogled my fat aunt so hard you nearly fell off your perch. And jealous, you bit me once right through my sweater, I still have the scar, just because I wasn't paying you enough attention. But I loved you most of all because you showed clearly that you loved freedom and were pure of I have to do this and I mustn't do that, and even when everything was topsy turvy, even though you were locked up countless times, you remained yourself and still called them blockheads and bladderbrains no matter how self-importantly they puffed out their chests. Now I have some idea of the country you came from, and I can understand your fits of melancholy and sadly sitting staring with your beak in your feathers. The winters here are such unhappy murky seasons. The endless free forests, the obsessive beat of the music, the hotchpotch of people. Yes, I understand your longing for home. And now you're rotting in the canal. It's cold again. The dogs dragged your body around for a while. Freedom wins no respect in a bourgeois house. And finally you went in a style befitting your origins, hunger and grandeur. Over there, too, the bodies of rebels are sometimes dragged around. It isn't so strange. It's just bitter for somebody who's in love. For me you remained the red and green ambassador from open skies. Our wings are clipped too, we too can count the bars of our cage, and polish them or detest them, but deep inside you gave me an unforgettable example of how to be unbreakably yourself. You paid for it. The price is not too high if in the end, on something important, you are right. That is not just hollow words. I can still say it playfully, but also with an iron echo: "Rule wild, rule free!"

[The following passage develops the idea, which we have just seen, that other people want the narrator to fill the social role they assign her and to conform unchangingly to the image they have of her:]

Two girls run through the street. In the city. They're in blue
uniforms, but that doesn't make them shy, no. They speak to each
other in a language they know. About taut little bras, shiny stockings
and click-clack high heels. Their femininity is almost brutally forcing
its way to the surface. But they still don't know themselves. Later,
in a few years, they will know the games and may take on the
modesty and haughtiness of priestesses. If they know what it is.
Only a few in the whole group of little bluebreasts will attain
self-knowledge, a reality that climbs above itself and makes a bed a
temple. The rest sink into fat around the hips, wrinkles and fancy
cakes and children and polishes and detergents. So only a few of
them. But the possibility is in all of them. At the traffic light where
everybody comes to a halt, Els shows her photo of "him." There he
is with his cheese spread smile behind the little plastic window in her
purse. In the other part is her streetcar pass, three letters and some
movie tickets. Next to the photo she's slipped in a scented sheet of
paper. Lilies of the valley, smells good. He's tall, a head taller than
she is, and every day they write each other a letter full of red-hot
declarations of love. That also is well known. An intense fire, a
newspaper that goes up in flames. Come a quarrel, and a few
smoke-blackened scraps of paper fall apart, drift down, and there's
room for a new fire. The fireworks of fifteen-year-olds. Halfway
across they're grabbed by a little old woman. Will we help her
across? Of course. In the knowledge and wealth of youth they take
on this responsibility. Look intently to left and right. Look after the
little woman as if she were an extended play record with a favourite
song on it.

Slowly they play ferry boat. Steer like a ferry through the
stream of traffic that they usually run through wildly. The woman
shuts her eyes and completely surrenders to them. Trusts us. And
suddenly I realize how risky this is. If I shut my eyes it's Els, the
comical young goat, who will be piloting us all alone between the
bumpers. Am I handed over like that, to whom? To somebody
unknown. We feel proud of ourselves, because the woman is old,
unsure of herself, pitiful. Do I feel proud of myself? No. I can't
shut my eyes and trust. Thank you, girls. Relieved, the little old
woman goes on her way. We go back to ours. Suppose, I say, we'd

let go of her. What would happen, eh? Els is shocked, forgets it at once and goes on talking about last Saturday and the party with Coke and beer in some garage. I am left thinking that we all want somebody, want to hold onto somebody so as to get across safely. That apparently our greatest need is to want to believe, with eyes closed, and to shuffle through life like that. Half asleep in somebody's arms. There are some who let themselves be led, and there are some who are always on the watch and spreading their arms out protectively. Not for the sake of domination, or balance, but the victim of that same dumb compelling instinct that makes the helpless person expose his vulnerability, relying confidently on the fact that surrender invites protection. Pioneers and guides are under compulsion like a mother who, whether she wants to or not, feels milk rise in her breasts when the baby cries to be fed and taken care of. It begins unrecognized, with helping an injured bird or a lame kitten, and it ends with old people and sick and unfortunate friends and children and the loved one. Is it not possible to cross over into the dangerous current, each setting out from his own shore, avoiding obstacles, turning corners, darting across the tracks, in order to meet on the refuge? And there in rest and love to slowly undress each other. There must be a resting point somewhere. Where things are not measured in terms of win and lose. This time also, as so often before and since, I feel alienated. Els is talking to me about a completely different planet. A human language. I don't understand you, she's saying, do you call that love, filling your letters with thoughts about politics and poets? And the books you two read, nothing will come of it! I have no way to reach her and the class of fifteen-year-olds.

And Dietrich far away, and knowing that our kisses weren't just a matter of trying out our mouths, and knowing that in our letters a deadly serious war was raging about how he experienced everything like a Wagnerian hero. And that the color of his eyes and the build of his shoulders were marks of his race and not of his sex. And that I loved him anyway, and wanted to love him, so I could be like the rest of them. And hopelessness. Because he didn't touch me, didn't approach me, but a woman such as he'd learned to expect women to be, because he wanted to do everything in the proper way. And because I can never figure out how things are supposed to be done. Because every time, for me, everything begins again, with everything at stake and unknown. Els doesn't understand it, I still don't understand it. To seem like a thing, to be a play that never gets a first performance, because I think plays only come to life on the stage. And yet I've tried so hard to find the group and the connection.

Again, years later, in the city. As it happens I'm in blue again, but not shy. I'm lost. Standing helplessly in the street, the houses like so many false teeth edging a sidewalk that's like greasy lips. In this mouth I've lost my tongue. Waiting to recognize something. When suddenly a little sister of Els, after all these years, comes around the corner. And I speak to her, asking for explanation and directions. She, I don't know her name, walks beside me in the same direction, our colored stocking legs move in step. Our hair blows in the wind. Again. We're almost there, we're there, she says. And then a little old gentleman with a filthy mongrel dog asks us if we can help him across the street. He picks the animal up in his arms. He wraps the leash around his hand. Halfway across I look at the dog. His ears back on his neck, he's burying his nose in the old man's jacket sleeve. His eyes are shut. Once across, the old guy thanks us, thank you girls. I look at the girl beside me. Wrong again.

The others never see me. Only the representation of something I have to be for them. A cliché.

So you, look at me well, look at me very carefully, explore very deep inside me, and know that at the end, when the heaving stops with a convulsive jerk and I am dead, nothing in your memory or your future can be recognized in me.

From *De confrontatie*

[Zoë starts to pull out the memories of her childhood:]

A greasy mess of streets. In my painful head a procession of suicide streets, forgotten streets, streets without end. The singsong of misery, the fishmonger's voice like a saw, cats eating the glassy fish-heads. A summer street, the ice cream vendor's bell. Vanilla and caramel. Girls with plaits, nine years old and not yet having periods, there is no cleft-calendar in their voices. I was a delicate child, my mother hated me irrationally and therefore violently. My father looked like Frank Sinatra, I always felt he would go out one day to buy a pack of cigarettes and never come back. And then the accursed street that I had to walk down twice a day in my sandals and the children from the slum apartments threw stones at me and yelled "Get some shoes!" And if I said anything about it at home, my grandmother gave me a shove with her knee and told me to hit them back, they won't touch you if they know they're liable to get beaten up. To school and back, but usually my mother thought of something else and sent me to the butcher's or the baker's. She would just be getting up when I came home, her face puffy with sleep, aggrieved and looking for any excuse to pick a quarrel. We were a fine decent family, so anything was possible, even if people did fight, it had to be done in a whisper. Nothing is more horrible than childhood sorrow, it is so absolute and nobody has to care about it.

What sort of a street was it, what sort of a life? A row of houses with little gardens in front and back. The rock garden in front, cabbages and lettuce in back. Dad still rode a bike in those days, but he wore a tie and his pant legs were folded under bicycle clips, as neatly as an umbrella. And Mom playing the fine lady, drinking coffee all afternoon. She got fat doing that, but an unhealthy blown up sort of fat. Later some verbal revolutionary talked to me at length about the white collar proletariat. Which just goes to show you can also find learned words to talk nonsense.

As you went further down the street it got wider, there was a greengrocer's, a baker's, a butcher's, a glazier and a savings bank, and at the end a doctor. After that, a section of new houses, which were all anyhow. There were people who wanted sunshine in their bedrooms, others wanted it in the kitchen, you could have whatever you wanted, they just turned the house around. The garage in front or in back, a sort of display window on one really awful house, glass panes set in lead, my grandmother's choice, you can look out undisturbed but nobody can look in. A brick house, inside and out, always cold. The new houses stood apart, didn't fit in with the village or the stores, and didn't fit in with each other either. There were still great patches of pasture and next to the house the farms began again, fields, cows, a canal. The house looked like an arrogant outpost of the new subdivision, out ahead of what was indeed completed a few years later. Asphalt, rubble stone and hortensias. Seen from the fields, to be honest, the house looked monstrous. Three storeys, a brick fortress, marble for the inside staircases, slate on the porch. And mirrors, a palace of mirrors. How can anybody live in a house whose thresholds haven't been worn down by forgotten feet? Where you can't lay your head in confidence because nobody else has fought the same battle before you. A human being is always following another one and there will be another one following after me. And there was the canal, a creation of military engineering, a stupidly straight highway of water, clear across the fields, for old fishermen in the summer, hours of patience for fish that tasted of mud, in the winter for children yelling on ice that never froze nice and smooth.

The flower nursery, now a heap of debris, the greenhouses collapsed, the windows smashed, the doors half torn off, the water tank empty and moldy, especially the water tank now, with fungus and lizards on the bottom. The abortion well, that I drowned them all in, time and time again. My grandmother, and my father and my mother, all of them down the well, just like the cat, Francis did it and immediately I knew I would never love anybody again, no man of that contemptible kind, the spaghetti smile and the clammy hands, and the cat pregnant and all, and my mother later in the kitchen with Francis and they were laughing about it yet.

That street runs right through me.

The asphalt road is black and broad in front of the greenhouses. The door of the big barn is half open. In the back of the delivery truck wooden boxes are being piled up, in them, wrapped in delicate tissue paper, are the flowers. Flowers, almost unbelievable, everything revolves around them, the misted greenhouses, the leaning chimney (the tower of Pisa) and the great water tank. The water is green, sometimes a minnow flits among the spiders and beetles. But mostly it's a gleaming motionless mass whose rise and fall you can only tell by the discolored sides of the tank. In the damp broody warmth of the greenhouses the carnations bend open on pale knobbly stems. A network of fine threads holds the pastel tints upright. The space between the greenhouses is taken up with little fields of narcissi. Easter.

A little girl comes hesitantly down the road to the flower nursery. She stands in front of the mongrel's kennel just as long as it takes for his nervous bark to change into a submissive whine. Everything is quiet at the noon hour, in front of the shed there are rubber boots, people are talking inside. It takes a while, but finally the door swings open and Renée comes out with a large tray of mussel shells on her hip. She throws the shells in a pit and stamps them down a bit at random with her plump feet. When she sees the little girl she takes her by the arm and leads her inside, almost like a friend. She's very friendly and guilty looking, is Renée, and she says everything twice, once in broken Flemish and once in fluent French. In the shed Francis and his father are still sitting at the table. It's so cramped in there that their knees touch. The little girl stands there a while, embarrassed and surprised, looking at them. The rough corduroy pants whose crotch always hangs too low like a double hole, a hen's ass, and the two pairs of knitted khaki socks in the rubber boots. Francis's father mumbles something and Francis laughs. The little girl likes being in the shed and also in the greenhouses or in the packing room with Renée. Renée sings as she packs the flowers, "Je suis seule ce soir" [I'm alone tonight] and sometimes Francis's father pats her arm or her butt. "Mon patron" [boss], Renée says, and Francis laughs again. Francis's mother has her own flower shop in town. The little girl's father took her along once on a visit to the hospital and first of all they stopped and bought flowers, Francis's mother was wearing an expensive brown dress and in a slow voice told Father things interspersed with French expressions and Oh!'s and

Oh là là!'s. Father nodded, looking wise and bored, and when he got home he remarked, they're a nice bunch across the road, I must say, keep the children away from there. But just then Francis came in the kitchen and her mother answered sourly, you get that sort of thing everywhere.

When the men crack a few more heavy jokes and stand up, their meal over, the little girl goes with Francis. He talks the whole time, sometimes more to himself than her, but she doesn't mind, she walks behind him over the slippery green paths in the greenhouses and carries a shoelace or a ball of string. Outside it's raining in angry squalls, the water streams over the glass roof and walls, it swishes and drips. The greenhouses are at blood heat, beads of sweat break out on your forehead. You can't see out, only the vague shadows of the other greenhouses loom.

When an unexpected hailstorm clatters down, Francis stops working and stares fixedly at the glass roof, the heating pipes quiver under the impact. Francis waves a hand at her, go away. But she stays with him, even though she's afraid the glass will break, she stands close to Francis and puts her hand in his. Francis is just eighteen. Now the rain is lashing the windows on all sides, the narcissi outside must have their heads bent over in the mud, if they haven't snapped and been ruined. Now they seem to hear somebody calling, far away as if from across the sea. Maybe Renée, getting worried, or is it her imagination? The light quivers in a green mist, the carnations' scent is heavy but they stand motionless, white and pink. Francis pulls her even closer to him, carefully, the way fishermen along the canal reel their lines in, he clutches her firmly, and with a violent yet controlled movement he pushes her hand into his pants pocket. They look at each other while the rattle of the hail abates and then suddenly stops. A spring rain falls, as gentle as balm. It clears up, a soft blue filtered light falls over the flowers. In his pants pocket Francis's fist now cautiously lets go of her hand and unfolds her fingers, then he presses his open hand over hers. It's warm in his pants pocket, warmer than in the greenhouse, it's as if her hand can see how dark it really is in there, and then she feels something hard that she doesn't know, pressing against her palm.

Francis's lips have just opened, her hand is caught between two pressures.

Now they can clearly hear Renée calling, surprisingly clear and close by. She tries to tug her hand loose. Her head just comes over the top of the carnations, and while she silently jerks and writhes she can see that it has stopped raining and the water is making streams down the glass and forming drops. Someone outside comes up to the door, they can hear the feet splash in puddles. Francis is no longer motionless, he is panting and suddenly he pulls her down, he falls on top of her like a heavy block, he corrects his position quickly by pulling her up, so that their heads are close together. The greenhouse door is pulled open and Renée calls their names in a questioning tone. A shock goes through the little girl, a cry is trying to get out. Francis is a heavy panting block from which strange eyes are staring at her, he opens his mouth and puts it over hers like a bell. Her cry vanishes, deadened in the strange space which at first remains passive then forms a sucking ring, and from its depths his tongue emerges and penetrates, at first just the tip but then big, much too big, into her mouth. She retches and cries, and vaguely hears the door shut. A cool draft swirls through the damp warmth and she doesn't know if Renée has gone back out or maybe Francis's father is coming closer in his big green rubber boots. She rears up wildly, but Francis keeps her pinned to the ground, under his armpits it's soaking wet and cold, he pins her hands against her sides with his arms. She is close to stifling in a smell of mussels. Then almost as quickly as it began it's over, three or four grunts, a strange spasm, he rolls over on his side and takes her with him, she almost rolls among the flower stems. Hastily she scrambles to her feet, her dress is all wet and green, on her thigh fine lines are imprinted from the ball of string that fell under her. Francis looks without seeing anything. Empty. He slowly smooths his hair with a muddy hand. But when she makes a movement to run away from him, he comes to and tries to grab her leg. She jumps back wildly and rushes, silently crying, through a maze of paths, stumbles, finds the door, outside the earth is steaming, the air is sharp and fresh and hurts the lungs, she runs down the asphalt road and there's Molly the cat, dapper on her white paws on top of a car. She stops and the cat stretches her front paws out and her tail in the air and comes over and rubs against her legs. She clutches the cat to herself, buries her face in the warm dry fur. But she gets an attack of hiccups, the cat is scared and scratches her and she wildly throws the creature away and shrieks: "Nasty cat, rotten creature!" As she turns and runs away she has a fleeting glimpse of Renée looking out of the packing room after her, looking frightened.

From *Marguerite*

[In the opening section, the narrator reflects on the picture in the museum at Arles, which looks just like her grandmother:]

She was never impressed by people, and seldom by things. A worthy successor to Queen Victoria, "we are not amused," but without the plush morality. Five foot three, fearless and gray, shoes, stockings, costume and hair. The eyes spoiled the whole picture, brown ironic devils. Marguerite. And she was my grandmother, very reluctantly to be sure, because I was like her, but without the eyes and without that gray. And from the moment she fished me out of the cradle, we danced an endless pas de deux, until in the end I came out on top and she lay six feet underground. Then she began to haunt me, I owed her an epitaph. And again I'm underneath, for the last time. After that we can forget each other without crying. No, the past doesn't spread open like a peacock's tail, it comes alive in bits and pieces, in fits and starts. You become a spectator of your own birth.

Blows that hit home. Dead? No, not death, because beyond death you have memory like a candle in your hand. A faint light that slowly goes out. But not painful. And for me, the only harm but an unconquerable one, the inability to write myself out of that moment of absolute loneliness. And maybe that isn't even the point any more.

But as T admitted, some time ago, shocked: "I saw my mother and I thought, But she's been dead for ten years! And I thought, for a dead person she's not doing badly." But that isn't what I meant. Well, it is, you could say of her that for a dead person she's not doing badly. The wretched years of slobbering are forgiven her and she lives again more and more, with an almost compelling irony. We aren't all lucky enough to be shot down at the peak of our flight. But in her case the decline was a disaster. It's hard to forgive anything in an exceptional person. I could stand seeing others become babies again. They told me that in her last days M clung anxiously to her daughter's skirts. The same daughter she was at loggerheads with all her life and whom she bullied so much that she drove her mad. I didn't care. But that she pissed and shit herself and stood there giggling, that was too much. A defeated enemy isn't an enemy any more. And we couldn't show our affection for each other in any other way. So, relief and no metaphysics over the grave. Now your parents, and then you would be free. All debts paid. It was spring. And no frogs jumping on the lid of the casket, as you read long ago in Gorki. It was done properly, with just as many candles and hymns as were considered necessary and were paid for. The priests' uncaring attitude and the routine way they did things, to be sure, was a bit rude, as if they did nothing else all day but ferry dear souls to the gates of eternity which swished open and shut. I would have liked to watch one of them die.

But perhaps they were so well trained that they held the mirror in front of their own lips, and when the mark of their last sigh had evaporated, they closed their eyes automatically like little box lids. Her husband wasn't there. Nobody remarked on it and it wouldn't have surprised her. The family stood around uneasily, a woman sobbed passionately. Nobody seemed to know her, but every time there was a funeral she appeared, in deepest black. The type of the professional mourner. It was an unforgettable moment when her four sons, those who had survived everything so far, walked in procession carrying the casket. All four held their fists in front of their crotch, their wedding tackle, undoubtedly chosen by her with that unfailing instinct for soundness of character, because they would look good in black suits, bareheaded, the glory of the good old days.

The Dalton brothers, I thought. A remarkable foursome, one a good head shorter than the one in front of him, and so on, the eldest being also the tallest. As if at their conception the parents had been a bit less enthusiastic each time. A good joke if you didn't know that between these four walked countless ghosts of others, children who had hardly lived at all or at most a few years, and then died, looking strange, like little yellow wrinkled old men. They had blamed her for it, of course. As if she had cast a spell on her own brood. And she was capable of a great deal, but not of that. And then the organ boomed out. In Paradisum.

We proceeded to the order of the day. She would have done things that way. Sentimentality was saved for the half hour with the novel serialized in the newspaper. A weakness I exploited mercilessly. Oh, so she could read! She could cry over all the sickly sweet stories about fallen girls. And I was a snotty brat who didn't understand anything! Then she wished she hadn't said that and chased me out of her room, grumbling. Did I leave her in peace? No, of course not. Till I couldn't stand it any more and bought her a book, and a classic at that. I was already a bit older then, or as she put it, my nose was beginning to stick out above the ears of wheat, and I even got her to promise to read it. But she never did. When I expectantly examined her, she admitted she'd given up halfway through. "I know all that stuff," she said. "It's all right for people who've never done anything."

I didn't understand, and asked her if she didn't think it was well written. "Too well," she answered, "you start believing it's true, and if you want to forget something you don't repeat it. The paper is entertainment. You can shed a tear over it, and you feel better." We never talked about books again, so far as I remember. Almost everything I know about her, of course, is what I remember and other people's stories. But you don't have to know everything in order to guess a great deal, and she was as remarkable as all the stories about her. Even so, I wish I knew more, there is too much that's obscure. And I would like to know why she was the way she was and not different. Not a boat that slips its anchor and drifts here and there, but a bird that deliberately escapes from its cage and fulfils itself in free flight. "If I hadn't been a woman," and then she would say no more. And it didn't occur to her that I wanted to be a woman, yet she was the one who showed me, however imperfectly, that it was possible to be a woman without becoming a victim. All my aunts accepted their fate, sighing and coquettish, but she fought to the last. And she wanted to forget where she came from, and I kept reminding her of it. Look at that place, small and almost forgotten. Flayed to the ribs, subdivided and polluted. You used to be able to find your way around there blindfolded, and now you discover in surprise that you're a stranger. The lovely river, feminine with its indolent curves and springy turf banks, now a shadow of its former beauty. She also was from that area, but she never talked about it, it was as if she had never been born or had parents. She seldom went back, she pretty well had to be forced to. I spent unforgettable years there and always remained attached to it, although with the years it is becoming more painful to go back. The past lives, but the frame in which it shows itself is often unbearable. No more poppies on the graves, just plastic chrysanthemums. And yet my early years are unforgettable, and the place plays a large part in them. It binds me to a doglike fidelity, and as always, fidelity is love for a ghost. You could do so much in a day then. I loved the summer warmth that lingered in the ground and the water after the sun had disappeared. Grass and trees, the difference between smooth and rough, and the two sensations. The view was never grandiose, the horizon was always plump and creased. Trees and little woods, a few houses, a church steeple, deceptive dwarf country. You couldn't see far, it was like the childhood years themselves, everything in your immediate surroundings became very important. And you developed a sort of respect for it, and a feeling of security. As if the whole Leie valley[2] were a sort of nest. It protected you against the cruelty of people, not the cruelty needed to live, but the cruelty that torments pleasure. An unwanted child is a sin against nature. Nobody can defend themselves against the line "you'd have been better off not being born." Especially not against the guilt feeling because you're alive after all. The bond between mother and child is sometimes as intimate as between a murderer and his victim. All the more so because they switch roles, each intending to survive the other. (H's problem: "Who would you be if you didn't exist?")

To have to accuse her of that. Three attempts at clandestine abortion, a delivery more like butchery, and then it's the wrong sex. Unforgivable. A monster begging for love. A tropical plant that should be in a hothouse, and carnivorous too if you don't watch it. You can't take that much worry in one lifetime, people have enough trouble looking after themselves. But the countryside is patient. That was the difference between my grandmother and me, the country that had spat her out took me in. And I have remained grateful to my stepmother. To her great annoyance. Because until now I have always wanted to live, even in the darkest moments, in fact especially then, and every time I see something die, even if it's only a bird or a rabbit, I feel deeply unhappy. There is no beauty whatever in death, and no death is ever fruitful. You can't understand how people can be so crazy about anything, except their well understood self-interest.

It's also incomprehensible why, despite everything, not least my obstinacy, every time things threatened to go completely wrong, she intervened. At the time I found it unforgivable of her to drag me away from my windmills and meadows and the greenhouses of the village. She was right, of course, that's what was always so intolerable; I had to get out of the children's room. "You're not a Vervloesem," she said, "you're a van Puynbroeck. It's time you began to understand that." And even then I thought that was a great injustice. I didn't want to be a Vervloesem or a van Puynbroeck. There was no reason to be either one. I wanted to be myself, in other words free! There was no landscape she could fit into, there was something bricklike about her, and actually you recognized her in houses, solid homes, schools, churches, maybe even cathedrals. It really wasn't surprising that she got interested in the construction business and made a good living at it. In the meantime she has turned me into a commuter. Constantly en route from the city to the country and back again. It isn't bad, I like being on the move. My love of nature was a constant source of amusement for her, and for my "dumb peasants" she felt nothing but contempt. For a while there was a picture hanging in her kitchen of an English professor chasing butterflies. He was running across the heath, wearing plus fours, long woolen socks and a tweed jacket. A pair of pince-nez on his nose and a sort of pith helmet on his head. In one hand he had a butterfly net, in the other a thick book, and on his back hung a funny little tin box with the lid open, which the butterflies were joyfully escaping from. The caption was "The Naturalist."

So she lies buried in the city and her husband in the country, the definitive outcome of a separation that lasted some fifty years. So you can reconcile yourself to the fact that their bones aren't rotting together. That was one of his last wishes, but nobody ever listened to him. As for her, skyscrapers rise on the edge of her burial plot, when you stand on the roof you can hardly see where she is.

From *De vermaledijde vaders*

[The opening section of part four is at once a description of the 1940 massacre of the inhabitants of the small village of Vinkt, and of the narrator's reactions when she is sent there, many years later (it is her birthplace), to record the survivors' memories of that war crime:]

The village may just as well be in Poland. In the Ukraine or in Normandy. Maybe in Gelderland. In Vietnam or Cambodia. Among the cedars of Lebanon or on the edge of the Sinai. But also in Flanders.

It may be called Lidice, My Lai, Oradour, Putten or Vinkt. Every village is suitable and all their names are unforgettable. A crossroads, a river or canal... Unexpected resistance, a bullet that hits a general's jacket, a bridge blown up... Any pretext can be seized on, any excuse will do. Incomprehensible but explainable.

The village is of all countries and all times. Even if it's a city and we call it Warsaw or Beirut. The story is the same. On the Oder or the Leie, the Mekong or the Litani. All rivers flow to the sea, as if they want to hide in water. Bodies floating... And the soldiers may wear gray or black uniforms, khaki or brown ones. They can sneak up or they can march in singing at daybreak. All soldiers are afraid and they all sing. Their name can be Kurt or John, Thy or Isi. They've forgotten. Only the women remember. All soldiers murder. And every man can be the wrong one.

There was a church, a mill and a convent. A café, and another café, a pigeon racers' association and a little school. There was a village square and a churchyard wall. The houses were small, except those of the lawyer and the priest. Those were considerably larger. From above you could see that the houses had been built along the arms of the crossroads. And that the farms spread out in a star shape in the fields around. The river wound past a little further away, and closer, bordered by leaning Carolina poplars, was the canal. A strange straight waterway through a landscape where everything bent, wound and twisted. A stranger would get lost in it. The people weren't rich but they were hardworking. To stay above the poverty line there was nothing else to do but work hard. The families had been connected by marriage for generations. Everybody knew everybody. A closed community. The pace of life was set by the seasons and the church calendar. They were attached to the soil. It seemed secure, it was cosy. They didn't like adventure. Any change met resistance. Emigration took care of discontent. People prayed to be spared illness, diseases of cattle and war...

***

In the merry month of May. Everything green. The wheat is coming up nicely. The prospects for harvest are good. A fertile smell of dung. Used in the best perfumes. But from May 10, 1940 onwards the village is in the Nevele-Meigem-Vinkt military sector, part of the Leie Line. The sun shone through the burning glass of history. On May 19 another order of the day was published: "forces definitely weaker than ours..."

It would have been better to talk about a steamroller. It's absolutely demoralizing. The invaders advance so fast that the refugees are trapped. Some want to go even further, to the sea, to France, to the other side of the world. Others are already turning back. In the village the barns, attics and cellars are full. The wildest rumors are going around. Meanwhile the cows have to be milked and the potatoes hoed. The bread has to be baked. Children are born, old folks want to die quietly. The king, son of the Knight King,[3] is staying in a Gothic castle and being served orchids with his breakfast by the attentive mistress of the house. The situation is critical. Are they going to dig in behind the Yser[4], like last time? Have the English landed? Are the French sending reinforcements?

On May 25 a breach is opened in the defenses. The Germans cross the Schipdonk Canal, a diversion canal of the Leie, and occupy Meigem. Immediately everything is done to close the breach. To block their passage to the coast and France. On the beaches of Dunkirk the soldiers are crawling towards the sea like tortoises that have just laid their eggs in the sand. Aircraft skim over their heads. It is of the utmost importance to complete the evacuation. Vinkt is at the crossroads. The village is defended by the Ardennes Rifles, "Les Chasseurs ardennais," and if you back them into a corner they can prove as dangerous as their emblem, the wild boar.

For three days fierce fighting, bombing, grenade attacks, artillery barrages. For three days, slaughter and looting. The enemy lose so many men, 748 dead, that they abandon any semblance of playing by the rules. Hundreds of dead, including some sixty officers and NCO's. The victorious progress stopped by a little nothing village?

First prisoners of war are used as human shields. Then civilians. It doesn't work. In the night of May 25 to 26, the defense is relieved and reinforced by a contingent of about three hundred men. And then there are the oak copses, the wheatfields, the stream called the Poekebeek. This charming landscape is deceptive. The enemy comes under fire from all sides. The farmyards are strategically located and are bitterly defended. At the entrance to the village, the convent serves as a fortress. The situation cries out for vengeance. Calls for total destruction.

The devastated village is taken on May 27 at about four in the afternoon. For the moment nothing worrying happens: the soldiers ask for food and drink and move on. But about half past six, other soldiers appear and organize a round-up. They use the well-worn slogan: "The civilians fired at us!" That was the cover for atrocities in 1914, too.

In the hamlets, people are flushed out of their hiding places and locked up in the churches of Meigem and Sint-Martens-Leerne. Women with babies, sick people in wheelchairs, old folks in wheelbarrows. Nobody is spared. The round-up is being conducted in the war zone and people are continually exposed to artillery fire and bombing. Accompanied with a hail of insults and blows from rifle butts. Constant repetition of the word Schweinhund, especially. Men are shot in front of their wives. Meigem is next to Vinkt, on the Schipdonk Canal, that's where the breakthrough occurred. Sint-Martens-Leerne is about seven miles away.

Eleven men are tied up with telephone wire and barbed wire, beaten up and run through with bayonets. In the temporary mass grave, a twelfth victim was later found, a man who was trying to go home. He was shot dead, the man with him managed to get away.

Houses are looted and set on fire. The little dots on the map where this happened are called De Spoele (The Spool), Kruiswege (Crossroads), Het Zwarte Huizeke (The Black House). In the church at Meigem, crammed full of people, the pastor is forced to announce that two hundred yards from there civilians armed with a German machine gun have opened fire on a German truck. A little later a loud explosion rocks the church. Witnesses saw the Germans carry boxes and barbed wire into the choir. They maintain that from there hand grenades were thrown into the church. Others speak of a direct hit on the roof. Twenty-seven dead and about forty seriously wounded. Indescribable chaos.

From the convent the soldiers drag out nuns, refugees, villagers and the people from the old folks' home. They had all sought refuge in the building's solid cellars. Women and children are parked in a nearby field. The men are driven down the village street at the double with their hands over their heads. Forty-five of them are shot. The first group, the old men, up against the walls of the convent and the old folks' home, the second group against the garden wall of the priest's house, and the third group near the butcher's shop. Some survive and groan. They are finished off during the night or the next day. The youngest victim is thirteen, the oldest ninety-one. Four get away. All the time soldiers pass by and take pictures of the bodies, kick them or, if they suspect someone is still

alive, shoot them. Of the four who survive, two hide under the
bodies and escape after dark, and the two others lie wounded beside
the bodies and are eventually put out of their misery.

Besides the collective executions, seventeen other people are
taken and shot here and there. People trying to go home, who
venture out of their hiding place, to take their animals somewhere
safe. Disarmed prisoners of war. But also an elderly couple aged
eighty-four and seventy-one, and their handicapped daughter, aged
thirty-two. The daughter, being obese, only dies after being hit by
several bullets. The neighbor woman suffers the same fate. All these
people allegedly shot at the Germans.

On May 28 the Belgian army surrenders. Immediately there
is a chaotic flood of refugees who want to go back home as soon as
possible. Those who come near Vinkt are taken prisoner and kept in
fields. It begins to rain. Brutality, harassment and threats. No food
or drink. Finally forced to watch while men have to dig their own
graves before being shot. A councillor begins to dig like an
automaton. A refugee, one of whose childen had picked up a spent
cartridge case to play with, refuses and throws down his spade. He
is punched and kicked before being shot. A father with two sons, one
son also refuses to dig his own grave and is mown down at once...

The orchard of a farm serves as an open air prison. General
Paulus comes and inspects it. "Shoot these Schweinhunde!" he yells
at the soldiers. Immediately a hundred or so men are separated from
the others and stood before a battery of machine guns. It's hours
before they are led away and locked up with others in the church of
Sint-Martens-Leerne. Three years later, after the fall of Stalingrad,
where Paulus is promoted to field marshal, stolen objects like
wedding rings and savings bank passbooks are sent back to the village
via the Red Cross.

Eight bodies turn up in various circumstances. Among them
are a child and a refugee who was hit in his hiding place. The
soldiers had noticed him and shot through the door. A peasant who
had thought he was safe after the capitulation and was heading for his
potato field. He was tied to the back of a cart and the horses were
driven off at a trot. After he had been dragged some distance in that

way they put a bullet through his head. A man who had gone out to see what was going on, and so on and so forth.

Lastly a hundred and eighteen hostages are locked up for three days in a chicken hatchery. A shed twelve feet wide and sixty feet long, most of which is occupied by an incubator and the cages. The men stand in the narrow aisles packed in like sardines. The windows are shut tight. Two days with nothing to eat or drink. The continual threat of being shot. Forced to applaud as communiqués of victories are read out. And to do gymnastics, lie down, stand up, Schnell! Schnell! The men are squeezed together and going crazy with fear and thirst. After they are released, the mayor, his secretary and the school principal are kept prisoner till May 31.

On June 3 all the remaining men are requisitioned to dig up and rebury people and animals. A hundred and one bodies are recovered, seventy civilians and twenty-three Belgian soldiers. It is hot and decomposition has already set in. A pestilential stench hangs over the scene. Identification is heartbreaking. The wives and family of the victims crowd around the mass grave. For many of them their worst fears are only confirmed now. There are no coffins to be had, so floorboards are used. On the other side of the wall between the churchyard and the priest's garden, some German soldiers have set up a bar. They've discovered the wine cellar.

All these events are photographed and filmed by the Germans. Photographers who developed the pictures made several prints and hid them. When the Germans come back to the village a few months later, they visit widows and bereaved families and show them the photos. "Do you remember?" They also have rings and other such things, which they had taken "as souvenirs." They seem proud of their deeds of valor. One soldier talks with relish about the "fat girl." He means the handicapped daughter. Another one forces people to stand in front of their destroyed houses so they can show their buddies what happened. Major Lohmann asks a widow if she knows how Lieutenant Bock died. She says she doesn't, and he maintains that the lieutenant was shot while pumping water, by the neighbor's wife. When the widow points out that her neighbor was a bachelor, the major goes away without a word.

The story of the civilians shooting at the Germans soon proves untenable, and besides the Vinkt affair is bad for propaganda. So they try to hush it up. And come up with a new version: the Ardennes Rifles supposedly disguised themselves as women and girls(!) so that the Germans would think they were being shot at by civilians. To reinforce this theory, a collaborationist lawyer and his helpers are sent to the village to "...cleanse the name of Vinkt of any stain..." On the pretext that the persons involved won't get a pension, they are pressured to sign a declaration clearing the Germans of all guilt and blaming everything on the Ardennes Rifles. The idea here is to play on the age-old antagonism between the Flemings and the Walloons. Nobody signs this declaration. The inhabitants of the village are what is hypocritically referred to as "uneducated people." Cunning reasoning and complicated turns of phrase supposedly go over their heads. They can get no further than "We saw what we saw!" Thanks to the photos and the visit of the Germans it was possible to identify the criminals. Most of them had been killed or gone missing on the Eastern Front. A few couldn't be traced. In the end Major Lohmann and Colonel Kuhner stood trial. They received life and twenty years respectively, at hard labor.

The village is a village again. There's a monument. There's an annual remembrance ceremony. Time is taking over. People don't forget things, but they speak of them less and less as time passes.

***

Stormy weather. Gusts of wind push the car this way and that. The windshield wipers can't cope with the downpour. In a submarine. The idea's enough to give you claustrophia. Listening to the motor through the violent rain and wind. "If you buy a secondhand car you're buying somebody else's problems." A voice from the past.

Underwater it's silent. Waving plants, fish with kissy lips. Soundless babble, bulging eyes, rounded mouths, as if sending smoke signals. The submarine bumps on the sandy bottom. The crew hold onto pipes and bunks. Look at each other, sweat pours from their foreheads. The beep beep of the sonar. Depth charges hit them. Das Boot. First see the movie, then read the book! A seagoing coffin. Not for me thank you, she thinks. The professional-looking tape recorder on the back seat. Should she have tied it down with the seat belt? Rumble. Are we going to have thunder and lightning too? The windows are misted up. No sign of the clear periods they called for. The sky is completely gray. The land of weather forecasts. She drives slowly. No point in trying to go fast. Hydroplaning. The river, tied-up boats rocking along the shores and docks. Always the feeling of crossing a border. Photo of Queen Elisabeth cruising on the Leie in the company of men of letters.[5] Gentlemen with hats and beards and pipes. Witty and gallant. A well-spoken court. At her feet like purring tomcats. Paper tigers.

The canal. Will soon be widened to accommodate strings of barges pushed by tugs. Trees have to be chopped down. The whole delta. Industrialization. Too many people. And all in the name of progress. Robber baron exploitation. The mentality. Makes you shrug your shoulders. Nobody expects things to stay unchanged. But when you do irreparable damage. Worn-out slogans to cover up corruption. These days you have to be a very special dead person to be sure your grave is safe. No time to rot in peace. A bit crazy to speak of the beauty of the landscape. Of the quality of life. As if we cling to our childhood years.

Nevele. From here she can find her way with her eyes shut. She has to. Ten yards visibility. Narrow roads, deep ditches. The house Cyriel Buysse was born in.[6] Our Zola! Sold to a chicken farmer. Brass plaque beside the door. Cyriel and his car. Got his peerage on his deathbed. A paper baron. Chose as his motto "In d'hope van vrede" (In the hope of peace). Good name for a bar. The name of the Loveling sisters fading over a garage. The Aunts. The Nightingales of Nevele. The Flemish Bröntes. And other such nonsense.

Anybody who had done anything wrong and could jump the Poekebeek, being then on the soil of Poesele, was free. A deep bed, a mini-river. You could drown in it. Full of sticklebacks before it was polluted. Turned out to be strategically placed. As she approaches Vinkt she goes as slowly as possible. Her first assignment is inevitably bringing her back to the place she wanted to write herself away from. Producer looks like Orson Welles. "A piece of living history." Any moment and all the witnesses will be dead. And they're your people, they'll talk to you. The usual manipulation. Looks as though she has to accept the inevitable. She parks in the empty space in front of the church. The certainty that she is noticed almost at once. That from now on everything she does will be watched and commented on. With an oilskin coat over her head, she runs to the common grave. The slate headstones gleam. A pietà with empty eyes: the mother of the martyrs. She starts to count the crosses, gets it wrong, starts over, gives up. Undecided in the rain. Across the street a woman is scrubbing the sidewalk. Soapsuds swirl away. The village is too quiet, the street is too wide. Her imagination must be coloring what she sees. Resolutely she rings the bell of the priest's house. It rings as it can only ring in empty hallways.

***

"You don't want to shout your sorrow from the housetops. And so you go crazy," says the woman with the joints lumpy from rheumatism. People with two voices. The ordinary one. And a contorted one, when they talk about that. Hoarse. Laborious. Trembling. The voices of people with the whooping cough. The needles of the tape recorder beat back and forth. Quiver.

The woman was the first at the opening of the mass grave and was lucky. She recognized him right away by his clothes. She'd darned his socks the week before. She was spared the uncertainty that other women lived with for days. "You know it but you can't believe it." There were soldiers all over the place, stamping their feet and yelling. "And we didn't understand why." With the muzzle of a rifle in your back, the men and women were separated. The little girl was the apple of her grandfather's eye. She didn't want to let go of his hand: "Grandpa, stay here!" The soldiers kicked the child away. The men were herded together at the double. Her husband turned around and waved. The villagers were in clogs. It isn't easy to walk on cobblestones.The refugees — the woman calls them "the strangers" — were in shoes. That's how you could recognize them afterwards. In the field there were neighbors and relatives. The men passed by. But the soldiers lined the road, so you only caught a glimpse of the procession. Shortly after that they heard the shooting. There were several bursts of fire. Women fell to their knees or hurled themselves at the soldiers. They were pushed back roughly. After that they were taken by all sorts of byways to the church of Sint-Martens-Leerne. The woman had to look after a nursing infant, her little daughter, and a senile mother-in-law of over seventy. There was still fighting. When shells came over the soldiers jumped into the ditch. But the people had to stand there on the road. "Helpless." They trudged on like sleepwalkers.

In the church there were some two hundred people. Nobody was allowed out. Some were scrabbling with their nails at the plaster walls. Others sat in a trance, praying. There was nothing to eat. Terrible thirst. They drank the water out of the font and the stinking liquid in the flower pots. People who had at first been shut up in the church at Meigem told what had happened to them. A flash and a thunderclap. Chairs and statues of saints knocked over and chunks of plaster fallen from the ceiling. Children yelling for their parents. Torn-off arms and legs. Dead people. Neighbors and relatives among them.

Sometimes it seemed that the soldiers were nailing the church doors shut, sometimes they seemed to be shooting at them. At every suspicious noise the people ran forward and crowded close to the altar to seek refuge. There were no toilets and people did their business in corners and behind pillars. "After a night and half a day we were released. I couldn't stand up any more. At a farm we got German bread for the first time. It looked dark and tasted sour. But we were glad to have it."

The house had been destroyed. For four years they lived in the barn. On a floor of bare earth. And in the evenings they went to sleep at the neighbors' house. They had set up a little carpentry business, she and her husband, but nothing of it was left. Hammers and tongs, even the nails had disappeared. To get by, she did the peasants' laundry. Warm water was a luxury. The woman holds out her misshapen hands. Her little girl had to look after grandmother.

She took the baby with her. He'd been born six weeks before war broke out. A quiet child. And he remained so. A colossus with an unworldly smile. Lets his mother talk. Calmly eats his bread and butter. He raises pet birds. Their chirping is in the background on the tape. The daughter is a little strange. A bundle of nerves, but they thought it'd get better when she got married. It didn't. She's just a child. One evening she grabs an iron and runs over to the neighbor's in back to hit the woman with it. The tv is always on full blast because she's deaf, but she always hears what she's not supposed to. It was a war movie. And what with the cardboard walls of the emergency housing, it was as if the shots were coming right through! (The doctor thinks it is correct to say that the percentage of heart disease and psychological disturbances is considerably higher here than the national average. But he couldn't put a figure on it. He's in a hurry. He's leaving soon for a developing country).

People ask why they stayed in the village, why they didn't move to the city, for example. "But we never had enough money. And what were we supposed to live on?" But the questions hit home. Why have we always stayed together? Or why did I let my daughter get married? "To do her some good. And because you don't know any better. Because you hope it'll stop one day." With the cheap loans you could get she started a little business. Enough to keep her head above water. She was thirty and strong. It's all gone. "Old and worn out before my time." She never even thought of remarrying. After what happened she couldn't have stood another man. And there were a lot of widows in the village. "What do I have in the world except my children?" Her husband lies under the monument with the others. That's hard, because now they'll never be together again. "Even in my grave I'll lie alone." But she accepts it. She could never have given him such a fine burial herself. There were three victims in the family. "My husband, his father and his brother." When they were dug up it was terrible. They kill them and stuff them in the ground. And when they find them, they make you come and recognize them. They're buried in rows, in a separate area, and after years and years apparently it's still only temporary. It's enough to drive you crazy. And more years go by and they put up a monument, and what are you supposed to do? You want something to be left. But you don't know what you're getting into. It's as if they can find no rest because their time had not yet come. And as long as they find no rest you can't forget. She was relieved when she saw how thick the new slabs were. And nobody had better come looking for anything or muck about with the graves. "They're dead, and not a day passes when I don't hear that bell toll!"

***

Didn't want to get into this. If the voices are going to sound like that... Handkerchiefs are pulled out... Began to clear my throat. To hum like a jamming station. Stop it, you! If you can't stand it just go outside, they said afterwards.

Ran zigzag across the road, threw myself into the ditches, hid in the wheatfields. They weren't going to get me! Hare across snowy fields. Run, stop, run. Rolls a few yards further. Spasms in the rump. Convulses and is stiff. Screams like a pig. Rabbit sitting motionless against the wall of its hutch. Protruding eyes. Quivering rib cage. I can even hear your little heart beating. They came this way... Dusty roads. Uneven worn cobblestones, convex in the middle. Every row of six or seven helmets that stuck up above the wheat was mown down.

Under the lean-to beside the kitchen door a bunch of birds were hanging to get high. Wings hanging down, heads slack. Fluorescent breast feathers. For that you get a feather in your hat!

Wails of love. Went down the hall on tiptoe as if you had been caught in the act yourself. The female cat cries out in pain during copulation. Tomcat has barbs on his dick. Question: what guy told you that one? He, aggrieved: It was a woman. Passionate man, always nice. Very fond of making love. Didn't seem to hate women. Cautious, of course. Didn't understand her. Afraid that one day her real self would emerge. That she would ask questions. Make demands. Impossible to explain love. As long as it lasts? No, a lot longer... A practical lesson in loving.

Loved the humming black alder tree. From spring to fall. From morning to evening. The bees. Even just before the storm, sharp flashes of lightning, descent into hell in the sky, buzz-buzz...

Sunday excursions to the war cemeteries. The prettiest gardens you could imagine. Between the endless rows of tombstones: roses, heather, climbing plants - not to mention the poppies. Something is in flower in every season. Plants from the dead men's countries. Inscription: "May the heavenly winds blow softly over that far and foreign grave..."[7]   "Look at all the boys lying here!" Elisabeth blows her nose. Nowhere else is the grass so springy. The moss so soft. And the silence that you'd like to mistake for peace. Lysenthoek, Vladslo, Tyne Cot Cemetery. Figures that make your head spin. A good place to hide, invisible among the ghosts. In the bare land, under the red beeches. Protected in the dunes. When the snow has covered the mounds of the graves, endless. Our footprints. Crackling kisses. Blinding flakes. Hold me tight. If they rise again. Wandering noiselessly through the walls. Infiltrate our houses. Or if the neutron bomb has already fallen. J'accuse. If it was only a movie... Imagination limps along behind reality. Would never have picked even one little flower. Afraid bony hands were clinging to the roots. The roses would smell of rotting. In the evening, standing shivering at the Menin Gate in Ypres. When the Last Post is sounded. Peering to see if any mud-caked figure comes stumbling up. But the ghosts in the plain are asleep. On the eleventh hour of the eleventh day of the eleventh month it was all over. War as a chain reaction.

"Once you've done it you keep on doing it." The man had a vulgar little laugh. Deflowering: a prosaic event. Who's afraid of the defenseless?

Photo of a shady orchard. They are standing in rows with their back to us. A soldier is kneeling to tie their hands. Another has them covered. The backs are bent from toil. They are wearing caps. Floppy peak, greasy sweatband, the crown hanging down. And the well-known hang of the pants. Sagging in the crotch, baggy at the knees. If you hang up a pair of pants like that in the evening, it will stay that shape. After they've been worn for a few days, they never lose it. How crushed they look. Helpless and broken. Once their voices rang out loud and lusty over the countryside. "Whoa!" The horse's name was Bella. And the photo under that one. They lie all tangled in front of the blood-spattered wall. Stiffened into strange positions. Their feet in clogs that look far too big.

For poaching a hare you could be thrown in the slammer. Youth was as short as it was intense. Once you were married you could work yourself to death. A glass of beer on Sundays. Just so long as you kept healthy! Eating was important. Nothing gourmet. Eating a lot can also be eating well!

Unnaturally wide street. As if a breach had been driven through the heart of the village. In some of the houses the tv is blaring away. Others are dark and as if abandoned. This May evening should be meaningful. Damp is seeping from the stones of the churchyard wall. Anybody who walks on that plateau in the posthumous silence will practise struggling against phenomena that suggest dread. Pursued by your own footsteps. Mom, what am I doing here? His lips as if just passing by. But arms around each other. Endless exploration of a mouth. When? Now? Yes. Now! Little monosyllables.

A cartload of flowers from the remembrance ceremony. They've never seen so many flowers. Not even at their weddings. Are there already little brown edges on the tenderest leaves? The soldiers, foaming at the mouth, were waiting for them on the village street. "They're waiting for us!" "They just want to scare us," said his brother in law. He knew that an officer would give the order. Watched the man with the peaked cap. The soldiers took aim. Instinctively the men drew back. Fire! He let himself fall. "The fifth one isn't dead!" A burst of fire which knocked him off his feet. Felt he wasn't mortally wounded. When he came to, there were two bodies lying on top of him. He heard somebody groan. A man who had been hit in the arms and legs. "Friend, let's run away together." "Can't walk." "I'll carry you." The man turned away moaning. Was shot through the head by an approaching soldier. He had gotten two or three hundred yards before they opened fire on him. Rolled in the stinging nettles, fled through a burning house and on to a farm where he jumped into the cesspit. He stayed in that stench all night and listened to the soldiers over his head smashing everything to bits. What you think of in moments like that, there's no way to explain...

In Monte Cassino, or Bastogne, the same gentlemen with the beginnings of a pot belly. Ceremony with a wreath and a minute of silence during which not a soul stirs. Then with relief, feet under the table for the fraternization meal. The war? Scheisse! Across the chicken with apple sauce the gentlemen look at each other with mutual respect. Fought hard but honorably. Toast to the fallen comrades. Young people are a headache and taxes should be done away with. Freedom is beyond price. Sometimes they still sing about the fatherland, the love that makes undaunted the final sacrifice, and the girl who sat faithfully waiting for him at home. A gentleman who gets sentimental when he's drunk starts to cry. Tends to takes things too hard. People clap him consolingly on the shoulders. It was war, and they were young, they knew not what they did. Respectfully they shake hands with their former adversaries. "I nearly got you," says one gentleman. "Yes, you came pretty close there," the man with the gold-rimmed glasses agrees. They climb stiffly into the bus. One less every year. Their wives didn't come along. It's more so for the boys...

From *De eerste steen*

[Lastly, from *De eerste steen* we translate a passage (p. 41-44) which vividly conveys the mixed emotions aroused in May by her experiences in Israel:]

Hagar and Yona had taken her into the desert. As eagerly as Tom Thumb, May had gathered glittering stones, but she wouldn't really have cared if they had left her there. They had driven fast through villages, stones had spat out from under their slipping tires and been thrown at them in handfuls. Boys jumped down from the slopes like dancing dervishes, women who looked either quarrelsome or despairing held their hands out, but when a child gave them two fingers and made as if to jump in front of the car, Yona had curtly ordered "Keep going!" and Hagar had stepped on the gas. May closed her eyes. Somehow the child jumped aside. When they got to the monastery, she felt ill. The mass of buildings was half buried in the rocks and half sticking out of them, a real fortress. Three grubby monks were on guard at the gateway and scattered, yelping like lapdogs, when Hagar and May walked up to them. Yona could go in, but when he laughingly asked "And the women?" the monks expressed their disapproval by spitting. "Slobs," said Hagar. May, who was in great need of a leak, was tempted to drop her pants and pee on their holy threshold. God and sex were one!

From every nook and cranny little boys had appeared like groundhogs, and their sharp eyes tried to weigh up the visitors. Should they serve them or rob them? Trust or murder? One of them stood staring in fascination at the bulky Czech revolver on Yona's hip. His index finger curled as if in his imagination he was pulling the trigger. Yona gave the boy a warning look, like a doctor trying to suppress a dangerous impulse in a patient. From the wadi a most horrible stench arose, the monks used the trickling stream as an open sewer.

"The odor of sanctity!" Yona said. May had to complete the climb down holding a handkerchief over her nose and gagging. In the rocks were holes which at one time hermits had withdrawn to, in order to become holy by starvation. May had visions of monks sitting above their own excrement, amid swarms of flies, talking gibberish like disheveled parrots on their perch, and imagining in their madness that they had left mortality behind.

The monastery sat high above the ravine, through the telescope May scanned the roofed terraces. Table and chair, a wooden bed, the simplicity of a monastic cell. From a frog's-eye view it looked marvelous. She would like to sit up there under an awning and let time glide by. The dunes and the monastery were one and the same landscape, hence the misunderstanding: eternity was within reach, but for things, not people.

When they had driven out of Jerusalem in the opposite direction, a few days before, in order to go through the hills down to the Mediterranean, May had been assailed by contradictory feelings.

There you had parasol pines, vineyards, wild anemones, cricket song and birdsong, and above all that, half hidden in the foliage, a house that May immediately wanted. But the view was spoiled by the stench rising from the valley. The stream was a sanitary canal for the sewers of the Holy City. The exhalations were so strong they left you gasping. It was as if you could see Heaven and smell Hell! As if above and below were indissolubly linked. People had not remained for long masters of the city they had built, they had very soon been captured by a dream that decayed into a nightmare. "The place where the king goes on foot," Poldine[8] used to say, it was her polite way of referring to the bathroom.

Even if stones fall into ruins, with time or through violence, the ruins remain standing to teach you a lesson: everything passes away, beginning with you. Thank the Lord for what you get and don't ask for too much, life is a gift horse and you don't want to look too closely into its stinking mouth.

As if accidentally, May had pushed away Hagar's hand, which was resting on her thigh. In that stench it was impossible to think of love or feel anything except disgust, and yet she was assailed by desire. Where it stinks it's hot! A practical joke of the gods. May didn't believe in poltergeists or earth rays, but damned or blessed, there was something about this place that made people embrace each other or reach for their knives.

At the first lookout point she had suddenly give way. Wave after wave, slope after slope of sand stretched out to the deceptive surface of the Dead Sea. A landscape that suggested emptiness, an emptiness sufficient unto itself where people could be no more than transient. A congealed ocean, ochre yellow and smelling like a gigantic cat litter. Serene in appearance but full of ruses and snares. Everything can be blown away like dust and the stones can walk. Dust lies like powder over the signposts, roads lead nowhere and suddenly stop. May stretched out her arms as if to embrace the world and hold it to her breast: "Let us build three tabernacles!"[9] Laughing, Yona pointed to the heap of rocks that perhaps marked the edge of somebody's property: "It is written: These stones are mine!"

Yona is Alida's husband, understanding, patient, but stubborn. At the Friday evening meal his wife serves him first, then he hands May, as his guest, a piece of the broken bread. Stocky, not fat, but with a belly. He makes a perfect sheepdog, something protective radiates from him, but also something hungry, like a silent grief, an incurable nostalgia. Inconceivable that this man would kill a child, and yet. He watches May attentively, as if he wonders what has led this strange bird to alight under his roof, what questions she's looking for the answer to, what story is pursuing her, what has driven her to the wall. Lord knows you come across wounded souls in Jerusalem. Besides, Yona is remarkably shy with women.

"He makes sure Alida gets whatever she wants, including in bed," Hagar had said, and May answered, hearing the echo of Poldine, "Oh, when did you lie between them?" A long forgotten melody comes to life somewhere in the back of her head, a little tune of regret that flows warmly down her spine and spreads out in her pelvis as desire. She turns away to hide her sudden blushing. Clumsily, as if he suspects he's in the way, Yona spread out a traveling rug for her so she can sit and look out over the desert, protected by the heap of rocks. He will withdraw and watch her from a distance, he understands that she just wants to be alone with this view. They're such fussy, even intrusive people, but they mean well. It doesn't all have to be said in so many words. May feels the shameless need to lean her head on Yona's shoulder and cry her eyes out. "I no longer recognize my country, my children are scattered and my mother died without knowing me, on what stone shall I lay down my head to rest?"[10]

NOTES to the Translation

1. The first selection describes the parrot. In the original, the encyclopedia is quoted in German, I have translated the passage directly from the novel; the last four words are in English.

2. The Leie River (in French, and in some English reference works, the Lys) rises in northeastern France and flows east and a little north, to join the Scheldt at Ghent.

3. Nickname given to Albert I (1875-1934, King of the Belgians 1909-34) for his valiant diplomatic and military efforts in the First World War. His son Leopold III (ruled 1934-51), on the contrary, was widely felt to have been less than firm in his resolve to have no dealings with the Nazis. In 1945 he withdrew to Switzerland, he was not allowed to return until 1950, and his return caused such uproar that he abdicated after a year. He was succeeded by his elder son, the present king Boudewijn I (Baudouin).

4. The Yser River runs northwards across West Flanders. It was the front line throughout the First World War and saw relentless fierce fighting. The Yser Monument, beside the river at Dixmude, is the focus of intense Flemish Catholic and nationalist emotion.

5. Elisabeth of Bavaria (1876-1965), wife of Albert I, Queen of the Belgians.

6. Cyriel Buysse (1859-1932), naturalist Flemish writer. Wrote, among other things, a powerful social drama *Het gezin van Paemel* (The van Paemel Family, 1903), which Monika van Paemel's family hated. Rosalie (1834-1875) and Virginie (1836-1923) Loveling, novelists, were Buysse's aunts.

7. In English in the original.

8. Poldine is May's grandmother.

9. Quotation from Matthew 17:4.

10. An imaginary quotation, we believe, in the style of the Old Testament prophets. The last part of it echoes Jesus's words: "The Son of Man hath no place to lay his head" (Matthew 8:20).

Bibliography

Primary works

Paemel, Monika van. *Amazone met het blauwe voorhoofd.* Amsterdam: Elsevier, 1971; rev. ed. Amsterdam: Meulenhoff, 1987.
_____. *De confrontatie.* The Hague: Nijgh and van Ditmar, 1974; rev. ed. Amsterdam: Meulenhoff, 1986.
_____. *Marguerite.* The Hague: Nijgh and van Ditmar, 1976; rev. ed. Amsterdam: Meulenhoff, 1985.
_____. *De vermaledijde vaders.* Amsterdam: Meulenhoff, 1985 (translated into French as *Les Pères maudits* [Arles, 1989]).
_____. *De eerste steen.* Amsterdam: Meulenhoff, 1992

Secondary works

Aken, Paul van. "Les romans de Monika van Paemel." *Septentrion* XVIII (2) 1989. 3-5. Reprinted in *Septentrion: le dialogue permanent.* Rekkem: Stichting Ons Erfdeel, 1990. 141-144.
Alleene, Carlos. "Monika van Paemel." *Schrijvers zijn ook mensen.* Amsterdam: Manteau, 1987. 155-167.
Janssens, Marcel, Marita de Sterck, and Luc Lannoy. Eds. *Geboekstaafd. Vlaamse Prozaschrijvers na 1945.* Louvain: Davidsfonds, [1991]. 199-201.
Kingstone, Basil. "Monika van Paemel." *Canadian Journal of Netherlandic Studies* XI ii (Fall 1990). 69-72.

Eva Gerlach

Myra Scholz-Heerspink

The awarding of literary prizes brings linguistic risks and challenges of its own. Rhetorical overload can easily drown out the quieter voices of poems, and the physical presence of the prize winner makes extensive biographical remarks seem at least pertinent, at times even pivotal. When Eva Gerlach was awarded the prestigious Roland Holst prize for her poetic oeuvre in 1988, the chairman of the jury avoided both these pitfalls. Respecting her preference for anonymity he refrained from any speculations about her personal past and present. And the single rhetorical flourish he added to his characterization of her work was obviously inspired by a close reading of her poems. "Poetic dwellings on stilts," he called them, "erected with conviction in the marshlands of everyday existence."[1] This compact metaphor suggests not only soundly crafted works of art but recurring themes in Gerlach's poetry as well: the need for form that rises above an always threatening chaos, and for a sense of dwelling in a setting ruled by time and inevitable processes of decay.

Gerlach's first volume of poems, *Verder geen leed* (1979, "No Other Damage Done") attracted a great deal of critical attention. Some of it, predictably, took the form of educated guesses about the person behind the pseudonym. Names of established Dutch writers were put forward; poetry of this quality, the reasoning went, could hardly represent a genuine debut. The poems that caused the stir are

Myra Scholz-Heerspink

for the most part made up of tightly constructed quatrains; virtually every line has its rhyme and underlying iambic meter. Monotony and sing-song patterns are kept at bay by natural speech rhythms and a liberal use of enjambment. Each poem presents a sharply drawn vignette, usually a childhood memory or dream image. The illustration on the cover of the volume suggests an artistic rationale behind these compact texts: Madame Blanchard is depicted in her fatal plunge from a hot air balloon against a background of gray Parisian roofs and ominous sky. The "No Other Damage Done" of the title appears to function as an ironic comment on the horror of the scene. Critics, in fact, repeatedly referred to the irony present in Gerlach's first volume. Since many of the poems deal with memories and fears of falling, the laconic language and highly finished form can be seen as a kind of ironic packaging of emotion.

"Tiger Moth," the title of the first section of the volume, draws attention to the poem in which a child, the "I" of the story, watches her elaborate model airplane fly magnificently, then crash. The feelings of let-down and tragedy remain outside the poem itself, which catches the fragments of the plane in a neat final rhyme. That the images of flying and falling have wider implications than the incidental disappointments of childhood becomes clear already in the first poem, with its memory of flying a kite in a graveyard. The rest of the volume bears this out, with analogues from nature (ants that grow wings and fail to use them) and — most importantly — from human relationships. The "you" in "You pushed me till the swing moved fast and high..." is obviously an adult, perhaps a parent figure, who has betrayed a child's confidence. Most poignantly this experience of total let-down comes through in a poem which explicitly names a father: "My father lived in a far-away land..." The grief that saturates multiple levels of memory is couched in sparse, matter-of-fact language and further distanced by the formal finesse of the quatrains.

This discrepancy between the experience of pain and its polished poetic expression can perhaps be explained as ironic technique. But a form which is at odds with content may also function in a different way. If immeasurable grief speaks from measured lines, if memories of broken faith appear in stanzas which make good their promise of rhyme, the poem as a whole may be saying more than its lexical content conveys. As Christopher Ricks put it in his defense of A.E. Housman: "rhythm and style temper or mitigate or criticize what in bald paraphrase the poem would be saying" (Ricks 163). Poetry in this case emerges as the sphere in which fragmentary, incoherent experience can be re-collected into an ordered whole.

Gerlach's frequent use of quotations suggests that, for her, formalized language does indeed function as a constructive force. Although much of the direct speech in her poems is simply part of jumbled everyday impressions, she often inserts lines from songs and children's rhymes; and these snatches of formulaic language exert a force all their own on the poetic material. In the poem about the laundry lady, for example, the first stanza is nearly comic in tone. The description of the physical appearance of the woman is matched by the helter-skelter rhythm of her mundane remark. In the second stanza the poem loses its ragged quality and the image turns serene through the shaping power of the woman's song. The last poem in the volume, "It's freezing...," also ends with a quotation from a song — not a Psalm this time, despite the despairing religious tone of the poem, but a rhyme from a children's game. The allusion is to a hypothetical situation, to the sense of release and joy that would be experienced if things were different. But the echo that lingers after the poem and the volume have come to a close, is that of carefree play rather than of the bleak "real" situation.

Regardless of the exact label attached to the function of strict form in Gerlach's earliest poetry — whether ironic, mitigating, or perhaps even incantatory — there can be no doubt that her preoccupation with structuring principles increased in her next three volumes. All poems in *Een kopstaand beeld* (1983, "An Upside-Down Image") consist of eight lines, but in a wide variety of constellations (3-3-2, 3-2-3, 8, 2-4-2, 4-4, 2-5-1, etc.). Since many of the poems are devoted to works of art, children's drawings and photographs, the capturing of momentary reality in some stable form here becomes thematic. At times the poetic treatment of the topic seems part of a dialogue begun in the literature of an earlier age. "Plate with Dragon," for instance, redirects the thrust of Keats's "Ode on a Grecian Urn;" here art is not credited with preserving transient beauty, but with taming and containing a destructive force. "Orphan Girls on their Way to Church" — titled after a painting in the Amsterdam Historical Museum — highlights the peculiar locus of human portraits between the life of a given moment and a static permanence that resembles nothing more than death. Never in this volume is artistic form offered as a patent remedy for the pain of impermanence. Form is explored from every angle — its power to deceive as well as to impose shape and create harmony. The isolated objects listed in "Vocabulary" may be hopeful or threatening, depending on the larger formal framework which they appear to be waiting for — just as lexical items depend on syntactic structures for meaning. Images, like the reflections in department store windows on a busy Amsterdam shopping street (in "People"), leave the reader in doubt about where to draw the line between appearance and reality, or even between the dead and the living.

There is nothing precious about this thematic preoccupation with form. Pain, in fact, is given a literally central place in the volume: the third of the five sections deals exclusively with hospitals, illnesses, and terminal cases. Here the undercooled language is most reminiscent of the earlier "falling" poems. Dispassionate bureaucratic expressions in "Clinic," for example, belie the intensity of the suffering. In this volume, however, the focus of pain has shifted from the "I" and its endless album of memories to anonymous faces in waiting rooms, strangers in the subway, the chronically ill. Although the past is not obliterated in a poem like "Season" — the father figure is associated with childhood pain — the dominant images are of new life, and the imperatives in the second half of the poem are benedictory. While the earlier "father" poem could be described as eloquent, this one calls up W.H. Auden's criterion for beauty in poetry: "a poem is beautiful or ugly to the degree that it succeeds or fails in reconciling contradictory feelings in an order of mutual propriety" (Auden 71). Form functions less as a foil in the later poem and more as a direct embodiment of "the predictable."

Quotations of formulaic language also appear repeatedly in Gerlach's second volume. In "Entropy" the warding off of both a child's bad dreams and the deterioration of a house is attributed to a singer of texts — here specifically of the thirteenth Psalm. Structurally the poem seems to rotate around the stable axis of the quotation. The simplicity and balance of form make this poem a kind of second-generation assault on chaos: older formulas bequeath their power to new verbal structures.

Dochter (1984, "Daughter") displays an even greater single-minded concentration on matters of form. Every poem consists of eight lines divided into two groups of five and three lines each. While the rhyme pattern between lines 2 and 7 varies from poem to poem, the first line invariably rhymes with the last. The organization of the volume as a whole obviously mirrors the micro-structure of the individual poems: five sections contain 3, 5, 8, 8, 5 and 3 poems each. Thematically the volume is focused on a single subject, the birth of a daughter and (roughly) the first year of the infant's life. The self-imposed structure serves as a kind of containing wall for the intense emotions felt by a mother toward her first child. There is fear that the prematurely born infant will not survive, but above all there is the ambivalence that grows out of an enormous sense of responsibility. The quotation by Thomas Blackburn which prefaces the volume sets the tone: "And have I put upon your shoulders then/what in myself I have refused to bear,/My own and the confusion of dead men." The awareness of a child's vulnerability in a world which by its very structure is fraught with risks accounts for a large part of the ambivalence. In the poem "The memory of pain..." the field of pathology offers chilling — and certainly far from arbitrary — metaphors to describe the growth of this awareness. With complex emotions like these always in the background, the volume avoids all sentimentality and greeting-card style joy. Yet a poem like "The dead are resurrected in my child..." does convey a sense of the miraculous; and "When half asleep and bitten into me..." shows through the smallest gesture how a mother is also given new life by a child. The world may be a fragile, almost flimsy place, but the experience of teaching language to a young child turns a parent into a kind of exuberant puppy ("World that I talk her into...").

The generally laudatory reception of *Dochter* revived the public debate about the poet's identity; from one quarter even came the assertion that this was undoubtedly a male writer using the mother-daughter theme as the ultimate mask for his identity. To put to rest once and for all any suspicion that coy games of this sort were being played, Gerlach agreed to be interviewed by a Dutch weekly magazine. It then became clear that anonymity was simply essential to her sense of being a writer; it was also a matter of conviction: "In principle every biography is a lie compared to the reality known as literature" (Gerlach 1985:48). Some biographical details did emerge from this interview nevertheless: a very real child was the subject of her third volume; "Entropy" in her second volume recalled an enormous decaying house from Gerlach's childhood and an unforgettable housekeeper; "The dead are resurrected in my child..." was written on the Dutch holiday commemorating the end of World War II; and the "father" who appears in so many of her poems could be any one of several father figures.

Not surprisingly, Gerlach's comments on her work proved more enlightening than biographical anecdotes. When asked about poets who had influenced her writing she mentioned the names of Donne, Quevedo and Achterberg, placing herself in a Dutch twentieth-century tradition which has its own place in a larger tradition of European poetry.[2] Several questions arose about her use of poetic form. The structure of "Entropy," with its 3-2-3 line arrangement, was, she explained, inspired by the shape of an hour glass. The interview also revealed that the principle behind the recurring 3-5-8 pattern in *Dochter* is that of the golden section — the division of a line such that the smaller segment is to the larger as the larger is to the whole. Two organizing principles inform the macro-structure of the volume: the golden section and mitosis, the biological term for cell division. What these remarks made clear is that poetic form in this volume has more than just the general significance of shape as opposed to shapelessness or chaos; specific forms here carry a symbolic charge intricately related to theme. "The volume is about the inability to coalesce, in various ways, but in any case imaged in that woman and her daughter...Every poem presents one of a number of possible ruptures" (Gerlach 1985:45ff). The split between the two parts of each poem, then, has its counterpart in the mother-daughter relation: "In no other relationship is the tension as great: wanting to be one and having to be two...or wanting to be two and having to be one" (Gerlach 1985:47). The "precarious balance" in "The sense of falling..." therefore applies not only to the general conditions of life in a risky world but also to the parent-child relationship with all its potential for see-saw movement. Perhaps their preoccupation with biographical issues prevented critics from seeing broader connotations of the volume's theme: according to Gerlach the mother and her child also represent an artist and her work. There, too, the relation is both intimate and uneasy.

If biography and "real" identities are not particularly relevant to the reading of poems, a consciously chosen fictional identity is. The name Gerlach, the interview revealed, was inspired by the name of a Dutch transport company. "I looked out of the window one day and saw a Gerlach moving van riding past. I liked the name, and what is a poet if not a mover of meanings? You take something out of reality and place it in a new context" (Gerlach 1985:45). Anyone on the lookout for such vans will have noticed that the Gerlach firm is also engaged in security transport. The heavily armored vehicles carry the term "Waardetransport" which, taken from its context, could mean not only "transport of valuables" but "transport of value(s)." Whether or not this was part of the original motivation, the reader is almost inevitably drawn into the ongoing poetic dialogue with haphazard objects and words.

The expectations for intricate poetic structuring raised by *Dochter* were more than met by *Domicilie* (1987, "Domicile"). A note on the dust-flap indicates that this volume, too, was conceived as a well-ordered whole: "*Domicilie* contains three times 24 answers — not very definitive ones — to the question 'How do death and life reside in each other?'" This is followed by a short sketch of the thematic contours of each of the three sections: "In the first series, 'The Hours,' an attempt is made to call back to life a person who has just died, by remembering her hour by hour. In the second, 'In Life,' an attempt is made to preserve a few memories. In the third, 'Domicile,' an attempt is made to settle into existence." A glance at the table of contents reveals that these are only the broadest outlines of the volume's structure. The middle section is itself divided into two types of poems: four longer poems printed in italics divide up shorter ones into groups of six, eight and six poems each. The third section presents its own uniquely puzzling arrangement, with many titles appearing twice.

The poems in the series "The Hours" show as much regularity of form as those of *Dochter*. All of them consist of eight lines, the first six interlocked by varying rhyme patterns, the last two always a rhymed couplet. The meter is consistently iambic pentameter. None of the poems have internal divisions into sections or stanzas. The homogeneity of this framework contrasts sharply with the welter of associations which crowd their way into the texts. The relationship between the "I" and the dead person was obviously one that extended over many years. Scenes from childhood therefore stand side-by-side with intense recent memories of caring for an aged woman during the last stages of her life. A certain merging of roles results at times: both grandmother and child appear as objects of care as well as caregivers. The close sense of identity comes about not only through the family relation, but through the acute realization of shared mortality, of the family tie between the exhaustion of the person providing care and the weakness of the dying. Grief is shown to be an intensely physical experience: bedsores fester in the memory, dentures grin from their glass of water, bedside drawers opened after the death reveal moldy food and handkerchiefs containing half-chewed mouthfuls of meat. As in "Entropy," the sturdy poetic form holds together images of general deterioration.

"The Hours," like Gerlach's earlier work, derives part of its stabilizing power from formulaic language. Since the central idea of the cycle is an attempted resurrection, it is hardly surprising that the New Testament supplies many of the images (e.g. the 153 fish and coals in "9 a.m.," the desperate "Eat my body then" of "5 p.m.") as well as quotations (e.g. "I come like a thief" in "7 a.m."). Perhaps the most effective use of formulaic language in the cycle is the simple imperative "Eat" which occurs twice in "1.a.m." In combination with the very ordinary "No complaints" (the original Dutch is probably closer to "no grumbling"), it is reminiscent of a parent reproving a child for making a mess of his dinner. But the echo from the liturgy of the Eucharist is unmistakable, as the force of this isolated word arrests the flood of repulsive images and introduces "quiet" into the poem, radically slowing the rhythm of the last two lines.

The New Testament allusions suggest other debts to traditional textual forms. The title of the cycle, besides underlining the passage of time, also recalls the medieval tradition of the "Books of Hours," devotional volumes consisting of prayers for lay persons to read at fixed hours of the day. Of the various cycles of prayers included in these books, the "Office of the Dead" offers the most illuminating parallels. The prayers of this Office, usually recited before the Requiem in a medieval funeral, are typically accompanied by miniatures depicting the raising of Lazarus from the dead and scenes from the life of Job (Wieck 1988:131ff). All nine lessons of the Office — lamentations about suffering and the transience of human life — are taken from the Book of Job. The images of decay in these texts are as uncompromising as those in Gerlach's cycle; her metaphor of flesh as a delicate woven fabric ("1 a.m.") particularly recalls Lessons III and IV (Job 10:8-12 and 13:22-28). The fact that some Books of Hours included a full cycle of 24 miniatures illustrating the Office of the Dead strongly suggests that the title and 24 vignettes of Gerlach's cycle are a quotation of this formal structure (Wieck 1988:134).

Further interpretive possibilities offer themselves once the symbolic potential of numerical structures, so important to the shape of *Dochter*, is taken seriously. Old traditions of number symbolism may play a role in "The Hours" that goes beyond the immediately obvious association of 24 with the hours of a day. Perhaps the passing of time is further reflected in the recurrence of the numbers six, traditionally associated with the six days of creation, and eight, the number of fullness and eternity. The total of 60 syllables in the first six lines of each poem could conceivably mirror the division of hours into minutes and seconds. There is, of course, a danger of over-interpretation here.[3] In view of Gerlach's admitted fascination with symbolic structures, however, a reader who allows for undogmatic associations of this kind will hardly be guilty of doing violence to the poetic text.

Despite the intricate structuring of the cycle, there is no easy sublimation of pain in the beauty of poetic form. The sense of grief grows more intense as the volume nears its end — an end which is itself a kind of second death, following as it does the second life, the

re-membering, of the deceased. The simple listing of items seen from
the window in "4 a.m." inexplicably conveys heartbreak. And
although "form" and "pattern" appear as lexical items in "5 a.m." the
prospect of grief finds such direct expression here that the formalities
in the poetry become completely inconspicuous. One critic went so
far as to call the last three lines of this poem the most dramatic
moment in Dutch poetry of his generation (Otten 4).

The phrase "in life" from the last poem of "The Hours"
serves as the title for the second section of *Domicilie*. The two types
of poems in this section suggest different types of memories: longer,
more persistent scenes that lend context and undertones to the shorter
vignettes which they frame. Since this section is not a cycle,
however, the individual poems invite a more independent reading.
Familiar from earlier volumes is, first, the compactness of poems like
"Neighbors" and "Heron" and, secondly, the way the satisfying form
contains — in both senses of the word — feelings of dissatisfaction and
restlessness.

Thematically the third section focuses on homes and houses,
the experience of moving to a new residence, and all the associations
ranging from imprisonment to secure dwelling that a house can
evoke. The compositional oddity of this section with its recurring
poem titles may be a formal metaphor for moving: familiar items are
transferred to new surroundings where they take on new identity, new
content. Longer forms are explored. While the language of a poem
like "Excluded" remains as terse as ever, the larger shaping principles
are images and an expansive flowing rhythm. The "new child"
mentioned in this poem seems to inspire a very different poetic form
from that of *Dochter*. Similar tendencies can be found in "Domicile,"
which constructs itself quite naturally from the rhythms of water birds
gathering for bread scraps and the solidity of a statuesque image. The
tone of this third section wavers between resignation and resolution
about dwelling in the here and now. Moments of reconciliation with
things as they are occasionally break through the web of contradictory
feelings. The oppressive neighborhood images of "Neighbors" and
"Heron," for example, give way in the last — formulaic — line of
"Settlement" to a redeeming empathy.

In her fourth volume, *De kracht van verlamming* (1988, "The Power of Paralysis"), Gerlach continues the exploration of longer forms. The first poem, which also bears the title of the volume, consists of irregular groupings of lines of widely varying lengths. The almost ragged visual impression of the poem is matched by the violent, jagged images of a car accident. Much about the content remains unclear: the identity of the "you" and of "those two," for example, but especially the order of the metaphorical relations. The fragmentary, indefinite quality of the text itself conveys a sense of shock. What emerges in the end is a double image of catastrophe and radical encounter, with phrases like "lost in each other, head over heels" recalling clichés of erotic love. The whole point of the poem seems to lie in its refusal to clarify which image is the metaphor and which the "reality." The title hints at a similar ambiguity. Paralysis is in the first place a powerfully destructive force, but the phrasing could also be taken to mean that the paralyzed state knows a power of its own. The title — part of a quotation which prefaces the poem — is taken from Dante's description of the peculiar punishment reserved for those who try to divine future events. Their heads have been turned around 180 degrees, forcing them to stumble blindly forward through all eternity, seeing only what lies behind them. The one short comment on the dust-flap of this volume indicates that looking backward is indeed a central theme: "*De kracht van verlamming* is once again about memory, but more directly than before." The first poem hints that the memories will focus on an experience of love and devastating loss. The question prompted by the title, then, is whether the power of such images is necessarily as relentless, as much beyond hope of being anything but destructive, as it is in Dante's hell.

This volume is dominated by images, some of them as elaborate and poem-filling as seventeenth-century conceits. For example, "Look!", with its call for a violent shaping of the self, bears a resemblance to one of John Donne's "Holy Sonnets," "Batter my heart..." Equally unsparing images of pain appear in a poem which actually quotes Donne in its title: "Death be not proud." The quotation owes part of its effectiveness to contrast: the low-key resignation of the last three lines of Gerlach's poem is a far cry from the vigorously defiant spirit of the Donne sonnet. Imagery changes as the volume progresses. The word "memory" appears more often as the intensity of individual memories seems to fade. As if to counteract the abstract quality of the term, Gerlach personifies it; memory is a "she" who visits the "I" in a variety of guises, often in frightening dream-like settings. Later in the volume all visual attention narrows to the qualities of stones — their solidity and permanence, but above all their enviable freedom from memory. The contrast between the "life" of stones and of vulnerable flesh and blood is explored in modes as different as the childlike narrative of "Story" and the more direct reflections of "On the Way."

Gerlach's most recent volume is *In een bocht van de zee* (1990, "By a Curving Shore"). As the prefatory quotation indicates, the title is part of a plaintive snatch of song from Chekhov's *Three Sisters*: "A green oak grows by a curving shore." The title reappears over the last poem in the volume, a vignette on the themes of death and new life drawn, in familiar Gerlach style, from fragments of ordinary conversation. Unlike any of the preceding volumes, this last one shows no obvious overall organization into parts or patterns. The poems present themselves in a variety of lengths and shapes, with scattered rhyme loosely binding lines which may or may not follow a given metric pattern. Many of the poems seem to represent a further stage of the structural exploration begun in the two previous volumes. The series "Memory, Longing" continues the personification of memory. The first two poems in the series, "She wears her hair in braids..." and "The horse kicked her...," invests the idea of memory with dense visual detail and a surrealistic kind of violence. The last poem in the series, "The nest...," with its natural images and simplicity of form, suggests something akin to the relief felt on waking from bad dreams.

Critical responses to Gerlach's later poetry have been mixed. The double tendency to heap images onto an abstract concept and to load simple objects with insinuated meaning recalls traditions of allegorical and emblematic poetry, and the reflex of the typical modern reader faced with patterns of association like these is simply to balk. Some of the brightest spots in *In een bocht van de zee* are the poems which further explore structures based on free-flowing rhythms. "Can vei la lauzeta mover," which opens the volume, recreates the plodding pace of a donkey, then uses it as a frame for a view of the totally other rhythm of larks. The conversational, freely associative style of "The Doorposts and the Narrow Windows" is reminiscent of "Excluded." Risks are taken here: almost hackneyed expressions of love open and close the poem; in between comes the everyday slamming of a gate accompanied by uncertain memories of loss, understatements of grief. Economy of imagery — one short glimpse of fast-flying swallows — matches the unpretentious tone.

In view of Gerlach's productivity and her relatively young age — that she was born in 1948 is the only piece of biographical information she has parted with willingly — her oeuvre can be expected to grow by several more volumes over the next decade. Just how a poetic talent will develop cannot be predicted with any certainty, but the six volumes which Gerlach has produced to date raise certain expectations. The large, perennial themes of suffering, memory, time, love and death will probably keep appearing in new formal settings, patternings which themselves will offer new possibilities for commenting on, mitigating or mending the brokenness of experience. What will probably not be forthcoming, despite all the past allusions to mother-daughter, father-daughter and grandmother-granddaughter relationships, is any thematic focus on issues of gender. Gerlach's poetry is not "topical;" it draws its themes neither from newspaper headlines nor from discussions in the social sciences. This says nothing, however, about its closeness to lived reality. As Helen Vendler pointed out so eloquently in a recent review article on the poetry of Adrienne Rich and Jorie Graham, the choice of topical themes can limit a poet's vision. If issues relating to social groups are central, the result may be an an allegorical mode of its own: portrayals of moral reality which tend toward the schematic and dualistic, with suffering neatly accounted for in terms of innocent victims and unredeemable victimizers (Vendler 50ff). In Gerlach's work, pain eludes patterns of analysis; it is all-pervasive, part and parcel of a shared predicament. Identity in a world with this fragile structure emerges not so much from roles played as from words spoken. Descriptions of fleeting scenes, incidental scraps of conversation are rescued from mundaneness and oblivion by incorporating them into poems which themselves are linked — through quotations, imagery, or structural principles — to age-old textual traditions. The result is a convergence of voices past and present, and the simultaneity makes for a sense of equality among the various speakers. Social roles appear as fluctuating and secondary compared to the staying-power of words.

NOTES to the Introduction

Thanks are due to Eva Gerlach and her publisher, the Arbeiderspers, Amsterdam, for permission to translate her work and publish the translations, as well as to the editors of *Dutch Crossing* (University College, London) which carried seven of the translations appearing in this chapter — some of them earlier versions.

1. Wam de Moor, quoted in "Eva Gerlach ontvangt Roland Holstpenning," *NRC Handelsblad* 9 June 1983.

2. Selections from the work of Gerrit Achterberg (1905-1962), whose themes of love and death are also woven into tight formal patterns, are available in English translation: *But This Land Has No End: Selected Poems*, trans. Pleuke Boyce (Lantzville: Oolichan Books, 1989), and *Hidden Weddings: Selected Poems*, trans. Michael O'Laughlin (Dublin: Raven Arts, 1987).

3. For a concise overview of various traditions of number symbolism, also of the interpretive pitfalls surrounding "formal numerology," see the chapter "Numerology" in Rivers.

Translations by Myra Scholz-Heerspink

From *VERDER GEEN LEED* ("No Other Damage Done")

Often I went to the graveyard, alone,
fat, to fly my kite. There the wind was best.
If the string sagged I jumped down from a stone.
I might be small, but I'd die like the rest,

the sexton said, "Someday you'll fly off with it."
A good kite that Dragon was, made the thing
myself. No Robber kite could ever get it;
fine grains of glass glittered around the string.

*****

Linen over a delicate frame. Double
wings, one above the other, open cockpit;
a motor that could run a good five minutes
on 1.5 cc's (a thimbleful of fuel).

Do-it-yourself scale model that I made dance
from where I stood; from semi-loops I sent
it into roll. My heart leaped at the flash
of sunlight on the fiercely yellow paint.

Faster than sparrows it flew, my *Tiger Moth*.
The tailspin started at three hundred feet.
I watched it spiral down like some dry leaf
and hit the field as bits of wood and cloth.

*****

It was evening when the ants grew wings.
Wave after wave they crawled out of the ground

and up the wall, where all they did was move
in clumsy circles. Later one or two

flew as far up as the awning, but found
it all too risky and retraced their route,
or fell. Soon many had flipped upside-down.
I also saw some gnawing at their wings.

*****

I had a special box (a *Schimmelpenninck,
Fine Assortment*)[1] for saving all the things
that frightened me. Lizards' tails, a snakeskin,
a long-horned beetle's blackish skeleton.

I'd look at them and they'd line up in rows
and march past me — one way only, no
halts, no turns. My life was in danger, too.
I never stopped growing out of my clothes.

*****

The laundry lady wore a felt hat when she ironed,
artificial freesias stuck out of both sides.
"You can't be too careful, before you know it you've caught
                                                        a cold."
I watched her from my chair beside the mangling board.

She loaded red-hot coals into the iron, then stood there,
feet planted wide apart, before the dampened clothes. "O
                                                        Lord
of all our souls," she sang, "Redeem Your children now."
                                                        The air
grew close, her head moved back and forth, steam hung
                                                above the board.

*****

My mother stands there on the dune, her clothes blown close
against her body, her hair streaming free.
She sees gulls swoop around the ships at sea
and flies away to them, Great Albatross.

I watch her go. "Just don't come back here, ever."
She taps the window, turns on lights, my mother
who kisses me, hangs up her coat and goes
to the big mirror to adjust her clothes.

*****

A house with little shutters, on the sea.
On the veranda sits a woman, staring.
"Your waves and billows have gone over me."
The wind gives her its bladder wrack and marram.

She still goes out beachcombing when the tides
are turning. Calfskin pumps on slick wet stones.

Hauls jetsam up between her knees. She writes,
"A donkey follows where its driver goes."

*****

My father lived in a far-away land.
He wanted to stay there. He never called.
I wrote his name with ballpoint in my hand.
When we were friends I couldn't write at all.

I still remembered riding on his shoulders,
and how I gripped his gray legs with my fists,
and how he said, "You've got to lend me something"
before he smashed my piggy-bank to bits.

*****

You pushed me till the swing moved fast and high.
Wind lashed my eyes as I swept forward, back
it pulled at them, trying, it seemed, to suck
them from my face. Down under I was blind,

above a hawk that hung in sky with free
view of the land: a forest with its clumps
of trees like reed, far towers like sails. "Jump"
you called. I jumped. Without you catching me.

*****

It's freezing. Grass is turning black. I don't
love you the way I used to, Lord. I know
you better, that must be why. This cold, though,
it's creeping round my heart. Come now, where are you?

If there were just some way to calculate
the chance of meeting you. The bank would break,

a jackpot hit, and we'd not care at all.
We'd run outside to sing "The Farmer in the Dell."

*****

From *EEN KOPSTAAND BEELD* ("An Upside-Down Image")

Orphan Girls on their Way to Church

They stand here in a row that reaches deep
inside the house. God's hand has rescued them
and placed them, shadowless, on this small square.
His hard Word stiffens every fold and pleat.
If He'd just call them back to life today!

For Him they'd break their ranks, the lips gone gray
from cold would start to whisper quietly;
they'd give the lie to death, and come to me.

Plate with Dragon

Jump, then. Your range is only one plate wide.

Go on, stick out all seven fiery tongues,
flap your wings high behind those wide-spread claws,
spray poison from your double snaky source,
but kaolin holds you in hardest white,
cobalt takes care to house you in two blues,
hot glazing fires have pressed your scales down smooth;

"God is eternal" says your other side.

Vocabulary

This is your eye. This is the sun. This cold
that tugs at you is draft from the open door.
This is water that's always just your size.

There on the fire is the kettle that sings
above four knobs for turning on the gas.
And here's the bread knife resting on its board.

Make sure that you remember all these things.
Tomorrow or today they'll have their say.

Entropy

She who banned evil from my sleep is dead.
Evenings she smelled of sweat, that is, of strength.

My heart, she sang, keep watch until the dawn.

Tall she stood in the kitchen eating bread.
How long, Lord, wilt thou hide thy face from me?

Among rubbish and dust she fought her way
against disorder and steady decay.
The house that kept resisting her is gone.

Clinic

In this room those on final lists are waiting,
each holding his insurance card. Across
a desk their numbers go on file because
eventually the costs will need defraying.

In folders alphabetically stored
pain turns into paper. News, sent in code,
of death, whose messages are few and brief
and usually delayed until we leave.

Season

My father, who could never stomach death,
lets hands that broke a yardstick on me touch
with different fingers newly germinated
green, curled beneath a sleeping cap of seed.

Make his heart light. Let him feel moved to greet
the predictable, keep it safe from wind
and watch the fruits till rottenness sets in.

He's had enough of doing what he hated.

People

I saw them in the Leidsestraat today,
behind me, mirrored in the glass of Metz
and Co. Thinner than ever, they
were easy to see through, most fragile, yet

the asphalt lay so firm beneath their feet
I had to turn before I recognized them.
They veered off quickly, unprepared to greet,
the only ones from whom no steam was rising.

From *DOCHTER* ("Daughter")

The sense of falling gives her such a fright
she flings her arms out wide and stays that way
till everything appears to be all right.
Our balance, daughter, how precarious
it is, each movement takes us by surprise,

under the constant threat of gravity
we open up our hands and shut our eyes,
a Moro reflex lasting all our lives.

*****

The dead are resurrected in my child.
Their heads hang limp still, groping fingers ask
for something in my arms that can be grasped;
they try their voices while I sing to them;
as hunger moves them to my breast their hands

find their support; now recognition trims

their pupils small as eyes from photographs,
all wide and blind, look up and into mine.

*****

When, half asleep and bitten into me,
she takes my hand and leads it to her cheek,
I feel prepared for every openness.
Three fingers placed in horizontal lines
beside her mouth are all that I possess.

I undergo her transplant quietly,
and take on form unknown before her time.
Body, reshaped, to what she wants to see.

*****

The memory of pain is altering
the happy blank page of her skin. Distrust
keeps swelling up inside her like a cyst,
larger with every hurt. Each scar has pressed
the unsuspecting tissue deeper down,

soft organs show first signs of weakening.
The thought, just breaking through, of powerlessness
is crippling her. She's vulnerable now.

*****

World that I talk her into, certainties
more firm and numerous than I possess.
She points and my tongue leaps, capers from this
to that, back and forth; nothing, all I know
I fetch and bring her without questioning.

Colorless, bleached-out flotsam, bare thought-thing,

unlikely flimsy framework that I clothe
for her with something that resembles sense.

*****

From *DOMICILIE* ("Domicile")

The Hours

7 a.m.
How still you lie, heart, gives a person a fright.
Do you know why. When you were dead and I
let your hand go you lay like this, cheek to
one side and from your braid some loosened white
beside your throat where swallowing had stopped.
Now don't be sad that I am waking you.
Here is your robe, coffee to refresh us,
yes I come like a thief, time is precious.

8 a.m.
Shall I wash you. Unbutton first. Poor bones,
what is this thing you're holding in one piece;
ash can with coatings of eau de colognes.
I'll smear some oil between your ribs. Sit up
now. Here, let me breathe air in through your nose,
start up new rhythm in your heart. You rub
the bone glue on your hip yourself, while I
move these raw bedsores over to the side.

9 a.m.
"Shopping list: fish, one hundred fifty-three
in all, bread and coals, bones, flesh, spirit, strength.
And tell the storekeepers if they miss me
that I am here and they're mistaken if

They think that it's all over now. Just say
that my accounts should be kept open." Lame
from life, weighed down by what I can't conceive,
I struggle back to where you wait for me.

10 a.m.
When you were still alive sheer fright marked you
as if with the most deadly pencil through
the thinnest blotter; under the refractive
surface you lay etched shakily in wood;
upset. Because I came and stood behind
your chair or stroked your hair as I walked by.
Look at me now, with your back bent to stay,
your hands flung upward, keeping you away.

11 a.m.
"You're spilling." Sugar glistened near the window
that looked out across black water. ("I'll stand
there with my bread." They didn't let you go);
the flies it drew I whisked off with one hand.
Bone, from the bridge to the tip of your nose,
rose parallel to that from ear to chin
as your breath would not give out yet, not give in.
The coffee steamed in thick white porcelain.

12 noon
A knife your life was; you who sharpened it,
then aimed at center point and threw, sit still.
World, sent back by your glasses, shrinks to fill
the thinnest thinkable streak of sunlight
that penetrates me now, like it or not.
Act blind then. You can see; some hidden spot
in time is where you're waiting, watching me;
each year I'll grow more like you. Just you see.

1 p.m.
Food, brought for you day after day, I found
all hoarded up in drawers beside the bed
that still refused to let your imprint fade.
Dry cake preserved in its sarcophagus,
fruit bitten into, scraps of meat spat out
in handkerchiefs, bread blanketed with moss.
It's time now, sit down. Eat. Be quiet. No
complaints. Eat. Live because I want you to.

2 p.m.
I don't believe you'll want to come back here.
But if you come, sit over there, assume
your old rebellious form again; unbending
as always, take your stand against surrender.
Sit there with mouth pinched shut alone in me
and listen. I don't care how ravaged you
drift back from ashes, alienated from
these things. Your chair is here, it's ready. Come.

3 p.m.
I'll do your hair. It should be neat you know.
Come, bend your head so I can comb it well.
Year after year thrust out from flaking skin;
my fingers touch your throbbing fontanel.
A higher knot? Brittle as dry brushwood.
Tighter? Roots, take up moisture to the end.
Wind it around your hand now. Strands that pull
away I'll pin down smooth against your skull.

4 p.m.
My body does a good impersonation,
can stand like you with shoulders bent, knees stiff
and feet apart. Each year the camera
that's guaranteed-to-norm and superfast
short-circuits when it measures lumination.
I stand against the dark and wave and laugh,

wearing your shoes, your glasses, hat and dress.
Easy; nothing to it. Just empty husk.

5 p.m.
What can I cook for you so you will eat
and live eternally. Ask what you like,
I'll make it, spoonful by spoonful I'll feed
you, though you'll give it back unsatisfied.
Eat my body then, the pains I go to;
let my flesh and my fat grow over you,
exhaust me, take my strength, use, demand, claim
me, but not as dry, self-consuming flame.

6 p.m.
Heart, all the pans dirty for one mouthful
of food, and even that did not go down.
The sense of waste and distaste I'll clear up:
counter that keeps me on my feet forever,
these dishes stacked for washing that will never
end, and — still resting in its glass of cloudy
water when progress of all kinds has been
dissolved — your dentures' fiercely scoffing grin.

7 p.m.
So here you are. Mist hovers at your feet;
come, drink a little faster. Tight-spanned skin
around your cup like sails before the wind;
haste drives some shape and form into your cheeks.
Curved garden, where the shadows wait for dark
with you. I'll put a shawl around your neck,
it's colder here than I'd have thought, inside.
We'll have to keep the gas fire on tonight.

8 p.m.
A country where you walked barefoot. At night
you went back there, ran screaming, naked through
rain beating down on you like sticks. Come now,

take off your slippers, the water's just right;
your nails need to be cut, your calluses
filed smooth. Never in all your dreams was this
your body that's pulling here above me
at its fibres. Sit still. You can't break free.

9 p.m.
Time, swing open and bring her into view.
She sits between hard armrests in her chair,
velour protects her from the setting sun.
The town is burning but she's unaware.
Don't mirror her, do what you have to do,
save her vision till her looking is done;
heavy with wind and with your own weight, cut
across the threshold, slam silently shut.

10 p.m.
A time when we took you for granted. You'd
cook, set the table in your dress of steam,
and sit until we'd finished all our food.
Young innocents you'd tell of wizards' tricks
and every night betray without a qualm
by leaving us, caressed and deep in sleep.
And now. Bent over your prone body, thoughts
of with what violence you wakened us.

11 p.m.
Did you call. I'll hold you, don't be afraid,
you don't have to go back, I'll stay here now,
yes I know how it was, they made you wait
there in the dark and with your ribs so tight.
Cough then. And spit it out. Air in, air out
we need, an open window. Listen, light
hissing of gas that flames behind the screen.
Now some damp cloths. Look, you can see the steam.

12 midnight
Your hands I would have liked to see, that dealt
out their caresses drily as their slaps,
but they were sheeted over. Someone else
had swelled your skin. Just your eyes, that never
could stand sun, still had their red familiar
rims. How you frowned past me once cataracts
were lifted from you. How you knew me blind.
"Come here, don't say your name, I know this time."

1 a.m.
If I didn't tire so fast, if all such
needs as air and food would let my body go,
if I could stay awake night after night
to work together thread by thread the light
soft weave that clothed you. If I did not grow
cold and stiff, had not forgotten so much,
if I were not a prisoner in skin
that works. Then yes. Then you'd be well again.

2 a.m.
Cheap market pottery from years ago;
the pattern, never much to look at, worn.
Dirt in the cracks. You weren't the cleanest sort.
Now let me brew the coffee that you ordered,
fresh bitter grind directly in the cup
with boiling water simply poured on top.
I know, you want much more than I'll be making.
No fuller, though. Just look at how you're shaking. .

3 a.m.
Is that comfortable, your legs are they cold,
would you like a heating pad on your lap.
How you twist and turn. No, nothing's put away.
Yes, that's dust, it will have to stay.
Come, keep your hands still now. Here's some cologne
on a clean handkerchief, it's for your trip.

Across the bridge at Arnhem in a black-
flagged limousine that will not bring you back.

4 a.m.

Come, we'll wait for death together. I'll hold
your hand tight and won't let it go again
as long as you live. Now look. Little spots
on the wallpaper, do you see them, sun
has hit the window; look there near the woods,
it's Goossen's horse, up to its belly in gold.
And apples, so many ripe on the tree.
At least two buckets for the notary.

5 a.m.

Where will you go now that the hour has come
when I'll leave you alone. What can I say
to you. I can remove your life from mine
but you can still be read like pattern in
my body. I'm cut to your size. The day
I have no more to ask you won't, as long
as I have form, come any nearer. Be
clear now; open up my mind. Comfort me.

6 a.m.

I set you down in all untruthfulness.
Under time past I come upon you as
if under crumbling skin — rank, thankless task,
for everything I touch I've lost. No longer
now will sleep place you inside me. In life
beneath bald hammering of finches' song
I turn the cover on my pen and know
I'm killing you. I am forgetting you.

Neighbors

Behind the glass their outline fills my view,
their movement through the house my day and night.
I've drifted into them, am sure as breath
of when and how they act. Speechlessly,

as in my body, I live in what they do.
They unfold strength, they open hidden seams,
they torture fabric, bearing down with weight
of irons in which I sigh like steam.

Heron

Evening. He stands behind their houses,
blind to borders, the one I want to follow.
Driven by hunger, he unfolds his neck

and strikes. Unseen by those who turn on lights,
wash children, talk about disasters. God,
take them away, make this place waste and void,
let him look out over water again
and teeming soul, as when it all began.

Excluded

Yesterday took the path under the railway bridge, past the
            sun three times with the new child,
up to where you can see the highway.

How you become divided, split
up among more and more lives,
like the sun setting on three ponds, over three bridges,
caught three times in mist, stretched out in water,
behind us, ahead of us.

Set fire to to a newspaper
under the bridge, but did not
become a child again,

older, if anything, eaten away
at the edges; illegible.

A cold bluish face in the pram. Picked her up
a moment, stood hair touching hair.
Put her down, went back
as always; a little later
maybe. No more stopping on the way.

Domicile

Complain then, complain
about your dried up life, scattered
by handfuls over the water,

complain then, complain and there
they come already, the swans, the greedy
hissing slow-moving, and turning, trumpeting
coots, eager for moldy crusts

and then the ducks! The ducks
proliferate at your feet
until you look like a statue on Sunday,

petrified on its pedestal,
carefully covered with moss, waiting
for the heads of dragons refracted in water and never
wanting to be freed from its base.

Settlement

Grass and rolled inside the blades and leaves, stalks
with headstrong blossoms, tangled skein of root,
strands separate and visible as dust,
gray dust collecting underneath the mat,

birds, their throats black, tearing with song,
worms and their deafening movements through ground

and garden after garden sharpest sets
of veins unfolding from the buds and now:
the neighbors turn on lights, put water on.

It must be time. Everywhere fire and flame,
I see their kitchen windows cloud, steam rise,
and through the damp their overhasty lives.
Keep them. Don't let their work be done in vain.

From *DE KRACHT VAN VERLAMMING*
("The Power of Paralysis")

The Power of Paralysis

> Forsa per forza già di parlasia
> Si travolse così alcun del tutto;
> Dante, *Inferno* XX

You had to go one way, I the other to get home.
Called something, looked back at me, I at you but a stream
of black swept your mouth away, your voice inside and for
a long
time I spent no more nights in thought of you

until against asphalt, one screaming next to me, one mute
against my shoulder, one deeper and
more defenseless, head in my lap,

I had to sing and sang
"the key is lost or broken — "

Saw you, saw from my head in the mirror your eyes.

Behind us, shrinking like lines you forget,
shake from your hair on getting up, the traffic lanes. "There"
you said, pupils suddenly smaller, and outside, tipped over,
those two, driven up to the steering wheel into each other.

So calm, blind to danger,

so lost in each other, head over heels,
so unintended and unswerving,
so sharply looking each other in the face.

Look!

Sun. Catch him whom I lose each night by day
in which I no longer walk with him and say

he must come here. Tell him
to bring his face once more down into me
with sharpest needles, tincture of iodine,
a feather dipped in acid of the caustic kind;
his mark then the etched out space.

His skin, each single hair,
his taut broad mouth,
must all be bitten into me,

so when his image wears away,
my body, but for fear, is all erased,
I'll have him still as closed eyes have the sun
through pain.

Death be not Proud

There was a tree there that moved
its bare pruned branches every time I looked;
more of it I couldn't see.
Sky all around it was shifting.

Left and right of you lay
your face like a wound
that, once it is slashed, keeps
closing, keeps opening again,

unwilling to heal for good.
Come pain and go then pain,
time's cut the pattern for me,
I am who I have to be.

Story

"Then stones turned into animals and the land
counted its wounds. Water and air were full
of eyes and mouths, the land began to send out shoots.

Animals animals come home, open and close
your wings, lie down while you still can
in the hollow that fits you so well.

Animals animals come home, swim two spades deep
down between the roots and keep yourselves small,
anyone who grew will soon be cut in two.

Tucked under a blanket of grass, the stones
lay quietly with cold, unmoving feet,
thinking how it was to be an animal."

On the Way

A stone as white as the days before time
switched off the light; gleaming near the ground,
unbroken, round. Never to be tossed aside,
something to carry in your mouth till dark,

almost, but not quite, making you choke.
(There is a kind of fish
that does this with its newcast spawn
until it gets too big and has to be let go
or otherwise be swallowed down.)

To stay the same,
not to grow anymore or to be grown
over. Wearing away and shattering
to sand, but to the eye a finished thing.

From *IN EEN BOCHT VAN DE ZEE* ("By a Curving Shore")

Can vei la lauzeta mover

Donkey-like passing the fields,
slowly, slowly, stop
when you find bits to eat.
Time and again feel the stick,

slowly pull at the cart,
balking just once or twice,

see how the larks
lose themselves in their flight.

From "Memory, Longing"

1

She wears her hair in braids, it's not allowed
to come undone. The air surrounding her
is thicker than anywhere else. Trees wait with their leaves
till she's passed by. Quiet and indecisive,
she keeps her arms wrapped round her neck
when we inquire about her favorite food.
There's something black about her, it seems
she wants to stand in shadows all day
long so that the cold she harbors won't
escape from her and flow away.

2

The horse kicked her last night, she still
bears the marks. Because he kept racing past
her window, around and around
the meadow he had eaten bare, snorting
and pounding with his hoofs, making
her dream again and again. Came
with her scarf to tie him to his fence
but he kicked her and looked
with his red eyes where flies
walk during the day
over to where she lay
among hard stubble, and went on
eating from the trees.

7

The nest, grass growing out of it.
mouthfuls of earth placed
one by one against small ends of world,

a hollow form for longing —
remember how you turned around in it.

The eggs, the fragile
folded things inside, beginning
of space, feathers behind membranes,
bulging, the air too much to bear.

The Doorposts and the Narrow Windows

Because that I loved you is sure.
The rest is not — whether you existed
and if you did, what color eyes, one moment green,
the next gray, once a swarm of swallows
shot up out of them. What kind. The fast ones,
that can't walk, mating takes place in the air.
How did it happen. You became
sick or something, taken away, there was a lot to do,
I had a new child I believe and forgot you
until I heard you last night, impossible hour,
come it's time. Leave everything behind, come outside,
I'm waiting for you at the gate.
But when I stood there, the latch
was loose, it was slamming in the wind
against the beam and I closed it well and walked back,
thinking of you, that godknows you really had
opened the gate, had stood there,
that I loved you and that the wood around
the hinges was showing signs of wear.

By a Curving Shore

A leaf was floating on the water.
Thin, yellow. Leaf like a little
hand grasping. You said, sometimes you

can cut a leaf in two, put it in the ground,
small plants start sprouting on the veins.

But, I asked, if it's salty from its stay
in the sea and half skeleton already?
Even then, you said, and you caught it,
stroked it, put it in your jacket pocket,
where it continued to crumble away.

NOTE to the Translations

1. A popular brand of Dutch cigars.

Bibliography

Primary Works

Gerlach, Eva. *Verder geen leed*. Amsterdam: Arbeiderspers, 1979.
_____. *Een kopstaand beeld*. Amsterdam: Arbeiderspers, 1983.
_____. *Dochter*. Amsterdam: Arbeiderspers, 1984.
_____. *Domicilie*. Amsterdam: Arbeiderspers, 1987.
_____. *De kracht van verlamming*. Amsterdam: Arbeiderspers, 1988.
_____. *In een bocht van de zee*. Amsterdam: Arbeiderspers, 1990.

Related Works

Auden, W.H. "The Virgin and the Dynamo." *The Dyer's Hand and Other Essays*. New York: Vintage, 1968. 61-71.
Gerlach, Eva. Interview. *Haagse Post* 23 March 1985. 44ff.

Otten, Willem Jan. "Wees niet bedroefd nu ik je wakker maak." (Review of *Domicilie*, by Eva Gerlach.) *NRC Handelsblad* 3 April 1987. CS 4.

Ricks, Christopher. *The Force of Poetry*. Oxford: Clarendon, 1984.

Rivers, Isabel. *Classical and Christian Ideas in English Renaissance Poetry*. London: George Allen & Unwin, 1979.

Vendler, Helen. "Mapping the Air." (Review of *An Atlas of the Difficult World: Poems 1988-1991* by Adrienne Rich and *Regions of Unlikeness* by Jorie Graham.) *The New York Review of Books* 21 Nov. 1991. 50-56.

Wieck, Roger S. *Time Sanctified: The Book of Hours in Medieval Art and Life*. New York: George Braziller; Baltimore: The Walters Gallery, 1988.

Maria Stahlie

Klaas van der Sanden

With the publication in this anthology of "Above Nature" and
"The Bitter Medicine," the young writer Maria Stahlie is, for the first
time, introduced to an American audience. Maria Stahlie, pseudonym
of Madelien Tolhuizen (b. 1955), is one of the most productive
women writers in contemporary Dutch literature. A quick glance at
her bibliography shows an impressive list of two novels, three
collections of short stories and three book translations, all of which
were published in the short time span of six years. Her work is
certainly too contemporary yet to produce a well-balanced assessment
of her place in Dutch literary history and, in light of the present
volume, writing by women in Dutch.[1] The critical inventory simply
is not there yet; literary history still has to catch up with Maria
Stahlie. Of course, all her books have been discussed in many a
positive review. Newspaper reviews, however, tend to assess new
works in such non-descriptive terms as "convincing," "a cunning play
of fiction and non-fiction," and "written in a smooth and fluent
style."[2] Clearly, they are not the most helpful for our present task.

Our task then could start with such a critical assessment. We
have to be careful though. Ideally, an introduction should not be a
one-way lecture where a supposedly more informed reader tells his
audience in great detail and supported by many quotations precisely
how the literary work should be read. Some influence will of course

result from any introduction, but it should primarily be an invitation. It should be the start of a process where the reader himself/herself engages with the work, its themes and his/her own reception of it in an informed manner. Stahlie's work cannot be simply consumed. Thematically, her work demands an active engagement, which has to include our own arguments of approach. What is offered here, then, is a theoretical background against which I propose to read Stahlie's work and which will, hopefully, prove inviting enough to encourage a critical reception of both stories and of the explication of the reading proposed here.

As a point of departure, I would like to refer to the polemically titled lecture "Who Are the Ghost-Riders in Literature-Land?" given by Dick Schouten, a writer, at the Dutch Studies Center, University of Minnesota, Minneapolis, on January 13, 1991. Schouten (who happens to be Stahlie's husband) referred to himself and Stahlie as a "closely cooperating writers' couple," which seems to justify the deliberate use of his opinions (quoted from the lecture, 2). Some caution is advisable, since this chapter appears, after all, in a book that purports to mark a tradition of "women writing." The danger exists namely, that I, as a male critic, will use another male voice to master the art of a woman writer. One justification is that one may take "closely cooperating" to mean that Stahlie herself cooperated on Schouten's lecture — even more so, since it served as an integral part of a lecture evening, where she herself read her story "The Bitter Medicine." Furthermore, however one describes Stahlie's work, it does not engage in hermeneutical gender politics. As a matter of fact, one cannot even classify it as "feminist" in a literary historical sense of the word. And that, in a way, does position Stahlie's work in contemporary literary history. If we respect the author's intention, we should not read it vis-à-vis the Dutch feminist literature that emerged in the 1970s and early 1980s with such writers as Renate Dorrestein, Hannes Meinkema, and others. On the contrary, Schouten-Stahlie label 99% of their contemporary Dutch colleagues-writers "ghost-riders," the Dutch term for those people who drive down the highway in the wrong direction. As a writers' couple, they claim that they "are heading in the right direction with our novels and short stories," because they do understand that "true literature doesn't want to convince the reader of a certain opinion" (4). Going even further in their rejection, in one sweeping motion they pretty much do away with most of post-war Dutch literature. They state that the "ghost-riders'" ignorance of "the true forces of literature" results in the choice of such subjects for their novels as, for example, "recollections of the war," "the daily life of contemporary women," "the effects of a Calvinist childhood," "superficial questions about language and reality," or, "what it means to be alive in the last decade of the 20th century" (7).

It is not uncommon, of course, for a writer to distance herself/himself from a previous generation of writers in order to position her or his own project. But Schouten and Stahlie obviously position themselves quite radically. For them, the question of the "true forces of literature" is based on renewed reflections on literature when it was still Literature with an upper-case "L" and on older functions of literature. In a move against the marginality of art and literature in modern society — the degradation of art into the realm of entertainment, to be enjoyed merely as a leisure time activity — they stress a meta-historical and universal function of the arts as a mode of expression of divine objects. "The true artists of old," they stated in "Ghost-Riders," "tried to discover what their presence was worth in light of the cosmos, in light of the creation of mankind, in light of a possibly unknowable objective" (2). Stahlie's work intends to do precisely that. It creates "doubles," images in which the artist sees herself reflected as in a mirror and which allow for a contemplation on the images on both sides of the mirror. As literature, her work wants to live up "to the old adage *Know thy self*" (2) and "to show the reader each and every niche of his self-knowledge" (4).

Hence literature becomes part and parcel of philosophical or even religious contemplation. Even a cursory reading of Stahlie's work will make it clear that "religious" should not be understood to mean that her work intends to celebrate the existence of some sort of divine being who created everything in a week or so. The contemplation is more complex than that. "Religious" here is defined in its etymological meaning as *relegere* — to gather anew, contemplate again and again — or as *religare* — to combine or unite in a new manner.[3] Literature is a process whereby the imagination as a creative faculty is confronted and confronts itself with its own infinite power to continually read new things into, combine and unite representations. This is a very important aspect of Stahlie's work and certainly the theme common to all her publications. Her work foregrounds the imagination as an awe-inspiring faculty of mind. It is in a very literal sense a question of positioning oneself in creation or of positioning the imagination vis-à-vis its own creations. At the same time, it is also a questioning of positioning as such. In a reflective move, where the literary project no longer has an external goal — remember: it doesn't intend "to convince the reader" — the imagination is faced with its own powers of creating and combining and, hence, positioning. And the imagination is awe-inspiring, because it is both creator and victim at the same time while unable to find a restful position in between. In the undirected-ness of play or the possibility of play going in many directions without being guided by an external finality, the self is forced in disorder. But maybe we are tackling the subject too fast; let us first take a quick look at the two stories that follow in translation, "Above Nature" and "The Bitter Medicine."

In both stories, the initial setting is a situation without any expectations: in the former a Jubilee, in the latter a short personal vacation. In that setting of no expectations, an uncertainty of fixing place jumps out at us. America is the "Land of Countless Lakes ... the Land of Ten Thousand Opportunities." Scattered impressions do not add up to a whole. In an attempt to capture the place, impressions are added up quasi-indefinitely and without inner connections. "One driving test, dozens of Vietnamese meals, hundreds of sky scrapers, thousands of squirrels, tens of thousands of impressions, hundreds of thousands of fall leaves and millions of snowflakes ..." constitute the situation. There is no sum total. The same is true of the writer's attempt to seize the nature of the petrified piece of wood in "The Bitter Medicine:" the addition of seconds to days, weeks, months, even years does not add up to an understanding of the stone's true age. Very gradually though, through the mind's rumination but almost against its will, connections are forced upon the imagination. There is a growing awareness that the mere addition process forces meaning upon the perceiver. This gradual path in "Above Nature" goes from "maybe coincidence," to "perhaps a coincidence," to "no doubt a coincidence," to "probably a coincidence," until finally the possibility of no coincidence is denied: "yet, no matter how one twisted and turned the events, it was no coincidence..." The same process is at work in "The Bitter Medicine:" if it had not been for the "mitigating circumstances," if the sign had not reminded the narrator, if her conference had not been so boring, if the sun had not been so hot, etc., she would not have looked for resemblances in the stones or, in other words, she would not have attributed meaning to them.

A new qualitative element is thus forced upon the narrator that derives from the purely quantitative addition of impressions in the stories — or, perhaps, we should stress two elements: meaning and force. Somehow these two elements are inescapably linked. And to complete the picture, there is a third element: fear. In "Above Nature," Maria becomes frightened when talking on the phone to Paulien, precisely at the point of "no coincidence," the point where meaningful connections cannot be denied anymore. This fear will not leave her until the end of the story, when finally the "spell" is broken and she regains her free will. Very much in the same vein, the narrator of "The Bitter Medicine" is haunted by the secret forces of the stone. It is this interplay of fear, force, and meaning and the question of how to position the self against (or among) them, that mark Stahlie's work as "sublime."

In order to explore this notion further and to map its implications, it is helpful to turn to the concept of the Sublime as it was rediscovered and redefined in modern aesthetics, especially by Immanuel Kant in his *Critique of Judgement*. When I consider Stahlie's work part of a literature of the sublime, I do *not* intend the sublime to be interpreted as a mere rhetorical device, or as the grand style that Boileau promoted in the seventeenth century as a device to exemplify more effectively the True, the Good and the Beautiful. The pathetic gesture is completely absent in Stahlie. Her stories and novels take place in every day settings, her style is almost down to earth. It is the experiences within the common settings that are sublime. Very much in the Kantian tradition of the sublime, Stahlie's work thematizes experiences of fear and force and meaning. Or, as Kant posited it, "sublimity does not reside in any of the things of nature, but only in our mind..."[4] To experience sublimity, the mind, indeed, has to represent nature as a source of fear, as having power over the self. "Nature considered in an aesthetic judgement as *might* ... is dynamically sublime" (Kant 109). In Kant's estimation, the sublime is opposed to the beautiful, in which the subject finds pleasure in unity and wholeness. The beautiful "conveys a finality in [the natural object's] form by making the object appear ... preadapted to our power of judgement" (Kant 91); thus, the beautiful connotes harmony, unity, just proportion, delineation. The subject's experience is a whole one, it has grasped the object in a way it feels is appropriate both for the object and itself. In the finality of the beautiful experience, the subject exerts control over the object. In the case of the sublime, the roles are reversed. The sublime connotes loss of control, and, faced with the formless or deformed, the self is faced with nature which it cannot comprehend as its own. Nature becomes a powerful other which "forces upon us the recognition of our physical helplessness as beings of nature" (Kant 111). We cannot measure ourselves against its omnipotence. Our faculties are incapable of rendering the representation of nature as a totality; the result is "a tempest in the depth of a chasm opened up in the subject."[5]

As one might expect, Kant does not leave the subject at that. A major part of his further efforts is reserved to regain his ground and to turn the loss into a gain. He does so in a very paradoxical move. Nature might be represented — or even has to be represented for it to be sublime — as a force with power over the subject, but it is *no dominion*. It is *not* a force "that is superior to our resistance of that which itself possesses might" (Kant 109). Within the sublime there is always a residue of resistance left that allows Kant to claim for the sublime a consciousness "of our superiority over nature within, and thus also over nature without us (as exerting influence upon us)" (Kant 114). He claims an elevated position for the subject above and beyond its loss; this position allows, in the end, for the turning of the negative into an even deeper and grander positive. Stretched to its limits, the imagination recoils upon itself and is raised "to a presentation of those cases in which the mind can make itself sensible of the appropriate sublimity of the sphere of its own being, even above nature" (Kant 112), that sphere being the realm of Ideas and Reason.[6] By transcending the merely sensible, the subject finds a "suprasensible destination" for itself. It discovers itself as the focal point of reason, of a finality (culture) in raw nature.

The sublime has to be read in the context of history, or better, as a critique of history as a project of modernity.[7] It problematizes the aporias of a strict and enslaving object rationality, in which nature is defined solely as pure objectivity. Nature has objective laws of its own, independent of any human relation to it. This positioning, the position the scientist takes vis-à-vis nature, is in and of itself a power game. For a scientist, increased knowledge of the laws of nature — thus the mere registering of what is supposedly objectively "out there" — is control of the laws. The laws are known only to be manipulated for one's own particular interest. Nature's basic "otherness" (*an sich*) becomes a mere "for me" (*für mich*).[8] Utilization is the highest criterion. Humanity, however, loses something in the process. It pays for the increase of its power with alienation from that over which it exercises its power. In a Marxist critique, one could point to the fact that this manipulation is performed in the interest of a particular class and to keep all others subject to those particular interests. In a sublime frame of mind, the critique is more fundamental than that, maybe even more existential. It questions the positioning as such. It flirts with and dares to pose the question of sheer "otherness," and a simplified "*für mich*" is not allowed.

Some have argued that the sublime, at least in the thrust of Kant's argumentation, is ultimately uncritical and even constitutes wishful thinking in its attempt at solving the basic oppositions.[9] There might be indeed, so the argument goes, something very critical about daring to confront a fundamental loss of meaning and about not allowing the mind to merely position itself outside of that loss, but a repositioning of the self over and above it would in effect mean eradicating the basic experience and making it instrumental in an even grander gesture of mastering. Imprisoning the sublime in a philosophical system would mean to render its terrible knowledge ineffective. To counter this argument, one might ask the question whether Kant could indeed close the box of Pandora that he had opened in the first place. The sublime feelings of pain and pleasure are not sublated in a new position of pleasure, but both are at the same time an integral and necessary part of its momentum.

Be that as it may. After all, we are not discussing Kant here but Maria Stahlie. It is sufficient for our purpose to observe that Kant at least attempts to make the basic experience of loss operational for something else. In my opinion, Stahlie's work seems to deny that possibility and would, therefore, add a new dimension to the notion of the sublime. Let me first recapitulate that, to do justice to Stahlie's work, one has to read her stories and novels as belonging to the (at least in its origin) very critical and maybe even anti-modern (but not necessarily conservative) tradition of the aesthetics of the sublime. Her work reflects on the "otherness" of nature and, while giving in to the inevitable momentum of these reflections, it discovers that nature does not exist *for* the subject but can actually exist in opposition to the interests of the subject. Seen in this context, Stahlie's work questions modernity.

The question then to be asked is: does Stahlie's work allow for even an attempt at a resolution? Can the subject claim a "suprasensible destination" for itself? As I have indicated, my answer would be, no. Her work revolves around the paradox that the only conclusion that the subject can draw is that it cannot draw a conclusion. The subject always finds that the final insight is the inexplicable. This is not to say that her stories and novels are open-ended, for there is always some kind of closure. But the ends are not resolution, but resignation. Every time, the protagonists have to step back and, as it were, come back to the daily nitty-gritty. Both stories translated here are good examples of this move: in both cases, reflections on the sublime state of the self are abandoned by an effort of the will. Yet, for remaining unresolved, the process will inevitably repeat itself. "Religion" is an on-going process. In other words, the stories in the last analysis do not allow for a new master discourse to master the feeling of loss. Stahlie's literature of the sublime, unlike Kant's project, does not in the end attempt to turn the forces that eradicate the self into a new historical philosophy of modernity. In that sense, Stahlie's project is even more critical than Kant's. In that sense too, one could, perhaps, call her sublime "female" versus a "male" project of the sublime as represented by the Kantian tradition.

For in its desire, Kant's sublime is historically directed at character building, and especially at the male character of the nation. In sometimes very surprising (and suspect) sentences, he calls the warrior the truly sublime person and war the most sublime state. Peace would only lead to "cowardice and effeminacy" and it "tends to degrade the character of the nation" (Kant 113). Erecting a master narrative, where one sublimely builds modernity, as it were, face to face with the enemy, can only be called a very male enterprise. Negating that possibility in the sublime, and using the same metaphor, can then be called "female." Thus, even though Stahlie is not engaging in "feminist" writing, she clearly has a place in this anthology of women's writing.

NOTES to the Introduction

1. For a historical overview of Dutch literary history see Ton Anbeek, *Geschiedenis van de Nederlandse literatuur tussen 1885 en 1985* (Amsterdam: De Arbeiderspers, 1990), which is the only literary history available for modern Dutch literature. For individual writers, the only other single reference work is Ad Zuiderent, Hugo Brems and Ton van Deel, eds. *Kritisch Lexicon van de Nederlandstalige literatuur na 1945* (Groningen: Wolters-Noordhoff, 1980-1989). Neither work mentions Stahlie.

2. See Janet Luis, "Maria Stahlie's roekeloosheid: Modder in de Mississippi," review of *In de geest van de monadini's* (*NRC/Handelsblad*, 8 December 1989); Lucas Ligtenberg, "Gestrande Nederlanders," review of *Verleden-Hemel-Toekomst* (*NRC/Handelsblad*, 6 May 1988) and "Miss Stap," review of *Unisono* (*NRC/Handelsblad*, 13 November 1987).

3. "Religion," *The Compact Edition of the Oxford English Dictionary* (1986 ed.).

4. Immanuel Kant, *The Critique of Judgement*, trans. James Creed Meredith (New York: Oxford Univ. Press, 1952), 114.

5. Gilles Deleuze, *Kant's Critical Philosophy: The Doctrine of Faculties*, trans. Hugh Tomlinson and Barbara Habberjam (Minneapolis: Univ. of Minnesota Press, 1984), xii.

6. "a feeling of the sublime postulates the mind's susceptibility for ideas...arising from the fact of its being a dominion which reason exercises over sensibility with a view to extending it to the requirements of its own realm (the practical)..." (*Critique of Judgement* 115).

7. Kant does speak of the sublime as being directed against the "predominance of a mere commercial spirit" and against "a debasing self-interest" (*Critique of Judgement* 113).

8. See Max Horkheimer and Theodor W. Adorno, *Dialectic of Enlightenment*, trans. John Cumming (1944; New York: Continuum, 1987), especially "The Concept of Enlightenment," 9ff. Some caution is advised in using this translation. Where Horkheimer and Adorno speak of an "*an sich*" of things, the translator speaks of "potentialities." But it is only in the "*für sich*" that potential is engendered. There is the possibility within the sublime of a negation of any potential — hence its extremeness.

9. See, for example, Hans Thies Lehmann, "Das Erhabene ist das Unheimliche: Zur Theorie einer Kunst des Ereignisses," *Deutsche Zeitschrift für europäisches Denken* 9 (10) 1989, especially 752-753.

Translations by Klaas van der Sanden and Maria Stahlie

"ABOVE NATURE"

Only two or three very old Israelites would still nod to each other in gratitude, should it come to their ears that a personal Jubilee had finally been granted to another human being. In days long gone by, Jubilees were exclusively intended to serve farmlands and serfs. Once every twenty-five or fifty years the fields remained untilled while the serfs were set at liberty. As if these arrangements still weren't enough cause for jubilation, a year like that cheerfully let off old debts and every pledge as well found its way back to the original owner. If ever there could be question of a new beginning, of a virgin conscience, it would be the year following such a Jubilee.

The abolition of slavery brought about the abolition of rural Jubilees, but on a much smaller scale they never have ceased to exist. There was no telling when this might happen, but every so many years somebody would be given the opportunity to live a personal Jubilee. Once in a great while, somebody would be allowed to experience a year without claims and without aims, a weightless and timeless Jubilee during which all old debts would be forfeited and no new debts could be made. And the prospect of such a year simply fell into my lap when Dick received an invitation from the Ministry of Culture to lecture, for a period of ten months, as a writer-in-residence at the University of Minnesota. I asked for and was granted a leave without pay from the large real estate agency where I had been working since time immemorial, and in a jubilant mood I followed my sweetheart to the United States of America, to the Land of Countless Lakes, to the Land of Ten Thousand Opportunities.

One driving test, dozens of Vietnamese meals, hundreds of skyscrapers, thousands of squirrels, tens of thousands of impressions, hundreds of thousands of fall leaves and millions of snowflakes later, I pressed my nose for the fourth day in a row against the glass wall behind which resided three lions. Two queens and one king. The only position I had seen the queens in was lying on their backs and thus they produced the in- and exhaling evidence of that theory that lions need an average of twenty hours of sleep a day. The King of the Jungle however mocked this rule of human invention by passionately pacing up and down, from pillar to post, along the glass wall behind which I stood. Every fifteen seconds his forehead crossed my forehead and then he looked at me, cross-eyed and perfectly blank. It was during these magical, empty moments — ten weeks after our arrival in America — that the euphoria brought about by a good Jubilee went to my head. It was only in the lion's den, in one of the indoor shelters belonging to the snow-flooded St. Paul Zoo, that I became a genuine outsider. I was outside everything: outside nature, outside Holland and outside America. A time difference of seven hours, 5,000 miles, a water-brimmed ocean and a thick covering of snow caught their real significance in the light radiated from the eyes of the King of all beasts who, if I could help it, wouldn't be in my way anymore for the rest of the jubilee.

Maybe it was a coincidence, but on the very day that we set foot in Minnesota, autumn broke out. Autumn in Minnesota can only be compared to an infernal gift from heaven. Luminous yellow, orange and red leaves clung unto their branches with all their might and, for weeks in a row, they lent the exuberant look of a Vincent van Gogh painting to the rolling landscape. In harmony with one of the oldest Indian customs, the sun added a little extra to the scene and issued an Indian Summer with mild temperatures and long evenings. Autumns in Minnesota fill Minnesotans with pride, and evening after evening one could find them on the wooden porches of their wooden houses. Ours too was a wooden house, and it too had a porch.

Perhaps it was a coincidence, but on the very day that we drove along the Mississippi from St. Paul to Winona, a wind rose that proved to be beyond the tenacity of the autumn leaves. A dense red, orange and yellow colored blanket covered the water surface and turned America's longest river into a sea of flames. In the midst of the flames, twelve big barges were pushed forward by a minuscule tug boat, and only God knew who was responsible for the sound of the little steam organ that left fragments of a song that was very well-known and unknowable to the mercy of the river.

No doubt it was a coincidence, but the very day that we visited "The House on the Rock" in the heart of Wisconsin's wilderness turned out to be the last day of the season and the only day in the year when visitors were allowed not just to look at the biggest carousel in the world, but to ride it as well: to the rhythm of marching music and blinded by countless sparkling red, yellow and orange lights, we spun round and round on the wooden tigers, elephants, zebras and lions.

Probably it was a coincidence, that in the Netherlands only medical specialists were on strike and that we knew no one with a medical specialty. We learned from the letters we received that the homeland marked time especially for us, and that for the months to come everyone would go on doing the exact same thing they were doing before we left Amsterdam. We were surprised to hear that Dutch newspapers never even mentioned the fact that American astronomers had stumbled across a statue of Elvis on Mars.

Yet, no matter how one twisted and turned the events, it was no coincidence that — five days before Paulien called — I came face to face with the Redeemer of the Animal Kingdom (surely the Judean Lion would applaud this comparison) so that in the nick of time I was allowed to experience, just for a moment, what the remaining days of my Jubilee would have looked like had it not been for Paulien's phone call on that third Sunday in November.

"Hahaha!" it sounded from the study where the writer-in-residence was preparing his classes for the next day. Dick had ten students who, if I was to believe him, clung to his every word as soon as he started to talk about medieval literature from the Low Countries.

"What's so funny?" I shouted jealously, but Dick didn't hear me. What was so funny about preparing lectures and why was the comedy I was watching not comical at all? I got up and walked to the study. "Only very odd people laugh out loud when they are all by themselves," I said while I opened the door. It was Sunday evening, nine fifteen.

"Tomorrow is going to be the Day of Truth. Tomorrow I'm going to reveal to my students that instead of a rogue, Tyl Uilenspiegel was a prophet."

"And when you had fabricated this thought, you burst into spontaneous laughter." I was still a bit testy because the film compendium was hardly ever right; *S.O.B.* a three star movie... excuse me while I puke!

"No, that didn't happen until I visualized Uilenspiegel devoting hour after hour to careful wrapping of a basketful of horse droppings."

"Oh?"

"Yes, one by one. And after that he took them to the market place to sell them as prophet's beads."

"As what?"

"As prophet's beads. Each and every pellet was supposed to have the power of endowing someone with the gift of prophesy. Normally, a bead was part of a rosary, but this time the future prophets were in for a more difficult task. They had to put the prophet's bead into their mouth and, chewing slowly, they had to consume it in its entirety. Only then the truth would become manifest ..." Dick started to chuckle again and looked at me with anticipation.

I forgot to join him in his chuckle. I was thinking of the huge lion's droppings that I had seen lying in one of the corners of the lion's den. If a dropping as small as a horse dropping could harbor some truth, then certainly a lion's dropping contained...it was then that the telephone rang. "I'll get it" I said, and only moments later I made it clear that I had been a citizen of America for ten weeks already. "Hello!"

"Maria? Paulien here..."

"Paulienchen!" I responded surprised. Both of us had followed with great admiration *Heimat*, the television series in eleven episodes in which close track was kept of a family coming from a small German village over a period of sixty years. There was a Maria as well as a Paulien in that family. "Do you realize what time it is?"

"Why, isn't it about nine o'clock where you are ... or is it?"

"Yes, where *we* are! But I hate to think about the time in Holland!"

"Oh, you're thinking about our time ... I couldn't sleep ... and I couldn't sleep because I have done something that is so awful, so terribly shameful..." Across the ocean, across the night, the Netherlands fell silent.

"Oh well, everyone is entitled to a few little mistakes in life," I said in a silly attempt to keep the conversation casual. I tried to shake off a faint pain that had crept up my left shoulder. "Take me for example. Even today ..."

"I'm not talking about 'a few little mistakes,' I'm talking about something awful, something terribly shameful," Paulien cut short my desperate move.

My left shoulder started to isolate itself from the rest of my body, a scary sensation which became even more prominent on account of the receiver that I held pinned between my right shoulder and my ear. With my free right hand I massaged the distressed body part. Dick followed my squirming with concern. I heaved a sigh.

"You can say that again," said Paulien, who took my sigh for a reply. And then Europe fell silent again.

"God, you're being secretive! Or rather creepy. You're being creepy." But I didn't know what frightened me more, Paulien or the mysterious twinges and cramps that crept up on me whenever someone threatened to appeal to my sense of duty. And at that, my shoulder made me painfully aware of the forty jubilant weeks I had still in store for myself.

Paulien started to giggle. "It will get even creepier ... but first you'll have to promise me that you won't take anything personally."

Jesus. It would be possible to take things personally! How in the world could this be, with Paulienchen in the *Heimat* and thousands and thousands of nautical miles between me and her ... I promised to take nothing, not one thing, personally. A stab running from the hollow of my knee to the hillock of my ankle underlined this solemn promise.

"All right then. Well ... the day before yesterday I sent you a letter, but I've been thinking and now I don't want you to read what's in it. I have done something of which I am tremendously ashamed and to make matters worse I've written it all down and sent it to you. I figured a confession would do me good, but that was an ugly miscalculation: I felt exactly twice as lousy as before the confession. And I'd already mailed the letter ... what it boils down

to is that I would feel at least 50% better if you'd promised me right
now that you won't open my letter ..."

"Gosh," I said. Paulien's request came as such a surprise that
I didn't even notice my left shoulder taking on its normal position
again.

"The letter has absolutely nothing to do with you," she added.
"It's just things about me. Anyway ... is it a promise?"

Cross my heart and hope to die! This was what I called a
promise after my heart. It would be no effort at all to make my best
friend 50% happier and that very same effort would prove that
nothing could possibly go wrong with Jubilees once they had started.
Not only did I promise to leave the letter unopened, I would destroy
it as only unopened letters could be destroyed: eyes closed I would
tear it into the smallest conceivable shreds and to top it all off I would
hold a burning match to the heap of paper. *What are friends for, huh?*
When soon after Paulien hung up, everybody was feeling relieved.
Not even a minute later though, my Days of Jubilation belonged to
the past.

All in all, how much does a letter weigh? In a weightless year
twenty grams may make a scale tip. All in all, how many days does
it take a letter to go from the Netherlands to Minnesota? In a timeless
year seven days may take 10,080 minutes. While I waited and waited
and waited the snow kept falling intermittently, the supermarkets kept
running 24 hours a day and seven days a week (10,080 minutes, week
in week out), the bright blue bags with *The New York Times* kept
finding their way to our wooden porch, the sixty television channels
kept buzzing, and even Dick continued to prepare class after class. As
if nothing had happened!

Of course I wouldn't betray Paulien's confidence. If she
didn't want me to read that letter, surely she had her good reasons.

Of course I would read that letter. Obviously Paulien was in
trouble, and both her letter and her phone call should be understood
as a cry for help. Indeed, who but I was in a better position to turn
her cry of distress into a cry of jubilation?

Excuses, excuses ... even though the address on the envelope
spelled out my name, I should ignore the letter, or better yet, trample

and burn it. Some books are better left unread, there were mysteries one shouldn't try to resolve and there were private matters even a best friend should stay away from.

Noble as I suddenly seemed to be, I shouldn't however take lightly that it was to *me* that she had sent her letter. And even though Paulien had sworn that her confession had nothing to do with me, there was absolutely no guarantee that she was speaking the truth. A cornered rat was the mother of invention ... if the letter was about me, I had every right to break the seal.

What was wrong with me? Promises were made to be cherished, not to be crushed ... in the days after Paulien's phone call I had crushed so much snow into submission that there were presently four snowmen on our lawn. They were the immobile materializations of my mobile conscience. It was cold in Minnesota and the sun didn't stand a snowball's chance in hell. The first snowman was standing there exactly as superior and white and virginal as when I first built him. The second snowman consisted of two big balls and one small ball which I had rolled together in a line and which were meant to represent a reclining figure. Two lumps on top of the middle ball took care of the identification of the individual as a sunbathing woman. The third snowman didn't consist of different segments, but was destined to be a kind of pillar in which I had carved a face. A man of character is as good as his word ... and the fourth snowman, I hesitate to admit it, the fourth snowman had been saddled with two heads.

It was inevitable: I started to guess. It was possible to link everything and everybody to Paulien. Whether I was in a museum or in a grocery store, whether I watched television or played frisbee in the snow, every detail seemed to contain an allusion to the alarming contents of the letter that surely but slowly was closing in. Looking worrisome, I walked the aisles in the supermarket, entrapped by the congested shelves. The huge boxes which for ten weeks had given me the thrills of actually roaming about in the Land of Cockaigne, now gave me the chills. I was reminded of the fits Paulien broke into between the ages of twelve and eighteen, outbursts in which she stuffed herself with food and puked it all out again: she stuffed and she puked, and then she stuffed and she puked some more ... until her outside couldn't remember her insides anymore. The oblivion she thus brought about, formed the excuse for the inexplicable behavior that made her do things she could never recall afterwards. Others, however, did remember. Paulien's grandma, a rich witch with a moustache, never really got over the punch in the face which Paulien gave her for her 76th birthday. And in junior high, in the eighth grade, our English teacher was as innocent as a new-born baby when Paulien raised her hand and declared aloud that she was pregnant ... by him. The outbursts had ebbed away after graduation but what if the tide had turned again? No wonder she didn't want me to know! And should I take action now that I knew anyway? A searing pain in my side gave me wings and taking off with just a few of the groceries I should have brought, I jumped into our Chevrolet Citation and flew back to our wooden house where I informed Dick about my apprehensions.

"Why work yourself up like this? I'm sure everything will sort itself out in time. Probably the problem is a completely harmless one. Something in the order of subscribing to *Reader's Digest* ... " Clearly Dick had things on his mind other than the confessions of Paulien. Uilenspiegel was everything Paulien was not: a man, a mirror of wisdom, a prophet, a master at meddling as only a fool can be a master at meddling. And nothing could stop the fool from meddling with my affairs: "An idiot may pose more questions in an hour than a wise man can answer in seven years."

Why didn't he mind his own business? You'd think he had a monopoly on truth. *No sirree!* In a touchy mood I started to read the newspaper. A baby froze to death in his own house because it had slipped his parents' minds that they had given birth to a son only six weeks ago. Paulien too had to deal with children on a regular basis, with her brother's children, and *boy*, if ever someone was forgetful it was she. At least three of her bikes stood rivetted to forgotten bridge railings in Amsterdam. She never forgot to carefully lock them, though. Just like she would always firmly lock her front door ... which reminded me of the old Russian man in St. Paul who had been a captive in his own house after he had locked himself in, couldn't find his keys anymore and was taken for a fool by those who came to rescue, when he first called out for help and then refused to open the door. And what was I to think of the story about the singles club that was joined by three men who were found out to be HIV positive after they had presented themselves as inverse vampires by sinking their teeth into the necks of their dancing partners? Paulien had responded to personal ads before! Why on earth didn't those newspapers mind their own business? I limped to the window and came face to face with my snowmen. Why didn't those snowmen mind their own business?

"Dick!" I called out in anger, and when he showed up to see what was bothering me, I said: "You know what? I am going to read that letter. If she didn't want me to read it, she shouldn't have sent it to me ..."

"Attagirl," Dick said enthusiastically.

"Christ, you are a sorry excuse for a big help!"

Paulien and I shared a collection. Normally the collection would be displayed in the attic at home, but now that I was in America it had moved to Paulien's living room. This was no big deal because the collection was a small one, even though we had been collecting since we were fifteen. Five cigarette butts, a piece of band aid with a black hair attached to it, a pair of old shoes, a shot glass, two coffee cups, a nail, a Mars bar wrapper, a crumpled paper towel ... we had no trouble understanding why among insiders our collection had come to be known as "The Sordid Collection." We, however, were of a different opinion. What in the world could be sordid about a Kevin Coyne cigarette butt or about a piece of band aid that once covered a cut on the shinbone of Ruud Gullit?[1] We collected those unique items, from which our idols had derived some relief. Comfort, protection, strength, convenience ... even idols were in need of these supports, and of this our collection took advantage.

Our collection also gained by the efforts of sympathetic friends and it was especially Paulien's ex-neighbor, presently living in Bussum, whom we held in high regard, because in her enthusiasm for our collection she knew no limits: late one night she fished a pair of *Beatle boots* worn to the thread from the trash can belonging to the Kees van Kooten mansion.[2] However, we had to be careful not to include every offering in our collection. As in any group consisting of more than ten persons, there was some riff-raff in our circle of friends too, mocking individuals who came out with a rigid hanky that allegedly had been of excellent use to David Byrne. We never were able to see the humor of it, and we showed ourselves to be particularly humorless whenever the fraud was less obvious, like the time when Dick came home from a visit to his publishing house and with a mysterious smile presented us with a coffee cup that had some brown sugar caked onto it. Only after three years — three years in which the cup had taken up a prominent place in our collection — did he reveal that instead of Gerrit Komrij,[3] he himself had been drinking from the cup. And when immediately after his confession, I went to the kitchen to thoroughly rinse the cup, he even had the nerve to be offended.

"So I am not one of your idols?" he asked, genuinely hurt. "That is really nice! I'll dedicate another novel to you ..."

There were more people who didn't quite grasp who was an idol and who was not. In particular the elderly were slow in that respect. I couldn't possibly get it into my mother's head that not every celebrity automatically was an idol as well, and that our collection would be anything but enriched by a napkin used by our mayor Ed van Thijn. To Paulien and myself our collection meant a confirmation of our friendship. We had shared the same taste for eighteen years already, a taste we blatantly revealed through coffee cups and cigarette butts. In America, I had instantly become a fan of the stand-up comedian Steven Wright, and though Paulien didn't know him yet, I was sure that she would be a sucker for his absurd jokes and for the crushed beer can I had succeeded to lay my hands on after his show in Minneapolis. "Suppose there was no gravity," he had said while dropping the beer can on the floor, "all the birds would be hanging in the air after they had died."

As the days went by and the mailman, who turned into our street every day at 12:30 pm, brought letters from my brother, Dick's mother, the publisher and one of my college friends, but not from Paulien, I became more and more convinced that something had happened to our collection. I knew Paulien well enough to know that she wouldn't hire a cleaning lady who, in her urge to clean, would mistake the irreplaceable cigarette butts and coffee cups for mere cigarettes and coffee cups. But I also knew her to be very impressionable, and especially the last couple of years she sometimes had pushed things a bit far in trying to adjust herself to the different men she had gotten involved with. Obviously this time she had gone too far. By the day Paulien's letter was due, I had neatly listed the points in question. That my mind had been making odd leaps in its initial attempts to explain Paulien's behavior, I now credited to the bad start my imagination had suffered. One should try to remain rational, even under pressure. My reconstruction of events looked like this: at the urgent request of some new man in her life, she had thrown away the complete collection; then the new man had moved on and regrets had moved in; on an impulse, she had confessed the whole thing to me in a letter, but this too she soon came to regret; she was afraid I would draw the conclusion that she was taking our collection less seriously than I did, and that is why she had decided to spend the remaining months of my absence reproducing each and every lost relic; finally she had called me with the request to leave the letter unread. It was as simple as ABC, or as we would say in the Netherlands: *a child could do the laundry.* I presented Dick with my watertight theory.

"Watertight," he agreed.

Honking his horn, the mailman brought his little jeep to a standstill at the end of the street, and less than fifteen minutes later — we were living in the very last house — I held Paulien's letter in my hands.

During the next three days, I often took Paulien's letter in my hands. But I didn't open it. And even though I didn't destroy it, I was quite pleased with myself. Who wouldn't kill for a friend like me, I pondered while taking long walks in the melting snow — for something funny was going on in Minnesota. The last time this had happened was in 1934. The night after I received Paulien's letter, the thaw had set in, and in the days that followed, it kept on thawing. Everything was leaking and dripping in St. Paul. Of all my snowmen only the pillar was more or less holding up in the twelve degrees Celsius which the coldest winter state of America also proved to have in reserve. With my hands in the pockets of my open parka, with my left hand loosely around Paulien's letter in my left pocket, I walked around the lake of Como Park, I crossed the fields of Como Park, and I roamed the woods of Como Park, but for some reason it was only after three days that I decided to visit the Zoo in Como Park.

Once there, I was suddenly in a hurry. Without even casting a glance into the deep pit where during the winter, under extreme temperatures, the Siberian Tiger proved to be the real Ruler of the Jungle, I walked straight to the building in which the lions were wintering. The pen of the restless lion and his two ever-resting spouses was in the back of the building. I wasn't surprised about the complete absence of visitors, it is usually quiet in a zoo during the winter. The shock I experienced when I found out that the lion's den was vacant, was accompanied by a severe cramp in my side. In an attempt to find relief I clutched Paulien's letter, but the pain didn't disappear. Clearly, the lions had been let outside now that the snow was almost gone. In one of the corners of the lion's cage, I was able to discern three big droppings. Eighteen carat prophet's beads. If I would slowly consume them, the truth would be revealed. But without eating them, without even smelling them, just by looking at them, I was still able to extract enough prophetic power to realize that I was completely wrong as far as Paulien was concerned. Whatever it said in that letter, it had nothing to do with our collection. And the lion's droppings, undisturbed by any wrapping, radiated yet another message: it was of major importance that I read Paulien's letter. I shut my eyes with all my might. Who was I kidding? Prophet's beads only existed in the dreams of Tyl Uilenspiegel. The stabbing pain in my side was still there and I decided to get some fresh air. I noticed that I had crumpled the letter and was holding it like a ball in my hand. Suddenly I knew what I really had to do. Just like the tigers, the lion's had their own open air pit. Not even a week ago Dick and I had thrown snowballs at the tigers who, just to be on the safe side, attacked the splattering snowballs with loud growls. This time I would throw a paper ball at the lions, and if the male was just as restless in his pit as behind glass, then little would remain of the letter. Clutching my side with my right hand and the letter with my left, I trotted to the lion's pit. And there he was, lying on his back in the sun, his eyes closed and his paws stretched out. This was not a king, this was just some lazy cat. I took the letter from my pocket, smoothed it out and ripped it open. High above the lion's den I started to read.

The smell of burning drew Dick from his room. When I came home, I kept on walking straight to the kitchen where I tore up Paulien's letter in an ashtray. To make quite sure that it would catch fire I had added some more paper. Four burning matches would do the job. The paper was burning like a torch, but I knew this could no longer help me.

"Is that Paulien's letter?" Dick asked. He was standing next to me and looked in disgust at the flames. When I nodded, he asked: "Well?"

"Well what?"

"I mean: well? Is the effect of the flames purifying? Do they singe away the bad spots on your conscience?"

"I read the letter," I then said as flatly as I could. The flames were devouring the last pieces of paper. Grimacing I tried to shrug my shoulders. My whole body was in a knot.

"You didn't!!!" Dick seemed to be genuinely shocked. And he had been the one telling me all week not to make a fuss, to just open the letter and get it over with. After all, it was addressed to me, wasn't it?

"It was addressed to me, wasn't it?" I repeated his argument. "But I wish I had never listened to you ... "

"Oh, now I am to blame ... it wasn't me, though, who read the letter!"

With a fork I poked around in the brittle black scraps of paper. The flames had completed their job and extinguished themselves. "Then I won't tell what was in it."

"Maybe I am to blame just a little bit," Dick prompted. "Yeah ... come to think of it ... everything is my fault. Definitely."

"Paulien is going to move," I commenced.

"Christ, no wonder she cringes with shame!" Dick said, but even to him it was clear that this wasn't all.

"She is going to move to the country. To a hole called Balkbrug. Situated somewhere between Zwolle and Hoogeveen."

"Then she might as well move on to Kingdom Come straight away."

"That was the alternative," I said, glad that Dick had brought up the angle himself. "She wrote she would die for sure if she didn't move to Balkbrug."

"That makes sense ..." Dick muttered.

"Surely you know how impressionable she is? Well, I don't understand why I didn't think of it before, I don't understand how for years I simply overlooked it ..." I shook my head in disbelief. My contorted neck protested. "Did I ever tell you that, when we were still in high school, for a while we were spellbound by so-called spiritualist games ... we kind of flirted with the unknowable and had a couple of ridiculous contacts with some innocent spirits ... through the letters of the scrabble game, of course. You remember? You have to put all the letters of the alphabet in a circle on a smooth table. Then you put a glass upside down, right in the middle ..."

"Yes, I remember and then the spirit crawls under the glass and by sliding from one letter to the next it spells out all kinds of messages ..." Dick said. "But you never told me you used to play these games."

"I haven't? Anyway, there was a time when we played the game practically every afternoon. And one fine day, things went wrong. We got in touch with the wrong spirit."

"What do you mean, the wrong spirit?"

"Oh, just an evil spirit ... but let's not talk about that now, I'll tell you all about it some time. Looking back, the whole thing seems quite funny ... anyway, we never again played the game with the scrabble letters. I mean, *I* haven't. I didn't want to have anything to do with it anymore. But apparently, the event made an even deeper impression on Paulien."

"So you were impressed by it too?"

"Oh yes. I was very susceptible at the time. And that is why, from then onwards, I kept away from it. There are things one shouldn't try to unravel."

"Like Paulien's letter," Dick said, returning to Paulien.

"The letter said that over the years she had been in contact with the inexplicable, without ever breathing a word to anyone about it. There was no mention of spiritualism, but all the more of fortune tellers, somnambulists, telepathists, or whatever those swindlers call themselves. Every time she felt bleak, she had herself hypnotized or her fortune told or even worse. And again and again the supernatural sessions left her in a haze, even bleaker than before."

"And yet the supernatural kept calling her?"

"Yes, she was convinced that somehow there had to be more to life, and she looked for it in the indiscernible. Until recently, however, she never carried out in real life the metaphysical advice that came to her through that menagerie of impostors." And again I shook my head, to emphasize the fact that all of this truly touched me. I sat down at the kitchen table. On the lawn slowly but surely the pillar snowman was also melting.

"Until recently," Dick repeated.

"Until recently ... almost three weeks ago, Paulien was brought down by the flu. Her temperature was running sky high and according to herself, this caused a short-circuit in her mind. She felt more alienated from herself than ever before. She was lying in bed, listening to the radio. It was Sunday, 12 noon, and *Veronica* was on the air.[4] The station lived up to its sensation-loving image: they had hired a clairvoyant who was able to conjure up crystal clear visions by telephone, and who gave striking advice to those who called in. Many listeners were dumbfounded by the insights the man volunteered in his broad Hague accent."

"Yeah ... Paulien would know a haguiologist when she heard one," Dick said in an attempt to breach my serious account.

I decided to ignore his remark. "Paulien has her telephone next to her bed. She dialed the number a *Veronica*-voice bellowed into the ether every five minutes. She just had to wait about four minutes and then she was on the air, live."

"Jesus Christ ..." Dick laughed in disbelief.

"Before she was able to explain that she had these bleak moods, the swindler told her in his Hague accent that he could see that she was feeling bleak again. He also told her that she had the flu. But, he said, this flu had nothing to do with her bleak mood. He dealt with his listeners at a staggering pace and in less than two minutes he had assured her that he had seen her very clearly in a vision. In the vision, she was in the company of two lovely little children, she looked very happy, and all this was to take place in a village by the name of ... he had to concentrate for no more than three seconds ... in a village known by the name of Balkbrug. But woe would befall her if she stayed in Amsterdam. So now she is moving to Balkbrug."

"Jesus Christ ..." Dick said. This was no longer a laughing matter.

Paulien and I were seniors in high school when all of a sudden everyone got involved in spiritism. Nobody knew what had instigated the craze, but everyone just happened to know someone who could pass for a medium. It may very well have been a coincidence that these mediums possessed a scrabble game as well as a glass. The medium we knew was called Jacqueline van Eyck. She was also a senior but in a different high school and her mother was friends with Paulien's mother. Moreover, at that time, Jacqueline's mother was one of the few mothers who had a full-time job. After school, often not much later than 3 p.m., six of us used to accompany Jacqueline to her house. The scrabble letters had been prepared at lunch time, neatly laid out on a smooth glass table while right in the middle a solid lemonade glass was itching to be possessed by a spirit. To the left of the glass was spelled *no* and to the right *yes* so as to spare the spirit unnecessary running from letter to letter when responding to simple yes/no questions.

The sessions were merry ones. Nobody really believed there actually was a spirit under the glass, and yet ... the glass made moves we couldn't account for. The game with the spirits was scary in the same way horror movies were scary. And the ambiance was in sync with the atmosphere: in broad daylight we closed the curtains and lit candles. The burning of incense was not required but it didn't hurt either. We all sat down around the table and put our index fingers on the glass. And then the medium began: "Is there a spirit present in this room ..." We could only wait and hope. Nobody was allowed to move. Now and again one of us couldn't help giggling, but this was always cut short by a deadly glance shot by the rest of us. "If a spirit is present in this room, could he then reveal his presence by moving the glass to *yes*? Please?" The thing was not to annoy the spirit, we were to remain polite at all cost. And eventually the glass always set out to move. Now we were in for the real treat. Jacqueline posed the questions and we posed our questions through her.

"What is your name?"

And off the glass went, sometimes it ran so fast that our fingers could hardly keep up with it. "M-A-R-C-E-L-L-O G-I-O-B-E-R-T-I." Or: "J-U-L-I-A P-I-E-R-S-O-N." It seldom occurred that we had a Dutch spirit in our glass but this was never a problem, all spirits were able to speak all languages. The questions were posed along established lines. First of all we wanted to know when the spirit had lived and where, what he had died of and whether he had had a good life. And when we had humored the spirit sufficiently by making him talk a great deal about himself, things would really get interesting. The time had come for the future.

"Can you tell us whether all of us will pass our final examination?"

"N-O-T A-L-L."

"Who won't?"

"P-E-T-E-R."

And even though nobody really believed there was a spirit under the glass, a sigh of relief escaped the group, while Peter continued to stare at the glass in dismay. "Who has been pushing the glass?" he asked offended. Practically every session, someone accused someone else of exerting some pressure on the glass. And once I tried to give the spirit a hand myself. This I did after the question: "Which one of us will go furthest in the world?" With all my might I tried to push the glass toward the M, but something or someone was stronger than me and the answer was: "S-T-E-F-A-N." Stefan was six foot two and an ace at weight lifting.

Only once had Jacqueline posed the question that in fact had been brewing all the time: "Which one of us is going to die first?"

The glass sort of shuddered on the spot, but then stopped moving altogether. It was after this session that Paulien suggested we should seek contact with the supernatural by ourselves from now on. She figured that by then we had gained so much experience that we had become mediums ourselves. And moreover, with only the two of us involved, we would know for sure that nobody was manipulating the glass.

The next day was Saturday and we were planning to go to the pub in the evening. Paulien ate dinner at our house and after dinner we went upstairs to my room. Once there, Paulien got a plastic bag filled with scrabble letters from her purse and she nodded towards the water glass on my sink. Without speaking a word we laid the whole thing out on the low table that was in the middle of my room.

We didn't close the curtains and the lights were on as we sank to our knees and put our index fingers on the bottom of the overturned glass. Before we could utter a word, the glass started moving. This never happened when we were with Jacqueline, but why didn't we stop?

"Come on, let's stop," I said, but didn't remove my finger from the glass.

Paulien shook her head. "What is your name?" she then asked.

"L-E-A-V-E M-E A-L-O-N-E," the glass spelled like lightning.

I knew it wasn't me who had pushed the glass and wavering between suspicion and fright, I looked at Paulien. Paulien looked startled. "Who are you?" she insisted all the same. And then she remembered the courtesy rule: "Could you tell us who you are?"

At first the glass didn't respond, but then it started to run again: "Y-O-U W-I-L-L R-E-G-R-E-T Y-O-U W-E-R-E E-V-E-R B-O-R-N." This was getting beyond a joke. I tried to remove my finger from the glass, but I couldn't do it. The glass had taken over. "I W-I-L-L H-A-U-N-T Y-O-U T-O T-H-E G-R-A-V-E." And only then was I able to free my finger. As soon as I let go, the glass stopped moving. Her finger still glued to the glass, Paulien looked at me with huge eyes. The glass had spent its fury.

"Did you do that?" she asked after having cleared her throat.

"I didn't do anything. Did you?"

"Me neither," Paulien said, obviously very scared.

We agreed to never meddle with the supernatural again. We also agreed to forget this evening. After this we never again referred to it. I never forgot the event, but as the years went by, the memory became more and more earthly. Finally, I was almost sure that the subconscious had nothing to do with the supernatural.

The thaw persevered. On the 5th of December, even the most obstinate remnants of snow had disappeared and all of the Midwest was in a jubilant mood. Records were broken. The meltwater formed some compensation for the hot dry summer Minnesota had endured. Nature solved everything all by herself. It was the 5th of December and in the Netherlands too a jubilant mood dominated. At 2 p.m. Minnesotan time, Saint Nicholas's eve was in full swing across the ocean. I didn't believe in Saint Nicholas anymore, just like I would never again believe in Jubilees. How could I have ever thought that weightless and timeless years really existed, that on very rare occasions years without claims and without aims were still being granted: Jubilees during which all old debts would be forfeited and no debts could be made.

Old debts and new debts, the days after I had read Paulien's letter were crammed with them. Why had I never paid attention to Paulien's bleak moods ... or rather, why had I always put them down to more tangible causes, like some lingering affair or some problem at work. I was her best friend and it had never occurred to me that Paulien needed a reason to live. And even if I had known this, I would have never thought that she'd search for this reason in less tangible spheres. All the time I had been convinced that, apart from a few peculiar details, we had an awful lot in common. I took for granted that we held the same outlook on life, the same taste ... didn't our sordid collection produce solid evidence of our concord? And now it turned out that while fate had shown me its teeth in a smile, it had shown its teeth to Paulien in a growl. While I chose never again to meddle with the supernatural, she obviously didn't have a choice. While I was being jubilant in the upper parts of America, Paulien had hit rock bottom in Europe's Lowest Countries.

Promises, promises, they were to be cherished, not to be crushed ... my body was given a taste of its own medicine: twinges crushed my side, cramps crushed my neck muscles and nerves crushed my stomach. I had crushed my promise. In spite of Paulien's express request not to read the letter, I had read it anyway. I had betrayed her confidence and there was nothing I could do about it. And what was even worse, there was nothing I could do about it either. Paulien was living in a different part of the world, in the future, in different spheres even. The only thing I had was the telephone. I tried every conceivable moment in her days as well as mine, but nobody answered. Maybe she had moved to Balkbrug already ... fleeing from the Amsterdam house where her old telephone was ringing and ringing. And maybe it was even for the best that I couldn't reach her, because instead of reassuring her, I would have made things worse. I had put myself in the paragon of a no-win-situation.

Dick wasn't much help either. In his eyes, Paulien had lost it. In spite of his fascination for the magical side of medieval literature and society, he couldn't begin to sympathize with someone who allowed dark and hysterical powers to spoil her earthly life. According to him the world was crawling with swindlers who tried to take advantage of human hysteria. "People like Uilenspiegel didn't cease to exist with the end of the Middle Ages," he explained his sneering attitude towards Paulien. "They are still alive and kicking and they still deal in many ingenious ways. And their only motivation is to enrich themselves. Time and again they appeal to the credulity of their receptive victims. Disgusting!" And if I understood him correctly, his disgust was meant for the credulous sooner than for the Uilenspiegels of this century. It wasn't Paulien who worried Dick, it was me. "You don't look well," he said. "You know what? Why don't we go away for a couple of days? Perhaps it will put everything in a different light."

For a moment I was in doubt, but then I decided that it was a good idea. It wasn't that I expected to see things differently after staying away from our wooden house for a couple of days, but who knows, maybe a change of environment would inspire me. Maybe a new environment would dictate to me just what to do. And that is why, a good two weeks after Paulien's phone call, we were driving on Highway 35, heading for Minnesota's neighboring state, Iowa. Iowa is to Minnesota what Belgium is to the Netherlands and there must be at least as many Iowa jokes around as jokes on Belgians, but just like Flanders surpasses the Netherlands in more than one respect, Iowa surpasses Minnesota with regards to its Effigy Mounds. In Minnesota too, effigy mounds have been raised alongside the river, prehistoric burial mounds raised by native Americans, but these are just random elevations and not, like in Iowa, mounds in the shape of birds and bears. Most of these mounds are so large that it is impossible to discern their shapes on the ground. High up in the sky, high above nature, birds and gods alone were allowed to follow the string of enormous bears and birds winding its way through the landscape, only high above nature could one discern what had never been intended for human eyes.

On our way to the Effigy Mounds we were largely unaware of what was awaiting us. We had just picked the closest natural monument on a map and had set off in our Chevrolet Citation. Before an end had come to my days of Jubilation, I could hardly think of a bigger thrill than driving the American highways with my brand new American driver's license in our fully automatic American car, mile after mile after mile ... but this time it started to get on my nerves after 45 minutes. I got sulky. And in spite of Dick's tireless efforts to cheer me up, I was sulking even more when we arrived at the entrance of the park many hours later, at 4 p.m. to be precise (23 Dutch time, a point in time unknown in America). The very first sign we stumbled across advised all visitors during the winter season to leave the area before 5 p.m. Nice going: six hours of driving for just one hour of visiting.

"Look at that sun," Dick said when we were standing at the foot of a steep path. Through the bare black branches of trees, much higher up, a yellow lit sky was visible.

"Exactly the same sun as at home," I said. This was not true, but I didn't feel like abandoning my bad mood just yet. We started climbing and passed two burial mounds of which a little sign claimed that they had the shape of huge bears. This we couldn't check as we were at about the same height of the mounds. Even in this elevated woody environment all snow had disappeared and were it not for the black trees against the yellow sky, we could have sworn it was springtime. But now it was clear that we were at the beginning of a long winter, surrounded by a spooky landscape composed of mass graves. Moreover, time was getting short: before 5 p.m. we had to be out of the ancient nature preserve or else ...

We continued our climb and all of a sudden, without being forewarned, we were standing on the edge of a precipice, high above the Mississippi. It was the widest and most beautiful view we had ever set eyes on and at exactly the same moment we heaved an awestruck sigh. With this vista within reach, it was no wonder that the Indians thought it to be proper practice to never be able to get an overall view of the true shapes of their huge burial mounds. The gods had bestowed upon nature what could never be equaled by man. The mounds were a nice try and had favorably impressed the gods, but they were absolutely no match for the Mississippi River Valley that glistened with majesty in the yellow light of the evening sun. And while I was standing there, high above the river, it came to me: I shouldn't try to contact Paulien, I should try to get hold of *Veronica*. On Sunday morning, 12 noon Dutch time, I should see to it that the clairvoyant would be exposed on the air, live.

Just to be absolutely sure, I set the alarm at 4:30, but this was merely going through the motions, because I had decided not to go to bed until after the telephone call with *Veronica*'s in-house prophet. Our tiny black and white television had the capacity of sixty channels and I picked those movies and programs that would bring me into the right mood. I watched *The Untouchables*, I saw a program in which the role of the CIA in the slaying of President Kennedy was discussed, I watched the weather predictions for the whole world for the next ninety days, I saw *The Great Santini* and an interview with Bette Midler. And then it was 4:30 pm. Dick was awakened by the alarm I had set, just to be sure.

"Something nice on the tube?" he asked in a groan when he came out of the bedroom. He pretended to have dragged himself out of bed just for the television, but I knew he'd never want to miss my telephonic performance.

"Na ..." I said, all American. The telephone was standing next to me and the number, which my mother had managed to get, was glowing crystal-clear in my mind. I was ready. The countdown to zero had started two days ago. It had not been difficult to come up with a scheme that would unmask the magnetopath as the psychopath he was. Still two days to go, one day to go, seven hours, three hours, thirty minutes...

"Shall I make some coffee?" Dick asked while nodding at the empty wine bottle.

"Why?"

Dick shrugged and walked back to the bedroom where household sounds clearly gave away that he was putting his clothes on. Twenty minutes to go ... In silence I started to count. "If I were you, I wouldn't call before 5:10," Dick said as he entered the living room again.

"I'm going to call at 12 noon sharp, I don't want to be late, in case there is a line ... who knows, maybe there is a real run on the seer every Sunday ... " By then I was quite nervous. Ten minutes to go, eight, five, ... now! "Can you dial the number for me, Dick? It might bring luck." And I enumerated the long number which Dick punched in dutifully. I had to wait for a moment to get through, but then, at the other end of the world, in Hilversum,[5] the telephone started to ring in the right rhythm. The line was not busy.

"There is more between heaven and earth ..." a girl's voice full of confidence announced.

"Eh, hi ... I would like to speak to the clairvoyant on the program," I blurted.

"What is your name, please ..." the girl said in the exact same tone of voice in which she had assured me that there was more between heaven and earth.

"Oh, excuse me. My name is Maria Stahlie."

There was a rustling sound at the other end of the line. "And your problem is ..." The exact same tone again. Maybe she was under hypnosis.

"I am having these recurring, inexplicable dreams about ..." I started, but then I was cut short.

"One moment, please." More rustling sounds got through to me. Was she checking some sort of blacklist, to see if my name was on it? "Mr. Van Vliet will be with you in a moment. Don't hang up, please ..." I heard a little click at the other end of the line.

"They have put me on hold," I whispered to Dick in a fluster. "They are going to put me through to Van Vliet. But I have no idea who this guy is. I'm sure clairvoyants don't go by the name of Van Vliet." I started to giggle.

"Ssst," Dick hushed.

And then, much sooner than I had imagined I got through. "Yes please, Ms. Stahlie, you're on the air." His broad Hague accent betrayed him. I had a direct connection with the disturber of my Jubilee. The swindler had to be swindled, Tyl Uilenspiegel was in for a nasty surprise.

"Lately I'm having the very same dream over and over again, and now I wonder whether this means something, I mean, maybe it is a dream with a special message..."

"Hold on, hold on ... our contact is still quite blurry, I cannot quite sense you. Are you calling from far away?"

He was bluffing. The bluffer had to be bluffed. "Would Balkbrug be too far away for you?"

"Ah, now I can sense you. Please go ahead."

"At least once every week I'm having this dream in which I am building these snowmen," I started. "I'm building four of them at the same time in the dream, but each time when I try to lug a head on top of one of the body balls..."

"I'm in it, I'm in it ..." Van Vliet called in a hurry. "I see a white plain. Is that correct?"

"That is exactly right," I replied. Some seer, I was talking about snowmen and all he came up with was a white plain. "But in my dream I can never get a single head on top of one of these snowmen. Sure enough, they stay put for a moment, but as soon as I go to the next snowman, they roll on the ground again." Dick gave his thumbs up. He thought I was doing a fine job.

"I can see them rolling, those heads ..." Van Vliet said. "I'm in the dream now — let me see, let me see ... are you married?" he then asked and before I could answer he urged me: "Come on, come on, there are more people in line."

I pointed at Dick and said: "Yes."

"And what about your stool?"

"Excuse me?"

"You see, I can see large droppings in this empty room. Do you eat enough oatbran? Hold your horses, wait a moment ... that is not the stool of a human being, this is the stool of a ..."

"... lion," I completed his sentence to my own amazement. I grabbed Dick's arm and pinched hard.

"Yes, those are lion's droppings. Is your husband's sign Leo?"

"No, his sign is Virgo." So here he was completely wrong. "That fits as well. That fits the image too, a Virgo often lives under the disguise of a lion ... I can see a little church now. Is there a church close to where you live?"

It was impossible that he could recognize as such the gospel church across from our house. This church was situated in an ordinary house and only a small cross above the door could give it away. Chance and luck were the only qualities this Uilenspiegel had based his act upon. I decided to contradict him. "No," I said. "The church at Balkbrug is just at the other end of the village."

"Right, I can see that now. And the vague figure I held for your husband gets clearer as well ... it is a young woman, with curly black hair ... is your hair black?

Paulien's hair was black and curly. And Paulien's sign was Leo. "Dark blonde," I replied, because I didn't want to leave at the mercy of this creepy man the real color of my hair. "But what's all this got to do with my dream?"

"I've got the complete picture now," Van Vliet said. "The rolling heads are a warning..." He started to breathe heavily. "... You are on the verge of being caught, you are on the edge of a precipice ... oh! what a magnificent view!!!" he suddenly exclaimed. "This light, this river ..." There was a fraction of silence at the other end of the line and then he said: "I lost all contact. I advise you to change your situation drastically. Maybe it is for the best if you move. I cannot say more. I hope you will act upon my advice." And before I could utter one more word, I was cut off.

"He hung up." I said bewildered to Dick.

Maybe Uilenspiegel was a true prophet after all? I didn't present Dick with this question but asked it in all seriousness to myself. The droppings, a lion, a little church, Paulien and the magnificent view ... could all this still be coincidence? I had told Dick that the man spoke in commonplaces while making vague allusions to general predicaments. And then he needed me to fill in the details, like the droppings being a lion's instead of human, before he could get new information from his crystal ball! The man was a fraud, and a cheap one at that ... Dick had had a wonderful time during the conversation and the only thing he regretted was that it was over before I could get around to the actual exposure. He didn't know, however, that I had gotten around that as well. For a very short moment, I had seen myself exposed: frightened and completely under the spell of the inexplicable. For a very short moment, I wanted to know it all. But then with a click the clairvoyant cut off not only the connection but also the spell and I was a person with a free will again.

     For the second time in my life I chose to give the supernatural the cold shoulder, but I realized that a third time around I wouldn't be let off this lightly. Third timer's luck didn't apply to those who had stolen a glance from above nature ... like Paulien ... Paulien ... I hoped she had not been listening to the radio and thus would never know that I had opened her letter. There simply were things one'd better not know.

     America was the Land of Ten Thousand Opportunities. One of those opportunities was to get a driver's license within a month's time. Another opportunity was to see a lion in the eyes without risking stepping into its mouth. I had seen enough, I had been on the edge of a precipice and had seen the Mississippi from above nature. In the remaining months of my Jubilee, I wouldn't tempt third timer's luck anymore and I would leave the remaining opportunities of Minnesota alone. Seven hours of time difference, 8,000 kilometers, an ocean filled to the brim with water and a winter beyond imagination would ceaselessly remind me to keep every sail down.

"THE BITTER MEDICINE"[6]

During my flight back to Amsterdam, I had calculated how much time it would take for two hundred million seconds to pass. Roughly. An hour covers 3,600 seconds and a day 86,400, so far my mental arithmetic added up to the exact number, but from that point onwards I made a slapdash job of it: one million divided by 86,400 makes about eleven and a half, and two hundred times eleven and a half makes 2,300. Two hundred million seconds account for two thousand and three hundred days, which means for more than six years and three months...the multi-colored stone that wasn't any bigger than a fist and that through its form bore a strong resemblance to the roaring man in the painting *The Bitter Medicine* by Adriaan Brouwer,[7] the multi-colored stone I had brought back with me from the United States and that I intended to give as a present to my sweetheart twenty five days after my arrival in Amsterdam, that multi-colored stone...wasn't two hundred million seconds old but two hundred million years. It was purely out of respect for the stone's age that I rented, on my arrival at Schiphol Airport, a small locker in which I left the prehistoric gem behind to allow it to simmer down until the moment was right to present Dick on his birthday with a nondescript little key.

Once in a while our government will pump money into a worthy cause, and once in an even greater while our government is seized by a whim and starts pumping money into the dissemination of Dutch culture in foreign countries. Thus it could occur that I was invited to a conference in Phoenix, Arizona, along with several other ex-writers-in-residence—Dutch writers who for a period of ten months had been lecturing at an American university. Why of all cities Phoenix had been chosen as the most likely spot on earth to hold a conference about the dissemination of Dutch culture in foreign countries, will probably remain a riddle forever. Phoenix is, apart from a few Islamic cities, the hottest desert city in the world. It is surrounded by a chain of mountains which is why the hot air never manages to escape and forms in the summertime the main obstacle for temperatures to drop, even during the night, below the point of 30 degrees Celsius. The conference on the dissemination of Dutch culture in foreign countries took place in the last week of July, and maybe this was why tempers never even thought about running high. Those present put every bit of energy into the maintenance of their own body temperature, and while sprawled on their wooden seats they were only capable of registering the drops of sweat on the brows of those rendering their speeches, while these speakers, for their part, made no effort whatsoever to keep up appearances: in lackluster short presentations they began to doubt whether it was of any use at all to disseminate Dutch culture in foreign countries. Along with the rest I heaved a sigh of sheer relief when the last speaker had performed his task and when everyone was allowed to go his own way.

I rented a colossal car in which the air conditioner was in such perfect working order that it made more noise than the engine, and I drove straight to the northeastern part of Arizona where The Petrified Forest has been for the last two hundred million years. On my route to this national park I came to believe that in Arizona car engines are running thanks to air conditioners, instead of the other way around...you had to believe something when you were driving all alone in a landscape where dark red, orange and brown tones produced a mass of stone-dead evidence that the desert was anything but an inexhaustible source of yellow sand. The roads were endless and empty, the air conditioner roared, and the car ran on. Everything was as it should be, except I was driving the car on my own this time and not like eighteen months before together with Dick. Eighteen months ago Dick and I had covered the same route, from Phoenix to The Petrified Forest, only then we hadn't been aware of the fact that we were about to be confronted with our own mortality by the most bizarre and awe-inspiring natural phenomenon in all of America.

The Petrified Forest, the wood that turned into stone, is not a forest in the generally acknowledged sense of the word. It is a piece of desert in which millions of years full of floods, landslides and other forms of erosion have caused quite a few tree stumps and slices of tree trunks to come to the surface. They are not ordinary tree trunks, the ones that are now scattered over the landscape by the hundreds and at definite random. Today a desert, but 225 million years ago a vast swamp in which fish and reptiles had the time of their lives, a swamp where trees and plants were shooting up like weeds. At a time when natural disasters didn't even exist, the vast swamp was swamped with natural disasters. Trees were felled and got buried under thick layers of mud, sand and silicon-rich volcanic ashes. Because of the absence of oxygen and because of the fact that each and every tree cell drowned itself in mineral-rich water, a unique alchemistic tour de force was allowed to take place, a tour de force that went against nature and turned the tree trunks into their opposites: cell by cell the wood became colorful stone, cell by cell nature proved the impossible to be possible. And today? Today, in the never-ending sunlight of Arizona, yellow, orange and red shades bounce off the two hundred million year old tree trunks, tree stumps and tree splinters, while at the same time darker shades of blue lend depth to the bewitched wood, a depth affording just a glance behind the scenes of the unfathomable number of years that have passed since the creation of the petrified forest.

"Removal of petrified wood prohibited" it said every ten yards on life-size signs in The Petrified Forest. I don't think it would have even occurred to me to take a stone back home with me, had there not been such explicit warnings that I shouldn't. I also presume that the stone that looked so much like the man in Adriaan Brouwer's painting would still be in its original spot in Arizona if only the conference on the promotion of Dutch culture abroad had been more exciting. And then of course there was the sweltering sun, that mind-troubling sweltering sun...under these and other mitigating circumstances I started to look for a nice specimen among the splinters and the smaller stones.

Eighteen months ago Dick and I had traveled the beaten path that had been set out in The Petrified Forest, from north to south—exactly as had been intended by the designers of the park. Then we had started off at the visitors' center, and by the way of a spectacular string of mountain highlights we ended up at the museum. But this time I started at the museum, which may have contributed as well to the fact that I felt nothing but excitement when I picked up the petrified double of *The Bitter Medicine* and slipped it into the pocket of my loose-fitting jeans after having cast a few quick glances around me.

The Petrified Forest hadn't changed a bit since a year and a half ago, since a century and a half ago, since fifteen million years ago.... At my leisure I drove from scenic view to scenic view and I saw in succession intact tree trunks, half tree trunks and rows of sparkling slices in which the growth rings had been replaced by minerals; I saw white-red plains dotted with fragments and splinters, I visited the ruins of pueblos where prehistoric Indians had once lived, and along with four other tourists I stared at the rock face where incomprehensible symbols made some essential statement about a prehistoric event. Finally, under the sizzling sun, I took a stroll among the shattered pieces. Removal of petrified wood prohibited...Removal of petrified wood prohibited ...Removal of petrified wood prohibited...enough already! I started to search among the fragments. It didn't take long before I noticed that practically every stone, through its fantastic shape, looked exactly like something else. This brought back in memory a visit Dick and I had made to a famous cave in the bowels of a mountain, a cave in which a waterfall seemed to originate from a void and to disappear into thin air. In this cave timeless centuries had formed stalactites, stalagmites and other rock formations. A number of these formations were lit by little spotlights and had been given a title: "Bacon and Eggs," "Potato Chips," "The Holy Family," ... and sure enough, the stones bore a striking resemblance to Joseph, Mary and the infant Jesus.

As soon as I spotted "The Bitter Medicine," in between two stones that for a change resembled nothing at all, I knew this was the stone I was going to take home with me. And at the same instant I knew where the stone would have to go once I had smuggled it out of the country: I would give it to Dick, my sweetheart after all, as a present for his 35th birthday. *The Bitter Medicine* was one of his favorite paintings, and likewise it was true that eighteen months ago he had been dumbfounded by the ancientry and the magnificent display of color in The Petrified Forest. Who could think of a better way to combine cultural and natural forces in one? Contemplating it for a while, the resemblance between the stone and the man in *The Bitter Medicine* seemed to be almost uncanny. In the painting a man roars in disgust because he has just gulped down a far too bitter medicine. The stone as well had its mouth wide open in disgust, and come to think of it, once a piece of wood, 200 million years ago this stone had digested such a bitter medicine that out of sheer dread it had turned into its opposite.

With my hand around the stone in the pocket of my jeans I visited the visitors' center and it was there that I saw the stones in the showcases, the stones that sooner or later had been sent back by persons who had ended up regretting their theft because it had brought them nothing but tough luck, misfortune and a bad conscience. As if "The Bitter Medicine" had never been in my pocket, I read several of the accompanying letters. Never before in my life had I been a thief; when I was still in high school I never even had the guts to look up from my test paper for fear of being accused of cheating and here I stood, with my hand around a two hundred million year old stone that I was about to snatch away from its only true habitat, and I was reading the letters of the penitents with heartfelt amusement. Jerry Cohen from New York wrote that the stolen stone gave him such a guilty conscience that his entire life was being unsettled by it. Suzie Mullins knew for sure that every bit of bad luck she had experienced during the last few years could be attributed to the magic fossilized stone she had been displaying on her mantlepiece. Each letter spoke of strange incidents, of regret and of pangs of remorse...but with my hand around "The Bitter Medicine" it never even occurred to me to go and put back the stone while I still had the chance. The bitter medicine had turned me into my opposite, the chicken had changed into a daredevil, and at the entrance of the park I dared the ranger by meeting his question with a reckless "no." No, I had not taken any petrified wood from the Park, why, wasn't that prohibited?

The aircraft that took me back to Amsterdam didn't crash, and still not ashamed of my theft I put away my stone in a small locker in Schiphol.

Dick was disappointed that I hadn't brought him a present from America. "What's the use of staying home all by myself if it doesn't pay off somehow..." he said gloomily, and it was obvious that I had temporarily come down in his estimation. But I never even flinched, knowing for a certainty that my time was still to come. On his birthday Dick would find out that not even in Arizona had he been out of my thoughts.

In the days upon my return I couldn't help thinking, over and over again, about the two hundred million year old stone that was sitting there in the dark, waiting for someone to open the door of its new dwelling place. I remember having read somewhere that very old objects, when snatched away from their natural habitat and exposed to new circumstances, were susceptible to the museum disease. In some museums tin goblets returned to dust as soon as temperatures dropped below 13 degrees Celsius. In other museums handles dropped off stone jugs because, after a stay of numerous centuries in the dark, they suddenly woke up in a brightly lit showcase. Who knows, maybe my stone couldn't handle the dark anymore? It was this idea that stuck in my mind and in the end I had no other choice but to go to Schiphol and see for myself if "The Bitter Medicine" was still in one piece.

At Schiphol the holiday season was in full swing and on my way to my locker no less than three times a luggage trolley bumped into my left ankle. But when I slipped the key into the lock of the small locker I forgot all pain. Nor did I pay any attention to the cursing man who, right behind my back, discovered that he had lost his sports bag. The door that hid the stone from the outside world opened smoothly and there it was, exactly as I had left it...or was it? Was I wrong or had the colors really become more brilliant? The blues in particular seemed to be fiercer than I remembered. I got the stone from its locker and studied it carefully. No, it was probably because of the lights in Schiphol that the colors looked slightly different. I focussed my attention on its shape. And then I knew, or rather, I didn't know anymore. How could I ever have thought that this stone was the spitting image of the man in *The Bitter Medicine*? True enough, with a little good will a profile could be distilled from its forms, and having done so the indentation below could be nothing but a screaming mouth. But this mouth didn't scream in horror because it had just downed the most disgustingly bitter medicine, no, the silent scream it hollered was very clearly a scream of aggression.

No use to beat around the bush: the stone's mouth craved for revenge. As if it was a burning poop I had in my hands, I let go of the stone and threw it back into its locker, swiftly closing the door behind it. Then I cast a few nervous glances around me, because it felt like I was being observed. But no one paid any attention to my fumbling with the locker. The running, stumbling, bumping and panicky crowd needed all its attention to just take care of itself.

There were three possibilities. Very possibly there was nothing at all wrong with the stone, and thus the stone would still be the same old striking look-alike of the man in Adriaan Brouwer's painting. Then there was a possibility that the dreaded museum disease had brought about the slight shift in the looks of the stone. And the third possibility really was too odd to be true and should have been ruled out in advance: the stone's expression had changed because it had been snatched away from its natural habitat after a period of two hundred million years. Its revenge would be sweet, that's what the ancient stone wanted to bring across with its battle-cry, sweeter than the bitterest of medicine.

Of course I didn't take the idea of the avenging stone altogether seriously, but nevertheless it had lost its colorful attraction. As the days passed I felt more and more discouraged to present Dick on his birthday with the little key to the locker. All of a sudden I wasn't quite so sure whether he would appreciate the fact that especially for him, I had upset a two hundred million year old combination of circumstances. The stone was, together with all the other pieces in The Petrified Forest, an essential part of the landscape that might have been older than the moon... no, fat chance my sweetheart would have any idea what to do with his birthday present. And having reached this conclusion, it dawned upon me as well that I'd better not confront him with the three theories I had scraped together concerning the changed looks of the stone. Besides, Dick wouldn't think the third theory strange at all: wasn't it true that there were, all over the world, hundreds of people who had experienced a touch of the fossilized wood's bewitching qualities? I thought of the letters that were being displayed in the showcases of the visitors' center in The Petrified Forest, and slowly but surely I became afraid.

Should I send the stone back to Arizona, or should I dump it in an Amsterdam canal? There were moments when I thought the best thing would be just to leave it there in its locker, just to leave the decision about the stone's fate to someone else...and then there were moments when I resolved to proceed with the original plan: surely my superstition was making a fool out of me!

Had Schiphol always been in the news this often? Journalists dressed up as temporary workers had proven that the surveillance of the airplanes was not worth a tinker's cuss. If you were out to stick a bomb under a plane, no one would stop you. The entire ground crew was infuriated by this accusation and threatened to go on strike. They would show the world how easy it was to stick a bomb under an airplane! In response to the strike threat, management threatened to hire more temporary workers, a threat that in its turn awoke all the air crews: for sure there would be, among the new temporaries, someone who had been inspired by the journalists, indeed, if ground crew and management weren't willing to live up to their responsibilities there would be no further flights. On top of all this bickering the holiday season was breaking many records. Not only were there more travellers than ever before, but there were also many more planes than ever before taking off late or not taking off at all. Continually suitcases were being sent to the wrong destinations. A current affairs program had in its summer special an item about those unhappy vacationers whose pockets had been picked and who found themselves, just before boarding, without tickets and without money. And was it really a coincidence when a 56 year old man had a heart attack while storing his bag in a locker?

I came around once and for all when, three days before Dick's birthday, I read in the newspaper that there had been a near-miss at Schiphol. On its way to the runway the wing of a plane had brushed a lawn mower, and in the process one of its fuel tanks had been missed by a hair's breadth. This could no longer be a coincidence, this preposterous near-hit had been a warning. The stone's activity would become more and more powerful, I saw this very clearly now. One should think twice before transferring a two hundred million year old stone to a new environment. A stone like that had more experience of life than even God. The accident between plane and lawn mower contained a warning that only I could understand. If I did not take away that stone immediately, if I did not instantly find a destination for my bitter medicine, then... then a disaster was likely to happen at Schiphol. Stung into action I took my bike, and I raced to the railway station.

Three quarters of an hour later I was standing, panting and legs trembling, in front of the small locker in which fate was being tempted. Would the stone have changed even more, would its expression have become even more ferocious? True enough, I didn't dare to open the locker's door. But there was no way I could leave the little gem behind in the airport. Then a terrible truth got through to me. If I truly believed in the stone's magic forces — and by now I could no longer fool myself into believing that I didn't — I would have no place left to go with it. I had to take it from its locker, or else a disaster would take place at Schiphol. But then what? It was as if the bitter medicine got more malevolent the longer it was forced to do without its natural habitat. I couldn't send the stone back to The Petrified Forest either, because only God knew what would happen underway. And I could hardly leave it behind in a deserted place: in the long-run deserted places were always brought to life again, and the two hundred million year old stone had all the time in the world. It was obvious that I was tied to my bitter medicine, there was nothing I could do but take the stone back home and wait and see...there was nothing I could do.

Today Dick's birthday is long gone. I have given him a leather soccer ball for a present, and never breathed a word about the stone that now has been lying for two months on the bottom of the aquarium in my study. All the fish are still alive, but even so I do not have the courage to throw the stone away or to send it back to Arizona. Although today I attribute the incidents at Schiphol to sheer, sheer coincidence, I have decided to play it as safe as possible. Most of the time, on the bottom of the aquarium, the scream resembles the scream of the man who has just swallowed a bitter medicine. But sometimes, through a ripple in the water or maybe even through a minute shift in the stone's expression, I can see again the cry for revenge, and it is in these moments that I realize that for the time being there is nothing left for me to do but to butter up to a piece of wood that two hundred million years ago turned into its opposite.

NOTES to the Translations

1. A famous Dutch soccer player.

2. A famous Dutch social critic, comedian and television personality.

3. Dutch poet, anthologizer and literary critic.

4. Not a person but the name of a Dutch radio and television broadcasting corporation specializing in popular, commercial programming.

5. City in the Netherlands, between Amsterdam and Utrecht, and radio and television broadcasting center.

6. Translation by Maria Stahlie.

7. Flemish painter (1605/6-38); spent several years in Haarlem, Holland (probably as a pupil of Frans Hals) before returning to Antwerp, where he died. Brouwer is especially famous for his vibrant and colorful genre-scenes of low-life as well as for his superb landscapes. A technical virtuoso, he was much admired by Rembrandt and Rubens, who both collected his work.

Bibliography

Primary Works

Stahlie, Maria. *Unisono*. Amsterdam: Bert Bakker, 1987 (novel).

_____. "De Monadini's." *De Held* 1988 (short story, published previously).

_____. "Boven de natuur." *De Held* 1989 (short story, published previously).

_____. *Verleden-Hemel-Toekomst*. Amsterdam: Bert Bakker, 1988 (collection of short stories).

_____. *In de geest van de Monadini's*. Amsterdam: Bert Bakker, 1989 (collection of short stories).

_____. "En die tong, dat was ik." "Literaire Bijlage," *Vrij Nederland* October 1989 (short story, first publication).

_____. "De haarbos van de heilige." *Liefdes Letterland: Erotische verhalen*. Amsterdam: Contact, 1989 (short story, published previously in *Hollands Maandblad* 1987).

_____. "Het bittere drankje." *25 onder 35: Nieuwe verhalen van jonge Nederlandse en Vlaamse schrijvers*. Eds. Jessica Durlacher, Peter Elberse and Joost Zwagerman. Amsterdam: Bert Bakker, 1990 (short story, first publication).

_____. *De sterfzonde of de ingebeelde dode*. Amsterdam: Bert Bakker, 1991 (novel).

_____. "De obsessie van Wally van Asten." In *Een schrale troost: Verhalen van vrouwen over mannen*. Amsterdam: Contact, 1991 (short story, first publication).

_____. *De Vlinderplaag*. Amsterdam: Bert Bakker, 1993.

Translations by Maria Stahlie

Lurie, Alison. *The War between the Tates*. Maria Stahlie, trans. *De oorlog van de Tates*. Amsterdam: Bert Bakker, 1987.

Moore, Lorrie. *Self-Help*. Maria Stahlie, trans. *Hoe word ik een andere vrouw?* Amsterdam: Bert Bakker, 1986.

Wolff, Tobias. *The Barracks Thief*. Maria Stahlie, trans. *De Kazernedief*. Amsterdam: Bert Bakker, 1987.